THE STORY OF THE FOURTH ARMY

IN THE BATTLES OF THE HUNDRED DAYS, August 8th to November 11th, 1918

BY MAJOR-GENERAL SIR ARCHIBALD MONTGOMERY
K.C.M.G., C.B.,
GENERAL STAFF, FOURTH ARMY

With a Foreword by
GENERAL LORD RAWLINSON
G.C.B., G.C.V.O., K.C.M.G., A.D.C.

The Naval & Military Press Ltd

Published by

The Naval & Military Press Ltd

Unit 10, Ridgewood Industrial Park,

Uckfield, East Sussex,

TN22 5QE England

Tel: +44 (0) 1825 749494

Fax: +44 (0) 1825 765701

www.naval–military-press.com

www.military-genealogy.com

GENERAL SIR HENRY RAWLINSON.
(*Commander of the Fourth Army.*)

THE STORY OF THE
FOURTH ARMY

IN THE BATTLES OF THE HUNDRED
DAYS, AUGUST 8th to NOVEMBER 11th, 1918

BY MAJOR-GENERAL SIR
ARCHIBALD MONTGOMERY
K.C.M.G., C.B.,
GENERAL STAFF, FOURTH ARMY

With a Foreword by
GENERAL LORD RAWLINSON
G.C.B., G.C.V.O., K.C.M.G., A.D.C.

HODDER AND STOUGHTON
LIMITED   LONDON

DEDICATED

TO

THE SOLDIERS FROM GREAT BRITAIN, IRELAND, AND THE DOMINIONS WHO BY THEIR
SELF-SACRIFICE AND DOGGED DETERMINATION IN DEFENCE, AND THEIR INITIATIVE,
RESOURCE, AND UNEQUALLED GALLANTRY IN ATTACK, TURNED DAYS OF
DISASTER AND ALARMS INTO WEEKS OF SUCCESS AND VICTORY.

" If you can force your heart and nerve and sinew
   To serve your turn long after they are gone,
And so hold on when there is nothing in you
   Except the will which says to them, ' Hold on ' :
         *   *   *   *   *
If you can meet with triumph and disaster
   And treat these two impostors just the same :
         *   *   *   *   *
Yours is the earth and everything that's in it,
   And—which is more—you'll be a man, my son ! "

                              —RUDYARD KIPLING.

FOREWORD

By

GENERAL LORD RAWLINSON, G.C.B., G.C.V.O., K.C.M.G., A.D.C.

THERE is no period in the history of the Great War which is of such transcendent interest to the soldier as that covered by this book. It is not too much to say that the events which took place in France during August, September, and October, 1918, constitute the greatest military triumph the world has ever seen.

This book, which is written by a soldier for soldiers, gives the first detailed account of any of the battles of the hundred days, and, for this reason, will be most valuable to all students of military history. The moment the armistice was signed steps were taken to lay the foundation of this work whilst events were still fresh in the memories of all who were directly concerned in the operations. As is well known, no written record of a fight can produce the mechanical accuracy of a cinematograph, but every possible endeavour has been made to avoid error and ascertain the truth. The numerous maps, photographs, and sketches have been the subject of especial labour and attention. They will not only enable readers who are unacquainted with the actual terrain to form some idea of the tactical features of the ground and to realise the truly formidable nature of the obstacles which confronted the troops, but will also serve as a permanent record of the general aspect of the country as it appeared in 1918. That such a record is needed will have been apparent to all who have visited the battlefields since the armistice. The growth of vegetation has already obliterated to a great extent the scars of war, and before long the reconstruction of villages and resumption of cultivation will have so far transformed the landscape as to completely change the war aspect of the terrain.

At the end of July, 1918, the opposing forces on the western front, after four years of unprecedented battling, still confronted one another without any decisive advantage having accrued to either side. The great German offensive of 1918 had no doubt failed, but the effect on the moral of the German Army, consequent on its failure, and combined with the result of the " wearing down " battles of 1916 and 1917, was still concealed from the world. We learn from the Ludendorff Memoirs that he himself dreaded, and had indeed suspected, a weakening in the German moral before this date, but to the world at large, as well as to the leaders of the Allied Armies, no reliable indication had so far been forthcoming.

Preparations were even being made in Allied Countries for the production of military material to enable the war to be continued not only throughout 1919 but into 1920. The Fourth Army victory in front of Amiens on August 8th, with its tale of some 16,000 prisoners and 400 guns, was the first indication of the true state of affairs in the enemy's camp. It restored permanently to the Allies the priceless weapon of the initiative, and aroused in the hearts of all the Allied Armies the confident hope that victory might be won in 1918. From evidence now available it is clear that our success on August 8th induced consternation at German General Headquarters. It caused Ludendorff to tender his resignation to Hindenburg, and produced from the Kaiser on August 14th a direct order to Secretary of State von Hintze to open peace negotiations.[1]

Though at the time these facts were not revealed to us, Marshal Foch quickly realised that as a result of the battle of Amiens the moment for a general offensive had arrived. It was his continued pressure on all fronts throughout August and September, that above all other factors brought triumph to the Allied Armies on the western front. The success of the Australians at Mont St. Quentin and Péronne, one of the most brilliant attacks carried out during the whole war, was further proof in early September that the resisting power of the enemy had declined considerably. It was not, however, until the third week in September when our Fourth, Third, and First Armies were confronted by the formidable defences of the Hindenburg Line, and the Canal de l'Escaut, that the momentous decision had to be taken as to whether it was worth while to accept the risk of one more supreme effort.

There were those who doubted if the capture of these positions, defended as they were by the flower of the German Army, was possible, and I confess that, when in the early part of September I was asked my views on this point, I hesitated to give an answer, until we had fought our way to within striking distance of this great defensive system. However, when by the 21st September this had been accomplished, I gave it as my considered opinion that the capture of the Hindenburg Line was possible and that an attack on it offered good chances of success. No doubt there was a risk of failure. There always is, and at this particular moment failure might have had serious consequences, but, on the other hand, success would mean a speedy and victorious termination of the war and the saving of thousands of lives, to say nothing of millions of money.

It is the essence of good strategy to force your enemy to fight in such a position that, whereas failure may cost you dear, success will bring disaster upon him. The positions of the Allied Armies on the western front at the end of September, 1918, fulfilled these conditions. What wonder then that military leaders with the genius and foresight of Foch and Douglas Haig declared emphatically for the immediate continuance of the offensive. That they were right in their judgment is abundantly clear from the fact that the first peace note was actually dispatched to the President of the United States on October 5th,[2] though Ludendorff states that " the events of the 29th September and succeeding days did

[1] " My War Memories," by Ludendorff, Vol. II., pp. 684 and 687   [2] *Ibid.*, p. 730.

not compel the Germans to sudden and momentous decisions."[1]   Whatever he may say, the sequence of events and dates, and the evidence of the great victories won between St. Quentin and Cambrai during the last week of September, 1918, are overwhelming.

It is probable, as he clearly points out, that the increasing danger of the situation on the western front had been withheld by the German Government from the German people.   When, therefore, the nation was suddenly confronted at the beginning of October with disaster, irretrievable and immediate, it is not surprising that the people turned against their Kaiser's Government and brought down the whole edifice of Empire with a crash.   The unexpected rapidity with which the armistice was forced upon the enemy is thus to some extent explained, for it was the direct consequence of overwhelming defeat on the field of battle, suddenly revealed to a nation utterly unprepared for such a reversal of fortune, and at the same time shaken physically and morally by the efficacy of our blockade and the far-reaching effects of our propaganda.

It has been contended by some that the armistice was premature—that in another few weeks the German Army would have been forced to lay down their arms and surrender unconditionally.   I do not hold this view.   It is true that, in so far as the fighting troops of the Allies were concerned, a pronounced moral ascendency had been established in all the Allied Armies throughout the whole western front, and was daily increasing.   Owing, however, to the thorough and systematic manner in which the Germans had destroyed all railways, roads, and bridges during their retreat, it was a physical impossibility for at least the British Armies, and I think for any of the Armies, to continue their advance rapidly and in strength, and to immediately follow up their successes. Had they done so, they would have starved.

Turning to the composition of the Fourth Army during the period covered by this book, it is interesting to note that it consisted of men drawn from almost every part of the British Empire.   Australians, Canadians, South Africans, as well as British and Americans.   Several of the British divisions engaged had been decimated during the retreat in March, only four months previously, yet they commenced the offensive on August 8th and fought right through till November 11th, a fine example of that great British characteristic of " never knowing you are beaten." The dogged determination of the British divisions, backed by a fighting spirit which was beyond all praise, will be ever memorable as one of the main factors of the Fourth Army success.   The Dominion troops won a reputation second to none ; the Australians by their skill and cunning as well as by their surpassing gallantry, the Canadians by their bold tactics and invincible will to conquer.   The South Africans more than maintained the fighting reputation they had gained while with the 9th Division.   All units, no matter from what corners of the earth they came, struggled gallantly and in unison to beat the hated enemy.   Of particular interest is the fact that forming part of the Fourth Army during some of the most bitterly contested battles of this period, and in no way behind their comrades in gallantry and dash, were the men of the

[1] " My War Memories," by Ludendorff, Vol. II., p. 719.

II American Corps from Illinois, New York, Carolina, and Tennessee, names that conjure up memories of the fierce battles nearly sixty years ago during the civil war between the North and South, in which men of the English-speaking race were likewise fighting to the bitter end for a cause which they were convinced was just. The gallantry and dash of these American troops will never be forgotten by their comrades of the Fourth Army.

It would be impossible to select for special praise any particular branch of the service, when all carried out their share and co-operated so effectively to the common end, but no factor did more to bring about success than the close and skilful co-operation with the infantry, of the various arms—cavalry, artillery, machine-gunners, engineers, the Air Force, and last but not least the tanks. There is always a tendency on the part of a new service like tanks, aeroplanes, or even machine-guns, when first employed in a general action, to think that they can win the battle " on their own," and it is a matter of time and careful training to get each arm to exert its maximum effort, not independently but in combination. To ensure this is no easy matter, but I attribute the success of the battles of the hundred days chiefly to three paramount factors : First, the unity of purpose and whole-hearted co-operation of all concerned ; secondly, the combined tactics of all the fighting services based on the lessons of four years of war ; and thirdly, the invincible will to conquer of every officer, non-commissioned officer, and man.

I should like in conclusion to acknowledge the devoted work that has been done by the Fourth Army Staff, and particularly by Maj.-Gen. Sir A. A. Montgomery, not only in the compilation of this book, no small labour in itself, but by the invaluable assistance he and they rendered to me during these " Battles of the Hundred Days." No Commander has ever been better served by his Staff, and I know that, in the opinion of the Corps and Divisional Commanders who served in the Fourth Army during this momentous period, the Army Staff won both the respect and affection of the lower formations by their helpfulness and consideration in times of sunshine and of cloud. It is not too much to say that our general success during the hundred days, and the smoothness and efficiency with which the Army machine worked as a whole, was largely due to the knowledge, efficiency, and tact of the Staff Officers at Army Headquarters.

RAWLINSON,
General.

GOVERNMENT HOUSE,
  ALDERSHOT,
    December, 1919.

PREFACE

This story has been compiled from the excellent accounts of the operations which have been written by the staffs of the corps and divisions which served in the Fourth Army during the hundred days, supplemented by verbal information given by individual officers, and from the records of the Fourth Army during that period. Though in narrating the events of a period so crowded with incident there must of necessity be many omissions, this book will, it is hoped, be of interest to all who shared in the victories of the Fourth Army, victories which, in three months of hard and continuous fighting, carried it from within sight of Amiens over the frontiers of France near Avesnes. It is thought, moreover, that the impressions left at the time on the minds of those who took part in operations of such importance will be of interest to the military student and of value to the future historian when a complete history of the World War comes to be written.

It is much regretted that it has not been possible to give the narrative of the doings of the II American Corps in so much detail as in the case of the other corps. This is due to the fact that the II American Corps left the Fourth Army soon after the Armistice to join the American Army, and that the reports received from it and from the 27th and 30th American Divisions did not furnish so many details as those sent in by the British, Australian, and Canadian Corps.

The following officers of the Operations and Intelligence branches of the General Staff of the Fourth Army have taken a very large share in the compilation of this story and in the production of the battle maps which accompany it :—

> Lt.-Col. R. M. Luckock, Royal Lancaster Regiment,
> Lt.-Col. V. Vivian, Grenadier Guards,
> Captain R. C. Berkeley, Rifle Brigade,
> Captain C. Q. Taplin, Australian Imperial Forces,
> Captain D. W. Furlong, Royal Berkshire Regiment,

and to them my sincere thanks are due.

They are also due to Lieut. E. C. Gardiner, Devonshire Regiment, attached to the General Staff, Fourth Army, who drew and prepared a large number of the maps for reproduction.

To Major A. M. Gillies, Head of the Fourth Army Printing and Stationery Services, for his help as regards the provision of photographs to illustrate the story, and to the Australian Imperial Force Publication

Department and the Canadian War Records for their kind permission to reproduce the photographs, taken by their special artists, to illustrate the part that the Australian and Canadian Corps took in the operations of the Fourth Army. To Captain F. E. Hodge, Royal Artillery, Fourth Army Artillery and Trench Mortar School, for the excellent sketches, which at much trouble to himself he has drawn especially for this book. To Sir Charles Close and Lt.-Col. W. J. Johnston, R.E., of the Ordnance Survey, Southampton, for the interest and trouble they have taken in the reproduction of the maps. To Major J. Ewing, 6th King's Own Scottish Borderers, and Lt.-Col. Cuthbert Headlam, for their assistance in checking and editing the narrative, and for many valuable suggestions. Nor must the clerks and draughtsmen of the Fourth Army Staff be forgotten, some of whom delayed their demobilisation in order to help.

This is a soldier's story of the achievements of officers and men, many of whom gave their lives or sacrificed their health in the cause of their country, and it is proposed to devote any profits that may be derived from its sale to augmenting the funds which have been raised for assisting those gallant officers who have been disabled during the Great War, to whom the British Empire owes a debt that it can never repay, and by whom the British Army has been set an example that it can never forget.

A. A. MONTGOMERY,
Major-General.

WARGRAVE,
 CAMBERLEY,
  October, 1919.

NOTE.—The titles of infantry battalions are given in full in the Orders of Battle in Appendix F, but in order to save space in the narrative the words " battalion " and " regiment " have been omitted, *e.g.*, the 7th Battalion The Queen's Royal West Surrey Regiment, 2nd Battalion Royal Dublin Fusiliers, and 1/5th Battalion Royal Warwickshire Regiment are referred to as the 7th The Queen's, 2nd Royal Dublin Fusiliers, and 1/5th Royal Warwickshire.

It will be noticed that in some cases the names of places, especially of woods and farms, are shown in English and French on the same map. This is due to our maps being in course of revision at the end of the war, but the work had not been completed. In order to avoid confusion the names of all places referred to in the text in their English form have been similarly shown on the maps which form the second volume of this book.

CONTENTS

CHAPTER I

INTRODUCTORY

Maps 1 and 2

CHAPTER II

PREPARATIONS FOR THE OFFENSIVE

Maps 1, 2, and 3

CHAPTER III

THE BATTLE OF AMIENS; THE ATTACK OF AUGUST 8TH

Maps 2 and 3 ; and Panoramic Photograph 1

CONTENTS

CHAPTER VII

THE ADVANCE TO THE HINDENBURG LINE, SEPTEMBER 5TH–28TH

Maps 1, 2, 4, 8, and 9 ; and Panoramic Photographs 4 and 5

CHAPTER VIII

THE STORMING OF THE HINDENBURG LINE, SEPTEMBER 29TH

Maps 2, 8, and 10 ; and Panoramic Photographs 6 and 7

CONTENTS

CHAPTER IX

CHAPTER X

CHAPTER XI

CHAPTER XII

THE CROSSING OF THE SAMBRE AND OISE CANAL, AND THE EVENTS LEADING UP TO THE ARMISTICE, NOVEMBER 1ST–11TH

Maps 1, 2, 16, and 17

CHAPTER XIII

CONCLUSION

APPENDICES

ILLUSTRATIONS AND MAPS

SKETCHES

By Captain F. E. Hodge

DIAGRAMS

MAPS
(*In map case*)

PANORAMIC PHOTOGRAPHS

PHOTOGRAPHS

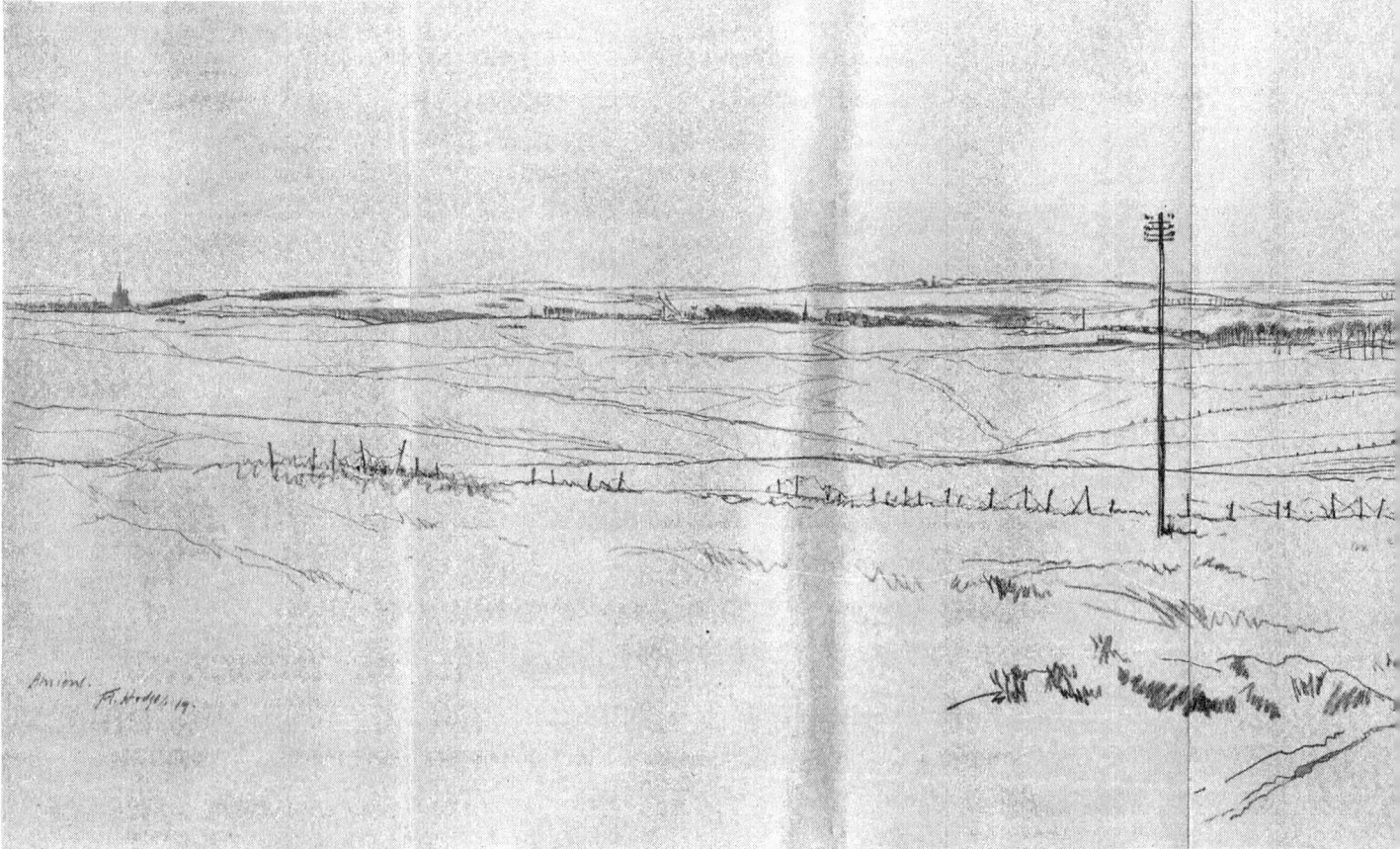

Amiens Cathedral   Glisy   Daours   Allonville   Aubigny   Hallue Valley

Panorama looking north-west

Poplars on Amiens—Albert road   Lahoussoye and
               Fouilloy   Bois D'Escardonneuse   Corbie Church

Villers Bretonneux—Corbie road

from VILLERS BRETONNEUX

THE STORY OF THE FOURTH ARMY

CHAPTER I

INTRODUCTORY

Maps 1 and 2

The value of moral—Human nature—The situation in front of Amiens at the end of March, 1918—The loss of Villers Bretonneux, April 24th—A comparison with the Waterloo campaign—The recapture of Villers Bretonneux—Events on other parts of the Western front in April, May, June, and July—The first signs of the weakening of the moral of the German Army—The situation on the Fourth Army front after April 24th—The Australians—The capture of Hamel on July 4th, and its lessons—Plans for a counter-offensive—The surprise attack on August 8th—The Third and Tenth French Armies and the Third British Army join in the offensive—The complete loss of the initiative by the Germans—The British moral—The First British Army extends the front of attack to the north—The crisis of the counter-offensive, September 26th-29th—The capture of the Hindenburg Line—The crossing of the Selle and Sambre rivers—German demoralisation—The Armistice—General Ludendorff and German moral.

ALTHOUGH the story of the Fourth Army in the Battles of the Hundred Days, strictly speaking, begins with the attack on August 8th, the events of the previous four months had such an important bearing on the subsequent operations that something more than a passing reference to them is essential.

While it is now realised that the moral effect of the successful attack of the Fourth Army on August 8th directly influenced the fighting spirit of the whole of the British Army in France, it is not

The value of moral

so generally known that this victory could not have been won without the steady and continuous offensive of the Australian Corps throughout the months of April, May, June, and July. To its remarkable achievements during these months may be attributed to a very large extent the increase in moral, which was necessary in order to make the battle of August 8th a complete success, or even a possibility.

The incalculable value of moral stands out as the greatest of the many lessons that are impressed on us by the period from March 21st to the Battle of Amiens and the months that followed. We most of us remember Napoleon's dictum that " in war moral force is to the physical as 3 to 1," but it has been the good fortune of few soldiers to witness so remarkable an example of the truth of this maxim.

As Col. Henderson tells us [1]—" Human nature, the paramount

[1] " The Science of War." " Notes on Wellington," p. 101.

consideration of either tactics or strategy, remains unaltered. The art of generalship, the art of command, whether the force be large or small, is the art of dealing with human nature." And again,[1]

Human nature " the first thing is to realise that in war we have to do not so much with numbers, arms, and manœuvres as with human nature. What did Napoleon find in the history of the campaigns of Alexander, Hannibal, and Julius Cæsar ? Not merely a record of marches and manœuvres, of the use of entrenchments, or of the general principles of attack and defence. No, he found in those campaigns a complete study of human nature under the conditions that exist in war, human nature affected by discipline, by fear, by the need of food, by want of confidence, by over confidence, by the weight of responsibility, by political interests, by patriotism, by distrust, and by many other things."

Those who followed the anxious days of March and April, 1918, the dawn of brighter days in May and June, and the final fulfilment of their hopes in August, September, and October, have seen these things for themselves. These months will live in military history for all time. They are yet one more proof of the great Corsican's knowledge of men and war, and a lasting testimony to the value of Col. Henderson's writings.

It will be remembered that the Fifth Army, attacked by overwhelming odds on March 21st, had, in spite of a determined resistance, been driven

The situation in front of Amiens at the end of March, 1918 back to the neighbourhood of Amiens. It had suffered heavy losses, the men were physically exhausted after ten days of continuous marching and fighting, and for the time being their moral had been seriously affected. But they were not a beaten army. They required rest and sleep, and, when they obtained these, it was astonishing to see how quickly they recovered, and thus demonstrated once again the indomitable spirit of the British soldier.

On March 28th, when the Fifth Army Headquarters were relieved by the Fourth Army Headquarters,[2] the situation about Amiens was found to be extremely critical. Not only had all reserves been absorbed into the firing line some days previously, but a considerable part of the actual firing line itself consisted of a force,[3] rapidly improvised from elements of different units and in many cases under strange officers, hastily thrown together in the emergency to oppose the enemy's further advance. The Germans continued to press forward, but, fortunately, the greater part of the Cavalry Corps and the 9th Australian Brigade arrived to reinforce the Fourth Army, and brought the enemy's advance to a halt until April 4th and 5th, when a strong German attack drove back our line once again to a point on the eastern outskirts of Villers Bretonneux. Here, thanks principally to the timely arrival of three more Australian brigades, the line remained stationary until April 24th, on which date the enemy made his final attempt to capture Amiens.

Attacking after a heavy bombardment and assisted by tanks, the

[1] " The Science of War." " Lessons from the Past for the Present," p. 174.

[2] The Fourth Army Headquarters were re-formed for this purpose under General Sir Henry Rawlinson, who, for the previous six weeks, had been the British Representative of the Supreme War Council at Versailles.

[3] Known as " Carey's Force."

VILLERS BRETONNEUX, AS SEEN FROM THE GERMAN LINES.

By kind permission of the Australian Government.

Germans in the early hours of the morning succeeded in capturing Villers Bretonneux. The possession of this village and of the neighbouring high

The loss of Villers Bretonneux, April 24th ground enabled the Germans to obtain direct observation down the valley of the Somme almost as far as Amiens, and of part of the Hallue valley. It was a tactical locality of vital importance to the defence of Amiens, and, in German hands, constituted a direct menace to the junction between the French and British Armies.

Just as in the Waterloo Campaign of 1815 the separation of Wellington's and Blücher's Armies, and their defeat in detail, was the paramount

A comparison with the Waterloo Campaign object of Napoleon's strategy, so in March and April, 1918, the best means, by which the Germans could hope to gain a decisive victory, lay in forcing the British and French Armies asunder at the outset of the campaign.[1]

As soon as the news of the loss of Villers Bretonneux reached Army Headquarters, Sir Henry Rawlinson decided to retake the village at all costs, and every available reserve at his disposal was employed for this purpose. These were little enough, and consisted of the 13th and 15th Australian Brigades, the 54th Brigade of the 18th Division reinforced by a battalion of the 58th Division, and two battalions of the 8th Division.

All the battalions of the 8th, 18th, and 58th Divisions employed had already suffered severely during the retreat, especially in experienced officers, and had had little or no time to absorb the drafts of young soldiers they had received. Moreover, heavy concentrations of Yellow Cross gas[2] on Villers Bretonneux and L'Abbé Wood had caused severe casualties to the 8th and 58th Divisions on April 22nd.

The counter-attack, which was organised by the III Corps at very short notice and under great difficulties, was launched at 10 p.m. on the

The recapture of Villers Bretonneux same day as the attack, and was executed in a most brilliant manner in spite of the darkness. It was greatly assisted by the determined manner in which the 5th Australian Division had maintained its position all day on the high ground immediately north of Villers Bretonneux. This division had learnt one valuable lesson of the March fighting, that, if part of a defensive line is forced back, it is essential for the rest of the line, and especially that part on the flanks of the breach, to hold firm. " Conforming," or " withdrawing," so as to straighten the line was not part

[1] As regards this, there are several questions which are of intense interest, but which it is at present impossible to decide with the information as yet available.

First, what degree of importance did General Ludendorff actually place on the separation of the French and British Armies ?

Secondly, how near did the Germans come to the attainment of this object ?

Lastly, instead of putting in large reserves to follow up the German success on the Lys on April 9th, would it have been possible for General Ludendorff to have directed his reserves against Amiens early in that month, and, if so, would he have achieved his purpose ?

Future historians will doubtless find an ample field for discussion on these points when further evidence from the German records is available. It would appear, however, that in changing his strategic objective in April, General Ludendorff committed an error which eventually brought about his undoing, and at the same time saved the Allies from a situation which might well have cost them the war.

Since this story was written, General Ludendorff's Memoirs have been published, but they do not appear to give a satisfactory answer to these questions.

[2] Commonly known as " Mustard Gas."

of its programme.   It realised that, if the flanks of the breach hold firm, the enemy who has penetrated has both his flanks exposed and is at the mercy of a well-organised counter-attack ; also, that the force that has broken through cannot receive efficient artillery support, owing to the ignorance of its gunners as to the exact position of the infantry they are supporting.

As the result of this brilliant counter-attack, carried out by the Australians and well supported by the divisions of the III Corps, the village of Villers Bretonneux was recaptured together with 900 prisoners, and Amiens was saved.   This is an excellent example of the value of a counter-attack delivered with all available forces before the enemy has had time to establish himself and organise the defence.   Hesitation and delay would have permitted the Germans to establish themselves firmly in their newly-won positions, their artillery would have been ready to rake all approaches to the village, and daylight on the 25th would have found the position practically impregnable against the limited forces which were at the disposal of the Fourth Army Commander.

Unfortunately, the First French Army, which had lost the village of Hangard at the same time as we had lost Villers Bretonneux, was unable to launch its counter-attack in conjunction with that of the III Corps. For various reasons it was postponed until next morning.   In spite of the greatest gallantry and self-sacrifice on the part of the troops engaged, it failed, and Hangard village remained in German hands until August 8th.[1]

The attack on April 24th was the last attempt made by the Germans to break through the defences of Amiens, and, although this front was prepared and maintained as an offensive one for some time, false strategy and more attractive objectives on other parts of the front relieved the Amiens area from any further hostile pressure.

Meanwhile, the German attack on the Lys, which had begun on April 9th, continued and drew in the enemy's available reserves.   As

Events on other parts of the Western front in April, May, June, and July

each fresh division made its appearance in the northern theatre, so did it become more and more evident that the enemy did not intend to press his menace at Amiens, and the spirits of the troops in this area continued to rise in proportion to the opportunities for rest and training thus afforded.

On May 27th, the great German offensive in Champagne was launched, followed on June 9th by an attack towards Compiègne from the Montdidier direction.   Both were brought to a standstill after the first successful rush.

Then ensued an anxious period of waiting until it was possible to discover on which portion of the Allied front the next great German onslaught would be delivered.   As time went on, it became evident that it would be directed against the French on either side of Rheims.   During this period our information was excellent, and it soon became clear, from the preparations that were being made, that every man and gun that could be made available would take part in this decisive attack, on

[1] This counter-attack was carried out by the famous Moroccan Division, consisting of four regiments, and of which the Foreign Legion formed a part.

The RED CHATEAU at VILLER

L'Abbé Wood

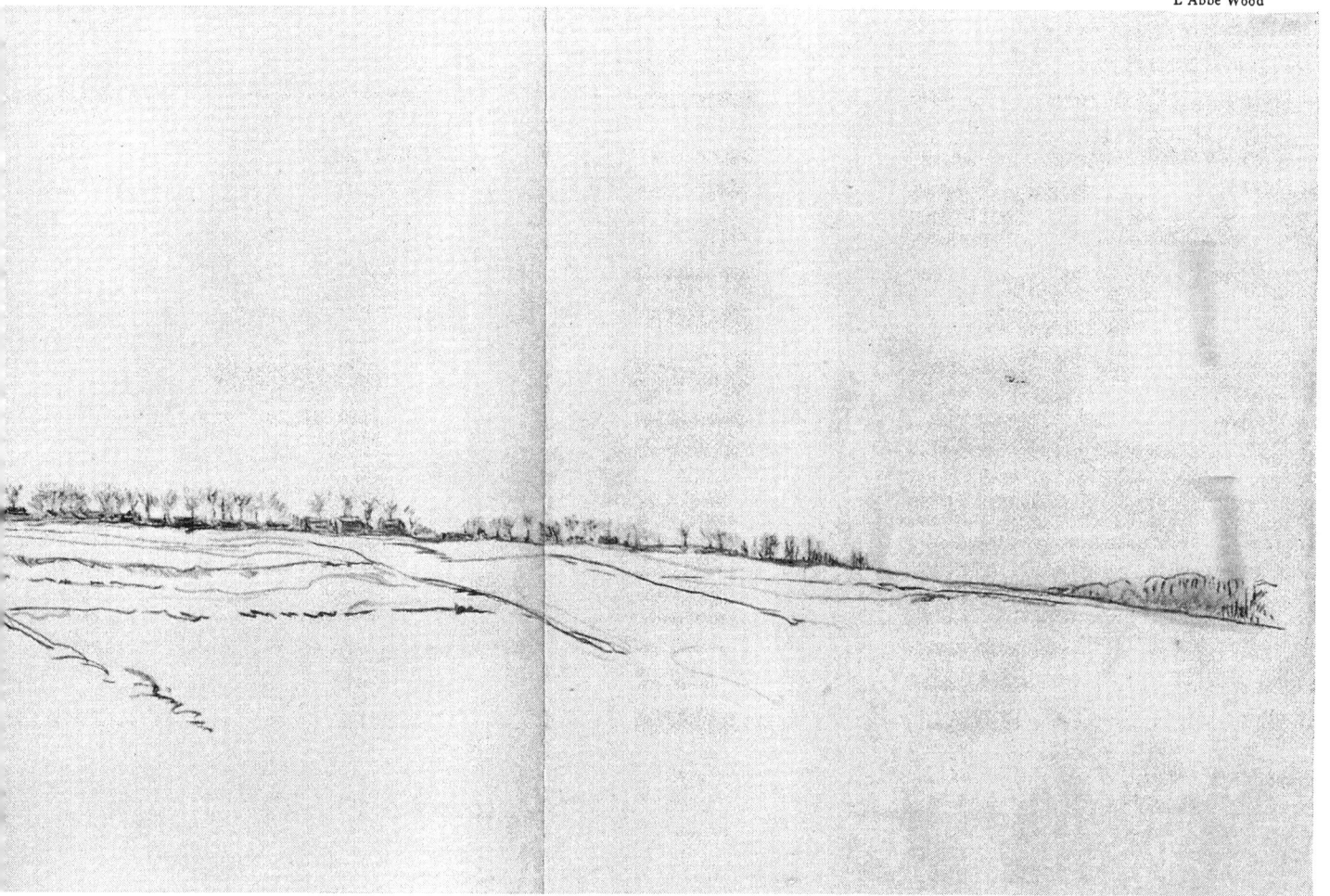

BRETONNEUX from the CORBIE road

which the Germans were about to risk their all, and that other fronts would be correspondingly weakened. General Foch [1] made his dispositions accordingly.

On July 15th the blow fell. How General Gouraud foiled the offensive east of Rheims, how the Germans, at first successful west of Rheims, succeeded in crossing the Marne, and how on July 18th General Mangin's counter-attack from the direction of Villers Cotterets Forest drove the enemy back in confusion over the Marne, is now well-known history.

It was clear to those who had watched the course of events and had studied the losses and the state of moral of the German Army that the **The first signs of the** crisis was over and that the time for the Allied counter-**weakening of the moral** offensive was approaching, if indeed it had not already **of the German Army** arrived. Moreover, the Germans, in addition to serious errors in strategy, had made the fatal mistake of underrating their opponents, and especially the power of recuperation of the British Army. Although acting perfectly correctly in weakening their forces on other fronts so as to mass all available reserves for their main attack, they had made no serious effort to improve their defences on the weakened portions of the line. In front of Amiens their defences were especially weak, and nothing had been done to improve them, although it might well have been realised that this omission gave the Allies an opening for a counter-stroke of which it was more than probable that full advantage would be taken.

Meanwhile, on the Fourth Army front, the situation after April 24th had rapidly improved, and, thanks to the indefatigable labours of officers **The situation on the** and men, the defences of Amiens had daily grown in **Fourth Army front** strength. Long lines of trenches and innumerable belts **after April 24th** of wire and machine-gun dug-outs covered all the country between Albert and Amiens. Battalions had improved in strength and training. The whole of the Australian Corps, with the exception of the 1st Australian Division, which was still up in the north, had by now joined the Fourth Army and held the sector from south of Villers Bretonneux to the Ancre, whilst the III Corps, consisting of the 18th, 47th, and 58th Divisions, held the remainder of the army front to just north of Albert. The weather was fine; the men when out of the line could enjoy good fishing and bathing in the Somme, and they were afforded excellent opportunities for rest, training, and recreation.

The Australians, always inquisitive, seldom idle, and with the greatest contempt for " Fritz," very soon began a series of inroads into the German lines which had a very important effect on **The Australians** subsequent operations. These minor operations and raids, some fourteen in number in May and June, met with encouraging success. Not only did they gradually improve the position of our line and give us many prisoners, but they established a moral superiority over the Germans that was to be of the greatest value in the future. No sooner had the Germans dug and wired a new front

---

[1] He was created Marshal of France on August 10th.

and support trench than, under a surprise barrage, the Australians captured them and repulsed any attempt at their recovery. The Germans had perforce to begin all their work over again and construct a new front line, which, in its turn, before long passed into the possession of the Australians.

Towards the end of June, the situation had so much improved that Sir Henry Rawlinson decided that the Australians should undertake an operation on a somewhat larger scale. This had for its objective the capture of the village of Hamel and Vaire Wood, together with an important ridge east of these two localities. The capture of this ridge, he considered, would materially improve our line by giving it more depth, would furnish us with better observation, and would deny to the enemy observation of much of the Somme valley. Moreover, he considered that the attack would test not only the strength of the enemy's defences, but also the state of the German moral, which was already under considerable suspicion. It would further form a good trial run for an offensive on a still larger scale, should it be desirable to carry out such an operation finally to disengage Amiens. A most important factor, however, at that time was the question of man power. In this respect the situation was serious, and it was not advisable, nor even possible, for us to incur heavy casualties. Fortunately, the terrain about Hamel was almost ideal for the employment of tanks, and, by using these in the closest possible touch with the infantry, it was hoped that casualties would be reduced to a minimum. Sir Henry Rawlinson decided, therefore, to attack on a very wide front, compared with those adopted in the offensives of 1916 and 1917, and to employ as few infantry as possible in the firing line. Six battalions attacked on a front of 6,000 yards[1] supported by sixty tanks, whose task it was to deal with whatever opposition might escape the barrage. The success of the operation, and the number of casualties incurred, would, it was felt, very largely depend on the degree of surprise attained. As the German defences were known to be weak, and there was little wire, no preliminary bombardment was considered necessary, and, in consequence, it was possible, with due precautions, to carry out all the preparations up to the moment of assault without attracting attention.

The attack, which came as a complete surprise, was delivered at dawn on July 4th and was entirely successful. Four companies of the

The capture of Hamel on July 4th, and its lessons 33rd American Division were attached to the attacking Australian battalions and added further glory to the American flag on Independence Day. All objectives were gained with astonishingly small loss, and all counter-attacks were easily driven off. The Australians had outfought the Germans at every point.

This operation conclusively proved several important points, which, up to that time, had been in doubt. It became clear that the German infantry, even though it had not been subjected on July 4th to the terrors of a preliminary bombardment, was no longer the formidable foe in defence

[1] 1,200 to 2,000 yards was looked upon as a suitable frontage to allot to a division in the offensives of 1916 and 1917.

AN AUSTRALIAN PLATOON RECEIVING INSTRUCTIONS FROM ITS COMMANDER PRIOR TO AN ATTACK.

By kind permission of the Australian Government.

AUSTRALIANS, AND AMERICANS OF THE 33RD (ILLINOIS) DIVISION, RESTING
NEAR CORBIE ON THEIR WAY UP TO THE LINE ON JULY 3RD.

that it had been in 1916 and 1917, and that the German defences, judged by previous standards, did not count for much. It was also obvious that, under the conditions obtaining on the Fourth Army front, a well organised attack, carried out by determined men and supported by tanks well trained with the infantry beforehand, had every chance of breaking right through the enemy's defences. Lastly, it proved that, given the element of surprise, an attack of this nature could be successful without incurring the heavy losses to which we had become accustomed in previous years.[1] It was a good omen for the future.

By July 16th there were good grounds for thinking that the last great German effort would definitely fail, and that the opportunity for a successful counter-offensive by the Allies would

Plans for a counter-offensive shortly arise. Everything indeed appeared to favour an early offensive, and it was certain that the Germans, after the failure of their great attack in Champagne on July 15th, would be in a state of despondency.

For an offensive, the object of which was to gain a decisive success, there was probably no sector on the whole Allied front which presented such favourable conditions at that particular time as that held by the Fourth Army. The situation, both as regards the forces opposed to us and the terrain, was ideal for an attack on a large scale. Moreover, if successful, the attack was bound to have very far-reaching results and was, therefore, well worth considerable risks, for it would render Amiens safe once and for all, and thus secure the junction of the British and French Armies. Further, it would directly threaten the communications of the German Armies facing the First and Third French Armies. In the light of after events the correctness of these forecasts has been clearly proved.

The plan for an attack on the Fourth Army front was submitted to General Headquarters on July 17th, was approved by Sir Douglas Haig, and received General Foch's approval a week later with some minor modifications which will be referred to later.

So far as one can judge, no surprise has ever been more complete than was that of the Germans on August 8th. It is astonishing that this should have been so, for, between July 30th and

The surprise attack on August 8th August 8th, the Cavalry Corps of three divisions, fourteen divisions of infantry, over 2,000 guns, and some 450 tanks were concentrated east of Amiens on a front of about ten miles, within striking distance of the unsuspecting von der Marwitz,[2] who commanded the opposing German Army.

The actual attack, carried out on the same lines as the attack of July 4th, though on a much larger scale, went without a hitch. The cavalry, after its many disappointments in previous offensives, at last found its opportunity. The Germans were swept off their feet

[1] The actual casualties incurred on July 4th were 1,030, while the prisoners taken amounted to 1,472.
[2] General von der Marwitz commanded the Second Army ; General von Hutier commanded the Eighteenth Army immediately to the south of the Second Army. They were the two commanders who had been most successful in March, and General von Hutier was also the victor of Riga.

and never really recovered from the overwhelming nature of the disaster.[1]

The attack of the Fourth Army assisted the First French Army to capture the important high ground north of Moreuil. This, together with the further success of the First French Army, as it advanced on the right of the Fourth Army, enabled the Third French Army, and then the Tenth French Army, to press forward in turn. On August 21st, when the advance of the Fourth Army reached the level of Albert, the Third British Army widened the front of attack to the north, and from then onwards continuous pressure was kept up along almost the whole of the British, and the greater part of the French and American fronts.

The Third and Tenth French Armies, and the Third British Army join in the offensive

The additional impetus given to the offensive by the participation of the Third British Army not only resulted in the capture of Bapaume and the turning of the Somme defences from the north, but also greatly discouraged the already dispirited troops of the enemy, and added enormously to the difficulties and embarrassments of the German Great General Staff. The enemy had now lost the initiative beyond all hope of recovery, and was forced by our successes to carry out an extensive withdrawal of his forces from the Lys salient. Reserves were flung into the line piecemeal, as our attacks developed, without time or consideration for their most useful employment.

The complete loss of the initiative by the Germans

---

[1] It is interesting to note the great importance General Ludendorff attaches in his Memoirs to this attack of August 8th. " August 8th," he says, " was the black day of the German Army in the history of the War. . . . Early on August 8th in a dense fog, that had been rendered still thicker by artificial means, the British, mainly with Australian and Canadian divisions, and French attacked between Albert and Moreuil with strong squadrons of tanks, but for the rest, in no great superiority. They broke between the Somme and the Luce stream deep into our front. The divisions in line at that point allowed themselves to be completely overwhelmed. Divisional staffs were surprised in their headquarters by enemy tanks. . . . The exhausted divisions that had been relieved a few days earlier, and that were lying in the region south-west of Péronne were immediately alarmed and set in motion by the Commander-in-Chief of the Second Army. At the same time he brought forward towards the breach by any means all available troops. The Rupprecht Army Group dispatched reserves thither by train. The Eighteenth Army threw its own reserves directly into the battle from the south-east and pushed other forces forward in the region north-west of Roye. On an order from me the Ninth Army too, although itself in danger, had to contribute. . . . By the early hours of the forenoon of August 8th I had already gained a complete impression of the situation. It was a very gloomy one. I immediately dispatched a General Staff officer to the battlefield in order to obtain a view of the condition of the troops. . . . Six or seven divisions, that were quite fairly to be described as effective, had been completely battered. Three or four others, together with the remnants of the battered divisions, were available for closing the broad gap between Bray and Roye. . . . The wastage in the Second Army had been very great. Heavy toll had also been taken of its reserves, when these were thrown in. In the case of some divisions the infantry had had to go into the line straight out of their motor lorries, while their artillery was lined up elsewhere. Units were badly mixed up. It was to be foreseen that a further number of divisions had become necessary to reinforce the Second Army, even if the enemy should not attack again, a prospect upon which we could not count with any assurance. Owing, in addition, to the deficit created by the number of prisoners taken from us, our losses had reached such proportions that the supreme command was once more faced with the necessity of having to disband a further series of divisions in order to furnish drafts. Our reserves were diminishing. As against all this there had been an only uncommonly slight expenditure of strength on the part of the enemy. The relative man-power had shifted appreciably further to our disadvantage. . . . All we could do was to put off the inevitable. We had absolutely to be prepared for a continuation of the enemy's attacks. He had been allowed to score too cheaply. . . . August 8th marked the decline of our fighting power, and, the man-power situation being what it was, it robbed me of the hope of discovering some strategic expedient that might once more stabilise the position in our favour. . . . The war would have to be ended."

See " My War Memories, 1914–1918," by General Ludendorff. Vol. ii, p. 679 *et seq.*

Upon our own troops in other parts of the line the record of these rapid and brilliant successes had a most inspiriting effect. Until

The British moral

August 8th the general feeling among officers and men was that the complete repulse of the enemy and the preparation for a triumphant campaign in 1919, by which time the weight of the rapidly increasing American Army would have turned the scale definitely in our favour, was the most that could be hoped for. Officers and men now saw with amazement that the enemy was being driven back almost as rapidly as he had advanced, and hopes ran high that the enemy's defeat would be complete before the end of the year. Local enterprises were accordingly undertaken against the enemy with eagerness and vigour, and it became clear that the demoralisation and depression of the enemy had spread far beyond the zone covered by the operations of the Fourth and Third Armies.

The results of the Battles of Amiens and Bapaume gave the opportunity for the First Army to join in the onslaught. Accordingly, on

The First British Army extends the front of attack to the north

August 26th, the battle was extended north to the Sensée and Scarpe, and on September 2nd the difficult and formidable Drocourt–Quéant line was brilliantly stormed, and the enemy thrown into precipitate retreat.

Under the combined and continuous pressure of the three armies the enemy, fighting tenaciously but unsuccessfully, was driven back to the strongly fortified zone of defences known as the Hindenburg Line, which was his main line of resistance, and upon the maintenance of which his hold on France and Belgium depended.

The crisis of our counter-offensive had now been reached. The inability of the Germans to check the advance, and the accumulating

The crisis of the counter-offensive, September 26th–29th

evidence of their growing demoralisation and disorganisation, proved conclusively that the time had come for the Allies to deliver the decisive blow without delay. Marshal Foch and Sir Douglas Haig lost no time in taking advantage of their opportunity. Four convergent and simultaneous attacks were delivered between September 26th and 29th.

In the Argonne and to the east, the French and American forces attacked the enemy and pressed them steadily back in the direction of Mezières. In Flanders, the Passchendaele Ridge, the scene of so much laborious and bitter fighting in 1917, was crossed in one day by the Belgian forces and the Second British Army under the command of King Albert.

The main and most critical attack was that delivered by the First, Third, and Fourth Armies against the Hindenburg Line. The attack

The capture of the Hindenburg Line

was a magnificent success and opened the way for the rapid and complete defeat of the enemy.

With the breach in the Hindenburg Line the enemy lost his last and most strongly prepared position, and he had no alternative but to withdraw his forces along the entire front. From now onwards, he endeavoured to make use of semi-prepared and natural positions to resist our advance for a period sufficiently long to enable him to carry out his withdrawal in good order.

c

Our troops, however, flushed with constant success and eager to transform the defeat into a rout, pursued the retreating enemy with the

The crossing of the Selle and Sambre rivers

utmost vigour and determination. Against the dash and resolution of our men no obstacles were of any avail. The battles on the Selle and Sambre rivers brought only new victories to our arms, and the Lys failed to check our progress in Flanders.

The embarrassment and bewilderment of the German Great General Staff increased daily. All reserves were used up. Many of the German

German demoralisation

battalions could not be relied upon to fight, and even in the case of the machine-gunners, hitherto the back-bone of the defence, the will to resist had vanished. After November 4th the withdrawal became a rout. In the words of Sir Douglas Haig's Victory Despatch, " The enemy was falling back without coherent plan in widespread disorder and confusion."

The destruction of the German Army was only averted by the signing of the armistice on November 11th. When a stroke of the pen put an end

The Armistice

to hostilities, the town of Mons, whence had begun the epic retreat of the " Old Contemptibles " in the autumn of 1914, was, by a fitting coincidence, once more in British hands. The forces of the enemy were still on foreign soil, but the utter demoralisation of his army is clearly evidenced by the terms which Germany was forced to sign before the armistice was granted. The armistice was, in fact, a capitulation, and is the best testimony to the value of the series of successes which began with the victory of August 8th.

NOTE TO CHAPTER I.—GENERAL LUDENDORFF AND GERMAN MORAL

As has been pointed out in this chapter, there was a feeling in the Fourth Army during July that the German Army had reached its limit of endurance, and that the bubble of its invincibility only required pricking. August 8th and the days that followed strengthened the impression and caused it to spread throughout the British Army. General Ludendorff's Memoirs confirm it. Seldom has the commander of large forces admitted defeat, and given the reasons for such defeat, in clearer language. The German High Command had lost all hope of victory, all hope even of staving off inevitable disaster. When those in supreme command are overcome with such feelings of despair as are expressed by General Ludendorff, then the forces which they control are indeed lost. History teaches us that it is the spirit of the commander almost more than anything else which affects the moral of an Army. It was the unconquerable spirit of Frederick the Great in the face of disaster that saved Prussia from destruction in the Silesian Wars, and again in the Seven Years' War. It was the magnetism of Napoleon that kept the half-starved, ragged conscripts of 1814 in the field so long against five or six times their number. Again, it was their wonderful faith in Lee's genius that maintained the moral of the Confederate soldiers, even when the enemy was within a few miles of Richmond. When one reads these Memoirs of General Ludendorff and thinks of the great commanders of the past, can one be surprised that the moral of the German Army was crumbling, that the officers had lost faith in their men, and the men in their officers ?

To students of Col. Henderson's " Stonewall Jackson " and " The Science of War," the story of August 8th and the subsequent three months' fighting will appeal with especial force. It bears out those imperishable maxims of war that Col. Henderson devoted his unique literary powers to impressing on the minds of British officers. " Wellington knew well," he says,[1] " that the issue of battles lies in the hearts of men—in the heart of the Commander even more than in the heart of the soldiers—and that human nature, even when disciplined, is peculiarly susceptible to a strong, sudden, and sustained attack." And again a few pages later,[2] " What could be more valuable than to have learned so thoroughly, that its application has become instinctive, the following principle. Always endeavour to mystify and mislead your enemy whether you are attacking or defending ; if you can surprise your enemy's General, his army is already defeated."

[1] " The Science of War," " Notes on Wellington," p. 97.
[2] *Ibid.*, p. 102.

GROUP TAKEN AT THE HEADQUARTERS OF THE FOURTH ARMY, AT FLIXECOURT, ON AUGUST 13TH, 1918, ON THE OCCASION OF THE VISIT OF HIS MAJESTY THE KING.

1. General Sir Henry Rawlinson, Commanding Fourth Army
2. General Debeney, Commanding First French Army
3. General Weygand, Chief of the Staff to Marshal Foch
4. Marshal Foch, Commander-in-Chief of the Allied Forces
5. His Majesty the King
6. Lieutenant-General Sir Herbert Lawrence, Chief of the Staff to Field-Marshal Sir Douglas Haig
7. Major-General H. C. Holman, D.A. and Q.M.G. Fourth Army
8. Field-Marshal Sir Douglas Haig, Commander-in-Chief of the British Armies in France.
9. The Lord Stamfordham, Private Secretary to His Majesty the King
10. Major-General C. E. D. Budworth, G.O.C., R.A., Fourth Army
11. Major-General R. U. H. Buckland. Chief Engineer, Fourth Army
12. General Petain, Commander-in-Chief of the French Armies in France
13. Major-General A. A. Montgomery, General Staff, Fourth Army
14. Sir Derek Keppel, Equerry to His Majesty the King
15. General Fayolle, Commanding the Group of French Armies in Reserve

British official photograph.

CHAPTER II

PREPARATIONS FOR THE OFFENSIVE

Maps 1, 2, and 3

The situation in the middle of July on the Fourth Army front—The concentration of troops—The reorganisation of the front prior to the attack—The nature of the country—The hostile defences—The strength and moral of the enemy—The strategic objectives of the attack—Secrecy, the basis of the plan of attack—The conditions affecting the plan—The frontage of the attack—The objectives—The synchronisation of the attack—The allotment of tanks—The rôle of the cavalry—The rôle of the Royal Air Force—The rôle of the artillery, engineers, and Machine Gun Corps—The issue of maps and photographs—The danger of hostile gas shelling during the assembly of troops—Minor hostile attacks on August 3rd and August 6th—The assembly of the troops—The forming up of the infantry—The hour of " zero "—The confidence of the troops.

THE belief that the conditions on the Fourth Army front were extremely favourable for the carrying out of a successful offensive on a large scale had been growing rapidly since July 4th. In addition to the moral superiority which had been attained by the Australians over the enemy, the German divisions on this front were known to be weak in numbers. Scarcely one had more than 3,000 effectives in its ranks, with the correspondingly lowering result on their fighting spirit that almost always accompanies reduced strengths ; nor was there any considerable body of reserves behind this front. There were no well-organised systems of defence, and, judging by those captured by the Australian Corps on July 4th, the German trenches were badly constructed, and were protected with little wire. Lastly, the terrain was extremely favourable for an offensive with a distant objective limited only by the physical powers of endurance of horse and man. The country was open and undulating ; the hard soil, with chalk very near to the surface, rendered it particularly favourable for tanks and cavalry. The chances of the successful employment of these arms were further increased by the absence of shell craters and by the dry weather of the preceding months. The observation available from our positions was excellent and favoured our artillery action ; good artillery positions were numerous, and the general lie of the country afforded covered lines of approach, which favoured a surprise attack.

On July 17th, Sir Henry Rawlinson submitted to the Commander-in-Chief his proposals for the attack, and on July 23rd, after some discussion, the plan[1] was approved, with some minor modifications, by

[1] The original proposal put forward by Sir Henry Rawlinson was that the Fourth Army should take over from the French as far south as Moreuil, and should carry out an attack on the whole of this front from Moreuil to Morlancourt. He considered that, for reasons of secrecy,

11

Sir Douglas Haig and General Foch. It was decided that the First French Army on the right should participate in the attack with the Fourth Army, and, to ensure close co-operation, General Foch placed the First French Army directly under the orders of Sir Douglas Haig. On July 26th Sir Henry Rawlinson received instructions from the Commander-in-Chief to press on the preparations for the attack, the date of which was fixed for August 10th, but subsequently advanced to August 8th.

At the end of July, the Fourth Army was composed as follows :

The III Corps, comprising the 12th, 18th,[1] 47th, and 58th Divisions, together with the 33rd American Division, which was attached for training but had not yet been in the line.

The concentration of troops

The Australian Corps,[2] comprising the 2nd, 3rd, 4th, and 5th Australian Divisions.

The 3rd Cavalry Division.

The 5th Brigade, Royal Air Force, comprising eleven squadrons.

The 5th Brigade, Tank Corps, comprising three battalions, two of which had taken part in the operations at Hamel on July 4th.

The artillery in the army, which totalled about 1,000 guns, consisted of 23 field artillery brigades, 13 garrison artillery brigades, and 10 long-range siege batteries.

By August 8th, the Fourth Army had been reinforced by five infantry divisions (1st Australian, 1st, 2nd, 3rd, and 4th Canadian), two cavalry divisions (1st and 2nd), six squadrons of the Royal Air Force, nine battalions of tanks, together with another 1,000 guns, the final strength and distribution being :—

The III Corps : Commanded by Lieut.-Gen. Sir Richard Butler.
    12th, 18th, 47th, and 58th Divisions, with the 33rd American Division attached.
The Australian Corps : Commanded by Lieut.-Gen. Sir John Monash.
    1st, 2nd, 3rd, 4th, and 5th Australian Divisions.
The Canadian Corps : Commanded by Lieut.-Gen. Sir Arthur Currie.
    1st, 2nd, 3rd, and 4th Canadian Divisions.
The Cavalry Corps : Commanded by Lieut.-Gen. Sir Charles Kavanagh.
    1st, 2nd, and 3rd Cavalry Divisions.

simplification in the co-ordination of the hour of attack, barrages, etc., it would be preferable to have the whole arrangements in the hands of troops of one nationality. Past experience had shown that, with the best will in the world on both sides, a combined attack by French and British troops was always more difficult to co-ordinate and keep secret than one which was entirely in the hands of a French or British Commander, controlling only his own troops. Sir Henry Raw-linson suggested that General Debeney, commanding the First French Army, should employ his available troops towards his right, and that, when the British attack had been successful and had thrown the German defence into confusion, General Debeney should attack northwards from the direction of Montdidier. He considered that this plan would, if successful, lead to greater strategical results. General Foch decided against this proposal, as he considered that better results would be obtained by a joint attack by both armies from the same direction.

[1] The 12th and 18th Divisions, though in the III Corps area, were earmarked for general reserve in case of emergency. They were released from general reserve at the end of July.

[2] The 1st Australian Division was still in the north, where it had been sent early in the spring to reinforce the Second Army during the Lys battle, and had greatly distinguished itself in the fighting round Hazebrouck.

The 5th Brigade, Royal Air Force:
    15th (Corps) Wing, six corps squadrons.
    22nd (Army) Wing, eight scout squadrons; three bombing
        squadrons.
The 3rd, 4th, and 5th Brigades, Tank Corps:
    12 Tank Battalions, of which eight were equipped with Mark V,
        two with Mark V star, and two with whippet tanks.

The large majority of the additional units and formations, which were concentrated during the eight days prior to the attack, were moved into the area by train; the cavalry, whippet tanks, and a portion of the artillery moving by road. Altogether about 230 special trains for personnel and guns, as well as upwards of 60 special trains for ammunition, were run into the Fourth Army area, in addition to the ordinary supply trains for food and engineer material. If it is remembered that only two railway lines were available, one along the coast via Etaples and Abbeville and the other via St. Pol and Doullens, that all movements from detraining stations had to take place during the hours of darkness, and that the utmost secrecy had to be maintained by all concerned in the moves, the amount of work thrown on the administrative services will be fully realised. The fact that the concentration was carried out and that the formations moved into their places of assembly without a hitch and entirely unsuspected by the enemy, was not the least remarkable feature in the story of the battles of the hundred days.

In addition to the troops already mentioned, the 17th, 32nd, and 63rd Divisions were assembled close behind the battle front, in general reserve in the hands of the Commander-in-Chief, in order to maintain the fight and to take full advantage of any success gained. Other divisions were also held in positions of readiness in rear of the remainder of the British front, with a view to their being moved to the battle front as circumstances required. By August 8th, the 17th Division was concentrated behind the Australian Corps, the 63rd Division behind the III Corps, and the 32nd Division in rear of the Canadian Corps. Of these three divisions, the 32nd Division was subsequently released from general reserve and placed at the disposal of the Canadian Corps, the 17th Division was employed to hold a portion of the line on the front of the Australian Corps for a few days during a lull in the fighting, whilst the 63rd Division was not used on the front of the Fourth Army.

On August 1st, the front held by the Fourth Army extended from Monument Wood, just south of Villers Bretonneux, where junction was made with the First French Army, to the high ground north of Albert, where the Fourth Army joined the Third Army; the total front being about 21,000 yards. The front was held by two corps; on the south the Australian Corps held from the southern boundary to the river Ancre, and the III Corps thence to the junction with the Third Army. Before the attack it was necessary to take over about 7,000 yards of front from the First French Army, and to readjust the corps boundaries of the Australian and III Corps. On the night of July 31st, therefore, the III Corps

The reorganisation of the front prior o the attack

extended its front southwards and took over as far as the Somme. This addition to the III Corps front included the high tongue of land about Morlancourt, on which so many of the successful enterprises of the Australian Corps had been carried out during the preceding months. In fact, as lately as July 29th, the Australian Corps had advanced its line on a front of 2,500 yards, capturing the important ground overlooking Morlancourt and adding considerably to the depth of the defence of the plateau. During the nights of July 31st and August 1st the 4th Australian Division took over from the First French Army as far south as the Amiens–Roye road inclusive. This extension of the front by the two corps already in the line must undoubtedly have assisted in giving the enemy a false sense of security, as the natural inferences to be deduced therefrom were the relief of French troops for employment on the Champagne battle front and a change to a passive attitude on the part of the Australian Corps, which had thus had its front very considerably extended.

At the beginning of August a withdrawal by the enemy in the neighbourhood of Albert to the east bank of the Ancre gave indications that rumours of an attack on our front might have reached him. These fears, however, were shortly allayed, when it was ascertained from prisoners that the withdrawal was only local, and that it had been carried out in order to avoid the difficulties of supplying troops on the far side of the marshy ground astride the Ancre.

The main features of the ground over which the attack of August 8th was made are the valleys of the Luce and the Somme, the dominating heights between the Avre and the Luce, the wide plateau between the Luce and the Somme, and the flat-topped high ground north of the Somme. North of the Somme the ground presents many difficulties. The high ground, for the first 3,000 yards east of the line we then held, is slightly undulating and offers few natural obstacles until Tailles Wood and Gressaire Wood are reached. The northern slopes fall comparatively gently down to the marshy valley of the Ancre, but the southern slopes of the plateau, leading down to the Somme, are steep and broken by a series of well-defined gullies or re-entrants. The ground is very rough, and, with the steep slopes, constitutes a serious obstacle for tanks. The village of Sailly Laurette lies hidden in one of these re-entrants on the northern bank of the Somme, whilst further east there is a steep gully, the slopes of which are in summer covered by the thick foliage of Malard Wood. Still further east is the village of Chipilly, built on the steep western slopes of the Chipilly spur, which is a dominating feature of the Somme valley, commanding it as far west as Corbie. Beyond the Chipilly spur the Somme winds its way to Péronne in a series of bends, the high ground in the vicinity of each bend forming an outstanding tactical feature and hiding in turn the villages of Etinehem, Bray-sur-Somme, and Suzanne, each of which played a conspicuous part in the early stages of the battle.

The Somme itself is well known in the history of the Great War. For purposes of commerce it has been canalised, the old river

The nature of the country [marginal note]

Malard Wood

From Morlancourt

To Sailly Laurette

MALARD WOOD FROM THE NORTH-WEST.

Oblique air photograph.

Proyart

Mericourt-sur-Somme

Chipilly

Cerisy

Malard Wood

THE SOMME VALLEY AND THE CHIPILLY SPUR

To face page 15.

No. 8.

Valley of the Luce

Demuin

Hangard

A.3.AE.O.200.
GRP 26·7·18·7

THE VALLEY OF THE LUCE AT HANGARD.

Oblique air photograph.

To face page 15.

Domart

Amiens-Roye road

Hourges

Rifle Wood

Valley of the Luce

THE HIGH GROUND BETWEEN THE LUCE AND THE AVRE, FROM WEST OF DOMART.

flowing by the side of the canal through marshy swamps, the whole thus forming an obstacle which can only be crossed by causeways and bridges.

Between the Somme and the Luce, the country is generally flat and open, with numerous villages and woods, scattered about at wide intervals. In this part of France a distinctive feature of the country is the absence of outlying farms and houses. The villages for the most part consist of groups of farms interspersed with the shops necessary for supplying them with commodities. Buildings are distinctly poor, the greater part of the granaries and cattle stalls being constructed of " wattle and daub." The villages are, in nearly every case, surrounded by orchards and trees; consequently at a distance they often present the appearance of small woods, from which, however, the church steeple standing out above the trees generally distinguishes them.

The Luce forms a difficult obstacle. The stream itself is not wide, but on either side there are broad marshes, which restrict the movement of troops to the normal crossings shown on the map. The only bridge in our lines was that at Domart; while, of the two which lay within the enemy's lines, the one at Hangard was broken, the other at Demuin was intact.

In the angle formed by the Luce and Avre the high ground between Moreuil and Demuin overlooks the valleys of both rivers and gives good observation on to a large part of the Gentelles–Cachy plateau, on which a very large number of our batteries were posted. It also includes Rifle Wood, a position of great natural strength.

It has already been mentioned that the enemy's defences were not formidable. The front system consisted of very roughly dug trenches, with few communication trenches and no dug-outs of **The hostile defences** any strength. Beyond the enemy's front system the only defences in existence were the old Amiens defences dug in 1915 and 1916. These defences were divided into two systems, the inner and the outer defences, of which the outer defences had been made the more complete. The inner defences ran northwards in a series of disconnected posts from Mezières along the eastern face of a deep re-entrant; crossing the Luce near Demuin, they continued in a northerly direction through Marcelcave to our front line in the vicinity of Hamel village. The outer defences, which were in a more advanced state, were complete with front and support trenches and numerous communication trenches and were protected by a thick belt of wire on the eastern side. They crossed the Amiens–Roye road just east of Le Quesnel, about 13,000 yards from our front line at Hourges, and thence ran in a general northerly direction to the Somme, which they crossed near Etinehem. North of the river the line reverted to a series of posts running along the eastern edge of Gressaire Wood and Tailles Wood, whence it curled gradually north-westwards to the Ancre, about 4,000 yards south of Albert.

These defences, having been carefully sited for the defence of Amiens, provided a well-defined objective, which could be easily recognised by the troops on reaching it and would also afford them a good line to hold prior to a further advance. The wire was thick, but was sited on the far side of the defences to protect them against an attack from the east, and it had suffered from time and weather. Between the inner and outer defences of Amiens there was little to stop the advance; small posts and trenches, lightly wired, had been made by both sides during the fighting in March and early April, and most of these were easily discernible on the excellent air photographs available.

East of the Amiens outer defences there were no organised defences as far as the Somme. In the neighbourhood of the Somme, however, the country, as the result of the battles of 1916, was covered with shell-holes and partially dismantled wire, which, being overgrown with rank grass and thistles, might be expected to retard the advance of the infantry and render the employment of cavalry and tanks almost impossible. As it turned out, the existence of this shell-crater area, the near edge of which ran approximately from Le Quesnoy-en-Santerre, through Lihons and Foucaucourt, to Frise, had an important influence on the later stages of the battle.

From the above it will be seen that the enemy had entirely neglected to strengthen his position by means of entrenchments, and it is interesting to note that General Ludendorff at the time ascribed the success of our operation in a great measure to the slackness and apathy of the garrison in the use of the spade.[1]

The Fourth Army had been confronted for some time past by seven divisions in line between the Luce and Albert. Of these the 13th, 41st, and 233rd[2] Divisions had been in line for one month, the 43rd Reserve and 54th[2] Reserve Divisions for one month and a half, and the 109th Division for three and a half months. The 27th Württemberg Division, which was fresh and a good

The strength and moral of the enemy

[1] In an order issued by German General Headquarters on August 11th, a copy of which order was captured during our advance, General Ludendorff said :—

"According to the report of the officers sent by G.H.Q. into the area of operations of the Second Army, the reasons for the defeat of the Second Army are as follows :—

"1. The fact that the troops were surprised by the massed attack of the tanks, and lost their heads when the tanks suddenly appeared behind them, having broken through under the protection of natural and artificial fog.

"2. The fact that scarcely any positions or obstacles worth mentioning existed, either in the forward battle zone, or in the villages and broken ground farther back, to make a methodical resistance possible there.

"3. The fact that the available artillery, allotted to the battalions at rest and to the reserve at the disposal of the higher command was wholly insufficient to establish fresh resistance with artillery support against the enemy who had broken through, and against his tanks.

"The following conclusions are drawn from these facts :—

"1. As I have already ordered in my tele-writer message Ia. 9718, Secret op. of the 8th August, considerably more must be done to obtain information regarding the enemy's intentions by taking prisoners, watching the ground by means of special observation posts, report centres, aerial reconnaissance and listening sets, as owing to the present situation we must also expect surprise attacks on other fronts. The closest vigilance is necessary at daybreak and in the early hours of the morning, as surprise attacks usually begin at this time, and because a certain lassitude is often prevalent among the men in the morning, after the strain on their nerves and endurance during the night. The supervision of the troops at this time is especially necessary, in view of our late experiences. Sufficient has been said on my part with regard to the organisation of infantry and artillery in depth.

"2. Far more must be done than has hitherto been the case in the construction of trenches and in the construction of defences against tanks. The dislike of the troops for trench digging must be combated by all means possible.

"3. The principle that troops, even if they are enveloped, must, if necessary, defend their battle zone for days, to the last round and to the last man, if they do not receive any further orders, appears to have been forgotten."   [2] North of Morlancourt.

fighting division, had only been brought down from the Lille area a few days before in order to carry out an attack in the Morlancourt sector on August 6th.[1] It was not, however, proposed to attack along the whole of the army front; hence, on that part of the front selected for our offensive, namely from the Amiens–Roye road to Morlancourt, it was estimated that we should be opposed by six divisions. These divisions were, it was believed, distributed as under :—

South of the Luce ..	..	225th Division (Prussians).
Hangard Wood Sector	..	109th Division (East Prussians).
Villers Bretonneux Sector ..		41st Division (East Prussians).
Accroche Wood Sector	..	13th Division (Westphalians).
Astride the Somme	..	43rd Reserve Division (Guard Corps Depôt).
Morlancourt Sector	..	27th Division (Württembergers).

In consequence, however, of the advance of the Canadian Corps being in a south-easterly direction, it was certain that soon after the start of the attack the Canadians would come in contact with the 14th Bavarian Division. The above divisions belonged to three corps, namely the LI Corps holding south of the Luce, the XI Corps from the Luce to just south of the Somme, and the XIV Corps thence northwards. All the above corps formed part of the Second German Army commanded by General of Cavalry von der Marwitz.

With regard to the enemy's reserves, it was anticipated that the Germans would be able to reinforce the front with eight divisions by the evening of August 11th. This number was an under-estimate, as will subsequently be seen.

From the examination of prisoners, captured by our troops during the period between July 18th and August 8th, it was ascertained that General Mangin's victory on July 18th had seriously affected the moral of both officers and men. Moreover, according to prisoners recently returned from Germany, the moral of civilians had been also very adversely affected. The ability of the French to carry out such a successful counter-stroke, after repeated assertions that the whole of the French reserves were exhausted, had seriously shaken the confidence in the German High Command, not only of the army, but also of the German people.[2]

[1] See page 26.
[2] The following order, issued by General Ludendorff on August 4th, shows how necessary he must have considered it to raise the drooping spirits of his troops even before he received the news of the attack on August 8th :—

" C.G.S. of the Field Army. G.H.Q.,
Ia. No. 9670. op. 4/8/18.
" I am under the impression that, in many quarters, the possibility of an enemy offensive is viewed with a certain degree of apprehension. There is nothing to justify this apprehension, provided our troops are vigilant and do their duty.
" In all the open warfare operations in the course of their great defensive battle between the Marne and the Vesle, the French were only able to obtain one initial tactical success due to surprise, namely that of July 18th, and this success ought to have been denied them. In the fighting which followed, the enemy in spite of his mass of artillery, was unable to obtain the lightest tactical advantage ; and yet, far from occupying prepared positions, our troops were fighting in open country and were merely holding the positions which they had chanced upon at the end of a day's battle. All the enemy's attacks broke down with sanguinary losses. It was

D

The initial object to be attained by the operations of the Fourth Army and the First French Army was to disengage Amiens and the Paris–Amiens Railway by seizing the Amiens outer defences on the line Hangest-en-Santerre–Harbonnières–Mericourt-sur-Somme, at the same time establishing a strong flank to the north of the Somme by the capture of the Chipilly spur and the high ground south of Morlancourt. Such an operation, if successful, would ease the situation enormously at the junction of the allied armies, and would render Amiens safe from bombardment.

The strategic objectives of the attack

As the preparations progressed, however, it became apparent that the situation offered such favourable opportunities for greater results that General Foch decided to enlarge the scope of the operations by employing French troops further to the south. On August 5th the Fourth Army received orders that, if the initial attack was successful, the operations should be continued by pushing south-eastwards in the direction of the line Roye–Chaulnes with the least possible delay, thrusting the enemy back in the direction of Ham and thus facilitating an attack by the French from the front between Noyon and Montdidier.

The basis of the whole plan was secrecy, and the first essential, therefore, was to ensure that the knowledge of the contemplated operation should be in the possession of as few persons as possible. At the first conference, held by Sir Henry Rawlinson on July 21st at Fourth Army Headquarters at Flixécourt, only the Chief Staff Officer and Artillery Commander of the Fourth Army, and the Commanders and Chief Staff Officers of the Canadian and Australian Corps, together with a representative of the Tank Corps, were present. Subsequent conferences were held every few days, but in different places, so that the constant gathering of commanders would be less likely to attract attention. The numbers attending the conferences gradually increased as the date of the attack approached and it became necessary for more officers to be consulted. The principle followed was for staffs and formations to be informed as late as possible, but in sufficient time to ensure that complete preparations could be made.

Secrecy, the basis of the plan of attack

The first intimation given to divisions of the proposed operation was on July 31st, and on August 4th the Army Commander held a conference

---

not the enemy's tactical successes which caused our withdrawal, but the precarious state of our rearward communications.

" The French and British infantry generally fought with caution ; the Americans attacked more boldly but with less skill. It is to the tanks that the enemy owes his success of the first day. These, however, would not have been formidable if the infantry had not allowed itself to be surprised, and if the artillery had been sufficiently distributed in depth. At the present moment, we occupy everywhere positions which have been very strongly fortified, and we have, I am convinced, effected a judicious organisation in depth of the infantry and artillery. Henceforward, we can await every hostile attack with the greatest confidence. As I have already explained, we should wish for nothing better than to see the enemy launch an offensive, which can but hasten the disintegration of his forces.

" Commanders and men must be imbued with a bitter determination to conquer, both in the defensive as well as in the offensive. This is a consideration which must not be lost sight of during training. Hence, we must not, under the present circumstances, neglect the organised defensive by devoting ourselves too exclusively to offensive tactics ; generally speaking, the organised defensive is the more difficult. It is the latter, in fact, which imposes the greatest test upon the spirit of the troops.

" (Sgd.) Ludendorff "

at the Cavalry Corps Headquarters at Auxi-le-Château, at which he explained his plans to the divisional and brigade commanders of the Cavalry Corps. The result of this secrecy was that the troops in the firing line were not acquainted with the Army Commander's intentions till about thirty-six hours before " zero." [1]

As the Canadian Corps had been kept in reserve and had not been involved in the March fighting, the enemy would certainly expect an early offensive wherever it was identified. The first problem, therefore, was to camouflage the move of the Canadian Corps from the First Army, on which front the 1st and 4th Canadian Divisions had recently gone into the line, to conceal their presence in the Fourth Army area until the last possible moment, and to draw off the enemy's attention elsewhere. With this object two Canadian battalions, two Canadian casualty clearing stations, and the Canadian wireless section were moved by General Headquarters to the Second Army and took over a portion of the line in the vicinity of Kemmel Hill, a very important tactical feature, which the enemy had captured, and which he would naturally expect that we should be anxious to regain. No Canadian troops were placed in the front line on the Fourth Army front until just before " zero " on " Z " day.

It was realised that the large concentration of troops in the back areas would become known to a number of junior officers and other ranks of the administrative services and railways who must necessarily assist in the move. This was bound to result in a great deal of discussion as to the object of the movement, and rumours of it might reach the enemy through his secret service in time to give him warning. Fortunately, an excuse was forthcoming. In accordance with the orders of General Foch, a British corps had been held in reserve west of Amiens, behind the junction of the Fourth Army and the First French Army. This corps, the XXII, had recently been moved south to assist the French armies on the Marne front. As soon as the concentration began to become known it was allowed gradually to leak out that the Canadian Corps, together with a brigade of tanks, a squadron of the Royal Air Force, and a powerful force of heavy artillery, was taking the place of the XXII Corps and was being concentrated west of Amiens ; also that this force was to be ready to reinforce the junction of the French and British Armies, or to move south against the flank of any hostile advance on the French front. At the same time, in order to cause confusion of thought, a rumour, previously in circulation, that the Canadian Corps would relieve the Australian Corps was not denied. The result of all these conflicting reports was that opinion in England and at the bases was about equally divided between Ypres, Arras, and Champagne as the destination of the various reinforcing formations, but whether they were for offensive or defensive purposes was not known.

In order to ensure concealment from hostile observation, all movements whether by road or rail were undertaken at night, and aeroplanes patrolled the army area by day to report any unauthorised movement. Everything also was done to indicate the continuance of normal conditions, and

---

[1] " Zero " was the term in use to describe the hour at which the assault would be launched, and " Z " day the day of attack.

work was actually continued on our rear defences up to the evening of the day prior to " Z " day.[1]

With regard to the artillery, it was all-important that the enemy's suspicions should not be aroused by an increase of fire prior to the attack. In order to ensure surprise all registration of guns and previous bombardment were prohibited, except in accordance with the normal artillery activity on the front. In order to support the advance of the infantry with a creeping barrage, accurate registration of the supporting artillery is essential, and, however carefully guns may be calibrated and their positions resected, it is always advisable to check calculations with a few rounds in order to ensure that there shall be no error. In consequence, programmes were carefully worked out giving the times at which guns should fire and the number of rounds to be fired, so that, even though the amount of artillery in the line had been doubled, the enemy should not appreciate it. No work on positions likely to be visible by aerial observation was permitted, the guns being camouflaged and remaining silent.

The precautions taken were fully justified in the result, and the success of the operation must be attributed in no small degree to their faithful observance.

With the exception of the Cambrai offensive in November, 1917, the operations in view differed in certain main essentials from any which

The conditions affecting the plan

had been undertaken in 1916 and 1917. In the battle of the Somme in 1916, at Arras and Messines in April and June, 1917, and at the third battle of Ypres in July, 1917, the attacks were launched against organised defensive systems of great depth, provided with dug-outs, and, in 1917, with

---

[1] In order to bring home to every officer, non-commissioned officer, and man in the Fourth Army his personal responsibility for maintaining absolute silence in regard to what was going on around him, the following pamphlet, known as " Keep your mouth shut," was issued to all ranks and pasted into the official small books carried by every officer and man :—

" KEEP YOUR MOUTH SHUT ! "

" The success of any operation we carry out depends chiefly on surprise.

" DO NOT TALK.—When you know that your unit is making preparations for an attack, don't talk about them to men in other units, or to strangers, and keep your mouth shut, especially in public places.

" Do not be inquisitive about what other units are doing ; if you hear or see anything, keep it to yourself.

" If you hear anyone else talking about operations, stop him at once.

" THE SUCCESS OF THE OPERATIONS AND THE LIVES OF YOUR COMRADES DEPEND UPON YOUR SILENCE.

" If you should ever have the misfortune to be taken prisoner, don't give the enemy any information beyond your rank and name. In answer to all other questions you need only say, ' I cannot answer.' He cannot compel you to give any other information. He may use threats. He will respect you if your courage, patriotism, and self-control do not fail. Every word you say may cause the death of one of your comrades.

" Either after or before you are openly examined, Germans, disguised as British officers or men, will be sent among you or will await you in the cages or quarters or hospital to which you are taken.

" Germans will be placed where they can overhear what you say without being seen by you.

" DO NOT BE TAKEN IN BY ANY OF THESE TRICKS."

A copy of an order, issued by the 54th Reserve Division on or about August 21st, was captured by the 47th Division. An extract from which ran as follows :—

" The Examination presented great difficulties, as the prisoners, especially those of the 23rd London, were apparently excellently schooled in the way they should behave if taken prisoner, and gave very clever evasive answers. The captured sergeant refused absolutely any information."

concrete " pill-boxes " ; moreover, these systems were in all cases protected by belts of strong wire. The situation, therefore, necessitated a preliminary bombardment of considerable duration, which at once indicated to the enemy not only the approximate front, but also the approximate date of attack. Strategical surprise under such conditions was therefore impossible. At Cambrai, on the other hand, a surprise attack was successfully launched against a strongly fortified position, but here the ground lent itself exceptionally well, not only to the concealment of the artillery, but, more important still, to the employment of large numbers of tanks. In August, 1918, the conditions as regards the ground on the Fourth Army front were very similar to those at Cambrai, and in addition the attack was to be made, not against a strongly organised position, but against one on which little work had been expended and which the enemy continued to regard as an offensive front. A strategical surprise was, therefore, possible. It was, in consequence, decided that there should be no artillery bombardment previous to " zero." The next factor that had to be carefully considered was the question of man-power. Our losses in March and April both in men and material had been very heavy, and, although the material had in a large measure been replaced, the provision of men, especially trained men, caused grave anxiety. It was essential, if the offensive was to be prolonged and produce large strategical results, that economy in men should be looked upon as of outstanding importance. The experiences of the Australians at Hamel on July 4th had, it was hoped, provided the solution of the problem by the employment of comparatively few infantry lavishly supported by tanks and artillery.[1]

During the previous six months, owing to the brilliant success of the Cambrai attack, the expansion of the Tank Corps had been rapid. Not only had the numbers of tanks available largely increased, but the tanks themselves had been improved very materially in pace, ability to manœuvre, and in mechanical efficiency and reliability. Apart from this, the training of the personnel both tactically and mechanically had been put on a sound footing, and the Corps, as a whole, had reached a high state of efficiency.

The front on which it was decided to attack extended from near Moreuil on the south, as far as the Ancre on the north, a distance of about 30,000 yards. Of this, the front from the Amiens–Roye road inclusive to the northern limit of attack was allotted to the Fourth Army, and was subdivided among the three corps as follows :—

The frontage of the attack

Canadian Corps.—From the Amiens–Roye road to the Villers Bretonneux–Chaulnes railway (both inclusive), a total of 7,500 yards as the crow flies, and about 9,500 along the British front line.

[1] Previous to the Hamel operations, the Australian battalions, which were to carry out the attack, had been very carefully trained, not only with tanks, but with the actual tank units which were going to work with them in battle. With tanks, even more if possible than with artillery, close liaison with the infantry is essential to success, and the results of the fighting at Hamel emphasised very clearly the value of this training. Every effort was therefore made in the time available to ensure that as many battalions as possible should carry out exercises with tanks before the battle commenced. This was possible with the Australian and III Corps troops which had been with the Fourth Army throughout the summer, but could only be carried out in a minor degree with the Canadian Corps, owing to its having so recently joined the army.

Australian Corps.—From the Villers Bretonneux–Chaulnes railway (exclusive) to the Somme, 7,500 yards.

III Corps.—From the Somme to the Ancre, 7,000 yards.

North of the Ancre the front of the III Corps was to be held defensively as far as the northern limit of the army front on the high ground north-west of Albert. On the right of the Fourth Army, the Commander of the First French Army allotted the front from Moreuil to the Amiens–Roye road to the XXXI French Corps, on the right of which again the front was to be held defensively until such time as the situation should develop with the advance of the Fourth Army. To the Australian and Canadian Corps, assisted by the cavalry, fell the honour of carrying out the main attack, whilst the XXXI French Corps on the right and the III Corps on the left formed the defensive flanks.

The final objective [1] to be reached in the main attack, if possible on the first day, was the Amiens outer defence line, which has been previously described. At the furthest point this objective entailed an advance of 14,000 yards, whilst the average distance from the "starting line" [2] was about 10,500 yards. Even if strong opposition were not encountered, the mere distance to be traversed would entail considerable fatigue to the infantry, which would necessitate the relief of the leading bodies of infantry at different stages in the advance. The Canadian Corps solved this problem on the left by forming up two divisions on comparatively narrow fronts and arranging for brigades of the same divisions to "leap-frog" [3] each other; on the right by placing one division on a wider front and "leap-frogging" a reserve division through it. The Australian Corps solved it by disposing two of its divisions on wide fronts and then "leap-frogging" two reserve divisions through the front line divisions. The principle was the same in both these methods.

The advance was to be made by bounds from objective to objective. The first bound covered a distance of between 3,500 and 4,000 yards, that is to say, approximately the limit of range at which an effective field artillery barrage could be maintained without moving the guns forward. It was also anticipated that a very large number of the hostile batteries, which had been located in the Cerisy-Gailly–Warfusée-Abancourt valley, were within this distance and would be captured in the first bound.

The advance from the first objective to the second objective covered a distance varying from 2,000 to 5,000 yards, and was arranged so as to

[1] The objectives are shown on Map No. 3, " The attack of August 8th," as follows :—
    Green line—First objective for all corps.
    Red line—Second objective for all corps.
    Blue line—Third objective for the Australian Corps.
    Blue dotted line—Third objective, or line of exploitation, for the Canadian Corps.

[2] The " starting line " is the line from which the infantry assault is launched. It is also often called the " jumping off " line.

[3] " Leap-frogging " is the term applied, in an attack against more than one objective, to the method of advance whereby the leading unit or formation captures the first objective and then halts, whilst the second unit or formation passes through it and attacks the next objective. Should there be a still further objective, the second unit then remains on the second objective whilst a third unit passes through it and attacks the third objective. The term was introduced to distinguish this method of dealing with a succession of objectives from that previously in use, to which the leading unit or formation went right through to the furthest objective.

bring the leading troops to a favourable line for consolidation, should a further advance on the first day be impossible. The advance of the infantry and tanks from the first to the subsequent objectives was covered by mobile groups of artillery. These were specially detailed to infantry brigades beforehand, and held in readiness to advance in support of the infantry as soon as the forward movement began. To give time for this artillery to move forward, and for the " leap-frogging " troops to reach their positions for the next advance, it was arranged that there should be a halt of two hours after the capture of the first objective on the Canadian and Australian Corps fronts before the advance was resumed.

The advance to the first objective was synchronised along the whole of the Fourth Army front. The French troops, however, which were to co-operate on the right, had no tanks to assist them, **The synchronisation of the attack** and their advance was therefore timed to begin forty minutes after that of the Fourth Army, in order that the enemy's positions in front of them might be subjected to an artillery bombardment. After the initial assault it was only possible to synchronise the successive advances of the Australian Corps and those of the two northern divisions of the Canadian Corps, as the attacks of the III Corps and of the southern division of the Canadian Corps were necessarily independent, on account of the rough nature of the ground in the case of the former, and of the difficulties presented by the crossing of the Luce in the case of the latter.

Ten battalions of heavy tanks were available.[1] Four of these battalions were allotted to the Canadian Corps, four to the Australian Corps, and one to the III Corps; the remaining **The allotment of tanks** battalion, which had recently been employed with the First French Army, being held in army reserve. The total number of fighting tanks available on August 8th was 456, of which 96 were whippet tanks.

The rôle given to the cavalry was to push through the leading infantry of the Canadian and Australian Corps as soon as opportunity offered, and, taking advantage of any opening that might occur, to **The rôle of the cavalry** secure the Amiens outer defences and hold them until the arrival of the infantry. Subsequently the cavalry was to move south-eastwards in the general direction of Roye and Chaulnes, with a view to cutting the enemy's communications and to easing the situation in front of the French. In order to ensure that no opportunity of passing through the infantry should be missed through the

---

[1] Two kinds of heavy tanks were employed : the Mark V and the Mark V star. The Mark V tank was exceptionally handy to manœuvre, being able to twist and turn with a rapidity which a year before would have been thought impossible. The Mark V star tank was similar in armament and in its mechanism to the Mark V, but was six feet longer, this extra length having been given to it with a view to enabling it to span a wider trench, and also to enable it to be used as a carrier for infantry or machine-guns. It had, however, by this increase in length lost the power of quick manœuvre and thus became an easier prey to the enemy's anti-tank guns. In both the Canadian and Australian Corps one battalion of Mark V star tanks was assigned the task of carrying infantry or machine-gun detachments to the final objective. On arrival, the detachments were to have been disembarked and to have held the position gained until the arrival of the remainder of their units. As it turned out, the detachments in most cases were unable to withstand the fumes and the heat of the engine, and, disembarking shortly after the start, followed the tanks to the objective on foot.

cavalry not being in the closest touch with the infantry, the 3rd Cavalry Division was placed temporarily under the orders of the Canadian Corps Commander, and one brigade of the 1st Cavalry Division under those of the Australian Corps Commander. This arrangement was to continue until such time as these bodies of cavalry had passed through the infantry, when they were again to come under the direct command of the Cavalry Corps Commander. Two battalions of whippet tanks, capable of moving at a rate of about seven miles an hour, were allotted to the Cavalry Corps. Of these, one company (sixteen tanks) from each battalion was detailed to accompany the leading troops of the 1st and 3rd Cavalry Divisions respectively, their rôle being to assist the cavalry in exploiting any success which might be gained.[1]

The control of the air throughout the days of preparation was of the greatest importance, if the enemy were to be kept in ignorance of the

The rôle of the Royal Air Force

forthcoming attack. For some weeks prior to August 8th the Royal Air Force was busily employed in ensuring a mastery over the enemy's aeroplanes, a work in which it was entirely successful. The number of hostile aeroplanes engaged in long distance reconnaissance was small, and only very few of the enemy's machines crossed the line and operated over our forward area. When they did succeed in doing this, they were prevented by our anti-aircraft defence and aeroplane line patrols from obtaining any useful information or doing any serious damage. It was essential to maintain this supremacy throughout the battle. To achieve this the Army Commander had at his disposal the 5th Brigade, Royal Air Force, consisting of the 22nd (Army) Wing of eight scout squadrons, the 15th Wing of six corps squadrons, and three other squadrons for bombing. He could also rely on the assistance of the scout squadrons of the 9th Brigade, Royal Air Force, from General Headquarters, and on that of seven bombing squadrons lent by other Army Wings.

The six corps squadrons of the 15th Wing were allotted as follows: the 35th and 5th Squadrons and the 3rd Australian Squadron worked with the III, Canadian, and Australian Corps respectively. The 8th Squadron worked with the Tank Corps, and the 6th Squadron with the Cavalry Corps. The remaining squadron, the 9th, was allotted the duty of keeping the machine-guns of the III and Australian Corps supplied with small arm ammunition on the second and third objectives.[2]

The duty of the corps squadrons was to keep the formations with which they were working supplied with information regarding the progress of the attack, and to carry out such additional tasks as were required of them, e.g. drowning the noise made by the tanks when assembling, forming smoke screens, and observing for the artillery. The eight scout squadrons of the 22nd Wing were to be employed exclusively in bombing and engaging with their machine-guns suitable targets on the ground on the whole army front. The scout squadrons of the 9th Brigade were to maintain constant patrols at a high altitude over the battle front. The objectives

---

[1] See Appendix K. "The Adventures of a whippet tank on August 8th."
[2] Ammunition was dropped from the aeroplanes to the troops in the ordinary S.A.A. boxes (containing 1,000 rounds) by means of small parachutes especially designed for this purpose.

of the day and night bombing squadrons were the railway centres at Chaulnes, Roye, Nesle, and Péronne, the crossings over the Somme, and the roads and billeting areas which the enemy was likely to use.

It is not possible to describe in detail the work allotted to the Artillery, Engineers, and Machine Gun Corps, nor adequately to record the important part played by these arms during the whole course of the operations which began on August 8th. Although little mention is made of the individual work of units of these arms in this narrative, yet their work went on continuously with little respite, and their infantry comrades are fully aware of what they owe to their devotion and skill.[1]

The rôle of the Artillery, Engineers, and Machine Gun Corps

Broadly speaking, for the attack on August 8th the artillery was allotted two tasks. The first, to be carried out by about one-third of the total number of guns available, was to form a creeping barrage,[2] covering the advance of the infantry. The second, in which all the remaining guns were to be employed, was the bombardment of every locality known to harbour hostile guns, thus preventing the enemy from either using or removing them, whilst the long-range guns also dealt with the villages and other localities suspected of being assembly places for German reserves. At " zero " the creeping barrage was to fall 200 yards in front of the infantry " starting line " and then pause for three minutes while the infantry closed up under its protection. The barrage was then to be lifted 100 yards every two minutes until it had advanced a further 200 yards, after which it was to slow down to lifts of 100 yards every three minutes until it had moved forward a total of 1,000 yards from the line on which it originally fell. From then onwards, up to the limit of range of the guns, it was to advance at the rate of 100 yards every four minutes. The object of gradually reducing the rate of advance of the barrage was to enable the infantry to keep close to it, and thus gain full benefit from the protection it afforded.

In order to supply the staffs of formations and the fighting troops with full information regarding the ground over which the attack was to take place and the nature and condition of the enemy's defences, a large number of special maps and photographs had to be printed and circulated. This entailed an immense amount of work on the photographic section of the Army Printing and Stationery Services, and on the Field Survey Battalion.

The issue of maps and photographs

It was the task of the former to reproduce, to piece together as mosaics, to distribute to the fighting troops and the headquarters of formations, and in some cases to enlarge, the photographs taken by the Royal Air Force.[3] Some idea of the amount of work involved will be gathered from the fact that, between August 1st and 6th, 37,825 whole plate photographs, 1,840 enlargements, and 4,500 mosaics were issued

---

[1] For details as regards the organisation and tactics of the Machine Gun Corps, see Appendix J.

[2] See map No. 18, which illustrates the system of the creeping barrage.

[3] Both vertical and oblique photographs were taken from the air. Vertical photographs covering a large area were pieced together and then cut up into smaller areas to suit the requirements of the various divisions. These mosaics were particularly valuable when used in conjunction with the oblique photographs covering the same areas, and were used practically as maps.

E

to the troops, many being distributed to company, platoon, and section commanders. The difficulty experienced was not so much the numbers of photographs to be taken as the shortness of the time available in which to reproduce them. This was due to the necessity for keeping the attack secret for as long a time as possible.

The work thrown on the Field Survey Battalion was equally great. It began in their case on July 29th, and within ten days 160,000 maps were issued to the troops, while 119,300 special maps were printed. The work of the Field Survey Battalion, however, was not confined to maps, as the arrival of artillery units new to the area necessitated much work in the field, including the fixing of positions for 128 new batteries.

A serious danger to be feared during the days prior to the attack was a hostile bombardment with Yellow Cross gas. On several occasions

The danger of hostile gas shelling during the assembly of troops during the preceding months the enemy had caused heavy losses and consequent disorganisation to our troops by means of concentrated bombardments of this gas. Although not so lethal as the other kinds of gas, it was a much more difficult type to combat, owing to its smell being so slight, and to the consequent difficulty found by the troops in realising in time the danger to which they were exposed. Moreover, its effects were often not experienced until many hours later. In addition, Yellow Cross gas did not disperse, but hung about for many days, especially in woods and enclosed places, and, in the event of heavy gas shelling, experience had shown that the only effective remedy was to move the troops from the affected area. Prior to the attack, when the whole area must of necessity be thick with troops and batteries, this would be obviously impossible without causing great confusion and altering the dispositions of troops just at the moment when it was least desirable to do so. In order to reduce the risks, therefore, L'Abbé Wood and other areas which had constantly been subjected to gas shelling in the past were avoided as much as possible. Arrangements were also made to open a heavy counter-battery fire on any hostile gun positions from which gas should be fired, and, for this purpose only, on the night preceding the attack, all available guns, whether they had recently arrived in the area or not, were specially authorised to fire should the enemy open a gas bombardment.

Two incidents which occurred shortly before the attack caused no little anxiety as to whether the enemy would thereby obtain information

Minor hostile attacks on August 3rd and August 6th regarding our impending operations. In the early morning of August 3rd an Australian post on the Amiens–Roye road at Hourges on the south bank of the Luce was captured, and the enemy succeeded in taking prisoner a sergeant and four men. Inquiries were at once set on foot, and it was ascertained that not only was the garrison of the captured post ignorant of our plans, but that the men had been overheard only the day before discussing the prospects of another long spell in the line owing to their having taken over a new front. Three days later, soon after dawn on August 6th, before the divisional reliefs consequent upon the extension of the III Corps front down to the Somme had been completed, the enemy attacked on a front of about 4,000 yards. The attack was made south

To face page 26.

Rifle Wood

German Front Line

British Front Line

To THENNES

HOURGES

R Luce

Domart

From HANGARD

DOMART AND THE HOURGES BRIDGEHEAD.

Oblique air photograph

ASSEMBLY AREAS OF AUSTRALIAN CORPS PRIOR TO AUG. 8ᵀᴴ

Not to Scale: Distances are only approximate

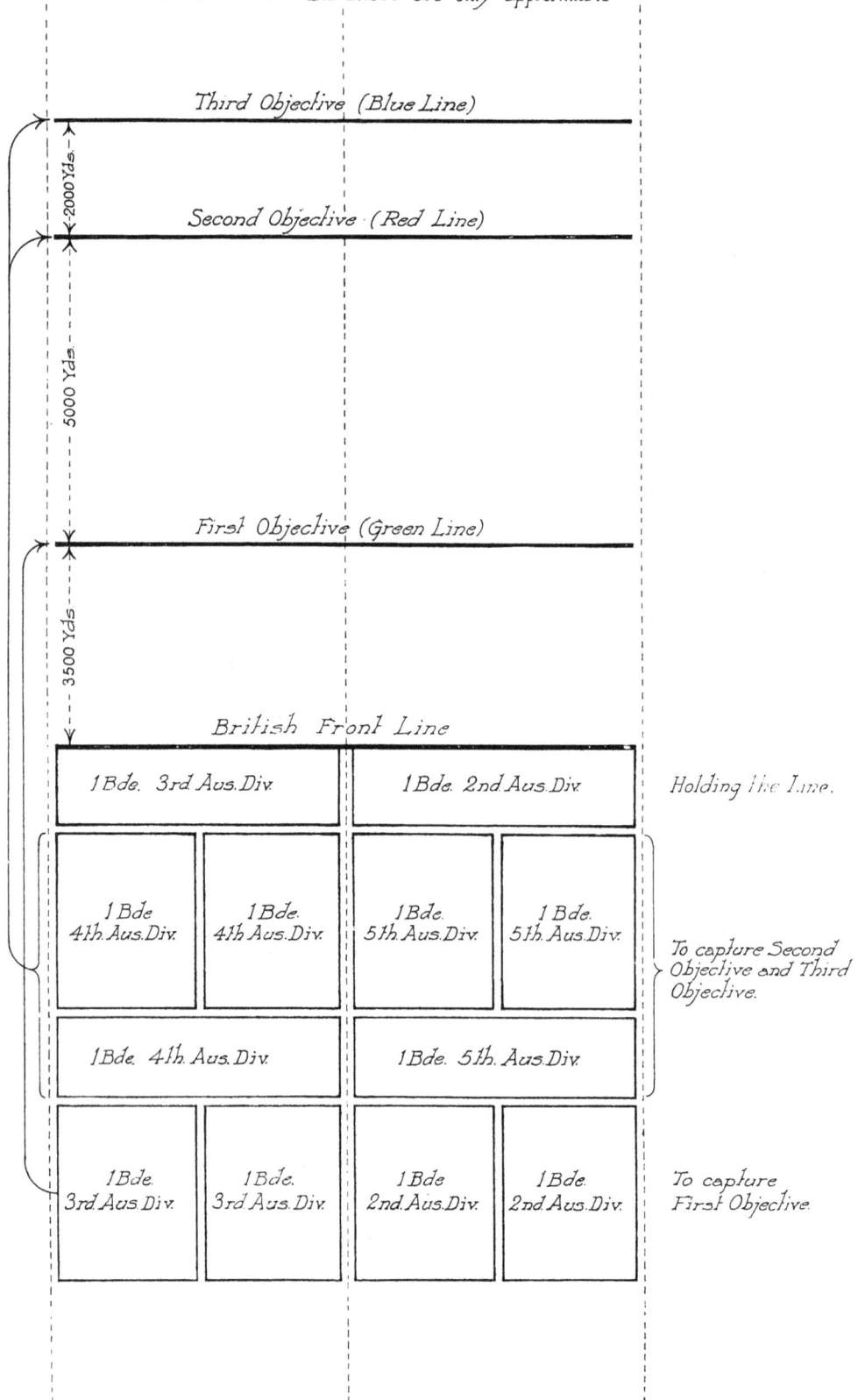

Third Objective (Blue Line)

← 2000 Yds →

Second Objective (Red Line)

← 5000 Yds →

First Objective (Green Line)

← 3500 Yds →

British Front Line

| 1 Bde. 3rd Aus. Div. | 1 Bde. 2nd Aus. Div. | Holding the Line. |

| 1 Bde 4th Aus. Div. | 1 Bde. 4th Aus. Div. | 1 Bde. 5th Aus. Div. | 1 Bde. 5th Aus. Div. | To capture Second Objective and Third Objective. |

| 1 Bde. 4th Aus. Div. | 1 Bde. 5th Aus. Div. |

| 1 Bde. 3rd Aus. Div. | 1 Bde. 3rd Aus. Div. | 1 Bde. 2nd Aus. Div. | 1 Bde. 2nd Aus. Div. | To capture First Objective. |

of Morlancourt against the positions which had been gained by the 5th Australian Division on July 29th.   The 18th Division, which was holding the sector, was at the time actually engaged in carrying out an inter-brigade relief, always a most unfortunate moment at which to be attacked, as the scheme of defence must necessarily be temporarily disorganised, and the communications blocked by the incoming and outgoing troops.   The attack was carried out by the 27th Württemberg Division, which had been brought down hurriedly from the Lille front with a view to stopping the rot which had set in owing to the offensive policy of the Australian Corps.   The Württembergers succeeded not only in penetrating our lines to a maximum depth of 800 yards, but also in capturing some 200 prisoners, including some artillerymen engaged at the time in establishing forward dumps of ammunition ready for the guns when they were brought into position for the offensive.   Luckily, either these prisoners did not know of the contemplated operations owing to the system of secrecy that had been in force, or, if they did, none of them disclosed what they knew.[1]   The next morning an attack by the 18th Division partially restored the situation and resulted in the capture of 70 prisoners.   These operations of necessity caused a local dislocation of plans on the front of the III Corps, since they affected the " starting line " of the infantry, and consequently the artillery programme.   They also reduced both the strength and vigour of the troops which were to be used in the main operations, and caused the enemy to be much more on the alert than on other parts of the front.   The general situation, however, was in no way affected.

The assembly of the infantry, owing to the large numbers of troops of all arms in the forward zone, entailed very careful staff arrangements and good march discipline, to ensure that everything worked smoothly and without undue fatigue to the men.   As the divisions of the Australian and III Corps were already east of Amiens, only comparatively minor readjustments were in their case required, but, even so, the assembly of the troops of these two corps was no easy matter, as a brief explanation of the forming up of the Australian Corps will show.

The assembly of the troops

In view of the distance to which it was proposed to penetrate, and of the great depth of the infantry formations throughout the attack, the assembly of the infantry of the Australian Corps was organised in such a manner as to reduce, to the greatest extent possible, the distance to be covered by the 4th and 5th Australian Divisions, which were detailed for the capture of the most distant objectives.   They assembled, therefore, in areas between those occupied by the 6th and 10th Brigades of the 2nd and 3rd Divisions, which were holding the line at " zero," and the areas occupied by the remaining four brigades of those two divisions.   The 6th and 10th Brigades were not to take part with their divisions in the attack on the first objective, but were to be collected and brought into

---

[1] The records of the examination of these prisoners by the German Intelligence, as well as that of the five Australians, were found amongst German documents subsequently captured.   From a study of these examinations it is clear that the Germans obtained no useful information or inkling of our attack.   This fact reflects the greatest credit on the manner in which our prisoners avoided giving information to the enemy which could be of use to him.

reserve after the whole of the attacking troops had passed through them, subsequently moving forward to rejoin their divisions. At " zero," therefore, the attacking troops of the 2nd and 3rd Australian Divisions were to pass through the assembly areas of the 5th and 4th Australian Divisions, and then through the brigades of their own divisions which were holding the line. The relative positions in which the divisions were disposed for forty-eight hours before " zero " is shown diagrammatically in Diagram I. This arrangement, while it achieved its object, necessitated very good control and accurate work on the part of the commanders and staffs, and the fact that all went according to plan is a testimony to the organising ability and discipline of the Australian Corps.

The divisions of the Canadian Corps had to be moved up gradually from their concentration areas, which extended far to the west of Amiens, and units had to be timed to reach their assembly positions at the appointed hour.

Arrangements for the forward movement of the reinforcing artillery were even more difficult ; not only was there a vast amount of traffic on the roads which impeded their movement, but, in the case of that of the Canadian Corps, it had to share the positions on the Gentelles plateau with the French artillery.

The assembly of the tanks was no easy matter, owing to the necessity for all movement taking place at night and for their being hidden away or camouflaged by daylight. In addition, the noise of over 400 tank engines droning away behind the army front was certain to be heard by the enemy unless arrangements were made to cover it. This was carried out by the Royal Air Force, which, for the four or five nights previous to the attack, kept several machines flying over the line. On the night of August 6th the tanks were moved up in groups to their preparatory positions, which, in most cases, had to be reached across country and were sited some two or three miles behind the front line. On the night of the 7th they were moved up to their assembly positions about 1,000 yards behind the infantry " starting line," and there deployed into the exact positions from which they were to advance in the early morning of the 8th. The exact route of every tank was minutely reconnoitred beforehand, obstacles were removed, and in many cases tape lines to guide the drivers were laid out.[1] It speaks volumes for the efficiency of the officers and men of the Tank Corps that almost every tank detailed for the initial attack arrived to time and in its allotted position.

The Cavalry Corps, which had been concentrated in the valley of the Somme between Amiens and Flixécourt, closed up into close billets and bivouacs just west of Amiens on the night of August 6th, and, on the night of the 7th, started at dusk and marched through Amiens to its assembly position on the open ground in the fork between the Villers

[1] Only one untoward incident marked the assembly of the tanks. One company of supply tanks which had been allotted to the 5th Australian Division was assembled in an orchard in the vicinity of Villers Bretonneux. During the afternoon of August 7th a lucky shot during a hostile area shoot in this vicinity struck one of the tanks carrying petrol, setting it on fire. The fire thus caused attracted the attention of the hostile gunners, and the enemy immediately subjected the orchard in which the tanks were concealed to a heavy concentrated bombardment, destroying almost the whole company of 25 tanks and their loads. The incident caused some uneasiness, as it was thought the enemy had discovered the presence of the tanks.

Enemy's front line

STARTING LINE

about 270'

1st. Wave; Leading Coys of each Bn. form 1st. Wave in two lines of skirmishers about 30 yards apart.

2nd. Wave; Formed in small section columns.

3rd. Wave; Formed in small section columns.

4th Wave; Formed in small section columns the M.G's. and T.M's. detailed to go forward with attack will accompany this Wave, also Bde. Forward Signal Party.

5th Wave; Carriers from each Coy. in small columns.

Tape lines continued forward to give direction at commencement of advance.

C. Bn.

A Coy.

B Coy.

C Coy.

D Coy.

B. Bn.

A. Bn.

1st Wave

2nd Wave

3rd Wave

4th Wave

Carriers

British Front Line

British Support Line

Track C Bn.

B Bn.

A Bn.

Note:— Guides and Markers thus ►
Tapes and Pegs

DIAGRAM SHOWING THE FORMING UP OF A BRIGADE FOR A TRENCH-TO-TRENCH ATTACK.

To face page 29.

Bretonneux and the Roye roads. The two battalions of whippets, which had arrived from the vicinity of Doullens on the night of the 6th and had assembled under cover of the trees in the outer boulevards of Amiens, joined the column as it passed. The column of three cavalry divisions was a very long one, and only one road out of Amiens was available. Only the most careful timings, therefore, and the strictest march discipline enabled them to reach their assembly positions by " zero " (4.20 a.m. August 8th). Forward of the assembly positions the mass of guns and infantry, which was crowded behind the front line, necessitated a special track being made by which the cavalry could advance without either interfering with the infantry, through whose reserves they would have to pass, or masking the artillery. This track was not made until the night of the 7th and was very expeditiously constructed by the engineers of the Cavalry Corps, assisted by a battalion of American engineers.

After the marshalling of the infantry divisions and brigades in their allotted assembly areas, there remained yet another preliminary measure to be taken which required care and accuracy. This

The forming up of the infantry

consisted in the laying out of the tapes from which the leading infantry was to start off to the attack.[1] An example of a method of forming up a brigade is shown in Diagram II. Before " zero " the units were led up to their positions by guides, and were met on the tape line by markers who had gone up in advance. Once in position the troops were not to move off their alignment until the assault began.

" Zero " was fixed for 4.20 a.m., just over an hour before sunrise. This hour was chosen so that the infantry could break the crust of the

The hour of " zero "

enemy's defence under cover of darkness, and also in order that there should be sufficient light, before they had gone more than a few hundred yards, to enable them and the accompanying tanks to keep their direction.[2]

The preceding pages will give some idea of the difficulties that had to be overcome, and of the magnitude of the task placed on the shoulders of the commanders and staffs of all formations in pre-

The confidence of the troops

paring for this operation. There were, however, very few novices in the art of mounting an attack, and, in spite of the short time available for completing the preliminary arrange-

---

[1] In laying out such tapes, certain considerations have to be borne in mind :—

1. It is essential that the troops should advance straight to their front, as a change of direction during the assault nearly always leads to loss of direction and consequent disorganisation.

2. The distance to be traversed by the infantry before reaching the enemy's front line must not be too far.

3. The forming up position should be, if possible, on the enemy's side of the area on which the hostile protective barrage is usually put down.

4. The necessary preliminary arrangements must not be observed by the enemy, or he will receive warning of the impending attack. To ensure this, strong patrols should be pushed out in front to cover the preparations.

[2] The decision as to the hour of attack must always be difficult, especially when infantry attack with the aid of tanks, as the requirements of the two arms must often be antagonistic. Cover from view is desirable to protect a tank from hostile anti-tank fire, but a tank is valueless unless it has sufficient light to keep its course and use its armament. For the infantry, on the other hand, darkness is usually preferable in order to neutralise the enemy's machine-gun defence and to avoid the risk of being caught in daylight in their assaulting positions, which must often be in the open. The hour chosen was a compromise between the various claims, and subsequent events proved the choice to have been quite satisfactory.

ments, all was ready by the evening of August 7th.   It only remained to hope for fine weather.

And so the morrow was eagerly awaited.   Never before in the war had the prospects of a great success seemed brighter, and nothing could have exceeded the confidence in success which was felt by all ranks of the Fourth Army from the highest to the lowest.   Nothing on August 7th was more remarkable than the spirits and supreme confidence of all the troops, to whatever arm they belonged.   It may be said without exaggeration that so strong was this feeling, so high the moral, and so fixed the determination to reach the furthest objectives at whatever cost, that the Battle of Amiens was really won before the attack began.

CHAPTER III

THE BATTLE OF AMIENS; THE ATTACK OF AUGUST 8TH

Maps 2 and 3; and Panoramic Photograph 1.

A summary of events on August 8th—The plan of attack of the Canadian Corps—The attack of the 3rd Canadian Division—The Franco-British liaison force—The advance of the 1st and 2nd Canadian Divisions to the first objective—Their further advance to the second objective —The advance of the 4th Canadian Division to the third objective—The capture of the third objective by the 1st and 2nd Canadian Divisions—The result of the day's fighting by the Canadian Corps—The Australian Corps plan of attack—The advance of the 2nd and 3rd Australian Divisions to the first objective—The capture of the second objective by the 4th and 5th Australian Divisions—The Armoured Cars—The advance of the 4th and 5th Australian Divisions to the third objective—The result of the day's fighting by the Australian Corps—The action of the Cavalry Corps—The III Corps plan of attack —The disposition of the troops at " zero "—The attack on the first objective—The advance against the second objective—The result of the day's fighting by the III Corps —The work of the Royal Air Force—The attack by the First French Army—The situation on the Fourth Army front on the evening of August 8th—The orders for August 9th.

THE night of August 7th was fine, and the inactivity of the enemy's artillery confirmed the view that he was in ignorance of the coming blow.

A summary of events on August 8th No untoward event marred the assembly of the troops, and, except north of the Somme, the curse of gas was absent.

Punctually at 4.20 a.m., with the first gleam of dawn of a typical August day, the storm broke, and the British Army, which only a few months before was in danger of defeat, had begun its march to the Rhine. The first to start were the tanks, which, leaving their position of assembly about 1,000 yards behind the infantry "starting line" some minutes before " zero," had to time their advance so as to arrive close up to the artillery barrage at the moment it fell. At " zero " our artillery opened, and the creeping barrage fell 200 yards in front of the infantry "starting line," and was then lifted according to the prearranged time-table.[1]

For some days previously the sound-ranging sections [2] and flash-spotting observation posts,[3] sited well forward, had been engaged in locating

---

[1] See page 25.

[2] These sections, which formed part of the Field Survey Battalion, were supplied with very delicate instruments which measured to the minutest fraction the pace at which sound travelled, and, by a very ingenious and accurate method of recording the noise of an explosion from several positions some distance apart, could locate the position of hostile guns when they fired. Sound-ranging was one of the many innovations which the discoveries of science introduced during the war.

[3] These observation posts, scattered along the front, located the direction of the flashes of hostile guns by visual observation, and, by taking cross bearings from two or more posts, were able to locate the exact position of any particular gun when it fired.

the enemy's battery areas in conjunction with the Royal Air Force. Consequently, the moment the assault began the enemy's batteries, especially those in the valley south of Demuin, around Wiencourt-l'Equipée, and in the Cerisy-Gailly-Warfusée-Abancourt valley, were deluged by a hurricane bombardment and neutralised to such an extent that the hostile artillery retaliation was almost negligible.[1] That the fire of the heavy artillery was most effective was also proved by the number of dead horses found lying in and about the enemy's battery positions.

There was a thick mist in the early morning which did not clear completely until nearly 10 o'clock. Although this assisted us very materially by concealing from the enemy the launching of the attack, it made it difficult for the infantry and tanks to maintain direction. Moreover, communications were rendered difficult both for the enemy and ourselves, and visual signalling was impossible. For the same reason, the work of the contact aeroplanes co-operating with the infantry was at first much restricted owing to the poor visibility, and early news of the attack was slow in coming through.

South of the Somme the enemy was taken completely by surprise, and all opposition was quickly swept aside by the impetuosity of the Canadian and Australian advance. By 6.20 a.m. the first objective on the greater part of Canadian and Australian Corps fronts had been reached, and, after the pause of two hours arranged to allow the troops destined for the next advance time to get into position, the assaulting waves again went forward.

Nothing could stop the infantry and tanks, and the cavalry, eagerly grasping the longed-for opportunity, went through. From that moment the issue of the day was never in doubt; thousands of prisoners and hundreds of guns were captured. The disorganisation and rout of the enemy were complete, and it was only distance and fatigue which caused a halt on the final objective given to our troops for the day. North of the Somme our advance was not so rapid. The enemy clung tenaciously to the woods and gullies and gave ground only after determined fighting.

Sir Arthur Currie's plan, drawn up in circumstances of considerable difficulty,[2] was to attack on a front of three divisions, the 3rd Canadian Division on the right, the 1st Division in the centre, and the 2nd Division on the left. Owing to the difficulties of the ground on

---

[1] The fire of our heavy artillery on all villages east of the second objective and south of the Amiens–Chaulnes railway, with the exception of Le Quesnel, ceased at 10.50 a.m., six and a half hours after " zero," so as to fit in with the infantry and cavalry programme ; on the latter village it ceased an hour later.

[2] Owing to the shortness of the time available between the arrival of the Canadian Divisions in the area and the date of the attack, the Canadian Corps had little time in which to complete its arrangements. The ground, which was new to the corps, had to be reconnoitred, and the plans for the attack had to be made simultaneously with the concentration of the troops in the area. This task, already sufficiently formidable, was made yet more difficult by the fact that, for purposes of secrecy, it was necessary for the 4th Australian Division to continue to hold the front line until just before "zero." On August 4th, the Canadian Corps took over its sector of attack from the Australian Corps, and, during the next three days, completed the relief of the Australian troops in the support area. It was not, however, until the early hours of August 8th that Canadian troops relieved the 13th Australian Brigade in the front line, the actual relief being completed and the Australian troops withdrawn into reserve at 2.10 a.m., a little over two hours before " zero." On relief, the 13th Australian Brigade moved to Aubigny to join the 1st Australian Division.

Villers-aux-Erables

Hollon Wood

Mazieres

Rifle Wood

Enemy Front Line Trenches

Amiens-Roye road

Hourges

V. Oblique. P. de yes Dohaet 237/430

RIFLE WOOD.

French oblique air photograph.

the right, it was desirable that the attack between Rifle Wood and Demuin, both inclusive, should be carried out by one formation. This front com-

The plan of attack of the Canadian Corps

prised nearly half of the whole of that allotted to the Canadian Corps, and it was considered that a whole division would be required for its capture. The task was allotted to the 3rd Canadian Division, the division, however, was only required to carry the attack as far as the second objective (red line), after which the 3rd Cavalry Division and 4th Canadian Division were to pass through and capture the third objective (blue dotted line). The ground on the left half of the corps front did not present the same difficulties, and it was divided between the 1st and 2nd Canadian Divisions, which were ordered to carry the attack through to the third objective (blue dotted line). Of the four battalions of heavy tanks detailed to co-operate with the Canadian Corps, one battalion of Mark V tanks was allotted to each of the three leading divisions, and a battalion of Mark V star tanks to the 4th Canadian Division to be employed in carrying forward Lewis and machine-gun teams to the third objective.

On the right of the Canadian attack an Independent Force was formed under Brig.-Gen. Brutinel, the commander of the Canadian Machine Gun Corps. This force consisted of the 1st and 2nd Canadian Motor Machine Gun Brigades, the Canadian Cyclist Battalion, and one section of medium trench mortars mounted on lorries. The rôle assigned to it was to pass through the 3rd Canadian Division, form a flank to the corps by making good the line of the Amiens–Roye road between the second and third objectives, and support the cavalry should it be able to advance beyond the third objective.

The ground, which it was the task of the 3rd Canadian Division, commanded by Maj.-Gen. L. J. Lipsett, to capture, consisted of a

The attack of the 3rd Canadian Division

plateau intersected by some deep ravines which ran down to the Luce. The river, which protected the northern flank of the plateau, was an unfordable obstacle with very marshy ground on both banks, the marsh being in places as much as 200 yards wide. On the enemy's side of the river we only held the small bridgehead at Hourges, and this was completely dominated from the German trenches on the forward slopes of the plateau. These slopes, however, were slightly convex, so that an advance of about 1,000 yards from the bridgehead at Hourges would secure dead ground. The difficulty was to assemble troops and tanks in this small bridgehead, and to deploy them outwards from such a cramped position.

Maj.-Gen. Lipsett decided to mass the 9th Canadian Brigade in the bridgehead before " zero," at which hour a portion of it was to advance rapidly, seize the edge of the plateau, and thus secure dead ground in which the brigade could deploy. The remainder of the brigade was then to move round eastwards along the river under the edge of the plateau and outflank the enemy's defences. When the 9th Brigade had captured the first objective (green line), the 7th Brigade was to pass through and carry on the advance to the second objective (red line) on the whole divisional front. The 8th Canadian Brigade was to capture Hangard, and,

F

operating along the north bank of the Luce as far as Demuin, was to assist the right flank of the 1st Canadian Division.

The 3rd Canadian Division was assisted by the 5th Mark V Tank Battalion, of which two companies, each consisting of fourteen tanks, were allotted to the 9th Brigade, one company of fourteen tanks to the 8th Brigade, and six tanks to the 7th Brigade.[1] One of the tank companies allotted to the 9th Brigade was assembled during the night of August 7th on the south bank of the Luce, having, by permission of the 42nd French Division, crossed the river before " zero " by the bridge at Thennes, which was outside the 3rd Canadian Division boundary. The other company assembled on the north side of the river close to the bridge at Domart. It was not considered advisable for this company to cross the river before " zero," as the danger of the enemy hearing the noise of the engines crossing the bridge, which was less than 1,000 yards from his lines, was too great. In spite of the difficulties caused by the lack of crossings over the Luce and by the bad approaches to the bridges, the assembly of the troops and tanks was carried out in silence and without a hitch. The Australians were relieved, and the Canadian troops were in their starting positions by 4 a.m.

All the tanks started from their assembly positions eight minutes before " zero " ; at " zero " the artillery barrage opened, and the infantry, keeping well up to it, advanced to the assault. The particularly heavy mist which hung over the Luce valley, while undoubtedly helping to reduce our casualties, made it very difficult for the troops to keep direction. The 9th Brigade on the right attacked with the 43rd, 116th, and 58th Battalions from right to left in the front line, and with the 52nd Battalion in support ; the 8th Brigade, which had a smaller front and a more limited objective, attacked with the 1st Canadian Mounted Rifle Battalion leading, and the 2nd C.M.R. Battalion in support ; the 4th and 5th C.M.R. Battalions were held in divisional reserve. The hostile barrage, which did not come down until about five minutes after " zero," was rather wild and not particularly heavy, though Domart bridge, as had been expected, received a great deal of attention. Luckily, the soil on each side of the road at this point was very marshy, and the effect of the shells bursting on the soft ground was very much localised.

The task of the 43rd Battalion on the extreme right of the 9th Brigade was a particularly difficult one. Owing to the glacis slope running down to the Luce from the edge of Rifle Wood, a direct attack would probably have been very costly. The 43rd Battalion, therefore, moved eastwards a short way along the Luce and enveloped the wood from the north.[2] Detachments entered the wood soon after 5 a.m., but it was not until

---

[1] In addition four supply tanks for carrying engineer material, ammunition, and stores were allotted to the division, of which two were allotted to the 7th Brigade, which had the furthest distance to go, and one to each of the other two brigades.

[2] The care and thoroughness with which subordinate commanders worked out their detailed arrangements for the attack are well illustrated by the accompanying sketch, which shows the plan of the 43rd Battalion for the capture of Rifle and Hollan Woods. While one company made a direct frontal attack, the remaining three companies moved to the north. These three companies then swung to the south in succession, one company attacking Rifle Wood from the north, another company similarly swinging round on Hollan Wood from the same direction, and the last company making straight for Vignette Wood, which was known to contain a battery of guns.

ATTACK OF THE 9TH CANADIAN BRIGADE

AUGUST 8.1918

E.G. Gardiner.

DOMART

HANGARD

DEMUIN

HOURGES

52nd Bn.

58th Bn.

116th Bn.

43rd Bn.

8th Can. Bde. Attack

Boundary with French

Original Front Line

R. Luce

Bode

Held by 8th Bn. Tr.

Elbe Tr.

1 (3 Plns.)

Rifle Wood

2

1 Pln.

1 Pln.

1 Pln.

1 Pln.

116th Bn.

Andrea Ravine

Inter-Allied Platoon

3

Hollon Wood

Moreuil Wood

Hamon Wood

Vignette Wood

4

58th Bn.

116th Bn.

FIRST OBJECTIVE

43rd Bn.

To Roye

On Right   43rd Cdn. Bn.
In Centre   116th .. ..
On Left   58th   .. ..
Reserve   52nd   .. ..

Companies of 43rd Cdn Bn are numbered in the order
of employment

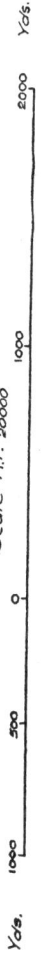

Scale R.F. 20000

Yds.   1000   500   0   1000   2000   Yds.

CANADIAN ENGINEERS FILLING IN THE CRATER BLOWN BY THE
GERMANS IN THE BRIDGE AT HANGARD.

By kind permission of the Canadian Government.

No. 13.

CANADIANS CAPTURING A GERMAN GUN NEAR MEZIÈRES.

By kind permission of the Canadian Government.

7.30 a.m. that the machine-gun nests were disposed of, and the wood finally captured. Hangard fell into the hands of the 8th Brigade without difficulty, and by 6.10 a.m. Demuin was occupied by the 58th Battalion.[1] About 6.15 a.m. the 116th Battalion, by a turning movement, drove the enemy from the Rifle Wood–Hangard road, thus assisting the 43rd Battalion to clear Rifle Wood. By 8.30 a.m. the 9th Brigade had captured Hollan Wood, the 8th Brigade had reached its objectives, while the 7th Brigade, which had followed up the 9th Brigade, was advancing eastwards from Rifle Wood to its starting position for the advance to the second objective. A gap of eighteen feet was found in the bridge at Hangard, but it was promptly repaired by the Canadian Engineers, and by 11 a.m. was ready for the passage of field artillery.

The advance from the first to the second objective met with little resistance, many guns and prisoners were taken, and by 12 noon the whole of the second objective within its divisional boundaries was in the hands of the 3rd Canadian Division.[2] This completed the task of the division for the day, and the 4th Canadian Division began to pass through on its way to the third and last objective of the Canadian Corps (blue dotted line).

During the advance it was of the utmost importance that close touch should be kept by the 3rd Canadian Division with the left of the First French Army, especially as the latter was attacking forty minutes later than the Fourth Army. This was successfully accomplished by an international liaison force which was commanded by a French officer and consisted of 30 men of the 42nd French Division, with one mitrailleuse, and a platoon of the 43rd Canadian Battalion. The liaison force thus formed acted under the orders of the officer commanding the 43rd Battalion. It proceeded along the southern edge of Rifle Wood and assisted in the capture of Hollan Wood.

The Franco-British liaison force

Simultaneously with the 3rd Canadian Division, the 1st Canadian Division, under the command of Maj.-Gen. A. C. MacDonnell, and the 2nd Canadian Division, under that of Maj.-Gen. Sir H. E. Burstall, in the centre and on the left of the corps front respectively, advanced under cover of the barrage. The frontage allotted to both divisions was practically equal and was about 2,500 yards wide at the " starting line," narrowing down to 1,500 yards and 2,000 yards respectively on the final objective (blue dotted line). Each division attacked on a front of one brigade, resuming the advance, as each successive objective was reached, with fresh brigades which " leap-frogged " the brigades which had carried out the previous attack. In the centre the 1st Canadian Division detailed the 3rd Canadian Brigade and the 4th Mark V Tank Battalion, consisting of forty-two tanks, to capture the first

The advance of the 1st and 2nd Canadian Divisions to the first objective

---

[1] It was during this advance that Corporal Harry Miner, 58th Canadian Battalion, 2nd Central Ontario Regiment, so distinguished himself. See Appendix E, No. 37.

[2] In this attack the 3rd Canadian Division completely defeated the 225th (Prussian) Division, which was withdrawn the following day, having lost in prisoners alone 44 officers and 1,732 other ranks. The Canadians also captured men of the 14th Bavarian Division and 192nd Division, but the greater part of these divisions was opposed to the French.

objective. This brigade was reinforced by two battalions, one from each of the reserve brigades, to ensure sufficient weight being available to break the enemy's main line of resistance without delay. Regardless of hostile posts which held out, the forward troops pushed on boldly and quickly, leaving these strong points to be dealt with by the troops who followed them.[1] As a result of these tactics, fighting was at one time going on simultaneously between Morgemont Wood and Aubercourt, an area more than 2,000 yards in depth. In Hangard Wood a strong hostile post at first checked a company of the 13th Canadian Battalion, but Corporal H. J. Good dashed forward alone and killed several of the garrison, the remainder then surrendering.[2] The western portion of the wood was speedily cleared with the aid of tanks, as was also Morgemont Wood, where a post with eight machine-guns was captured. The strongest resistance offered by the enemy was in a trench running across the divisional front just west of Aubercourt, and covering some of his main artillery positions. Thence the advance met little opposition, and the first objective was reached within the scheduled time at 6.20 a.m.

On the left the 2nd Canadian Division attacked with the 4th Canadian Brigade leading, assisted by two companies of fourteen tanks each of the 14th Mark V Tank Battalion. In the initial stages of the advance considerable resistance was encountered by the 19th Battalion from a trench about 1,000 yards east of the "starting line," but this was quickly overcome with the timely aid of the supporting tanks, which accounted for many nests of machine-guns. The co-operation of the 7th Brigade of the 2nd Australian Division on the left of the Canadians was also most effective. The Amiens–Chaulnes railway, the boundary between the Canadian and Australian Corps, had been strongly organised for defence, and there were many instances of the Australians assisting the advance of the 2nd Canadian Division with Lewis gun fire, as well as by sending small parties of infantry to assist in the capture of machine-gun posts along the railway, and of similar assistance rendered to the Australians by the 2nd Canadian Division.

Soon after 6 a.m., when the heavy artillery lifted off Marcelcave, the 19th and 21st Battalions, parties of which had worked round to the north of the village, rushed it from the north and west. Heavy fighting occurred in the southern portion of the village, but, with the assistance of the tanks, the infantry succeeded in capturing the whole of it by 6.45 a.m., together with a large number of prisoners. Meanwhile, the mist was lifting and the enemy's field artillery and anti-tank guns, stationed east of the village, directed a heavy fire on our tanks over open sights. This unfortunately resulted in heavy casualties to the tanks and their personnel, but, to compensate for this, the 5th Brigade Canadian Field Artillery and the 2nd Battalion Canadian Machine Gun Corps gave such efficient close support to the advance that the 19th and 21st Battalions reached their objectives by 6.55 a.m., and somewhat later Cancelette Wood ravine was captured by the 18th Battalion. By 7.45 a.m. the first objective

---

[1] The capture of one of the strongest of these posts was achieved practically single-handed by Private John Croak, 13th Canadian Battalion, Quebec Regiment. See Appendix E, No. 13.
[2] See Appendix E, No. 19.

To face page 37.

No. 14.

A 4.2 INCH HOWITZER BATTERY CAPTURED BY THE CANADIANS ON AUGUST 8TH.

By kind permission of the Canadian Government.

had thus been secured along the whole front of the 2nd Canadian Division.

As soon as the leading brigades of the 1st and 2nd Canadian Divisions had reached the first objective, the creeping barrage was halted, and a protective barrage was put down a few hundred yards **Their further advance to the second objective** in advance of the captured positions in order to deal with any possible hostile counter-attacks. During the pause of two hours previously arranged, the 1st and 5th Canadian Brigades closed up and, passing through the brigades on the first objective, formed up ready to continue the advance. At 8.20 a.m. the artillery lifted its fire, and the advance was renewed. The troops of the 1st Brigade went forward without difficulty as far as Ignaucourt and Lemaire Wood. Hostile machine-guns holding the western edge of Lemaire Wood disputed our advance, but were forced to surrender their positions when shelled by the supporting field artillery. On the right of the attack the Canadians came under heavy direct fire from the hill north of Cayeux. The village was, however, taken at a rush, and by 11.30 a.m., after some resistance on the southern edge of Ruisseau Wood and on the high ground north of Cayeux, the second objective had been gained without further difficulty along the front of the 1st Canadian Division. On the left the 5th Brigade encountered little resistance from the enemy's infantry, but a stubborn defence was put up by a large number of machine-guns scattered throughout the area. Many of these machine-guns were concealed in the standing crops, and had to be dealt with one by one by the infantry and tanks, as their positions were not sufficiently defined for the artillery to engage them with success. On the other hand in Pieuret Wood, where our advance was held up for a short time by the fire from nests of machine-guns, the field artillery was of great assistance and very soon drove the enemy from the wood towards Wiencourt-l'Equipée. By this time the gradual improvement in visibility materially assisted the enemy's machine-gunners in engaging our troops, and consequently a number of casualties were suffered when crossing the crests of the ridges during the advance.

Little opposition was encountered in Wiencourt-l'Equipée, but there was heavy fighting in and around Guillaucourt, which was effectively shelled by the Canadian field artillery, assisted by three guns and two howitzers captured from the enemy in Pieuret Wood. By 12.10 p.m. Guillaucourt had been captured, and the 5th Canadian Brigade moved forward to its objective. Soon after this the second objective was reached on the whole front of the 2nd Canadian Division.[1]

At 5.20 a.m., exactly an hour after the attack began, the 4th Canadian Division, under the command of Maj.-Gen. Sir David Watson, began its

[1] In this attack the 1st and 2nd Canadian Divisions were opposed, contrary to expectation, by two divisions, namely, the 117th and the 109th, the latter being in process of relief by the former. This was fortunate for us, as, first, we found the enemy in a state of disorganisation owing to the relief, and, secondly, our attack practically overwhelmed two divisions, one of which would, but for the fact of this relief, have been available as a reserve in back areas. Both these divisions suffered heavy losses, 48 officers and 1,810 other ranks of the 117th, and 25 officers and 869 other ranks of the 109th being captured. These divisions were withdrawn from the line on August 11th and 12th respectively, and the 109th division was shortly afterwards disbanded. One regiment of the 41st Division was also in this area.

advance and moved forward to the general line of the Hollan Wood–Demuin road. It had been detailed to pass through the 3rd Canadian Division, **The advance of the 4th** and, following up the 3rd Cavalry Division, to secure **Canadian Division to** the third objective. The 1st Tank Battalion, which **the third objective** was attached to this division, consisted of thirty-four Mark V star tanks, each of which carried one machine-gun and two Lewis gun detachments. The tanks were to precede the infantry, and, having reached the third objective, were to disembark the detachments, which were to hold that line until the arrival of the infantry.

It was not possible to foretell the exact hour at which the division would pass through the 3rd Canadian Division on the second objective, but, as soon as news was received that the second objective had been captured, Maj.-Gen. Watson issued orders for the advance to begin; at 12.40 p.m. the leading brigades with the tanks passed through the 3rd Canadian Division. The advance was made with the 11th Brigade on the right, the 12th Brigade on the left, and with the 10th Brigade and the 4th Battalion Canadian Machine Gun Corps in support.

About three hours before the 4th Canadian Division began to advance from the second objective, the 3rd Cavalry Division had passed through the 3rd Canadian Division, with the Canadian Cavalry Brigade leading. The Canadian Cavalry Brigade captured Beaucourt village and reached the outskirts of Beaucourt Wood, which was found strongly held. A gallant attempt to gallop the wood was not successful. When the 11th Canadian Brigade arrived on the scene, the Canadian Cavalry Brigade was holding the eastern edge of Beaucourt village, but all attempts to advance beyond this were held up owing to machine-gun fire from Beaucourt Wood, which swept the open ground over which the advance must be made. The commanding officer of the 54th Battalion, after a daring personal reconnaissance, realised that no further headway could be made until the wood was taken, and that unless it was taken at once the advance of the whole brigade, and also of the division, was in danger of being checked. Notwithstanding that the wood was outside his own line of advance, he decided to attack it. No artillery, trench mortar, or machine-gun support was immediately available, but without any hesitation he deployed two platoons of his reserve company, and at a given signal led his men to the assault. Despite the entire absence of cover and the deadly intensity of the enemy's machine-gun fire, the gallant survivors effected an entry into the wood. At this moment the 102nd Battalion most opportunely arrived, and, with the assistance of the 72nd Battalion of the 12th Brigade, which attacked simultaneously from the north-west, succeeded in clearing the wood by 4.30 p.m. after stiff fighting, and in establishing a line on its southern edge.

South of Beaucourt Wood the ground was very open and devoid of cover ; consequently, when attempts were made to push forward to Le Quesnel, the Canadians suffered a considerable number of casualties from machine-gun fire from Fresnoy-en-Chaussée and the outskirts of Le Quesnel. As the resistance increased towards the evening it was decided to postpone the attack on Le Quesnel until next morning, and our line was consolidated on the eastern edge of the plateau north of Fresnoy-en-Chaussée and along the southern edge of Beaucourt Wood.

On the left of the 4th Canadian Division advance, the 12th Brigade, upon emerging from the Péronne and St. Quentin woods, came under heavy fire, chiefly from the right front, where the enemy had many machine-guns posted on the edges of the woods and in the chalk pits. The opposition was finally overcome by successful co-operation between a company of the 78th Battalion, the 13th Battery of Canadian Field Artillery, four or five tanks of the 1st Tank Battalion, and a medium trench mortar, during which the company of the 78th Battalion was handled with conspicuous skill by Lieut. Tait.[1] The 12th Brigade then pressed forward and by 6.15 p.m. had occupied the final objective.

In the meantime, about 11.15 a.m., while the 2nd Canadian Division was employed in clearing Guillaucourt, the 9th and 2nd

The capture of the third objective by the 1st and 2nd Canadian Divisions Cavalry Brigades of the 1st Cavalry Division, which had followed closely behind the infantry, passed through and reached the Amiens outer defences south of the railway. Behind them on the right, the 2nd Canadian Brigade, which had assumed the lead in the 1st Canadian Division, started from the second objective at 11.30 a.m.; advancing rapidly, it cleared Caix and arrived at its final objective about 1.15 p.m. On the left the 6th Canadian Brigade, detailed to carry forward the advance of the 2nd Canadian Division to the final objective, was at 1 p.m. in position east of Marcelcave waiting for orders to move through the 5th Brigade. These orders were not received until 2.30 p.m. owing to the difficulties which had been experienced by the 2nd Canadian Division in maintaining its communications. By 4.30 p.m., however, the 6th Brigade had passed the second objective, and, advancing without meeting any resistance, arrived at the final objective on the Amiens outer defences at 5.35 p.m.

As the result of the day's fighting, the Canadian Corps had captured the villages of Hangard, Demuin, Aubercourt, Marcelcave,

The result of the day's fighting by the Canadian Corps Beaucourt, Ignaucourt, Cayeux, Wiencourt-l'Equipée, Guillaucourt, and Caix, and had secured the whole of its objectives except on the right, where the enemy still stubbornly defended the village of Le Quesnel. On the left the 2nd Canadian Division had penetrated the enemy's territory to a depth of 14,000 yards, and had established connection with the Australian Corps on the Amiens outer defences south-east of Harbonnières. On the right the Independent Force had done fine work during the day and had materially assisted the advance of the left of the XXXI French Corps, especially in the capture of Mezières. At nightfall the Canadian Corps was in touch with the French on the Amiens–Roye road north of Fresnoy-en-Chaussée. One hundred and fourteen officers, 4,919 other ranks, and 161 guns were captured by the Canadians, together with several hundred machine-guns and large quantities of war material.

The manner in which the Canadian Corps, in spite of the short time it had had for preparation and of the difficulties it had to overcome on its

[1] See Appendix E, No. 42.

right, carried out the task allotted to it on August 8th will always rank as one of the finest performances accomplished by this famous corps during the Great War.

On the left of the Canadians, the Australian Corps was to attack between the Amiens–Chaulnes railway and the Somme. Sir John

The Australian Corps' plan of attack

Monash decided that the operation should be carried out on a front of two divisions. He detailed the 2nd and 3rd Australian Divisions, on the right and left respectively, to capture the first objective, on reaching which there was to be a pause of two hours in the advance. This pause was arranged to give time for the 5th and 4th Australian Divisions to pass through and capture the second and third objectives, the latter including the Amiens outer defences. It was synchronised with a similar pause of two hours in the advance of the 1st and 2nd Divisions of the Canadian Corps. The 1st Australian Division, which had only arrived from the north on August 7th, was held in corps reserve about Allonville and Daours.[1]

At 4.20 a.m. the 2nd Australian Division, under the command of Maj.-Gen. C. Rosenthal, and the 3rd Australian Division,

The advance of the 2nd and 3rd Australian Divisions to the first objective

under that of Maj.-Gen. J. Gellibrand, attacking with the 7th and 5th, and the 9th and 11th Brigades, respectively, moved steadily forward under the barrage towards their objectives. Each attacking brigade was allotted one company of twelve tanks of the 2nd and 13th Mark V Tank Battalions, of which, generally speaking, sections were sub-allotted to battalions.[2] Notwithstanding the heavy mist which, combined with the smoke shell and the dust raised by the barrage, made the maintenance of direction difficult, the attack was driven home with great energy. The resistance met with was generally weak, hostile machine-gun nests and strong points causing the only difficulties. One of these strong points which was temporarily holding up the advance was dealt with by Lieut. Alfred Gaby, 28th Australian Battalion, who, single-handed, compelled the surrender of 50 Germans with four machine-guns.[3] Some stout-hearted Germans in the neighbourhood of Warfusée-Abancourt put up a good fight, but an encircling movement by the infantry assisted by tanks soon resulted in their capture, together with a 5·9-inch battery complete with its officers. It had been expected that the capture of Accroche Wood, which lay just within the enemy's lines, would prove a difficult task, but the surprise of the enemy was so complete and the fog so dense that the garrison, which was a large one, was overwhelmed and driven by our barrage into its dug-outs, from which for the most part it emerged only to surrender. At different points, where the ground was more difficult, the rate of advance,

---

[1] Owing to the fact that the 13th Australian Brigade had been ordered to hold the Canadian Corps front of attack until the early morning of August 8th, the 1st Australian Brigade had been lent to the 4th Australian Division to replace it. The 4th Division, on August 8th, therefore consisted of the 1st, 4th, and 12th Brigades, whilst the 1st Division consisted of the 2nd, 3rd, and 13th Brigades.

[2] One supply tank, loaded up with ammunition and engineer stores of all kinds, was also allotted to each infantry brigade.

[3] See Appendix E, No. 18.

To face page 40.

PRISONERS CAPTURED BY THE AUSTRALIANS PASSING BURNING DUMPS IN THE CERISY-WARFUSÉE VALLEY.

By kind permission of the Australian Government.

owing to the density of the mist, was slower than had been expected, and the infantry was unable to keep close up to the barrage. The dangers resulting from this were neutralised, however, by the good work of the tanks which were of the greatest possible assistance in attacking strong points, thus enabling the infantry to capture them at small cost.

On the right a liaison force of two infantry companies was given the task of ensuring the maintenance of touch with the 4th Brigade of the 2nd Canadian Division, which also detailed a party for the same purpose. As a result the closest touch and excellent co-operation were maintained throughout the advance.

By 6.20 a.m., or soon afterwards, the whole of the first objective had been captured; the creeping barrage was then halted, and the protective barrage was put down while the infantry reorganised.

During the pause on the first objective the 5th Australian Division, under the command of Maj.-Gen. Sir J. J. T. Hobbs, and the 4th Aus-

The capture of the second objective by the 4th and 5th Australian Divisions

tralian Division, under that of Maj.-Gen. E. G. Sinclair-Maclagan, which had been following behind the 2nd and 3rd Australian Divisions, passed through them, the 15th, 8th, 12th, and 4th Brigades leading, from right to left, and took up their positions ready to continue the advance at 8.20 a.m. There were attached to each of these four brigades a brigade of field artillery and a section of an engineer field company, the whole forming a brigade group under the infantry brigade commander. The field artillery of these two divisions had previously been assisting in the barrage which covered the advance to the first objective, but had kept its gun teams handy, and, directly the infantry had reached the first objective, it limbered up and moved forward to join its brigade groups. Each division was given thirty Mark V tanks, which had not been engaged in the first phase, from the 2nd, 8th, and 13th Tank Battalions, and was also given one and half companies of the 15th Tank Battalion, equipped with Mark V star tanks, to carry machine-gun and Lewis gun detachments. These tanks advanced close in rear of the attacking brigades, ready to move forward to the third objective as exploiting detachments as soon as the second objective had been reached.

Meanwhile, behind the attacking divisions the 1st Cavalry Brigade, with sixteen whippet tanks, moved up in the closest touch with the infantry, ready to dash forward the moment the opportunity arrived. The 17th Armoured Car Battalion, consisting of twelve cars, also moved up as soon as the crews, helped by the 5th Australian Pioneer Battalion, had repaired the road sufficiently for the cars to pass.

Punctually to time, at 8.20 a.m. the advance to the second objective began. The enemy's artillery retaliation on the front of the 5th Australian Division was slight, and, shortly after leaving the first objective, the infantry came upon the enemy's battery positions. In the majority of cases the detachments had already abandoned their guns, but in some cases they stuck manfully to their positions and only surrendered when the batteries were captured at the point of the bayonet. On the right just east of Marcelcave, a battery of 5·9-inch howitzers was encountered firing at the infantry over open sights. One company of the 57th Battalion, 15th

G

Brigade, manœuvred to attack the howitzers, while a tank drove straight at the battery, only to be knocked out at forty yards' range before reaching it. Meanwhile, a second tank worked round the flank, and, as soon as it was discovered, the enemy jumped out of their gun-pits and surrendered. The village of Bayonvillers was not attacked frontally until after it had been outflanked by the leading battalions. The 58th Battalion, assisted by six Mark V tanks, was given the task of " mopping " it " up," [1] which was accomplished without much difficulty. By about 9 a.m. the leading battalions of the 5th Australian Division had reached the second objective, and about a quarter of an hour later the 1st Cavalry Brigade pushed its advanced guards through the right brigade of that division.

On the left the 4th Australian Division was almost equally successful, but, as the attack of the III Corps had not been able to progress as rapidly as that of the Australians, the enemy's artillery and machine-gun fire from the Chipilly spur, north of the Somme, caused casualties among the infantry and unfortunately knocked out a large number of tanks. In spite of the severity of this fire, the attacking units advanced in good order, meeting with some resistance on the right from Lena Wood. This was speedily overcome, and several guns were captured. Prisoners came in freely throughout the advance, and many field and heavy guns and howitzers fell into our hands. In many localities machine-gun nests were encountered; these were either dealt with by tanks or quickly outflanked and rushed by the infantry. By 10.30 a.m. the 4th Australian Division had reached the second objective all along its front.

Shortly before the second objective was reached, the 17th Armoured Car Battalion, seeing that there was little resistance to the advance, went through the infantry along the main Amiens–Brie road, and after passing through a light artillery barrage, succeeded in obtaining excellent targets. After reaching La Flaque the crews of the armoured cars inflicted heavy casualties on the enemy by shooting down the valley west of Foucaucourt. The road here soon became blocked with hostile transport, the drivers of which, taking alarm at the sight of the cars, lost control of their animals, and many of the vehicles collided and fell across the road. The armoured cars then turned north and south to Proyart and Framerville. At the latter place many of the enemy were killed, much of his transport was destroyed, and the hostile rear services were thoroughly disorganised. At Proyart the armoured cars surprised some of the staff of the LI Corps Headquarters snatching a hasty meal, apparently ignorant that the battle had come so near. Their surprise was short-lived, for fire was opened on them through the windows of the room in which they were sitting. It was an unlucky chance that the Corps Commander had left in his car only about half an hour before the arrival of the armoured cars. The cars then patrolled the area until dusk, greatly adding to the enemy's demoralisation.

[1] " Mopping up " is a term commonly used to describe the clearing of trenches, dug-outs, fortified posts, etc., in which the enemy continues to hold out after the leading waves of an attack have passed.

ARMOURED CAR TEMPORARILY HELD UP BY FALLEN TREES ON THE VILLERS BRETONNEUX–BRIE ROAD.

By kind permission of the Australian Government.

Chipilly

Chipilly Spur

Cerisy-Gailly

Somme Canal

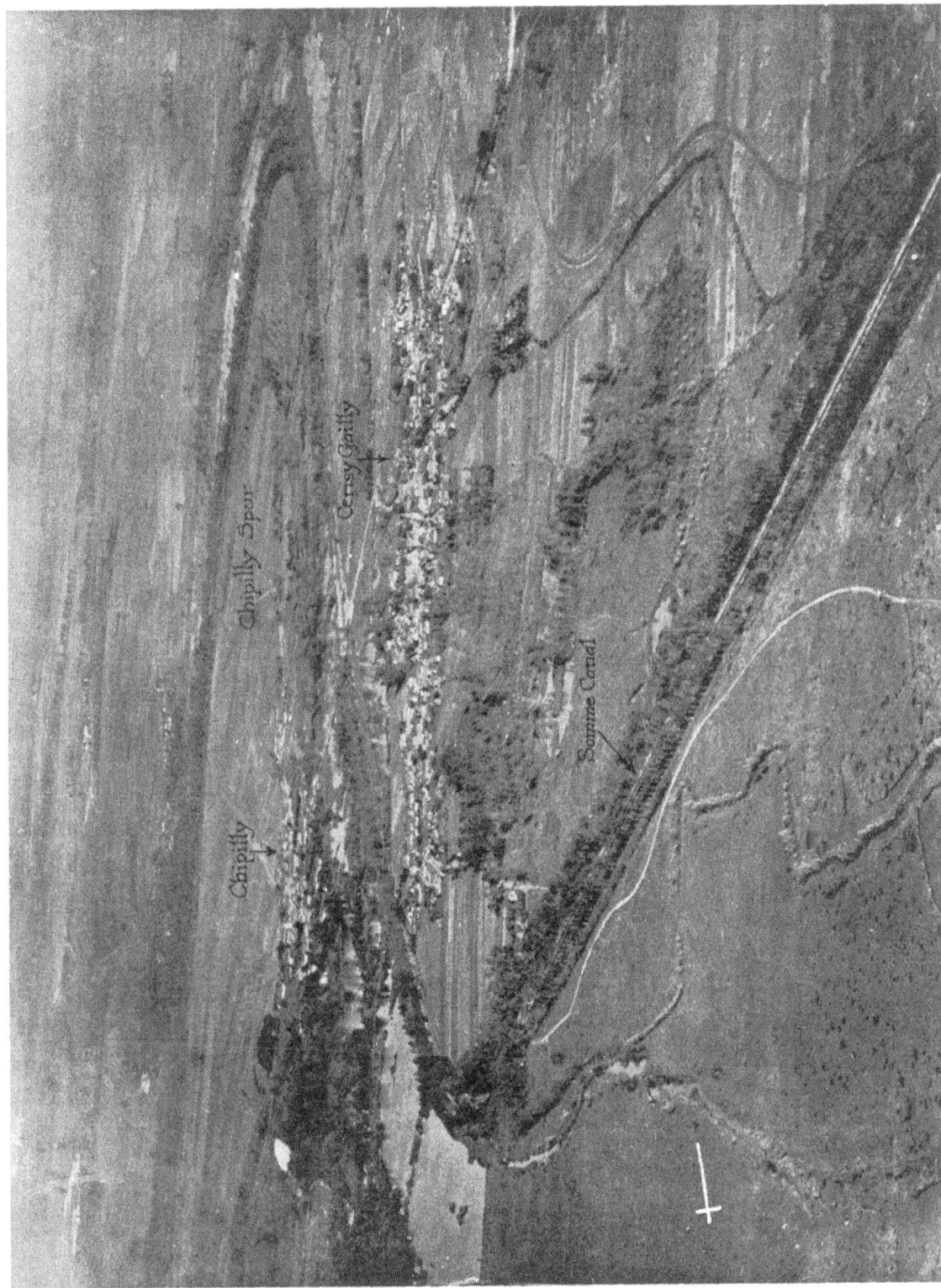

CHIPILLY AND CERISY-GAILLY.

Oblique air photograph.

So rapid had been the advance to the second objective that the Mark V star tanks, which had been detailed to follow up the cavalry to the Amiens outer defences, were not able to come up in time, and the 15th and 8th Brigades of the 5th Australian Division, and the 12th and 4th Brigades of the 4th Australian Division, after a short interval for re-organisation, decided to push on without them. The 15th Brigade and its attendant tanks, having "mopped up" Harbonnières and hoisted the Australian flag on the church tower, arrived at the third and final objective without difficulty about 10.30 a.m., the 8th Brigade reaching it about half an hour later. The brigades of the 4th Australian Division, owing to the losses incurred from the hostile fire on the left flank, were not ready to advance as early as those of the 5th Australian Division. They moved off from the second objective about 11 a.m. and again incurred heavy casualties, as the enemy had brought more guns into action on the north bank of the river. Taking advantage, however, of the folds in the ground and of all other available cover, and making light of the enemy's machine-gun defence, the division pushed gallantly on, using clever enveloping tactics, and soon after noon reached the final objective. As the troops on the extreme left were exposed to enfilade fire and to fire from their rear, the flank of the left battalion was swung back south of Mericourt-sur-Somme. As soon as it was seen that the advance north of the river was checked, the 1st Brigade, which had been held in reserve to the 4th Australian Division, established an outpost line along the southern bank of the Somme west-wards from Morcourt.

The final result of the day's fighting by the Australian Corps was the capture of the whole of the objectives allotted to it, except a small portion on the extreme left. The villages of Warfusée-Abancourt, Lamotte-en-Santerre, Bayonvillers, Harbonnières, Mor-court, Gailly, and the greater portion of the village of Cerisy-Gailly had been taken, and touch had been established on the right with the Canadian Corps. On the left, however, a junction with the III Corps had not been effected, the situation north of the river still being obscure.

One hundred and eighty-three officers, 7,742 other ranks, with 173 guns and numerous machine-guns, trench mortars, and anti-tank rifles were captured during the day, whilst the casualties of the corps were not only very slight, but were much less than the number of prisoners taken.[1] Never had the Australian Corps had such a successful day, and, as it was the first time it had been in action as a corps of five divisions, the result was especially satisfactory both to it and to its commander, Sir John Monash. Moreover, not only their careful preparation for the attack itself, but all their labour and persistent offensive tactics of the previous three months were reaping a splendid harvest.

[1] In this attack the Australians were opposed by the 41st (East Prussian) and 13th (West-phalian) Divisions on either side of the Amiens–Brie road, as well as by elements of the 108th and 43rd Reserve Divisions, which were relieving each other astride the Somme. So severely were the 108th and 43rd Reserve Divsiions handled in this and the subsequent days' fighting that they were both shortly afterwards disbanded.

Before describing the attack of the III Corps north of the Somme, it is necessary to give a more detailed account of the dashing work done by the Cavalry Corps in the main attack on the opening day of the Battle of Amiens.

The action of the Cavalry Corps

At " zero " the troops of the Cavalry Corps, having passed through Amiens, were concentrated in the triangle formed by the Villers Bretonneux and Roye roads east of Longueau. At 5.20 a.m. the heads of the 1st and 9th Brigades of the 1st Cavalry Division (1st, 2nd, and 9th Brigades), commanded by Maj.-Gen. R. L. Mullins, were about one mile north-east of Cachy. The 3rd Cavalry Division (6th, 7th, and Canadian Brigades), commanded by Maj.-Gen. A. E. W. Harman, was also well forward just west of Cachy, with the Canadian Brigade leading. The 2nd Cavalry Division (3rd, 4th, and 5th Brigades), commanded by Maj.-Gen. T. T. Pitman, was in reserve at the road junction east of Longueau. Following the Canadian Corps as it advanced, the 3rd Cavalry Division was confronted with the difficulty of crossing the Luce, but, owing to the successful reconnaissance carried out by the cavalry patrols which had accompanied the infantry, and to the excellent arrangements made for crossing trenches, the Canadian Cavalry Brigade started to cross at Ignaucourt at 9.20 a.m.

At this time the two leading brigades of the 1st Cavalry Division were astride the Villers Bretonneux–Chaulnes railway near Marcelcave, with the 9th Cavalry Brigade south of the railway following the 2nd Canadian Division, and the 1st Cavalry Brigade north of the railway in rear of the 5th Australian Division. The remaining brigades of the 3rd and 1st Cavalry Divisions were following close behind, and the 2nd Cavalry Division, with the reserve whippet tanks, was massed on the plateau between Cachy and L'Abbé Wood.

The 3rd Cavalry Division, having crossed the Luce at Ignaucourt, passed through the infantry. On approaching Beaucourt, which was held by the enemy, two parties of the Canadian Cavalry Brigade worked round to the north and south of the village. The southern party, consisting of two troops of Strathcona's Horse, reached the Amiens–Roye road without difficulty, and penetrated as far as Fresnoy-en-Chaussée, where 125 prisoners were captured. The further advance of this party was, however, held up south-west of Beaucourt Wood. The northern party, consisting of the Royal Canadian Dragoons with eight whippets, was also checked north-west of the wood. The whippet tanks came into action in support, but were unable to reach the wood on account of the fire of the enemy's field guns. Beaucourt village was captured by the main body of the Canadian Cavalry Brigade with great dash, but it was unable to advance east of the village. The situation in front of Beaucourt Wood remained unchanged until the arrival of the 11th Brigade of the 4th Canadian Division, which passed through the Canadian cavalry and captured the wood later in the day.[1]

On the left of the Canadian Cavalry Brigade, the 7th Cavalry Brigade pushed forward south of Cayeux and carried the wood south of the village at the gallop, taking 200 prisoners. It then gained the high ground south

---

[1] See page 38.

No. 18.

THE CAVALRY DISMOUNTED NEAR FRAMERVILLE.

By kind permission of the Australian Government.

of Caix in the next bound and captured another 100 prisoners, five machine-guns, and six heavy guns. The 7th Cavalry Brigade was followed by the 6th Cavalry Brigade, which, after passing through Cayeux Wood, advanced in a southerly direction towards Le Quesnel. Hostile machine-guns in Beaucourt Wood and Le Quesnel checked the right of the brigade, but the left pushed forward in conjunction with the 7th Cavalry Brigade, and by 2.35 p.m. had occupied the Amiens outer defences, which it held until the arrival of the 4th Canadian Division.

Hearing of the resistance encountered in Beaucourt Wood, Sir Charles Kavanagh ordered two brigades of the 2nd Cavalry Division forward from corps reserve with a view to their assisting the left of the 3rd Cavalry Division by moving north of the Luce; the successful advance, however, of the 7th Cavalry Brigade enabled the 3rd Cavalry Division to reach its objective on the left unaided.

Meanwhile, the 1st Cavalry Division passed through the infantry of the 2nd Canadian and 5th Australian Divisions when they reached the neighbourhood of Guillaucourt and Bayonvillers. The 1st Cavalry Brigade, north of the railway, advanced rapidly to Harbonnières, which it enveloped, moving north and south of the village. The 5th Dragoon Guards from the 1st Cavalry Brigade then pushed on towards Vauvillers, but, finding it strongly defended, masked it with one squadron and swung round to the north between it and Framerville. During this movement the regiment captured a train full of reinforcements, securing 600 prisoners and a battery of guns. The opposition now became too great to allow of a further advance eastwards, and in consequence the 1st Cavalry Brigade, about noon, moved southwards to help the 9th Cavalry Brigade, which, operating south of the railway, had encountered considerable opposition from enemy machine-guns between Caix and Guillaucourt. Avoiding these machine-guns, the 9th Cavalry Brigade gained the valley south of Harbonnières and, working up the valley, had by 1 p.m. reached the Amiens outer defences south-east of Harbonnières, on the right of the 1st Cavalry Brigade. In order to secure the third objective east of Caix, the 2nd Cavalry Brigade, which had followed up the advance as far as Guillaucourt, was ordered at 1 p.m. to secure Caix and the Amiens outer defences east of that village. This was successfully carried out in conjunction with the 2nd Canadian Brigade, and touch was established with the 7th Cavalry Brigade on the right, and with the 9th Cavalry Brigade on the left, on the line of the final objective. The 1st Cavalry Division endeavoured to make further progress, but patrols from the 2nd and 9th Cavalry Brigades found Vrély and Rosières-en-Santerre strongly occupied.

When it was found that their assistance was not required, the two brigades of the 2nd Cavalry Division, which had been sent forward to reinforce the 3rd Cavalry Division, advanced north of the Luce and crossed the Amiens outer defences with the object of exploiting the enemy's disorganisation to the full. They found, however, that the line Beaufort–Warvillers–Vrély–Rosières-en-Santerre was strongly held by the enemy's reinforcements, chiefly machine-guns, and they were unable, therefore, to make any serious progress. During the night of August 8th the 2nd Cavalry Division relieved the 3rd Cavalry Division.

The cavalry on August 8th did much useful work. In addition to the large number of prisoners, guns, and material which it actually captured, its rapid advance and the bold manner in which it had been handled had a very marked effect on the enemy's moral. It was the first occasion on which, since the war began, the cavalry in France had been able to move rapidly across open country against a beaten enemy, and reap the fruits of a successful infantry and tank attack.

The III Corps' plan of attack

The task that had been given to the III Corps in the operations was to secure the Amiens outer defences between the Somme and the Ancre, as a flank to the main attack of the Canadian and Australian Corps south of the Somme. Owing to the difficulties of the ground, which have already been described, it was not considered possible for this task to be completed on the first day of the offensive, and a less distant objective was in consequence decided upon for August 8th. Sir Richard Butler's plan was to attack with three divisions. On the right, the 58th (London) Division, under the command of Maj.-Gen. F. W. Ramsay, and the 18th (Eastern) Division, under that of Maj.-Gen. R. P. Lee, were to attack shoulder to shoulder, with the right of the 58th Division making liaison on the Somme with the left of the Australian Corps. The 36th Brigade from the 12th (Eastern) Division was attached to the 18th Division to take the place of the 54th Brigade, which had been involved in the hostile attack by the 27th Württemberg Division on August 6th. On the left, and north of the 18th Division, after a gap of 500 yards on which no attack was to take place, the 12th Division, less the 36th Brigade, under the command of Maj.-Gen. H. W. Higginson, was to attack on a front of 2,000 yards. It was to capture a portion of the slopes leading down to the Ancre, with the idea of encircling Morlancourt in conjunction with the attack on the right and thus compelling the enemy to evacuate the village.

The attack was to be carried out in two phases. In the first phase, the 58th Division, of which two battalions of the 175th Brigade were retained in corps reserve, and the 18th Division were to capture the first objective, which included Sailly Laurette and Malard Wood. In order to give the troops of the 58th Division a straight run at Malard Wood, it was very important that the attack on Sailly Laurette should be successful. The capture of this village was, therefore, to some extent regarded as a separate and preliminary operation, and a battalion was specially detailed for the purpose. After an hour's halt on the first objective, to enable the "leap-frogging" troops to get into position, the second phase was to begin. This phase entailed the capture of the second objective, which included the Chipilly spur, Gressaire Wood, the southern portion of Tailles Wood, and the Brickyard; the line to be reached bending back thence to the "starting line" on the left of the 18th Division front.

For these operations three companies of tanks of the 10th Mark V Tank Battalion (twenty-two tanks) and twelve supply tanks were available. Of these, one company was allotted to the 58th Division, and two companies to the 18th Division; of the supply tanks the two brigades

CERISY

PERCOURT

HAMEL-CERISY ROAD →

Somme Crossing
at Q.14.2.8.

SAILLY LAURETTE.

SAILLY LAURETTE.

Oblique air photograph.

destined for the final objective had three each, while each of the other three brigades engaged had two each.

The disposition of
the troops at
"zero"
The III Corps was disposed at "zero" as follows :

Main attack.

58th Division—right attack—
  174th Brigade for first objective (Green line), and
  2/10th London (from 175th Brigade) to attack Sailly Laurette.
  173rd Brigade (less 1 Battalion) for second objective (Red line).
  1 Company, 10th Mark V Tank Battalion.
  1 Battalion (173rd Brigade) ⎱
  1 Battalion (36th Brigade) ⎰ In reserve.
18th Division—left attack—
  36th Brigade (less 1 Battalion) ⎱ for first objective
  and 1 Battalion (55th Brigade) ⎰   (Green line).
  53rd Brigade for second objective (Red line).
  2 Companies, 10th Mark V Tank Battalion.
  54th Brigade   ⎱
  55th Brigade (less 1 Battalion) ⎰ In reserve.

Subsidiary attack.

12th Division—
35th Brigade.
37th Brigade (in reserve).

Corps reserve.

175th Brigade (less 1 Battalion).
1/1st Northumberland Hussars.[1]
50th Battalion Machine Gun Corps.

Defensive front.

47th Division and 130th American Regiment.

Under Army Headquarters.

33rd American Division, less 1 Regiment.

Owing partly to the uncertainty as to the exact position of the front line on the 18th Division front, due to the hostile attack on August 6th,
and partly to the darkness of the night and some hostile gas shelling, great difficulties were encountered in launching the attack.[2] Nevertheless, a good start was made in the thick mist, which, here as elsewhere, enveloped the battle-field. A powerful artillery barrage of 350 guns, as well as the fire of some 200 heavy howitzers and long-range guns, supported the infantry and tanks

---

[1] Each division was allotted one troop from the 1/1st Northumberland Hussars.

[2] The task of the 36th Brigade was made especially difficult by the fact that it was only placed at Maj.-Gen. Lee's disposal on August 7th to replace the 54th Brigade. It had, therefore, no time for previous reconnaissance of the ground. In spite of this the brigade was ready on the "starting line" by 3.30 a.m.

of the 18th and 58th Divisions. On the attack being launched it was found that the enemy's barrage was not formidable, but the hostile infantry, and especially the machine-gunners, resisted the advance with determination. At the time that the 174th Brigade was due to be in possession of Sailly Laurette and Malard Wood, the village had been taken, but the hostile posts in the wood were still uncaptured and for some hours continued to offer resistance. As was to be anticipated, the uncertainty of the position on the front of the 18th Division at " zero " made the advance of the 36th Brigade more difficult, and, at the moment when it should have been on the first objective, the situation was obscure and caused some anxiety. By 9 a.m., however, the position had been made good, partly by the troops originally detailed for the task, and partly by the 53rd Brigade moving up on its way to the second objective.

On the left the subsidiary operation of the 12th Division, which was carried out by the 7th Norfolk and the 9th Essex of the 35th Brigade, went entirely according to plan and completed the success of the first phase of the attack.

The second phase of the attack proved a more arduous task. On the right the 173rd Brigade was strongly opposed from the western slopes of the Chipilly spur by portions of the 108th and 43rd Reserve Divisions, which, as has already been stated,[1] were relieving each other astride the Somme.

The advance against the second objective

Our troops, advancing towards the second objective, on emerging from Malard Wood were met by heavy machine-gun fire from Chipilly and the Chipilly spur, and during August 8th it was not found possible to advance our line beyond the eastern outskirts of the wood, except for some small parties which worked their way forward in the first attack.

On the left the 53rd Brigade had some hard fighting before it reached its starting position on the first objective. From there the left of the brigade pushed on against considerable opposition. The 7th Royal West Kent on the left, and the battalion commander and about eighty men of the 10th Essex in the centre, reached a line running south-eastward from the Brickyard; the 8th Royal Berkshire, on the right of the 10th Essex, advanced along the northern edge of Malard Wood, but was unable to reach its objective, and parties of the enemy with machine-guns, working westward from Gressaire Wood, were thus able to attack the advanced troops of the 53rd Brigade in flank and rear. These advanced troops were in consequence compelled to withdraw, and only isolated detachments of our troops remained between the first and second objectives.

Meanwhile, on the extreme left of the III Corps, the 12th Division had, as already described, gained the whole of its objective, and, except in the case of the 1/1st Cambridgeshire on the right, the position which had been reached was maintained. This battalion was forced back, but, attacking again at 12.15 p.m., was completely successful in regaining the lost ground.

The eight hours' fighting of the morning, although yielding a substantial measure of success, had not given us all the ground we wanted, and

[1] See note to page 43.

The CHIPILLY Spur from the

e Canal.

Swamp west of Canal.

Morcourt Church.

CERISY—MORCOURT road.

in particular the Chipilly spur.   That such should have been the case was due partly to the stubborn resistance with which the enemy met the

The result of the day's fighting by the III Corps attack, and for which he must be given full credit, and partly to the fact that the infantry was not able to establish satisfactory co-operation with the tanks.   The mist in the early morning and the gas shelling during the night were probably the principal causes for this lack of co-operation between the two arms.   Careful arrangements had been made beforehand for rendez-vous between tanks and individual infantry units, in many cases verbally, directly between the officers in command of the units concerned.   These arrangements, unfortunately, could not be carried out.   Neither the 173rd Brigade nor the 53rd Brigade, whose rôle it was to go forward from the first to the second objective, found tanks awaiting them on the first objective as expected.   The 36th Brigade began operations without tanks. The 174th Brigade was more fortunate, as its tanks arrived to time and were of the greatest assistance in securing the first objective on the 58th Division front.   On the corps front as a whole, however, the two arms seem to have been by force of circumstances compelled to work independently.   It must also be remembered that the ground in the III Corps sector, cut up as it was by deep ravines from the Somme valley in the south and from the Ancre on the north, was a far less favourable area for tanks to operate in successfully than were the areas of the Australian and Canadian Corps south of the Somme.

The remainder of August 8th was fully occupied on the III Corps front in clearing up the ground gained, and in dealing with counter-attacks.   One such counter-attack, which was delivered early in the day by the 27th Württemberg Division and forced the advanced troops of the 18th Division round the Brickyard to withdraw, has already been mentioned.   During the afternoon the artillery was called upon on three occasions to deal with hostile concentrations, and on each occasion was able to prevent the attack from materialising.   The " mopping up " of the captured territory was, however, a more arduous matter, as parties of the enemy continued to hold out in Malard Wood after its capture, and a considerable time elapsed before their resistance was overcome by the 58th Division.   As a result of the day's fighting the first objective on the front of the 58th and 18th Divisions, and the final objective of the 12th Division, had been captured.   While the casualties had been com-paratively heavier than in the main attack south of the river, they were by no means excessive and compared favourably with the large number of prisoners taken, which totalled 2,388, including 75 officers.   About forty guns, together with numerous machine-guns and other material, were also captured.   It was unfortunate that the III Corps, which had to advance over such difficult country, should have found the enemy expecting a counter-attack on account of the success of his operation on August 6th.   The element of surprise, which helped us so much on the rest of the front, was, therefore, to a great extent lacking on the front of the III Corps.   When the spirited nature of the enemy's resistance, the difficulties the 18th and 58th Divisions encountered, and the fact that they had been heavily engaged on many occasions earlier in the

H

year,[1] are taken into account, the manner in which these divisions, largely composed as they were of young and only partially trained soldiers, endeavoured to carry out their task was worthy of all praise.

Throughout the battle most valuable work was performed by the Royal Air Force. During the early morning flying was restricted by the thick mist, but directly the weather cleared our aeroplanes could be seen everywhere hovering over the enemy's territory at various altitudes searching for prey. Apart from the usual artillery and contact patrol work, two, and sometimes three, scout squadrons flew over each corps front, engaged solely in attacking the enemy's troops and transport from low altitudes. Flying very low, which, even in trench warfare, is extremely dangerous on account of the machine-gun fire from the ground, our aeroplanes completed the demoralisation of the enemy by attacking his retiring troops and transport with bombs and machine-gun fire, and by shooting gun teams in the act of withdrawing the guns. Early in the morning, some low-flying aeroplanes discovered an 11-inch long-range railway gun, which had been used in the bombardment of Amiens, busily firing, although our infantry was advancing within about 1,000 yards of its position. Swooping down close to the gun our airmen dropped a number of bombs on it with such effect that, when the troops of the 5th Australian Division arrived on the spot, they found the whole gun crew of about twenty men either killed or wounded. We lost on August 8th about forty aeroplanes, many of which were brought down by machine-gun fire from the ground. The results obtained, however, were well worth the losses incurred.[2]

As soon as the advance began our observation balloons were pushed well forward with the greatest rapidity. They obtained much useful information and performed valuable service in directing the fire of the mobile artillery.

At 5 a.m., forty minutes after the attack of the Fourth Army was launched, and just as the infantry of the 3rd Canadian Division was entering Rifle Wood, the troops of the First French Army advanced to the assault. Their attack was preceded by a very heavy artillery bombardment of the enemy's position, which began at 4.20 a.m., up to which hour only normal artillery activity had been permitted. The attack against the commanding ground in the angle between the Avre and the Luce was made by two divisions of the XXXI French Corps, while a third division was told off to capture the town of Moreuil. The enemy resisted stubbornly, but was gradually driven back and Moreuil Wood captured, thus securing the flank of the Fourth Army. The French advance then continued until the villages of Villers-aux-Erables and Mezières were reached. At the former village some British tanks had been detailed to co-operate with the French should they require assistance, but the tanks were unable to come up in time. The Canadian Independent Force, however, co-operated with the French most successfully and assisted them in the

The work of the Royal Air Force

The attack by the First French Army

---

[1] They both suffered severely in the March retreat.
[2] The pluck and endurance of our airmen are well illustrated by the story of Captain Felix West, 8th Squadron, Royal Air Force. See Appendix E, No. 48.

THE 11-INCH NAVAL GUN ON RAILWAY MOUNTING CAPTURED BY THE
ROYAL AIR FORCE AND AUSTRALIANS ON AUGUST 8TH.

By kind permission of the Australian Government.

No. 21.

FRENCH AND CANADIAN TROOPS ON THE ROYE ROAD.

By kind permission of the Canadian Government.

SOME OF THE GUNS TAKEN ON AUGUST 8TH.

British official photograph.

No. 23.

SOME OF THE PRISONERS CAPTURED ON AUGUST 8TH.

British official photograph.

capture of both Villers-aux-Erables and Mezières, which were in French hands by 1 p.m.

By the end of the day the First French Army had made valuable progress and, though Fresnoy-en-Chaussée was still in the enemy's hands, Moreuil and Plessier-Rozainvillers were in the possession of the French, and the junction of the Allies was assured by the Canadian Independent Force. As a result of the fighting about 150 officers, 3,000 other ranks, and a number of guns were captured by the French.[1]

On the evening of August 8th the situation on the Fourth Army front was most satisfactory. The main attack south of the Somme had

The situation on the Fourth Army front on the evening of August 8th been successful almost beyond the most sanguine expectations, and the Canadian and Australian Corps had reached their final objectives, except for a small portion on their extreme northern and southern flanks. The losses of these two corps had been exceptionally light, the largest capture of prisoners and guns taken on any one day during the war on the western front had been made, and, in addition, the enemy's troops were thoroughly demoralised. Prisoners from eleven different divisions had been captured by the Fourth Army, there were few hostile reserves immediately available, and the prospects of further success on the following day were extremely bright.

Orders were accordingly issued by Sir Henry Rawlinson for the advance to be continued next morning with a view to reaching the

The orders for August 9th general line Roye–Chaulnes–Bray-sur-Somme–Dernancourt. The Canadian Corps was to establish itself on the general line Roye–Hattencourt-Hallu. The Australian Corps, conforming in the first instance with the advance of the Canadian Corps, was to establish itself on the general line Lihons–Framerville–Mericourt-sur-Somme, while the III Corps was to secure the Etinehem spur and the high ground north of it, joining up with the original front line at Dernancourt, and forming a strong defensive flank to the army. When the III Corps reached its objective, the Australian Corps was to swing forward to the general line Lihons–Chuignolles. A study of the map will show that the main advance would thus be on the Canadian Corps front in a south-easterly direction, Special emphasis was laid in the army orders on the importance of the III Corps attaining their objective, and of securing the left flank of the army. The hour of the Canadian attack, with which the Australian Corps was to conform, was left to the discretion of the Canadian Corps Commander, while north of the Somme the III Corps Commander was authorised to fix the time for launching his own attack. The Cavalry Corps was ordered to operate on the right of the army front so as to assist the Canadian Corps in gaining its objectives and to facilitate the advance of the First French Army.

---

[1] In this attack prisoners were taken from seven German divisions, of which the 14th Bavarian Division, which also lost severely to the Canadians, suffered the heaviest casualties.

CHAPTER IV

THE BATTLE OF AMIENS (*continued*), AUGUST 9TH—11TH, AND THE EVENTS OF AUGUST 12TH—21ST

Maps 1, 2, 3, and 4

August 9th ; the Canadian Corps—The capture of Le Quesnel—The action of the 2nd and 1st Cavalry Divisions—The advance of the 3rd, 1st, and 2nd Canadian Divisions—The Australian Corps—The III Corps operations—The attack on the Chipilly spur—The situation on the night of August 9th—The re-allotment of front between the Australian and III Corps—The orders for August 10th—August 10th ; the Canadian Corps ; the Chilly and Le Quesnoy operations—The Australian Corps ; the advance on Lihons—The attacks astride the Somme by the 3rd and 4th Australian Divisions and the 131st American Regiment—The complete occupation of the Amiens outer defences by the III Corps—The orders for August 11th—August 11th ; the Canadian Corps—Heavy hostile counter-attacks—The Australian Corps ; the capture of Lihons—The general situation on August 11th ; the Army Commander's conference—A lull in the battle—Events from August 12th–16th—August 17th ; instructions from General Headquarters—The progress of the First French Army, August 11th–20th—The reorganisation of the front of the Fourth Army—The German dilemma—The results of the Battle of Amiens.

IT was originally intended that the general advance on the front of the Canadian Corps should begin at 10 a.m. on August 9th. The 3rd,

August 9th : the Canadian Corps

1st, and 2nd Canadian Divisions were to attack, the 3rd Division passing through the 4th Division after the latter had captured Le Quesnel. Owing, however, to the difficulties of communication and other causes, the general forward movement did not begin till 11 a.m., and in the case of some brigades not till 1 p.m. As a result, the fighting was of a very disjointed nature throughout the day, the attacks of the various divisions and brigades starting at different times. Some of the attacks were covered by artillery or supported by tanks ; others were carried out by infantry without the support of the other arms, but, whatever the circumstances, the troops engaged carried out their tasks with great determination, in spite of the fatigue consequent on the exertions of the previous day.

When the Cavalry and Canadian Corps began their advance, the enemy's defence was very uneven in character. For instance, in Rosières-en-Santerre and Vrély the defence was very determined until the afternoon, while other villages were secured with little or no fighting by the cavalry, which started ahead of the infantry. During the day the enemy, who was very disorganised, attempted to fill the gaps in his line by bringing up reinforcements by 'bus and lorry, but there were few, if any, serious attempts at a counter-attack.

A CANADIAN ARMOURED LORRY GOING INTO ACTION ALONG THE ROYE ROAD ON AUGUST 9TH.

By kind permission of the Canadian Government.

It will be remembered that the cavalry and the 4th Canadian Division had met with determined resistance in Le Quesnel on the previous evening, and that Sir Arthur Currie had decided to postpone the capture of the village until the early hours of August 9th. During the night the village was heavily bombarded, and at 4.20 a.m. the 75th Battalion of the 11th Canadian Brigade attacked under cover of an artillery barrage. Almost at once the battalion came under heavy rifle and machine-gun fire from the village and from the high ground to the south of it, and the advance of the leading troops sustained a temporary check from the fire of a strong nest of machine-guns situated at the western entrance to the village. This resistance was overcome by the prompt initiative of the commanding officer, who himself led a detachment against the machine-guns and succeeded in killing the machine-gunners and capturing all the guns. As a result of this gallant action, the enemy's resistance weakened sufficiently to enable the whole battalion to advance and capture the village.[1] In order to secure the whole objective, our men had to advance beyond Le Quesnel, and several parties of the enemy were encountered in the wood south-east of the village.[2] By 11 a.m. all resistance was overcome by the infantry, assisted by the fire of the trench mortars of the Canadian Independent Force.

The capture of Le Quesnel

Pushing forward in advance of the infantry, the 2nd Cavalry Division captured Folies, but was checked by machine-gun fire in the wood west of Beaufort, and was not able to advance until the village was captured by the 1st Canadian Division in the afternoon. The 2nd Cavalry Division then, working round Warvillers and Vrély which were left to the infantry to deal with, pushed on towards Méharicourt, and by dusk had reached the western outskirts of Maucourt. Further north the 1st Cavalry Division almost immediately encountered formidable opposition from the newly-arrived 119th Division north-west of Rosières-en-Santerre, and made no progress. It suffered heavy casualties in the several gallant attempts made to advance, both from machine-gun fire from near the railway north of the village, and from artillery which was very active in this neighbourhood. All attempts to advance north of Vrély were unsuccessful until that village was captured by the 2nd Canadian Division. At nightfall the 1st and 2nd Cavalry Divisions were relieved by the infantry of the Canadian Corps and withdrawn to the vicinity of Cayeux for the night.

The action of the 2nd and 1st Cavalry Divisions

The Canadian Independent Force, working in close touch with the 2nd Cavalry Division, the infantry of the 3rd Canadian Division, and with the French, was fighting along the Amiens–Roye road very successfully all day. It passed the night between Arvillers and Bouchoir.

The advance of the 3rd, 1st, and 2nd Canadian Divisions

Advancing at noon, the 8th Canadian Brigade of the 3rd Division reached Folies at 4.20 p.m. After having co-operated with the French

[1] Le Quesnel had on August 8th contained a German divisional headquarters, and, although the staff had escaped, much valuable material was secured.

[2] From the examination of prisoners captured in this action, it was found that the leading troops of the 1st Reserve and 82nd Reserve Divisions had arrived on the battlefield, which accounted for the increasing opposition met with in this sector.

in their attack on Arvillers, the brigade advanced against Bouchoir, which it captured after heavy fighting, and established an outpost line for the night east of the village. It was then in touch with the French east of Arvillers, and was supported by the 7th Brigade which had moved up close behind it.

Further north, starting at about 1 p.m., the 1st Canadian Division had captured Beaufort by 3.30 p.m., and, after some severe fighting, occupied the villages of Warvillers and Rouvroy-en-Santerre before dusk.[1] It established outposts east of Rouvroy-en-Santerre in touch with the 3rd Canadian Division to the south, and with the 2nd Canadian Division to the north near Méharicourt.

When they began their advance about 11 a.m. on the left of the Canadian Corps, both the 6th and 5th Brigades of the 2nd Canadian Division were unsupported on either flank, and met with strong opposition. This weakened appreciably as the advance of the 1st Canadian Division to the south, and that of the 5th Australian Division to the north, developed. The 2nd Division then pressed on and, largely owing to the bravery and initiative of Lieut. John Brilliant of the 22nd Canadian Battalion,[2] captured Vrély. Rosières-en-Santerre was also secured, and Méharicourt fell to a combined attack of the infantry and the 9th Cavalry Brigade.

The 6th Brigade, which had suffered heavy casualties, was now reinforced by a battalion of the 4th Brigade, and the advance continued. By 9 p.m. the 2nd Canadian Division had established an outpost line 500 yards east of Méharicourt and 1,000 yards east of Rosières-en-Santerre, in touch with the 1st Canadian Division at Méharicourt, and on the north with the 1st Australian Division on the railway.

As the result of the day's fighting the Canadian Corps had made another deep advance all along their front and had captured eight more villages, together with many prisoners.

The task allotted to the Australian Corps was to advance its line between the Amiens–Chaulnes railway and the Amiens–Brie road, and, refusing its left, to protect the flank of the advance of the Canadian Corps. It was originally intended that the 1st Australian Division should pass through the right brigade, and the 2nd Australian Division through the left brigade, of the 5th Australian Division which was holding the line on a two-brigade front. Owing, however, to its late arrival on the battlefield on August 8th and the long approach march which followed, the 1st Australian Division was unable to reach its assembly position in time to co-operate with the advance of the Canadian Corps. Consequently, the 5th Australian Division was ordered to continue the advance, assisted by seven tanks of the 8th Mark V Tank Battalion. This division captured Vauvillers by 1 p.m. without the assistance of an artillery barrage.

The Australian Corps

---

[1] It was in this fighting that Sergeant Zengel, 5th Battalion Saskatchewan Regiment, and Corporal Coppins and Private Alexander Brereton, 8th Battalion (90th Rifles), Manitoba Regiment, showed such splendid gallantry and initiative. See Appendix E, Nos. 50, 12, and 6.
[2] See Appendix E, No. 7.

A TANK DEALING WITH A GERMAN MACHINE-GUN POST ON THE RAILWAY NEAR LIHONS.

By kind permission of the Australian Government.

To face page 55.

CREPFY WOOD.

At 1.40 p.m. the 2nd Brigade of the 1st Australian Division, passing through the 5th Australian Division, reached its starting position, and carried on the advance towards Lihons, supported by fourteen tanks of the 2nd Mark V Tank Battalion. The 7th and 8th Battalions, which led the advance, immediately encountered heavy machine-gun fire from the left flank, which was much exposed owing to the postponement of the attack of the 2nd Australian Division to a later hour. Considerable opposition was also encountered on the other flank from isolated machine-guns north of Rosières-en-Santerre, and it was found necessary to divert two companies to attack them.[1] Later in the afternoon the enemy was found to be holding in strength some trenches on the western slopes of Lihons Hill,[2] where he had posted a number of machine-guns and supported them with field guns placed in forward positions. The direct fire of these field guns across the open played havoc with the tanks, which were in consequence unable to give the requisite support to the infantry. The battalions in the front line were then reinforced, and a footing on the western slope of the hill was secured. The consolidation of the line gained was begun, and covering patrols pushed out during the evening and night to cover working parties. Some of these patrols advanced beyond Crépey Wood and occupied a portion of the trench system running through the western outskirts of Lihons.[3]

In the meantime, the 2nd Australian Division had advanced through the left brigade of the 5th Australian Division, and at 4.30 p.m. attacked Framerville with two brigades, the 7th Brigade on the right and the 5th Brigade on the left. The enemy's machine-guns in the outskirts of the village contested the advance, but their opposition was eventually overcome by the determination of the Australians, who succeeded in occupying the village and captured over 300 prisoners.

During the course of the day's fighting the Australian Corps secured 500 prisoners. Large numbers of the enemy were also killed, particularly by the troops of the 1st Australian Division, who themselves suffered fairly heavy casualties.

During the night of August 8th the situation on the front of the III Corps remained unchanged, except on the right, where the advanced

The III Corps operations   parties of the 58th Division were withdrawn to the eastern edge of Malard Wood. The three divisions of the III Corps, which had been engaged in the heavy fighting of the 8th, were not considered sufficiently strong to gain the objective without further assistance. Sanction was therefore obtained for the employment of the 131st Regiment of the 33rd American Division, which it had not been intended to employ in offensive operations, and which was in billets near Heilly on the Ancre, some distance behind the

---

[1] The heroism of Private Robert Beatham, 8th Australian Battalion, greatly facilitated the advance of his battalion. See Appendix E, No. 4.

[2] Lihons Hill, which was intersected with trenches, the remains of the old French defensive system of 1916, was a position of great natural strength of which the village of Lihons, situated on its summit, was the key. The ground rises in a gradual slope to this point from all sides for a considerable distance, while the surrounding country is particularly open, and the whole position is admirably adapted for defence.

[3] The 1st Australian Brigade rejoined its division during the day, and was held in divisional reserve.

battlefield. It had been originally intended to resume operations on the III Corps front early in the morning of August 9th, but, on account of the impossibility of moving up the American troops in time, " zero " was postponed until 5.30 p.m. The Etinehem spur was excluded from the objectives for the day.

For the main operation against Gressaire Wood, Tailles Wood, and the Amiens outer defence line extending from Tailles Wood northwards to Dernancourt, the 131st American Regiment, the 175th Brigade (less the 2/10th London) of the 58th Division, reinforced by the 8th London and 5th Royal Berkshire from the 174th and 36th Brigades respectively, and the 37th Brigade of the 12th Division were employed from right to left. Twelve tanks of the 10th Mark V Tank Battalion were allotted to the 58th Division, and eight tanks to the 12th Division. The Americans were placed under the orders of the commander of the 58th Division. In conjunction with this attack, the 174th Brigade, less one battalion, the 173rd Brigade, and the 2/10th London of the 175th Brigade were to attack Chipilly and the Chipilly spur, and thereby protect the right flank of the Americans and clear the left flank of the Australians.

The advance of the 174th and 173rd Brigades was strongly opposed by the enemy, and as a result the right American battalion suffered heavy casualties from hostile fire on its right flank. The brigades reached the sunken road running north from Chipilly, but were unable to make any further progress in face of the hostile enfilade machine-gun fire from the terraces north of Chipilly. However, the 2/10th London succeeded in working its way through Chipilly and along its northern edge, and attacked the enemy machine-gun posts on the terraces in flank and rear. The battalion was then held up for a time by machine-gun fire from the valley north-west of the Chipilly spur, but a company of Americans went to its assistance, and helped to drive the enemy out of the valley. The enveloping movement was eventually successful, and the enemy was driven from the terraces. This success brought about the capture of the whole of the Chipilly spur.

The main attack against Gressaire Wood, Tailles Wood, and the Amiens outer defences, in a north-easterly direction was launched on a front of about 7,000 yards, and was completely successful. Although the Americans had to double for the last mile in order to reach their assembly positions in time, they advanced to the attack in fine style. Led by their commander, Colonel J. B. Samborn, the Americans swept everything before them, and the German resistance collapsed. So precipitate was the retreat of the enemy that a German battalion commander fled from his dug-out, abandoning his orders, maps, and telephone switchboard. The Americans were so impetuous that they outstripped the British on the left, and it was due to them that the objective was so quickly and rapidly gained on the front of the 58th Division.

On the left of the 58th Division the 12th Division had been stoutly opposed near Morlancourt by heavy machine-gun fire, but the devoted heroism of Sergeant Thomas Harris of the 6th Royal West Kent, who

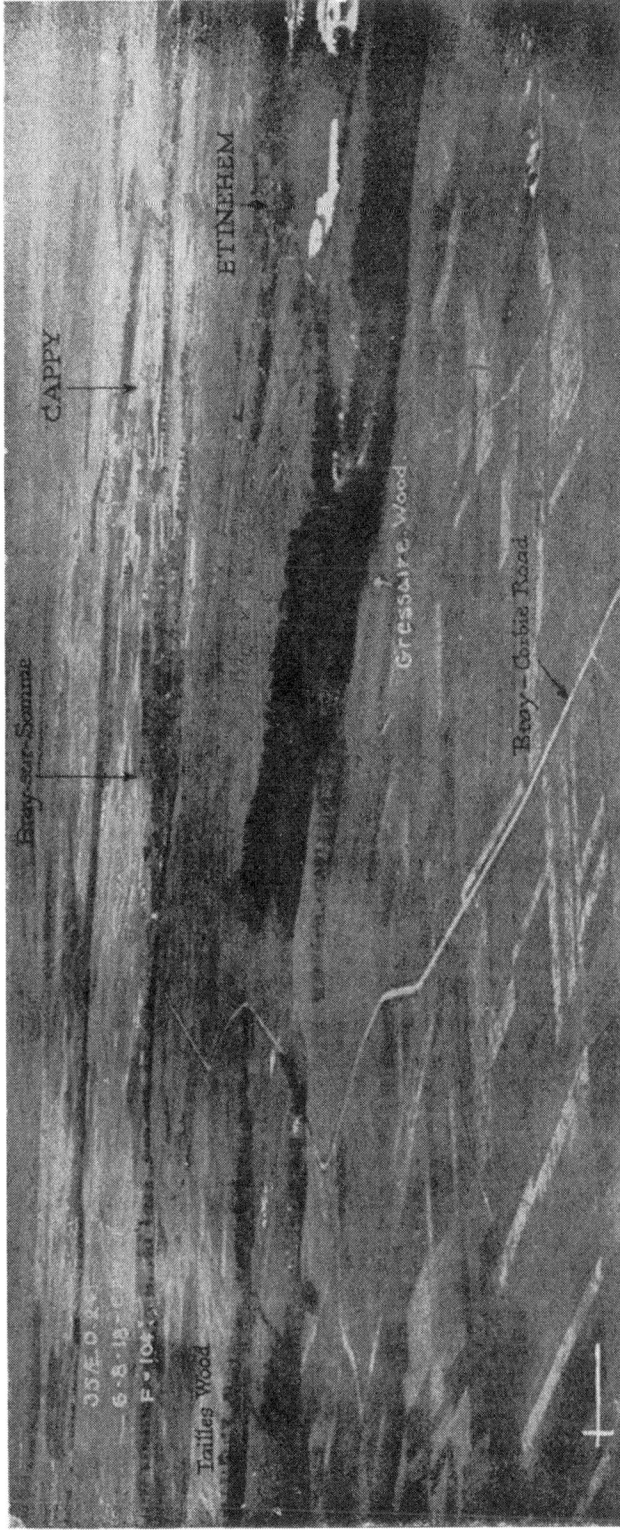

CAPPY

ETINEHEM

Bray-sur-Somme

Gressaire Wood

Bray—Corbie Road

Taillos Wood

GRESSAIRE WOOD.

Oblique air photograph.

A LARGE DUMP OF ENGINEER MATERIAL CAPTURED AT ROSIERES.

By kind permission of the Canadian Government.

was killed while rushing hostile machine-gun posts, prevented the advance from being checked.[1]   Ultimately, after obstinate fighting, the division secured all objectives, except that part of the Amiens outer defences which lies south-west of Hill 105.

The result of the day's fighting was another big advance on the whole army front, extending to as much as 9,000 yards in the south.   The

The situation on the night of August 9th

line we had now reached ran approximately Bouchoir– Rouvroy-en-Santerre – Méharicourt – Framerville – Mericourt-sur-Somme (exclusive) – Gressaire Wood – Tailles Wood–Dernancourt.   On the right of the Fourth Army the First French Army had also made progress and reached the general line Pierrepont– Arvillers.

Large additions had been made to the tale of prisoners, guns, and material, and, although the enemy's resistance was felt to be stiffening, no counter-attack in any strength had so far materialised. Troops from six more hostile divisions had been encountered, the 1st Reserve, 82nd Reserve, 107th, 119th, 233rd, and 243rd, making a total of seventeen German divisions engaged by our twelve divisions in the two days' fighting. No information had yet been obtained from prisoners or from other sources as to any line of defence which the enemy proposed to occupy, or even whether such a line was to be east or west of the Somme.   On the other hand our casualties, except in a few cases, had not been severe, and, with the exception perhaps of two of the divisions of the III Corps, all the divisions in the army were fit to continue the operations.   In addition, the 32nd Division, which had been released from general reserve and allotted to the Canadian Corps, had so far not been employed. During the evening orders were issued by Sir Henry Rawlinson to the Cavalry, Canadian, Australian, and III Corps to continue the advance towards the general line Roye–Chaulnes– Bray-sur-Somme–Dernancourt. It was still felt that, if the determined pressure exerted on August 8th and 9th was continued, the enemy's resistance might be definitely broken down. The chief difficulty with which we had to contend was the very broken ground which had now been reached. It was most unsuitable for the employment of tanks and cavalry, and favoured enormously the enemy's delaying tactics and his lavish use of machine-guns in the defence.

Notwithstanding the successful advance of the III Corps on August 9th, the junction between it and the Australian Corps south of the river

The reallotment of front between the Australian and III Corps

was not satisfactory. While the Somme itself afforded a well-defined line of demarcation, it was found that the tactical interdependence of the slopes on each side of the river made it an unsatisfactory boundary. Sir Henry Rawlinson therefore decided to place the Australian Corps astride the Somme and to make the Corbie–Bray-sur-Somme road the inter-corps boundary. Instructions to this effect were accordingly issued, and the 131st American Regiment was transferred from the III to the Australian Corps.

The same objectives were given to the three corps for August 10th as had been given them for the previous day, that is to say, the

[1] See Appendix E, No. 22.

I

approximate line Roye – Chaulnes – Bray-sur-Somme – Dernancourt, the objective for the Australians, however, was extended to include the Etinehem spur. The 3rd Cavalry Division was detailed to work with the Canadian Corps, the 1st and 2nd Cavalry Divisions being held in reserve.

The orders for August 10th

During the night of August 9th, the 32nd Division, under the command of Maj.-Gen. T. S. Lambert, moved up in close support of the 3rd Canadian Division, ready to pass through on the right. At 4.20 a.m. the 8th Canadian Brigade, assisted by four tanks, advanced on Le Quesnoy-en-Santerre, and, after encountering heavy machine-gun fire which was overcome with the assistance of the tanks, captured the village and established a line on its eastern edge. Thence the advance continued, and the trench area north-east of the village was occupied by 9.30 a.m. Soon afterwards the troops of the 32nd Division, who had followed close on the heels of the Canadians, passed through them, and, in spite of strong opposition and the very difficult nature of the ground, advanced our line to the western outskirts of Damery and Parvillers. On the right of the 32nd Division the Canadian Cavalry Brigade endeavoured to push forward with the object of securing the high ground north and east of Roye, while a brigade of the 2nd Cavalry Division moved in the direction of Nesle.[1] Owing to the hostile machine-gun fire and the difficulties of the ground, which was intersected by old trenches and belts of wire hidden by the long grass, cavalry action was found to be impossible. At nightfall, therefore, the whole Cavalry Corps was withdrawn into reserve to localities in the valley of the Luce, where water was more plentiful.

August 10th ; the Canadian Corps ; the Chilly and Le Quesnoy operations

On the left of the 32nd Division, the 4th Canadian Division passed through the 1st and 2nd Canadian Divisions and attacked at 10.15 a.m., the hour of assault having been postponed to allow the tanks, of which nineteen were eventually mustered, time to get into position. The village of Fouquescourt was allotted as objective to the 10th Brigade, while Chilly was the objective of the 12th Brigade. Unfortunately, owing to the hostile artillery fire, very few tanks were able to cross the Rouvroy-en-Santerre–Méharicourt road, many being destroyed by direct hits, and of those that escaped this fate the greater part were "ditched" in the intricate ground. While the tanks were suffering so severely in their self-sacrificing efforts to assist the infantry, the situation from the standpoint of the assaulting troops was the reverse of satisfactory. Confronted with a more determined and organised resistance, they were obliged to attack in the open over level fields with comparatively little artillery support and without assistance from the tanks. It was only after very severe fighting, in which all ranks displayed the greatest gallantry and determination, that the enemy's resistance was overcome and a footing established in Maucourt and on the high ground south of Fouquescourt. At a later stage of the fighting three tanks arrived at Fouquescourt and rendered valuable assistance in the capture of the village, which was completely in the

---

[1] The 1st and 2nd Cavalry Divisions had been ordered forward from reserve, as very optimistic reports were received during the morning as to the demoralisation and retirement of the enemy. These reports proved to be exaggerated.

MARK V TANKS ADVANCING ACROSS THE OPEN NEAR LE QUESNOY.

By kind permission of the Canadian Government.

No. 30.

CANADIAN CAVALRY RESTING ON AUGUST 10TH.

By kind permission of the Canadian Government.

Auger Wood

Crepey Wood

German Hospital

CREPEY AND AUGER WOODS.

Oblique air photograph.

A TRENCH NEAR LIHONS, CAPTURED BY THE AUSTRALIANS ON AUGUST 10TH.

By kind permission of the Australian Government.

hands of the 44th Canadian Battalion of the 10th Brigade by 5 p.m. The 50th Battalion on the left of the 10th Brigade then pushed on and reached the railway south-west of Hallu, but the enemy still held out east of Fouquescourt.

On the front of the 12th Brigade desperate fighting took place in Chilly about noon, but by 12.30 p.m. the 72nd Battalion had cleared the village. The 78th Battalion then passed through and, taking advantage of the enemy's temporary demoralisation, captured Hallu without much opposition. Further north the attacking troops of the 85th Battalion found great difficulty in advancing on account of heavy machine-gun fire from Lihons, which at that time had not been captured by the Australians. Finally, however, the 85th and 38th Battalions cleared the country as far as the Chilly–Lihons road.

Open warfare tactics were impossible owing to the way in which the ground was broken up by the old trench system, of which the enemy took the fullest advantage. There was, therefore, an enforced and very unwelcome reversion to trench warfare, involving slower progress and more numerous casualties. At 3.30 p.m. the 119th German Division [1] began to develop a counter-attack from the north-east against the exposed flank of the 78th Battalion which had pushed forward to Hallu. The attack was brought to a standstill within fifteen yards of our trenches. Regardless, however, of the heavy losses sustained in this counter-attack, the enemy made a further attempt at 7.30 p.m. For the second time he was beaten off, leaving many dead in front of our trenches, the result of well-controlled and effective rifle and Lewis gun fire, in which the battalion headquarters took a by no means unimportant part.

On the left of the Canadian Corps the 1st Australian Division, with the 2nd Brigade on the right and the 3rd Brigade on the left, renewed the advance at 8 a.m., at which hour it was originally intended that the Canadians should also attack. The 1st Brigade was in reserve. The objectives of the division included Crépey and Auger Woods.

The Australian Corps; the advance on Lihons

The advance was only covered by a thin artillery barrage, and the right flank of the advance was exposed, with the result that severe fighting took place before the Australians reached a line running roughly north and south through the eastern end of Crépey Wood. The wood itself was still held in force by the enemy, and formed a pocket in our line. It was eventually captured by a company of the 10th Battalion after very bitter fighting. All the defenders were either killed or captured, and posts were established on the eastern edge ; the company of the 10th Battalion, when it had completed its task, was reduced to twenty of all ranks.

During the afternoon two determined counter-attacks were made on the left of the 1st Australian Division. The first was driven off with heavy loss to the enemy ; the second succeeded, after some of our posts east of Crépey Wood had been totally destroyed by artillery fire, in gaining a footing in the wood itself. Our troops on the flanks of the hostile attack closed in, and thus isolated the Germans who had penetrated into the wood ; these refused to surrender and fought to the last man. Once more

---

[1] This division arrived to reinforce the Second German Army on August 9th.

there was a bitter struggle in the wood from which the Australians emerged triumphant, over 90 of the enemy's dead being counted after the fight was over. In the evening it was decided to consolidate the position gained, with a view to making adequate preparations for the renewal of the attack next day.

During daylight on August 10th the remainder of the Australian line south of the Somme remained almost unchanged, except for a small advance on the right of the 2nd Australian Division north of Crépey Wood; during the night of the 10th, however, considerable progress was made about Etinehem.

The command of the right divisional front of the III Corps between the Bray-sur-Somme–Corbie road and the Somme passed to the Australian Corps at 10 a.m. on August 10th. Early in the evening of the same day the 3rd Australian Division relieved the portion of the front held by the 4th Australian Division south of the Somme. Thus, on the night of August 10th the Australian Corps front was held, from right to left, by the 1st, 2nd, and 3rd Divisions south of the Somme, and by the 4th Division, to which the 131st American Regiment was attached, north of the river.

The attacks astride the Somme by the 3rd and 4th Australian Divisions and the 131st American Regiment

The village of Etinehem itself was of no tactical importance, being tucked away in a small re-entrant on the northern bank of the Somme. North-west of the village the ground rose steeply towards Tailles Wood, while to the north the re-entrant, in which the village itself lay, developed into a crescent-shaped valley with gentle slopes in the vicinity of the Bray-sur-Somme–Corbie road. On the east Etinehem was dominated by the high ground which rises steeply from the river to the bluff overlooking Bray-sur-Somme. In many ways the Etinehem spur resembled that east of Chipilly, and, as regards observation of the Somme valley, constituted an important tactical feature which it was most necessary to secure prior to any advance south of the river. In conjunction with the operation for the capture of Etinehem, it was decided to encircle Mericourt-sur-Somme, clear up the ground formed by the bend in the river between Mericourt-sur-Somme and Etinehem, and gain the ridge east of Proyart. North of the Somme the attack was carried out by the 13th Brigade, which had rejoined the 4th Australian Division, and the 131st American Regiment, and, south of the river, by the 9th and 10th Brigades of the 3rd Australian Division. The tactics employed both north and south of the river were almost entirely identical, a silent encircling movement under cover of darkness.

On the 13th Brigade front the 50th and 49th Battalions, supported by tanks, advanced at 10 p.m. in an easterly direction along the Corbie–Bray-sur-Somme road and the river road to the south, one battalion moving along each road. The southern battalion, the 50th, encircled Etinehem, which it captured and " mopped up." The northern battalion, the 49th, attacked down the Etinehem spur, secured almost the whole of it, and on the left formed a defensive flank along the Bray-sur-Somme–Corbie road as far as the junction with the III Corps at the cross roads about 500 yards east of Tailles Wood.

ETINEHEM AND THE SOMME MARSHES.

Oblique air photograph.

THE SOMME CANAL NEAR MERICOURT WITH A PONTOON BRIDGE BLOWN UP BY THE GERMANS
IN THE FOREGROUND.

By kind permission of the Australian Government.

South of the Somme Mericourt-sur-Somme was occupied with slight opposition, but further south the operation was not so successful. The 10th Brigade, which was to carry out the first part of the operation, advanced along the main Amiens–Brie road early in the evening, supported by tanks. Its object was to encircle Proyart from the south, and thus establish itself on the high ground east of the village. Unfortunately the enemy discovered this movement and, by heavy shelling of the forward area and some effective bombing, caused considerable confusion and heavy casualties; as a result the operation had finally to be abandoned.

On the front of the III Corps a hostile counter-attack, at about 3 a.m. on August 10th, resulted in a temporary withdrawal of our line at the junction of the 58th and 12th Divisions east of Tailles Wood, but the ground lost was promptly regained. Strong patrols from the 58th and 12th Divisions advanced during the morning and were closely supported by strong detachments. By 10 p.m. the whole of the Amiens outer defences had been secured from the Bray-sur-Somme–Corbie road to Dernancourt. The new line was consolidated during the night and thereafter held in its entirety.

The complete occupation of the Amiens outer defences by the III Corps

On the evening of August 10th orders were issued by Sir Henry Rawlinson, acting on instructions from General Headquarters, for the attack to be continued on the 11th with the object of pressing the enemy back on to the Somme, and securing the crossings between Offoy, about four miles east of Nesle, and Bray-sur-Somme. The left of the First French Army was at the same time directed on Ham. The objective allotted to the Canadian Corps was the river line between Offoy and St. Christ; and that allotted to the Australian Corps the line of the river from St. Christ to Bray-sur-Somme. The bulk of the cavalry was ordered to assist the Canadian Corps, while one brigade was attached to the Australian Corps. The III Corps was ordered to maintain a defensive flank on the north on the line of the Amiens outer defences.

The orders for August 11th

The enemy's counter-attacks during the 11th, and the severe fighting which ensued, proved that the hostile resistance was stiffening and prevented any progress being made. Owing to the increase of hostile artillery fire, the difficult nature of the ground, and the lack of tanks and sufficient artillery support, the Canadian attacks were cancelled by Sir Arthur Currie early on the 11th, after consultation with Army Headquarters. The attack of the 32nd Division, however, against Damery and Parvillers was launched at 9.30 a.m., before the cancelling order reached the troops. It was checked by strong machine-gun fire and heavy wire, and at 11 a.m. orders not to press the attack were received.

August 11th; the Canadian Corps

About 12 noon, after a heavy bombardment, the enemy launched determined counter-attacks against Chilly and between Damery and Fouquescourt. In the vicinity of Hallu our troops were seen withdrawing from the village, and the situation for a time was obscure. It subsequently transpired that the enemy had concentrated in Hallu Woods and had attempted to

Heavy hostile counter-attacks

work round the flanks. The 50th Battalion, in view of the enemy's concentration, threw back its left flank and the hostile attack was thus anticipated. When, therefore, the Germans advanced in mass formation, they afforded an exceptionally good target for the 50th Battalion and the 78th Battalion on its left. The attack was completely repulsed by the combined fire of all available guns, machine-guns, and rifles, and the enemy suffered very heavy casualties, the ground in front of our trenches being strewn with the German dead.

Later in the evening our advanced troops in the vicinity of Hallu were withdrawn to the main line in front of Chilly, in order to avoid unnecessary casualties. Meanwhile, the enemy's attack south of Fouquescourt met with partial success, but an immediate counter-attack by the 32nd Division succeeded not only in restoring the situation, but in advancing the line to the western outskirts of Damery. Throughout the remainder of the afternoon, the enemy's attacks in the area east of Le Quesnoy-en-Santerre continued with unabated vigour. Although supported by intense concentrations of artillery fire, they were all beaten off, and our line remained intact. While the losses sustained by the enemy in these attempts to arrest the victorious advance of the Canadian Corps were very severe, especially in the 79th Reserve and 119th Divisions, those sustained by the Canadian Corps were by no means light, and it became necessary to relieve the 32nd and the 4th Canadian Divisions. On the night of August 12th, therefore, the 32nd Division, holding the Damery–Parvillers sector, was relieved by the 3rd Canadian Division, and the 4th Canadian Division by the 2nd Canadian Division on the Chilly front.

After the heavy fighting of August 10th Maj.-Gen. T. W. Glasgow, commanding the 1st Australian Division, realised that the period of semi-open fighting had temporarily passed. He also saw that on the old Somme battlefield, covered with its complicated systems of trenches, a definitely organised attack would be necessary in order to capture the important tactical locality of Lihons Hill, to retain which the enemy would be certain to employ all his available resources. He decided to cover the advance of the infantry with a creeping barrage moving at the rate of 100 yards in three minutes, and to employ such tanks as were available to lead the attack, the infantry following immediately in rear of them.

At 4 a.m., the hour fixed for the attack, it was foggy and dark, but the conditions were otherwise favourable. Owing to the fog, only one tank was able to reach its position by " zero " ; the remainder lost direction in the intricate ground, although the majority of them succeeded in catching up the infantry later in the morning. The attack, which was undertaken by the 2nd and 3rd Brigades, with the 1st Brigade in reserve, was at once met by very heavy machine-gun fire, which luckily, owing probably to the fog and darkness, was very wild and entirely failed to check the Australians. By 5.15 a.m. Lihons and Auger Wood had been captured, and our troops were well down the east side of the hill.

The tactical value of the position had not been over-estimated, and the 1st Australian Division was now in possession of a commanding

The Australian Corps ; the capture of Lihons

LIHONS.

ridge, from which a fine view was obtainable over the enemy's positions to the north, south, and east.

The Germans promptly attempted to recover the lost ground, and at 6 a.m., employing the 5th Bavarian Division and the newly-arrived 38th Division, began a series of powerful counter-attacks against the 1st Australian Division. At 8.30 a.m. one of these counter-attacks broke the line, and parties of the enemy, working down behind our position on the hill towards Crépey Wood, for a time made our hold on the hill precarious; the Australians, however, fought with the greatest tenacity and succeeded in beating off all attacks with heavy loss to the Bavarians. By the evening our hold on the whole position was firmly established, and a dashing and hard-fought operation of great tactical importance was brought to a successful conclusion. The 2nd Australian Division also made considerable progress. It captured Rainecourt and advanced its line to near Herleville, keeping touch with the 1st Australian Division north of Lihons.

At 3 p.m. on August 11th Sir Henry Rawlinson held a conference of Corps Commanders at Villers Bretonneux, and discussed the general The general situation on situation. From all the reports which had been received August 11th; the Army it was quite evident that the enemy's resistance had Commander's conference stiffened, and that he had been able to bring up fresh troops and to reinforce his shattered artillery. In addition, he was holding the western edge of a broad belt of country admirably suited for defence, which was difficult for the infantry to advance over, and practically impossible for tanks or cavalry. It was now certain that the Germans had decided to make a stand west of the Somme, but whether this was only a temporary effort to cover a withdrawal across the river, or was a new defensive line which they were determined to hold to the last, was not yet clear. On the other hand, all our divisions had been engaged in the battle. The troops had performed wonders; twenty-four hostile divisions had been engaged and defeated by thirteen of our divisions and part of one American division; but it was realised that, in the stress of modern battle, with its never-relaxing strain on nerves and sinews, there are limits to human endurance. For many days the infantry, machine-gunners, and artillery had been continually on the move, and most of the units had been in action several times. The tanks had been fully employed since the battle began on August 8th, and the constant strain of continued action, especially on August 10th, when the majority of the tanks operating with the Canadian Corps were constantly under heavy artillery fire, had begun to tell on the crews. The tanks themselves, too, had suffered considerable wear and tear, and required overhauling and refitting before they could be used again. Our casualties certainly had so far been light—as compared with the number of prisoners taken and the losses inflicted on the enemy; we had achieved the maximum of result with the minimum of loss, but the situation as regards the supply of reinforcements did not permit of risks being taken. It had, moreover, not been possible up to date to bring up all the heavy artillery, and to supply it with ammunition. In addition to these considerations, previous experience had shown that, once the first impetus of an offensive was over and the enemy had been able to reorganise his defences, infantry attacks, even with the co-operation of tanks, became more and more costly. This was chiefly because it was difficult to avoid making them more or less disjointedly and on narrower fronts, and also because the available artillery support was bound to be considerably less than in the initial attack. Experience had definitely shown that, if casualties were to be avoided, it was essential for the infantry to attack on a wide front, well supported by artillery, and in the closest co-operation with the tanks. Sir Henry Rawlinson, therefore, decided that no attempt should be made to force the position by independent effort on the part of formations, nor until we could bring into action our overwhelming strength in artillery.

As a result of the conference, instructions were issued on August 11th that for the time being only minor alterations were to be made in the line, and that such alterations should be designed to assist **A lull in the battle** in obtaining a good "starting line" for a general attack which was fixed for August 15th. For the moment, therefore, the advance was checked. Owing to the difficulties which had to be surmounted in moving forward the heavy artillery, and to the time taken to make the necessary reliefs of divisions, this date was first postponed for twenty-four hours and subsequently "sine die," but ready to be undertaken at twenty-four hours' notice.

On August 12th the whole of the Cavalry Corps was withdrawn into reserve in the valleys of the Luce and the Avre.

Events from August 12th–16th On the front of the Canadian Corps reliefs were carried out, and patrols were pushed further towards Damery and Parvillers, but this gain of ground was not made without considerable hostile opposition. The fighting in places was very strenuous, as is proved by the fact that two Canadians, Sergeant Spall, Princess Patricia's Canadian Light Infantry, and Private Dinesen, 42nd Battalion, Quebec Regiment, won the Victoria Cross in the fighting near Parvillers. Sergeant Spall deliberately gave his life in order to extricate his platoon from a most difficult situation. Private Dinesen was the outstanding man in his company during ten hours' hand-to-hand fighting, which resulted in the capture of over a mile of strongly garrisoned trenches.[1]

The enemy's resistance, as had been anticipated, gradually increased, and was particularly strong on the front of the Canadian Corps,[2] where the famous Alpine Corps had made its appearance on August 11th. Here the enemy carried out a number of local counter-attacks, which were supported by heavy concentrations of artillery fire from field and high velocity guns, large quantities of gas shell being employed. Undeterred by these attempts of the enemy to regain the initiative, the 3rd Canadian Division succeeded in capturing Damery and Parvillers on August 15th. The German artillery retaliation was exceptionally severe, and was shortly afterwards followed by a counter-attack delivered by the 121st Division and the Alpine Corps. This was successfully repulsed, 200 prisoners and

[1] See Appendix E, Nos. 40 and 16.
[2] Nine fresh divisions had come in against the Canadian Corps since the 8th.

40 machine-guns being captured, and casualties, estimated at 1,500, were inflicted on the enemy.

Further north the Australian Corps materially improved and straightened the line between Lihons and the Somme by a series of local actions carried out by the 2nd and 5th Divisions. Numerous prisoners were captured, and the enemy was allowed no rest.

On August 12th, just before it was relieved, the 3rd Australian Division secured Proyart. In the attack on this village Sergeant Statton, 40th Battalion, armed only with a revolver, rushed four of the enemy's machine-gun posts in succession. This had an inspiring effect on the troops, who cheered him as he returned, and his daring exploit enabled the battalion to gain its objective.[1]

North of the Somme the Liaison Force[2] and the III Corps[3] also harassed the enemy. At dawn on August 13th a successful attack was carried out by the 13th Australian Brigade, whereby the whole of the Etinehem spur, a part of which had been retaken by the enemy on the 11th, was recaptured with 200 prisoners and a large number of machine-guns. On the same day the 12th Division established a footing on Hill 105.

While this continual pressure was being maintained on the enemy, the preparations for the general attack, which had been planned along August 17th; instruc- the front of the Canadian and Australian Corps, were tions from General still going forward. On August 17th,[4] however, in-Headquarters structions were received from the Commander-in-Chief that the attack was not to take place in view of the heavy losses which an attempt to capture such a strong position might involve. The Canadian Corps was to be withdrawn into general reserve, the First French Army would extend its front northwards to compensate for the withdrawal of the Canadians, and the 33rd American Division was to leave the Fourth Army in order to rejoin the American Army.

The Commander-in-Chief had decided that the next big British attack should be made on a part of the line where the Germans were not so fully prepared, and that the Fourth Army should mark time until a more favourable opportunity should arise for continuing its advance. It was hoped that in the interval we should be able to find out whether the enemy meant to hold his ground west of the Somme, for which purpose he would have to reinforce that front with both men and guns, or whether he would retire across the river, in which case we should gain a further advantage without loss. If he adopted the first alternative, an attack

---

[1] See Appendix E, No. 41.

[2] On August 12th, in order to relieve the 4th Australian Division for a well-earned rest, a provisional formation known as the Liaison Force was formed under the command of Brig.-Gen. E. A. Wisdom, commanding the 7th Australian Brigade. This force took over the front from the Somme to the Bray-sur-Somme–Corbie road, and its task was to ensure complete liaison between the Australian and the III Corps. It was composed of the 13th Australian Brigade and the 131st American Regiment, with the necessary auxiliary troops. This force was broken up on August 20th on relief by the 3rd Australian Division, and the troops composing it returned to their formations.

[3] On August 11th the command of the III Corps had been taken over temporarily from Sir Richard Butler by Lieut.-Gen. Sir Alec. Godley, the commander of the XXII Corps.

[4] The gist of these orders was communicated verbally to Sir Henry Rawlinson by General Headquarters before August 17th.

K

from the north in the direction of Bapaume, would place his troops west of the Somme in a very precarious position.

The Fourth Army, meanwhile, was not to remain idle, as it was essential that the enemy should not realise what the next move was to be. He must be made to expect an attack at any moment, and every method of gaining ground, which could be employed without incurring serious losses, was to be undertaken. These instructions entailed no change in the army policy, and the harassing of the enemy by minor operations was maintained until August 21st, the day prior to the opening of the second phase of the battles of the hundred days. On August 21st our line had reached approximately Damery–La Chavatte–Fransart–Chilly–Lihons–Rainecourt–Proyart–Etinehem and along the Amiens outer defences to Dernancourt.

During the period from August 11th to August 20th, the First French Army, operating south of the Amiens–Roye road on the right flank of the The progress of the First French Army, August 11th–20th Canadian Corps, had made good progress and advanced its line to within machine-gun range of Roye. This advance was materially assisted by the Third French Army, which on August 10th attacked south of Montdidier in a north-easterly direction, and finally effected a junction with the First French Army north-east of that town.[1] The advance of the First French Army automatically shortened the front held by the French. This enabled the French High Command to withdraw from the line the Third French Army, which held the front between the First and Tenth French Armies.

When the instructions came from General Headquarters on August 17th for the withdrawal of the Canadian Corps, it was holding a front extending from Damery to just south of Lihons, with two divisions in line and two in reserve. It was to be withdrawn as soon as possible and placed in general reserve; later it was to be transferred to the First Army on the Arras front, where it was eventually to take part in a further attack. In accordance with these orders the 2nd, 3rd, 1st, and 4th Canadian Divisions, in the order named, were gradually withdrawn and concentrated in the Longueau area, being subsequently moved by rail to the First Army. The withdrawal of the Canadian Corps necessitated a considerable shortening of the front held by the Fourth Army, if it was to maintain its offensive attitude. It was arranged, therefore, by Sir Douglas Haig with Marshal Foch, that the front of the Canadian Corps should be taken over by the First French Army. The first half of the relief, that of the 3rd Canadian Division, began on the night of August 19th and was completed on the morning of August 22nd. On this date the Canadian Corps Headquarters were withdrawn, and moved by road to the First Army area, while the front of the 4th Canadian Division came temporarily under the command of the Australian Corps Commander. The second phase, which involved the relief of the 4th Canadian Division, did not begin until August 23rd and was completed on August 27th.

The 33rd American Division was rejoined, about August 20th, by

---

[1] Until August 16th the First French Army was under the orders of Sir Douglas Haig, but at 12 noon on that date it reverted to the command of General Fayolle, commanding the Group of Armies of the north and north-east.

CANADIANS ON A MARK V TANK BEHIND OUR LINES.

By kind permission of the Canadian Government.

the 131st and 132nd American Regiments from the Australian Corps, and was concentrated at Poulainville, prior to moving by rail on August 23rd to join the First American Army in the French zone near Verdun. The 33rd American Division had been training with the Fourth Army for several months, and the first action in which any of its troops had taken part had been with the 4th Australian Division at Hamel on July 4th. From its commander downwards, the officers and men who composed it had gained the respect and admiration of all by their gallantry in action, their keenness, and their determination to miss nothing during their training that would help them to beat the Germans.

Before further operations could be carried out by the Fourth Army, it was essential that as many as possible of the divisions that it was going The reorganisation of to retain should be given a short period of rest in order the front of the Fourth to regain their full fighting efficiency. All the divisions Army of the Australian Corps were given short periods of rest between August 12th and 23rd. In order to do this, the 17th Division, released temporarily from general reserve, was employed to hold the line from the Amiens–Brie road to the Somme between August 12th and 16th, after which it again reverted to general reserve.[1] On August 17th the 32nd Division was transferred from the Canadian to the Australian Corps.

On the morning of August 22nd the situation on the Fourth Army front was as follows :—

The Australian Corps held a frontage of 23,000 yards, extending from Fransart to the Bray-sur-Somme–Corbie road, with five divisions in the line—4th Canadian, 4th Australian, 32nd, 5th Australian, and 3rd Australian —from south to north, and with three divisions in reserve, the 1st Canadian, 2nd Australian, and 1st Australian. The length of front held by the III Corps, which extended from the Bray-sur-Somme–Corbie road to just north of Albert, remained unchanged. There were three divisions holding the line—the 47th, 12th, and 18th—from south to north, with the 58th Division in reserve.[2] On this date it was estimated that the Fourth Army was opposed by eleven divisions, of which five, including the Alpine Corps, might be reckoned to possess more than the average fighting spirit. Apart from those divisions which the enemy had withdrawn exhausted from the battle, he was believed to have five divisions in reserve.

The enemy opposite the Fourth Army was obviously in an extremely awkward situation. He was faced with two alternatives : either to reinforce the troops west of the Somme and The German dilemma build up a new defensive line, taking full advantage of the existing trenches and wire, or to retire east of the Somme to his old reserve line of 1917 and make use of the river as an obstacle to our advance. At first it was not apparent which of these alternatives he would adopt. The danger he would incur by endeavouring

---

[1] During its time in the line the 17th Division did not take part in any operations, but sustained a number of casualties from hostile gas shelling, which at times was very severe. Its fighting efficiency was not, however, affected.

[2] The 18th Division had been withdrawn from the line on August 10th and brought round to relieve the 47th Division, which was holding the line opposite Albert. The latter division, under the command of Maj.-Gen. Sir G. F. Gorringe, had then taken over the part of the line held by the 58th Division on the night of August 13th and 14th.

to make a stand with an obstacle such as the Somme behind him was obvious, especially in view of the further severe drain on his resources in men and material which such a course would entail. On the other hand, we had to remember that the enemy had held a similar position for four months in 1917, and that he must realise that any further retirement was bound to have a lowering effect on his already shaken moral. Circumstances, however, since 1917 had changed considerably, and the question of economising man power at this time was of even greater importance to the enemy than to ourselves. Faced with the heavy losses consequent on the failure of his spring and summer offensives, in which he had cherished the hope of gaining a decisive victory, he was now confronted with the menace of the increasing strength of the American Army. It became evident, therefore, that the enemy, if pressure was applied, must withdraw east of the river.

Before passing to the next phase of the operations, it may be of interest to consider the results of the Battle of Amiens, in order to appreciate

The results of the Battle of Amiens

its influence in determining the ruthless offensive policy of the Allied Armies, which ultimately achieved one of the most decisive victories in history and the final defeat of Germany.[1]

From the opening of the battle on August 8th to its conclusion on August 11th, the Fourth Army penetrated the enemy's defences to a maximum depth of twelve miles, forcing the enemy back to the borders of the old Somme battlefield, where there existed practically no accommodation for his reserve troops, and where the roads were exceedingly poor.

During the period of fighting from August 8th to 21st, 23,064 prisoners and 400 guns of all calibres, with many hundreds of machine-guns and trench mortars, were captured. In addition, large ammunition dumps, enormous quantities of engineer material, and a considerable amount of rolling stock were secured. Such heavy losses in prisoners naturally compelled the enemy to throw in reserves.[2] These he could ill afford to spare in view of the wide extent of the allied offensive which at this time extended from Rheims to Albert.

From the identification of the German divisions, it was ascertained that Prince Rupprecht's reserves, numbering thirty-six divisions early in July and destined for a big attack in the Ypres salient, were rapidly being drawn into the battle. On August 16th he retained only nine divisions in reserve available for employment between the sea and Albert.[3]

The result of the attack of August 8th also immediately influenced events as far south as the Oise. On August 8th the battle front lying between the rivers Luce and Oise was held by the First and Third French Armies, whose sectors lay respectively north and south of Montdidier. On that date the First French Army, by its advance in co-operation with

---

[1] As already pointed out, this story was written before General Ludendorff's Memoirs were published.

[2] By the evening of August 21st, twenty-seven different hostile divisions had been engaged by the Fourth Army, many of which had been heavily defeated, and withdrawn to rest or disbanded.

[3] Prince Rupprecht's offensive had apparently been definitely postponed about July 20th, and from that date his reserves had been steadily withdrawn southwards, first to the Marne front to meet General Mangin's offensive of July 18th, and later to the Somme to meet our attacks.

No. 37.

PRISONERS ARRIVING AT THE ARMY CAGE ON THE AMIENS–DOULLENS ROAD ON AUGUST 8TH.

British official photograph.

the Canadians, threatened to cut off the retreat of the German troops in the Montdidier salient. It thus facilitated the attack of the Third French Army, when it was launched on August 10th between Montdidier and the Oise. This compelled the enemy to beat a hurried retreat on a front extending from Chevincourt, six miles north of Compiègne, to Gratibus, three miles north of Montdidier, that is to say a distance of twenty-five miles, and to an average depth of approximately 9,000 yards.

The moral effect of the battle of Amiens was of even greater importance. In the first place the battle demonstrated that the British forces had lost none of their fighting qualities, in spite of the reverses sustained in the enemy's March and April offensives. It proved that the British Army was as capable of carrying out a big offensive as it had been in 1916 and 1917, in spite of the heavy casualties it had suffered. Before August 8th there were many, not only in the German Army, but among the French, and even in our own Army and in England, who doubted this. On the other hand, it showed the German High Command that the German infantry was no longer of the same quality as that which had resisted so determinedly during the five months of the Somme battle of 1916. Even the machine-gunners had deteriorated. A brief inspection of the prisoners streaming westwards sufficed to dispel any doubts that might have been entertained as to the condition of the enemy's moral. The physique of the men was fairly good, and their power of endurance still high, but many expressed evident pleasure at being captured and thus being relieved of the necessity of fighting a losing game. In several cases new arrivals were greeted with cheers by parties which had been captured earlier in the day. A more thorough examination of the prisoners showed that there was a prevalent conviction among both officers and men that Germany could not win the war.[1] One reason for this was that they had realised, during

---

[1] Various orders issued by German General Headquarters and lower formations during this period are of interest, of which two examples are perhaps worth quoting :—

Extract from an order of the Second Army, dated 25/8/18.

It passes all comprehension that inconceivable rumours have been spread about behind the front during the last few days by people who have lost their nerve. People with anxious temperaments see everywhere squadrons of tanks, masses of cavalry, and dense lines of enemy infantry. It is in fact high time that our old battle-tried soldiers spoke seriously to these cowards and weaklings, and told them of the deeds that are achieved in the front line. Tanks are no bogey for the front line troops, who have artillery in close support. For instance, a battery-sergeant-major with his gun destroyed 4 tanks ; one battery destroyed 14 ; and a single division in one day 40. In another instance, a smart corporal climbed on to a tank and put the crew out of action with his revolver, firing through an aperture. A lance-corporal was successful in putting a tank out of action with a hand grenade.

The English cavalry, which has been engaged many times, has been shot to pieces and reduced to a skeleton force by our infantry and artillery. Our riflemen and machine-gunners never had better targets.

With regard to the enemy's infantry, stress must again be laid on the fact that in most cases they have only received drafts of 18-year old men. Therefore there are no reasons for any panic. On the contrary, the troops in the front line have never before considered themselves victors in the way that they do at present.

This Army order is to be read out to all units.

                               (Sd.)   Von der Marwitz,
                                            General.

Extract from an order of the 2nd Guard Division, dated 27/8/18.

According to reports received by Army Headquarters the infantry of other divisions in the battle hardly made any use of their rifles. The whole defence had been left to the machine-guns

the French offensive on the Marne front in July, that American troops in large numbers had arrived in the battle area, had given a very good account of themselves, and had thus proved in the most forcible manner that the unrestricted " U " boat campaign had failed.

The conservation of man power constituted a very important feature of the battle. Between August 8th and August 21st we had lost 1,423 officers and 25,856 other ranks, killed, wounded, and missing; the enemy's losses in prisoners alone during that period amounted to some 23,000, while his losses in killed and wounded were known to be very heavy.

This was a satisfactory balance sheet, and, if the same proportion of losses could be maintained, it was certain that we should be able to outlast the Germans in the final struggle.

and artillery. A large number of cases have also been substantiated in which companies of infantry have passed through the artillery lines, and have taken no notice of the request of the artillery to protect them. The strongest and severest measures will be taken to prevent conduct which points to such neglect of duty. By order of the Army, artillery officers are empowered to ascertain and report the name of any unit and commander refusing protection to the artillery. Men who come back from the front and are met by the military police without their arms are to be punished by court-martial.

Subordinate commanders are to use every opportunity for the delivery of controlled rifle-fire. Control is to be exercised by regimental and battalion commanders. In this respect, I particularly call attention to the special necessity in defensive warfare of having reliable non-commissioned officers behind the front. On every occasion, it must be made absolutely clear to the men that their rifles are their best means of defence, and that the attacking enemy must be shot down.

(Sd.)   Von Freideburg.

CHAPTER V

THE ADVANCE TO PÉRONNE, AUGUST 21ST—30TH

Maps 2, 4, and 5

August 21st ; the opening of the second phase ; the general policy—The III Corps plan of attack for August 22nd—August 22nd ; the artillery support—The attack by the 47th and 12th Divisions—The capture of Albert by the 18th Division—The advance of the 3rd Australian Division—The German counter-attack in the Happy Valley—August 23rd ; the operations of the Australian Corps south of the Somme—The general plan of attack—The first phase of the Australian Corps attack—The second phase—The third phase ; the capture of Chuignes —The action of the 32nd Division—The capture of Tara and Usna Hills—August 24th ; the capture of Bray-sur-Somme and Bécordel-Bécourt by the Australian and III Corps—The situation on the Fourth Army front on the night of August 24th—The readjustment of the Australian Corps front south of the Somme—August 25th ; the capture of Ceylon Wood and Fricourt—Our artillery policy—The enemy's retirement in front of the Third Army—The events of August 26th—The action of the hostile artillery—August 27th ; the renewal of the pressure south of the Somme—The co-operation of the First French Army with the Australian Corps—The events north of the Somme—The capture of Trones Wood by the 18th Division— The events of August 28th—The events of August 29th ; our troops reach the banks of the Somme south of Péronne—The advance north of the Somme on August 30th.

IN his despatch of December 21st, 1918, Sir Douglas Haig has explained his reasons for extending the front of attack northwards to the area between the Somme and the Scarpe in the following

August 21st ; the opening of the second phase ; the general policy
words :—

" The enemy did not seem prepared to meet an attack in this direction, and, owing to the success of the Fourth Army, he occupied a salient the left flank of which was already threatened from the south. A further reason for my decision was that the ground north of the Ancre River was not greatly damaged by shell fire, and was suitable for the use of tanks. A successful attack between Albert and Arras in a south-easterly direction would turn the line of the Somme south of Péronne, and gave every promise of producing far-reaching results. It would be a step forward to the strategic objective St. Quentin–Cambrai. . . . It was arranged that on the morning of August 21st a limited attack should be launched north of the Ancre to gain the general line of the Arras–Albert railway, on which it was correctly assumed that the enemy's main line of resistance was sited. The day of August 22nd would then be used to get troops and guns into position on this front and to bring forward the left of the Fourth Army between the Somme and the Ancre. The principal

71

attack would be delivered on August 23rd by the Third Army and the divisions of the Fourth Army north of the Somme, the remainder of the Fourth Army assisting by pushing forward south of the river to cover the flank of the main operation. Thereafter, if success attended our efforts, the whole of both Armies were to press forward with the greatest vigour and exploit to the full any advantage we might have gained."

The centre of gravity of the British offensive was, consequently, transferred for a time from the front of the Fourth Army to that of the Third Army north of Albert. At 4.55 a.m. on August 21st, Sir Julian Byng launched eight divisions against the enemy's defences between Grandecourt, five miles north of Albert, and Moyenneville, seven miles south of Arras, on a front of some 16,000 yards.

News of the battle was eagerly awaited by the Fourth Army, as it was known that, if all went well on August 21st, offensive operations were to be resumed on the Fourth Army front between the Somme and Albert on August 22nd as a preliminary to a general advance on Péronne. Early news was received that Beaucourt, Achiet, and Courcelles had been captured with 2,000 prisoners, and that the enemy was holding the line of the Albert–Arras railway very strongly. This was a satisfactory beginning, and no doubt was felt that the enemy's resistance would soon be broken, and his troops compelled to retire.

There were at this time indications that the Germans were contemplating a withdrawal in front of the First Army south of the Scarpe. Moreover, although the enemy was fighting very stubbornly against the Third Army north of Albert, the moral and general condition of his troops along the whole of the Allied front was now known to be such that, if bold and resolute tactics were adopted, his total collapse appeared probable. This was fully realised at General Headquarters, and an order was issued by Sir Douglas Haig on August 22nd to all Army Commanders defining a ruthless offensive policy designed to achieve the final downfall of the German Armies.[1] The efforts of the Fourth Army for the next

[1] " I request that Army Commanders will without delay bring to the notice of all subordinate leaders the changed conditions under which operations are now being carried on, and the consequent necessity for all ranks to act with the utmost boldness and resolution in order to get full advantage from the present favourable situation.

" The effect of the two very severe defeats and the continuous attacks to which the enemy has been subjected during the past months has been to wear out his troops and disorganise his plans. Our Second and Fifth Armies have taken their share in the effort to destroy the enemy and already have gained considerable ground from him in the Lys sector of our front. To-day the Tenth French Army crossed the Ailette and reports that a Bavarian division fled in panic, carrying back with it another division which was advancing to its support.

" To-morrow the attack of the Allied Armies on the whole front from Soissons to Neuville Vitasse, near Arras, is to be continued. The methods which we have followed hitherto in our battles with limited objectives, when the enemy was strong, are no longer suitable to his present condition. The enemy has not the means to deliver counter-attacks on an extended scale, nor has he the numbers to hold a continuous position against the very extended advance which is being directed against him. In order to turn the present situation to account, the most resolute offensive is everywhere desirable. Risks which a month ago would have been criminal to incur ought now to be incurred as a duty.

" It is no longer necessary to advance in regular lines and step by step. On the contrary, each division should be given a distant objective which must be reached independently of its neighbour, and even if one's flank is thereby exposed for the time being. Reinforcements must be directed on points where our troops are gaining ground, not where they are checked. A vigorous

Becordel

To Contalmaison

Bellevue Fm

To Bray-sur-Somme

Cathedral

ALBERT AND THE GROUND TO THE SOUTH-EAST.

Oblique air photograph.

ten days were, therefore, directed towards Péronne, in co-operation with the advance of the Third Army on Bapaume, and with that of the First French Army on Ham.[1] Thus the second phase of the operations of the Fourth Army in the battles of the hundred days, which opened with the attack of the III Corps between the Somme and the Ancre on August 22nd, formed part of the general advance of the Allied Armies from Soissons to the Scarpe.

As a prelude to any renewal of the advance north of the Somme, it was necessary to eject the enemy from the trench system which he was holding opposite the Amiens outer defences. This system, although only recently established, was well organised and was supported by a substantial weight of artillery. It was also necessary, in order to enable the V Corps on the right of the Third Army to advance east of the Ancre, that the enemy should be driven out of the positions in and around Albert which he had been holding for the past four months. Since August 6th our patrols had occupied positions in the western portion of Albert, but had been unable to drive the enemy from the remainder of the town. North of Albert the swampy reaches of the Ancre were impassable except by means of bridges and causeways; these would have to be constructed if an advance was to be made across the river by the V Corps. As the construction of these bridges would involve considerable labour, time, and casualties, it was decided first to clear Albert, and then to pass troops of the V Corps through the town in order to turn the enemy's positions east of the Ancre from the south.

On August 22nd the III Corps was to attack between the Bray-sur-Somme–Corbie road and Albert inclusive, whilst, on the right of the III Corps, the 3rd Australian Division was to advance its

The III Corps' plan of attack for August 22nd

left in order to protect the right flank of the attack. The immediate object of the operation was to secure the high ground which lies north of Bray-sur-Somme, east of the well-known Happy Valley, and between the Chalk Pit and Bécordel-Bécourt, also the western slopes of Shamrock and Tara Hills. The task of securing the high ground east of the Happy Valley, and between the Chalk Pit and Bécordel-Bécourt, was allotted to the 47th and 12th Divisions, their final objective representing an advance of some 3,000 yards. There was also an intermediate objective for these two divisions about 1,000 yards west of the final objective on the western slopes of the Happy Valley. On the right Maj.-Gen. Gorringe, commanding the 47th Division, detailed the 141st Brigade to capture the first objective. The 142nd Brigade in support was then to "leap-frog" the leading brigade and secure the final objective; the 140th Brigade was in reserve. The 12th Division, under Maj.-Gen. Higginson, operating on a

offensive will cause hostile strong points to fall and in due course our whole Army will be able to continue its advance. This procedure will result in speedily breaking up the hostile forces and will cost us much less than if we attempted to deal with the present situation in a half-hearted manner. The situation is most favourable. Let each one of us act energetically and, without hesitation, push forward to our objective."

[1] These three towns were important road junctions and of considerable strategical value to the enemy, as is apparent from a study of the Somme campaigns of 1916 and 1917, wherein they played a most conspicuous part and represented the main centres of the enemy's resistance.

L

slightly broader front, employed the 35th and 36th Brigades, attacking side by side, to capture both objectives, with the 37th Brigade in reserve. Orders were issued for all ground gained to be consolidated and organised for defence in depth, as it was possible that a temporary halt might have to be made on this line, until a further advance by the Third Army should threaten the enemy's communications.

The task of the 3rd Australian Division on the right of the 47th Division was to ensure the security of the southern flank of the III Corps by advancing its left to the high ground immediately north of Bray-sur-Somme. This necessitated an advance of approximately 2,000 yards, and the task was entrusted to the 9th Australian Brigade.

On the left, the crossing of the Ancre between Dernancourt and Albert, and the clearing of Albert, presented numerous difficulties. This task was assigned to the 18th Division. Maj.-Gen. Lee decided to employ the 54th Brigade to secure the ground between Méaulte and Albert; the 55th Brigade to complete the capture of Albert and secure the southern portion of Tara Hill, and Shamrock Hill; the 53rd Brigade was retained in divisional reserve.[1]

In order to ensure that no opportunity should be missed of pressing forward on the heels of the enemy, should he show further signs of withdrawal, the reserve brigades were organised ready to assume the rôle of an advanced guard if the situation so demanded. In addition, a force of two squadrons of the III Corps Cavalry, supported by six whippet tanks and one troop of Australian Light Horse attached to the 3rd Australian Division, was organised for the purpose of pushing forward as far as the small woods on the high ground north of Suzanne, some 4,000 yards beyond the objective allotted to the 47th Division.

Sir Alec. Godley retained the 58th Division in corps reserve, but instructed Maj.-Gen. Ramsay to move one brigade at " zero " to an assembly position in rear of the 18th Division, and two brigades to a position just west of Morlancourt.

The preparations for the attack were made with the utmost effort to ensure secrecy. There was no preliminary bombardment other than the normal harassing fire which was maintained until " zero." Nevertheless, the enemy appears to have discovered that trouble was brewing. This was proved not only by the statements of prisoners, but by the weight of the enemy's counter-preparation during the night of August 21st. This bombardment was especially heavy at 4 a.m. on the morning of August 22nd, only forty-five minutes before " zero," when a considerable quantity of gas shell was fired, making it necessary for our troops to adjust their gas helmets. The assembly was not, however, seriously hampered.

At " zero," which had been fixed for 4.45 a.m., the barrage from 250 guns came down 200 yards in front of the leading waves of the 47th and 12th Divisions. This was the signal for the assembled infantry and tanks of these divisions to advance under cover of a creeping barrage, moving

---

[1] As soon as Albert had been cleared of the enemy, the 38th Division, under the command of Maj.-Gen. T. A. Cubitt, which formed the right of the V Corps, was to pass through the town and operate in a north-easterly direction.

forward at the rate of 100 yards every four minutes. The 18th Division moved forward covered by the fire of four brigades of field artillery, which fired on centres of resistance, and pro-

August 22nd; the artillery support

vided a dense smoke screen designed to conceal the movements of the attacking troops and tanks. A smoke screen was also placed on the high ground which formed the objective, thus depriving the enemy of valuable observation points.

The 47th and 12th Divisions, each supported by ten Mark V tanks, made good progress. The enemy's resistance was not formidable, with

The attack by the 47th and 12th Divisions

the result that by 6.45 a.m. the whole of the inter-mediate objective, about 2,000 yards from the " starting line," was in our possession, except at one point near the Filiform Tree close to the boundary between the two divisions. Here a party of Germans stubbornly defended the crest of the rise and defeated all attempts to dislodge them.

The barrage was halted for ten minutes covering the intermediate objective, before moving forward again in advance of our troops to the final objective. Once again the infantry surged forward, but found its progress more strongly opposed. On the front of the 47th Division small parties of the enemy, concealed by the numerous folds in the ground on the eastern slopes of the Happy Valley, checked our advance, and were only " mopped up " after hard and stubborn fighting. Some of these parties in the northern end of the valley also helped to stiffen the resistance offered earlier in the morning in the vicinity of the Filiform Tree, and no further progress was made at this point. Elsewhere the 47th Division reached the final objective. The 12th Division succeeded in clearing the whole of Méaulte, and secured the high ground along the Bray-sur-Somme–Albert road south-east of the village, but, as with the 47th Division, its further progress was checked by the party of Germans, who clung desperately to the position near the Filiform Tree. Thus, at the close of the first phase of the battle, the 47th and 12th Divisions had secured their objectives except in the vicinity of the Filiform Tree.

As soon as the 47th Division reached the final objective, the two squadrons of corps cavalry moved forward to carry out their rôle of exploitation. The moment they left the shelter of the Happy Valley and appeared over the crest of the rise which our troops were consolidating, heavy artillery and machine-gun fire was directed upon them. It at once became apparent that the situation was not suitable for the employment of mounted troops, and the cavalry was therefore withdrawn. Unfortunately, or perhaps fortunately, the whippet tanks, which should have accompanied the cavalry, were unable to move forward in support owing to mechanical trouble and other causes, and consequently did not take part in the action. Even if they had moved forward with the cavalry, it is very doubtful whether they would have been able to render any assistance, as the enemy was completely ready and prepared for our attack.

On the left, the 18th Division, assigned the difficult task of clearing Albert and its environs of the enemy, was assisted by four Mark V tanks. On the evening of August 21st strong patrols of the 54th Brigade had succeeded in crossing the Ancre at dusk, and had gained a footing on the Albert–Méaulte road, south of Albert and north of Vivier Mill.   This very well executed enterprise simplified the task of the 54th Brigade, as it to a great extent rendered unnecessary the difficult, and probably costly, operation of forcing the passage of the Ancre and its marshes in the face of strong opposition.

The capture of Albert by the 18th Division

Following on the brilliant patrol work of the 54th Brigade, came the gallant achievement of the 55th Brigade, which carried out the difficult operation of dislodging the enemy from his well-concealed and strongly-defended posts in the ruins of Albert.   It was work which could not be hurried, and required exceptional thoroughness and individual initiative. The operation for capturing the town was divided into three phases.   The first phase began at 4.45 a.m., when a heavy bombardment was directed on the whole of that portion of Albert which lies east of the Ancre.   This bombardment lasted for an hour, during which time the 8th East Surrey worked its way through that part of the town which lies west of the river. For the second phase, the bombardment was lifted on to the strong points on the eastern outskirts, where it remained stationary until 6.45 a.m., while the 8th East Surrey cleared the town east of the river.   In the final phase the bombardment was lifted clear of the town.   By 9.10 a.m. the 8th East Surrey had overcome the enemy's resistance and was in complete occupation of Albert.

Meanwhile by " zero," under cover of the patrols, the 11th Royal Fusiliers and three companies of the 6th Northamptonshire, of the 54th Brigade, had silently assembled east of the Ancre along the Vivier Mill– Albert road.   The remainder of the latter battalion, which had been unable to cross the Ancre south of Vivier Mill, fought its way forward to the western exit of Méaulte, which it reached a little before 5.30 a.m.   A quarter of an hour later, the two attacking battalions swept forward from the line of the Vivier Mill–Albert road, under cover of a creeping barrage, supported by the four Mark V tanks which had been allotted to the division.   The enemy was holding his position with pairs of machine-guns disposed in depth along the front; over 80 of these were captured, and many more destroyed by shell fire.   By 8 a.m. the 6th Northamptonshire had gained the slopes of Shamrock Hill, and was in touch with the 12th Division east of Méaulte.   On its left the 11th Royal Fusiliers, after meeting with strong opposition from the direction of Albert, Bellevue Farm, and Shamrock Hill, had reached a line 500 yards east of Bellevue Farm.   About 10 a.m. the 7th The Buffs, of the 55th Brigade, which was supporting the attack of the 8th East Surrey on Albert, debouched from the town and endeavoured to advance towards Tara Hill, but was unable to proceed beyond the eastern outskirts of the town owing to the severity of the machine-gun fire.   During the afternoon a company of the 2nd Bedfordshire, supporting the attack of the 54th Brigade, moved through the advanced troops and secured the summit of Shamrock Hill, from which the German machine-guns had been particularly active.

Starting at " zero " and keeping close up to the barrage, the 9th Australian Brigade, operating on the right of the 47th Division, advanced

To face page 76.

BRITISH INFANTRY IN ALBERT ON AUGUST 22ND.

British official photograph.

.

AUSTRALIAN PIONEERS DIGGING-IN ON THE HIGH GROUND OVERLOOKING BRAY, WHILE THE ENEMY STILL HELD THE VILLAGE.

By kind permission of the Australian Government.

to the first objective, a distance of about 1,000 yards from the
"starting line." The enemy's resistance was quickly
overcome, and the advance was so rapid that many
machine-guns were captured before the crews could
bring them into action.[1]

The advance of the 3rd Australian Division

After a halt of an hour on the first objective, the advance of the
Australians was resumed. This halt had allowed the enemy time to shorten
his artillery barrage, which caused a number of casualties, but, in spite
of this, the final objective was gained by 8.30 a.m. In this latter stage
of the attack the troops of the 47th Division, which were operating immediately on the left of the 9th Brigade, diverged too much to the left,
probably on account of the resistance encountered in the Happy
Valley, and a company of the 34th Battalion of the 9th Brigade was in
consequence sent forward to strengthen the left flank. This company
succeeded in capturing the Chalk Pit, where it was relieved later in the
day by troops of the 47th Division. While these operations were in
progress the 3rd Australian Pioneer Battalion, which was holding the
Etinehem spur from the Bray-sur-Somme–Corbie road to the river,
advanced our line to the Crucifix, from which point the whole of the village
of Bray-sur-Somme was under observation.

In order to reap full advantage from the success gained by the
III Corps and the 3rd Australian Division, orders were issued by Sir
Henry Rawlinson, on the evening of August 22nd, for a combined attack
to be made by the III Corps north of the Somme, in conjunction with an
attack by the Australian Corps south of the river. The attack by the
Australian Corps had already been arranged for the early morning of
August 23rd. Sir Alec. Godley accordingly issued orders for an attack
to be launched on the whole front of the III Corps on the 23rd, but a
change in the situation, caused by a German counter-attack in the Happy
Valley on the afternoon of the 22nd, necessitated a modification of his
plans, and it was finally decided to carry out the attack only on the
northern part of the front held by the 18th Division.

Throughout the afternoon of August 22nd the enemy shelled the
Happy Valley and the high ground to the east of it, where the advanced
troops of the 47th Division were digging in. Unfortunately the crescent-shaped formation of the high
ground east of the Happy Valley had necessitated the
troops on the right of the 47th Division taking up a position in a semicircle,
and this minimised the effectiveness of the protective barrage. At
5.30 p.m. the shelling increased in volume, and the enemy in considerable
strength attacked the 142nd Brigade of the 47th Division. Although
the consolidating troops offered a stout resistance, they were forced to
withdraw west of the Happy Valley, finally taking up a position along the
Bray-sur-Somme–Albert road. On the extreme right of the 142nd Brigade,
two companies of the 22nd London held their ground for some time, but were
finally forced to withdraw, thus leaving the flank of the 3rd Australian
Division dangerously exposed. After a hard fight the Chalk Pit was

The German counter-attack in the Happy Valley

---

[1] A German battalion commander and his staff, captured in the fight, could speak of nothing
but the rapidity with which our men were upon them and surrounded their machine-guns.

secured by the enemy, but was recaptured almost immediately by a company of the 33rd Battalion of the 9th Australian Brigade. This company, in conjunction with the two companies of the 22nd London, then formed a defensive flank along an underspur running into the Happy Valley. Reserve machine-guns were sent forward to take up positions on the high ground immediately north of the Bray-sur-Somme–Corbie road, and the 140th Brigade was pushed forward as a further reserve to provide against contingencies, but no further attack developed. The enemy placed a number of machine-guns in the Happy Valley, the fire of which intermittently swept the area held by the 3rd Australian Division north of the Bray-sur-Somme–Corbie road, and was a constant source of trouble to reinforcements and ration parties moving forward to the front line.

On account of this check, and owing to the casualties suffered by the 142nd Brigade, the 47th Division was unable to continue the attack on August 23rd, as had been originally intended. The 175th Brigade of the 58th Division was moved up from corps reserve, and was placed at the disposal of Maj.-Gen. Gorringe for the relief of the 142nd Brigade. This relief was effected on the night of August 22nd, and the relief of the 47th Division by the 58th Division was completed on the morning of August 24th.

South of the Somme, no untoward incident interfered with our plans, and the attack of the Australian Corps, with the 32nd Division on the

August 23rd : the operations of the Australian Corps south of the Somme

right and the 1st Australian Division on the left, was carried out on a front of four miles, extending from Herleville to the Somme. The 5th Australian Division, which was holding the sector immediately south of the Somme on the night of August 22nd, remained in position until the assembly of the 1st Australian Division was complete, when it was withdrawn into reserve.

Sir John Monash decided to carry out the attack, the object of which was the capture of the general line Herleville–Chuignes–Square Wood, in

The general plan of attack (see Map 5)

three phases. The objectives of the first phase included Herleville and Chuignolles, and the Plateau Woods and the Arcy Woods. Here the enemy had constructed an organised defensive system since August 12th, and, although these defences were by no means formidable, a certain amount of resistance was to be expected. Sir John Monash considered, therefore, that ample artillery and tank support must be provided, and that a carefully organised attack must be prepared by the 32nd Division and the 1st Australian Division. In the second phase the line to be reached ran along the foot of the eastern slopes of the Chuignolles Valley, from near Chuignes to the Somme. This attack was to be carried out by the 1st Australian Division without artillery assistance, as no serious opposition was expected. Finally, the third phase, the execution of which was dependent upon the success of the preceding phases, involved an attack by the 1st Australian Division against the high ground east of the Chuignolles Valley, as far as the Chuignes–Cappy road and the western outskirts of Cappy. The objective also included the village of Chuignes.

On the right, Maj.-Gen. Lambert detailed the 97th Brigade for the attack on Herleville. On the left, Maj.-Gen. Glasgow employed the 2nd and 1st Australian Brigades, operating on the right and left respectively, while the task of capturing the final objective was allotted to the 3rd Brigade.[1]

The field artillery barrage covering the initial advance of the infantry to the first objective was furnished by fifteen field artillery brigades, six of which were to support the advance of the 32nd Division, and nine that of the 1st Australian Division. A smoke screen was placed on the Bray-sur-Somme spur north of the Somme, but, contrary to the usual custom, smoke shells were not employed in the barrage to define the various stages of the advance. Throughout the operation the task of the heavy artillery, in addition to the requisite counter-battery fire, was to keep the crossings over the Somme at Cappy and Eclusier under a steady fire, and to bombard selected targets in the vicinity of Foucaucourt and the roads further east.

Twelve tanks of the 8th Mark V Tank Battalion were detailed to co-operate with the 32nd Division in the attack on Herleville, while the 1st and 2nd Australian Brigades were each allotted twelve tanks from the 13th and 2nd Mark V Tank Battalions respectively. In addition, each attacking brigade was allotted three tanks of an older type for carrying forward additional ammunition and supplies. By dawn on August 22nd all the tanks had been assembled within 3,000 yards of the front line, and at 9.30 p.m. that night they moved forward to their "starting line," which was approximately 1,000 yards in rear of that of the infantry.

The attack, which was timed to start simultaneously with that of the 18th Division against Tara Hill, was launched at 4.45 a.m. on the morning of August 23rd. As soon as the artillery barrage, which was in all respects excellent, came down, the infantry moved forward followed by the tanks. The latter were well up to time with the exception of those supporting the 2nd Australian Brigade, which were a little late in arriving at the "starting line," and only succeeded in catching up the infantry at a later stage of the advance.

The first phase of the Australian Corps attack

On the 32nd Division front the 2nd King's Own Yorkshire Light Infantry and 10th Argyll and Sutherland Highlanders of the 97th Brigade attacked Herleville, and the village was soon in our possession. Heavy fighting occurred near the church, where the enemy was in considerable strength and fought with determination.

On the 1st Australian Division front the assaulting troops of the 2nd and 1st Australian Brigades, keeping close up to the barrage, made good progress and quickly overran the enemy's outpost line. South of the Amiens–Brie road considerable opposition was encountered by the 2nd Brigade in the neighbourhood of the St. Denis Woods, where it was difficult for the troops to advance as the ground was broken by a deep gully and sunken roads. The St. Denis Woods were strongly defended, and enfilade machine-gun fire from the southern portion of the St. Martin Woods delayed their capture for a short time, until the timely arrival of

---

[1] The 32nd Division, in the first phase, attacked on a front of 2,000 yards, and the 1st Australian Division on a front of 5,000 yards.

the tanks enabled the infantry to clear them. Further north it took some time to "mop up" the large expanse of the St. Martin Woods, but, as this work was done chiefly by the supporting troops, the advance was not delayed, and the 2nd Brigade was able to keep well up to the barrage and made good progress.

At 5.15 a.m. the infantry of the 1st Brigade was entering the Matto Woods, after having overcome the enemy's resistance on the outskirts with the assistance of a tank. Robert Wood, which was strongly held, was surrounded by our troops, and the enemy surrendered freely. In the sunken road between the Matto Woods and Robert Wood many Germans surrendered to the 1st Brigade without attempting to fight. Chuignolles was surrounded and "mopped up" with the effective assistance of the tanks, and almost immediately afterwards Chuignolles Wood fell into our hands. Owing, however, to the heavy machine-gun fire which was encountered, it was found necessary to make a temporary withdrawal to its southern outskirts. On the extreme left of the 1st Brigade German machine-guns caused trouble from the outset of the attack, and it was only after stiff fighting that our troops reached their objective.

It had been arranged for the barrage to halt at 5.30 a.m. for fifteen minutes some distance short of the first objective, to ensure that the infantry should not lose it. When this hour arrived the situation was well in hand, and the infantry was almost everywhere in touch with the barrage. At 5.45 a.m. the barrage was again lifted, and the advance to the first objective was resumed. The troops of 32nd Division pushed forward, and the 2nd King's Own Yorkshire Light Infantry gained its objective on the right without difficulty, but considerable opposition was experienced on the left from the fire of machine-guns posted in the Herleville Woods. One of these copses was held by 50 Germans who were surrounded, and eventually surrendered to three of our men after the officer in command had been shot.

Owing to the increasing opposition met from the Herleville Woods, the troops of the 2nd Australian Brigade on the right began to lose the impetus of their initial attack, and the advance became slower. The splendid leadership of Lieut. William Joynt of the 8th Battalion, however, here stood the 2nd Australian Brigade in good stead. Realising that the men of the leading battalion had lost all their officers and had become disorganised, Lieut. Joynt rushed forward across the open from his own battalion, under very heavy fire, to join them. Having got the men under cover of some dead ground, he re-formed them, and linked them up with his own men. A personal reconnaissance showed him that the fire from the Herleville Woods was holding up the whole advance. Without any hesitation he dashed forward, calling on the men to follow him. By sheer force of example he inspired them to make a brilliant bayonet charge, which was successful in reaching and entering the woods.[1] Although fighting in the Herleville Woods continued most of the day, by 7 a.m. the 2nd Brigade had worked through or round them and had reached the first objective. The 1st Brigade similarly met with determined resistance from the high ground north-east of the St. Martin Woods,

[1] See Appendix E, No. 28.

To face page 81.

THE 15-INCH GUN CAPTURED BY THE AUSTRALIANS IN THE ARCY WOODS.

By kind permission of the Australian Government.

THE COUNTRY NEAR CHUIGNOLLES, WITH FROISSY BEACON IN THE BACKGROUND.

By kind permission of the Australian Government.

but the attack was resolutely pushed home, and, with the admirable co-operation of the tanks, the high ground which constituted the objective at this point was secured.

At 7 a.m., although the first objective had been gained, the 1st Australian and 32nd Divisions had lost touch with each other, and a gap of some hundreds of yards existed between them, through which the enemy was endeavouring to force his way. A company of the 8th Australian Battalion, however, was at once moved up, and succeeded in filling the gap and regaining touch.

The second phase, which really became merged into the first phase, consisted of a number of small attacks against the numerous small woods and copses north-east of Chuignolles, without *The second phase* the support of an artillery barrage. The opposition was very local, and by about 7 a.m. the whole area inside the second objective was clear of the enemy.[1]

The attack on the third objective was carried out by the 3rd Australian Brigade which advanced in artillery formation, with the 12th and 9th Battalions leading, the 11th in support, and the 10th *The third phase; the capture of Chuignes* in reserve. The Germans, who were under the impression that our advance had come to an end, were holding this high ground in considerable strength. At 2 p.m. the 12th and 9th Battalions deployed west of the Long Woods and Luc Wood, and advanced through the 1st Brigade and across the valley, under cover of a creeping barrage provided by three field artillery brigades which had been pushed forward rapidly during the early phases of the advance. The high ground overlooking Chuignolles, and at the Marly Woods and Froissy Beacon, was stormed, and the enemy fell back in confusion to Garenne Wood and Square Wood. On the left, however, the enemy's artillery fire was heavy and caused the 9th Battalion numerous casualties, and the 10th Battalion, from reserve, was sent up to protect the left flank of the advance. The 11th Battalion, which during the advance had followed in close support of the 12th Battalion, was employed in the actual capture of the Marly Woods and Froissy Beacon. Turning due north, while the 12th Battalion continued its advance, this battalion attacked the enemy in flank and took him completely by surprise.[2]

Meanwhile, the 12th Battalion reached the outskirts of Garenne Wood, which was held too strongly to permit of its being captured by a frontal attack. An enveloping movement was, therefore, carried out, and resulted in the capture of the wood with seventy prisoners. At the same time Square Wood was secured, and our troops were able to follow the retreating enemy to within 400 yards of Cappy. One company, after penetrating as far as the village itself, eventually withdrew without difficulty.

During this fighting the remaining brigades of the 1st Australian Division had not been idle. The 1st Brigade, under cover of the barrage which supported the attack of the 3rd Brigade, gained possession of

[1] In the Arcy Woods there was found a 15-inch gun on a huge mounting. The gun, which was one of those employed for bombarding Amiens, had been either blown up intentionally or accidentally destroyed by a premature explosion.

[2] Although capturing over 100 prisoners, the total casualties of the 11th Battalion for the day amounted to two.

M

Chuignes, and of the spur and small valley immediately south of the village. The 2nd Brigade on the right pushed forward patrols, but, owing to the number of casualties the brigade had suffered during the earlier stages of the advance and to the resistance offered by the enemy, very little progress was made.

While the 97th Brigade of the 32nd Division was attacking the enemy's positions around Herleville, the 96th Brigade on its right, under
The action of the 32nd Division cover of the creeping barrage which was extended to the south as far as Lihons, pushed forward strong patrols and succeeded in advancing the line 500 yards south of Herleville.[1]

During this very successful day's fighting the 1st Australian and 32nd Divisions again greatly distinguished themselves by skilful leadership, intelligent use of the ground, and the dash and gallantry of all ranks. The 1st Australian Division secured 2,596 prisoners, 23 guns, and 167 machine-guns, and the 32nd Division 311 prisoners and many machine-guns.

Before the V Corps on the right of the Third Army could make any progress, it was essential to capture the Tara Hill–Usna Hill
The capture of Tara and Usna Hills ridge, astride the Albert–Bapaume road, and thus secure the flank of the V Corps. Consequently, after consultation with Maj.-Gen. Cubitt, commanding the 38th Division, Maj.-Gen. Lee arranged for the 53rd Brigade, which had been in reserve on August 22nd, and which he reinforced with the 7th The Queens, to attack this ridge at dawn on August 23rd in conjunction with the 113th Brigade of the 38th Division. The latter brigade was to move through Albert and attack Usna Hill, after deploying east of the marshy reaches of the Ancre immediately north of Albert. In order to make it possible to assemble the 113th Brigade, the 55th Brigade, which was holding Albert, advanced its line about 500 yards during the night astride the Albert–Bapaume road. This allowed the 113th Brigade sufficient space from which to debouch from the eastern exits of Albert. The assembly positions of the latter brigade to the north of the town were reached with some difficulty, as the troops had in some cases to wade waist high through the swamps east of the Ancre. At 4.45 a.m., after overcoming all difficulties, the 53rd Brigade on the right assisted by six Mark V tanks, and the 113th Brigade on the left formed up with its back to the floods, launched a frontal attack against Tara and Usna Hills and captured the ridge by 6 a.m.

These operations improved our position very materially and gave us a good footing on the slopes of the high ground overlooking Albert. This high ground, it was realised, would be our next objective, as soon as the advance of the Third Army towards Bapaume began to threaten the rear of the enemy's position on the Longueval–High Wood–Pozières ridge, and as soon as the remainder of the troops of the III Corps were ready to advance.

---

[1] The 4th Australian Division also made incursions into the enemy's lines, in one of which Lieut. McCarthy, 16th Australian Battalion, took 5 machine-guns and 50 prisoners almost single-handed. See Appendix E, No. 32.

On the evening of the 23rd, as the result of the success gained during the day, Sir Henry Rawlinson issued orders for the pressure to be maintained along the whole army front north of the Somme.

The capture of Tara and Usna Hills, on the morning of the 23rd, concluded the initial phase of the operations north of the Somme, and the remainder of the day was spent in consolidating the position and in organising for a further advance. As the weather was perfect and the moon full, it was decided to vary the tactics, and to attempt an advance by night all along the front north of the river.

August 24th; the capture of Bray-sur-Somme and Bécordel-Bécourt by the Australian and III Corps

Prior to the attack Bray-sur-Somme and La Neuville-les-Bray, as well as the centres of hostile activity east and south of these places, were harassed with artillery fire. Taking advantage of this opportunity, the 3rd Australian Pioneer Battalion, as soon as it was sufficiently dark, crossed the river south of Bray-sur-Somme by bridges, which it had thrown across the night before, and by midnight had cleared La Neuville-les-Bray and the peninsula formed by the bend in the river.

The main attack by the 3rd Australian, 47th, 12th, and 18th Divisions, in the order named from south to north, started at 1 a.m. in brilliant moonlight. On the right the 40th Australian Battalion attacked the village of Bray-sur-Somme. It encountered opposition on the outskirts of the village, and after experiencing some difficulty in maintaining touch and direction in the village, succeeded in establishing a line along the eastern edge. One hundred and twenty-five prisoners and 22 machine-guns were captured in Bray-sur-Somme, as well as a large dump of timber and ammunition and three loaded trains which were taken in the railway sidings.

To the north of the Australians the troops of the 47th and 12th Divisions advanced without difficulty, except in the centre, east of the Filiform Tree, where, as on the 22nd, the attack was at first held up by a strong post of the enemy. It was not until the operations had been in progress for two hours that the hostile artillery fire became at all heavy, but, from 3 a.m. until 8 a.m., the ridge east of the Happy Valley was heavily shelled with high explosive and gas shell. At 8 a.m., the enemy launched a strong counter-attack, the concentration for which was luckily observed by one of our aeroplanes and at once reported. Our artillery promptly responded to the call, and, with the aid of the scout aeroplanes which were patrolling in the neighbourhood, and which attacked the enemy with bombs and machine-guns, the counter-attacking troops were overwhelmed before they could approach our lines.

Further north the troops of the 12th Division succeeded in capturing the hamlet of Bécordel-Bécourt, and established themselves without difficulty on the high ground south-east of the village. Working in conjunction with the right of the V Corps, whose first objectives were Ovillers-la-Boisselle and La Boisselle, the 18th Division advanced against Chapes spur. By 5 a.m. it had captured the spur and thrown out a defensive flank facing south, north of Bécourt Wood. The La Boisselle crater, which had been blown on the first day of the Battle of the Somme over two years before, afforded the enemy a strong locality of which he made full use. He held on to this position until 8 p.m., when a brilliant attack by the 8th Royal Berkshire finally dislodged him, and resulted in the capture of 250 prisoners and several machine-guns. During the day strong patrols " mopped up " Bécourt Wood, and cleared the northern end of Sausage Valley in conjunction with the 38th Division.

During the morning there were signs that the enemy was about to begin a general withdrawal north of the Somme. He evacuated the commanding position on the ridge east of the Filiform Tree, which had been the cause of so much trouble to the 12th Division during the early hours of the morning. Patrols of this division then occupied the position and pushed forward several hundred yards beyond it, thereby reducing to a certain extent the sharp salient formed by the advance of the 47th Division east of the Happy Valley.

During the fighting from August 22nd to August 24th the enemy had on the whole offered a stout resistance to our advance. On the **The situation on the** 22nd portions of three divisions participated in the **Fourth Army front on** counter-attack, which resulted in the recapture by the **the night of August 24th** enemy of the Happy Valley. It also transpired that the attack of the 18th Division in the vicinity of the Sausage Valley, on the morning of the 24th, had forestalled by one hour a counter-attack by detachments of three German divisions, the object of which was the recapture of Tara Hill. This resistance, at first sight, naturally conveyed the impression that the enemy contemplated making a determined stand.

Throughout the three days' fighting, however, no new hostile divisions had been identified, and the enemy's reinforcements were all drawn from those divisions which had been already engaged in the battle since August 8th. This, combined with the fact that aeroplane photographs taken on August 22nd disclosed new trenches on the eastern side of the Somme south of Falvy and north from Voyennes,[1] and also a report from the French further south that digging was in progress east of the Canal du Nord between Noyon and Nesle, proved fairly conclusively that the enemy contemplated a retirement to Péronne, and that the resistance offered was only of a temporary character, to stem our advance until his defensive preparations could be completed.

During August 24th, after the failure of the German counter-attack east of the Happy Valley, there were more and more signs of demoralisation amongst the enemy's troops north of the Somme. The pressure of the Third and Fourth Armies was evidently too strong, and, if it could be increased, or even maintained without relaxation, there was every reason to believe that the enemy's arrangements for an orderly retirement behind the line of the Somme could be upset, and that he would be compelled to retreat before they were complete. Consequently, in accordance with the policy contained in Sir Douglas Haig's instructions, which appear at the beginning of this chapter,[2] orders were issued that all formations should spare no effort to harass the enemy's withdrawal, and should allow him no respite.

---

[1] North-east and east of Nesle respectively.
[2] See note to page 72.

No. 43.

SIR DOUGLAS HAIG CONGRATULATING CANADIAN TROOPS A FEW DAYS AFTER THE BATTLE OF AUGUST 8TH.

By kind permission of the Canadian Government.

To face page 85.

To Maricourt and Péronne

Billon Wood

To Bray-sur-Somme

Bronfay Farm

Carnoy

from Fricourt

The Loop

CARNOY AND BILLON WOOD.

Oblique air photograph.

South of the Somme, the night of August 24th was remarkable for a very heavy hostile concentration of gas shell fired on the front of the

The readjustment of the Australian Corps front south of the Somme

Australian Corps. It was particularly severe on gullies and woods, and on the extreme right in the vicinity of Lihons. This bombardment came at a most unfortunate time, as the XXXVI French Corps was in process of relieving the 4th Canadian Division south of Lihons, and the 4th Australian Division on a portion of their front between Lihons and Lihu. Moreover, on the same night the 32nd Division was extending its front southwards as far as Lihu, thus releasing the whole of the 4th Australian Division from the line. The unavoidable movement of troops, consequent on these reliefs, led to a large number of casualties both amongst the French troops and in the 4th Australian Division. The gas concentration was unusually dense and drifted over the area of the 32nd Division, which also suffered a number of casualties.

On relief, the 4th Canadian Division was concentrated in the Longueau area and quitted the Fourth Army on August 27th. The whole Canadian Corps had now left the army. By its determination and gallantry it had taken a large share in the successes of the Fourth Army on August 8th and during the following days. The Fourth Army's loss was, however, the First Army's gain, and the Canadians later took a prominent part in our successes further north.

In accordance with the general plan of operations, the advance of the Fourth Army was continued on August 25th north of the Somme

August 25th; the capture of Ceylon Wood and Fricourt

in conjunction with that of the Third Army, while the troops south of the river contented themselves with improving their positions and preparing for a further advance.

At 2.30 a.m. the III Corps, with the 3rd Australian Division on its right, advanced without any preliminary bombardment or creeping barrage; the artillery, when called upon to do so, supporting the infantry by engaging fleeting targets and centres of resistance. The 3rd Australian Division, advancing on a two-brigade front, met with little resistance as the infantry climbed the open slopes of the Bray-sur-Somme spur, on the eastern edge of which stands Ceylon Wood, until the old trench system on its crest was reached. Here small parties of the enemy endeavoured for a short time to check the advance, but by dawn the ridge had been gained, and a position established along the top of the cliffs overlooking the river northeast of Cappy, and along the western edge of Ceylon and Trigger woods. North of the Australians the 58th Division, advancing on a front of two brigades, and the 12th Division on a front of one brigade, although slightly delayed at the start by the heavy ground mist, met with little opposition on the plateau south-west of Carnoy and Mametz, but the 58th Division was checked opposite Billon Wood. Further north again the 18th Division, advancing on a two-brigade front, and in touch with the 38th Division of the Third Army, made good progress. The Fricourt mine craters were taken soon after daylight by the 18th Division, and, by 10 a.m., patrols had cleared Fricourt and Bottom Wood and were approaching Mametz Wood, the scene of so much hard fighting in July, 1916. There was now no doubt that the enemy was in full retreat along the whole of the front north of the Somme, and was retiring in bounds protected by rearguards. The enemy's artillery activity was limited to the fire of a few long-range high-velocity guns firing at extreme range, which harassed some of the forward roads, and to that of a small number of field guns which he employed to support his rearguards. These guns were well handled and, firing over open sights from the many small woods that are scattered over the area, caused our infantry considerable trouble. The advance, however, pressed on, and Billon Wood was captured by the 173rd Brigade. By nightfall our line had also been advanced east of Mametz and along the eastern edge of Mametz Wood, whence it was continued by the 38th Division. During the day over 500 prisoners were captured.

In conjunction with the advance north of the Somme, the left brigade of the 1st Australian Division moved forward at 4 p.m. under cover of an artillery barrage. Considerable opposition was encountered, but the line was advanced to a depth of approximately 500 yards, between Chuignes and the river.

At this stage of the operations the withdrawal of the enemy's guns and transport over the shell-crater zone of the old Somme battlefield was restricted to a few roads, all of which, as well as the crossings over the Somme, which were not numerous, were well known to us. South of the river the main road junctions which the enemy was obliged to use were those at Villers Carbonnel, Barleux, and Herbecourt, while those north of the river were at Cléry-sur-Somme, Maurepas, and Combles. The main river crossings were at Péronne, Brie, and St. Christ. These road junctions and crossings, therefore, were kept constantly under the fire of our long-range guns, both 6-inch and 60-pdrs. The guns were pushed well forward regardless of risk, in one instance to the extent of coming under machine-gun fire, and the roads were shelled with shrapnel and high explosive with instantaneous fuses.[1] The success achieved by this policy was afterwards apparent by the number of dead horses and abandoned vehicles on the roadside.

Our artillery policy

On the left of the Fourth Army, as the result of the continued pressure of the Third Army from Albert to Neuville-Vitasse (south-west of Arras), the enemy became very disorganised and began to withdraw on August 24th. The troops of the Third Army pursued the enemy with untiring energy, forcing back his rearguards step by step. By the evening of the 25th a considerable advance had been realised, and the villages of Contalmaison, Martinpuich, Le Sars, Favreuil, Sapignies, and Behagnies had been captured. Bapaume, the immediate objective of the Third Army, was strongly defended by the enemy.

The enemy's retirement in front of the Third Army

In spite of the fact that some of our troops were becoming exhausted, especially those of the III Corps, which had been almost continually

---

[1] These fuses were used so as to avoid damaging the roads themselves, which would be of great importance to us later

AUSTRALIANS CLEARING A DUG-OUT NEAR CAPPY ON AUGUST 26TH.

By kind permission of the Australian Government.

No. 46.

MONTAUBAN

British official photograph.

engaged under difficult conditions since August 6th, there was no

wish or intention to relax the pressure, as all ranks were imbued with the determination to pursue the beaten enemy.

Immediately south of the Somme the 1st Australian Division resumed the advance at 6 a.m. on August 26th with strong fighting patrols. Batteries of field artillery were pushed well forward to support the advance, and were chiefly employed in dealing with machine-guns. By clever use of the ground the 2nd Brigade secured the woods east of Chuignes, and reached the western outskirts of Fontaine-les-Cappy. On the left the village of Cappy was cleared by the 3rd Brigade, and by nightfall the line had been advanced 2,000 yards east of the village. Further south an attempt, made by troops of the same division, to advance astride the Amiens–Brie road was not successful, as Foucaucourt was strongly defended by machine-guns which had been well sited with an admirable all-round field of fire.

Meanwhile, north of the river, the III Corps and the 3rd Australian Division had not been idle. During the night and early morning the Australians advanced in conjunction with the 58th Division, and by 8.30 a.m. had captured Suzanne. The enemy made little attempt to check the advance against the village itself, but, when our patrols debouched from its eastern outskirts, they encountered heavy fire from the machine-guns posted on the high ground on the east of, and overlooking, the village. During the afternoon, however, the enemy was driven back from this position after some hard fighting, in which forty prisoners were captured and over a hundred Germans killed. The 3rd Australian Division then established its line forward of the crest of the ridge which runs from the west of Vaux Wood to Maricourt. Further north the three divisions of the III Corps moved forward at the same hour as the Australians. Each division employed one brigade as advanced guard, one in support, and one in reserve. The 58th Division was directed on Maricourt and Support Copse, the 12th Division on the Maltz Horn Farm knoll (north of Hardecourt-aux-Bois), and the 18th Division on Trones Wood. At first the enemy's resistance was fairly strong, but it was apparent that our troops were only being opposed by rearguards. On the right the 58th Division advanced to within some 500 yards of Maricourt; in the centre the 12th Division captured Carnoy; and on the left the 18th Division gained possession of Montauban together with sixty prisoners. The enemy defended this village successfully with machine-guns, until the advance of the 38th Division on the left enabled the machine-gunners of the 18th Division to bring their fire on to Montauban from Marlboro' Wood. This flanking fire was of the greatest assistance to the infantry, and the prisoners asserted that it made retreat impossible.

After the capture of Montauban, the 18th Division prepared to advance with the 55th Brigade as advanced guard. Patrols approached Bernafay Wood, but, when the enemy was found to be holding the wood in considerable strength, it was decided to establish an outpost line east of Montauban, and to attack Bernafay and Trones woods the next morning. Meanwhile, the 58th and 12th Divisions were unable to make any further progress, and in the evening formed an outpost line west of Maricourt and east of Carnoy.[1]

Since August 22nd the artillery activity of the enemy had fluctuated considerably, but, as a general rule, the volume of fire was never great

The action of the hostile artillery

and conveyed the impression that the Germans were employing comparatively few guns, the fire of which was continuous and distributed over a wide front. The successful attack of the Australian Corps south of the river on August 23rd necessitated the withdrawal of the enemy's batteries to the east of Cappy, and into the wooded district north-west and south of Estrées. After the attack, his high-velocity guns were particularly active and harassed our forward communications assiduously, whilst any attempt we made to advance provoked fairly heavy retaliation, but more during the later than during the initial stages of the attack.

From August 24th to 26th the fire of the enemy's guns increased considerably south of the Somme, in which part of the battlefield his field artillery was well distributed in depth.[2] During this retirement there were three noticeable features in the tactics employed by the Germans in the withdrawal of their artillery. First, a retrograde movement of the guns was usually prefaced by an intense bombardment, doubtless for the purpose of using up all the ammunition dumped near the artillery positions. Secondly, the withdrawal of the field guns was covered by the increased activity of the high-velocity and heavy guns, and " vice versâ." Lastly, the bold and skilful handling of sections and single guns, by which they essayed to cover the retirement of the infantry and to delay our pursuit. This last feature was well illustrated on August 25th and 26th when our infantry, advancing towards Maricourt and astride the Somme, met with considerable opposition from field guns firing from the copses and woods which abound in this area. On this occasion trench mortars in some cases kept up the bombardment after the field guns had been withdrawn.

The successful advance of the 1st Australian Division against Cappy on August 26th concluded, for the time being, the operations of this

August 27th ; the renewal of the pressure south of the Somme

division, and on the night of August 26th it was relieved by the 5th and 2nd Australian Divisions. On completion of the relief the front of the Australian Corps, south of the river, was held as follows : the 32nd Division from Lihu to south of Foucaucourt ; the 5th Australian Division from south of Foucaucourt to Fontaine-les-Cappy, exclusive of the village ; the 2nd Australian Division from Fontaine-les-Cappy inclusive to the Somme. Each division held the front line with one brigade, and kept one brigade in support and one in reserve. The Australian Corps, in order to maintain continuous pressure on the enemy and to avoid heavy losses, decided to carry forward the advance with strong fighting patrols. These tactics

[1] From prisoners captured during the day it was ascertained that the enemy had reinforced the front opposite the III Corps with three new divisions, the 2nd Guard, the 87th, and the 232nd, which had not been previously engaged in the battle.

[2] The sound-ranging sections located the German field artillery in positions from 2,000 to 8,000 yards behind the front line.

were begun at dawn on the morning of August 27th, and considerable progress was made, as in many parts of the front the enemy's forward positions were found to have been vacated.

On the right of the Australian Corps the First French Army had received indications from prisoners and other sources that the enemy *The co-operation of the* contemplated a general retirement opposite its front. *First French Army with* In consequence, in order to anticipate the enemy's *the Australian Corps* withdrawal, the First French Army pushed forward along its whole front simultaneously with the Australian Corps. South of Chaulnes the enemy's resistance was slight, and Roye was captured without difficulty. Chaulnes itself, however, which, up to the beginning of the Battle of Amiens, had been one of the enemy's most important railheads in this area, was strongly defended, and all attempts to capture it during August 27th failed. Some progress was made north of Chaulnes by the French in conjunction with the 32nd Division, and, although the enemy offered determined resistance, most of the woods north of Chaulnes were captured during the afternoon. The 32nd Division also gained possession of Vermandovillers.

The patrols of the 8th Brigade of the 5th Australian Division were checked at the outset of their advance by the fire of machine-guns holding the trenches round Foucaucourt. The artillery at once placed a heavy concentration on the trenches and on the ruins of the village, while the infantry of the 8th Brigade enveloped it under cover of the bombardment, and forced the enemy to surrender. Thirty-five prisoners and sixteen machine-guns were captured in Foucaucourt. Meanwhile, the 6th Brigade, which was the advanced guard brigade of the 2nd Australian Division, also encountered some resistance; machine-guns, hidden in a small wood, caused a temporary check. By evening, however, the Australian patrols had penetrated to within a few hundred yards of Dompierre and Frise, and had gained touch with the 3rd Australian Division on the river just north of Vache Wood. As the result of the day's fighting the Australian Corps south of the Somme held the general line Vermandovillers–Foucaucourt–Fontaine-les-Cappy–Vache Wood.

North of the river some troops of the 3rd Australian Division advanced during the night, and, by 3 a.m. on August 27th, had secured Vaux Wood *The events north of the* and the spur south of the village of Vaux, thereby *Somme* obtaining observation up the valley of the Somme almost as far as Péronne. Long-range machine-gun fire from the direction of Maricourt had been the chief difficulty with which the Australians had to contend, but heavy casualties were avoided by the skilful manner in which company and platoon commanders selected covered lines of advance.

At 8 a.m. the 11th Australian Brigade, co-operating with the 58th Division on its left, pushed forward along the bank of the river towards Fargny Mill.[1] The mill was captured during the morning, but the enemy,

---

[1] It was during these operations that Lce.-Corp. Bernard Gordon, 41st Battalion, captured, almost single-handed, 2 officers, 61 other ranks, and 6 machine-guns. See Appendix E, No. 20.

N

supported by fire from the high ground to the north, still held on to the greater portion of Fargny Wood.

Meanwhile, the advance of the III Corps met with varying success. Against an opposition which was never inconsiderable, the 58th and 12th Divisions pressed forward some 4,000 yards, and captured Maricourt and the important Maltz Horn Farm knoll after strenuous fighting.

On the left the 18th Division found itself faced for a second time with the problem of capturing Bernafay and Trones woods.[1] When Sir Alec Godley issued instructions for the attack on these woods, it was believed that the high ground round Longueval and Delville Wood was in the hands of the 38th Division, and that in consequence the left flank of the attack would be secure. Maj.-Gen. Lee, therefore, planned that the attacking troops should advance along the northern divisional boundary [2] on a front of about 1,000 yards, and that, after reaching the eastern edge of the northern portion of Trones Wood, they should turn southwards and clear the remainder of Bernafay and Trones woods from the north.

The capture of Trones Wood by the 18th Division

At 4.45 a.m. the artillery barrage opened, and the 8th Royal Berkshire and the 7th Royal West Kent of the 53rd Brigade, which had formed up without difficulty, advanced. Almost immediately the former battalion was taken in flank by machine-gun fire from the Longueval ridge, notwithstanding which, the attacking troops gallantly pressed on and, despite severe losses, secured the northern portion of Trones Wood.

Two companies, which had been detailed previously for the task, then wheeled to the south, and, advancing through Bernafay Wood and the southern portion of Trones Wood, cleared the whole of these woods and the intervening ground. Unfortunately the left flank south of Longueval was so weakened by casualties, that an immediate counter-attack by the enemy at about 6.30 a.m., from the direction of Delville Wood, forced our troops out of the northern portion of Trones Wood. This was followed, about an hour later, by a heavy counter-attack against the southern portion of Trones Wood by a fresh battalion, belonging to the 2nd Guard Division, which had been brought forward during the night of August 26th. This counter-attack succeeded in forcing our troops out of Trones Wood, but, thanks to the gallantry of the officers and men of the 53rd Brigade, it was checked west of the wood.

Owing to our losses and the intermingling of units, an immediate counter-attack to recover the lost ground was considered inadvisable, preparations were, however, at once put in hand for a deliberate counter-attack to be made with adequate artillery support. From 7.30 p.m. to 8 p.m. a bombardment with artillery of all calibres was placed on the southern portion of Trones Wood, and a well-planned attack was launched at 8 p.m. by a force of two composite companies of infantry, formed from all three battalions of the 53rd Brigade, under the commander of the 8th Royal Berkshire. The wood was strongly defended by a battalion of the Emperor Francis Joseph's Prussian Guards. A bloody hand-to-hand

---

[1] In July, 1916, the 18th Division had taken a prominent part in the capture of these localities.

[2] This boundary ran approximately due west and east through the Quarry just north of Trones Wood.

conflict ensued, which resulted in the gallant survivors of the 53rd Brigade emerging from the eastern edge of Trones Wood, tired but victorious. In clearing the wood of its battle débris over 50 of the enemy's dead and 40 machine-guns were found, and, in addition, 73 prisoners were captured.[1] By this time the 38th Division, on the left of the 18th Division, had advanced to the Longueval Windmill and the western edge of Delville Wood, thus securing the left flank of the 18th Division in Trones Wood.

During the night of August 27th the 53rd Brigade, somewhat exhausted after its successful exertions during the day, was relieved by the 54th Brigade. No advance was made by the 18th Division on August 28th, and the 38th Division on the left also had a brief rest.

Although the Australian Corps and the III Corps needed no urging or encouragement, orders were issued on the evening of August 27th for the advance to be continued on the 28th. The Aus-tralian Corps was given Péronne, and the III Corps Bouchavesnes and St. Pierre Vaast Wood, as objectives.

The events of August 28th

Early in the morning of the 28th the First French Army, on the right of the Australian Corps, entered Chaulnes and, pressing vigorously forward, forced the enemy to withdraw more rapidly than he intended, with the result that by midday he was in full retreat along the whole front from Noyon to Chaulnes. The French, taking advantage of the enemy's confusion, pushed forward cavalry patrols, which succeeded in reaching the Somme south of Epenancourt. Attempts to capture Noyon failed on the 28th, but, on the following day, the enemy's resistance ceased, and the town was entered. On the evening of the 28th the First French Army was established along the general line of the Canal du Nord from the north of Noyon as far as Rouy-le-Grand, thence along the western bank of the Somme to Epenancourt.[2]

In conjunction with the rapid advance of the First French Army on the 28th, the 32nd Division pushed patrols forward at dawn, and, meeting with little resistance, occupied Ablaincourt, Soyécourt, and Déniécourt. During the afternoon, however, opposition was encountered north of Marchelpot, and at Berny-en-Santerre. This opposition grew stronger towards dusk, and it became apparent that the 32nd Division would be unable to advance further that evening without incurring considerable casualties. Consequently an outpost line was established east of Gener-mont and west of Berny-en-Santerre, while the French formed a flank facing north from Epenancourt to Marchelpot.

Further north the 5th and 2nd Australian Divisions were more stubbornly opposed, but, by dint of vigorous exploitation, they had realised a big advance by the end of the day. On the right, the 5th Australian Division moved forward, with the 8th Brigade as advance guard, and gained touch with the enemy's rearguards early in the morning. The enemy withdrew behind a screen of machine-guns, supported by some

---

[1] Although not of such long duration as in July, 1916, the struggle for Trones Wood had been no less bitter. It was a commanding position, giving good observation over the country to the eastward, which the enemy could ill afford to lose ; its occupation by us, together with that of the important knoll to the south of it, was of great tactical importance.

[2] The Canal du Nord runs from Noyon to Nesle. It is not shown on Map 2, but the northern end of it, near Nesle, is shown on Map 4.

cyclists. The village of Fay soon fell into our hands, and the line moved steadily forward until the outskirts of Estrées were reached. The resistance stiffened momentarily in front of this place, but it was overcome by 1.45 p.m.[1] A general line was then established in some old trenches east of Estrées, where, owing to the broken nature of the country and the maze of trenches and wire, a temporary halt was made, while patrols moved forward to reconnoitre the ground towards Belloy-en-Santerre. The advance was resumed later in the afternoon, and the infantry, although the men were beginning to show signs of fatigue, pressed on and, by 9 p.m., had captured Asevillers. The advance was checked in front of Belloy-en-Santerre by machine-gun fire from the copses west and north-west of the village, and, as it was by this time almost pitch dark, an outpost line was formed south-west and west of Belloy-en-Santerre and east of Asevillers.

On the left of the 5th Australian Division the 2nd Australian Division advanced on Dompierre and Frise. Although the enemy offered some resistance at Dompierre and at Triangular Wood, he was quickly driven out of these places, and two field guns were captured in the village. On the extreme left, the advancing infantry met with strong opposition at the village of Frise, but, after half an hour's intense bombardment by the field artillery, the village was captured. The maze of trenches west of Mereaucourt Wood again, however, held up the advance, and the clearing of these trenches and the wood took some time ; eventually the wood was surrounded and captured with 50 prisoners and 15 machine-guns. Meanwhile, patrols on the right of the division had occupied Becquincourt, and had advanced over 1,000 yards beyond the village. Our line was finally established for the night west of Herbecourt and along the eastern edge of Mereaucourt Wood.

The 3rd Australian Division, which had pushed on to Curlu and the marshy reaches of the Somme to the south of that village, finally cleared the peninsula north of Frise and established an outpost line on the high ground east of Curlu. On the left of the 3rd Australian Division the 58th and 12th Divisions pushed forward strong fighting patrols to secure Hardecourt-aux-Bois. The enemy defended the ruins of this village stubbornly ; it was, however, eventually surrounded and captured after a severe struggle, and the high ground north and south of the village was also secured.

Considerable progress had been made on the front of the Fourth Army during the day, and the general impression was that the opposition, which in the south was weak, gradually stiffened towards the north. The enemy, it seemed, intended to hold a bridgehead about Péronne as long as possible, in order to enable him to withdraw the accumulation of guns and transport, which had been gradually pressed into the angle formed by the bend of the river, and to allow of more time for the destruction of all the crossings over the Somme at and near Péronne.

The advance was resumed along the whole front of the army during the night of the 28th, and early in the morning of the 29th. On the

---

[1] During this advance an 8-inch howitzer was captured in Touffu Wood, and a train consisting of 20 carriages and 30 trucks was secured intact in the valley north of the wood.

Anvil Wood   Mont St. Quentin   Moat and ramparts of Peronne

PERONNE and MONT ST

agar Factory   Peronne, with Somme in front   Peronne—Nurlu road   Bussu

QUENTIN from LA MAISONETTE

extreme right, the enemy's resistance was negligible, and the 32nd Division gained the western bank of the Somme without experiencing any difficulty, effecting a junction with the First French Army about 1,000 yards south of Cizancourt. On the left of the 32nd Division the 5th Australian Division captured Belloy-en-Santerre, Villers Carbonnel, and Barleux without opposition, but was checked for a short time by machine-guns defending the high ground overlooking Eterpigny on the west. It was evident that this was only a temporary stand, made to cover the retreat of the last remnants of the enemy across the river, for by 9.20 a.m. our patrols had gained the river bank, and had some good shooting at the last parties of the enemy as they crossed the river. Not to be restrained, a strong patrol of the 8th Australian Brigade set out in pursuit and crossed the canal at Eterpigny, returning with 20 prisoners. Operating immediately south of the Somme, the 2nd Australian Division continued the advance. On the right the 6th Brigade, although the men were suffering from physical fatigue and want of sleep, had captured Herbecourt and Flaucourt by 7.30 a.m. The 7th Brigade then passed through and advanced on La Chapelette and Biaches. On the left the 5th Brigade occupied Feuillères.

The marginal note: The events of August 29th; our troops reach the banks of the Somme south of Péronne

The Somme was a formidable obstacle, and, if the Germans succeeded in retiring across it and destroying the bridges after them, we should be confronted with great difficulties before bridgeheads could be established on the eastern bank. East of the general line Flaucourt–Feuillères, moreover, the ground fell away to the river both to the north and the east, and all movement east of this line could be observed from Mont St. Quentin and from the high ground east and south-east of Péronne, while the terrain was a maze of old trenches and wire. These factors added to the difficulties of forcing a passage at this point.[1] There was just a possibility that, by following close on the enemy's heels and taking advantage of his confusion, a crossing might be made over one or more of the existing bridges before the enemy had time to destroy them. Sir John Monash and Maj.-Gen. Rosenthal knew well the importance placed by the Army Commander on securing the bridges intact, and the 2nd Australian Division made a determined attempt to force a passage without delay before the bridges could be destroyed. The 7th Brigade on the right was given as its objective the high ground south-east of Péronne, and the 5th Brigade on the left the Mont St. Quentin heights. Two battalions of the latter brigade were to attempt to cross the river west of Halle, while the remaining two battalions were to cross by the causeway in the river bend at Ommiécourt-les-Cléry.

On the right the 7th Brigade gained the canal bank by 9.30 a.m., meeting with only slight resistance at La Maisonette from machine-guns

---

[1] Every detail of the ground round Péronne on both banks of the river was known to the commander and staff of the Fourth Army.

The Fourth Army had fought over the same ground during the early spring of 1917, and the same problem of how to force a crossing had confronted Sir Henry Rawlinson when the Germans began their retreat to the Hindenburg Line in March of that year. The first troops to reach the eastern bank on that occasion had been those of the 48th Division. They had secured Biaches and La Maisonette, and then, forcing a crossing where the embankment of the Canal du Nord crosses the Somme south-west of Halle, had seized Mont St. Quentin.

which were covering the enemy's withdrawal across the river. Small parties on the left of the brigade worked round behind these machine-guns, causing the enemy to abandon his guns and make a rapid retirement. Our patrols found all the crossings blown up except the railway bridge at La Chapelette. Repeated attempts were made to force a crossing at this point, but they were all unsuccessful on account of the enemy's machine-gun fire; at 2.30 p.m. the enemy succeeded in blowing up the bridge, and further attempts to cross at this point had to be abandoned. On the left the 5th Brigade met with no more success. Encountering little resistance in the advance to the canal, three companies of the 18th Battalion crossed the canal by means of the footbridge of the lock at the bend in the canal south-west of Ommiécourt-les-Cléry, and had established themselves on the northern bank by 9 a.m. South of this point all crossings on the brigade front were destroyed. The 18th Battalion attempted to push forward, but was unable to make any progress owing to heavy machine-gun fire from Ommiécourt-les-Cléry, Cléry-sur-Somme, and the high ground east of the latter village. Consequently, it was decided to make no further attempt to continue the advance, until Cléry-sur-Somme had been captured by troops operating on the northern bank of the river.

In the meantime, north of the Somme the 3rd Australian Division, advancing in conjunction with the 58th Division on the right of the III Corps, had cleared the broken ground in the vicinity of Hem, but was held up on the ridge west of Cléry-sur-Somme by the enemy's vigorous machine-gun fire. Further north the troops of the III Corps realised a considerable advance during the day. In the vicinity of Maurepas the opposition offered by the enemy's rearguards checked the advance of the 58th and 12th Divisions for some time. Maurepas itself was ultimately cleared after some stiff fighting, but the enemy, who held Le Forest in strength, prevented our making any further progress. On the extreme left the 18th Division moved steadily forward throughout the day in co-operation with the 38th Division of the Third Army. Guillemont was captured, and, after a short struggle, our line advanced to the eastern outskirts of Combles. Strong nests of machine-guns in the vicinity of Priez Farm for the time being rendered a further advance impossible.

During the evening and early part of the night the enemy's resistance west of Cléry-sur-Somme slackened, and by 10 p.m. the village was in our hands, except for a few houses on the eastern edge. The enemy counter-attacked several times during the night, and the eastern portion of the village changed hands several times.

During the 29th the Third Army had made good progress and had captured Bapaume.

On the morning of August 30th the attack north of the river by the 3rd Australian Division was continued. On the right the enemy's **The advance north of** resistance was strong enough to prevent our infantry **the Somme on August** from advancing beyond the limits of Cléry-sur-Somme **30th** until the evening. On the left, however, less resistance was encountered and satisfactory progress was made. The line was

No. 47.

48. V. 3712
62c. I. 26.27.32.33
3.5.18-14

St. Radegonde

PÉRONNE

River Somme

Fbg de Bris

La Maisonette

La Chapelle

Somme River

Railway Bridge intact

River and marshes of the Somme

Flamicourt

PÉRONNE AND ITS SUBURBS.

Vertical air photograph.

eventually advanced to Cléry Copse and to the western edge of Road Wood.

At dawn on the 30th the 58th and 47th Divisions[1] resumed the advance on the right of the III Corps. The 58th Division advanced to the western edge of Marrières Wood, meeting with more and more vigorous opposition as the advance progressed, and an unsuccessful attempt to seize the wood about midday showed that the enemy held it in considerable strength as part of his main line of defence. Similarly, on the left the 47th Division pressed forward, meeting increased resistance until the line Marrières Wood–Priez Farm was reached at 7.30 a.m. Patrols were pushed forward towards the Bouchavesnes–Rancourt road, but were met with machine-gun fire, and were forced to withdraw. Meanwhile, with its right held up at Priez Farm, the 18th Division made no attempt to advance during the day, but contented itself with consolidating its position east of Combles, touch on the left being maintained with the V Corps north of Bouleaux Wood. North of the Somme, the enemy's defence had hardened considerably.[2]

[1] The 47th Division relieved the 12th Division in front of Le Forest during the night of August 29th.

[2] The action of the Australian Corps south of the Somme on August 30th will be described in the next chapter, as it forms an important part of the story of the capture of Mont St. Quentin and Péronne.

CHAPTER VI

THE BATTLE OF MONT ST. QUENTIN, AUGUST 30TH—SEPTEMBER 2ND, AND THE EVENTS OF SEPTEMBER 3RD AND 4TH

Maps 4, 6, and 7

The situation on August 30th—The forcing of the river crossing; the Australian Corps plan—First phase; August 30th; the seizure of a bridgehead south-east of Cléry-sur-Somme—Second phase; August 31st; the attack on Mont St. Quentin by the 5th Australian Brigade—The advance of the 6th Australian Brigade—The action of the 3rd Australian Division and the III Corps—September 1st; the attack continued—The 14th Australian Brigade enters Péronne—The capture of the village of Mont St. Quentin by the 6th Australian Brigade—The advance of the 3rd Australian Division—The operations of the III Corps; the attacks of the 58th and 47th Divisions—The 18th Division attack—The situation on the evening of September 1st—September 2nd; the exploitation of success—The attack of the 5th Australian Division—The attack of the 2nd Australian Division—The operations of the III Corps—The events of September 3rd and 4th—The results of the Battle of Mont St. Quentin—The general situation on September 4th.

ALTHOUGH the Australian Corps had reached the banks of the Somme on the whole of its front from St. Christ to Cléry-sur-Somme by the evening of August 29th, all attempts up to the evening of the 30th to secure a bridgehead on the right bank east of Cléry-sur-Somme had been foiled by the enemy's machine-gun defence. Between Marrières Wood and Morval the III Corps had been opposed during the 30th by six divisions, which had maintained a resolute resistance. For the first time, moreover, since August 22nd distinct signs were noticed that the enemy's batteries were being grouped and organised for vigorous defence; the hostile shelling also had increased. It was clear, therefore, that the enemy intended to make a determined stand on the line of the Somme as far north as Péronne, and thence along the heights of Mont St. Quentin, Frégicourt, and Morval.[1]

The situation on August 30th

---

[1] The following order, captured later in the advance, shows that these premises were correct:

119 Inf. Div.   Div. H.Q.,
   Ia No. 4056. Secret.   29/8/18.
Instructions for the Conduct of the Defence in Winter Positions.

   Fighting will be conducted for the retention of the main line of resistance. All available effectives will be employed for this purpose, with the exception of an emergency garrison in the artillery protective line, which must not be employed forward of this line.

   In the main line of resistance, the defence must be organised in such a manner as to ensure, by means of infantry and machine-gun fire, the prevention of a crossing of the Somme valley by the enemy. Single machine-guns (including heavy machine-guns) must be pushed forward in front of the main line of resistance to the river bank, so as to have undisputed command of the river, especially at favourable crossing places (machine-guns on the banks). The machine-

Mont St. Quentin Wood

Mont St. Quentin Village

MONT ST. QUENTIN from

Ruins of Feuillaucourt   Anvil Wood   Halle

the BAPAUME-PERONNE road

All the crossings over the river had been destroyed, and the forcing of the passage of the river, with its marshes from 400 to 500 yards broad, presented a difficult problem.   A frontal attack had little chance of success, and would in any case be costly against the enemy's machine-gun defence.   Furthermore, it was doubtful if a sufficiently strong force could be passed across to resist the counter-attacks which the enemy would undoubtedly deliver against it.

Sir Henry Rawlinson, therefore, determined to turn the enemy's position on the line of the Somme, and to seize the high ground north of the Cologne river from Buire Wood to Nurlu.   Orders were accordingly issued on the evening of August 30th, for the III Corps to attack this position from the west, and for the Australian Corps simultaneously to force a crossing of the river at as many places as possible at, and north of, the Péronne railway bridge.   The Australians were then to attack the Buire Wood–Nurlu position from the south-west, working up the three ridges which ran down to the river from Buire Wood, Aizecourt-le-Haut, and Epine de Malassise.   South of Péronne the Australian Corps was to confine itself to seizing any opportunity that offered of gaining a footing on the east bank of the river.   As the advance towards the Buire Wood–Nurlu position progressed, the Australian Corps, pivoting on Péronne, was to form a flank facing south-eastwards along the high ground north of the Cologne river.

The commanding height of Mont St. Quentin, north of Péronne, was the key of the position.   It was a veritable bastion, the capture of which would enable us to enfilade the enemy's positions covering the river to the south and threaten the safety of his whole line.   If it could be seized by a coup de main, not only would the rest of the task given to the III and Australian Corps be much simplified, but much time would be saved.   Time was the ruling factor in the situation.   It was of the greatest importance that no respite should be given to the enemy's tired troops, and that they should be allowed no time in which to improve a position of great natural strength, and thus increase the difficulties of an already formidable task.

The position of Mont St. Quentin, however, was an extremely strong one, and its slopes, covered with thick belts of wire and intersected with the remains of the old trench systems, afforded great possibilities for a stout and prolonged defence.   From the ruins of the village on the western slope of the hill, the   country for a considerable distance lay exposed

guns in the river bank emplacements must be permanently manned, but should only open fire in the event of a hostile attack.   Shell-proof emplacements are not necessary ; the chief requisite is adequate concealment.

Patrols must be pushed forward into the Somme valley by night, in order to obtain early intimation of any attempt on the part of the enemy to cross the river.   Attempts by the enemy to effect a crossing are to be expected.   By skilful patrolling it should be possible to annihilate any hostile detachments which may attempt to reconnoitre the conditions of the river valley with a view to effecting a crossing, and to bring in prisoners from them.

The troops must on no account allow themselves to be lulled into a sense of security by the fact that the Somme forms an obstacle to the possibilities of an enemy advance.   A determined enemy will carry out an attack at this point simply for the reason that it is least expected.

The enemy must be prevented from gaining a foothold on the eastern bank of the Somme at all costs.   Demolition detachments must be sent out each night until the bridges have been thoroughly destroyed, and the remaining portions removed.   Portions which cannot be reached must be destroyed by medium minenwerfer fire.

O

to the enemy's observation and fire. Every movement on the stretch of river marsh from Péronne to near Cléry-sur-Somme could be observed, and the passage of the river presented the same difficulties as it did further south. The examination of prisoners revealed that the German High Command had issued instructions that the Mont St. Quentin area was to be defended at all costs, and, to ensure the position being held, had entrusted its defence to the 2nd Guard Division.

Sir John Monash fully realised the importance of seizing Mont St. Quentin at once. He had held a conference of his divisional commanders on the evening of the 29th, and, anticipating his orders, had made his plan. Moreover, some of the preliminary moves had been completed. He had decided that Mont St. Quentin must be taken from the direction of Cléry-sur-Somme, and that Péronne could then be captured by troops entering it from the north-west. To the 2nd Australian Division was allotted the task of attacking Mont St. Quentin, while the capture of Péronne was entrusted to the 5th Australian Division. Maj.-Gen. Rosenthal selected the 5th Brigade, under Brig.-Gen. E. F. Martin, for the attack on Mont St. Quentin, while Maj.-Gen. Hobbs detailed the 14th Brigade, under Brig.-Gen. J. C. Stewart, for the capture of Péronne. The operation was planned to be undertaken in two phases. The first phase, beginning on August 30th, involved the seizure of a bridgehead south-east of Cléry-sur-Somme by the 5th Brigade, which was to move along the north bank of the river through the area of the 3rd Australian Division. The second phase comprised the assault of Mont St. Quentin, and the capture of Péronne and the high ground east of that town.

On the night of August 29th the 2nd Australian Division held the front from Eterpigny to the bend in the canal south-west of Cléry-sur-Somme with the 7th and 5th Brigades, on the right and left respectively. Early on the morning of August 30th the 17th, 18th, and 20th Battalions of the 5th Brigade were withdrawn from the line, and by 7.15 a.m. were concentrated near Mereaucourt Wood. Although the withdrawal had been carried out in daylight these battalions suffered no casualties. The 19th Battalion was left in the line covering the brigade front.

At 10.30 a.m. the approach march to Cléry-sur-Somme began, and the column moved off with the 20th Battalion leading, followed by the 17th and 18th. Crossing the river at Feuillères, where the bridge had been repaired, the column proceeded eastwards along the north bank of the river. As it was difficult to ascertain the exact situation in the vicinity of Cléry-sur-Somme, the troops of the 5th Brigade took the precaution of making as much use as possible of the existing trenches. This precaution was well repaid, as the enemy was found to be holding the trench system north and east of the village. By 9 p.m. these trenches had been cleared of Germans, and the 17th Battalion, following behind the 20th, debouched from Cléry-sur-Somme; the 18th Battalion remained in the village in reserve. In the short time available, it had not been possible to arrange a creeping barrage, but artillery fire was maintained on areas and objectives selected by the infantry commanders

Bapaume — Peronne Road

MONT ST. QUENTI

from the south-west.

according to their requirements. The advance progressed satisfactorily, and by 10.30 p.m. a line had been established in the old trench systems from the river near the western end of Limberlost Wood to a point south of Berlin Wood—a suitable position from which the attack could be launched next morning. During this fighting 120 prisoners and 7 machine-guns were captured.

A bridgehead had now been established, and reconnaissances revealed that the bridge at Ommiécourt-les-Cléry could be made passable for troops. This work was immediately put in hand, and the 19th Battalion was ordered to cross the river by means of this bridge at 3 a.m. on August 31st.

In order to enable the 2nd and 5th Australian Divisions to carry out the second phase of the operations, it was necessary for the frontages of these two divisions to be substantially decreased. This was effected on the night of August 30th by an extension northwards of the front held by the 32nd Division as far as Lamire Farm, and the side-slipping of the 5th Australian Division as far as Sword Wood. The 6th and 7th Brigades of the 2nd Australian Division were concentrated in the old trench system south of Mereaucourt Wood and at Flaucourt, and were thus in a position to support the operations of the 5th Brigade. The 5th Australian Division held its front with the 15th Brigade, and retained the 8th and 14th Brigades in readiness for the capture of Péronne.

In the early hours of August 31st the 19th Battalion crossed at Ommiécourt-les-Cléry, and by 4 a.m. the 5th Brigade was ready in **Second phase; August 31st; the attack on Mont St. Quentin by the 5th Australian Brigade (see Map 6)** the position from which the attack was to be launched. The 19th Battalion was on the right, the 17th in the centre, and the 20th on the left; the 18th Battalion was held in reserve in the eastern portion of Cléry-sur-Somme. While our troops were assembling, the enemy opened machine-gun fire from Park Wood, but this was promptly dealt with by a company of the 17th Battalion.

Supported by five brigades of field artillery and one brigade of heavy artillery, the attack started at 5 a.m., the 19th Battalion being directed on the trenches between Anvil Wood and Mont St. Quentin village, the 17th on Mont St. Quentin village, and the 20th on Feuillaucourt. The 19th Battalion made good progress until it reached the rising ground south-west of Mont St. Quentin village. Here our men, who were on the line Save Trench–Galatz Alley–Agram Alley, encountered heavy machine-gun fire from the direction of Anvil Wood, the Aerodrome, and St. Denis. From the two former places hostile field guns were also firing at point blank range, and further progress was impossible until our artillery could deal with this opposition. The Germans made several counter-attacks, which were repulsed, but the 19th Battalion suffered considerable casualties from the fire to which it was exposed. Meanwhile, the 17th Battalion in the centre had overcome all resistance, and at 7 a.m. two of its companies were established on its objective east of Mont St. Quentin village. On the left, also, the 20th Battalion had reached its objective, and had captured Feuillaucourt. Only a few of the enemy were found in the ruins of either of these villages, but large numbers were observed retiring eastwards. The attack of the 5th Brigade had evidently come as a complete surprise. Unfortunately, on the left of the 5th Brigade, the attack of the 3rd Australian Division, which was designed to capture the high ground which lies south of Bouchavesnes and just west of the Mont St. Quentin–Bouchavesnes road, had been unable to progress beyond the first ridge, with the result that a gap existed between the 3rd Australian Division and the 20th Battalion which had occupied Feuillaucourt.

Shortly after 7 a.m. a determined counter-attack, preceded by heavy shelling and supported by a battery of field artillery, developed against the 17th Battalion, which was holding Mont St. Quentin village. The main attack was launched from a north-easterly direction, simultaneously with a subsidiary attack from east of the village. Our troops sustained heavy losses, and, as many of the officers had become casualties, our line was withdrawn to the trench system just west of the Péronne–Bouchavesnes road. The enemy launched five successive bombing attacks against our new positions, which were all successfully beaten off. At this time the situation between Mont St. Quentin and Feuillaucourt was very obscure, and at 9 a.m. the 18th Battalion from reserve in Cléry-sur-Somme was moved up in close support. One of its companies was sent up to reinforce the junction of the 17th and 20th Battalions, and two companies to reinforce the right flank of the 19th Battalion, which was held up in front of Anvil Wood. The opposition from Anvil Wood, however, was still very determined, and only a slight advance was realised by the reinforcing troops.

At 11.20 a.m., although the situation between Mont St. Quentin village and Feuillaucourt had been cleared up, the 20th Battalion, which was holding Feuillaucourt, was still out of touch with the troops of the 3rd Australian Division on the left. During the afternoon the enemy, taking advantage of this gap in our line, worked round the north end of the village, and gained a position which threatened the exposed flank of the 20th Battalion. As this battalion was subjected to enfilade fire from both field guns and machine-guns, it was withdrawn from Feuillaucourt, and subsequently held the line of Oder Trench, 500 yards west of the Péronne–Bouchavesnes road.

Meanwhile, as the advance of the 5th Brigade had made good progress, and the bridgehead had been extended eastwards, the 6th Brigade started

The advance of the 6th Australian Brigade

to move from its concentration area north-east of Herbecourt at 11.30 a.m. with the object of extending our gains towards Péronne. The brigade crossed the river by a temporary bridge at Buscourt, and, moving along the north bank through Cléry-sur-Somme, about 4 p.m. advanced in artillery formation towards Park Wood and Halle. The 23rd Battalion acted as advanced guard, and was followed by the 24th and 21st; the 22nd was left in reserve west of Cléry-sur-Somme. Although the advancing troops came under machine-gun fire from Prague Trench when passing through Halle and Park Wood, the fire was not sufficient to check their advance. By 5 p.m. Florina Trench was cleared, it was not found possible, however, to effect a junction with the

From Mt. St. Quentin

Aerodrome

Anvil Wood

Johannes Trench.

To St. Radegonde

Florina Trench

Wire

Wire

ANVIL WOOD AND FLORINA TRENCH.

Oblique air photograph.

GAPS IN THE WIRE THROUGH WHICH THE AUSTRALIANS HAD TO PASS WHEN ATTACKING ANVIL WOOD.

By kind permission of the Australian Government.

AUSTRALIAN INFANTRY MOVING UP A TRENCH PREVIOUS TO ATTACKING MONT ST. QUENTIN.

By kind permission of the Australian Government.

right of the 5th Brigade. One company of the 23rd Battalion succeeded in fighting its way as far as the church north of Ste. Radégonde Wood, but was not able to maintain its position there, and withdrew to Florina Trench. While the advance of the 6th Brigade was in progress, the 19th Battalion, on the right of the 5th Brigade, had improved its line north of Anvil Wood.

During the morning of the 31st the 14th Brigade of the 5th Australian Division also crossed to the north side of the river with a view to carrying out the task assigned to it of attacking Péronne from the north-west. It was obliged to cross at Buscourt, the Ommiécourt-les-Cléry crossing having by then become impassable owing to the intensity of the hostile artillery fire. As, however, the 5th Brigade had not been able to maintain its position east of Mont St. Quentin, it was impossible for the 14th Brigade to carry out the operation against Péronne. It was, therefore, concentrated in the shelter of the valley east of Cléry-sur-Somme, together with two field artillery brigades, reaching this position by 8.30 p.m. While this movement was being carried out, the enemy's artillery was shelling the area east of Cléry-sur-Somme and the banks of the Somme to the south unceasingly. This did not, however, stop the steady flow of companies moving in Indian file to their assembly positions. At one time the bank of the river between Cléry-sur-Somme and the canal by Lost Ravine swarmed with troops, gathered well under the side of the steep bank, playing cards, smoking, and waiting for the word to move on. In front of them the shells falling in the river threw up great spouts of water, while behind them, on the slopes of the hill, the hostile barrage fell with great regularity and precision, but luckily well clear of the thickly packed troops. It was an anxious time, although fortunately there were few casualties.

As the result of the day's fighting our line at 8.30 p.m. was held along Florina Trench by the 6th Brigade, and thence past the brickworks north of Anvil Wood, along Gott Mit Uns Trench, Deus Trench, Elsa Trench, Moineville Alley, and Oder Trench by the 5th Brigade. From there to a point on the Canal du Nord east of Freckles Wood, where rested the right of the 3rd Australian Division, there was a gap of about 1,000 yards along the Canal du Nord.

The attack on Mont St. Quentin by the 5th Brigade, with only hastily arranged artillery support and without a creeping barrage, ranks as one of the most notable examples of pluck and enterprise during the war. Confronted with the task of storming a very strong position defended by picked troops, this brigade, comprising only 1,800 fighting troops, overcame every difficulty and gained a footing on Mont St. Quentin, which it maintained in spite of the enemy's numerous counter-attacks.

It was a soldiers' battle, throughout which the physique, individuality, and bravery of the Australians were always conspicuous. There were only about 1,200 men in the three leading battalions when they attacked, and it is doubtful if at the end of the day there were more than 600 men covering a front of 4,000 yards. Owing to the intense hostile fire, and with men so widely scattered, control by company officers was well nigh impossible, but the fighting spirit of the men carried them through. This spirit is well expressed by the exhortation of an officer who was heard to shout down the line at a critical moment in the fight " Come on, boys, let's do it in the good old ' digger ' fashion."

On the left of the main operations against Mont St. Quentin, the front of attack was extended by the 3rd Australian Division and the

The action of the 3rd Australian Division and the III Corps

58th and 47th Divisions of the III Corps. At 5.42 a.m., forty-two minutes after the advance of the 5th Brigade had started, the 10th and 9th Australian Brigades on the right and left respectively, with the 11th Brigade in support, advanced against the high ground west of the Mont St. Quentin–Bouchavesnes road. The 10th Brigade, after reaching the crest of the nearest ridge, established itself on the line held by the enemy before their big retirement in 1917. It was unable, however, to maintain its position on the further crest, with the result that a gap existed [1] between its right and the left of the 20th Battalion of the 5th Brigade. The 9th Brigade captured Road Wood, crossed the Mont St. Quentin–Bouchavesnes road, and captured the important locality of Quarry Farm.[2] Later in the day the enemy launched a strong counter-attack against this position, which drove our troops out of the farm, but the enemy's attack was checked at the Old Quarry south of Bouchavesnes. During the day the 3rd Australian Division captured a large number of guns, the detachments of which fought most stubbornly and in many cases were bayoneted at their guns.

At 5.30 a.m., twelve minutes before the advance of the 3rd Australian Division began, the troops of the 58th and 47th Divisions of the III Corps moved to the attack. The 58th Division had some hard fighting before it was able to gain possession of Marrières Wood, which was stubbornly defended. By the evening the division had established a line on the high ground west of the Mont St. Quentin–Rancourt road overlooking the village of Bouchavesnes.

The 47th Division was even more successful. Its troops, comparatively fresh after a four days' rest, went straight through and by 8.30 a.m. had gained Long Wood, just west of the Mont St. Quentin–Rancourt road, with the left of the division thrown back to the eastern edge of Arderlu Wood south-west of Priez Farm. Patrols were then pushed forward towards Rancourt, where the enemy was located holding a trench line from north of Bouchavesnes to Priez Farm. A little before noon the enemy launched a strong counter-attack down the valley south-west of Rancourt; but this was driven off by rifle and machine-gun fire, except at one or two points where a short hand-to-hand encounter took place, which ended in our favour. The chief feature of the enemy's resistance throughout the day was the retaliation from his heavy guns, which shelled the whole of the front of the III Corps and the country for some distance in the rear.

On the extreme left flank of the Fourth Army the 18th Division did not attempt to advance, as it was known that the enemy was holding the

---

[1] See page 100.
[2] In this attack Private George Cartwright, 33rd Battalion, single-handed, put out of action the crew of a machine-gun that was holding up his battalion in Road Wood, and thus enabled the advance to be continued. See Appendix E, No. 9.

Priez Farm–Frégicourt position in strength; it was decided to post-pone the attack until the next day, when the Third Army would be able to co-operate by making a simultaneous attack on Morval.

The results of the day's fighting had been very satisfactory. Good progress had been made in the attempt to turn the enemy's defences on the line of the river, and it was felt that, if the initial advantage that had been gained could be utilised without delay, the operation would be crowned with complete success.

As is always the case in hand-to-hand fighting, the casualties had been heavy, and the 5th Australian Brigade had suffered severely in the struggle round Mont St. Quentin. Maj.-Gen. Rosenthal, therefore, decided that the 6th Brigade, which had been moved forward during the 31st in rear of the 5th Brigade, and one battalion of which was holding Florina Trench, should complete the capture of Mont St. Quentin. On the right it was arranged with the 5th Australian Division that the 14th Brigade should take over Florina Trench during the night, and should attack simultaneously in a south-easterly direction so as to clear the area west of Péronne and capture the town. On the left the 3rd Australian Division and the III Corps were to continue their operations, in co-operation with the 38th Division of the Third Army on their left.

In trench warfare, when there is severe fighting, it is as a rule impossible to locate definitely the exact positions of the leading troops until after dark. The battle of the 31st had been no exception, and the furthest positions reached by our troops were not definitely known. Conferences were held by the commanders of the 2nd and 5th Australian Divisions about 10 p.m. on the 31st, at which it was decided to continue the attack at 6 a.m. next morning. An earlier hour would have been preferred, so that the approach march could be made in the dark, but this was impossible, as sufficient warning could not be given to the troops. It was nearly midnight before the conferences broke up, and in the six hours remaining before " zero " the orders had to reach the troops, the troops had to be moved to their starting positions, and artillery programmes had to be made out and passed down to batteries. There was no time to spare. Luckily, as with Sir John Monash and Maj.-Gen. Rosenthal on the 29th, Brig.-Gen. Robertson, commanding the 6th Brigade, had anticipated his orders.[1] Brig.-Gen. Stewart's arrangements were also rapidly made, and during the morning the 14th Australian Brigade moved south from its assembly position east of Cléry-sur-Somme and took over Florina Trench from the 23rd Battalion of the 6th Brigade. The last part of the approach march was carried out under artillery fire, as the enemy's guns opened in reply to the fire of the artillery of the 2nd Australian Division which began at 5.30 a.m., half an hour before " zero." The 54th

September 1st ; the attack continued

---

[1] Originally ordered to be prepared to extend the front of attack by advancing his brigade on the south of the 5th Brigade, Brig.-Gen. Robertson realised during the afternoon that the situation would not permit of this plan being carried out. He thought it more likely that he would be required to go through the 5th Brigade in the morning and complete the capture of Mont St. Quentin village. At 4 p.m., therefore, he met his commanding officers, discussed the latter operation with them, and issued warning orders. At midnight when the divisional conference broke up, he only had to give his final instructions to his commanding officers, who were waiting outside the conference. Several hours were thus saved.

Battalion assembled with its right on the river without difficulty, but the 53rd Battalion on its left was unlucky enough to find a portion of Florina Trench in the enemy's possession.   Fierce hand-to-hand fighting ensued amidst thick belts of wire and broken ground before the battalion reached its "starting line."   The 6th Brigade, which assembled on a two-battalion front, the 23rd Battalion on the right and the 24th Battalion on the left, had a similar experience.   The 23rd Battalion moved across from Florina Trench, which it had been occupying since the afternoon of the 31st, and met with strong opposition in the southern end of Gottlieb Trench, which was to be its "starting line" for the attack.   The advanced patrols of the battalion were held up here by German posts, and the company commander of the right company sent off his runner, Pte. MacTier, to ascertain the cause of the delay.   MacTier worked along the trench until he found a German post ; this he bombed, threw the hostile machine-gun over the parapet, and killed the crew.   Further on he found a second post, which he dealt with similarly, but unfortunately, when jumping over the parapet to make further investigation, he was killed by a bullet from a third post.[1]   This gallant action considerably assisted the assembly of his battalion, which, however, only completed the clearing of the trenches a few minutes before "zero."

There had been no time to arrange for a creeping barrage to cover the advance of the infantry, and heavy concentrations of artillery fire were, therefore, placed on known and suspected points of enemy resistance, this fire being lifted on to fresh targets at fixed times as our advance progressed.   Four brigades of field artillery south of the Somme supported the advance of the 5th Australian Division, while the attack of the 2nd Australian Division was supported by five brigades of field artillery north of the river, and by three brigades on the south.   To each division was allotted one brigade of heavy artillery.

With its right on the Somme, the 14th Brigade moved forward at 6 a.m., coming immediately under heavy enfilade machine-gun fire from the direction of Mont St. Quentin.   By 6.45 a.m. the

The 14th Australian Brigade enters Péronne 54th Battalion, having cleared Ste. Radégonde village and wood without difficulty, had reached the causeway leading over the moat surrounding Péronne, which the enemy blew up as they retired into the town.   On the left the 53rd Battalion, with portions of the supporting battalions, which had become involved in the fighting near the "starting line," met with considerable opposition from the enemy holding Anvil Wood.   The "mopping up" of this wood took a long time, and was much hampered by machine-gun fire from the direction of St. Denis and the Sugar Factory.   Quickly grasping the situation, three privates of the 53rd Battalion, under heavy artillery and machine-gun fire, manned a captured field gun and silenced the machine-guns.[2]   Largely as the result of this gallant action, Anvil Wood was cleared of

---

[1] See Appendix E, No. 33.

[2] This gun had previously been captured by Pte. William Currey of the same battalion, who during the early stages of the advance, seeing that the gun was causing heavy casualties by firing over open sights at very close range, dashed forward and despite a withering machine-gun fire directed on him from either flank succeeded single-handed in capturing it, and killing the entire gun detachment.   See Appendix E, No. 14.

AUSTRALIANS CHARGING THE BRICK WALL ON MONT ST. QUENTIN ON SEPTEMBER IST.

By kind permission of the Australian Government.

the enemy, and the cemetery north-east of the wood captured by 7.30 a.m. All attempts to advance beyond the cemetery were checked by converging machine-gun fire from the ramparts of Péronne, and, as the left of the 53rd Battalion had lost touch with the 6th Brigade, it was decided not to push further forward until the situation had improved on that flank. One company of the 55th Battalion was moved up to form a defensive flank on the left of the 14th Brigade at the brickworks north of the cemetery. By 8.40 a.m. the 54th Battalion had succeeded in reaching the centre of Péronne, having crossed the moat north-west of Péronne by means of two narrow foot-bridges, in the face of heavy artillery fire and of sweeping machine-gun fire from the houses. Moving southwards through Péronne, the " mopping up " proceeded satisfactorily, and by 8.45 a.m. connection had been established with the 15th Australian Brigade at the causeway south of the town.[1] Péronne was now practically in our hands with the exception of the isolated north-east portion around the Faubourg de Bretagne.

The 6th Brigade moved forward simultaneously with the 14th Brigade. As the situation of the leading troops of the 5th Brigade was not clear at the time of the assembly of the 6th Brigade, the 23rd Battalion on the right formed up in Gottlieb and Save Trenches, and, in order to avoid the possibility of shelling any of our troops who might still be holding out in Elsa Trench, our artillery bombardment was placed just east of the Péronne–Bouchavesnes road. The result was that the leading troops of the 6th Brigade had to advance about 1,000 yards without close artillery support over ground in which there were small parties of the enemy still offering resistance. Although subjected to very heavy machine-gun fire from the direction of St. Denis and Péronne, and in spite of the fact that in two companies all the officers and all the sergeants except one became casualties, the leading troops of the 23rd Battalion with great determination pressed on and reached Elsa Trench, where some parties of the 5th Brigade were found. On the left the 24th Battalion, immediately it advanced, encountered the same heavy machine-gun fire. Notwithstanding this, skirting Feuillaucourt, the battalion reached a line east of the Péronne–Bouchavesnes road on which, owing to the intensity of the fire from Plevna Trench and the Canal du Nord, a halt had to be made.

The capture of the village of Mont St. Quentin by the 6th Australian Brigade

Orders were at once issued by Brig.-Gen. Robertson for a heavy bombardment of the enemy's position on the hill and in the village, after which a further advance was to be made. The 21st Battalion was also brought up from reserve to reinforce the 23rd Battalion. From 1 p.m. to 1.30 p.m. the village of Mont St. Quentin was bombarded by every gun and howitzer which could be made available, and at 1.30 p.m. the attack was renewed. Two companies of the 21st Battalion rushed the northern half of the village, and the 23rd Battalion the southern half, while at the same time the 24th Battalion advanced on the north of, and one company of the 21st Battalion on the south of, the village. A desperate struggle

---

[1] Corporal Hall and Corporal Buckley, 54th Battalion, greatly distinguished themselves during this advance and in the fighting in Péronne. See Appendix E, Nos. 21 and 8.

ensued.[1] The defenders were picked troops who fought hard, but the impetus of the first rush carried the advance to Mont St. Quentin Wood, which was captured, and our line established along its eastern edge. The 24th Battalion cleared Plevna and Koverla Trenches, and, on the extreme left, reached its objective in Tortille Trench, 500 yards south-west of Allaines. During the afternoon touch was gained with the 14th Brigade on the right, and, as the fighting had been exceptionally severe and the casualties heavy, no further advance was attempted. Machine-guns were pushed forward, and our line consolidated east of Mont St. Quentin village and wood, and along Koverla and Tortille trenches to the Tortille river.[2]

The pressure on the left of the 14th Brigade was somewhat relieved by the successful attack of the 6th Brigade, and fresh attempts were made to push forward east of the cemetery north of Péronne. Heavy machine-gun fire from the ramparts, however, again rendered all these efforts unsuccessful, until at 5 p.m. the 53rd Battalion advanced to the outskirts of St. Denis in spite of the enfilade fire to which it was exposed. At 6.30 p.m. the situation was unchanged; fighting was still in progress in the northern portion of Péronne; the Germans held the ramparts of the town and St. Denis in strength, and were also defending the sugar factory north-west of St. Denis. While these positions were still in the enemy's possession it was impossible to advance, and, as some parties of the 53rd Battalion had reached the neighbourhood of St. Denis, it was not possible for our artillery to open fire on these points of resistance. At 8.30 p.m., therefore, the advanced parties at St. Denis were withdrawn, and our line was established along the eastern outskirts of Péronne, and east of the cemetery to the Brickworks.

At 5 a.m., thus preceding the advance of the 2nd Australian Division by one hour, the 11th Brigade of the 3rd Australian Division continued the attack between the Canal du Nord and Bouchavesnes. The advance of the 3rd Australian Division On the right the 43rd Battalion met with strong resistance from the trenches north of Allaines, but by 6 p.m. it had secured the southern slopes of the spur north-west of that village, and was in touch with the 2nd Australian Division at the Canal du Nord 500 yards west of Allaines.[3] Good progress was made on the left by the 41st and 42nd Battalions, and, early in the afternoon, our line was established on the high ground south-east of Bouchavesnes. The position of the troops of the 58th Division was at this time a little obscure, and consequently one company of the 44th Battalion was moved to Quarry Farm to support the left flank of the 11th Brigade. Four hundred and five prisoners and 15 machine-guns were captured by the 3rd Australian Division during the day.

The operations on the front of the III Corps were very successful. On the right the 58th and 47th Divisions, attacking in conjunction with

---

[1] The conspicuous gallantry and initiative of Sergeant Lowerson, 21st Battalion, in this attack materially influenced the situation at a critical period. See Appendix E, No. 31.

[2] The machine-gunners of the 2nd Australian Machine Gun Battalion were of great assistance to the infantry in this attack, and Lieut. Towner's gallant behaviour did much towards ensuring success. See Appendix E, No. 43.

[3] Lce.-Corp. Weathers during this attack was instrumental in capturing 180 Germans and 3 machine-guns. See Appendix E, No, 47.

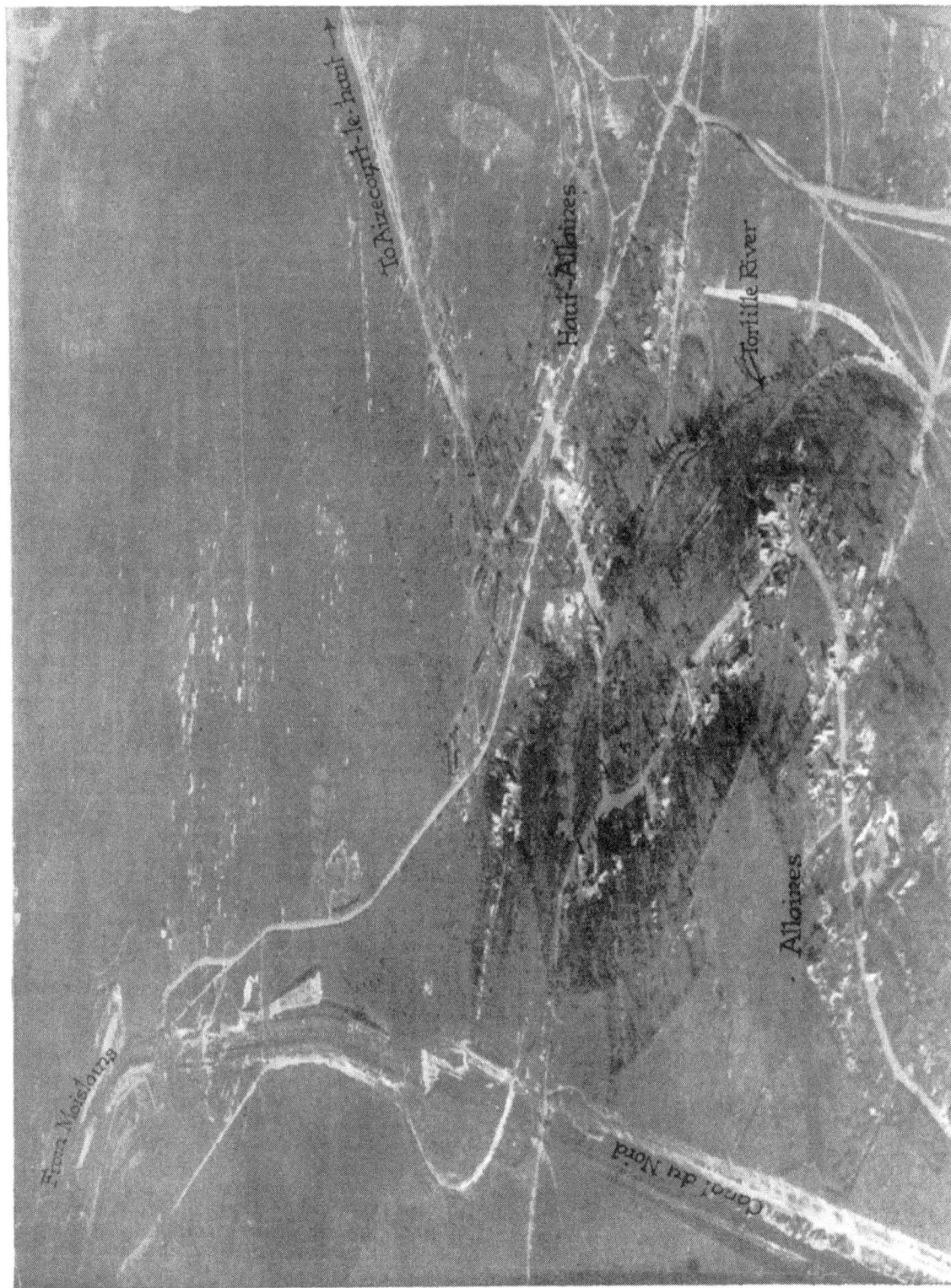

THE CANAL DU NORD, ALLAINES AND HAUT-ALLAINES.

Oblique air photograph.

the 3rd Australian Division, made good progress. The resistance offered to our advance was not so serious as that on the previous day, and the

The operations of the III Corps ; the attacks of the 58th and 47th Divisions hostile artillery retaliation was comparatively light.[1] Bouchavesnes was captured by the 58th Division, and Rancourt by the 47th Division, a considerable number of prisoners being taken in both places. By 11 a.m. the high ground east of Bouchavesnes had been gained, and the 47th Division had reached the south-western edge of St. Pierre Vaast Wood.

The task of the 18th Division on the left was to connect up the attack of the 47th Division on Rancourt with that of the 38th Division on

The 18th Division attack (see Map 7) Morval by the capture of the Sailly-Saillisel–Combles valley, across which the enemy held the line Priez Farm–Frégicourt–Haie Wood, all of which had been strengthened considerably during the past few days.

In order to avoid making a frontal attack against the enemy's position in the valley, Maj.-Gen. Lee decided to attack only the southern portion of the position opposite Priez Farm.[2] His plan was to push straight through to St. Pierre Vaast Wood on this part of the front with one battalion, and to mask the remainder of his front with the fire of artillery, trench mortars, and smoke. The leading battalion was to be followed by two others, which would in turn change direction, attack northwards and thus take the enemy's position in flank and rear. The attack, which was carried out by the 55th Brigade, was a complete success. The 8th East Surrey in the van, after capturing Priez Farm, where the fighting was very bitter, reached its final objective with comparatively little loss.[3]

Following behind the 8th East Surrey, the 7th The Buffs and the 7th The Queens moved through the area of the 47th Division, turned northwards, and successfully carried out their tasks, the latter battalion capturing 300 prisoners at Frégicourt, out of a total for the division of 700.

Not content with the brilliant success of these tactics, Maj.-Gen. Lee placed the 7th Royal West Kent at the disposal of the 55th Brigade, and at 7 p.m., after a brief struggle, this battalion captured Saillisel in conjunction with the troops of the 38th Division, whose objective was Sailly-Saillisel, the northern end of the same block of ruins which had been the scene of such hard fighting in the winter of 1916.

On the evening of September 1st the situation on the front of the Fourth Army was most favourable. The Australians had stormed the

The situation on the evening of September 1st enemy's positions on, and north of, Mont St. Quentin, and held the greater part of Péronne. The divisions of the III Corps had driven the enemy from his strong positions on the heights between Bouchavesnes and Morval, where he had undoubtedly intended to make a stand. Moreover, the enemy's losses

---

[1] This was probably because the enemy, when he was driven from his positions on the previous day, had been compelled to withdraw his guns well back owing to the lie of the ground.

[2] Priez Farm was actually in the 47th Division area, and the 8th East Surrey formed up south of the divisional boundary.

[3] Near Priez Farm a hostile strong post which held out was heavily bombarded by the 142nd Trench Mortar Battery of the 47th Division. Eventually the battery commander and one man went out and accepted the surrender of the whole garrison of 80.

had been very heavy, especially in the vicinity of Mont St. Quentin and Péronne, and in the neighbourhood of the Bouchavesnes ridge, Priez Farm, and Frégicourt.

Information obtained from prisoners showed that the front north of Péronne had been heavily reinforced at the expense of the front south of the town, where the enemy relied on the Somme to strengthen his position. His battalions were much below strength, and consequently a large number had been engaged. Thirty-four battalions of eight different divisions had been identified during September 1st; several machine-gun and pioneer battalions had reinforced the infantry battalions, proving conclusively that the enemy's situation in regard to reinforcements was precarious, and that his losses had been unusually severe.

During the night of September 1st the Australian Corps pushed the bulk of its field and heavy artillery across the river in order to support the advance of the infantry on September 2nd. On

September 2nd ; the exploitation of success the III Corps front, during the same night, the 58th Division was relieved by the 74th (Yeomanry) Division, under the command of Maj.-Gen. E. S. Girdwood, which had joined the Fourth Army on August 30th. Sir Alec. Godley decided to use this division to drive the enemy across the Canal du Nord, storm the Nurlu heights, and secure the high ground to the south of that village. The 47th and 18th Divisions, further north, were ordered at the same time to establish a defensive flank on the high ground north and north-east of Moislains, the 18th Division operating in conjunction with the 38th Division on the right of the Third Army.

In order to ensure the success of this plan it was necessary for the 2nd Australian Division to push forward with its left flank on the Canal du Nord, and secure the high ground around Aizecourt-le-Haut, so as to protect the right flank of the 74th Division as it advanced. Concurrently with these operations the 5th Australian Division was to seize the high ground from Doingt to Bussu, including the two prominent localities, Flacques Wood and Bacquets Wood.

The advance of the 5th Australian Division was entrusted to the 14th and 15th Brigades. The former employed the 56th Battalion, supported by two companies of the 55th, to work

The attack of the 5th Australian Division eastward north of Péronne, and the 54th Battalion to complete the " mopping up " of the north-eastern portion of the town. The latter brigade moved the 58th, 59th, and 60th Battalions across the Somme during the night by the causeway south of Péronne in support of the 14th Brigade. The 58th was ordered to assist the 54th in clearing Péronne, while the 59th and 60th were to support the attack of the 56th north of the town.

The attack, which was launched at 6 a.m., was preceded by half an hour's bombardment of the ramparts on the northern outskirts of Péronne, where a considerable amount of machine-gun resistance was anticipated. At " zero " the bombardment was lifted and directed on to various centres of resistance, which were kept under fire until attacked by the infantry. This preliminary bombardment provoked very heavy retaliation from the enemy's artillery, which continued throughout the operation.

To Nurlu

From Mt. St. Quentin

St. Denis

Bussu

Aerodrome

Anvil Wood

Forest Alley

To Haucourt

PERONNE

PÉRONNE, ST. DENIS, AND ANVIL WOOD.

Oblique air photograph.

Moving forward from their assembly positions at " zero," the troops of the 14th Brigade met with a withering fire from the ramparts north of Péronne and from St. Denis. Under this converging fire the advance sustained a temporary check, but the two companies of the 55th Battalion, from support, worked forward on the left and gained a footing in the Sugar Factory, and by 7.45 a.m. had penetrated to the Brickworks on the outskirts of St. Denis, thereby forcing the enemy to evacuate the village. By 10 a.m. the 59th Battalion of the 15th Brigade had pressed forward north of Péronne, and, supported by the 60th, held a line from the ramparts to the outskirts of St. Denis on the right of the 55th and 56th Battalions. About this time also the north-eastern ramparts of Péronne were cleared by the 54th Battalion, assisted by the 58th. In the afternoon patrols advanced across the St. Denis–Mont St. Quentin road, but, as numerous casualties were sustained in approaching St. Denis Wood, it was finally decided to take up a position west of the road. This was accordingly done, and at 6 p.m. a line was established by the 5th Australian Division along the south-eastern and eastern outskirts of Péronne, and about 100 yards west of the St. Denis–Mont St. Quentin road. In the course of the afternoon patrols, which endeavoured to force a passage across the river near La Chapellette, were unable to effect a crossing on account of the severity of the machine-gun fire from the eastern bank ; attempts to cross the marshes at Flamicourt were equally unsuccessful.

North-east of Mont St. Quentin the 2nd Australian Division attacked on the left of the 5th Australian Division, with the 7th Brigade operating on a three-battalion front. The attack was supported by seven brigades of field artillery which put down a series of standing barrages, each brigade being allotted an area on which to direct its fire. The heavy artillery co-operated by a bombardment of Allaines, Haut-Allaines, and other selected points in rear.

The attack of the 2nd Australian Division

At 5.30 a.m. the 7th Brigade passed through the 6th Brigade, which was holding the line, and advanced to the attack. Almost immediately, the 26th Battalion on the right encountered heavy machine-gun fire from the right flank, as the troops of the 5th Australian Division did not begin their advance until half an hour later. The troops on the extreme right of the brigade, therefore, after making slight progress, faced southwards and consolidated Koros and Kurilo Alleys, thus forming a defensive flank. On the left the 27th Battalion was also checked by machine-gun fire. As a result of this temporary check, the artillery barrage outpaced the infantry, and the fight developed into an infantry attack against numerous well-sited machine-gun nests held by determined men. Section leaders, however, showed splendid initiative and daring in dealing with these nests, and the advance was resumed.[1] After exceptionally heavy fighting Allaines and Haut-Allaines were finally captured, and about 600 of the enemy were seen retreating in confusion over the flat country north of Aizecourt-le-Haut.

[1] In one of these nests, situated in a mine crater near the Mont St. Quentin–Haut-Allaines road, 17 machine-guns and 2 trench mortars were captured.

At 7 a.m. a defensive flank, facing south-east, was established north of, and almost parallel to, the St. Denis–Aizecourt-le-Haut road up to within 1,000 yards of the latter village, while the 25th Battalion in the centre reached a line 700 yards beyond the Bussu–Haut-Allaines road. Immediately east of Haut-Allaines the infantry found itself under the fire of field guns firing over open sights, and established itself well clear of the village. On the left, north of Haut-Allaines, a gap existed in our line near the Canal du Nord, and, as the advance of the 74th Division north of the canal did not make the progress that had been anticipated, a defensive flank was thrown back through the northern outskirts of Haut-Allaines to Allaines. The position of the 7th Australian Brigade, forming as it did a sharp and narrow salient, was at first somewhat precarious, but additional machine-guns were pushed forward, and a good defensive position was established with the troops distributed in depth. At dusk the 43rd Battalion of the 11th Brigade of the 3rd Australian Division moved forward, established a post on the canal north of Haut-Allaines, and cleared the trenches near the canal north-west of Allaines, thus obtaining connection with the 7th Brigade on the right and with the 74th Division on the left, and closing the gap which had previously existed.

It had been a stiff day's fighting, for the enemy resisted stubbornly; in spite of this, the 7th Brigade had crossed the fire-swept slopes and had reached their objectives, capturing over 200 prisoners, 93 machine-guns, 8 minenwerfers, and inflicting heavy losses on the enemy.

North of the Canal du Nord the 74th and 47th Divisions, operating against Moislains, encountered a much more vigorous resistance than had been anticipated. Starting at 5.30 a.m. down the western slopes of the Tortille valley, the troops of the 74th Division at first made rapid progress. They advanced south of Moislains, crossed the Canal du Nord, and by 8 a.m. were advancing up the eastern slopes of the valley towards Nurlu. Shortly afterwards, however, a counter-attack, supported by the fire of machine-guns and artillery, drove our troops back over the canal and through Moislains, where there was heavy fighting. Eventually the troops of the 74th Division, much weakened by the enemy's counter-attack, were unable to maintain their hold along the western bank of the canal, and established a line of resistance along a trench line on the western bank of the Tortille. On the left of the 74th Division the 47th Division advanced about 1,000 yards, finally holding a trench running about 300 yards west of Moislains.[1] Meanwhile, the 18th Division, which was operating on the northern portion of the army front in conjunction with the 38th Division of the Third Army, was engaged in clearing up St. Pierre Vaast Wood. This work was successfully completed during the day; about 100 prisoners were captured, and Government Farm was occupied.

During the next two days our patrols made continuous efforts to gain ground east of Péronne and Mont St. Quentin, and to force the line of

The operations of the III Corps

[1] The attack of the 47th Division was much assisted by the courage and initiative of Private Jack Harvey, 1/22nd London, who, single-handed, compelled 37 Germans to surrender. See Appendix E, No. 23.

the Canal du Nord. Patrols of the 5th Australian Division gained a footing in Flamicourt on September 3rd, and, on the following day, cleared the village and gained possession of Chair Wood, which lies to the east of it. East of Mont St. Quentin the 2nd Australian Division gained a little ground, **The events of September 3rd and 4th** and advanced their left along the Canal du Nord slightly, but as the enemy's machine-gun fire was still very active, no serious effort was made to continue the advance.

All attempts made by the 74th and 47th Divisions on September 3rd to eject the enemy from Moislains and force a crossing over the Canal du Nord were unsuccessful, but, when the pressure was renewed on the morning of September 4th, although at first the resistance appeared to be as strong as ever, our troops succeeded in establishing posts on the farther side of the canal. By the evening Moislains had been completely cleared, and our line was firmly established east of the canal at the foot of the slopes leading up to the Nurlu heights. Meanwhile, on September 3rd the 18th Division pushed patrols through Vaux Woods, which met with very little resistance, as the Germans were in process of retiring in front of the V Corps on the left. By the evening of September 3rd the troops of the 18th Division were established along the western bank of the Canal du Nord. On the following day the progress of the V Corps, combined with the energetic action of our patrols, made Riverside Wood, east of the Canal du Nord, untenable for the enemy, and by the evening the 18th Division was firmly established on the eastern edge of the wood.

The battle of Mont St. Quentin may be said to have ended on September 2nd, when the Australian Corps had secured Péronne, St. Denis, Mont St. Quentin, and Haut-Allaines, and the III Corps **The results of the Battle of Mont St. Quentin** was in possession of the Bouchavesnes ridge and St. Pierre Vaast Wood. Mont St. Quentin and Péronne were the dominating features in the enemy's defences, and their capture by the 2nd and 5th Australian Divisions, very materially assisted by the action of the 3rd Australian Division, will always rank high amongst the many brilliant feats of arms performed by the Australians. They captured the position from the enemy's picked troops and maintained it against numerous counter-attacks.[1] The whole operation was a triumph for the Australian Corps. It was conspicuous for the excellent preparatory work of the commanders and staffs, as well as for the initiative, courage, and resolution of the regimental officers and men.[2] The spirit of the Australian soldier is well exemplified by an epitaph, which the visitor to the battlefield of Mont St. Quentin may still find inscribed on a small white cross roughly put together from timber collected from the ruins of the village :—

" Here lie six Boches.
They met a Digger."

The operations of the III Corps were also worthy of the highest

---

[1] In all, the enemy made fifteen counter-attacks to recover the position. He employed nine divisions in his attempt to stem the advance of the Australian and III Corps, and to prevent our troops crossing the Canal du Nord.

[2] In the three days' fighting round Mont St. Quentin the Australians captured 2,600 prisoners, including men from the 2nd Guard, 14th Bavarian, 21st, 38th, and 185th Divisions.

praise. The advance of the troops of this corps, from the capture of Albert on August 22nd until they crossed the Canal du Nord on September 4th, covered a distance, as the crow flies, of some fourteen miles, over the desolate shell-pitted area of the old Somme battlefields. The operations require to be studied in greater detail than is possible here before the magnitude of the task the troops were asked to perform, and the demands on the officers and men which such an advance in face of determined opposition entailed, can be fully realised. The spirit, however, of the young soldiers of the 12th, 18th, 47th, and 58th Divisions successfully overcame every difficulty, and well did they answer every call made on them, and uphold the best traditions of the British soldier by their cheerfulness and endurance.[1]

The situation as regards the German troops who opposed us was, from our point of view, very satisfactory, and, thanks to our Intelligence, we were kept well informed both as regards their future

The general situation on September 4th

intentions and their condition.

It had been ascertained from prisoners that the German withdrawal to the line of the Somme and the Canal du Nord had been timed to begin on August 24th. The enemy had started his retreat on that day in the Albert area, while he had evacuated Roye on August 26th. This retirement, especially south of the Somme, when once begun, had been very rapid. It had been, however, covered by rearguards, and it was evident from the number of counter-attacks delivered, especially north of the Somme, that the enemy had no intention, if he could prevent it, of allowing our troops to push forward faster than he wished.

Between August 21st and September 4th, however, in order to prevent a disaster, the enemy had been compelled to throw into the line fourteen more divisions ; of these the 2nd Guard, 14th Reserve, 25th, 83rd, 87th, 232nd, and 233rd Divisions were engaged for the first time, the remainder had been engaged in the battle before. This gave a total of thirty-three divisions which had opposed the Fourth Army between August 8th and September 4th, eight of which were engaged twice[2] ; against these the Fourth Army had employed sixteen divisions. The disorganisation of the German forces was extreme. Owing to our sweeping successes, the enemy had been forced to throw his reserve divisions into the line on widely separated parts of the front, regiment by regiment, as they arrived on the field of battle. For instance, in Bernafay Wood on August 27th, prisoners belonging to twenty-one different battalions of six different divisions had been taken, and again on September 1st between Péronne and Rancourt, prisoners belonging to thirty-four battalions of eight different divisions were captured. No troops could suffer such defeats as had the Germans without serious loss of moral, and ample evidence was forthcoming that this was affecting the German Army as a whole. Certain formations, indeed, had fought well, noticeably the 2nd Guard Division and the Alpine Corps, while the Machine Gun Corps still retained its high reputation. It was ominous

[1] The prisoners captured by the III Corps, between August 31st and September 2nd alone, amounted to over 2,300.

[2] 36,209 prisoners, of whom 838 were officers, had been captured since August 8th. Of these, 3,397 prisoners belonged to the 225th Division, 2,760 to the 117th Division, 2,557 to the 41st Division, and 2,483 to the 14th Bavarian Division.

OLD GATEWAY in PERONNE

"La Porte de Bretagne"

for the enemy, however, that on more than one occasion machine-gun crews had surrendered without firing. The situation, too, from the enemy's point of view, with regard to reinforcements was very serious. In July, as the result of their losses, the Germans had been compelled to disband two divisions, while in August nine more had been broken up. This, therefore, reduced the enemy's strength on the western front from 207 divisions, including four dismounted cavalry divisions, in June—the maximum strength to which he ever attained—to 198 divisions at the beginning of September; moreover, a number of battalions had been reduced from four to three companies.

The result of the battle of Mont St. Quentin left the enemy in a very difficult position in front of the Fourth Army now that the line of the Somme had been turned. It was obvious that the number of troops which had sufficed to hold the crossings over the river south of Péronne, would not suffice to hold a position of equal length further east without an obstacle such as the Somme in front of them, and that this part of the front, which had been denuded of troops to provide reserves for the counter-attacks further north, would have to be reinforced. Nor was this all, for the Third Army had made rapid and consistent progress during the last few days and had carried its advance well beyond Bapaume.[1]

The storming of the famous Drocourt–Quéant line by the First Army on September 2nd, and the advance of the French to Ham, had added still further to the enemy's difficulties. It appeared that, pivoting for the moment on the well-wired defences on the high ground about Nurlu, the enemy was continuing his retreat in front of the First and Third Armies, and that this retirement was to be followed later by a withdrawal in front of the Fourth Army and the French.

The enemy could not be allowed to carry out this manœuvre without interference, and, either the Nurlu heights would have to be captured, or the thin screen holding the Somme south of Péronne would have to be driven in.

In view of the strength of the enemy's defences on the Nurlu heights, and the losses that a premature frontal attack on such a strong position would entail, Sir Henry Rawlinson, decided, on September 3rd, while continuing to make every preparation for an attack on the Nurlu position, to attempt to force a passage over the Somme by a surprise attack at St. Christ, and so open up the crossing at Brie. This operation if successful, combined with an attack in a south-easterly direction from Péronne, would clear the line of the Somme and thus render feasible an eastward advance along the whole front of the Australian Corps south of the town. The Australian Corps at once began preparations to carry out these orders, but, before they were completed, the situation had developed, and the enemy had begun his retirement to the outer defences of the Hindenburg Line along the whole front of the Fourth Army. On the evening of September 4th the indications of this retirement became definite, and orders were issued for the III and Australian Corps to follow him up energetically with strong advanced guards.

---

[1] On the evening of September 4th the troops of the V Corps crossed the Canal du Nord between Manancourt and a point east of Hermies.

CHAPTER VII

THE ADVANCE TO THE HINDENBURG LINE—SEPTEMBER 5TH–28TH

Maps 1, 2, 4, 8, and 9; and Panoramic Photographs 4 and 5

The readjustment of the front—September 5th; the enemy in full retreat—September 6th and
7th; the pursuit—The co-operation of the Royal Air Force—The events of September 8th
—The situation on September 9th—September 10th; the fighting on the flanks at Holnon
Wood and Epéhy—September 11th; the arrival of the IX Corps; the readjustment of the
front—The general situation on September 11th—Sir Henry Rawlinson's proposals—The
proposals approved—September 12th to 17th; minor operations—The preliminary arrangements for the attack on September 18th—The objectives—The frontages of attack—The
artillery arrangements—The allotment of tanks—A summary of the Fourth Army attack
on September 18th—The assembly of the IX Corps—The first phase of the IX Corps attack
—The second phase—The result of the day's fighting by the IX Corps—The assembly of
the Australian Corps—The first phase of the Australian Corps attack—The second phase—
The third phase—The result of the day's fighting by the Australian Corps—The assembly
of the III Corps—The first phase of the III Corps attack—The 74th Division attack—The
18th Division attack—The attacks of the 12th and 58th Divisions—The second phase of the
III Corps attack—The result of the day's fighting by the III Corps—The situation on September 19th—The events on the IX Corps front on September 19th and 20th—The events
on the III Corps front on September 19th and 20th—The decision to attack the Hindenburg
Line; the Fourth Army reinforced—The readjustment of the front—The III Corps attacks
on September 21st–22nd—The IX Corps operations on September 24th—The pressure
maintained by the IX Corps on September 25th and 26th—The bombardment of the
Hindenburg Line begun on September 26th—Minor operations by the 27th and 30th
American Divisions on September 26th and 27th—The attacks of the Allied Armies on
other parts of the front—The situation on the Fourth Army front on September 28th.

WHEN orders were issued, late on September 4th, for the
Australian and III Corps to follow up the enemy, the Australian Corps
held the southern portion of the front of the Fourth

The readjustment of the front Army from south of Cizancourt, where it was in touch
with the First French Army, to the Canal du Nord
about 1,000 yards north of Haut-Allaines. The 32nd Division and the
5th and 2nd Australian Divisions held the line on this front from right
to left; the 1st, 3rd, and 4th Australian Divisions were in reserve.
The northern portion of the army front, to its junction with the
Third Army on the southern outskirts of Manancourt, was held by the
III Corps, with the 74th, 47th, and 18th Divisions in line from right to left,
and with the 12th and 58th Divisions in reserve. In the army area, but in
general reserve, were the IX Corps Headquarters and the 6th Division.

As the 2nd Australian Division was feeling the effects of the strenuous
work it had just accomplished, it was relieved on the night of September
4th. This was effected by the 74th Division and the 5th Australian

Division extending their fronts to the south and north respectively, and joining hands on the new inter-corps boundary, which ran east and west from north of Mont St. Quentin through Bussu and Roisel.[1]

The withdrawal of this division left the 32nd Division and the 5th Australian Division, each with two brigades in the line, holding the whole front of the Australian Corps. As, however, it was essential that the pursuit of the enemy should be maintained with unabated vigour in order to prevent him from destroying the roads and railways west of the Hindenburg Line during his retirement, the 3rd Australian Division, on the evening of September 5th, took over a portion of the line held by the 5th Australian Division, while the 5th Australian Division took over part of the 32nd Division front. On completion of this readjustment on September 6th the troops of the Australian Corps were organised for the pursuit; the 32nd Division on the right, as far north as the Brie–Vermand road; the 5th Australian Division in the centre, operating between the Brie–Vermand road and a line running east and west through Cartigny; the 3rd Australian Division on the left.

The whole front covered by the Australian Corps amounted to some 15,000 yards. This was too extensive for the troops at the disposal of the Australian Corps Commander, in view of the hard fighting which they had been through since August 8th, and of the losses they had incurred. It was, moreover, probable that, now the Somme had been passed, the weight of the enemy's opposition would be equally distributed along the whole front of the Fourth Army. This was represented to General Headquarters, and the Fourth Army was shortly afterwards reinforced by the IX Corps with four divisions, in order that the front of the Australian Corps might be reduced, and strong pressure be maintained against the retreating enemy.

The changes necessary on the III Corps front before the advance was resumed were not so extensive. During the night of September 4th the 18th Division was relieved by the 12th Division, which had been resting since August 30th, and moved into reserve for the first time since the commencement of the Battle of Amiens on August 8th. For the greater part of a month the 18th Division had been fighting incessantly and successfully, and had covered in its advance from the Ancre to the Canal du Nord a distance of approximately seventeen miles. The 47th Division remained with the Fourth Army until the evening of September 7th; it was then withdrawn to join the Fifth Army. This division also had taken a conspicuous part in the advance of the III Corps since August 22nd.

Early on September 5th the enemy began to retire along the front of the Australian Corps, covered by strong rearguards. On the right

September 5th; the enemy in full retreat rearguards of the 5th Bavarian and 119th Divisions defended the crossings of the Somme at St. Christ and Brie. Early in the morning, however, a platoon of the 15th Highland Light Infantry of the 32nd Division crossed the swamps of the Somme at Eterpigny undiscovered, and surprised one of the

[1] The 2nd Australian Division, on relief, was withdrawn to the vicinity of Cappy, where it remained for some weeks.

enemy's posts. This platoon was quickly reinforced by the remainder of the 14th Brigade, which cleared Brie and St. Christ after a stiff fight. The engineers and pioneers of the 32nd Division then carried out the construction of bridges at Brie and St. Christ with such skill and rapidity that, by noon on September 6th, not only the whole of the 32nd Division, but also a considerable number of French troops had crossed the river by these bridges. Meanwhile, advancing at dawn on the 5th, patrols of the 5th Australian Division worked forward under cover of a smoke screen and captured Doingt and Bussu after slight opposition. Further opposition was encountered, mainly from machine-guns and isolated field guns, which, although causing a temporary delay, did not impede the general advance to any great extent. During the day 150 prisoners were captured.

The III Corps also pressed forward at dawn on the 5th. The 74th Division on the right, and the 47th Division in the centre, advanced rapidly, seized Aizecourt-le-Haut, and cleared the ground east of the main Péronne–Nurlu road to the outskirts of Driencourt. On the left the troops of the 12th Division were subjected to a heavy gas concentration while forming up for the attack in the early morning. Nevertheless, they pressed on at daybreak, and, in spite of a number of casualties from machine-gun fire, succeeded by skilful manœuvring in making a considerable advance during the day. They penetrated the first system of trenches and wire of the Templeux-la-Fosse–Nurlu defences, and by evening had established themselves in the trenches on the western edge of Nurlu.[1] An attack, which was launched in the dark against Nurlu village, was unsuccessful, and provoked considerable retaliation from the enemy's artillery. A footing, however, had now been established on the Nurlu heights, which deprived the enemy of satisfactory observation for his artillery fire, and when the advance was resumed next morning Nurlu was occupied after slight resistance by the 12th Division.

The pursuit was resumed on September 6th, and very little resistance was encountered along the whole army front until the evening of September 7th. The 13th Australian Light Horse

September 6th and 7th ; the pursuit (see Ma Regiment and the Australian Corps Cyclist Battalion formed the advanced screen of the Australian Corps, while the Northumberland Hussars performed a similar duty for the III Corps.

The advance was closely supported by field artillery brigades, of which sections accompanied the advance guard battalions. The German rearguards were thus continually harassed, and the isolated machine-gun nests, left behind by the enemy in order to impede our progress, were in most cases destroyed, or forced to withdraw without fulfilling their mission. On the Australian and III Corps fronts the patrols of the 13th Australian Light Horse Regiment and the Northumberland Hussars maintained contact with the enemy's rearguards throughout his retirement.

Athies and Cartigny were entered early on September 6th, and by

---

[1] This area was defended by the newly arrived 6th (dismounted) Cavalry Division, prisoners being captured from regiments of each of its three brigades.

A SMOKE SCREEN THROWN ACROSS THE HILLS EAST OF PÉRONNE, TO COVER THE ADVANCE OF
AUSTRALIAN PATROLS ON SEPTEMBER 5TH.

By kind permission of the Australian Government.

To face page 116.

THE CAUSEWAY OVER THE SOMME AT BRIE, TAKEN FROM THE EAST BANK.

the evening of September 7th the advanced troops of the Australian Corps had established themselves along the high ground east of Beauvois, and thence through Villévécque, Soyécourt, and Bernes, and along the western slopes of the ridge east of Roisel. During the same period the III Corps effected an advance of some 4,500 yards, and captured Aizecourt-le-Bas, Longavesnes, and Liéramont during September 6th. Following this up on the 7th with the capture of Villers Faucon, Saulcourt, and Guyencourt, its advanced troops established an outpost line on the spurs 1,000 yards east of the Roisel–Épéhy railway as far north as Ste. Emilie, and within 1,500 yards of Epéhy and Peizières.

Meanwhile, on September 6th the First French Army entered Ham, and by the evening of September 7th had advanced to the St. Quentin Canal at St. Simon and Tugny, and was holding a line running northwards to Fluquières and Vaux (see Map 2). A number of prisoners and a few guns were captured in the advance, but in many parts of the battlefield the enemy withdrew so rapidly that touch was lost for several hours.

During our advance most valuable work was again accomplished by the 5th Brigade, Royal Air Force. The weather was ideal at this

The co-operation of the Royal Air Force

period, and our airmen made full use of their opportunity, flying over the battle area from dawn to dusk. On September 5th very few hostile aeroplanes were encountered, but on the following day a large number were engaged, eight of which were destroyed and five driven down out of control by our airmen. Early on the morning of the 6th several of the enemy's observation balloons were in the air around Epéhy observing for their heavy guns, and watching the movements of our troops. Within two hours of taking the air, these had all been destroyed or forced to descend by our airmen. The enemy's retreating troops also offered good targets for the machine-guns and bombs from our aeroplanes.[1]

The pursuit was renewed early on September 8th, but it soon became apparent that the enemy's resistance was stiffening. His artillery had

The events of September 8th

been withdrawn, and was apparently in position covering the general line Attilly–Maissemy–Jeancourt–Templeux-le-Guérard–Epéhy. South of the river Omignon the hostile shelling was chiefly from field guns and was dispersed over the forward area, but north of that river the enemy's heavy guns

---

[1] Magnificent work was performed by a flight of S.E. 5's of No. 84 Squadron under Captain Beauchamp-Proctor. On the morning of September 5th, this flight of six machines set out on an independent mission, with the object of doing as much damage as possible to the retreating enemy. Flying low round Roisel, small parties of the enemy were seen and engaged with machine-gun fire. The flight then proceeded from Roisel to Hancourt, and thence to Mons-en-Chaussée. No Germans were seen, but, while passing over Athies, our aeroplanes were fired on by a field gun in the open. Captain Beauchamp-Proctor dived at the gun, killing some of the crew with his machine-gun fire, while the remainder fled. Another of the airmen dropped a bomb on the limber, which scattered the drivers and killed some of the horses. One of the enemy attempted to escape on a horse, but was pursued and rolled over after a short burst of fire from Captain Beauchamp-Proctor's machine-guns. The flight, still flying very low, then pursued its course to St. Christ. Our infantry was seen advancing towards a hostile machine-gun concealed in a sunken road, at which Captain Beauchamp-Proctor, followed by his flight, at once dived and killed or dispersed the crew. Our troops were then observed to be pointing towards some trenches about 400 yards from them. Flying in the direction indicated Captain Beauchamp-Proctor and his airmen observed about thirty of the enemy attempting to leave the trench where they had been hiding. With the exception of five of the enemy, who were killed by the infantry, the flight accounted for the whole of this party. See also Appendix E, No. 5.

were also very active. In addition to the increased resistance of the enemy, there was a break in the weather, which, apart from a few showers, had been consistently fine since August 22nd. This change hindered the advance of the troops.

On the front of the Australian Corps very little progress was made. Patrols of the Australian Corps Cyclist Battalion entered Vermand during the morning without opposition, and found the enemy holding positions along the left bank of the Omignon at Marteville, Villecholles, and Maissemy, and on the high ground about Vendelles and west of Jeancourt. On the left of the Australian Corps front, the 3rd Australian Division advanced about 1,500 yards and secured Montigny Farm and Hervilly.

On the front of the III Corps patrols of the 74th Division almost immediately encountered strong opposition in the Villers Faucon area from troops belonging to the 56th Straf Kompagnie, one of the disciplinary companies which had been formed by the Germans from men condemned to various periods of imprisonment. In accordance with orders which it had received not to incur heavy casualties, the 74th Division did not attempt to press on, and halted on the line it had gained. On the left the 58th Division advanced against Epéhy and Peizières, and made some progress.[1] During the day patrols of this division entered the villages of Epéhy and Peizières[2]; they were, however, driven out again by determined hostile counter-attacks, which were delivered almost immediately by the Alpine Corps. The advanced troops of the 58th Division at the close of the day's fighting were established in an existing trench system on the southern and western slopes of the hill, while the enemy occupied a position on the western outskirts of Epéhy and Peizières, and showed indications of making a determined stand on what had been the British main line of resistance in the previous March.[3]

On September 9th the operations of the Australian Corps were limited to active reconnaissance. Patrols of the 3rd Australian Division

The situation on
September 9th

pressed forward east of Montigny Farm and through Hesbecourt; they succeeded in advancing 1,000 yards and in retaining the ground gained.

A counter-attack south-west of Epéhy, which was carried out by the Alpine Corps on the morning of September 9th, and resulted in the loss to us of a few lengths of trenches, was a further evidence of the increasing resistance on the front of the III Corps.[4]

On the morning of September 10th the 32nd Division, on the right

---

[1] Before advancing, the 58th Division extended its front southwards in order to take over the portion of the line which was held by the 12th Division. The latter division was then withdrawn into reserve. Later in the day the 74th Division shortened the line held by the 58th Division by extending its front 1,500 yards to the north.

[2] The high ground on which these villages are situated was very important to the enemy for the defence of the line he had taken up further south. (See Panoramic Photograph No. 5.)

[3] All the prisoners captured at this time reported that the enemy proposed to hold this line.

[4] During the week following the capture of Mont St. Quentin, the enemy had reinforced his front with six divisions, of which the 6th (dismounted) Cavalry Division and the Alpine Corps were probably the most formidable. He had also managed to withdraw the remnants of nine divisions, the intermingling of whose units had caused such indescribable confusion during, and just after, the Battle of Mont St. Quentin. These reliefs undoubtedly increased the enemy's power of resistance for the time being.

of the Australian Corps, advanced over the high ground east of Beauvois, and, meeting with little resistance except at Marteville, established posts in the south-west corner of Holnon Wood and in the outskirts of Marteville. The 5th and 3rd Australian Divisions, which were being relieved by the 4th and 1st Australian Divisions,[1] did not attempt to move forward.

September 10th; the fighting on the flanks at Holnon Wood and Epéhy

The III Corps on the 10th again attempted to force the enemy's position at Epéhy, in order to test the accuracy of the reports received, and to ascertain definitely whether the enemy's resistance was a rearguard action or an organised defence in depth. On the right, south of Epéhy and facing Ronssoy Wood, the 74th Division attacked at 5.15 a.m. and advanced about 1,000 yards. Our troops were, however, unable to maintain their hold, in face of the counter-attacks which were again launched against them by the Alpine Corps. They, consequently, withdrew to their starting positions, retaining only a few advanced posts, which succeeded in withstanding all further attempts of the enemy to force them back. On the left at the same hour an attack was launched by the 173rd Brigade of the 58th Division under cover of a creeping barrage, and supported by a concentration of heavy artillery fire on selected targets. Good progress was made at first, and our troops gained a footing in both Epéhy and Peizières, and even penetrated as far east as the railway. They were, however, driven back by an immediate counter-attack from the railway embankment, and were compelled to withdraw almost to their original " starting line." In the day's fighting 100 prisoners of the Alpine Corps were captured, and it was definitely ascertained that the enemy was holding Epéhy strongly with an organised garrison. This was a strong position, and it was clear that it could only be captured by a deliberate assault, supported by all available artillery and tanks.

At 11 a.m. on September 11th Lieut.-Gen. Sir Walter Braithwaite, commanding the IX Corps, took over command of the 32nd Division and the front it was holding between Holnon Wood and Vermand, both inclusive, from Sir John Monash. On the same day the 6th Division, commanded by Maj.-Gen. T. O. Marden, was transferred from army reserve to the IX Corps. The 1st Division, commanded by Maj.-Gen. E. P. Strickland, which was arriving by rail, was also placed at the disposal of that Corps. On September 19th the 46th Division, commanded by Maj.-Gen. G. F. Boyd, arrived and was also posted to the IX Corps.[2]

September 11th; the arrival of the IX Corps; the readjustment of the front

During the 11th, continuing its success in Holnon Wood, the 32nd Division gained a further footing in the south-western portion of this wood and occupied the greater portion of Attilly. Posts were also established in Vermand without opposition. During the night of the 11th the 1st Division relieved the left half of the front of the 32nd Division between Attilly and Vermand. Further north, the 4th Australian Division, in conjunction with the 1st Australian Division, made slight progress

---

[1] These divisions began to arrive from the rest areas on September 9th.
[2] The 1st, 6th, 32nd, and 46th Divisions remained with the IX Corps until the end of the campaign.

between Vermand and Hesbecourt. At first the resistance was only slight, and the 4th Australian Division reached the western outskirts of Jeancourt without difficulty. On the III Corps front, following on the fighting around Epéhy on September 10th, the enemy under cover of a heavy bombardment delivered a strong counter-attack against the right of the 74th Division on the 11th. This resulted in a withdrawal of some of our advanced posts, but entailed no further alteration in our line.

Meanwhile, on September 8th Sir Douglas Haig had called for a general report on the situation, with especial reference to the enemy's dispositions and moral, together with Sir Henry Rawlinson's opinion as regards the prospects of success of any future offensive operations on the front of the Fourth Army.

The general situation on September 11th

In reply, Sir Henry Rawlinson on September 11th reported that, as the result of the operations of the previous days, his troops were close up to, and in the centre had occupied part of, the old British reserve line of March, 1918, which included the localities of Holnon, Maissemy, Jeancourt, Hesbecourt, and Ste. Emilie.

East of this, he pointed out, the enemy possessed five distinct lines of defence.[1] The first of these, which the Germans had held against us for some time during their withdrawal in the spring of 1917, and which had then become the British main line of resistance, contained the important tactical localities of Fresnoy-le-Petit, the high ground south of Berthaucourt, Le Verguier, Grand Priel Woods, the high ground north and south of Hargicourt, Ronssoy–Basse Boulogne, and Epéhy–Peizières. These were all naturally strong positions, and had been very much strengthened with wire, trenches, and dug-outs both by ourselves and the enemy. This was the line the enemy was now holding in considerable strength, and he showed no signs of giving it up without a struggle. So long as it was held by the Germans we were denied all observation over the main Hindenburg Line.[2] Some 1,500 to 2,000 yards east of the first line, and likely to fall with it, was the old British outpost line, neither strongly wired nor offering any great difficulties to an attack from the west.

To the east of this again was a third line of defence, which in 1917 was the German outpost position to the main Hindenburg Line. It ran through Thorigny, Ste. Hélène, Buisson Gaulaine Farm, Ruby Wood, Quennemont Farm, Gillemont Farm, The Knoll, and Little Priel Farm. When constructed in 1917, this line was not intended to be held against an attack in force. The importance to us, however, of this line, on account of the observation it afforded over the main Hindenburg Line, was so obvious that it had been very materially strengthened, and had become part of the outer defences of the main Hindenburg Line. The enemy, moreover, had, as the result of our attacks in 1917, realised the advantage of defence in depth. He had prepared accordingly, and, given sufficient troops of reasonably high moral, he might, Sir Henry Rawlinson considered, be expected to hold the outer defences with determination.

---

[1] These five lines can best be seen on Map 10, on which all the trenches and wire are shown.
[2] This line was called the Siegfried Line by the Germans.

Next came the Hindenburg Line proper, of which the St. Quentin Canal and the Bellicourt and Le Tronquoy tunnels formed the chief features. This main line of defence was undoubtedly very strong, and there could be no hope of rushing it. Behind the main Hindenburg Line there was yet a fifth line, known as the reserve Hindenburg, or Le Catelet–Nauroy Line, which, although not so formidable as the main Hindenburg Line, was well wired and of considerable natural strength.

On the other hand, Sir Henry Rawlinson represented that the enemy's moral had without doubt much deteriorated. It was true that his infantry had fought well at Mont St. Quentin and Péronne, and later at Epéhy, but his severe defeat in the Battle of Amiens, his long forced retirement, and his heavy losses, which he had been unable to replace, had all told severely. His troops were much shaken, and their power of resistance had greatly depreciated.[1]

It was calculated that on the 11th the Fourth Army was opposed by seven divisions,[2] of which six were engaged for the second time, and that the strength in rifles in the line probably did not exceed 12,000.[3] It was estimated that, out of the twenty-one divisions that had been withdrawn from the line since August 8th, only five were immediately fit for active operations, and that their total fighting strength would not amount to more than 10,000 to 11,000 bayonets.

In view of the above, Sir Henry Rawlinson asked that he might be allowed to undertake with the least possible delay a definite operation on the whole front of the army to gain possession of the outer defences of the Hindenburg Line. Such an operation, if carried out at an early date, would deny the enemy any opportunity of reorganising his troops, improving his defences, or becoming familiar with the scheme of defence. Every day's respite given to the enemy was of inestimable value to him. Further, should it be decided to attack the main Hindenburg Line, our troops would need a short period of rest in which to reorganise their communications [4] before undertaking such an important operation. It would be advisable that this interval should take place after the capture of the outer defences of the Hindenburg Line, rather than before, so that advantage might be taken of it for reconnaissance, for the systematic organisation of the artillery arrangements, and for other important preliminaries, that would have to be carried out before an attack on a large scale could be undertaken.

In conclusion, Sir Henry Rawlinson submitted that, although he was inclined to think that an attack on the main Hindenburg Line on a wide front and with ample artillery support would be successful, he did

Sir Henry Rawlinson's proposals

---

[1] Some orders captured during the next few weeks give a good idea of the state of the German moral at this period. See Appendix H.

[2] These calculations proved to be approximately correct. There were, in fact, eight divisions opposing us on September 18th—the 25th Reserve, 79th Reserve, 119th, 1st Reserve, 5th Bavarian, 38th, 2nd Guard, and the Alpine Corps (from south to north).

[3] The strength of companies was known to be down to 25 in many cases, and none had a strength of more than 70.

[4] The railway had at that time reached Péronne, but beyond that all food and ammunition had to go forward by lorry, which caused a great strain on the roads, many of which were in bad repair.

R

not consider that he could give a definite opinion as to its practicability until the high ground then held by the enemy, and especially Holnon Wood, Le Verguier and the high ground north of it, the high ground about Cologne Farm, and the group of villages round Ronssoy and Epéhy had been captured. The possession of these positions would give us good observation over the main Hindenburg Line, which was essential before an attack against it could be contemplated, and would enable reconnaissance to be made of the best avenues of approach. An attack on these advanced positions would, moreover, be an infallible test of the enemy's power of resistance, which was after all the ruling factor, and by the result of it we should discover the probable chances of success of an attack against the main Hindenburg Line.

Sir Douglas Haig approved of Sir Henry Rawlinson's proposals. He authorised the launching of an attack by the Fourth Army at an
The proposals approved
early date with a view to capturing the high ground which gave observation over the Hindenburg Line, and he arranged for the attack to be extended northwards by the Third Army, and for the co-operation of the French to the south.

The task of the IX and Australian Corps for the next few days consisted in making preparations for the attack, and in advancing their
September 12th to 17th; minor operations
line, where it was to their advantage to do so, by vigorous action of strong fighting patrols. These tactics were employed with success. By September 13th the IX Corps had occupied the greater part of Holnon Wood and Villecholles, while the First French Army on the right had reached the outskirts of Roupy and Savy. On the night of September 13th the 6th Division relieved the remainder of the 32nd Division on the right of the IX Corps front.[1]

On the Australian Corps front the 1st Australian Division occupied Jeancourt on September 12th without meeting with much resistance. On the following day the 4th Australian Division advanced our line several hundred yards east of Bihecourt and Jeancourt, and secured the ridge between these two villages, capturing two officers and 96 other ranks.[2] The III Corps made no attempt to advance its line, although both our own and the enemy's artillery were very active. Our airmen were also fully occupied at this period, as the weather was generally fine with only a few occasional showers of rain. Seven of the enemy's observation balloons were attacked by our airmen and were all forced to descend, three in flames and one shot adrift.

With the exception of the final clearing of Holnon Wood by the 11th Essex of the 6th Division, and the capture of part of the high ground between Holnon Wood and Maissemy by patrols of the 1st Division, no infantry operations were undertaken on September 14th.

At 5.30 a.m. on September 15th the 1st Division continued its success by capturing Maissemy and the rest of the high ground to the

---

[1] The 32nd Division on relief moved back to the Corbie area for a well-earned rest after 26 days continuously in the line.

[2] These prisoners belonged to the 1st Reserve and 119th Divisions. The former division had just relieved the 21st Division, and was now engaged for the third time since August 8th.

south-east of it against slight opposition ; 78 prisoners of the 25th Reserve and 79th Reserve Divisions and 20 machine-guns were taken.   On the same date the 4th Australian Division seized the spur south-west of Le Verguier, thus weakening the enemy's hold on this important village. Infantry action on September 16th on the army front consisted only of some slight advances on the part of patrols.   On the other hand, our airmen were extremely active and successful.   During the day, fourteen hostile machines were destroyed and five shot down out of control, while we lost only three machines.

On September 17th, in order to improve its " starting line " for the attack on the outer defences of the Hindenburg Line, the 6th Division, on the right of the IX Corps, employed the 18th Brigade to attack Holnon village and Badger Copse in co-operation with the 34th Division of the First French Army.   The 18th Brigade encountered strong opposition on the edge of Holnon Wood, and suffered heavy casualties from artillery and machine-gun fire.   By 11 a.m. the 11th Essex had secured Trout Copse, and later on Badger Copse ; Holnon village changed hands several times during the day, and at night it was doubtful who held the village. The French, after much opposition, secured the right flank of the IX Corps by the capture of Savy Wood.

On the rest of the army front, except for some desultory shelling, all was quiet on the 17th.

In the meanwhile, on receiving Sir Douglas Haig's permission to carry out the attack, orders had been issued on September 13th defining

The preliminary arrangements for the attack on September 18th   objectives, the inter-corps boundaries and those of the army, and giving the allotment of tanks to corps. On receipt of these orders the IX, Australian, and III Corps commenced their preparations.   Aeroplane photographs of the enemy's defences to a depth of 4,000 yards were taken, and were distributed throughout formations to all officers and non-commissioned officers taking part in the operations.   As in the preparations for August 8th, every provision was made to ensure secrecy.   Final instructions were issued by Sir Henry Rawlinson on September 14th, giving the nature and rate of advance of artillery barrages, the length of halts in the advance of the barrage, and other details, and also fixing the date of attack as September 18th.   By the evening of September 17th all arrangements had been completed, and " zero " was fixed for 5.20 a.m.

The attack was to be carried out along the whole of the front of the Fourth Army, in conjunction with the XXXVI French Corps of the First

The objectives   French Army to the south, and the two southern corps of the Third Army to the north.   The operation was to be undertaken in three phases.   The first phase included the capture of the enemy's first line of defence[1] or the old British main line of resistance, and special importance was placed on securing Selency, Fresnoy-le-Petit, Le Verguier, the Grand Priel Woods and the high ground north of them, Ronssoy–Basse Boulogne, and Epéhy–Peizières. The objectives of the second phase coincided in many places with the

[1] See page 120.

enemy's second line of defence, or the old British outpost line. It included the villages of Gricourt, Berthaucourt, and Pontru, Ascension Farm, Villeret, Cologne Farm, Malakoff Farm, Sart Farm, Tombois Farm, and Little Priel Farm.

The third phase, or phase of exploitation, depended upon the collapse of the enemy's opposition, and consisted of gaining a footing in the last of the outer defences of the Hindenburg Line. This entailed the capture of Thorigny, Pontruet, Buisson Gaulaine Farm, Quennemont Farm, Gillemont Farm, and The Knoll. It was not expected that this line would necessarily be reached on the first day of the operations, but it was considered probable that, in the event of the attack being successful on September 18th, vigorous exploitation would shortly afterwards result in this objective being secured.

The front on which the Fourth Army was about to attack was approximately fourteen miles in width, and extended from Holnon village to just north of Peizières. The IX Corps front extended from the south-eastern outskirts of Holnon to a point 500 yards north of Vadencourt, some 7,000 yards in all. The 6th and 1st Divisions were in line on the right and left respectively, the former holding 3,000, and the latter 4,000 yards. In the centre of the Fourth Army the Australian Corps held a front of 7,000 yards, from the northern boundary of the IX Corps to the Cologne river immediately west of Templeux-le-Guérard. This was divided equally between the 4th Australian Division on the right and the 1st Australian Division on the left. The III Corps continued the line to a point about 500 yards north-west of Epéhy, where it was in touch with the V Corps of the Third Army. This front of about 7,000 yards was held by the 74th, 18th, 12th, and 58th Divisions, from right to left. The 74th Division was allotted rather more than 2,000 yards, the 18th Division rather less than 2,000 yards; the 12th Division, immediately in front of Epéhy, held over 2,500 yards, and the 58th Division on the extreme left about 700 yards.

The frontages of attack

There was to be no preliminary bombardment, reliance being placed, as on August 8th, on the effect of surprise, a powerful artillery concentration including intense counter-battery work, and the assistance of tanks at points where the resistance was expected to be most pronounced. A creeping barrage, provided by 750 18-pounder guns and 228 4·5-inch howitzers, was to cover the advance of the infantry to the first objective. This barrage was to be lifted 100 yards after two minutes, after which it was to advance at the rate of 100 yards every three minutes until it had moved forward 1,300 yards from the infantry " starting line," after which it was to advance at the rate of 100 yards every four minutes until the first objective was reached. It would then form a protective barrage for one hour, after which it was again to be moved forward at the rate of 100 yards every four minutes as far as the second objective. The barrage in the second phase of the attack would be less dense than in the first phase, as, after the protective barrage on the first objective had ceased, a number of batteries were to move forward to new positions, under divisional arrange-

The artillery arrangements

ments, with a view to assisting in the third phase of the attack; their fire would thus be lost during the second phase.[1]

The 2nd Tank Battalion had been allotted to the Fourth Army for this operation and was sub-allotted to corps as follows :

The allotment of tanks

"C" Company of six   tanks to the IX Corps.

"B"   ,,   ,, nine   ,,   ,,   Australian Corps.

"A"   .   ,,   ,, eight   ,,   ,,   III Corps.

It was necessary to economise tanks to the utmost, in view of the probability of an attack being carried out against the main Hindenburg Line in the near future, for which a large supply of tanks would be essential. Corps were, therefore, instructed to limit the employment of tanks to assisting the infantry attacks against certain strong points of resistance, and to forbid them to advance east of the first objective.[2]

In accordance with these instructions, out of the six tanks allotted to the IX Corps, four were detailed to deal with an important trench system north of Selency called the Quadrilateral, and two were to assist to clear Badger Copse and attack Fresnoy-le-Petit. Of the nine tanks with the Australian Corps, five were earmarked to clear Le Verguier and the trench systems north and south of it, in co-operation with the 4th Australian Division, and five for the attack on Hargicourt, Villeret, and the high ground around Cologne Farm, in co-operation with the 1st Australian Division. The III Corps allotted four tanks to the 18th Division to assist in the attack on Ronssoy–Basse Boulogne and Ronssoy Wood, and four tanks for the operations against Epéhy and Peizières. The 5th Brigade, Royal Air Force, was ordered to co-operate with the 2nd Tank Battalion in the arrangements for masking anti-tank guns with smoke bombs, and for the usual low-flying aeroplanes to drown the noise of the tank engines during their assembly. To supplement the small number of tanks available, the 1st and 4th Australian Divisions constructed a considerable number of dummy tanks, by means of which it was hoped to increase the demoralisation of the enemy and make him disperse his anti-tank fire.[3]

The assembly of the infantry took place almost without incident, except on the right of the IX Corps. Although the early part of the **A summary of the** night was fine, it was raining heavily when the attack **Fourth Army attack on** was launched at 5.20 a.m. ; later the rain ceased, and **September 18th** a dull cloudy day followed. The light was bad ; the ground was soft and slippery, and consequently not suitable for the tanks, of which a certain number were " ditched " in the deep sunken roads and high embankments.

The enemy's resistance varied considerably. It was perhaps most determined in front of the III Corps and on the right and centre of the IX Corps; as a result, these two corps were unable to gain all their

---

[1] In addition to, and in close co-operation with, the artillery barrages, machine-gun barrages were arranged by all corps.

[2] The 1st Australian Division was permitted to use its tanks as far as the second objective as it included Cologne Farm, which was known to be strongly defended.

[3] These dummy tanks, though excellent imitations of real tanks, were not as successful as would have been the case had the weather been dry, as the mud quickly clogged the wheels and rendered the dummies immobile. Even so they drew a good deal of hostile artillery fire.

objectives, although considerable progress was made in each case.[1] On the Australian Corps front the initial opposition was also strong, and it was not until the crust of the defence had been broken by the rapidity and impetuosity of the Australian advance, that the enemy began to surrender freely and in large numbers. The Australians made a remarkable advance, and by the evening had established themselves in close proximity to the line of exploitation, the objective of the third phase of the attack.

By 5 a.m. the 6th Division, on the right of the IX Corps front, was assembled with the 71st and 16th Brigades in the line, and the 18th

The assembly of the IX Corps

Brigade in support. The uncertainty as to the position of the troops of the 71st Brigade in the neighbourhood of Holnon village, and the enemy's shelling on this portion of the front, rendered the assembly and forming up of the troops of the 6th Division very difficult. On the left the 1st Division formed up for the attack without incident, the 1st Brigade being on the right, the 2nd Brigade on the left, and the 3rd Brigade in reserve.

In spite of the sodden ground caused by the heavy rain, fair progress was made when the troops moved forward at " zero," except on the

The first phase of the IX Corps attack

right of the 6th Division. Here the advance was slow, as, from the moment the attack started, considerable machine-gun fire was encountered from Selency, the Quadrilateral, and Fresnoy-le-Petit ; also from Round Hill and Manchester Hill, to the south-west and south of Francilly–Selency respectively, positions which the French on the right of the IX Corps were unable to secure.[2] The hostile artillery shelling was heavy ; the advance of our troops was made down bare slopes swept by enfilade as well as frontal fire, and was much impeded by wire; while the drizzling rain, accompanied by mist, obscured the landmarks and made it difficult to keep direction. In consequence, the 71st Brigade made little progress, and the struggle about Holnon village and Selency continued. The 16th Brigade on the left was at first checked in front of Fresnoy-le-Petit, but had occupied it by 8.40 a.m. Later in the day our troops were forced to withdraw from the village. Only two of the four tanks allotted to the 6th Division succeeded in coming into action ; these, finding that the infantry was held up by fire from the Quadrilateral, headed straight for the seat of the trouble. Here very strong opposition was encountered. One tank became " ditched," and the other, after engaging the enemy and inflicting heavy casualties, burst into flames and had to be abandoned. The gallant survivors of both tanks then held a

---

[1] An incident which is worth recounting occurred on the right of the III Corps front. Owing to an error in the synchronisation of watches, some machine-guns opened fire too soon. This mistake, however, enabled the waiting infantry to realise fully the intensity of the covering fire they were receiving from machine-guns. Some of our men stated that the noise of this fire resembled the tearing of a huge sheet of calico, while others compared it to the firing of a million rifles. It can, therefore, be imagined what effect was produced, not only on the enemy but on the attacking infantry, when the noise of the fire of these comparatively few machine-guns was augmented at " zero " by that of 1,488 guns and over 300 machine-guns.

[2] These two localities " Round Hill " and " Manchester Hill " had played an important part in our retreat in March, 1918. They had, prior to the German offensive, been organised as strongholds, or redoubts, each holding a complete battalion provisioned for forty-eight hours. Although completely surrounded, Manchester Hill held out in March for many hours. Both positions were very strong and dominated the surrounding country.

Lehaucourt→

Levergies

Sycamore Wood→

Sequehert

Le Tronquoy

Thorigny

Cornouillers Wood

Gricourt

Flame Copse

Flat Iron Wood

Marroniers Wood

Cartigny Woods

Fresnoy-le-Petit

Dean Copse

Dee Copse

Otter Copse

Badger Copse

FRESNOY-LE-PETIT AND GRICOURT.

Oblique air photograph.

portion of trench a little in rear of their disabled tanks until relieved later by the infantry.

Meanwhile, further north the 1st Division made good progress. The 1st Brigade on the right was somewhat delayed by machine-gun fire from the valley north of Fresnoy-le-Petit and from the trenches north-east of that village, but, with the assistance of the 2nd Brigade, which had reached the first objective at 7.30 a.m., the 1st Brigade secured its objective by 8.15 a.m. The IX Corps had thus secured the first objective from Fresnoy-le-Petit northwards to its junction with the Australian Corps.

The advance towards the second objective from Fresnoy-le-Petit northwards was resumed at 8.30 a.m., but, as further progress south of Fresnoy-le-Petit seemed doubtful, the 71st Brigade

The second phase   formed a defensive flank in order to secure the flank of the advance against any counter-attacks which might be launched from the direction of Selency and the Quadrilateral. On the right of the 1st Division progress north-east of Fresnoy-le-Petit was very slow in the face of considerable opposition, and the line was only advanced a few hundred yards beyond the Fresnoy-le-Petit–Berthaucourt road. On some parts of the front the barrage gradually outstripped the infantry, and any attempt to advance had, therefore, to be made without its assistance. The left of the 1st Division, however, made good progress and kept well up to the barrage. Berthaucourt was captured at 10.30 a.m., and the 2nd Brigade, keeping in touch with the Australians on its left, captured the second objective at 11 a.m. The troops of the 4th Australian Division at this stage, finding that the resistance in front of them was slight, had continued their advance beyond the second objective. In order to maintain touch with them, the troops of the 2nd Brigade advanced towards Ste. Hélène and established themselves just west of that hamlet.

At 3.30 p.m. the enemy launched several determined counter-attacks against the left of the 6th Division at Fresnoy-le-Petit, and against the right of the 1st Division south of Berthaucourt.[1] North of Fresnoy-le-Petit these counter-attacks were repulsed by rifle and machine-gun fire, but the situation around Fresnoy-le-Petit became very involved. Fighting continued also throughout the afternoon on the front of the 6th Division, especially round Holnon village and Selency, no further progress was, however, made. Meanwhile, the French division on the right of the 6th Division had been held up in front of Francilly–Selency, which added to the difficulties of the 6th Division; the 2nd Life Guards Machine Gun Battalion, attached to the 6th Division, was, therefore, disposed in depth on the high ground near Holnon in order to secure the safety of the right flank.

When darkness set in our line ran along the eastern edge of Holnon village, where a junction was established with the French, north of Selency, through the western outskirts of Fresnoy-le-Petit, with a few posts in

---

[1] These counter-attacks were carried out by three battalions of the 197th Division (a Jäger formation), which had been sent forward in 'buses, leaving Maretz (6 miles south-west of Le Cateau) at 10 a.m., to reinforce the 79th Reserve Division.

the village, thence due north, keeping just west of Pontruet and Ste.
Hélène, near which village the 1st Division was in touch with the
The result of the Australians. As the result of the day's fighting, the
day's fighting by the IX Corps had captured 18 officers, 541 other ranks,
IX Corps 8 field guns, and numerous trench mortars and machine-
guns. The casualties had unfortunately been comparatively heavy, owing
chiefly to the determined resistance offered by the 25th Reserve, 79th
Reserve, and part of the 197th Divisions.

In spite of the rain and the muddy state of the ground, the 1st and
4th Australian Divisions completed their assembly in good time. Of the
nine tanks supporting the infantry, eight succeeded
The assembly of the in reaching the " starting line." On the right of the
Australian Corps Australian Corps the 4th Australian Division assembled
for the attack with the 12th Brigade on the right, the 4th
Brigade on the left, and the 13th Brigade, disposed along the
spur south-west of Vendelles, in reserve. The 12th Brigade was
to attack on a one-battalion front throughout the advance;
the 48th Battalion carrying out the attack against the first, the 45th
against the second, and the 46th against the third objective. The 4th
Brigade was to attack the first objective on a three-battalion front,
the 13th and 15th Battalions passing round Le Verguier, while the 16th
" mopped up " the village. The two former battalions were then to
continue the attack on the second objective, after the capture of which,
the 14th Battalion was to " leap-frog " them and carry out the exploitation to the third objective.[1]

On the left of the corps front the 1st Australian Division was disposed
for the attack with the 3rd Brigade on the right, the 1st Brigade on the
left, and the 2nd Brigade in reserve. The 1st and 3rd Brigades were
to attack the first objective, each on a front of two battalions. The
remaining two battalions of each brigade were then to " leap-frog " the
leading battalions, capture the second objective, and, if possible, secure
the third objective.

The infantry advanced to the attack at " zero," keeping close behind
the barrage, which was excellent and so dense that the enemy in many
The first phase of cases " went to ground " and became an easy prey for
the Australian Corps our infantry. The hostile artillery retaliation to our
attack barrage was light and scattered, causing very few
casualties. On the right of the 4th Australian Division the 12th Brigade
encountered some fire from machine-gun nests, but these were promptly
outflanked and put out of action by the 48th Battalion.[2] On the front
of the 4th Brigade, however, Le Verguier proved a more difficult task.
The enemy had established a number of strong machine-gun posts among
the ruins of the village, and these posts, owing to the smoke of the barrage,
were difficult to locate. This was a disadvantage to the 16th Battalion,
which had been detailed to " mop up " the village, but a distinct advantage
to the 13th and 15th, as it helped to conceal their movements from the

[1] For details of the machine-gun dispositions to support the attack of the 4th Australian
Division, see Appendix J and Map 19.
[2] In this advance the capture of an important German machine-gun post by Private James
Woods, 48th Battalion, and three men enabled touch to be gained with the troops on the right.
See Appendix E, No. 49.

AUSTRALIANS ADVANCING CLOSE UP TO THE BARRAGE ON SEPTEMBER 18TH.

By kind permission of the Australian Government.

No. 58.

AUSTRALIAN RESERVES WATCHING THE BARRAGE CREEPING UP THE SLOPES TOWARDS
THE OUTER DEFENCES OF THE HINDENBURG LINE ON SEPTEMBER 18TH.

By kind permission of the Australian Government.

enemy. In the hope of checking the advance, the Germans fired blindly in a westerly direction, but the 13th and 15th Battalions moved round the flanks, where they were apparently not expected.[1] The 16th Battalion then proceeded rapidly with the " mopping up " of the village, which yielded 450 prisoners belonging to the 1st Reserve and 119th Divisions, 60 machine-guns, and several field guns. By 7.35 a.m. the whole of the first objective on the front of the 4th Australian Division had been secured.

On the left the 12th, 11th, 2nd, and 4th Battalions of the 1st Australian Division, which were leading, met with considerable opposition at several points, chiefly on the 3rd Brigade front. Heavy fighting took place in Brosse Wood and in the trenches on the western outskirts of the Grand Priel Woods, where the garrison fought with great determination, and refused to surrender until all the machine-guns were silenced and their crews killed. The resistance from Carpela Copse and Fervaque Farm ceased as soon as these places were outflanked. The Grand Priel Woods, however, caused considerable difficulty ; here the resistance was very determined, and severe fighting ensued before they were captured. About this time a tank,which had been unable to keep up, arrived and, advancing through the barrage, silenced some machine-guns concealed in the sunken roads and trenches south-west of Villeret. The action of this tank helped to break the back of the enemy's resistance in front of the 3rd Brigade, and the first objective was secured along the whole front of the 1st Australian Division, the 1st Brigade having reached it earlier in the morning without difficulty.

At 8.30 a.m., after halting for an hour covering the first objective, the barrage was again moved forward on the Australian front, and the attacking troops advanced. On the front of the 4th The second phase Australian Division the 45th, 13th, and 15th Battalions of the 12th and 4th Brigades had by 9.50 a.m. reached the second objective and captured a large number of prisoners. The 1st Australian Division experienced less resistance than during the first phase of the battle. When the advanced troops of both the 3rd and 1st Brigades, which were now found by the 10th, 9th, 1st, and 2nd Battalions, encountered some opposition at Villeret, and in the trench systems north and south of it, one of the tanks rendered timely assistance and largely contributed to the eventual capture of Villeret. The troops of the 1st Brigade also cleared the maze of trenches about Cologne Farm in spite of the heavy fire from the high ground round Quennemont Farm. Thus the second objective was quickly secured on the whole of the divisional front.

The protective barrage remained stationary for fifteen minutes to cover the reorganisation on the second objective, and then ceased about 10 a.m. By this time some batteries of field The third phase artillery had moved forward and were in action in previously selected positions, from which they were able to support the further advance of the infantry.

---

[1] It was during this advance that Sergeant Gerald Sexton of the 13th Battalion displayed great gallantry and was in a large measure responsible for the success of his battalion. See Appendix E, No. 39.

S

The 4th Australian Division pushed forward two battalions, the 46th Battalion from the 12th Brigade and the 14th from the 4th Brigade, but communication with the 1st Division of the IX Corps on the right was difficult, and the 46th Battalion found its right flank in the air. Undeterred, however, by the machine-gun fire which was enfilading it from its right, the 46th Battalion pressed forward and reached the sunken road running northwards from Ste. Hélène, where it was joined later by troops of the 1st British Division. On the left of the advance the 14th Battalion was very successful; it obtained a footing in the outer defences of the main Hindenburg Line, and immediately commenced to exploit its gains by bombing down the trenches. In face of the small number of our attacking troops, the enemy's resistance was now found to be strengthening, and it was, therefore, decided to wait until the darkness had set in before launching an attack, under cover of a barrage, to capture the rest of the third objective on the divisional front. A hot meal was served while the men were waiting for the order to advance in the sunken road which runs northwards from Ste. Hélène. At 11 p.m. the barrage fell, and the 46th Battalion on the right and the 14th on the left, advancing from the sunken road, gained a firm footing in the outer defences of the main Hindenburg Line. By 1 a.m., therefore, on September 19th the whole of the third objective on the front of the 4th Australian Division had been captured; in this attack alone 300 prisoners and numerous machine-guns were taken. This night attack of the 14th and 46th Battalions was a fine performance in view of the distance already covered and of the strenuous fighting during the day.

When the artillery barrage, covering the troops of the 1st Australian Division on the second objective, ceased at about 10 a.m., the 10th and 9th Battalions of the 3rd Brigade, moving forward in conjunction with the troops of the 4th Australian Division, secured a footing in the trenches north of Buisson Gaulaine Farm and gained practically the whole of the Cologne Farm ridge. Heavy machine-gun fire from the direction of Quennemont Farm, however, prevented a further advance of the left of the 1st Brigade, and at the end of the day the 1st Australian Division held the greater part of the outer defences of the Hindenburg Line from its junction with the 4th Australian Division at Buisson Gaulaine Farm to Malakoff Farm, where connection was established with the 74th Division of the III Corps.

As the result of the day's fighting, the Australian Corps had penetrated the enemy's defences to an average depth of 5,000 yards on a frontage **The result of the** of four miles. The Australians were now well established **day's fighting by the** in the outer defences of the main Hindenburg Line, **Australian Corps** and held a position which necessitated some reorganisation by the enemy of his plans for its defence. All the strongly fortified localities in the old British line of resistance had fallen, and the captures amounted to 4,243 prisoners, 87 guns, over 300 machine-guns, and about 30 trench mortars.

A comparison of the number of troops engaged, the prisoners captured, and the casualties incurred in this operation, is of particular interest. The attacking strength of the 1st Australian Division was 2,854, that of the

A TYPICAL GERMAN TRENCH NEAR COLOGNE FARM.

By kind permission of the Australian Government.

No. 60.

GERMANS SURRENDERING TO THE AUSTRALIANS ON SEPTEMBER 18TH.

By kind permission of the Australian Government.

4th Australian Division 3,048. In both cases this excludes the reserve brigades, which were not engaged. The prisoners captured by the former amounted to 66 officers and 1,634 other ranks, as compared with 490 casualties, and by the latter to 99 officers and 2,444 other ranks, as compared with 532 casualties. These figures speak for themselves, and demonstrate not only the skill and gallantry displayed by the infantry, but also the moral effect of the tanks and the accuracy of the artillery and machine-gun support. The chief resistance came from the enemy's machine-guns, and the fact that this was overcome with so few casualties indicates that it was a battle in which success was to a great extent due to the initiative of subordinate commanders.

Sir Richard Butler, who had resumed command of the III Corps on September 12th, originally intended to attack with three divisions, but, owing to the strength of the enemy's defences and the large area of the villages to be " mopped up," he finally decided to attack with all four divisions of his corps.

The assembly of the III Corps

In addition to those caused by the rain, the difficulties of assembly on the night of September 17th were increased by a considerable amount of gas shelling on battery positions and assembly areas. Nevertheless, the infantry was assembled up to time and without confusion. Unfortunately, however, only six tanks, out of the eight allotted to the III Corps, succeeded in reaching the " starting line " by " zero " ; three of these were to operate with the 18th Division against Ronssoy and Basse Boulogne, and three with the 12th and 58th Divisions against Epéhy and Peizières.

On the right of the III Corps the 74th Division was assembled, with the 230th and 231st Brigades in line on the right and left respectively, each strengthened by one battalion from the 229th Brigade. Two battalions of each of the two leading brigades were allotted the task of going right through to the third objective, the remaining battalions were to follow in support and " mop up " the ground gained. In the centre the 18th and 12th Divisions were allotted the formidable task of capturing Ronssoy, Basse Boulogne, and Epéhy. An important feature on this part of the front was the basin lying in the triangle Ronssoy–Epéhy–Ste. Emilie. It was decided to avoid this basin in the initial attack, and that the 18th Division should attack south of the spur running from Ronssoy to Ste. Emilie, while the 12th Division attacked west of the spur running from Epéhy to Ste. Emilie. After the capture of Ronssoy and Epéhy, the attacking troops were to wheel inwards and roll up the enemy's main line of defence, which was on the ridge joining these two villages. The 18th Division employed the 54th Brigade, strengthened by one battalion of the 53rd Brigade, to capture Ronssoy, Basse Boulogne, and the first objective ; the 55th Brigade was then to advance through the 54th Brigade and secure the second objective. The 53rd Brigade, less one battalion detached with the 54th Brigade, was held in divisional reserve. On the front of the 12th Division the 36th Brigade, less one battalion, was assembled on the right, and the 35th Brigade on the left facing Epéhy, for the advance to the first objective. In rear of these brigades, with orders to move through them and secure the second objective, was concentrated the 37th Brigade, with one battalion of the 36th Brigade attached.

On the extreme left of the III Corps the 58th Division employed the 173rd Brigade to capture Peizières and the first objective, after the capture of which it was to be " squeezed out " by the advance on its right of the 12th Division, as the latter moved forward to the second objective. The remaining two brigades of the 58th Division were retained in corps reserve.

Serious opposition was encountered by the troops of the III Corps almost from the moment the advance began. It is almost certain that
The first phase of the attack did not take the enemy by surprise, although
the III Corps attack the actual hour of the attack may not have been known.[1]
The thick mist and rain, in which the attack was launched, may have been responsible for the measure of surprise attained, but, although advantageous in this respect, they were otherwise a disadvantage, as the bad light rendered it difficult for the infantry and tanks to keep direction at the beginning of the attack. The enemy's artillery retaliation to our bombardment was comparatively light and came chiefly from high velocity guns, the field guns having been previously withdrawn. The aspect which the fighting assumed differed from the operations carried out by the III Corps over the old Somme battlefield. Manœuvring on a large scale against prominent tactical features was impossible, owing to the complicated trench systems of the old British main line of resistance in which the fighting took place during the whole day. Every section of trench was stubbornly defended by either a machine-gun or a few of the enemy's infantry. The fighting consisted of countless section, platoon, and company actions for the possession of these trenches and fortified posts. The chief feature of the battle was the tenacity displayed by our officers and men in holding on to the ground they had gained, and the determination with which they continued their endeavours to secure all their objectives.

The 74th Division made more rapid progress than the divisions on its left. The 230th Brigade moved forward, keeping close touch with the
The 74th Division 1st Australian Division on its right. Under cover
attack of the artillery barrage and the fire of the 74th Machine
Gun Battalion, this brigade captured Templeux-le-Guérard and cleared the quarries north-east of the village, where twelve heavy machine-guns were captured with slight loss. The garrison of the quarries was overwhelmed by the rapidity of our advance.[2] That the enemy failed to hold on to such a strong position was due, partly to the excellent covering fire afforded by the 74th Machine Gun Battalion, and partly to the dense ground mist, which impeded the enemy's observation and thus restricted his fire. The 231st Brigade on the left also made good progress, and by 9 a.m. both brigades of the 74th Division were established on the first objective.

[1] A prisoner captured on September 17th stated that an attack was expected on the morning of the 18th. This information was confirmed when the enemy subjected the forward and battery areas to a concentrated gas bombardment on the night of September 17th.

[2] Forty men of the 5th Bavarian Division, who came out of a dug-out later in the morning, surrendered to an unarmed groom who had taken his horses to the quarries for shelter.

Quarries

Templeux-le-Gerrard

Templeux Wood

Road Villers-Faucon

TEMPLEUX-LE-GUERARD AND THE QUARRIES.

Oblique air photograph.

The advance of the 18th Division proved to be more difficult. The 7th Royal West Kent, attached to the 54th from the 53rd Brigade,

The 18th Division attack

led the attack, keeping well under the barrage. It advanced through the southern portion of Ronssoy Wood and the village of Ronssoy, and was then " leap-frogged " by the 2nd Bedfordshire, which reached the first objective up to time. The northern portion of Ronssoy Wood was cleared by the 6th Northamptonshire after stiff fighting, and a footing was gained in Basse Boulogne.[1] By 10 a.m. the trench system round Quid Copse, some 500 yards short of the objective on the left, had been secured, but it was not until some hours later that the whole of Basse Boulogne village, in which the enemy held numerous small posts, was " mopped up " with the assistance of two tanks. The 54th Brigade was now in touch with the 74th Division on the right on the first objective, but had not yet been able to connect up with the 12th Division on the left. Owing to the continuance of the fighting in the southern part of Basse Boulogne, not only the supporting battalions of the 54th Brigade, but also some of the troops of the 55th Brigade, which was due to pass through the 54th Brigade and attack the second objective, were drawn into the fight.'

On the front of the 12th Division the 9th Royal Fusiliers and the 7th Royal Sussex, of the 36th Brigade, operating immediately south

The attacks of the 12th and 58th Divisions

of Epéhy, made good progress and succeeded in clearing the railway embankment south-east of the village. The troops of the 7th Norfolk and 9th Essex of the 35th Brigade, however, experienced determined opposition immediately on reaching the western outskirts of Epéhy and lost touch with the barrage. Even when the leading two battalions were reinforced by the 1/1st Cambridgeshire, it proved a difficult matter to dislodge the Alpine Corps from the village, which it had been told to hold at all costs, and casualties were severe on both sides. The tanks, supporting the attack, lost direction in the mist and were mistaken for hostile tanks by some of our troops; this caused some confusion. At 9 a.m. Maj.-Gen. Higginson decided to stop the barrage from moving beyond the first objective, as it was evident that the division would not be able to continue the advance beyond the first objective, until time had been allowed for reorganising the troops.

With great determination the troops of the 35th Brigade pushed slowly through Epéhy, where strong resistance was met with, especially from a few posts, including Fisher's Keep, which still held out, and from Germans who had hidden in the cellars.[2]

On the left of the 12th Division the 173rd Brigade of the 58th Division made a good start at " zero," the 2/2nd London leading, and by 10.20 a.m. had cleared Peizières of the enemy except for one post. On attempting to continue to move forward to the first objective, the right flank was found to be exposed owing to the slow progress of the 12th Division in Epéhy; a defensive flank was, consequently, formed astride the railway.

[1] The courage and initiative of Lce.-Corp. Albert Lewis, 6th Northamptonshire, largely contributed to the successful advance of his battalion. See Appendix E, No. 30.

[2] The village was not finally cleared of Germans until after midnight on September 18th. Fisher's Keep held out till 7.45 p.m. on the 18th when only 17 unwounded survivors remained of the garrison of 3 officers and 45 other ranks

While the 18th and 12th Divisions were engaged in the heavy fighting around Basse Boulogne and Epéhy, the attacking battalions of the 74th

The second phase of the III Corps attack (see Map 9)

Division moved forward towards the second objective shortly after 9 a.m. The 230th Brigade on the right, keeping in close touch with the Australians, gained its objective at 10.30 a.m. On the left the 231st Brigade was not so fortunate, although a considerable advance beyond the first objective was made. The slow progress of the 18th Division, east of Ronssoy, made it necessary to form a defensive flank along the sunken road running south-east from Basse Boulogne, known as the Bellicourt road. Thus, although the second objective was gained on the right of the 231st Brigade as far north as Benjamin Post, prolonging the line held by the 230th Brigade, the resistance encountered at Benjamin Post prevented any further advance being made.

Meanwhile, very confused fighting was still in progress in Basse Boulogne. This delayed the assembly of the troops of the 55th Brigade which were to pass through the 54th Brigade for the second phase of the attack, and had caused some of them to be drawn into the fight in the village. By the time the assembly was completed the artillery barrage had moved on too far to be of any assistance, and, as the enemy's resistance round Lempire and east of Basse Boulogne had increased considerably, only a slight advance was made by the 55th Brigade. Maj.-Gen. Lee decided to postpone any further attempt to advance until the troops could be reorganised, and arrangements could be made for adequate artillery and machine-gun support.

Consequently, about mid-day the situation on the front of the III Corps was that the 74th Division was established on the second objective on the right, with its left thrown a little back; the 18th Division held a line east of Basse Boulogne and Quid Copse, north of which it joined with the 12th Division; this division prolonged the line along the railway east of Epéhy; while the 58th Division was established well east of Peizières, but had not succeeded in maintaining connection with the 21st Division on the right of the V Corps, which, attacking further north, had captured Chapel Crossing and Gauche Wood.

About 5 p.m., by which time the whole of Basse Boulogne had been cleared of the enemy, the 18th Division renewed the attack towards the second objective, including Lempire, Yak, and Zebra posts, moving forward this time under a creeping barrage. The 55th Brigade pressed forward and succeeded on the right in approaching the second objective at certain points, but the left of the division made only slight progress. The enemy had brought up fresh troops, and held X, Y, and Z copses in strength with machine-guns, which enfiladed the infantry advancing against Lempire, Yak, and Zebra posts.[1] By 7 p.m. it was clear that, so long as

---

[1] From prisoners captured during the afternoon it was ascertained that the strong resistance encountered by the 18th Division in Lempire and from X, Y, and Z copses, was due to the fact that the 121st Division had been hurried forward from Maretz, starting at 7 a.m. on the 18th. On arrival at Bony the division had debussed, and had counter-attacked at 5 p.m. with the object of regaining Basse Boulogne, Ronssoy, and the original front line held by the enemy on the morning of the 18th. Although, therefore, its attack had not been successful, the 55th Brigade had to its credit the repulse of a fresh division and the breaking up of a hostile counter-attack

the enemy held these positions, it would not be possible for our men to retain the ground gained on the right, and accordingly a withdrawal to the line of the Bellicourt road was ordered and carried out by 9 p.m.

Earlier in the afternoon the troops of the 35th Brigade and the 5th Royal Berkshire continued the advance of the 12th Division east of Epéhy, with the object of securing the line of the first objective. They made considerable progress and captured Malassise Farm. The 5th Royal Berkshire did especially good work and was fighting during most of the night. In conjunction with this attack, the troops of the 58th Division endeavoured to establish themselves in Poplar Trench on the line of the first objective, but were unsuccessful.

By nightfall, beyond the capture of Benjamin Post, which was skilfully enveloped from the north by the 74th Division, a slight advance by the 18th Division east of Basse Boulogne, and the withdrawal of the troops of the 12th Division from Malassise Farm, our line had undergone no material change since midday.

As the result of very severe fighting, the III Corps had captured the strongly fortified villages of Ronssoy, Basse Boulogne, Epéhy, and The result of the Peizières, which had been held by two crack German day's fighting by the divisions, the Alpine Corps and the 2nd Guard Division. III Corps The III Corps had also captured 2,300 prisoners, 10 guns, and numerous machine-guns and trench mortars.

On the morning of September 19th the weather was still overcast, and a high wind was blowing. The Australians, in the centre of the army front, had now gained practically the whole of their The situation on objectives of the 18th, and devoted the next two days September 19th to consolidation and to adjusting their line at certain points with a view to improving observation. All attempts by the enemy to drive in some of the forward posts established by the Australians were unsuccessful.

On the flanks of the army, on the other hand, neither the IX nor the III Corps had reached all their objectives on September 18th. The attack was, therefore, continued on the fronts of these two corps on the morning of September 19th, as it was essential that all objectives of the 18th should be secured as early as possible, with a view to future operations.

On the IX Corps front the 6th and 1st Divisions endeavoured to gain ground round the Quadrilateral, Fresnoy-le-Petit, and east of The events on the Berthaucourt. The 6th Division, attacking with the IX Corps front on Sep- 71st and 16th Brigades, encountered even greater tember 19th and 20th resistance at the Quadrilateral and at Fresnoy-le-Petit than on the 18th, and was unable to make any progress. Similar attempts by the 1st Division, east of Berthaucourt, were checked by heavy machine-gun fire; on the other hand a counter-attack, launched against the 1st Division at Berthaucourt at 8 a.m., was completely repulsed. The 34th French Division, operating on the right of, and in conjunction with, the 6th Division, attacked Manchester Hill during the morning, but was unsuccessful. The situation at Round Hill still hung in the balance. The enemy was now holding naturally strong positions about Francilly–Selency, at the Quadrilateral, and at Fresnoy-le-Petit, and it was quite evident that he did not contemplate relinquishing them without a determined struggle. Moreover, after three days' severe fighting, the men of the 6th Division, in whose case the battle had begun on the 17th, were beginning to feel the strain.[1] Sir Walter Braithwaite, therefore, decided not to attempt any further attack, until preparations could be made for one on a larger scale, supported by organised artillery and machine-gun barrages. Throughout the remainder of the day fighting of a desultory nature continued on the whole of the IX Corps front, several bombing encounters taking place in the neighbourhood of Fresnoy-le-Petit.

During the night of September 19th the troops of the 6th Division finally gained possession of Holnon village, which for three days had been the scene of continuous fighting and had changed hands several times.

Except for persistent hostile shelling of Holnon Wood, and for a small attack by the enemy against Berthaucourt which met with no success, September 20th passed quietly.

During the night of September 18th the 58th Division, on the left of the III Corps, had succeeded in gaining the northern part of Poplar Trench, and the 12th Division had secured Tétard Wood. *The events on the III Corps front on September 19th and 20th* On the morning of September 19th an operation on a larger scale was carried out by the 18th and 12th Divisions to secure Lempire village, Lempire, Yak, and Zebra posts, and the trenches along the southern slopes of the Catelet valley, including Braeton Post, south of Little Priel Farm. This operation, which was carried out chiefly by means of bombing attacks along the trenches, met with partial success. The 18th Division encountered heavy machine-gun fire from X, Y, and Z copses, which had given so much trouble in the fighting of the previous day, but, after a struggle, Lempire village was cleared, and Lempire, Yak, and Zebra posts were secured. The 12th Division captured May Copse and Malassise Farm, and our line was advanced 1,000 yards beyond Old Copse; touch was, however, lost with the 18th Division on the right, and was not regained until the next day.

September 20th was remarkable for the number of more or less isolated, and at the same time hotly contested struggles, which took place for the possession of small lengths of trenches. The enemy in front of the 18th Division evacuated X, Y, and Z copses, thereby indicating that he had given up the idea of regaining Ronssoy and Epéhy. These small posts were occupied, but, beyond advancing our line to Sart Farm, little further progress was made by the 18th Division. The enemy had taken up new positions in the old British outpost line, and held Braeton Post and the trenches around Little Priel Farm in strength. Although the 12th and 58th Divisions gained some ground, they were unable to capture the whole of their objectives, as the Alpine Corps defended every post, trench, and copse with great stubbornness.

The fighting of the past three days had now brought the III Corps to within a short distance of the outer defences of the main Hindenburg Line. On the right the 74th Division had gained a footing in these defences,

[1] The 6th Division had had a very trying and difficult time, as, owing to the French being unable to advance, the right flank of the division was constantly enfiladed.

To face page 137.

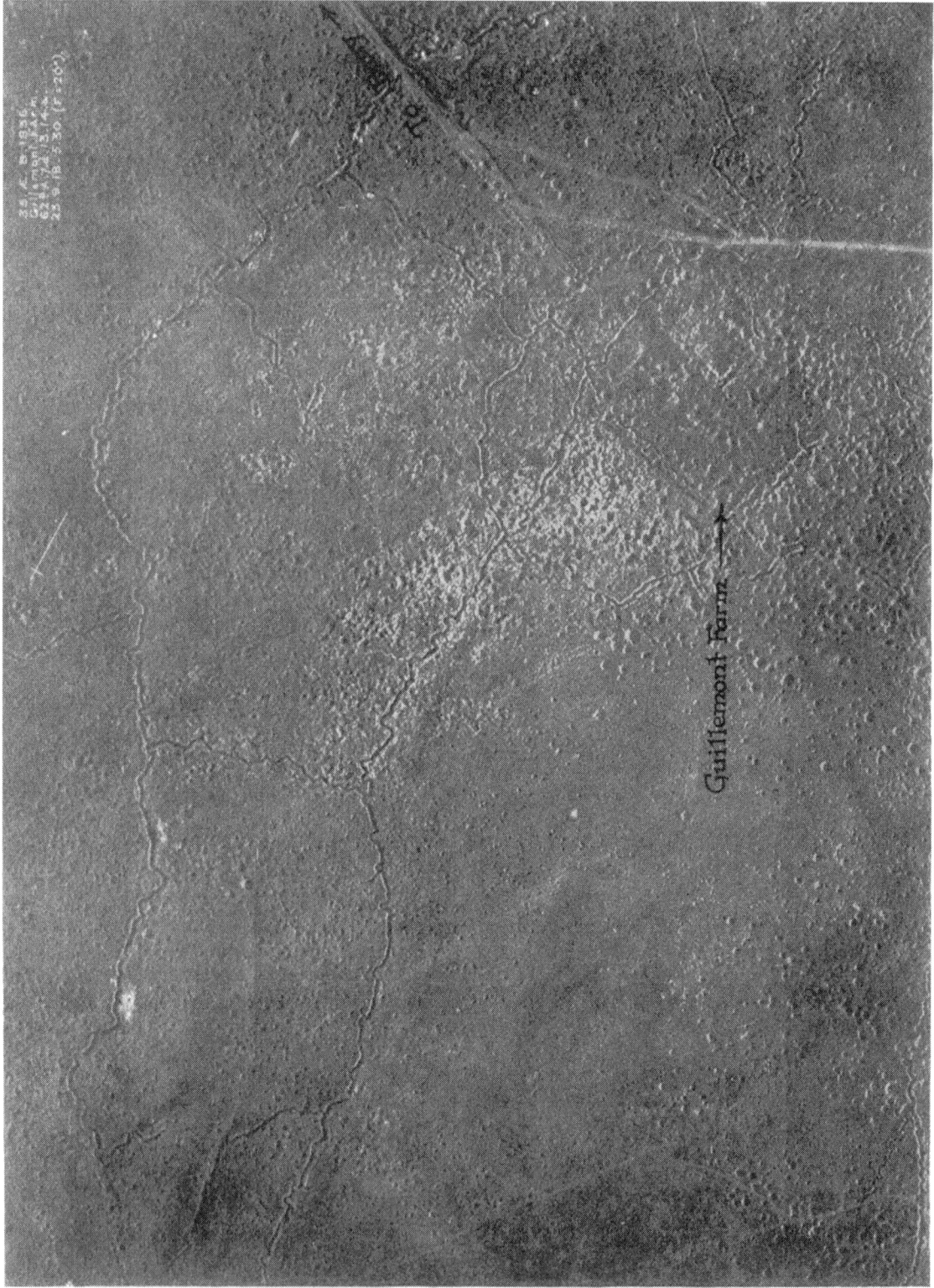

Guillemont Farm →

GILLEMONT FARM, SHOWING THE RESULT OF THE SHELLING TO WHICH IT HAD BEEN
SUBJECTED BOTH IN 1917 AND IN MARCH AND SEPTEMBER 1918.

Vertical air photograph.

but the 18th and 12th Divisions, at the beginning of their task, were confronted with formidable redoubts such as Duncan Post, Tombois Farm, Braeton Post, and Little Priel Farm, all of which played a prominent part in the fighting of the next few days. It now became clear that another organised attack would have to be made, if we wished to make further progress on the III Corps front. Preparations for this were at once begun, as it was essential that we should gain the whole of the enemy's outer defences as early as possible, especially the important localities of Quennemont Farm, Gillemont Farm, and The Knoll. The chief importance of these places to us was that, so long as they were held by the enemy, it would be very difficult to move our artillery sufficiently far forward for it to be able to support our attacking troops with an efficient barrage beyond the main Hindenburg Line. After careful consideration, Sir Henry Rawlinson decided that they must be secured, even though this involved a preliminary operation of some magnitude.

Meanwhile, after the success of the British attacks on September 18th, and of the American attack on the St. Mihiel salient on September 12th, it had been decided between Marshal Foch and Sir Douglas Haig that four convergent and simultaneous offensives should be launched by the Allies, one by the Americans west of the Meuse in the direction of Mezières, the second by the French west of the Argonne in close conjunction with the American attack and in the same direction, the third by the British on the St. Quentin–Cambrai front in the general direction of Maubeuge, the fourth by the Belgian and Allied forces in Flanders in the direction of Ghent.

The decision to attack the Hindenburg Line ; the Fourth Army reinforced

The most important and critical of these attacks was the one to be undertaken by the British Armies against the Hindenburg Line.[1]

On September 22nd the following orders for the British attack on the St. Quentin–Cambrai front were issued by General Headquarters—

" The First Army will attack on ' Z ' Day (September 27th) with a view to capturing the heights of Bourlon Wood in the first instance. It will then push forward and secure its left on the Sensée River and operate so as to protect the left of the Third Army.

[1] In the words of his despatch of December 21st, 1918, Sir Douglas Haig's views were that—

" The results to be obtained from these different attacks depended in a peculiarly large degree upon the British attack in the centre. It was here that the enemy's defences were most highly organised. If these were broken, the threat directed at his vital systems of lateral communication would of necessity react upon his defence elsewhere.

" On the other hand, the long period of sustained offensive action through which the British Armies had already passed had made large demands both upon the troops themselves and upon my available reserves. Throughout our attacks from the 8th August onwards our losses in proportion to the results achieved and the numbers of prisoners taken had been consistently and remarkably small. In the aggregate, however, they were considerable, and in the face of them an attack upon so formidably organised a position as that which now confronted us could not be lightly undertaken. Moreover, the political effects of an unsuccessful attack upon a position so well known as the Hindenburg Line would be large, and would go far to revive the declining moral not only of the German Army but of the German people.

" These different considerations were present to my mind. The probable results of a costly failure, or, indeed, of anything short of a decided success, in any attempt upon the main defences of the Hindenburg Line were obvious ; but I was convinced that the British attack was the essential part of the general scheme, and that the moment was favourable. Accordingly I decided to proceed with the attack. . . ."

T

" The Third Army will operate in the direction of the general line Le Cateau–Solesmes. It will attack on ' Z ' Day (September 27th) in conjunction with the First Army and will press forward to secure the passages of the Canal de l'Escaut so as to be in a position to co-operate closely with the Fourth Army on ' Z ' + 2 day (September 29th). The Third Army will assist the Fourth Army with counter-battery work on the enemy's guns in the region La Terrière–Villers Outréaux.

" The Fourth Army, protected on its right flank by the First French Army, will deliver the main attack against the enemy's defences from Le Tronquoy to Le Catelet, both inclusive, operating in the direction of the general line Bohain-Busigny. The bombardment will commence on ' Z ' day (September 27th) and the assault will be delivered on ' Z ' + 2 day (September 29th)." [1]

On receipt of the above orders, Sir Henry Rawlinson issued his own orders for the attack ; these will be explained in the next chapter. [2]

The following reinforcements were placed at the disposal of the Fourth Army :

The XIII Corps Headquarters, with the 25th, 50th, and 66th Divisions.

The II American Corps Headquarters, with the 27th and 30th American Divisions.

Before proceeding with the narrative of events after September 20th, it will be well to relate very briefly the distribution of these

The readjustment of the front reinforcements, and the consequent changes in dispositions which resulted between September 21st and 25th.

On September 20th orders were issued by Sir Henry Rawlinson for the readjustment of the Fourth Army front, which was to commence on the night of September 21st ; as the result of it the boundaries and dispositions of troops prior to the attack on the main Hindenburg Line would be as follows :—

The IX Corps would have the 6th, 1st, and 46th Divisions in line, from right to left, and the 32nd Division in reserve, on a front of some 10,000 yards from the junction of the Fourth Army with the First French Army, immediately north-west of Francilly-Selency, to a point on the ridge just south of Buisson Gaulaine Farm. This necessitated the relief of the 4th Australian Division by the 46th Division.

The combined Australian and II American Corps would have the 30th and 27th American Divisions in line, the 5th and 3rd Australian Divisions in support, and the 2nd Australian Division in reserve, from the northern boundary of the IX Corps, just south of Buisson Gaulaine Farm, to opposite The Knoll ; a front of 8,000 yards, practically facing the Bellicourt tunnel. This necessitated the relief of the 74th, 18th,

[1] The dates in brackets were not in the original order, but were fixed afterwards. The Franco-American attack in the direction of Mezières was to take place on September 26th, and the Allied attack in Belgium on September 28th.

[2] It must be understood that there were two attacks in view—the preliminary attack against the outer defences of the Hindenburg Line on the III and IX Corps fronts, and the main attack against the Hindenburg Line itself on September 29th. The Army Commander's orders, referred to here, only dealt with the preparations for the main attack, but preparations for the preliminary attack by the troops already in the line were going on simultaneously.

and 1st Australian Divisions by American troops. The whole of the
Australian and American troops were to be under the command of Sir
John Monash, with whom General Read, commanding the II American
Corps, would work in the closest touch ; the reason for this arrangement
will be explained later.

North of the Australian and II American Corps, the III Corps, shortly
to be reduced to two divisions owing to the departure of the 74th and
58th Divisions to another army, would hold a narrow front of 3,000
yards to the northern boundary of the Fourth Army east of Peizières,
with the 12th Division in line and the 18th Division in reserve.

The XIII Corps, with the 25th, 50th, and 66th Divisions, would be in
army reserve.

This redistribution was to be complete by September 25th.

The readjustment was carried out as ordered. On September
19th the 46th Division was transferred to the IX Corps and concentrated
in the Tertry area.[1] On the night of September 21st this division took
over the line from Berthaucourt to a point just south of Buisson Gaulaine
Farm, relieving the 4th Australian Division and a portion of the 1st
British Division. On relief, the 4th Australian Division was moved to
a rest area near Amiens. The 1st Division was now able to side-slip
southwards and thus shorten the front of the 6th Division. This enabled
the IX Corps to hurry on with their preparations for securing the high
ground between Selency, Fayet, and Fresnoy-le-Petit, which it was
desirable to capture as a preliminary to the attack on the main
Hindenburg Line.

On September 22nd and 23rd the 27th and 30th Divisions of the
II American Corps commenced to arrive in the Fourth Army area by 'bus
and train, and were concentrated in the Tincourt and Haut-Allaines areas
prior to going into the line on the Australian Corps front. On the night
of September 23rd the 30th American Division relieved the 1st Australian
Division in the line from a point just south of Buisson Gaulaine Farm
to Malakoff Farm. On relief, the 1st Australian Division was moved
back to a rest area near Abbeville.[2]

On September 23rd the arrangements necessary to enable the 27th
American Division to take over the remainder of the new front of the Australian Corps were completed, and on the night of September 24th this
division relieved the 74th and 18th Divisions. On relief, the 74th Division
was transferred to the Fifth Army, and the 58th Division to the First Army.
The command of the front of the composite American and Australian
Corps passed to Sir John Monash at 10 a.m. on September 25th.

While these moves in the forward area were in progress, the XIII
Corps, commanded by Lieut.-Gen. Sir Thomas Morland, arrived
in the Fourth Army area from the Fifth Army, and took over the
25th Division, commanded by Maj.-Gen. J. R. E. Charles, the
50th Division, commanded by Maj.-Gen. H. C. Jackson, the 66th
Division, commanded by Maj.-Gen. H. K. Bethell, and the 18th

[1] Tertry is about 4 miles west of Holnon Wood.
[2] Although they did not realise it, the 1st and 4th Australian Divisions had fought their
last, but not least successful, battle in the Great War.

Division from the III Corps. Of these, the 18th and 50th Divisions were both in the III Corps area, and the 25th and 66th, with the XIII Corps Headquarters, were in army reserve near Albert, ready to move up as soon as required.[1]

To resume the narrative of the attacks on the outer defences of the Hindenburg Line. Little of importance occurred on the front of the IX Corps and on the southern half of the Australian Corps front between September 21st and 23rd. There was a small hostile attack near Berthaucourt on the evening of the 22nd, which was easily repulsed.

The III Corps attacks on September 21st–22nd

On the front of the III Corps, however, there was much activity. It had been decided on the 20th to make an organised attack against the enemy's advanced positions at Duncan Post, Tombois Farm, Braeton Post, and Little Priel Farm, which he was holding very strongly, and then without delay to secure Quennemont Farm, Gillemont Farm, and The Knoll, the capture of which would place the whole of the outer defences of the Hindenburg Line, north of Bellenglise, in our possession.

In order to attain this object, an attack was launched on the morning of September 21st along the whole front of the III Corps, assisted on the right by the 1st Australian Division, which captured Ruby Wood, and gained a footing in Malakoff Wood, capturing 51 prisoners. At the same time the V Corps of the Third Army attacked the trench system running due south from Villers Guislain.

On the front of the III Corps the 74th Division was given as its objective Quennemont Farm, Quennet Copse, and Gillemont Farm; the 18th Division was given The Knoll; the 12th Division Braeton Post and Little Priel Farm; and the 58th Division the trench systems round Dados Loop, north of Little Priel Farm. Four tanks of the 2nd Tank Battalion were detailed to assist the 74th Division, and seven tanks of the same battalion the 18th Division. The assault was delivered at 5.40 a.m. under cover of a creeping barrage. Before " zero " the enemy's artillery fire was severe; it increased when our barrage fell at " zero," and remained heavy all day. The action which ensued lasted during the whole of September 21st and continued throughout that night with unabated violence until the early hours of September 22nd.

On the right, the 74th Division reached both Quennemont Farm and Gillemont Farm, in addition to Quennet Copse and Cat Post.[2] The tanks assisting this division were unable to give any assistance, as two broke down before reaching the " starting line," and the remaining two

---

[1] These four divisions remained in the XIII Corps until the end of the campaign.
The 25th Division had just been reformed from battalions drawn from the 7th, 23rd, and 48th Divisions in Italy.
The 50th Division was composed of battalions brought from Egypt and Salonika, in June, since when they had been training and undergoing treatment for malaria.
The 66th Division was composed of the South African Brigade under Brig.-Gen. Tanner, and two brigades composed of battalions which had come from Egypt and Salonika, at the same time as those of the 50th Division, and had since then been training and undergoing treatment for malaria.

[2] The enemy, however, found his way back into Cat Post through a gap which then existed between the 74th and 18th Divisions. This post was recaptured during the night by the 10th King's Shropshire Light Infantry in a very gallant manner, together with 200 prisoners and 30 machine-guns, although the battalion had been reduced by that time to under 200 men.

were put out of action by hostile artillery fire early in the day. The 18th Division secured Duncan Post and Doleful Post, but, on approaching The Knoll, the attack broke down before the annihilating fire of the machine-guns holding that locality and Tombois Farm. Five of the seven tanks which supported the attack were put out of action at various stages of the advance, and only one reached The Knoll. Those of the crews of these tanks, who had the good fortune to return from the fight, reported that the machine-gun fire had often been so heavy that they had been unable to work their guns. Before this machine-gun fire was encountered, the 53rd Brigade of the 18th Division had succeeded in pushing forward to Egg Post, but was almost immediately counter-attacked and driven back. While this fighting was taking place, the 12th Division gained a footing in Braeton Post, and the attack of the 58th Division reached a line some 300 yards short of Dados Loop.

From this time onward the enemy's resistance became even more determined. The troops of the 230th Brigade were ejected from Quennemont Farm by a counter-attack, and eventually held a line slightly in advance of their original " starting line." The troops of the 231st Brigade, which had succeeded in reaching Gillemont Farm, held out until 2 p.m., and then fell back to the general line which was being consolidated; the troops of the 18th Division, which had succeeded in penetrating to Duncan Post and Doleful Post, were forced to withdraw. The 12th Division was unable to advance further on account of heavy machine-gun fire from Little Priel Farm and Heythorp Post. By 5 p.m. it was clear that the objectives assigned for the day's operations could not be gained without fresh impetus, although attempts were still being made to push forward.

Exhibiting the same splendid spirit that they had shown all through their advance, the troops of the III Corps refused to admit defeat without another attempt to gain their objective. In spite of the heavy fighting and the many disappointments which the 21st had yielded, all ranks realised the imperative necessity of pressing forward and allowing the enemy no respite. At 12.15 a.m., therefore, on September 22nd the attack was resumed, and the troops advanced in the bright moonlight without much difficulty. The artillery supplied the requisite support by putting down a creeping barrage.

By daylight on the 22nd the 74th Division again held Cat Post; the 18th Division had secured Duncan and Doleful Posts; the 12th Division had captured Heythorp Post and Little Priel Farm; and the 58th Division Dados Loop. Some further progress was made later in the day, when Braeton Post was again captured. During the afternoon of the 22nd the enemy launched several counter-attacks; one against the 74th Division just south of Duncan Post, and another against the 18th Division in the vicinity of Doleful Post; these were driven off with heavy loss to the enemy. In the evening, following on the repulse of another counter-attack from the direction of Gillemont Farm, in which our artillery caused heavy losses to the attacking infantry, the 11th Royal Fusiliers of the 18th Division, taking advantage of the confusion amongst the retreating enemy, left its trenches in pursuit and captured a strong point with 80 prisoners near Duncan Post, which had been holding them up all day.[1] Thus the bitter fighting of the past forty-eight hours had placed the III Corps in possession of a large part of the important positions which had been its objectives since September 18th.

During the next few days a number of small operations were undertaken by the 18th Division with a view to improving our line by capturing Tombois Farm and Egg Post, but without success. Further north the 12th Division, which had relieved the 58th Division on the night of September 23rd, was driven out of Dados Loop by a hostile counter-attack. Although the enemy also made persistent efforts to regain the posts he had lost, the line remained practically unchanged till the III Corps was relieved by the Americans on the night of September 24th.

It was important for the IX Corps both to gain observation over the main Hindenburg Line, and to improve the position on its right flank, prior to the general attack on the 29th, and Sir Walter Braithwaite devoted all his attention to attaining these objects. The IX Corps, therefore, resumed operations on the morning of September 24th against Selency and the Quadrilateral, which had been causing the 6th Division so much trouble, and also against Fresnoy-le-Petit and the high ground north of Gricourt. A fresh battalion of Mark V tanks, the 13th, was allotted to the IX Corps for this attack. The right flank was to be secured by the First French Army, which was to attack Francilly-Selency and Manchester Hill.

The IX Corps operations on September 24th

The attack was launched at 5 a.m. On the right the 6th Division, supported by eight tanks, moved forward towards Selency, the Quadrilateral, and the high ground north of the latter place. The 1st Division in the centre pressed forward through Fresnoy-le-Petit, and also south and north of the village towards the high ground about Mont Needle and the hook-shaped ridge north of Gricourt. Twelve tanks assisted the attack of the 1st Division, and were employed to reduce the enemy's resistance in Fresnoy-le-Petit and in the wood north-east of the village. Simultaneously the 46th Division on the left attacked Pontruet and Ste. Hélène.

Although the attack was apparently expected by the enemy, satisfactory progress was made on the whole of the corps front, except on the right at the Quadrilateral and Selency. Here, as on previous occasions, the enemy offered a stout resistance and checked the advance early in the day. By 8 a.m., however, the 6th Division had gained a footing in the trench system immediately west of Selency and in the western and northern portions of the Quadrilateral. The neighbourhood of the Quadrilateral was the scene of continuous bombing throughout the day. At nightfall, there were still some Germans in the Quadrilateral itself, and a German post still held out south of the Quadrilateral between the right of the 6th Division and the French. A well executed moonlight attack, carried out by the 1st Leicestershire of the 71st Brigade about 11 p.m., secured the post south of the Quadrilateral.

In the centre the 1st Division made good progress. Fresnoy-le-Petit was cleared by the 3rd Brigade, but heavy fire from machine-guns

[1] The stout resistance made in this area was partly accounted for by the reinforcement of the Alpine Corps and 2nd Guard Division by the 232nd Division.

holding Marronniers Wood was then encountered. Outflanking these machine-guns, the 3rd Brigade pushed on to its objectives west and south of Gricourt and secured them by noon. The machine-guns at Marronniers Wood held out until finally overcome at 5 p.m., when 5 officers and 130 other ranks were captured in the wood.

On the left front of the 1st Division the 2nd Brigade met with resistance at Cornouillers Wood, and sustained numerous casualties from machine-gun firing from positions in Pontruet, which the 46th Division had been unable to capture. Nevertheless, some of the brigade reached the high ground of the objective north of Gricourt, only to be practically annihilated by artillery fire, and by enfilade machine-gun fire from Pontruet. In this fighting the 1st Northamptonshire of the 2nd Brigade particularly distinguished itself in a very difficult position. A trench line between Gricourt and Pontruet was consolidated and held, despite numerous hostile counter-attacks to regain it. At one time, when counter-attacked by a force of over 400 of the enemy, the garrison, consisting of men of the 2nd Royal Sussex, finding themselves temporarily short of ammunition, moved a Lewis gun out in front of the trenches, and, under cover of its fire, delivered a bayonet charge which completely routed the enemy and succeeded in securing 50 prisoners.[1] The 2nd Royal Sussex was later reinforced by the 2nd King's Royal Rifle Corps, which also did excellent work in repulsing the enemy's counter-attacks.

Although Gricourt itself had not been given as one of the objectives for the day's operations, the 3rd Brigade captured it in the afternoon under cover of a hastily arranged bombardment. This operation by the 3rd Brigade, following on the capture of Fresnoy-le-Petit, was a fine performance. Ably planned at short notice by the brigade commander, it was executed with great skill and determination, and well exemplifies the value of initiative by subordinate commanders. This success was followed at dusk by a local attack by the 2nd Brigade, which regained the high ground north of Gricourt.

The failure of the 46th Division to secure Pontruet has already been mentioned. On the left, however, this division cleared Ste. Hélène without difficulty. Its efforts to secure Pontruet were redoubled, when it was found that the possession of this village was so important for the success of the 1st Division attack, and by 8 a.m. the northern portion of the village had been captured together with a large number of prisoners;[2] the enemy, however, still held the southern portion. At 7.30 p.m. the 46th Division made a further attempt to capture the southern portion of Pontruet, but was again unsuccessful.[3]

On the right of the IX Corps the XXXVI French Corps captured all its objectives except Manchester Hill, and secured the village of Francilly-Selency, together with 200 prisoners.

---

[1] These men belonged to two regiments of the 11th Division, which had been alarmed in its rest billets three hours before " zero " and hurried to the front. This division carried out three counter-attacks in the Gricourt area during the day and assisted in the defence of Pontruet.

[2] It was in this attack that Lieutenant John Barrett, 1/5th Leicestershire, so distinguished himself. See Appendix E, No. 3.

[3] The total captures of the IX Corps during the fighting on the 24th exceeded 1,500 prisoners.

Taking advantage of the success attending the fighting of September 24th, the 6th Division pushed forward strong fighting patrols during the night towards Selency and the Château. By 10.30 a.m. on the morning of September 25th, the enemy's main resistance had been overcome, and the patrols were making good progress. Meanwhile, fighting was still in progress among the maze of trenches constituting the Quadrilateral, but by 6 p.m. the whole of it was in our hands, and Selency and Château Wood had also been secured. Although counter-attacked severely north of Gricourt during September 25th, the 1st Division retained all the ground it had gained on the 24th, and improved its position.

The pressure maintained by the IX Corps on September 25th and 26th

The situation on the right of the IX Corps front was further improved on the morning of September 26th, when the 6th Division established our line well east of Selency and the Quadrilateral, and the French captured Manchester Hill. Thus the right flank of the Fourth Army was secure, and sufficient observation of the main Hindenburg Line had been gained.

Meanwhile, the preparations for the attack to be launched against the main Hindenburg Line on September 29th were well in hand. At 10.30 p.m. on September 26th the preliminary bombardment for the attack by the Fourth Army on the main Hindenburg Line began with " BB " gas shell,[1] which was used until 6 a.m. on the 27th, after which high explosive and shrapnel were employed.[2] This bombardment continued without intermission until " zero " on the 29th.

The bombardment of the Hindenburg Line begun on September 26th

During the night of September 26th the 30th American Division improved its position at certain points with a view to securing a better " starting line." Further north the general line of Quennemont Farm–Gillemont Farm had been selected as the " starting line " of the 27th American Division. As, however, in spite of great self-sacrifice and gallantry, the troops of the III Corps had been unable to capture this line before being relieved, it devolved on the 27th American Division to secure it. In order to attain this object, the 27th American Division, assisted by one company of tanks of the 4th Mark V Tank Battalion, attacked at 5.30 a.m. on September 27th, under cover of a powerful artillery barrage. Determined opposition was encountered from the 54th German Division, which had just relieved the 232nd Division, and a very involved situation supervened. Throughout the morning the fighting was most severe, as the enemy launched strong counter-attacks whenever any gain of ground was achieved by the Americans. In the afternoon the situation slightly improved, but all attempts to ascertain the exact situation failed, com-

Minor operations by the 27th and 30th American Divisions on September 26th and 27th

---

[1] The " BB " gas was almost identical with the German Yellow Cross, or " Mustard," Gas.

[2] It was originally intended that the preliminary bombardment should begin at 6 a.m. on September 27th (see Sir Douglas Haig's orders on page 138), but when it was found that 30,000 gas shell, the first consignment of shell filled with our new gas, would arrive from England in time and could be made available, it was arranged that the forty-eight hour bombardment with high explosive and shrapnel should be preceded by a gas bombardment lasting eight hours and beginning at 10 p.m. on the 26th.

munication with the leading troops being almost impossible. Subsequent events, however, showed that although small parties of the 27th American Division had reached their objective and gallantly maintained themselves there, the line as a whole was not materially advanced by the day's operations.

Meanwhile, good news had been received from other parts of the allied front. On September 26th and 27th the French and American

The attacks of the Allied Armies on other parts of the front Armies had attacked on both sides of the Argonne between the Meuse and the Suippe, and had taken over 8,000 prisoners. The difficulties, however, of the country and the communications rendered further advance slow, and gave the enemy time partially to recover and reorganise. The Third and First British Armies had attacked on September 27th on a front of thirteen miles, between Gouzeaucourt and the Sensée river, had made excellent progress, and had taken 10,000 prisoners. On September 28th the advance of these two armies was continued, and their troops established themselves on the east bank of the Canal de l'Escaut at Marcoing. The enemy, however, made most determined efforts to prevent the Third and First Armies from extending their bridgeheads on either side of Cambrai. The Canal de l'Escaut formed a very formidable obstacle and rendered a further advance most difficult. That this would be so had been fully realised by General Headquarters, and the attack of the Fourth Army on September 29th was intended to turn the flank of the enemy's defences on the Third and First Army fronts, and enable a general advance to be continued. On September 28th the British, French, and Belgians, under the command of King Albert, had also attacked between the Lys and Dixmude and had met with complete success; transport difficulties, however, as in the case of the Americans and French, prevented a rapid advance after their initial victory.

The Fourth Army had now been fighting for 51 days, driving the enemy from position to position. During this period it had employed

The situation on the Fourth Army front on September 28th 19 divisions to defeat 41 German divisions. The enemy's losses in prisoners alone, since August 8th, amounted to 46,500, including 1,100 officers, while our casualties in killed, wounded, and missing had reached 72,000.

That the enemy intended to hold the Hindenburg Line to the utmost of his power and resources there was no reason to doubt; not a single trench rumour of a further retirement reached us from prisoners. It was estimated that our attack on the 29th would be opposed between Le Tronquoy and Vendhuile by seven divisions, and that this line could be reinforced within 72 hours by six more divisions from reserve.[1] The moral of the German troops, after their severe defeats, had undoubtedly much deteriorated and would continue to do so with every fresh retirement, but there still remained a considerable number of stout-hearted machine-gunners who could cause us much trouble, and there were certain regiments, and even divisions, that retained a good fighting spirit. The moral of our

---

[1] Actually eight divisions were encountered : the 2nd, 8th, 11th, 54th, 75th Reserve, 79th Reserve, 121st and 185th Divisions ; six more joined in the battle within seventy-two hours : the 2nd Guard, 21st, 25th Reserve, 84th, 119th, and 221st Divisions.

own troops was continuing to rise every day with the consciousness of superiority over the enemy, and it was further increased by the arrival of the fresh British and American divisions which had reinforced the army since the 18th.

We were undoubtedly face to face with a very strong position; but all ranks realised the far-reaching issues of the result of the forthcoming attack, and, as on August 8th, there existed in the army the will to conquer, and the confidence in victory, that foreshadow success.

FOURTH ARMY HEADQUARTERS ESTABLISHED IN A CAMOUFLAGED CAMP AT ETERPIGNY, NEAR PÉRONNE, IN SEPTEMBER, 1918.

CHAPTER VIII

THE STORMING OF THE HINDENBURG LINE, SEPTEMBER 29TH

Maps 2, 8, and 10; and Panoramic Photographs 6 and 7.

The German defences—The preparations for the attack—The communications—Secrecy—The temporary amalgamation of the Australian and II American Corps—The frontages of attack —The objectives—The co-ordination with flank armies—The artillery—The preliminary bombardment—The ammunition supply—The allotment of tanks—The special mission of the 5th Cavalry Brigade and the armoured cars—The rôle of the Cavalry Corps—The assembly of the troops—The assault—The IX Corps ; the action of the 1st Division—The capture of the first objective by the 46th Division—The advance of the 32nd Division to the second objective—The result of the day's fighting by the IX Corps—The Australian-American Corps ; the attack of the American divisions—The 30th American Division—The 27th American Division—The action of the 5th Australian Division—The action of the 3rd Australian Division—The armoured cars—The III Corps operations—The situation of the III Corps at dusk—The result of the battle—The orders for September 30th.

THE Hindenburg Line was selected and organised for defence in the latter end of 1916, and the work was continued during the spring of 1917. It was the direct result of the battle of the Somme, as it was to this line that the Germans retired in March, 1917, in order to shorten their line and make good the losses suffered during their defeats of the preceding summer and autumn. It was first discovered and photographed, by the 4th Brigade, Royal Air Force, in February, 1917, thus confirming vague rumours of its existence received from refugees repatriated by the enemy through Switzerland.[1] Since March, 1918, when the British Army had been driven back, the Hindenburg defences had been unoccupied and more or less neglected.

The German defences

In addition to our previous knowledge of the line, further valuable information had been acquired. On August 8th a defence scheme, complete in every detail, for the Hindenburg Line between the Oise and Bellicourt, was captured at a German Corps Headquarters. This document was undated, but was evidently drawn up early in 1917.[2] That the original

---

[1] The country and nature of the defences were well known to the commander and staff of the Fourth Army, under whose direction careful reconnaissances of the line from St. Quentin to Havrincourt had been carried out between April and July, 1917.

[2] This document, in addition to showing all the trenches and wire, gave the position of every battery, its calibre, barrage lines, and observation posts ; the position of all sound-ranging and flash spotting sections ; the location of every artillery and infantry headquarters and of all battle stations ; and that of every dug-out, both concrete and otherwise, and of every machine-gun emplacement. It also revealed to us the rear organisation, that is to say, the divisional sectors ; ammunition and supply dumps ; railheads ; billets and camps, specifying the accommodation for men and horses ; the signal communication and electric power installations ; and the selected places for balloon sheds and landing grounds.

policy for the defence of the Hindenburg Line was one of rigid defence, is clearly shown in the following extracts from this document :

" The Siegfried Line makes full use, along extended stretches, of the front line of defences afforded by the Bellicourt–St. Quentin Canal. . . . The strength of these defences, increased as it is by inundated areas, the very extensive possibilities of mutual flanking support by the different sectors, and the, generally considered, good artillery observation render the line very strong. Added to this is the advantage that the Siegfried Line, having been reconnoitred without interference from the enemy, and plans having been drawn up for its occupation by troops of all arms, a systematic withdrawal from the outpost positions can be effected.

" The Siegfried Line is considered to afford the most favourable conditions for a stubborn defence by a minimum garrison. It is therefore adapted to the requirements of obstinate close combat.

" Its position, behind the natural defences offered by the Bellicourt–St. Quentin Canal, affords the enemy free use of many favourable points of observation close in front of it. The use of these points by the enemy must be hindered as long as possible. For this reason outposts will be established before the Siegfried Line with the object of maintaining contact with the enemy and obstructing his reconnaissance. These will retire on the Siegfried Line before an enemy attack. It is the duty of the Command to prevent any decisive action being fought further forward than the first line of defence of the Siegfried Line which is prepared for a stubborn defensive. It must be clearly understood by units of all arms that the battle will be fought from the first line trenches of the Siegfried Line."

It must, however, be remembered that, since this document was written, the superiority, under modern conditions, of defence in depth over a rigid defence had been universally recognised. There is little doubt that this change in policy, to a certain extent, altered the plans for occupying the line previous to our attack, and added to the confusion and disorganisation of the enemy.

The attack of the Fourth Army involved the surmounting of two widely different types of obstacle. In the southern half of the front, where the St. Quentin Canal runs through open country, the enemy's main defence line was sited east of the canal, which provided a naturally formidable obstacle on its immediate front. The trenches in this part of the line were not so formidable as in the northern, or tunnel, sector. Along the whole length of the canal bank, however, concrete machine-gun emplacements had been constructed to enfilade the wire, which was erected along the inside slopes of the western bank. Moreover, in order to keep the water at a sufficient depth, the canal had been dammed at Bellenglise ; in consequence, the canal bed south of the village was dry for a certain distance.

In the northern half of the front, where the St. Quentin Canal runs through the Bellicourt tunnel, the main defences, also of an extremely formidable nature, were sited on the western side of the canal tunnel,

To face page 149.

Hargicourt—Bellicourt road

No. 64.

WIRE AT BELLICOURT

THE THICK BELTS OF WIRE DEFENDING THE BELLICOURT TUNNEL.
The gaps made by our guns can be seen in the foreground.

No. 65.

Spoil heap

Entrance to Tunnel under construction.

Bellenglise

22.N.3199.
10·5·17-4

G34.b0.4.

St Quentin Canal

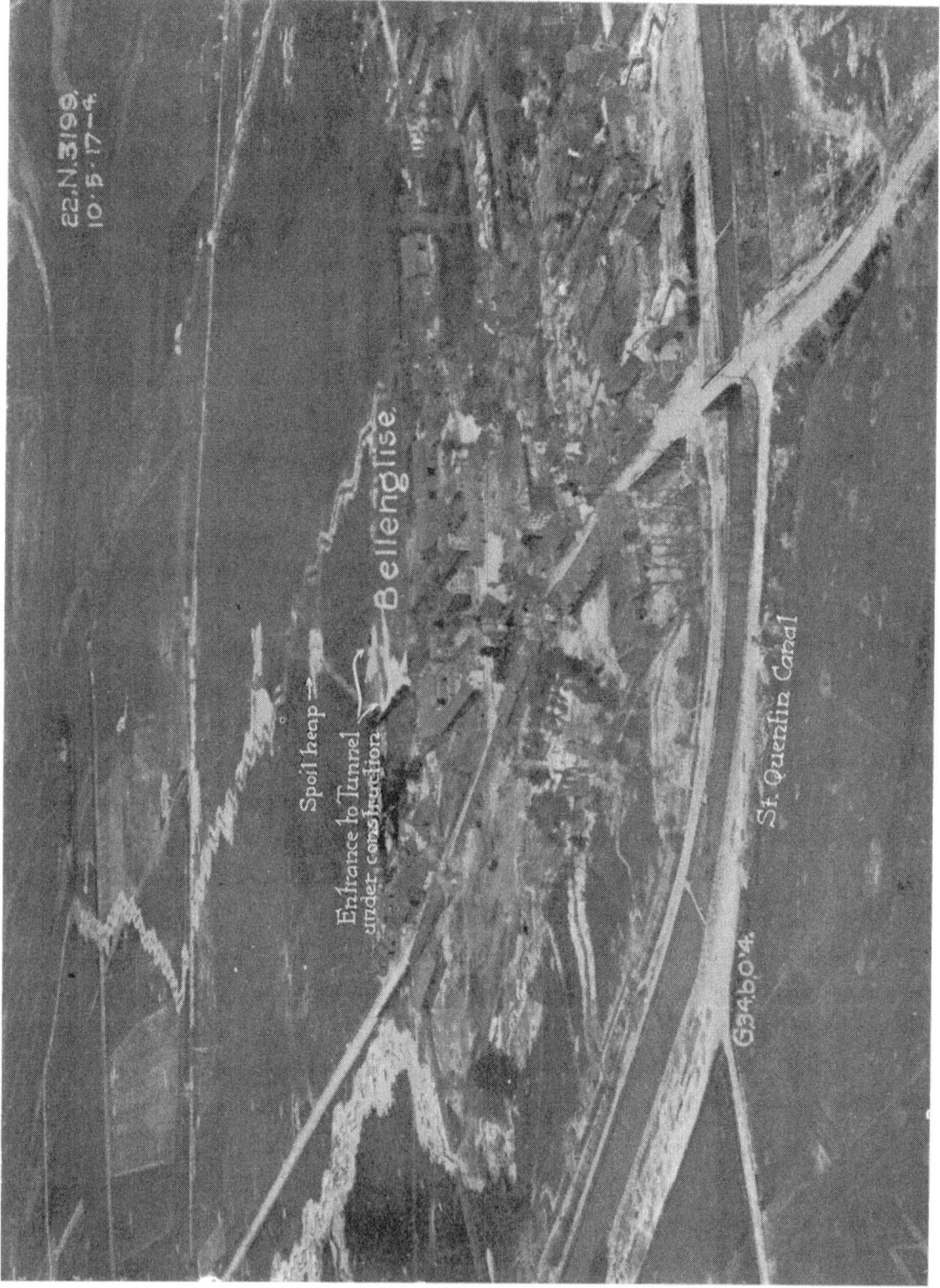

BELLENGLISE, SHOWING THE UNDERGROUND TUNNEL IN COURSE OF CONSTRUCTION.

Oblique air photograph, taken in May, 1917.

and consisted of two or three strong lines of trenches, each protected by several thick belts of wire. Furthermore, the tunnel itself, which was connected by passages with the ground level, provided good cover for reserves. Besides these main defences, numerous trenches had been constructed at various points to counteract local weaknesses, or to take advantage of the lie of the ground and give a good field of fire. The villages of Bellenglise, Bellicourt, and Bony had been strongly fortified.

The whole scheme, combining, as it did, the skilful use of the ground with artificial aid in the shape of wire, dug-outs, and machine-gun emplacements, and with the judicious disposition of field and machine-guns, had undoubtedly resulted in the creation of a very strong defensive position, which well merited the reputation attached to it. A study of the defence scheme, however, showed that the German High Command fully realised that there were weak points in the position, and this was confirmed by the manner in which the enemy was fighting for every inch of ground in his outer defences. One serious drawback to the Bellicourt tunnel defences was the fact that the high ground about Quennemont Farm, Gillemont Farm, and The Knoll, when no longer in German possession, gave magnificent observation over them, and also provided the necessary cover for artillery to approach to close quarters for the purpose of dealing with the belts of wire that protected the defences. Another weakness was the salient at Bellenglise, which, overlooked as it was from the high ground both to the south and north-west, was very vulnerable to the converging fire of artillery. Further, owing to the configuration of the ground, it was difficult for the enemy, once the outer defences were lost, to find positions, not under hostile observation,[1] in which to place his artillery or collect his reserves for counter-attack. Full advantage of these weaknesses was taken in drawing up the plan of attack and in allotting the objectives.

Behind the main Hindenburg Line there was only one single line of trenches to arrest our progress. This line, of which the wiring was not complete, ran from Lesdins to Le Catelet, passing west of Magny-la-Fosse and Nauroy.[2] It is true that there was another line further east, namely the Masnières–Beaurevoir–Fonsomme Line ; this, however, was 5,000 to 6,000 yards away from the main Hindenburg Line, and was too far distant to play any part in the defence of the canal.[3]

Such, then, was the nature of the defences opposed to us. It has fallen to the lot of few commanders to be provided with such detailed information as to the nature of the enemy's defences as was furnished by the German memorandum and maps already referred to.

The orders issued by Sir Henry Rawlinson on September 22nd [4]

[1] By constructing underground tunnels, especially a very extensive one between Bellenglise and Magny-la-Fosse, the Germans had overcome to a considerable extent the difficulty of massing supports and reserves presented by the lie of the ground. The captured plans, corroborated by prisoners' statements and photographs, had, however, revealed to us the exact position of these tunnels and of their exits ; with this knowledge in our possession, they became to the Germans a source of weakness rather than of strength.

[2] Usually called the Hindenburg reserve, or Le Catelet–Nauroy, line.

[3] Opposite the Fourth Army front the northern part of this line was called the Masnières—Beaurevoir, and the southern part the Beaurevoir—Fonsomme Line.

[4] See page 138.

defined the general plan of attack, and were amplified on subsequent

The preparations for
the attack
days by a series of instructions dealing with the details of the operation.

The preliminary arrangements for the attack were, generally speaking, identical with those for August 8th, but the IX Corps, in addition, had to make special preparations for crossing the canal. For this purpose 3,000 life-belts were obtained and issued to the storming troops, as were also a few light portable boats and a number of ladders for scaling the banks of the canal. On the day prior to the attack these were tested with success on the banks of the Somme.

Much work had to be carried out to improve the forward communications, which were practically non-existent. Roads, rapidly constructed in each divisional sector, were definitely allotted to

The communications
infantry, artillery, and tanks, and were clearly marked by signboards throughout. Units with distant objectives were given priority on certain roads between prescribed hours. Pioneer battalions and road construction companies were told off to improve certain roads as the attack progressed. Furthermore, the IX and III Corps made special arrangements for the repair of the bridges over the canal at Bellenglise and Vendhuile, as soon as those places should be accessible. Railway construction was also pressed on with the utmost energy, as it would be impossible to maintain our ammunition supply to the guns unless the railway reached Roisel and Montigny Farm before the bombardment commenced.

It was decided that, as the enemy would necessarily expect an early attack on the St. Quentin–Vendhuile front, a strategical surprise of the

Secrecy
nature of that of August 8th was out of the question. A tactical surprise, however, would still be possible, that is to say the date and hour of our attack might be kept from the enemy until the assault was actually launched. As regards this question, it must be remembered that the conditions obtaining on August 8th and those on September 29th were radically different. In the former case the enemy's wire and defences were practically non-existent, and no wire-cutting or destruction of strong points and machine-gun emplacements was required. Moreover, the Germans early in August still had a considerable number of divisions in reserve in the western theatre, which they could send to reinforce the Amiens front if they received warning of the attack. A strategical surprise was, therefore, all important on August 8th in order to attain a decisive success at small cost, whilst a preliminary bombardment would not have materially contributed to the success of the attack, and might, by destroying all chance of surprise, have involved its failure. On September 29th, on the other hand, we were face to face with very strong defences. These included numerous belts of wire, concrete emplacements, and defended villages, all of which must be subjected to a very heavy bombardment prior to the assault, if they were to be captured without prohibitive losses; on the canal front, south of Bellicourt, it was not possible to employ tanks. A strategical surprise, moreover, was no longer essential; in fact, such was our superiority in men and moral, in artillery, tanks, and aeroplanes that it would positively

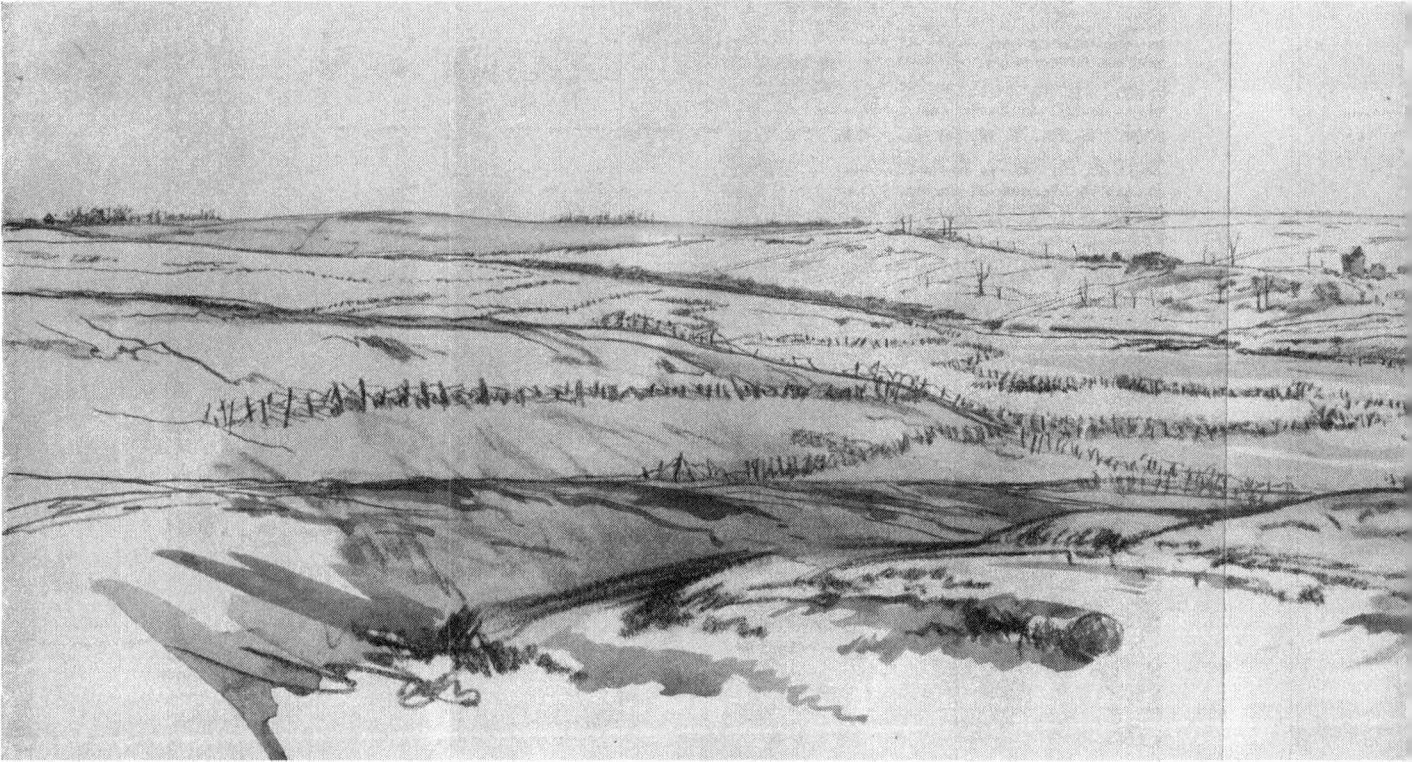

Nauroy   Etricourt   Magny la Fosse

BELLENGLISE and th

Bellenglise, and the canal embankment immediately in front of it   Le Tronquoy

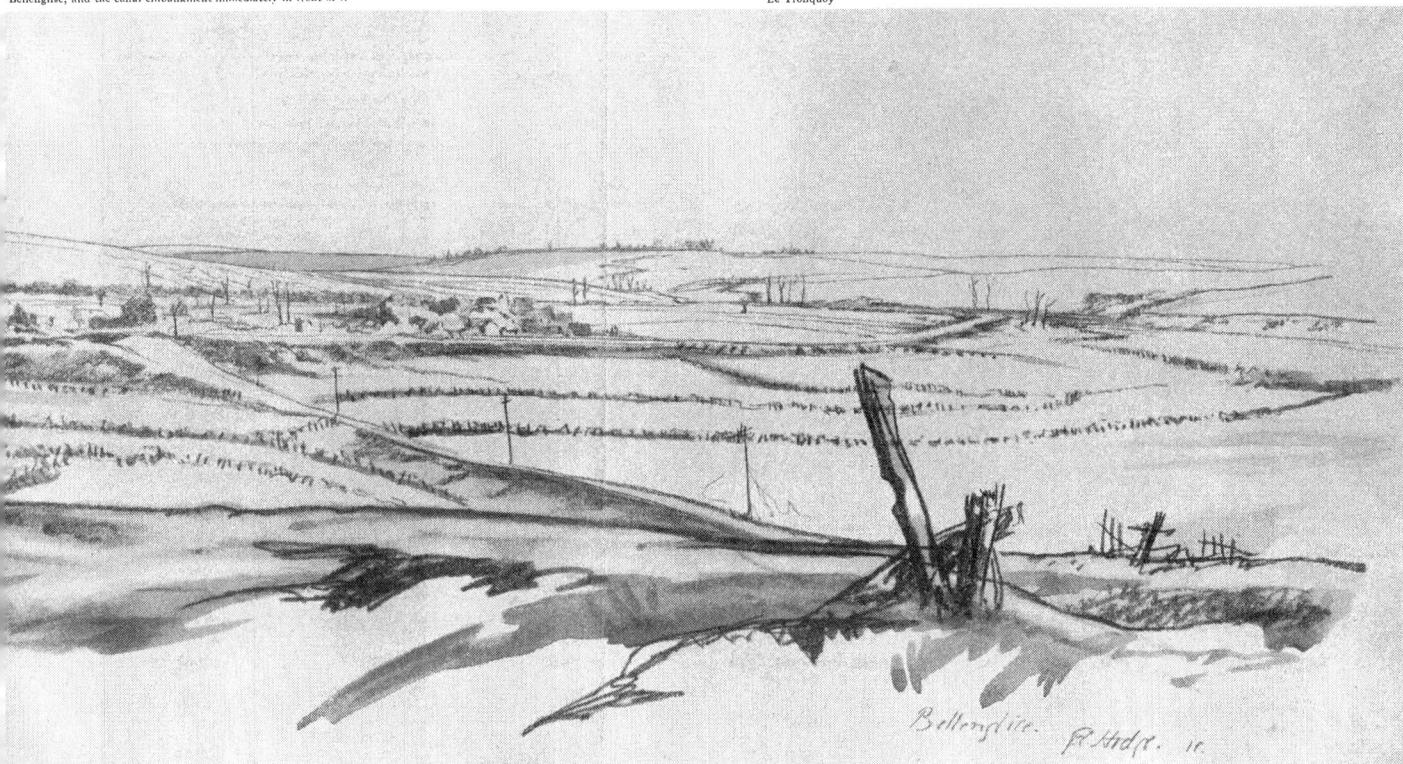

Bellenglise.

ST. QUENTIN CANAL

be to our advantage if the enemy could be induced to increase the number of troops holding the line, as his losses would be all the heavier, and the result of the attack all the more decisive. A tactical surprise, however, would undoubtedly result in reducing our casualties, and all efforts were devoted to attaining it. The necessity of maintaining the strictest secrecy with regard to the projected operations was therefore impressed on all ranks, and orders were issued that all movement of troops and transport in an easterly direction, on and after September 23rd, should take place at night.

The place of honour in the assault on the tunnel defences of the Hindenburg Line was allotted to the troops of the II American Corps,

The temporary amalgamation of the Australian and II American Corps supported by three Australian divisions. Neither the American divisions nor the II American Corps had, however, any American artillery at their disposal, and, in consequence, all the artillery, both heavy and field, to support the attack of the 27th and 30th American Divisions, was supplied by the Australian Corps or from army resources. The corps signal organisation of the II American Corps had not been completed, and such personnel as was available had had no experience of the difficulties of signal communication in battle. Further, neither General Read, the II American Corps staff, nor the 27th and 30th American Divisions, had as yet had the experience of organising and mounting an attack of such magnitude, and on the results of which so much depended.

It was, therefore, decided that, for the operation of breaking the Hindenburg Line, the 27th and 30th American Divisions should be affiliated to the Australian Corps and work under the direction of Sir John Monash and his staff, though in all other matters remaining under General Read's direct orders. The Americans would thus benefit by the extensive war experience of the Australian Corps, while maintaining the administrative unity of the II American Corps. The arrangement was no doubt somewhat complicated, and might have led to difficulties, but for the loyalty of General Read and his subordinates, and the tact of the Australians. The II American Corps established its headquarters close to those of the Australian Corps, and was thus able to keep in close touch with the situation. On September 24th, in order further to facilitate co-ordination, an Australian mission was formed and attached to the II American Corps. The object of this mission was to ensure that all American formations and units should be thoroughly acquainted with the methods of the Australians, and understand the orders they received. The personnel was carefully selected from all branches of the staff and from all arms, so that there should be an Australian officer, or senior non-commissioned officer, with every American unit down to a company of infantry.

The front on which the Fourth Army launched its attack extended from Selency to Vendhuile, a distance of twelve miles. On the right, on

The frontages of attack a front of 10,000 yards, the IX Corps was to attack from Selency to near Buisson Gaulaine Farm. The main attack of this corps, against Bellenglise and the canal north of it, was to be launched by the 46th Division, with the 32nd Division in support, while the 1st Division, operating between Gricourt and Bellenglise and keeping west of the canal, was to maintain touch with the 46th Division and press forward towards Thorigny and Le Tronquoy. South of Gricourt the 6th Division, though not taking an active part in the main attack, was to try to gain ground eastwards.

In the centre the Australian–American Corps prolonged the front to near Tombois Farm, a distance of some 8,000 yards. On this front, the 30th and 27th Divisions were to assault the tunnel defences around Bellicourt and Bony respectively, with the 5th and 3rd Australian Divisions in support, and the 2nd Australian Division in reserve.

On the left the III Corps held the remainder of the army front, some 3,000 yards, with the 12th Division in line and the 18th Division in reserve. Although not taking part in the main assault of the Hindenburg Line, its mission was, nevertheless, very important. It was to secure the left flank of the Australian–American Corps by capturing the high ground south-west of Vendhuile, and later, when the Americans had crossed over the tunnel, by clearing Vendhuile and the area west of the canal in that vicinity.

To the south of the Fourth Army the First French Army was to extend the attack as far as Essigny-le-Grand, operating on a front of six miles. To the north, the V and VI Corps of the Third British Army were to co-operate by attacking between Vendhuile and Marcoing.

The first objective, or green line, extended from the northern entrance of the Le Tronquoy tunnel to the northern entrance of the Bellicourt tunnel, passing east of Lehaucourt, Magny-la-Fosse and **The objectives** Nauroy, west of Mont St. Martin, and thence round the eastern and northern outskirts of Gouy and Le Catelet. It entailed the storming of the canal and tunnel defences from Bellenglise to Vendhuile and the forcing of the Hindenburg reserve, or Le Catelet–Nauroy, Line, which would mean an advance by the IX Corps and the 27th and 30th American Divisions of 4,000 to 5,000 yards.

When this objective was gained, the Americans were to swing north and south; to the north, with a view to cutting off the enemy holding Vendhuile, thus facilitating the task of the III Corps; to the south, in order to gain touch with the bridgehead to be established by the IX Corps at Bellenglise.[1] This exploitation would also protect the flanks of the 5th and 3rd Australian Divisions, as they moved through the American divisions towards the second objective.

While the first objective was being consolidated, and while the American divisions were engaged in exploitation, the IX Corps and the 5th and 3rd Australian Divisions were to continue the advance to the second objective, or red line. In the case of the IX Corps, this was to be carried out by the 32nd Division, which was to " leap-frog " the 46th Division and secure the tunnel defences at Le Tronquoy and the high ground round Levergies. This involved an advance beyond the first objective of from 2,000 to 4,000 yards. At the same time the 1st Division, still operating west of the canal, was to secure Thorigny and gain touch with the 32nd Division at Le Tronquoy. The 5th and 3rd Australian Divisions, after " leap-frogging " the Americans, were to capture the Masnières–Beaurevoir–

_____
[1] The extent of this exploitation is shown on Map 10 by the green dotted line.

BELLICOURT and the wire

Entrance to Tunnel

Bellicourt

ront of the HINDENBURG LINE

Fonsomme Line from east of Joncourt to Guisancourt Farm and to exploit further east to Wiancourt and Beaurevoir, an advance of from 4,000 to 5,000 yards beyond the first objective. It was expected that, even if our troops did not reach all the objectives, they would probably gain a footing in the Masnières–Beaurevoir–Fonsomme Line on the first day.

It had been decided that St. Quentin itself was not to be attacked by the First French Army, and that the French should cross the canal north and south of the town. In order to assist the

The co-ordination with flank armies

advance of the XV French Corps, which was on our immediate right, across the canal immediately north of St. Quentin, arrangements were made for this corps to have a right of way through the IX Corps area. It was also arranged that, as soon as the Le Tronquoy tunnel had been captured by the 32nd and 1st Divisions, the French were to take over the front held by the 6th Division from Selency to Gricourt. Then, when the whole of the 1st Division had passed over the Le Tronquoy tunnel, the French were to be given access to the Fresnoy-le-Petit–Thorigny–Le Tronquoy road, until such time as they were able to establish a passage over the canal at Lesdins. After crossing the tunnel at Le Tronquoy, the XV French Corps was to advance eastwards and south-eastwards within its boundary, in order to safeguard the right of the Fourth Army and turn the enemy's position about Lesdins.

On the northern flank of the army it was desirable that the 38th Division on the right of the V Corps should cross the canal and operate in a north-easterly direction, thus facilitating the passage over the canal of the other divisions of the V Corps. It was accordingly arranged that the 38th Division should have the right of way over Vendhuile bridge, as soon as it had been captured and repaired by the III Corps.

In order to give the necessary volume of fire for the preliminary bombardment, which was to destroy the defences, cut the wire, and demoralise the garrison of the Hindenburg Line, 44

The artillery

brigades of field artillery, 21 brigades of heavy artillery, and 4 long-range siege batteries were placed at the disposal of the army. These amounted in all to 1,044 field guns and howitzers, and 593 heavy guns and howitzers.

In the gas bombardment, which opened at 10 p.m. on the 26th and was maintained intermittently until 6 a.m. on September 27th, 6,336 howitzer and 26,101 18-pdr. " BB " gas shell were fired.

The preliminary bombardment

This gas bombardment took the form of concentrations of fire on localities of activity, such as headquarters and groups of batteries, as experience, gained from studying the enemy's methods, had shown that a bombardment with Yellow Cross gas was most efficacious when limited in this manner and not distributed promiscuously over a large area.

At 6 a.m. on September 27th the artillery began to fire the remainder of its programme, which was continued until " zero." This consisted of vigorous counter-battery and harassing fire, the cutting of lanes in the enemy's wire, and a sustained bombardment of selected strong points and defended localities. The bulk of the artillery was disposed around Hargi-

x

court and Lempire, where the configuration of the ground was more adapted to the grouping of batteries than it was farther north and south; there was also a big group at Le Verguier. Owing to atmospheric conditions, which curtailed photography and observation, it was impossible to locate the positions of hostile batteries with accuracy, but, nevertheless, our counter-batteries dealt with them effectively and were successful in reducing the enemy's fire. The subsequent examination of his gun positions revealed a satisfactory percentage of direct hits. The harassing fire was particularly good, and, as the result of it, the enemy's communications were cut in many places, and in numerous cases he was unable to send up either rations or reinforcements.

The wire-cutting was carried out principally by 4·5-inch and 6-inch howitzers using instantaneous fuses; where it was feasible 6-inch Newton mortars were used. In some places the wire was entirely swept away; in others, lanes were cut through it, or it was severely damaged. Generally speaking, however, it was due less to the preliminary bombardment, and more to the demoralisation of the enemy, to the help of the tanks, and to the effective artillery covering fire, that our infantry was able to penetrate the wire defences on the day of the attack.

The destruction of the deep tunnels and dug-outs was beyond the power of the artillery, and was not attempted, but their entrances and exits were subjected to heavy and unexpected concentrations, especially on September 29th. On the same day the telephone exchanges and the defended localities of Bellenglise, Nauroy, Bellicourt, and Bony were treated to a particularly heavy shelling, which reduced them to heaps of rubble. The sides of the canal were hit at frequent intervals, and ramps of débris formed, up which the attacking infantry was able to scramble. The use made of enfilade fire proved remarkably effective.

Provided as he was with substantial cover from shell fire, the enemy's losses in killed from the bombardment were probably not great, but it undoubtedly drove the defenders into their deep dug-outs and tunnels, so demoralising them that a large proportion failed to man their defences when they were attacked.

The task of supplying over 1,600 guns with the requisite ammunition was by no means light. It must be realised that it had to be brought forward and dumped while the preliminary fighting was actually in progress, and additional difficulty was caused by the unavoidably late running of trains on the newly opened line to Templeux-le-Guérard. Each day as many as fifteen ammunition trains had to be cleared, their loads of ammunition being moved forward by lorries, which, as often as not, were delayed by the congestion on the roads due to the movement of troops and supplies. When it is stated that from September 26th to October 4th 1,299,467 rounds of artillery ammunition were expended, the magnitude of the task of supplying the ammunition for an attack of this nature becomes apparent.

The existence of the canal necessarily limited the zone of activity of the tanks, and, for this reason, the majority were employed in conjunc-

tion with the Americans and Australians on the tunnel front, where the
numerous belts of wire, and the strength of the
defences, rendered the support of a large number of
tanks essential.

The allotment of tanks

The Fourth Army was allotted the 3rd, 4th, and 5th Tank Brigades
and the 17th Armoured Car Battalion for the operations. These were
sub-allotted, the 3rd Brigade to the IX Corps, the 4th Brigade to the
American divisions, and the 5th Brigade and the 17th Armoured Car
Battalion to the Australians. Only a portion of the tanks allotted were
to be engaged on the first day of the battle, as experience had shown the
necessity of keeping a large reserve in hand for subsequent days' fighting.
Consequently, in the IX Corps only the 9th Mark V Tank Battalion of
twenty-four tanks and one company of nine whippet tanks were to be
employed on the first day. Of these, sixteen Mark V tanks were to assist
the 46th Division in securing the first objective, and eight Mark V and the
nine whippet tanks were to support the advance of the 32nd Division
to the second objective. Their employment depended on the 30th
American Division securing the tunnel defences round Bellicourt, as it
had been arranged that all these tanks should cross the tunnel south
of that village, and, moving along the east bank of the canal, should join
their respective divisions in the advance eastward. In the case of the
4th and 5th Tank Brigades supporting the American and Australian
divisions, their tasks, although possibly more difficult, were straightforward. The 4th Tank Brigade, comprising the 1st, 301st American, and
4th Tank Battalions, all of which were either Mark V or Mark V star,
was to assist the American divisions to gain the first objective.[1]

The employment of the tanks of the 5th Tank Brigade, except such
tanks as were held in corps reserve, was to be governed by the principle
that each tank unit, in liaison with a definite body of infantry, should
undertake a specific operation. It was, therefore, definitely laid down
by Sir John Monash that on no account were tank units of this brigade,
on the completion of their mission, to be attached to another formation
without reference to the Australian Corps Headquarters. From the
point of view of the Tank Corps, this policy was welcomed as being the
one likely to produce the best results, as it gave the tank brigade and
battalion commanders a chance of husbanding resources, a most important
consideration. The 5th Australian Division was allotted twenty-four
tanks of the 8th Mark V Tank Battalion and eight whippet tanks of the 3rd
Battalion, and the 3rd Australian Division twenty-four tanks of the 16th
Mark V Tank Battalion and eight whippets of the 3rd Battalion. The 13th
Mark V Tank Battalion, comprising twelve tanks, together with twelve
tanks from the 16th Battalion, formed the corps reserve. These were
to move up under orders from the 5th Tank Brigade, and keep in as close
touch as possible with the progress of the battle.

[1] The original intention was to employ the 1st Tank Battalion with the 30th American
Division against Bellicourt, the 301st American Tank Battalion with the 27th American Division
against Bony, and to retain the 4th Tank Battalion in reserve. For various reasons, however,
it was found necessary to change this distribution considerably, and finally all three battalions
were used on the 29th, thirty-three Mark V tanks supporting the 30th and thirty-four the 27th
American Divisions.

The general principles governing the employment of the tanks were the same as those observed on August 8th. The tanks engaged in the initial attack on the first objective were to leave their assembly position just before " zero," join the infantry on the " starting line," and move forward with them. The noise of the tank engines during assembly was to be drowned by aeroplanes flying at a low altitude over the battlefield. As each objective was secured, the tanks were to rally at previously selected localities, while, in the event of the attack not progressing satisfactorily, alternative rallying points were chosen further in rear.

The rôle of the whippet tanks, attached to the " leap-frogging " divisions for the attack on the second objective, was purely one of exploitation. They were to penetrate further into the enemy's territory than could be expected of the infantry, in order to demoralise him and thus influence the later stages of the battle.

As the roads east of the Hindenburg Line were known to be in a fairly good condition, it was decided, in the event of the attack making The special mission of satisfactory progress, to employ the 17th Armoured the 5th Cavalry Brigade Car Battalion supported by eight whippets of the 3rd and the armoured cars Tank Battalion to carry out a special mission. Supported by the whippet tanks, which if necessary could also assist to tow the cars over the shell area, the armoured cars were to push forward and demolish the railway line in the vicinity of Bohain and Busigny, thereby cutting the enemy's main communications. The whippet tanks were to escort them as far as Serain and Premont, and then " stand by " until assistance was required of them. The 5th Cavalry Brigade was placed at the disposal of the Australian Corps, with a view to working in conjunction with the armoured cars in the exploitation beyond the second objective.

With the exception of the 5th Cavalry Brigade, the Cavalry Corps remained under the orders of General Headquarters. Until the result of the attack of the Third Army on September 28th The rôle of the was known, Sir Douglas Haig could not determine Cavalry Corps on what portion of the front the cavalry could best be employed. On the evening of September 28th, seeing that there was no immediate prospect of the situation on the Third Army front being suitable for the employment of cavalry, the Cavalry Corps was moved into the Fourth Army area. It was, however, only attached for administration, and, for its tactical employment, was to continue to act, should the occasion arise, under the orders it had already received from General Headquarters.

These orders were :—

(a) To advance in the general direction of Le Cateau, securing the railway junctions at that place and at Busigny.

(b) To operate against the flank and rear of the enemy opposite our Third and First Armies.

(c) To cut the enemy's communications about Valenciennes.

In accordance with these instructions, the 1st and 3rd Cavalry Divisions were ordered by Sir Henry Rawlinson to concentrate in the Hervilly–

Hamelet–Boucly and the Bihecourt–Vermand–Caulaincourt areas respectively, so as to be ready to carry out their mission should the opportunity offer.

During the night of September 27th all the divisions taking part in the battle occupied their assembly areas, and the assaulting troops took **The assembly of the troops** over the line in their respective sectors. The final preparations were carried out without a hitch except on the northern half of the American front. Here, the failure of the 27th American Division to complete the capture of Quennemont Farm, Gillemont Farm, and The Knoll on September 27th rendered its final preparations for the attack most difficult. It was originally intended that the general line Quennemont Farm–Gillemont Farm should be the infantry " starting line," and the barrage maps had been worked out on this basis and issued to all concerned. To alter the barrage at the last moment would inevitably lead to confusion, and, even had it been possible to do so without jeopardising the success of the operation, the knowledge that parties of American troops, including a number of American wounded, still occupied portions of trenches in the vicinity of these farms and of The Knoll made it impossible to bring the barrage further back. After careful consideration, Sir Henry Rawlinson decided that the barrage line must remain as originally planned, that is to say on the east of the line Quennemont Farm, Gillemont Farm, and The Knoll, and that the troops of the 27th American Division should form up for the attack as near the barrage line as possible one hour before " zero," and, assisted by an additional number of tanks, should fight their way forward to the barrage line by " zero." Five-fifty a.m. on September 29th was selected as the " zero " hour, and headquarters of formations were so informed at noon on the 28th.

The early morning was fine but foggy, and was almost a replica of the morning of August 8th. The surface of the ground was soft and slippery **The assault** owing to the recent rains, but, as there had been a few days of fine weather previously, it was hard underneath. The tanks had reached the tank " starting line " during the night of the 28th. From here, those co-operating with the infantry in the initial assault moved forward just before " zero," in order to pass through the infantry on their " starting line " at " zero."

By 5.50 a.m. the infantry was assembled in its positions waiting for the signal, some in trenches, some in shell holes in No Man's Land, others in the shelter of sunken roads. The guns continued relentlessly battering the enemy's positions, and above the noise of the guns could be heard the drone of the tank engines moving forward in the darkness over the slippery ground. Persistent and distinct from the gun fire, and not unlike the drone of the tank engines, was the rhythmic throb of the aeroplanes patrolling overhead. Occasionally these dropped a bomb on the enemy's trenches.

At 5.55 a.m. the noise was appalling. The barrage had fallen 200 yards in front of the infantry and was moving steadily forward, invisible, except for the flashes, in the thick morning mist which hung over the battlefield. The tanks, followed by the leading waves of infantry, rumbled forward and became enveloped in the fog, which was by that time greatly intensified by the smoke of the shells. Shrapnel bursts filled the air, and machine-gun bullets whistled everywhere overhead. The attack was launched, and the fate of the battle now rested in the hands of the subordinate commanders.

On the southern flank of the IX Corps the 1st Division, employing the 3rd and 1st Brigades, began the difficult task of clearing the enemy from the ground east and north-east of Pontruet with **The IX Corps ; the action of the 1st Division** strong fighting patrols. The mission of the division was to secure the right flank of the 46th Division in its advance to the canal, to gain the high ground north of Thorigny, and join hands with the 32nd Division at the tunnel defences south of Le Tronquoy. The 1st Loyal North Lancashire and the 1st Black Watch of the 1st Brigade, the former battalion operating in close liaison with the right of the 46th Division, cleared the trenches west of the canal astride of the Bellenglise–Ste. Hélène road. The 3rd Brigade on the right sent forward the 1st Gloucestershire towards the high ground around Sycamore Wood. When this battalion had progressed about half a mile it encountered strong resistance from the enemy holding the trenches west of the wood, and, in accordance with the orders it had received, did not attempt to make a frontal attack, the wood being subsequently secured after dark from the north. Meanwhile, the 1st Black Watch, with the 1st Loyal North Lancashire in support, had swung round its left west of the canal and was clearing the trenches in the area as far east as the main St. Quentin–Cambrai road. The clearing of this maze of trenches was no easy task, and the fighting was severe, but the 1st Black Watch, and the 1st South Wales Borderers of the 3rd Brigade, were not to be denied, and early in the afternoon the high ground around Road Wood and the trenches between it and the canal were captured.

During the remainder of the afternoon, little progress was made by the troops of the 1st Division beyond the St. Quentin–Cambrai road, on account of heavy enfilade fire from the south, but connection was established with the 6th Division. This division, which had not been able to advance north of Gricourt, was relieved by the French during the night of September 29th, and went into corps reserve near Vermand.

The 46th Division advanced to the storming of the canal line and the capture of Bellenglise, with the 137th Brigade leading on a three-battalion **The capture of the first objective by the 46th Division** front. The 139th and 138th Brigades, each on a one-battalion front, were in rear of the 137th, on the right and left respectively, their task being to " leap-frog " the leading brigade and secure the first army objective (green line). One company from the leading battalion of each of the supporting brigades was detailed to " mop up " the area west of the canal. These battalions were also instructed to keep in close touch with the situation, in order to ensure that the 137th Brigade, having once crossed the canal, should run no risk of being outnumbered in the trench systems immediately beyond.

Under cover of the dense mist the 137th Brigade stormed the trenches west of the canal, killed most of the garrison, and reached the canal well up to time. The 1/6th South Staffordshire on the right

THE AREA OVER WHICH THE RIGHT OF THE IX CORPS ATTACKED ON SEPTEMBER 29TH.

Oblique air photograph.

THE ST. QUENTIN CANAL; ONE OF THE PLACES WHERE THE 46TH DIVISION CROSSED.

No. 68.

ANOTHER PART OF THE ST. QUENTIN CANAL, WHERE A CROSSING WAS
EFFECTED BY THE 46TH DIVISION.

To face page 159.

St Quentin Canal

BELLENGLISE, SHOWING THE EXITS FROM THE TUNNEL.   (The exits are marked thus : O.)

Vertical air photograph.

crossed the canal north-west of Bellenglise, finding little water in it. At first the Germans put up some resistance, but, after a number of our men had crossed, they surrendered freely. This battalion then advanced through Bellenglise and secured the tunnel entrances in the village, where some hundreds of prisoners were captured before they had time to offer any resistance. As a means of giving shelter, and thus avoiding casualties during a bombardment, these tunnels had served their purpose admirably, but, as our attacking troops reached them before they were cleared, they became a veritable trap for those who had taken refuge in them.

The 1/5th South Staffordshire and the 1/6th North Staffordshire, in the centre and on the left respectively, found a considerable depth of water in the canal, and the banks where they crossed were high. Swimming over first with ropes, the officers were soon joined by the leading waves of their men, who made use of life-belts, rafts, light portable boats, and in some cases of bridges which had only been partially destroyed by the enemy. At Riqueval Farm the bridge was found intact, although prepared for demolition. Some German pioneers were in the act of lighting the fuses to the demolition charges, but were prevented from doing so by the timely arrival of a company of the 1/6th North Staffordshire and an engineer detachment, who rushed the bridge. The bridge was saved, and some pontoon bridges were rapidly constructed ; these subsequently proved invaluable for pushing the supporting troops across the canal. Rapidly overcoming the resistance of the enemy holding the trenches east of the canal, the troops of the 137th Brigade penetrated a further 700 yards and captured a battery of four guns. At 8.20 a.m. the barrage was halted, and a protective barrage was formed, which remained stationary for the next three hours.[1] The leading battalions of the 139th and 138th Brigades were already across the canal and close in rear of the 137th Brigade, and, during this pause, the remainder of these brigades crossed.

When the barrage lifted at 11.20 a.m., the 139th and 138th Brigades " leap-frogged " the 137th Brigade and advanced against the first objective. The two companies of the 9th Tank Battalion allotted to these two brigades had successfully crossed the tunnel south of Bellicourt, and moved forward, one company with each brigade. By this time the dense mist, which had greatly assisted the attack of the 46th Division in its early stages, had thinned considerably, and the visibility was much improved. This enabled the enemy to bring effective fire to bear on our troops, and made the tanks an easy mark for hostile field guns. The leading battalion of the 139th Brigade was immediately subjected to intense enfilade fire from machine-guns, as well as from a battery of field guns situated on the high ground west of the canal. This battery also quickly put out of action the company of tanks which was co-operating with the 139th Brigade.

Although deprived of the assistance of these tanks, the brigade pushed steadily forward, keeping close to the barrage. On reaching the high ground west of Lehaucourt the whole attack was, however, held up by artillery fire from the front, and by machine-gun and rifle fire from the right flank. Realising that everything depended on the advancing

---

[1] See Map 18. "Barrage Map." This three hour protective barrage is "Protective B" on the map.

troops keeping close to the barrage, Lieut.-Col. William Vann,[1] commanding the 1/6th Sherwood Foresters, rushed up to the firing line and, with the greatest gallantry, led the whole line forward. The fate of the tanks had meanwhile been avenged by the enterprise of a party of men of the 139th Brigade, who, having crossed to the western bank of the canal, killed the detachments of the field guns which had destroyed the tanks. In this part of the field several attempts were made by the enemy to stem the tide of our advancing infantry, but in vain.[2]

On the left the 138th Brigade moved forward steadily, and by 12.30 p.m. was approaching Magny-la-Fosse. Until the mist lifted, communication with the 30th American Division on the left was difficult. When the visibility improved, it was seen that there were still Germans in Nauroy, and the left flank of the 138th Brigade was, therefore, refused. Similarly, the right flank of the 139th Brigade was in advance of the 1st Division west of the canal. In consequence there was a slight delay, when for a short time the infantry lost touch with the barrage; it was soon regained, and, assisted by the tanks which co-operated with the 138th Brigade, the advance of the 46th Division continued. Our troops had now reached the enemy's artillery positions, where the German gunners fought gallantly and continued firing their guns up to the last. Finally Lehaucourt and Magny-la-Fosse were captured, and by 3 p.m. the whole of the first objective had been secured on the front of the 46th Division.

Meanwhile, the 32nd Division had moved forward from its assembly area round Le Verguier, with the 14th and 97th Brigades leading on the right and left respectively, and with the 96th Brigade in reserve.[3] The leading brigades, with two batteries of field artillery, began to cross the canal at 3 p.m., the 96th Brigade remaining west of the canal. At about 4 p.m. the attacking brigades " leap-frogged " the 46th Division on the first objective, but the tanks allotted to the 32nd Division to co-operate in the attack were unfortunately unable to reach their rendezvous in time to take part in the advance. They were, therefore, concentrated near Magny-la-Fosse ready for the next day's operations.

The advance of the 32nd Division to the second objective

Although the advance of the 32nd Division met with determined resistance, it made good progress. At 6 p.m. the 15th Highland Light Infantry on the right of the 14th Brigade advanced against Le Tronquoy, covered by a light artillery barrage. Fighting ensued, but the village and the high ground and woods round it were captured. On the left of the 14th Brigade the 1st Dorsetshire was not so fortunate, the shelling and machine-gun fire on its front being very severe. Nevertheless, the battalion reached the second objective on its right, while its left was refused along Ecume Trench.

[1] This gallant officer, before the war, was Chaplain to Wellingborough School. See Appendix E, No. 44.

[2] One German officer, who was mounted, made three gallant attempts to rally the men of the 79th Reserve Division, but, after he and his horse had been killed, the enemy retreated in disorder.

[3] In order to ensure the closest co-operation between the 32nd and 46th Divisions the two Divisional Commanders established a joint headquarters on September 29th in a dug-out well forward.

For the same reason the right of the 97th Brigade was held up in the valley south-west of Levergies, and its left, exposed to heavy fire from the enemy's machine-guns posted south of Joncourt and on the southern slopes of Mill Ridge, was temporarily checked north-east of Magny-la-Fosse. At this time the left of the 32nd Division was temporarily out of touch with the Australians, of whom some troops of the 32nd Battalion reached the south-western outskirts of Joncourt about 6 p.m., but, finding themselves isolated, withdrew to near Etricourt. Machine-guns of the 32nd Machine Gun Battalion were, meanwhile, moved up the sunken roads north-east of Magny-la-Fosse, and swept the slopes of Mill Ridge with harassing fire, to such good effect that the fire of the enemy's machine-guns was neutralised, and the 97th Brigade was again able to move forward. The Lehaucourt Ridge was secured to within about 1,000 yards of Joncourt, and a flank was thrown back facing north, connection being established with the Australians near Etricourt.

By nightfall all three brigades of the 32nd Division were east of the canal; the 96th Brigade, which had moved forward during the afternoon, being in close support of the 14th and 97th Brigades. The artillery was also well up; one brigade of field artillery and one brigade of horse artillery had already crossed the canal and were in action 1,500 yards east of it, covering the 32nd Division, while two brigades of field artillery and a brigade of heavy artillery were crossing the canal on their way to reinforce them. The bridgehead at Bellenglise was therefore firmly established.

The success attending the operations of the IX Corps was primarily due to the dash and determination with which the troops of the 46th
The result of the day's fighting by the IX Corps Division pressed forward to their objective, and to the excellent leadership and initiative of the subordinate commanders. When their flanks were exposed, they exerted pressure where the enemy was weak and gave way, and only strengthened their flanks just sufficiently to safeguard them.

Not so dramatic, perhaps, but almost equally difficult and important in its results, was the work of the 1st Division on this day, as the safety of the right flank of the army depended on the success of its advance, which the enemy opposed throughout the day with the greatest determination.

The sector which had been considered in some ways the most formidable part of the Hindenburg Line on the army front had been captured at small cost on the whole of the IX Corps front. The enemy's defences had been penetrated by a deep wedge to a maximum depth of some 6,000 yards. This would form an excellent salient from which pressure could be applied to the north and south with every prospect of success, and the many months of work which the enemy had spent in constructing these defences had been rendered useless in a few hours. Over 5,100 prisoners,[1] 90 guns, and many hundreds of machine-guns and trench mortars

[1] Prisoners were captured from the 2nd, 11th, 75th Reserve, and 79th Reserve Divisions. Of these the 2nd Division, which was occupying the Bellenglise salient, suffered very heavily. The men on the whole had little stomach for the fight, their moral having been much lowered by our bombardment and by the consequent lack of food during the two days previous to our attack.

Y

were captured, the 46th Division alone accounting for 4,200 prisoners and 70 guns.[1] It was a great and well-deserved victory for Sir Walter Braithwaite and the IX Corps.

The 30th American Division on the right experienced little trouble in forming up on the " starting line." The 60th Brigade, disposed on a

The Australian-American Corps; the attack of the American Divisions

front of two regiments, formed up for the assault, with the 59th Brigade in reserve.[2] The 117th regiment of the 59th Brigade, which was to exploit to the south when the first objective had been reached, was in close support of the right flank of the 60th Brigade. On the left the 27th American Division, which was to advance an hour before " zero," experienced considerable difficulty in forming up on account of the uncertainty of the situation. It was intended that the 54th Brigade, which was to carry out the assault, should form up about 1,000 yards in rear of the barrage line, with the 53rd Brigade in reserve. The 105th Regiment of the 53rd Brigade, which was to exploit to the north when the first objective had been reached, was to be in close support of the left flank of the 54th Brigade. Owing to the difficult situation these dispositions were not carried out entirely as arranged.

The attack started well on the front of the 30th American Division. The infantry, keeping close up to the barrage, moved through the masses

The 30th American Division

of wire and trenches towards the Bellicourt tunnel, but the intricate nature of the trench systems, the confusion of wire, and the number of dug-outs were responsible for a certain loss of cohesion, with the result that, by the time the tunnel was reached, the barrage had been lost, and a good deal of the impetus had gone out of the attack. Nevertheless, Bellicourt and the southern entrance of the tunnel at Riqueval were captured. Beyond this line it is difficult to say how far the Americans penetrated. As they passed over and beyond the tunnel, it is certain that numerous groups of Germans, belonging to the 121st and 185th Divisions, emerging from their dug-outs and from the tunnel itself, offered a strong resistance to the advance of the 5th Australian Division following in rear of the Americans. In the excitement of their first big battle, fought as it was in a dense mist and thick smoke, combined with the difficulty of locating all the entrances to the tunnel and dug-outs, the " moppers up " of the 30th American Division appear to have gone on, instead of dealing with those of the enemy who had taken shelter during the initial advance.[3] Several parties of Americans penetrated beyond Nauroy and reached the first objective. When the smoke and mist had cleared, and these parties could see where they were, most of them joined the 5th Australian Division as it fought its way forward.

---

[1] The casualties of the 46th Division on September 29th were only 800.

[2] An American division is composed of two brigades; each brigade consists of two regiments of three battalions each.

[3] This was no new story. It had happened to the British and French many times in 1916 and 1917. Amongst several instances may be recalled the similar experiences of the Ulster Division at Thiepval on July 1st, 1916, and of the 30th and 55th Divisions at Guillemont in August of the same year, when the leading waves of the assault, after their first brilliant initial success, were cut off by the enemy coming out of his shelters in their rear.

Hargicourt—Bellicourt road

Front trench of the
Hindenburg Line

North end of
Bellicourt village

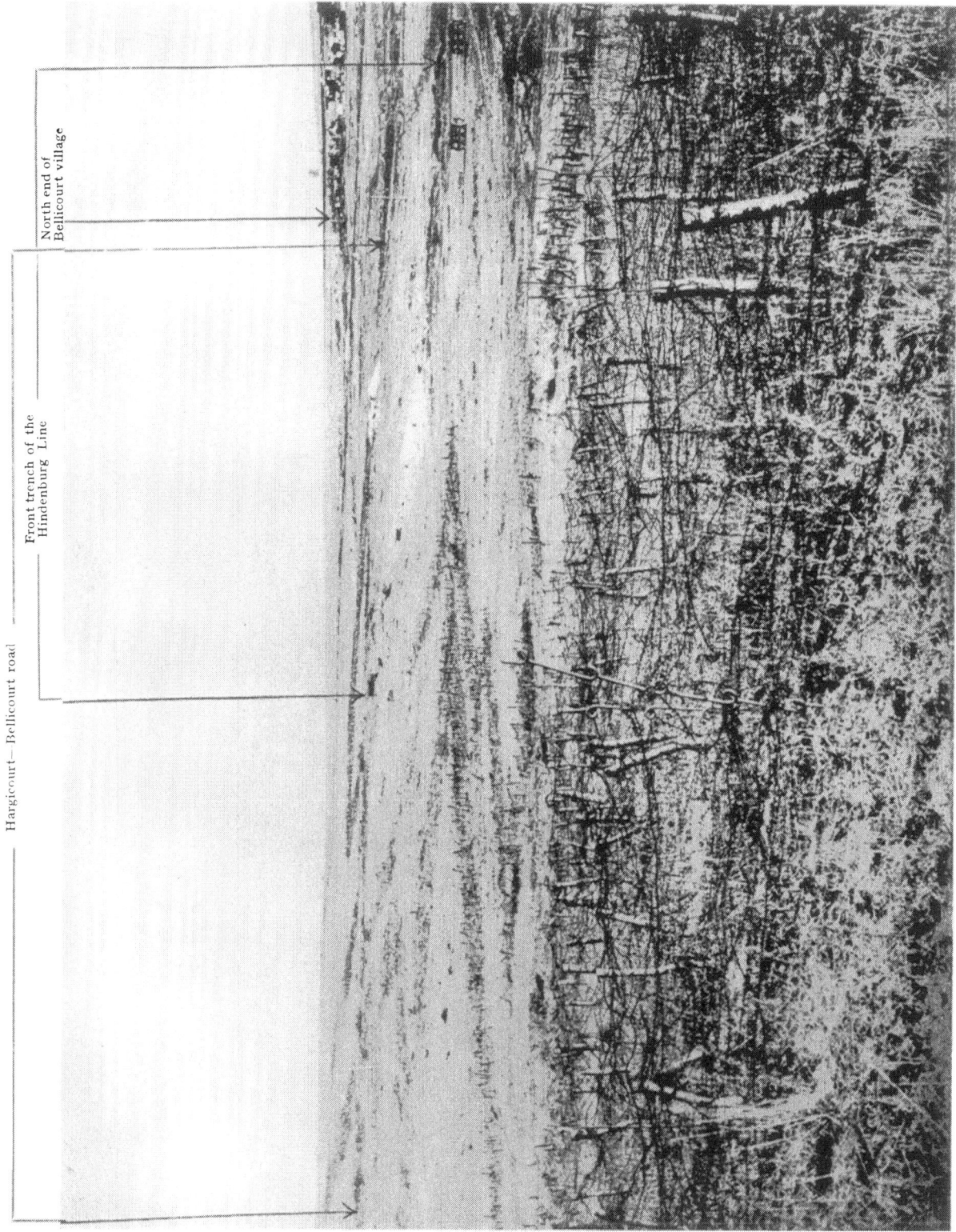

THE WIRE PROTECTING BELLICOURT.

To face page 162.

Portion of screen remaining in position

THE SOUTHERN ENTRANCE OF THE ST. QUENTIN CANAL TUNNEL AT BELLICOURT.

About 30 yards inside the tunnel a concrete dam was built up to the ceiling with loopholes for machine guns, and there was a movable wooden screen at the outer edge of the tunnel to conceal the dam.

From the outset the 27th American Division was beset with difficulties, which might well have daunted less gallant troops. Assisted by the tanks, which had been specially detailed to "mop up" the German defences round Quennemont Farm, Gillemont Farm, and The Knoll, the troops of this division advanced an hour before "zero" against these centres of resistance, while the barrage, for reasons given earlier in this chapter,[1] came down at "zero" east of these localities and 1,000 yards from the infantry "starting line." From the start the advance was strongly opposed by the enemy with the fire of numerous machine-guns, and of a number of field guns specially sited for dealing with tanks. Raking the open ground, over which the assaulting troops were forced to advance, the machine-guns wrought terrible havoc among the waves of advancing Americans. Of the thirty-nine tanks assisting the advance, twelve received direct hits, while seven more were "ditched." In one instance, seven tanks approached to within a hundred yards of Gillemont Farm, but were put out of action by the enemy as soon as they became visible through the mist, and only one tank succeeded in crossing the Bellicourt tunnel on this divisional front.

The 27th American Division

The gallant Americans gained a footing on The Knoll, but were subsequently driven off part of it by a strong counter-attack delivered by the 54th German division.[2] Some of the troops of the 27th American Division broke through the tunnel defences of the Hindenburg Line under cover of the mist and smoke of the barrage,[3] the main force of the attack was, however, expended against Quennemont Farm and Gillemont Farm, which were still held by the enemy when the 3rd Australian Division arrived on the scene.[4]

Moving from its assembly area round Hesbecourt and Ste. Emilie at 7 a.m., the 5th Australian Division advanced across country in artillery formation, with a view to reaching the original "starting line" of the 30th American Division by 9 a.m., and to "leap-frogging" the Americans on the first objective two hours later. The division was disposed with the 8th Brigade on the right on a two-battalion front, and the 15th Brigade on the left on a similar frontage. The 32nd and 29th Battalions led the 8th Brigade advance, with the 31st in support. The 57th and 59th Battalions led the 15th Brigade advance, with the 58th in support. The 14th Brigade was held in divisional reserve.

The action of the 5th Australian Division

In spite of the thick mist the tanks, followed by the Australian infantry, crossed the American "starting line" at 9 a.m. without incident, although there was considerable shelling. On approaching Bellicourt, the tanks encountered machine-gun fire from the outskirts of the village. Two tanks

---

[1] See page 157.

[2] Some troops of the 18th Division moved forward on the left of the 27th American Division to protect its left flank and reached The Knoll with the American troops.

[3] During the afternoon returning wounded reported that they had reached the Hindenburg Line, while aircraft reported the presence of ground flares near Gouy.

[4] The two American divisions were opposed in this attack by parts of four German Divisions, namely, the 54th, 75th Reserve, 121st, and 185th, all of which were in line between Riqueval Farm and the northern entrance to the Bellicourt tunnel. Of these, the 54th Division was fresh and put up a very good fight in the Bony area.

moved forward, and were followed immediately by the 32nd and 29th Battalions, which entered the village at 9.40 a.m. and proceeded to clear it of such Germans as still remained. Major Anderson Wark,[1] who commanded the 32nd Battalion, now found the situation somewhat critical; he at once went forward and obtained sufficient information regarding the situation in front to enable him to lead his command forward. During his reconnaissance he found 200 Americans, whose advance had been checked with heavy loss, and who were in consequence considerably disorganised. These Major Wark attached to his leading company, and thus reinforced the 32nd and 29th Battalions, having "mopped up" Bellicourt, pushed forward towards Nauroy. The mist now lifted, exposing the infantry and tanks to the view of the enemy holding the high ground round Nauroy, and the anti-tank guns concealed in the village quickly put the tanks out of action. In spite of this, the 32nd Battalion on the right, moving up the western slopes of the high ground, entered the southern portion of Nauroy; it "mopped up" this village and captured 50 prisoners. The 29th Battalion on the left reached the Le Catelet–Nauroy Line, but was unable to advance farther on account of the intensity of the fire which enfiladed their position from the direction of Cabaret Wood Farm. Shortly after noon the enemy's resistance strengthened,[2] and it became evident that there were no American troops in front of the 8th Brigade except small isolated parties. Moreover, by this time all except two of the twelve tanks supporting the brigade had been put out of action by direct hits or had been "ditched." The 8th Brigade Commander, therefore, decided to wait until 3 p.m., and then launch an organised attack.

On the left of the 5th Australian Division the 15th Brigade advanced steadily towards the American "starting line" without incident. Beyond this line progress was hampered by fire from machine-guns which had come into action as soon as the Americans had passed. Nevertheless, at 11 a.m., when the mist began to clear, the 58th Battalion, which had moved up in support between the 57th and 59th, had reached the tunnel north of Bellicourt. Here isolated groups of Americans were encountered, but they could give no information regarding the situation in front. A line was, therefore, formed on the west bank of the tunnel embankment, with the 57th Battalion on the right and the 58th in the centre. The 59th on the left had lost touch with the 57th owing to the mist, had swung too much to the left, and thus became mixed up with the 44th Battalion of the 3rd Australian Division. The 59th Battalion found great difficulty in reaching the Hindenburg Line owing to the enfilade and reverse fire which it experienced from machine-guns on the high ground round Quennemont Farm, where the enemy was still holding out; there were also isolated posts of the enemy still occupying portions of the Hindenburg Line. Some hard fighting ensued, but finally the support trenches about 500 yards west of the tunnel were cleared and held by a mixed garrison, comprising men of the 59th Battalion, one platoon of the 44th Battalion, and parties

---

[1] For details regarding Major Wark's splendid leadership, see Appendix E, No. 45.
[2] The line here had been reinforced by at least one battalion of the 21st Division from support.

NAUROY AND THE SURROUNDING COUNTRY.

Oblique air photograph.

of the 108th Regiment of the 27th American Division. Numerous bombing counter-attacks down the trenches from the north were repulsed, and touch with the 58th Battalion was regained on the tunnel. Reconnaissance beyond the tunnel revealed the fact that we had no definite line in front, except some posts which had been established by the troops of the 30th American Division. As the resistance in front of the 5th Australian Division had strengthened considerably during the past two hours, it was decided to continue the attack at 3 p.m. with the 15th Brigade as well as with the 8th Brigade, under cover of a creeping barrage.

At 3 p.m. the 8th Brigade, assisted by four tanks, all of which were put out of action almost at once, moved forward. The 32nd Battalion established touch with the troops of the IX Corps on the northern slopes of Knobkerry Ridge, north of Magny-la-Fosse, about 5.30 p.m. It then continued its advance and succeeded in reaching Joncourt, but, finding itself isolated, withdrew later to Etricourt, where it was in touch with the 32nd Division. The 29th Battalion on the left quickly gained the first objective on its front, although opposition was encountered from machine-gun posts on the high ground north-east of Nauroy. This battalion was compelled later to withdraw to the Le Catelet–Nauroy Line owing to its left flank being enfiladed from the north. The 31st Battalion, meanwhile, moved forward through Nauroy from support and advanced between the 32nd and 29th Battalions. It was, however, checked east of the village by heavy fire from the Sugar Factory and was unable to advance farther.

On the 15th Brigade front the 57th and 58th Battalions, reinforced by groups of the 30th American Division, also resumed the advance at 3 p.m. Four Mark V and eight whippet tanks took part in the operation, but unfortunately, within fifteen minutes of starting, all of the Mark V tanks and five of the whippets were put out of action. The lightness of our artillery barrage added to the difficulties of the infantry, as it permitted the enemy to man his machine-guns in the Le Catelet–Nauroy Line. Nevertheless, the 57th Battalion on the right managed to capture the Le Catelet–Nauroy Line on its front, and the 58th Battalion gained a footing in it further north. This left the enemy still in possession of the trenches in front of Cabaret Wood Farm, with the result that numerous bombing encounters took place. Although a portion of these trenches was cleared by the 57th Battalion, the 58th Battalion on the left was unable to make any headway on account of the enfilade fire from the north, and at 4.30 p.m. it withdrew, and formed a defensive flank from the Le Catelet–Nauroy Line west of Cabaret Wood Farm to the tunnel. This line was prolonged northwards along the tunnel for 200 yards, and then swung back to the sunken road 500 yards west of the tunnel, where a junction was effected with the 44th Battalion of the 3rd Australian Division. Later in the afternoon the 59th Battalion moved forward from the trench just west of the road and relieved the troops of the 44th Battalion.

Thus, at nightfall the 5th Australian Division, after a very severe day's fighting, was established on the high ground round Etricourt in touch with the IX Corps; it held Nauroy and the Le Catelet–Nauroy

Line as far north as Cabaret Wood Farm; thence it threw back a defensive flank to the tunnel to join with the 3rd Australian Division.

The 3rd Australian Division moved off from its assembly area round Ronssoy at 7 a.m. and, preceded by the tanks, advanced in artillery forma-

The action of the 3rd Australian Division tion towards the line Quennemont Farm–Gillemont Farm, which it expected to cross by 9 a.m. The 11th and 10th Brigades which were leading, each advanced on a two-battalion front, followed by the 9th Brigade. As soon as the leading battalions had crossed the original " starting line " of the 27th American Division, machine-gun fire was encountered from Quennemont Farm, Quennet Copse, and Gillemont Farm. At the same time the enemy's artillery fire was very intense, putting a number of the tanks out of action.

Although reports from wounded men, and later from the air, were received that the 27th American Division was through the Hindenburg Line and had secured its objective, it was obvious that the enemy was still holding strong localities behind the advanced troops of the American division, and that there would be considerable fighting before the first objective could be reached. Definite information regarding the situation of the troops of the 27th American Division could not be obtained, and observation was impossible owing to the thick mist which obscured everything.

It was essential, however, that the line Quennemont Farm–Gillemont Farm should be secured, and that the 3rd Australian Division should push forward and assist the Americans to reorganise and complete their task. It was known that the 30th American Division had captured Bellicourt, and the 9th Brigade was, therefore, ordered to hold itself in readiness to move at short notice southwards, with a view to assisting the easterly advance of the 11th and 10th Brigades by operating against the flank of the enemy's defences from the direction of Bellicourt. This move, however, did not take place on the 29th.

Throughout the remainder of the morning heavy fighting took place, the 54th and 121st German Divisions resisting our advance between Bellicourt and Le Catelet with determination. Two tanks secured the small spur immediately south of Quennemont Farm, but were put out of action shortly afterwards. Other tanks advanced against Quennet Copse, from which a number of machine-guns were causing our infantry considerable casualties. The tanks arrived at the copse to find that the enemy had surrendered, and that our infantry was in possession. Further north the infantry, working in close conjunction with the tanks, cleared South Gillemont Trench and gained the western edge of the farm. The mist was now lifting, visibility was decidedly better, and the shelling from the north had increased and was at this time very severe. The tanks, as they moved over the crests of the ridges, formed an excellent target for the anti-tank guns, and several were put out of action; their crews, however, removed the machine-guns from them and joined the infantry.

By noon no material progress had been made. The 44th Battalion on the right of the 11th Brigade was in touch with the 15th Brigade of the 5th Australian Division in the main trenches of the Hindenburg Line,

AUSTRALIANS MOVING ALONG A TRENCH NEAR GILLEMONT FARM.

By kind permission of the Australian Government.

but the remainder of the brigade was held up west of Quennemont Farm and in the trenches east of Quennet Copse. The 10th Australian Brigade continued the line to the north along South Gillemont Trench, then west of Gillemont Farm and across the Macquincourt valley to The Knoll, which was held by our troops. The enemy was beginning to work up the Macquincourt valley in small parties, and made repeated counter-attacks against The Knoll and the left flank of the 10th Brigade.

Maj.-Gen. Hobbs ordered the advance to be resumed at 3 p.m. by the 11th and 10th Brigades and tanks. The 9th Brigade was brought forward in close support of the 10th Brigade, with the object of protecting the left flank of the division from any attacks from the north. It was impossible to employ covering artillery fire for this attack, on account of the uncertainty of the situation with regard to the Americans. Consequently, when the infantry and tanks began to advance at 3 p.m., they were met by such a storm of shell and machine-gun fire that it was obvious that to continue the attack in daylight under these conditions was impossible. An advance of a few hundred yards, however, was made, and Gillemont Farm was captured. At about this time the enemy, as the result of continued counter-attacks, succeeded in gaining a footing on the eastern slopes of The Knoll, thus threatening the left flank of the 3rd Australian Division and the right of the III Corps. One battalion of the 9th Brigade, therefore, took up a position south-east of Tombois Farm at the head of the Macquincourt valley to prevent any further penetration.

While the fighting was in progress during the morning, the armoured cars, with their usual boldness, moved down the Hargicourt–Bony road to carry out their special mission. On approaching The armoured cars Bony they found that the enemy was still in occupation. Four armoured cars and four whippet tanks were put out of action by anti-tank gun fire. The remainder of the whippets and armoured cars were, therefore, withdrawn to a position of safety until the situation should allow them to carry out their allotted task.

The action of the III Corps was entirely dependent on the progress of the battle on its right. The 12th Division was disposed along the front of the III Corps, the 35th Brigade on the right and the The III Corps operations 37th Brigade on the left, with the object of securing the left flank of the army. It was not to undertake a gene al attack. but, whenever the situation permitted, was to endeavour to gain ground along the whole of its front and secure Lark Spur. The main operation on the III Corps front was undertaken by the 18th Division. This division formed up for the attack with the 54th Brigade in rear of the left of the 27th American Division near Sart Farm. When the latter division had advanced beyond The Knoll, the 54th Brigade was to swing to the north and secure Macquincourt Trench. The 55th Brigade was to assemble north of Ronssoy, and follow the 3rd Australian Division when it moved forward at 7 a.m. It was then to advance down the Macquincourt valley and establish a bridgehead across the canal at Vendhuile. This would in turn allow the 38th Division of the V Corps to cross the canal and advance northwards against the flank of the enemy's defences opposite the remainder of the V Corps. One battalion of the 37th

Brigade of the 12th Division was to form up west of The Knoll on the left of the 54th Brigade, with the task of securing the high ground 1,000 yards west of Vendhuile.

The III Corps attack was launched at " zero " and at first made good progress. By 1 p.m. the 54th Brigade had established itself in Macquincourt Trench overlooking Vendhuile; the 12th Division had advanced its line 1000 yards; on the left, however, the 37th Brigade was unable to push forward beyond Dados Loop. Up to this time the reports as to the progress of the 27th American Division had been most favourable, but information now began to be received which modified the earlier reports. Moreover, the right flank of the 54th Brigade was in some danger from the enemy's pressure up the Macquincourt valley.

As the Australians were held up in front of Gillemont Farm, the proposed advance of the 55th Brigade down the Macquincourt valley was impossible. Therefore, at 1.25 p.m. one battalion of this brigade was instructed to operate southwards from The Knoll against the trenches north of Gillemont Farm; the situation at this time, however, round ¡The Knoll and south of it, combined with the intensity of the enemy's artillery and machine-gun fire, made such an operation impracticable. Subsequently, the 55th Brigade strengthened the position round The Knoll by holding the trenches on its southern slopes, and joined up with the Australians on the right and the 54th Brigade on the left, the latter having thrown back a defensive flank from Macquincourt Trench. The 12th Division continued the line on the left of the 54th Brigade, at a distance of about 700 yards from the canal, connecting with the 33rd Division north of Dados Loop.

Such was still the situation at dusk. On the left no material progress had been made, and, in consequence, the right divisions of the Third Army

The situation of the III Corps at dusk were unable to advance. Moreover, the German artillery on the high ground about La Terrière was very well placed to harass the advance of our left flank, while, so long as the advance of the Third Army was held up, its own position was perfectly secure. As the result of the day's fighting, the III Corps had captured over 250 prisoners and was in possession of Macquincourt Trench and The Knoll, both of which were of considerable importance, as they protected the left flank of the Australian-American Corps.

Our total captures on September 29th amounted to over 5,300 prisoners, of whom 128 were officers. These came from 48 battalions of

The result of the battle twenty regiments of nine different divisions. In the IX Corps, whose attack had been a complete and far-reaching success, the casualties had been very light compared with the results achieved. It had every reason to be proud of the day's work, which was second to none amongst those recorded in this story. The American divisions, whose task under any conditions was far from easy, had been compelled by the events of the previous forty-eight hours to face a very difficult proposition. Only the most fearless and self-sacrificing troops would have faced the fire to which they were subjected from the moment the attack started, and it is to their undying credit that they achieved what they did and broke the backbone of the tunnel defences. The Australian troops engaged surmounted the difficulties which met them from the start with their usual determination and individual initiative in the face of unexpected situations, while the 18th and 12th Divisions showed that the continuous fighting in which they had taken part since August 8th had in no way damped their ardour. September 29th was perhaps the most trying day the tanks had experienced during all the battles in which they took part with the Fourth Army during the hundred days, but they earned the sincere gratitude of the infantry by their never-failing gallantry and self-sacrifice whenever they were called upon for assistance.

Such high hopes had been held of a sweeping and decisive victory on September 29th, that the check received at the northern half of the tunnel defences was for the moment the cause of some disappointment. It was soon realised, however, that, although we had not achieved all that was desired and expected, we had, nevertheless, inflicted a crushing defeat on the enemy. We had forced a wedge into his defences to a depth of some 5,000 to 6,000 yards on a front of about 10,000 yards, which would render his position a very difficult one, and, if a little more pressure was exerted, the whole of the tunnel defences would shortly be in our possession.

After discussing the situation on the northern half of the front with Sir John Monash and General Read, Sir Henry Rawlinson decided to withdraw the II American Corps for a short rest, and to carry on the operations with the IX, Australian, and XIII Corps on fronts of approximately equal widths, as soon as the situation on the tunnel had been cleared up by the Australian Corps, and the gap widened.

The orders for September 30th

On the evening of September 29th, therefore, orders were issued to the following effect :—The IX Corps was to secure the whole of the Le Tronquoy tunnel defences, with a view to allowing the XV French Corps to pass through as early as possible, to capture the high ground on the line Le Tronquoy–Sequehart–Preselles, and to push forward towards Joncourt, thereby assisting the advance of the Australian Corps. The Australian Corps was to endeavour to get into touch with the American troops who were believed to be in front of our main line, to capture Estrées and Folemprise Farm, and to secure the remainder of the Hindenburg Line as far as the northern entrance of the tunnel, and the Nauroy–Le Catelet Line as far as the southern outskirts of Gouy. The II American Corps was to withdraw its troops to a position in rear, as soon as relieved by the Australians. The III Corps was to occupy Vendhuile, and to give as much artillery assistance as possible to the Australian Corps. The XIII and Cavalry Corps were to remain in reserve in the positions they then occupied until the situation developed.

It was hoped to secure all these objectives within a short time, and to advance our line to within striking distance of the Masnières–Beaurevoir–Fonsomme Line, which could then be broken by another organised attack on a wide front.

z

CHAPTER IX

THE COMPLETION OF THE CAPTURE OF THE HINDENBURG DEFENCES, SEPTEMBER 30TH—OCTOBER 2ND, AND THE CAPTURE OF THE BEAUREVOIR LINE, OCTOBER 3RD—5TH

Maps 2, 10, 11, and 12

AT 8 a.m. on September 30th the 1st Division, operating west of the canal, attacked under cover of a creeping barrage. The 3rd Brigade on the right advanced against Thorigny and Talana Hill, whilst the 1st Brigade co-operated by moving along the low ground, with its left resting on the canal. Thorigny and Talana Hill were captured during the morning with little opposition, together with 300 prisoners of the 11th and the 79th Reserve Divisions. Early in the afternoon the 3rd Brigade linked up with the 14th Brigade of the 32nd Division on the Le Tronquoy tunnel; the 1st Brigade, crossing the canal, then relieved the 14th Brigade between Le Tronquoy and Levergies with two battalions.

At the same time the 32nd Division continued to press forward with strong patrols of the 14th and 97th Brigades, while the 15th Lancashire Fusiliers, of the 96th Brigade which was in support, attacked Joncourt from the south-west. In spite of strong resistance the line was advanced to close to the southern outskirts of the village, and connection was established with the 5th Australian Division. During the day the 14th Brigade completed the "mopping up" of the Le Tronquoy tunnel defences, and at 7.30 p.m., in conjunction with troops of the 97th Brigade, attacked Levergies, capturing the village with 400 prisoners.

September 30th; the advance of the IX Corps

No. 74.

22 N.3178.
10.5.17 — 4.

Levergies.

Railway.

Le Tronquoy.

LE TRONQUOY.

Oblique air photograph, taken in May, 1917.

During the night of September 30th preparations were made for the 14th Brigade to attack Sequehart; for the 96th Brigade to operate against Joncourt in conjunction with the 5th Australian Division, and to gain the Beaurevoir–Fonsomme Line round Chataignies Wood in co-operation with the 97th Brigade.

Meanwhile the 47th Division of the XV French Corps, which had relieved our 6th Division at Gricourt, had been ordered to attack towards the canal south of Le Tronquoy. Little progress was made during the afternoon of the 30th, but, on the morning of October 1st, the enemy's resistance weakened, and the canal was reached in the afternoon. The French then established connection with our 1st Brigade at Le Tronquoy, thus cutting out the 3rd Brigade of the 1st Division, which was withdrawn into reserve.

While the IX Corps was operating around Le Tronquoy and Sequehart, the Australian Corps was engaged in the difficult task of clearing the

The plan of operations of the Australian Corps remainder of the Hindenburg main and reserve lines. To add to the difficulties of the situation it was almost certain that isolated parties of Americans were still holding out in advance of our line, although their exact position was not known. This very much limited the action of our artillery.

The 5th Australian Division was ordered to attack with its right up the southern slopes of Mill Ridge, in conjunction with the attack of the 32nd Division, and with its left working northwards towards Gouy along Railway Ridge. The 3rd Australian Division was ordered to attack simultaneously northwards along the main Hindenburg Line and along the tunnel towards The Knob.

The 5th Australian Division attacked with the 8th and 14th Brigades, on the right and left respectively. The 8th Brigade made little head-

The attack of the 5th Australian Division way except on the right, where at 4 p.m. the 32nd Battalion advanced in conjunction with the troops of the 32nd Division. An appreciable advance was made south-west of Joncourt, and a footing was established on the southern slopes of Mill Ridge. On the left the 14th Brigade employed the 53rd Battalion supported by the 55th, and attacked in co-operation with the 11th Brigade of the 3rd Australian Division. In order to keep the battalions of the 14th Brigade free to continue the attack, the 15th Brigade, which was holding that part of the line, was instructed to take over from the 14th Brigade all ground gained by extending its left northwards.

The attack started at 6 a.m. and was supported by a barrage. Machine-gun fire was encountered from the outset from Cabaret Wood Farm, from the Le Catelet–Nauroy Line, and from the exits from the tunnel east of Bony. In spite of this, the 53rd Battalion made steady progress, and by 1 p.m., with the help of a company of the 55th Battalion, had cleared the Le Catelet–Nauroy Line northwards for a distance of 1,200 yards, and had repulsed several counter-attacks.[1] The 15th Brigade took

---

[1] In this attack Private John Ryan, 55th Battalion, displayed great bravery and initiative, and his action, when his officers and non-commissioned officers were disabled, saved a critical situation. See Appendix E, No. 38.

over the greater part of the Le Catelet–Nauroy Line captured by the 14th Brigade, but was unable to clear Cabaret Wood Farm.

The task of the 3rd Australian Division was rendered very difficult by heavy shelling from the north from the enemy's batteries on the high ground about La Terrière, and by machine-gun fire from round

The attack of the 3rd Australian Division

Bony. To the 11th Brigade, less one battalion, but strengthened by two battalions of the 9th Brigade, was entrusted the clearing of the Hindenburg Line north and south of Bony from the south. The attack was to be made on a one-battalion front, each battalion being given a portion of the Hindenburg Line and the tunnel to "mop up." As each battalion completed its task, the next battalion was to pass through it and continue the operation. In order to assist the 11th Brigade as it worked its way up the Hindenburg Line and the tunnel from the south, the 10th Brigade was to operate eastwards against the enemy's defences between Bony and the northern entrance to the tunnel, by means of strong fighting patrols. The 9th Brigade, which had been moved during the night of September 29th to the area between Gillemont Farm and Malakoff Wood, was, with its two remaining battalions and one from the 11th Brigade, to ensure that touch was maintained between the attacks of the 10th and 11th Brigades.

The night of September 29th was dark and cold, and the movement of the troops, and particularly that of the 9th Brigade, through the mud and without landmarks, was very trying. Notwithstanding this, the troops were assembled up to time on the morning of September 30th.

At 6 a.m. the attack of the 3rd Australian Division began simultaneously with that of the 5th Australian Division. The 44th Battalion of the 11th Brigade led the advance behind a creeping barrage which moved northwards searching the trenches of the main Hindenburg Line. Progress was steady but slow, as movement except along the trenches was almost impossible. The Germans fought stubbornly for the possession of each post and machine-gun position, and hand grenades, Lewis guns, and especially the bayonet, were all freely employed during this reversion to trench warfare. By nightfall the 11th Brigade had cleared the trenches northwards for about 1,000 yards and had gained a footing in the outskirts of Bony.[1]

During September 30th the 12th and 18th Divisions of the III Corps succeeded in driving the enemy across the canal at Vendhuile, and in

The action of the III Corps

clearing the village and the greater part of the area west of the canal. This materially assisted the 10th Brigade of the 3rd Australian Division, which was thus able to advance eastwards on October 1st without further fear for its left flank.

[1] During these operations the Australian Corps encountered another division from reserve, the 2nd Guard Division, which had been sent up hurriedly in lorries on the 29th, and its three regiments divided among the 21st, 185th, and 121st Divisions. From prisoners' statements it appeared that the 1st Guard Grenadier Regiment had received orders to counter-attack early on the morning of the 30th, but that our attack had forestalled it. The moral of this division was by now very bad, the men being dispirited at being brought into the line for the third time during September, it having been previously engaged against the 18th Division at Trones Wood, and against the Australians at Mont St. Quentin.

Beaurevoir

Bellevue Farm

Mont St. Martin

To Bellicourt →

Bellevue Valley

Guizancourt Farm

Gouy

Line of Canal Tunnel

BONY

BONY

Dirk Valley

BONY AND THE GROUND TO THE NORTH-EAST.

Oblique air photograph, taken in 1917.

Road to Hargicourt

BONY from the west.

SEQUEHART

Road to LEVERGIES

SEQUEHART.

On the morning of October 1st the IX Corps held its line thus : the 1st Division from Le Tronquoy to Levergies, with the 1st Brigade in the line. The 32nd Division held from Levergies to Joncourt, with the 14th, 97th, and 96th Brigades all in line from right to left, and with the 46th Division in support.

October 1st; the IX Corps operations; the 32nd Division attack

The attack on Joncourt was launched at 8 a.m. on October 1st under cover of a barrage. The 15th Lancashire Fusiliers of the 96th Brigade entered the village from the south, and the Australians from the west. There was little resistance, as most of the enemy had retired to the Beaurevoir–Fonsomme Line during the night, and only eight prisoners were captured.

The attack by the 32nd Division on the Beaurevoir–Fonsomme Line and Sequehart was not delivered until 4 p.m. This was a much more difficult operation, as the enemy's position on the high ground at Sequehart was one of great natural strength, and the Beaurevoir–Fonsomme Line at this point was well wired and strongly held.

The infantry, accompanied by sixteen tanks from the 9th Mark V Tank Battalion, advanced under cover of a barrage. Sequehart was captured with great dash by the 5/6th Royal Scots of the 14th Brigade with over 200 prisoners of the newly arrived 221st Division. The enemy, however, at once counter-attacked in strength, after shelling the village heavily, and drove the 5/6th Royal Scots back to the west of the village. Further north the 1/5th Border of the 97th Brigade encircled Chataignies Wood and entered Preselles, but the frontal and enfilade machine-gun fire, which was encountered from the Beaurevoir–Fonsomme Line, rendered it impossible for our men to retain the ground gained, and they were finally withdrawn to the railway cutting 100 yards west of the wood.

Complete success crowned the attack of the 96th Brigade on the left. The 2nd Manchester attacked with great gallantry, and was assisted by four tanks, while five tanks followed in rear to clear the trenches to the north of the objective. The battalion broke through the Beaurevoir–Fonsomme Line and, after stiff hand-to-hand fighting, cleared the line from Swiss Cottage to a point 1,400 yards south of it, capturing 210 prisoners of the 2nd and 241st Divisions.[1] In this attack the tanks rendered valuable assistance, although unfortunately three were hit just before " zero." In one of these tanks the whole crew except the officer became casualties ; picking up an officer and a man of the attacking battalion to work the machine-guns, the tank went into action and met with considerable success. The IX Corps had now gained a footing in the Beaurevoir–Fonsomme Line which would be of great value to it, and of this the enemy was fully aware. Repeated counter-attacks were made during the night against the left flank of the 96th Brigade, but the 2nd Manchester successfully maintained its position, with the assistance of a company of the 15th Lancashire Fusiliers which had been sent forward to reinforce it.

During the evening of October 1st patrols of the 5th Cavalry Brigade, which had been transferred from the Australian to the IX Corps, passed beyond the Beaurevoir–Fonsomme Line to test the strength of the enemy's

---

[1] The wire in front of these trenches was very thick, and the trench itself, although only one foot deep, contained numerous rifle and machine-gun pits.

defence. The village of Ramicourt and the ridge south of it were found to be strongly held with machine-guns, and the cavalry was withdrawn.

The 5th Australian Division made an organised attack on October 1st with the object of completing the capture of Mill Ridge, and, if the enemy's resistance showed any signs of weakening, of reaching the Beaurevoir–Fonsomme Line east of Joncourt and Estrées. This attack was carried out by the 8th Brigade on the right, the 14th Brigade, less two battalions, in the centre, and the 15th Brigade on the left.[1] It was launched at 6 a.m. in a thick ground mist, under cover of a barrage. On the right the 8th Brigade, assisted by two tanks of the 8th Mark V Tank Battalion, encountered only slight machine-gun fire, though the enemy's artillery fire was fairly heavy. The tanks rendered yeoman service, and Mill Ridge was captured by 7 a.m., whence patrols were sent out towards Joncourt. This village was entered from the west, and by 9 a.m. had been cleared with little opposition in co-operation with the 32nd Division. From here patrols attempted to reach the Beaurevoir–Fonsomme Line, but were unable to do so. Eventually, the 8th Brigade established a line on the north-eastern slopes of Mill Ridge between Joncourt and Estrées, about 400 yards from the Beaurevoir–Fonsomme Line which the enemy was holding in considerable strength.

In the centre the 56th and 54th Battalions of the 14th Brigade, on the right and left respectively, moved forward towards Estrées along the high ground south of Folemprise Farm, and by 7.30 a.m. the leading infantry had reached the outskirts of the village. Fifteen minutes later the advance was resumed by the 56th Battalion, which, with the assistance of eight tanks from the 8th Tank Battalion, cleared Estrées, taking a few prisoners [2] and some field guns.

The 15th Brigade attacked with the 59th, 57th, and 58th Battalions from right to left. All the battalions made a good start, and by 7.30 a.m. Cabaret Wood Farm and Cabaret Copse had been captured, and the line advanced to the vicinity of Folemprise Farm and Mint Copse. Strong patrols then went forward, and Folemprise Farm and Mint Copse were secured without difficulty. The enemy's shelling, however, was severe, and to avoid casualties our line was withdrawn behind the crest of the spur running north-west from Folemprise Farm, while only a few posts were maintained along the Estrées–Gouy road. Later in the afternoon the line of this road was consolidated, and subsequently handed over to the 2nd Australian Division.

While this fighting was in progress the 53rd and 55th Battalions of the 14th Brigade, which were astride of Railway Ridge, finding the enemy's resistance decidedly weakening, pushed forward and during the morning

[1] The 14th Brigade had taken over part of the front north of Nauroy during the previous night with two battalions, leaving its 53rd and 55th battalions holding the line on the left of the 15th Brigade.

[2] These prisoners belonged to the 119th Division, showing that yet another division had been thrown into the line. The division had arrived late in the evening of the 29th September, and had received orders to counter-attack should we succeed in capturing the front line positions. These instructions had, however, not been carried out, and the men had retired in the face of our attack. This division had only been relieved on the 20th September after suffering severely during our attack on September 18th.

occupied practically the whole of the ridge. Communication was then established by these battalions with the 15th Brigade in the Soult valley, and with the 3rd Australian Division in the Vauban valley.

On the front of the 3rd Australian Division the struggle had continued during the night of September 30th, and the pressure was maintained persistently on October 1st. Although considerably exhausted by the trench fighting, the troops of the 3rd Australian Division made good progress, and by 12 noon Bony, The Knob, the main Hindenburg Line, and the tunnel had been captured. The enemy still held Macquincourt Farm and was not ejected from it until the following night, when patrols of the 10th Brigade drove him across the canal. The 10th and 11th Brigades consolidated the ground gained during the afternoon and pushed forward patrols east of the tunnel and towards Le Catelet and Gouy.

On the night of September 30th, after the successful attack on Vendhuile, the 18th Division took over the whole of the III Corps front, relieving the 12th Division, which was transferred to **The III Corps relieved by the XIII Corps** the First Army by 'bus three days later. On the night of October 1st the 149th Brigade of the 50th Division relieved the 18th Division, which, on relief, moved back to a rest area near Amiens. At 12 noon on October 1st Sir Thomas Morland, commanding the XIII Corps, took over command of the front held by the 18th Division from Sir Richard Butler, and the III Corps Headquarters were transferred to the Fifth Army on October 3rd. Since March, the III Corps had been holding a sector of the Fourth Army front without a rest. During the months of April, May, June, and July it was busily engaged in supervising the construction of defences to cover Amiens. From August 8th onwards it had taken an important part in a period of almost continuous fighting, during which the III Corps with five divisions had engaged twenty German divisions, taking 13,700 prisoners and 150 guns. The outstanding feature of this period had undoubtedly been the powers of endurance of officers and men, and their cheerful response to the incessant demands made upon them.

During October 2nd the 1st Brigade of the 1st Division spent a trying and unsatisfactory day. Its rôle was to keep touch with the left of the 47th French Division, which was passing over the tunnel **October 2nd; the action of the IX Corps** at Le Tronquoy and attacking south-east, and also with the right of the 32nd Division on the Le Tronquoy–Sequehart ridge. On the right the French were unable to make any appreciable progress, while on the left the 32nd Division, after capturing Sequehart for the second time, had again been forced to withdraw. The result was that the 1st Brigade, without being actually engaged in the fight, sustained considerable casualties from shell fire. The excellent information, however, as to the situation on this flank of the army, which was sent in by the 1st Loyal North Lancashire and the 1st Cameron Highlanders during the day, was of the greatest value.

At 6 a.m. on the morning of October 2nd, the 14th Brigade renewed its efforts to capture Sequehart with the 5/6th Royal Scots. Once more the village was secured and 100 prisoners taken, but again a strong counter-attack by the 221st Division three hours later drove our men back to their original position on the western edge of the village.[1]   It was essential for the enemy to maintain his hold on Sequehart, which commanded all the ground to the east, south, and west.   He appreciated its great tactical importance, and realised that its capture by us would widen the breach already made in the Masnières–Beaurevoir–Fonsomme Line, which was his last prepared line of defence, and would also enable us to turn his positions north of St. Quentin.

At 8.30 a.m. on the 2nd the 97th Brigade employed one company of the 10th Argyll and Sutherland Highlanders in an attempt to extend our hold on the Beaurevoir–Fonsomme Line north of Preselles,[2] while simultaneously the 96th Brigade launched an attack against Ramicourt.   Both attacks were checked by the enemy's machine-gun fire.

As the result of the determined fighting by the 32nd Division during the past three days, the IX Corps had added materially to its previous success and had driven the wedge deeper into the enemy's position.[3] On the evening of the 2nd the IX Corps held a front of some 8,000 yards from Le Tronquoy to Swiss Cottage.   This line ran along the high ridge to Sequehart, along the western outskirts of that village, thence to a point 1,000 yards north-west of Preselles, from which point to Swiss Cottage we held the Beaurevoir–Fonsomme Line.   The 1st Division held from Le Tronquoy to just south of Sequehart, while the 32nd Division held thence to Swiss Cottage.

During the night of October 1st the 5th Brigade of the 2nd Australian Division relieved the 5th Australian Division between Joncourt and **The relief of the 3rd** Mint Copse.   No operations were undertaken during **and 5th Australian** the day on October 2nd, and that night the **Divisions** remainder of the 3rd Australian Division was relieved as far south as Mont St. Martin, by the 151st Brigade, of the 50th Division of the XIII Corps.   This left the 2nd Australian Division holding the Australian Corps front between Joncourt and Mont St. Martin.[4] On relief the 3rd and 5th Australian Divisions moved back to rest areas near Amiens.   They had successfully completed a most difficult operation, after four days of almost continuous fighting, and, like the 1st and 4th Australian Divisions, they had fought their last fight in the Great War.

The front of the Fourth Army was held on the night of October 2nd

---

[1] According to the German wireless, intercepted that day, the counter-attack was led in person by the Divisional Commander.

[2] During this attack the bravery and devotion of a sergeant and eight men of the company of the 10th Argyll and Sutherland Highlanders were in keeping with the best traditions of their regiment. This party entered some trenches which it was thought were already held by us, and from which it was to push southwards and join up with the troops attacking from the west.   But the enemy was holding this portion of the trench in considerable strength, and severe hand-to-hand fighting ensued.   The bodies of the sergeant and his eight men were subsequently found in the thirty yards of trench which they had cleared.   Eleven deserted machine-guns and 16 dead Germans proved the stubbornness with which the Highlanders had fought.

[3] With three British divisions the IX Corps had defeated portions of four divisions in the line and of four divisions from reserve.   Of the latter the enemy had hurried up reserve battalions belonging to both the 84th and 241st Divisions from the La Fère area, as well as the whole of the 221st Division from south of St. Quentin, and the 25th Reserve Division from close support in the Lesdins area.

[4] The 54th Battalion of the 5th Division remained in line until the morning of the 3rd between Mint Copse and Mont St. Martin.

Beaurevoir. Bridge. 18.

BEAUREVOIR

Brancourt le Grand   Wire of the Beaurevoir-Fonsomme line   Montbrehain   Beaurevoir Mill

BEAUREVOIR MILL

by the IX, Australian, and XIII Corps. The front of the IX Corps was held by the 1st, 32nd, and 46th Divisions;[1] that of the Australian Corps by the 2nd Australian Division; that of the XIII Corps by the 50th Division, with the 25th and 66th Divisions in support. Our line was within easy striking distance of the Masnières–Beaurevoir–Fonsomme Line. The breach made in the Hindenburg defences on September 29th had now been considerably widened, and these defences had been captured from Le Tronquoy to Vendhuile, while to the south our advance had enabled the First French Army to occupy St. Quentin and reach the line of the canal. During this time the left of the Third Army had captured Masnières, had secured the crossings over the canal between that village and the outskirts of Cambrai, and was continuing its attacks. The Canadian Corps also on the right of the First Army was making good progress north of Cambrai.

The situation on the evening of October 2nd

It was considered that one more determined attack would give us the Masnières–Beaurevoir–Fonsomme Line on the whole of the Fourth Army front. This would turn the enemy's defences in front of the right of the Third Army, thus enabling it to advance the whole of its line, while to the south it would enable the French to advance east of St. Quentin. Again, as in the case of the Mont St. Quentin operations and of the attack against the outer defences of the Hindenburg Line, time was of great importance. The enemy was still greatly disorganised as the result of the fighting since September 29th, and, by attacking him again on October 3rd, he would be prevented from either reorganising his troops or carrying out an orderly retirement.

Sir Henry Rawlinson had on October 1st decided to attack this line on October 3rd. He wished to secure the high ground about Mannequin Hill, the villages of Montbrehain and Beaurevoir, Prospect Hill, and the hill north of Gouy and Le Catelet. Orders for the necessary readjustment of fronts and the allotting of objectives had been issued on October 1st to the IX, Australian, and XIII Corps, and they had been making preparations for the attack. On October 2nd it was decided that " zero " should be 6.5 a.m. on the 3rd.

The orders for the attack on October 3rd
(see Map 11)

On the right the IX Corps, operating in conjunction with the First French Army, was to capture Sequehart and Ramicourt, and as a second objective was given Mannequin Hill and Montbrehain. For this attack, the 32nd and 46th Divisions were employed in the centre and on the left respectively; the latter division was to maintain touch with the 2nd Australian Division on the road between Joncourt and Wiancourt. To the 1st Division, on the right of the 32nd Division, was entrusted the rôle of maintaining touch with the First French Army. In addition, the 5th Cavalry Brigade was to follow the infantry [closely and seize any opportunity for mounted action which might arise. The Australian Corps, employing the 2nd Australian Division, was to capture the Masnières–Beaurevoir–Fonsomme Line north of Swiss Cottage and, if possible, Beaurevoir and Ponchaux. The XIII Corps allotted the difficult task of

The objectives and frontages of the attack

[1] The 46th Division relieved the 96th Brigade of the 32nd Division on the night of October 2nd.

A A

clearing Gouy and Le Catelet and of gaining Prospect Hill to the 50th Division.

While these operations were in progress, the Third Army was to co-operate by exploiting east of the canal towards Aubencheul-aux-Bois. To the south, Marshal Foch ordered the First French Army to press forward east and south-east from Le Tronquoy and so support the right flank of the Fourth Army, which for the past two days had been repeatedly counter-attacked from the south-east, these attacks being chiefly directed against the 32nd Division at Sequehart.

The IX Corps attack was launched at 6.5 a.m. under cover of a heavy barrage, and supported by sixteen tanks of the 5th Mark V Tank Battalion.

On the right the 1st Division held the front south of Sequehart with the 1st Brigade in the line and the 3rd Brigade in close support. Although no definite attack was to be carried out by the division, the 1st Brigade, in order to keep close touch with the French on the right and with the 32nd Division on the left, and to assist the 32nd Division which was attacking Sequehart from the north-west, was compelled to extend its left northwards. This resulted in the 1st Loyal North Lancashire becoming involved in the fighting in the south-eastern portion of Sequehart, where it repulsed an enemy counter-attack with the bayonet and captured 40 prisoners.

October 3rd ; the IX Corps attack ; the action of the 1st Division

The 32nd and 46th Divisions completed their assembly early in the morning of October 3rd and began their advance at 6.5 a.m. The 32nd Division attacked Sequehart from the north-west with the 14th Brigade, assisted by four Mark V tanks, and the Beaurevoir–Fonsomme Line north of Sequehart with the 97th Brigade. After hard fighting, the 5/6th Royal Scots, which had at its own request again been allotted this task, captured Sequehart and gained a footing in the trench line north of it, taking 200 prisoners. The enemy once more made a great effort to recapture Sequehart, and two counter-attacks were delivered by the 34th and 84th Divisions. Both counter-attacks were driven off, and all the captured ground was retained, partly owing to the prompt action of two companies of the 15th Highland Light Infantry, which, led by their battalion commander, swept through the village and cleared it with the bayonet; partly to the action of the 1st Loyal North Lancashire of the 1st Division; and partly also to the stubborn manner in which the 5/6th Royal Scots clung to the village it had three times captured.

The attacks of the 32nd and 46th Divisions

The line gained by the 32nd Division was finally established in touch with the 1st Division at Chardon Vert and with the 46th Division on the left. At 6 p.m. the enemy put down a heavy barrage on the area captured, and under cover of it attacked from the east and south-east, but was again repulsed with heavy loss by rifle and machine-gun fire.

The 46th Division attacked with the 137th Brigade on the right and the 139th Brigade on the left. Owing to the fact that the 32nd Division only held portions of the Beaurevoir–Fonsomme Line, it was decided that the 46th Division should form up on a track somewhat behind the line held, which could be found in the dark and which allowed a straight barrage to be put down, a most important factor, as many batteries had not been able to get into position before dark. The 32nd Division arranged to have its troops withdrawn behind the "starting line" by "zero." The arduous task of forming up on a dark night on unreconnoitred ground was successfully carried out, and at 6.5 a.m., supported by two companies of Mark V tanks, the infantry moved forward behind a good barrage. The 137th Brigade went through to its objective without a check and reached Mannequin Hill, but the 139th Brigade in advancing to Ramicourt, after penetrating the Beaurevoir–Fonsomme Line, found its left flank exposed, owing to touch being lost with the Australians, who were experiencing very severe opposition in the Beaurevoir–Fonsomme Line on the left. Two companies, however, were promptly moved forward to the left flank to link up with the Australians, and formed a protective flank through Wiancourt, where they captured about 200 prisoners.

The enemy attempted to hold Ramicourt, but was driven out of the village with the assistance of the tanks,[1] after which his resistance weakened, and the 139th Brigade, pushing forward rapidly, cleared Montbrehain and captured 1,000 prisoners and a battery of field guns.[2] In Ramicourt and Montbrehain over a hundred French inhabitants were found and sent back through our lines.

By 10.30 a.m. all the objectives allotted to the 46th Division, including Mannequin Hill and Montbrehain, had been gained. The division, however, had suffered heavy casualties, and about 1 p.m. our troops were driven off Mannequin Hill by a determined counter-attack.[3] This withdrawal caused a considerable gap in our line south of Montbrehain, and the troops of the 139th Brigade were slowly forced back out of that village by a second and even stronger counter-attack delivered by portions of the German 21st, 221st, and 241st Divisions. The 137th and 139th Brigades of the 46th Division now held a general line along the western slopes of Mannequin Hill, and east of Ramicourt and Wiancourt. The 138th Brigade, from reserve, was moved up in close support to the Beaurevoir–Fonsomme Line. At 6 p.m. the enemy, encouraged by his success, again attacked the 137th Brigade and drove it off the western slopes of Mannequin Hill. An immediate counter-attack regained the western slopes of the hill, but the enemy still held the eastern slopes ; the summit, on account of the severity of the fire, was at this time held by neither side.[4]

On the right of the IX Corps the XV French Corps had

---

[1] While operating south of Montbrehain a tank was exposed to the fire of 16 machine-guns holding a strong point. It destroyed all the crews of these guns before it was in its turn disabled by the enemy's artillery fire.

[2] Sergeant William Johnson, 1/5th Sherwood Foresters, here materially assisted the advance of his battalion by capturing two machine-gun posts single-handed. See Appendix E, No. 27.

[3] It was during this retirement that Lce.-Corp. Coltman, a stretcher-bearer of the 1/6th North Staffordshire, so distinguished himself by his courage and devotion to duty. See Appendix E, No. 11.

[4] The fighting in this operation had been severe, and the 46th Division had suffered considerable losses, especially in officers, but, in comparison with our casualties, those of the enemy must have been very great, as the 46th Division alone captured 2,000 prisoners. Since the morning of September 29th the 46th Division had captured 6,000 prisoners and over 70 guns at a cost of 2,500 killed, wounded, and missing.

attacked towards Fontaine Uterte at 10 a.m., but had been unable to gain much ground.

The action of the XV French Corps During the night of October 3rd the 126th French Division of the First French Army took over the southern portion of the IX Corps front as far north as Chardon Vert, thus relieving the 1st Division. This division was then withdrawn to the Vraignes area with the exception of the 3rd Brigade, which was placed temporarily at the disposal of the 46th Division.

On the night of October 2nd the 7th Australian Brigade took over the front from Folemprise Farm to Mont St. Martin from the 5th Brigade; The Australian Corps; the attack of the 2nd Australian Division the 6th Brigade, in reserve, was concentrated south of Nauroy. The 5th and 7th Brigades formed up for the attack each with two battalions in line. The leading battalions were to capture the Beaurevoir-Fonsomme Line, after which the two supporting battalions of each brigade were to "leap-frog" the leading battalions and capture the final objectives. The 5th Brigade was allotted eight tanks of the 13th Mark V Tank Battalion, and eight whippet tanks of the 3rd Battalion. Eight tanks of the 8th and 16th Mark V Tank Battalions assisted the 7th Brigade. The approach march of the tanks to the assembly positions was long and difficult, owing to the darkness and the number of trenches and shell holes, and only six of the Mark V tanks allotted the 5th Brigade arrived. These had to cover a distance of 8,500 yards.

At "zero" the barrage came down covering the "starting line" and remained stationary there for six minutes, after which pause it advanced at the rate of 100 yards every four minutes. The barrage was good, and the infantry started well up to it; the tanks, however, were late, though those that survived the approach march caught up the infantry later.

The 18th and 19th Battalions, on the right and left of the 5th Brigade front respectively, gained the support trench of the Beaurevoir–Fonsomme Line between 7.15 a.m. and 7.45 a.m., with the exception of 500 yards of trench immediately south of the Estrées–Genève road.[1] Here, the two inner companies of each of these battalions were unable to penetrate the thick wire in the face of heavy machine-gun fire, and no tanks had as yet arrived. These four companies were withdrawn to the sunken road east of Estrées, and the troops which were already in the support trench endeavoured to clear the trenches by working inwards from the north and south, but without success. The trenches were then subjected to thirty minutes' bombardment, after which two companies of the 19th Battalion attacked from the north and captured the trenches, together with 200 prisoners and 18 machine-guns.

Meanwhile, when the 18th and 19th Battalions had reached the support trenches of the Beaurevoir–Fonsomme Line on the flanks, the 17th on the right and the 20th on the left had passed through them. Only two companies of the 17th Battalion were able to go forward, as the remaining two companies had become involved in the struggle for the trenches which had held up the first attack. The advance of the 17th Battalion was checked

---

[1] Lieut. Joseph Maxwell, 18th Battalion, displayed fine leadership in this attack. See Appendix E, No. 35.

THE WIRE IN FRONT OF THE BEAUREVOIR LINE.

By kind permission of the Australian Government.

north-east of Wiancourt by machine-gun and artillery fire, but later it was reinforced by a company of the 19th Battalion and gained touch with the 46th Division on the right. The 20th Battalion, in passing through the Beaurevoir–Fonsomme Line, was deflected to the left by the machine-gun fire from the trenches which had held up the four companies of the 18th and 19th Battalions.[1] It advanced as far as the road junction near Beaurevoir Mill, but was forced to withdraw down the western slopes of the hill. Thus, owing to the advance of the 17th and 20th Battalions having been diverted outwards, there was a wide gap between them, which was further accentuated by the enemy's tenacious defence of La Motte Farm. Shortly before noon, however, after the Germans had been cleared out of the trenches east of Estrées, the four companies of the 18th and 19th Battalions advanced, captured La Motte Farm with the aid of two tanks, and filled the gap with a line of posts. By 2 p.m. the 5th Brigade held the general line Wiancourt–La Motte Farm with all four battalions in line, and with the 23rd Battalion of the 6th Brigade in close support.

On the front of the 7th Brigade the 25th Battalion on the right advanced about 500 yards and captured some enemy posts without difficulty; the 27th Battalion on the left met with some resistance, but reached the Torrens Canal. Both battalions were now close up to the Masnières–Beaurevoir Line, and, with the assistance of two tanks which had caught up the 25th Battalion, the line was captured. One company of the 27th Battalion encountered about 100 of the enemy lining a bank and firing at the troops of the 50th Division advancing on the left, but Lewis guns were promptly brought to bear on them, and, after 40 of the enemy had been killed, the remaining 60 surrendered. The whole of the support trenches of the Masnières–Beaurevoir Line on the 7th Brigade front had been secured by 8 a.m.; touch, however, had been temporarily lost with the XIII Corps north-west of Lormisset Farm.

At 8 a.m. the 26th and 28th Battalions " leap-frogged " the leading battalions, the 26th Battalion advancing towards Bellevue Farm, and the 28th Battalion working northwards up the Masnières–Beaurevoir Line. Bellevue Farm was captured, the dug-outs and cellars were cleared, and two field guns were secured just beyond the farm. With the Germans, however, still in possession of Beaurevoir Mill hill and the high ground north of Bellevue Farm, and also debouching from Beaurevoir, the position of the right of the 26th Battalion was very exposed. It was, therefore, withdrawn from Bellevue Farm, and gained touch with the 5th Brigade in the Kukri valley. The 28th Battalion reached the Beaurevoir–Gouy road with practically no opposition, but north of the road the opposition stiffened, and at 9.30 a.m. the advance was checked. Strong fighting patrols then moved north-east and endeavoured to reach Prospect Hill, but field guns firing from the vicinity of Guisancourt Farm, combined with machine-gun fire from Prospect Hill and Beaurevoir, prevented this manœuvre from being successful. During the afternoon attempts were made by both the 26th and 28th Battalions to push forward

---

[1] This was an interesting case of an exception to the general tendency of troops to be drawn in the direction from which fire is coming.

with the object of regaining Bellevue Farm and the intervening ground between it and Guisancourt Farm, but with only limited success, and the line was established from south-east of Bellevue Farm to the Masnières–Beaurevoir Line 500 yards south of Guisancourt Farm, where a junction was made with the 50th Division on Prospect Hill.

In view of the resistance offered to the advance of the 5th and 7th Brigades, Maj.-Gen. Rosenthal decided to employ the three battalions of the 6th Brigade which were still in reserve, in order to gain the high ground north-west of Montbrehain, and Beaurevoir Mill; the 22nd, 23rd, and 24th Battalions were, therefore, placed at the disposal of the 5th Brigade. The 21st Battalion, which had already reinforced the 7th Brigade, remained with it, and, as this brigade had reached most of its objectives, and an assault on Beaurevoir was not to be attempted that day, the 21st Battalion was not employed and remained in support at Folemprise Farm. The 22nd, 23rd, and 24th Battalions assembled in the Beaurevoir–Fonsomme Line north-east of Estrées during the afternoon. At 6.30 p.m. they advanced, and ten minutes later, when the barrage lifted, passed through the battalions of the 5th Brigade. By 8.30 p.m. all three battalions had secured their objective without difficulty and had joined up with the 46th Division north of Ramicourt.

The 2nd Australian Division during the day's operations had captured the Masnières–Beaurevoir–Fonsomme Line on a front of about 6,000 yards. The enemy's losses in killed were very heavy, and the prisoners captured amounted to 28 officers and 1,164 other ranks, belonging to the 21st, 25th, and 119th Divisions, together with 163 machine-guns and 11 field guns. Eleven Australian battalions, whose average fighting strength was 260 rifles, were engaged in the fighting; their casualties were not more than 1,000 killed, wounded, and missing.[1]

On the XIII Corps front the 50th Division had assembled for the attack with two brigades in line. The 151st Brigade on the right was

The XIII Corps; the attack of the 50th Division

disposed with the 6th Royal Inniskilling Fusiliers and the 4th King's Royal Rifle Corps in line, and with the 1st King's Own Yorkshire Light Infantry in close support. In addition, the 2nd Northumberland Fusiliers of the 150th Brigade was placed at the disposal of the 151st Brigade, and took up a position west of Mont St. Martin to ensure touch being kept with the Australian Corps. The 149th Brigade on the left had two of its battalions holding a defensive flank along the canal, and one in support near The Knob. The 150th Brigade, less one battalion, was held in divisional reserve near Bony.

The attack was successfully launched at 6.5 a.m. Moving forward through the mist, the infantry kept close up to the barrage, which advanced at the rate of 100 yards every four minutes. The 151st Brigade entered Le Catelet and Gouy before 7 a.m., but touch on the right was temporarily lost with the Australians who had reached Lormisset Farm. This was due to the deflection of the 6th Royal Inniskilling Fusiliers to the left.

---

[1] An unsolicited tribute to the skill and enterprise of the Australians was given by a German officer captured by the 25th Battalion, who exclaimed, " You Australians are all bluff ; you attack with practically no men and are on the top of us before we know where we are."

Prospect Hill

Le Catelet Wood

Tunnel Spoil-bank

Vauxhall Quarry

Gouy

The Knob

Le Catelet

Northern entrance to Tunnel

Knob Wood

Escaut River

Macquincourt Farm

Hindenburg Line

Canal

GOUY LE CATELET AND MACQUINCOURT FARM.

Oblique air photograph.

This Battalion had been allotted the task of capturing Prospect Hill, but it was caught in flank by machine-gun fire from Gouy, and the well-known tendency of all troops to be drawn in the direction from which fire is coming at once showed itself; the battalion swung round to the left and became involved in the fighting in Gouy. The Commanding Officer of the 1st King's Own Yorkshire Light Infantry quickly grasped the situation, and, showing sound judgment and initiative, immediately moved his battalion forward with all speed. It succeeded in catching up the barrage, and by 10 a.m. had secured Prospect Hill and joined up with the Australians. The 6th Royal Inniskilling Fusiliers and the 4th King's Royal Rifle Corps, meanwhile, pushed through Gouy and Le Catelet, and by 10.30 a.m., after some stubborn fighting, the 54th German Division was driven out of these villages, except for small parties which still lurked in the cellars and dug-outs. The objective had now been reached along the front of the 50th Division, except on the left centre where the situation was uncertain. Consequently, it was arranged that the artillery fire should lift off the high ground north of Le Catelet at 11.30 a.m., and that strong patrols should endeavour to seize it. Failing this, the two battalions of the 150th Brigade which had not as yet been engaged, were to capture the high ground during the afternoon. As the employment of these two battalions would have left the 50th Division without any reserves, one battalion of the 7th Brigade of the 25th Division was ordered up to the vicinity of Mont St. Martin.[1]

At 12 noon our line on Prospect Hill was firmly established and was continued along the northern outskirts of Gouy and Le Catelet to Macquincourt Farm. An hour later a strong counter-attack against Gouy was delivered by at least five battalions of the 21st Reserve Division, which had been brought down from further north for the purpose. This attack was made down the valley from Aubencheul-aux-Bois, and after a stiff fight the enemy succeeded in penetrating to the centre of Gouy. The 2nd Northumberland Fusiliers of the 150th Brigade was sent forward, and, forming up south of Gouy, soon drove the enemy out of the village. By 7 p.m. the 50th Division was firmly established north of Gouy and Le Catelet. The 150th Brigade then relieved the 151st Brigade on Prospect Hill and north of Gouy, the latter brigade being withdrawn into reserve about Bony.

As the result of the fighting on October 3rd, nine different German divisions had been engaged by the Fourth Army, of which two divisions had been brought up from reserve, and one had been brought

The result of the day's fighting down from the front of the Third Army. Fighting had been severe on most parts of the front, and the number of counter-attacks, five in all, showed that the enemy had received orders to hold the Masnières–Beaurevoir–Fonsomme Line at all costs. Evidence of a retirement, to be carried out shortly to a line further in rear, began to accumulate as prisoners were examined. An Alsatian prisoner, whose information was regarded as reliable, stated that railways and roads were being mined in the back areas, and that the bridges were

---

[1] This order was cancelled later, as Maj.-Gen. Jackson considered he had sufficient troops available.

being prepared for demolition at Le Cateau and Busigny. It seemed likely, therefore, that the more active resistance of the enemy during the day was intended to cover the preparations for a withdrawal.

Although we had gained a tactical victory on October 3rd, we had not compelled the enemy to withdraw in front of the right of the Third Army as we had hoped to do. This could only be accomplished by the capture of Beaurevoir, and by extending the salient which we had already made in the enemy's line. The 2nd Australian Division, however, was too weak in numbers to renew the attack on the same frontage as on October 3rd, and it was, therefore, arranged that the XIII Corps should extend its front southwards to the Torrens Canal immediately north of La Motte Farm. This front was taken over that night by the 50th Division with the 7th Brigade, which had moved up from Ronssoy to Quennemont Farm during the afternoon of October 3rd, the 74th and 75th Brigades moving respectively up to Mont St. Martin and Ste. Emilie from Moislains and Nurlu. The 7th Australian Brigade, when relieved, moved back into reserve near Nauroy.

Orders were issued on the evening of October 3rd for the attack to be continued on the 4th. The IX Corps was to seize Mannequin Hill and the high ground north-east of it; the Australian Corps was to make a small advance on the high ground north-west of Montbrehain, capture Genève, and support the right of the XIII Corps. The XIII Corps was to make the main attack; it was to capture Beaurevoir, to advance its line north of Prospect Hill, and to seize Guisancourt Farm and the high ground north of Le Catelet about La Pannerie South. It was arranged that the First French Army was to co-operate with this attack by an advance towards Fontaine Uterte.

The orders for the continuance of the attack on October 4th

On the front of the IX Corps no advance was made. On the night of October 3rd the 139th Brigade had been relieved by the 138th Brigade and 1/1st Monmouthshire (Pioneers), and, early on the morning of October 4th, the 137th and 138th Brigades were counter-attacked from the direction of Mannequin Hill; this forestalled our attack and kept our troops fully employed in repulsing it. At nightfall the 3rd Brigade of the 1st Division, temporarily attached to the 46th Division, relieved the 137th Brigade, while the 2nd Australian Division relieved the 138th Brigade, thus permitting the infantry brigades of the 46th Division to be withdrawn into reserve.

October 4th; the action of the IX Corps

In the centre of the army front the subsidiary attack by two battalions of the 6th Brigade of the 2nd Australian Division encountered machine-gun fire from the outset. For a short time touch with the 25th Division was lost, but was regained later by the 7th Australian Brigade moving up a portion of its support battalion. By 9 a.m. an advance of 1,000 yards had been made on the left, while on the right the line was moved forward to within 300 yards of the railway.

The action of the 2nd Australian Division

On the XIII Corps front Sir Thomas Morland's orders were for the 25th Division on the right to capture Beaurevoir by enveloping it from the north and south, and also to secure Ponchaux and Guisancourt Farm. The task of the 50th Division on the left was to capture the high ground north of Gouy and Le Catelet, between La Pannerie South and Richmond Quarry. It was intended that, if this attack was successful, the V Corps of the Third Army should push the 38th Division through Gouy to work northwards behind the Hindenburg Line towards La Terrière. Very little time was available for preparations, and consequently the assembly of the troops for the attack was a matter of some difficulty owing to insufficient opportunity for reconnaissance, the darkness of the night, and the heavy rain.

The attack started at 6.10 a.m. under a barrage, in a dense fog which continued until a late hour in the morning and precluded all observation. The right of the 7th Brigade of the 25th Division reached the high ground west of Ponchaux and was in touch with the Australians, but it suffered heavily from fire from Beaurevoir and Ponchaux and was forced to withdraw. Although the left of the brigade made some progress towards Guisancourt Farm, it was checked in front of Beaurevoir. It became clear early in the afternoon that the 7th Brigade was not strong enough to complete its task alone, and Maj.-Gen. Charles began his preparations for renewing the attack next day with stronger forces.

Meanwhile, the 50th Division had captured La Pannerie South; its left, however, was held up by machine-gun fire from Hargival Farm and Richmond Copse, and for some time no progress was made beyond the sunken road between Le Catelet and Hargival Farm. Later in the afternoon the enemy's resistance weakened on this flank, and by 6 p.m. the 149th Brigade had captured Hargival Farm. The 50th Division then established a line along the northern slopes of Prospect Hill through La Pannerie South to Hargival Farm, pending the arrival of the 38th Division of the V Corps, which was already on its way to pass through the 50th Division and continue the attack northwards.

While the fighting was in progress on the Fourth Army front, the First French Army resumed its advance south-east of Le Tronquoy. Attacking at 10 a.m. the XV French Corps entered the outskirts of Lesdins, but was checked by machine-gun fire from Flatiron Wood south of Chardon Vert. The troops west of the canal found the enemy's resistance weakening, and, pushing patrols across, captured Morcourt.

The attack on Beaurevoir on October 4th having been unsuccessful, it was decided to continue the attack on the following day, and to capture the village together with the high ground between La Sablonnière and Guisancourt Farm. Simultaneously, an attack was to be delivered on Montbrehain by the 2nd Australian Division. To enable this operation to be carried out, the 2nd Australian Division extended its front southwards during the night of October 4th as far as a point 1,000 yards south-east of Ramicourt, relieving the 138th Brigade of the 46th Division with the 2nd Australian Pioneer Battalion. The IX Corps was to assist the Australians with artillery fire, and to protect their southern flank by

B B

securing Mannequin Hill and the high ground south of Montbrehain by means of strong fighting patrols.

When they advanced on October 5th, the patrols of the IX Corps made some progress up the slopes of Mannequin Hill, but were unable
October 5th; the IX Corps at Mannequin Hill to secure the summit, with the result that the enemy holding the high ground south of Montbrehain subjected our infantry advancing through that village to enfilade fire.

The 6th Australian Brigade formed up for the attack on Montbrehain with the 21st Battalion on the right and the 24th Battalion on the left.
The capture of Montbrehain by the 2nd Australian Division The 23rd and 22nd Battalions were to hold the remainder of the divisional front to the north, and were to keep touch with the 25th Division south of Ponchaux. The 2nd Australian Pioneer Battalion was to support the 21st and 24th Battalions and protect their right flank as they advanced. The 18th Battalion of the 5th Brigade and the 27th Battalion of the 7th Brigade were placed at the disposal of the 6th Brigade Commander as a reserve against hostile counter-attacks, and by "zero" these two battalions were concentrated south and north of Wiancourt respectively.

The attack was assisted by twelve tanks of the 16th Mark V Tank Battalion, four each being allotted to the 21st, 24th, and the 2nd Australian Pioneer Battalions; eight brigades of field artillery supplied the creeping barrage, which covered the advance at the rate of 100 yards every four minutes.

The assembly was completed under fairly heavy shell fire, a certain amount of gas shell being employed, and at 6.5 a.m. the advance began. The 21st and 24th Battalions swept forward, the former followed by the pioneer battalion, which protected its right flank as the advance progressed. The tanks were late in arriving at the "starting line," and consequently the initial stage of the advance was carried out without their aid, though later, during the fighting in the village itself, they were of the greatest assistance. Machine-gun fire was encountered during the advance on Montbrehain until the village was entered. On the north-western outskirts of the village one strong point in particular, in a quarry which was held by over 100 men of the 241st Division and 40 machine-guns, offered a strong resistance, and was only captured by the 24th Battalion after a fierce struggle.[1] The 21st Battalion, keeping touch with the right company of the 24th Battalion, pushed forward through Montbrehain assisted by some tanks. It overcame the resistance of many machine-gun posts and finally established a line of posts clear of, and to the east of, the village. These posts were, however, withdrawn later on account of the severity of the enemy's shelling. Meanwhile, touch was temporarily lost between the companies of the 24th Battalion in the village, but steady progress was made, and touch was maintained with the company of the same battalion which was advancing north of the village.

While this fighting was in progress the 2nd Australian Pioneer Bat-

[1] The capture of this quarry was in a large measure due to the courage and leadership of Lieut. Ingram, 24th Battalion. See Appendix E, No. 25.

Bellevue Farm

BEAUREVOIR and BELLEVU

RM from the west.

talion, advancing in support of the right flank of the 21st Battalion, also met with considerable opposition. The battalion was accompanied by two tanks, which rendered it much assistance. While engaged in protecting the right flank of the 21st Battalion, the pioneers were subjected to heavy fire from Mannequin Hill and Doon Hill. In spite of this, they established a defensive flank south of Montbrehain through Neville's Cross, joining up with the IX Corps on the right and with the 21st Battalion on the left north-east of the village, and held it all day. Considerable assistance was also rendered to the 24th Battalion by a company of the pioneers, which had followed it through the village; realising the difficulties that the 24th Battalion was encountering, the company commander promptly filled the gap between its right and centre companies. The fighting in the village had been severe, and the casualties were considerable; consequently, the 18th and 27th Battalions were moved up from reserve, the former reinforcing the 21st, and the latter the 24th Battalion. By 4 p.m., with their assistance, the whole of Montbrehain was completely in our hands. Over 600 unwounded prisoners and 150 machine-guns were captured during the day, and of the former the 2nd Australian Pioneer Battalion could claim at least 300. These prisoners came from ten different regiments, thus again indicating the general state of the enemy's disorganisation along the battle front.

During the night of October 4th the 25th Division had strengthened its front by moving up the 74th Brigade into the line on the left of the 7th Brigade, while the 75th Brigade was concentrated in close support in the vicinity of the Masnières–Beaurevoir Line. During the night Beaurevoir was bombarded intermittently, but, although the houses were considerably knocked about, the majority of the cellars were undamaged.

The XIII Corps; the capture of Beaurevoir by the 25th Division

The attack of the 25th Division was launched at 6 a.m. under a powerful artillery barrage, five minutes before that of the Australians against Montbrehain. On the right the 21st Manchester, leading the attack of the 7th Brigade, and supported by four tanks of the 4th Mark V Tank Battalion, advanced through the southern outskirts of the village. On the left the 74th Brigade, assisted by four tanks of the 4th Mark V Tank Battalion, advanced against Bellevue Farm, Guisancourt Farm, and the northern portion of Beaurevoir, with the 9th Yorkshire, the 13th Durham Light Infantry, and the 11th Sherwood Foresters in line from right to left. Although the thick ground mist restricted observation, the attack started well, and good progress was made on the flanks. Beaurevoir was entered by the infantry of the 74th Brigade and by two of the supporting tanks; the enemy, however, was holding it in considerable strength, and a counter-attack from the north forced the 74th Brigade back to their "starting line," with the exception of some men of the 9th Yorkshire who held on to Bellevue Farm. At 12 noon Maj.-Gen. Charles decided to wait until dusk before renewing the attack, and, meanwhile, placed two companies of the 1/8th Royal Warwickshire at the disposal of the 74th Brigade in order to assist it in the capture of Guisancourt Farm. During the afternoon the 75th Brigade moved forward in order to make a direct attack on Beaurevoir after dark in conjunction with the 7th and 74th Brigades, which were to push forward on the flanks towards Ponchaux and Guisancourt Farm respectively.

At 6.30 p.m. the attack was launched and achieved immediate success. In the centre the 1/5th Gloucestershire and the 1/8th Worcestershire of the 75th Brigade passed through the 9th Yorkshire and the 13th Durham Light Infantry. The 1/5th Gloucestershire, not waiting for the barrage to lift, went right through Beaurevoir, taking the garrison completely by surprise, and dug itself in well east of the village. The 1/8th Worcestershire came under heavy machine-gun fire from the railway cutting on the west of the village, and its advance was temporarily checked. A critical situation was saved by the prompt action of the right platoon commander, who worked round the left flank of the enemy with his platoon and attacked the defenders of the railway cutting from the rear. This enabled the battalion to resume its advance, clear the northern half of Beaurevoir, and establish a line clear of the village on the left of the 1/5th Gloucestershire. On the right the 21st Manchester of the 7th Brigade captured the cemetery south-east of Beaurevoir, but was unable to reach Ponchaux; on the left the enemy still held Guisancourt Farm. At 4.10 a.m., however, on the morning of October 6th the farm, together with 195 prisoners, was finally secured by the 11th Sherwood Foresters and the two companies of the 1/8th Royal Warwickshire, owing to the initiative of the Commander of the 74th Brigade. This completed the difficult task which had been allotted to the 25th Division. Beaurevoir, with the three advanced posts of Beaurevoir Mill, Bellevue Farm, and Guisancourt Farm, formed a very strong natural position, considerably strengthened by wire and machine-gun emplacements. Although very much disorganised, the enemy put up a good fight, prisoners being taken from four different divisions, the 21st, 21st Reserve, 119th, and 121st. The performance of the 25th Division was all the more creditable as it had very short notice in which to make its preparations for the attack. Perhaps the outstanding feature of the operations was the daylight attack of the 1/5th Gloucestershire and the 1/8th Worcestershire, which finally captured Beaurevoir village.

During the early morning of the 5th the 149th Brigade of the 50th Division pushed patrols across the canal at Vendhuile and north of that

The advance of the 50th Division north of Gouy, and of the 38th Division of the V Corps village. These patrols, working in conjunction with patrols of the 33rd Division of the V Corps on the left, found Putney evacuated and reached Basket Wood. About midday the 38th Division of the V Corps, after crossing the tunnel defences of the Hindenburg Line near Bony, advanced northwards through Gouy and Le Catelet, and passed through the 50th Division near La Pannerie South. Orders were then issued by Sir Thomas Morland to the 50th Division to withdraw the 149th and 151st Brigades into rest, and to conform to the movement of the 38th Division, which had swung eastwards towards Aubencheul-aux-Bois. This was done, and by nightfall the 150th Brigade had advanced 500 yards beyond Vauxhall Quarry and was in touch with the 38th Division south of Aubencheul-aux-Bois.

The result of the day's fighting had been most satisfactory.

Although Mannequin Hill and the high ground north of it were not in our possession, Montbrehain, Beaurevoir, and Guisancourt Farm had been captured, while the V Corps was now rapidly extending the front of attack northwards on the right of the Third Army. During the day prisoners belonging to ten divisions had been captured, including some from a fairly fresh Saxon division, the 24th.

The result of the day's fighting

During the night of October 5th the 30th American Division moved forward from reserve and relieved the 2nd Australian Division in the Montbrehain sector. At 9 a.m. on October 6th the command of the Australian Corps front passed to Gen. Read, commanding the II American Corps. Subsequently all five divisions of the Australian Corps, with the exception of some of the artillery which remained up in the line with the II American Corps, were concentrated in areas west of Amiens for a long period of rest after six eventful months' fighting. The Australian Corps had begun to come into the line on the Amiens front at the end of March, 1918, and took a prominent part in finally checking the enemy's advance on Amiens. Then followed the series of successful minor operations which it undertook during April, May, June, and July, and which led up to the attack on August 8th. From August 8th—when the Australian Corps, together with the Canadian and III Corps, opened the offensive which had achieved such remarkable success—until October 5th, it had been almost continually attacking. Its advance had covered a distance of 37 miles, during which 116 towns and villages had been captured. Between August 8th and October 5th, the Australian Corps had captured 610 officers and 22,244 other ranks from 30 German divisions, and 332 guns.

The relief of the Australian Corps by the II American Corps on October 6th

Time dims many recollections; but the work of the Australians, their individual intelligence, good comradeship, and bravery will always remain a vivid memory to those who had the honour and pleasure of working with them.

During these operations the work of the 5th Brigade, Royal Air Force, had been as brilliant as ever. Much of it was achieved under bad weather conditions and in face of much stubborn opposition, especially on October 4th and 5th, on which days unusually strong and aggressive German fighting formations were sent over the lines. During the week commencing September 29th, in addition to invaluable contact and artillery patrols, more than 1,500 offensive flights were carried out; 31 enemy aeroplanes were destroyed and 8 were driven down out of control, while 13 enemy observation balloons were brought down in flames; 3,300 bombs were dropped on hostile transport, billets, dumps, railway centres, and headquarters, and upwards of 200,000 machine-gun rounds were fired from the air. The whole of this programme, which was carried on by day and night, was achieved with the loss of only 24 British machines.

The work of the Royal Air Force

The capture by the Fourth, Third, and First British Armies of the Hindenburg Defences on which the enemy had expended so much skill and labour, and which he had believed capable of defying any assault, was the

A review of the situation on October 6th

culminating point of the Allied offensive.   As stated in Sir Douglas Haig's Victory Despatch :

" The enemy's defence in the last and strongest of his prepared positions had been shattered. The whole of the main Hindenburg Line passed into our possession, and a wide gap was driven through such rear trench systems as had existed behind them.

" The effect of the victory upon the subsequent course of the campaign was decisive. The threat to the enemy's communications was now direct and instant, for nothing but the natural obstacles of a wooded and well-watered countryside lay between our armies and Maubeuge.

" Great as were the material losses the enemy had suffered, the effect of so overwhelming a defeat upon a moral already deteriorated was of even larger importance."

That the enemy had had no intention of relinquishing the Hindenburg Line without a desperate struggle is certain. Not only was this proved by documents subsequently captured, but by the attitude of the enemy during the bitter fighting between September 29th and October 5th. Within this period the Germans launched no fewer than thirteen counter-attacks, delivered principally against the flanks of the Fourth Army and depriving us for a short period of Sequehart, Montbrehain, Gouy, Le Catelet, and portions of the Beaurevoir Line. In these counter-attacks the enemy employed his reserve divisions freely. It was significant, however, that they had without exception been engaged previously on several occasions since August 8th.

The strenuous days between September 30th and October 5th had witnessed a prolonged struggle between the Fourth Army and the Second and Eighteenth German Armies. Our object had been to widen the gap made on September 29th ; theirs had been to narrow it, or, at any rate, to close it by retaining possession of the Beaurevoir Line. Thanks to the indomitable spirit of the British soldier, the Fourth Army had gained the day. The right of the Third Army was now able to cross the canal and increase very considerably the front of attack in the next phase of the operations.

By October 6th the enemy's situation was becoming desperate. Not only had he failed to prevent important strategical and tactical successes being gained by our troops, but he had suffered very heavy losses in men and material. During the operations, which included the capture of the Hindenburg and Beaurevoir Lines, the Fourth Army had captured 14,664 prisoners, including 307 officers, and 120 guns. The enemy had employed twenty different divisions against us, two of which were engaged twice, whilst we had only employed twelve divisions.

As regards the future, the Fourth Army was still astride the junction of the 18th German Army of von Hutier and the 2nd German Army of von der Marwitz, hence reserves belonging to both armies could be brought against us. These reserves were estimated at fourteen divisions, all of which had been previously engaged and were in various stages of exhaustion. Moreover, no fresh divisions from reserve had been brought against

FOURTH ARMY ADVANCED HEADQUARTERS ESTABLISHED IN A RAILWAY TRAIN AT MONTIGNY FARM, NEAR ROISEL, DURING THE FIRST TWO WEEKS OF OCTOBER, 1918.

By kind permission of the Australian Government.

the Fourth Army since September 24th, and it was difficult to see how the enemy could reinforce this front by fresh divisions while the Allied forces continued to advance on the whole front from the Argonne to Flanders.

What then were the enemy's intentions on the front of the Fourth Army? From the information obtained from air photographs and the personal reconnaissance of pilots of the 5th Brigade, Royal Air Force, it was ascertained that the enemy was not carrying out any work on defence lines, other than the digging of a few rifle pits here and there. All aerodromes west of the St. Quentin–Busigny–Cambrai railway had been evacuated. The large ammunition dumps at Fresnoy-le-Grand and Brancourt-le-Grand had been emptied, and numerous fires and explosions had been seen in villages and dumps between the front line and Busigny. These signs all tended to indicate an early retirement, and confirmation of this was obtained from the examination of prisoners. Also escaped British prisoners of war stated that on their way from Landrecies they had passed transport and guns, including heavies, moving eastwards, and that civilians were being evacuated from Le Cateau and from the areas as far back as Landrecies.

There was, however, the general situation to consider. As a result of their failure to hold the Hindenburg defences against the British troops, the Germans were compelled to withdraw their forces along the whole front from Lens to Armentières. In the south, in the vicinity of Rheims, they were retreating on a wide front, and in Flanders preparations for an extensive withdrawal had commenced. All this demanded time, and the safety of the German armies in France, therefore, depended on the ability of their troops in the centre to check the advance of the First French Army and the Fourth, Third, and First British Armies for a period long enough to enable a general withdrawal to be properly organised. A complete collapse in this part of the line could only mean overwhelming disaster for all the German Armies, and the enemy, therefore, would have to strive his utmost to stem our advance with such resources as remained to him.

Orders were received from General Headquarters on October 5th for a vigorous attack on a wide front, to be carried out by the Fourth
Sir Douglas Haig's and Third Armies on October 7th, before a new
orders for the con- defensive position further in rear could be organised
tinuance of the offensive by the Germans, while any success gained was to be
exploited by the cavalry.

The date of this attack was shortly afterwards postponed until October 8th.

CHAPTER X

THE ADVANCE TO LE CATEAU, OCTOBER 6TH TO 16TH

Maps 2, 12, 13, and 14

The nature of the country east of the Beaurevoir Line—The objectives for the attack on October 8th—The rôle of the cavalry—The allotment of tanks—Artillery action—The disposition of troops on the Fourth Army front on October 6th—The events of October 6th and 7th—October 8th ; the attack of the IX Corps—The attack of the II American Corps—The attack of the XIII Corps—The result of the day's fighting—The orders and objectives for the continuance of the advance on October 9th—October 9th ; the attack—The action of the cavalry—The capture of Honnechy—Further objectives ordered—The action of the armoured cars—The result of the fighting—October 10th ; the advance resumed ; cavalry action—The infantry advance—The attacks of the 25th and 66th Divisions on St. Benin and Le Cateau—The events of October 11th—The orders from General Headquarters for the continuance of the offensive—The preparations for the attack—The nature of the country ; the Selle—Le Cateau—The readjustment of the front—The dispositions of the troops—The objectives—Information regarding the enemy—The detailed arrangements for the attack.

ON the Fourth Army front our troops had now reached open country, where the enemy had no prepared lines of defence, and which bore few

The nature of the country east of the Beaurevoir Line
traces of the devastation of war. It consisted of open undulating ground devoid of hedges and free from wire, and was well suited to the employment of cavalry and tanks. The probable points of resistance, until the Selle was reached, were the villages, the small scattered woods north of Brancourt-le-Grand and Bohain, and the line of the railway running north and south, a short distance west of Bohain and Busigny. The villages were all intact, and were known to be in most cases still occupied by the civilian population, which had for over four years been in the power of the enemy.

The Selle, on which Le Cateau is situated, was likely to prove the most serious obstacle later on. It seemed from the map that it could be crossed without much difficulty anywhere from its source near Vaux Andigny as far as St. Benin ; between the latter village and Solesmes, however, it appeared probable that a crossing could only be effected at the fords or by bridges. The river was the obvious line behind which the enemy would make his first determined stand and endeavour to reorganise his forces. On the southern flank of this position, and south of Vaux Andigny, there were two woods of considerable size, Riquerval Wood and Andigny Forest.

On receipt of the orders from General Headquarters on October 5th,

LE CATEAU from th

Le Cateau Station   St. Benin

HONNECHY road

Sir Henry Rawlinson issued his orders for the attack on October 8th.
Two objectives, known as the first objective and the line

The objectives for the
attack on October 8th

of exploitation, were allotted to the IX, II American, and XIII Corps, each of which was to attack on a front of about 4,000 yards.

As its first objective, the IX Corps on the right was given Mannequin Hill, Beauregard Farm, and the high ground between Fresnoy-le-Grand and Montbrehain. If the First French Army, which was to attack simultaneously on the right, succeeded in capturing Fontaine-Uterte and Croix-Fonsomme, the IX Corps was to push on and occupy Mericourt, while the 5th Cavalry Brigade was to exploit towards Fresnoy-le-Grand and Bohain. If the First French Army should be unable to take these villages, the right of the IX Corps was not to advance beyond its first objective; its left, however, was to keep touch with the II American Corps and push on to Brancoucourt.

The II American Corps in the centre was allotted Brancourt-le-Grand and Vaux-le-Prêtre as its first objective, after the capture of which, it was to exploit towards Brancoucourt and Prémont, and secure the woods and copses between those two places.

The XIII Corps on the left was to seize a line which included Le Hamage Farm and Les Marliches Farm as its first objective, joining up with the II American Corps on the right on the Roman road from Estrées to Maretz, and on the left with the V Corps of the Third Army, which was to capture the village of Villers Outréaux. Its line of exploitation included Serain. " Zero " for the attack was to be at 5.10 a.m. on the 8th.

If the attack was successful, the cavalry was to be ready to move in the direction of Le Cateau and secure the railway junctions at that place and at Busigny. If the opportunity offered, it was to

The rôle of the
cavalry

operate against the flank and rear of the enemy opposing the Third and First British Armies and endeavour to cut his communications about Valenciennes. In order that no opening might be lost the cavalry was to keep close touch with the advancing infantry and tanks. It was left to Sir Charles Kavanagh, commanding the Cavalry Corps, to decide when to send the cavalry through.

For the operations one company of whippets of the 6th Tank Battalion was allotted to the IX Corps. The II American Corps was allotted

The allotment of
tanks

two companies of whippets of the 6th Tank Battalion, and the 4th and 301st Mark V Tank Battalions; of the latter one battalion was to assist in the attack on Brancourt-le-Grand and the other was to remain in corps reserve. With the XIII Corps were one company of whippets of the 3rd Tank Battalion and the 1st Mark V Tank Battalion; of these the latter was to be held in corps reserve.

The whippets were to follow closely on the heels of the infantry, and, after the protective barrage lifted off the line of the first objective, they were to push on independently to the line of exploitation, beyond which they were not to proceed.

The attack was to be launched under cover of a barrage, which was

c c

to come down at "zero" 200 yards in front of the infantry "starting line." The first lift was to be made three minutes after "zero," after which the lifts were to be made at three minute intervals up to and including the 12th lift; the barrage was then to be lifted every four minutes until the line of the first objective was reached. A protective barrage was to be maintained for thirty minutes covering the first objective, after which it was to cease; the further advance of the infantry and tanks being covered by specially detailed brigades of field artillery. The selection of targets for the heavy artillery was left to corps, but, as it was most important that the action of the cavalry should not be interfered with by the heavy guns, the II American and XIII Corps were each ordered to detail a special contact aeroplane, whose sole duty was to warn artillery units by wireless of the passage of the cavalry through the infantry. As an additional precaution, the headquarters of the leading cavalry brigade was to fire a special "golden-rain" signal rocket when the cavalry passed through. Moreover, orders were issued that the 14-inch guns should lift off Busigny at five hours after "zero," and that at the same time the 9·2-inch guns should cease firing, while the fire of the artillery under the command of corps was to be confined, as soon as the cavalry had passed through, to targets engaged by direct observation or in answer to calls from the air.

Artillery action

On October 6th the front of the Fourth Army was held as follows :—From Chardon Vert to Neville's Cross, just south of Montbrehain, by the IX Corps, with the 6th Division, reinforced by the 139th Brigade of the 46th Division, in line, and with the 46th Division, less the 139th Brigade, and the 5th Cavalry Brigade in support. From Neville's Cross to the Torrens Canal by the II American Corps, with the 30th American Division in line and the 27th in reserve. From the Torrens Canal to a point about 1,000 yards south of Villers Outréaux by the XIII Corps, with the 25th Division and 50th Division in line, and with the 66th Division in support. The Cavalry Corps, consisting of the 1st and 3rd Cavalry Divisions, was in reserve near the St. Quentin Canal.

The disposition of troops on the Fourth Army front on October 6th

The two days prior to the attack were occupied in completing the preparations, and only a few minor operations were carried out. On October 6th the 50th Division, working in co-operation with the V Corps, captured a portion of the Masnières–Beaurevoir Line between Guisancourt Farm and Aubencheul-aux-Bois, and secured a number of prisoners. On October 7th the 117th Regiment of the 30th American Division made an advance of about 500 yards; in this operation the Americans captured 150 prisoners of the 20th German Division, which was engaged on the Fourth Army front for the first time. On the same day a strong counter-attack against the French in the Morcourt area gave the enemy possession of some ground, which he retained until the following day.

The events of October 6th and 7th

On the front of the IX Corps the attack was to be made by the 6th Division, commanded by Maj.-Gen. Marden, assisted by the 139th Brigade of the 46th Division which was attached to it. The 16th and 71st Brigades

October 8th; the attack of the IX Corps

No. 80.

MONTBREHAIN AND BRANCOURT LE GRAND.

Oblique air photograph.

were in line from right to left, with the 139th Brigade keeping touch with the French on the right, and with the 18th Brigade in close support.

Launched under cover of a heavy barrage and assisted by the whippets, the attack met with immediate success, and the first objective was quickly gained. The only serious opposition encountered was experienced by the 16th Brigade from the fire of machine-guns in Mannequin Wood and the village of Mericourt. The whippets of the 6th Tank Battalion supporting this attack broke down; the crews made very gallant efforts to repair them under fire, but they were all put out of action by hostile artillery. By midday Mannequin Hill, Doon Hill, and Beauregard Farm had been captured, but an attempt of the 5th Cavalry Brigade at this period to break through just south of Brancourt-le-Grand and capture some field guns at Jonnecourt Farm was frustrated by the enemy's machine-gun fire. The French on the right were held up by machine-gun fire from Cerise Wood.

After some strenuous bomb fighting in the trenches of the Beaurevoir–Fonsomme Line east of Sequehart, the 1st West Yorkshire, which was attached to the 16th Brigade, secured Cerise Wood, where three officers and 190 other ranks of the 84th German Division surrendered, and shortly afterwards the village of Mericourt was rushed by the 16th Brigade. After the capture of Cerise Wood the French resumed their advance, and by 3.30 p.m. had gained possession of Fontaine-Uterte. At about the same time the resistance in Mannequin Wood was overcome by the 1st West Yorkshire, five officers and 193 other ranks being taken prisoner. By nightfall the IX Corps had reached the line of exploitation on the left, but had progressed little beyond the first objective on the right flank, as the French had been unable to keep pace with our advance. Over 1,200 prisoners of the 24th, 34th, 221st, and 241st Divisions and four field guns were captured during the day by the IX Corps.

The attack of the II American Corps was carried out with great dash by the 30th American Division with the 59th Brigade, with one battalion of the 60th Brigade attached, leading. The principal organised resistance came from Brancourt-le-Grand, which was, however, soon captured with the assistance of the 301st American Tank Battalion, and by 2.15 p.m. the attacking troops had reached the line of exploitation. In this satisfactory operation the Americans captured 30 guns and over 1,500 prisoners of the 20th, 21st, 208th, and Jäger Divisions, and the Cyclist Brigade.

The attack of the II American Corps

The XIII Corps employed three divisions, the 66th Division having come into the line on the evening of October 7th, between the 25th Division on the right and the 50th Division on the left. On the right the 7th Brigade of the 25th Division was to attack through Ponchaux, with its centre directed on the Serain Farms, and was to maintain connection with the II American Corps; the 74th and 75th Brigades were in reserve. In the centre the South African Brigade and the 198th Brigade of the 66th Division were to carry out the main attack, the objectives of which included the village of Serain; the 197th Brigade was held in reserve west of Beaurevoir. The advance of the left flank of the 66th Division was to be protected by the 151st Brigade of the 50th Division

The attack of the XIII Corps

As the V Corps had arranged to attack the village of Villers Outréaux at 1 a.m., four hours and ten minutes before the Fourth Army main attack was to be launched, the 50th Division was ordered to attack Villers Farm, a position just south-west of Villers Outréaux, from which the enemy could enfilade the Masnières–Beaurevoir Line both to the north and south, simultaneously with the V Corps. The 1st King's Own Yorkshire Light Infantry successfully accomplished this task, but the enemy's artillery retaliation inflicted heavy casualties on the 198th and South African Brigades while they were forming up for the main attack. In spite of this, thanks to the steadiness and discipline of the troops, the assembly was completed punctually and without confusion.

The attack was delivered with great vigour and met with immediate success. Some resistance at Ponchaux was quickly overcome, and the first objective was soon gained. The whippet tanks then pushed on towards the exploitation line, but most of them were put out of action by shell or anti-tank rifle fire; an attempt by the 2nd Cavalry Brigade to break through was also frustrated south-west of Maretz by hostile machine-gun fire. The infantry, meanwhile, made rapid progress, and Serain was captured with the assistance of the 1st Tank Battalion. The exploitation line was reached at 11 a.m., except on the left where the advance of the 198th Brigade was enfiladed by field and machine-gun fire from Villers Outréaux, which was not captured by the V Corps until later. After the capture of this village the left flank of the XIII Corps also reached the line of exploitation without any difficulty.

Sir Thomas Morland now issued orders for the 25th and 66th Divisions to establish themselves securely on the exploitation line and to send forward patrols to Elincourt, Avelu, and Pinon Wood, which they were to occupy if not strongly held by the enemy. No attempt, however, was to be made to capture them if this would entail heavy fighting; the 50th Division was at the same time ordered to concentrate north-east of Gouy in corps reserve.

At nightfall the line held by the XIII Corps ran just clear of the eastern outskirts of Prémont and Serain to the Elincourt–Malincourt road; over 1,200 prisoners and some guns had been captured during the day.

The attack had been an unqualified success. All objectives on the whole army front had been secured, and over 4,000 prisoners and 56 guns had been taken. Though the enemy still retained **The result of the day's fighting** sufficient cohesion to prevent the cavalry breaking through, his disorganisation was pronounced. Prisoners were captured from seventy-three different battalions of thirty regiments of fifteen divisions, in addition to artillery and machine-gun units of two other divisions and companies of the 2nd Cyclist Brigade.[1] During the afternoon the roads converging on Le

---

[1] The divisions encountered were the 2nd Guard, 8th, 20th, 21st, 21st Reserve, 24th, 30th, 34th, 38th, 84th, 119th, 121st, 204th, 208th, 221st (machine-gun units only), 241st (artillery only), Jäger, and 2nd Cyclist Brigade. Of these divisions the enemy had reinforced his line with the Jäger, 204th, 208th, and the 2nd Cyclist Brigade, the 204th having just arrived from Lorraine, while the 2nd Cyclist Brigade was being employed for the first time, since its arrival from Russia a few months previously.

Cateau were blocked with transport, and full advantage of this was taken by our airmen. Between 5.30 p.m. and midnight the German airmen made a most determined bombing attack against the area east of Beaurevoir on both sides of the main Estrées–Le Cateau road, in which the 1st and 3rd Cavalry Divisions were located. The Germans were evidently very nervous lest our cavalry should break through, and tried this means of preventing it. Although the bombing was extremely violent while it lasted our casualties from it were luckily light.

Sir Henry Rawlinson still hoped that, if our victory were followed up at once, the cavalry might be given the opportunity, denied to them on the 8th, of completing the rout of the enemy. Orders were accordingly issued for the offensive to be resumed at 5.20 a.m. on the 9th, in conjunction with an advance of the Third British and First French Armies.

The orders and objectives for the continuance of the advance on October 9th

The IX Corps was allotted the line of the railway between Fresnoy-le-Grand and Bohain as its first objective, including the village of Fresnoy-le-Grand; Bohain, a town of considerable size and importance, was to be its second objective. The first objective given to the II American Corps was the line of the railway between Bohain and Busigny Station, while the villages of Becquigny and Busigny were its second objective. Maretz was to be the first objective of the XIII Corps, and its second objective included the villages of Honnechy and Maurois. The distance to be covered by the XIII Corps was considerably greater than that to be covered by the other two corps; this was due to the long flank which the IX Corps was compelled to maintain in consequence of the difficulty experienced by the French in advancing north-east of St. Quentin. The 5th Mark V Tank Battalion was allotted to the IX Corps, the 4th and 301st American Mark V Tank Battalions and two companies of whippets to the II American Corps, and the 1st Mark V Tank Battalion and one company of whippets to the XIII Corps. The rôle of the cavalry was the same as for October 8th, and it was to be ready to seize any opportunity of breaking through.

At 5.20 a.m. on October 9th the attack was resumed along the whole front. On the right the IX Corps, with the 46th and 6th Divisions in the line,[1] had little difficulty in securing Fresnoy-le-Grand and Jonnecourt Farm. The enemy retreated rapidly before our advance, and by 3 p.m. the line of the railway, which formed the first objective, was secured. So vigorous was the advance of our troops that the enemy's resistance broke down, and the 9th Norfolk of the 6th Division captured Bohain without difficulty towards evening.[2] On our right the French secured Croix-Fonsomme.

October 9th; the attack

The II American Corps, with the 59th Brigade of the 30th Division leading, experienced only slight opposition from hostile rear-

---

[1] The 46th Division took over the right sector of the IX Corps front from the 6th Division on the night of the 8th. The 1st Division also moved further forward.

[2] Four thousand five hundred French inhabitants were liberated in this town, some of whom had been three days without food.

guards, and, advancing rapidly, occupied the villages of Becquigny and Busigny.[1]

Equal success attended the advance further north, where the XIII Corps advanced with the 25th Division on the right and the 66th on the left. Maretz was captured before 7 a.m. by the 75th Brigade of the 25th Division and the 199th Brigade of the 66th Division, and Elincourt and Pinon Wood by the 198th Brigade. Having secured Maretz, the advance was continued by the 25th Division on a two-brigade front, the 74th Brigade coming into line on the right of the 75th Brigade, while in the 66th Division the South African Brigade " leap-frogged " the 198th and 199th Brigades.

It was not until 9 a.m. that the enemy made any show of resistance; the advance of the 25th Division was then checked in front of the railway south-west of Honnechy, and a little later that of the 66th Division on the outskirts of Gattigny Wood.

Throughout the advance the cavalry had kept in close touch with the infantry. The 3rd Cavalry Division (the 6th, 7th, and Canadian

The action of the cavalry

Brigades) followed up closely, while the 1st Cavalry Division was in reserve, but ready to move forward at once, as the rapid retirement of the enemy in front of our advance seemed likely to offer an opportunity for their employment.

At 9.30 a.m. the 3rd Cavalry Division received word that the XIII Corps advance had been checked by machine-gun fire from the railway south-west of Honnechy. Thereupon a squadron of the 6th Cavalry Brigade went forward to Busigny and endeavoured to turn the position from the south, but this attempt had to be abandoned on account of the wired enclosures. Meantime the Canadian Cavalry Brigade, moving north of the main Le Cateau road, found the infantry held up by machine-gun fire from the western edge of Gattigny Wood and from Clary village. At 11 a.m. the Fort Garry Horse made a very dashing attack on the western edge of Gattigny Wood, and not only gained a footing in the wood, but passed through portions of it; this enabled the infantry to resume their advance. At the same time Lord Strathcona's Horse secured a small copse south-east of Clary, and, pushing forward, occupied Mont-aux-Villes Wood midway between Clary and Bertry. In these operations the Canadian Cavalry Brigade captured 230 prisoners of the 8th German Division, two field guns, and 40 machine-guns.

Meantime, the enemy clung tenaciously to the line of the railway south-west of Honnechy. Shortly before noon, however, more artillery arrived,

The capture of Honnechy

and arrangements were made for the railway and village to be attacked by the 25th Division under cover of a barrage. This attack was arranged by Maj.-Gen. Charles in co-operation with Maj.-Gen. Harman, commanding the Third Cavalry Division, who ordered the 6th Cavalry Brigade (3rd Dragoon Guards, 1st Royal Dragoons, and 10th Hussars) to encircle the village,[2]

---

[1] On reaching the first objective, the 60th Brigade " leap-frogged " the 59th Brigade and captured the second objective—Becquigny and Busigny.

[2] While the 10th Hussars were moving into position for the attack, they were observed by hostile aircraft and suffered considerable casualties from bombs and machine-gun fire.

while the Canadian Cavalry Brigade advanced north of Maurois with a view to seizing the high ground north-east of that village.

The concerted attack against Honnechy began at 2 p.m., and within forty minutes the village and the ground to the east of it were captured. Further north the Canadian Cavalry Brigade, after securing 42 prisoners and 5 machine-guns between Clary and Bertry, pushed forward north of Maurois.

In consequence of the slight opposition encountered by the troops during the morning, Sir Henry Rawlinson issued further orders about noon on the 9th. The IX Corps was ordered to secure the high ground north and south of Andigny-les-Fermes; the II American Corps was to push on to Molain, St. Souplet, and St. Benin, and seize the crossings over the Selle at these places; the XIII Corps was ordered to capture Le Cateau. The cavalry was to advance as rapidly as possible on Le Cateau, and then carry out the remainder of the mission allotted to it for October 8th.

Further objectives ordered

The IX and II American Corps did not gain much ground beyond their original final objective for the 9th.

In compliance with their instructions, the Canadian Cavalry Brigade moved forward, and by the evening had taken Troisvilles and occupied the high ground north-west of Le Cateau between Montay and Rambourlieux Farm. The 6th Cavalry Brigade, however, was unable to get to Le Cateau, as the advance was checked by strong opposition from the line St. Souplet–Reumont, which was occupied by parties of the 2nd Cyclist Brigade and by one of the newly arrived regiments of the 204th Division from Lorraine. The 7th Cavalry Brigade then advanced, driving the enemy from Reumont, and filled the gap between the 6th Cavalry Brigade south-east of Reumont and the Canadian Cavalry Brigade on the high ground overlooking Le Cateau. The Third Cavalry Division thus held a line from south-east of Reumont to Rambourlieux Farm along the high ground overlooking the Selle just west of Le Cateau, Montay, and Neuvilly, its left being thrown back along the road running from Neuvilly to Troisvilles. Late in the evening the infantry of the 66th Division arrived and relieved the cavalry, which bivouacked close in the rear of the positions they had captured. In the course of its operations the 3rd Cavalry Division had captured 450 prisoners, 10 guns, and between 50 and 60 machine-guns, but its experiences showed that the enemy's resistance was not yet completely broken, as it had not been possible to make any advance except by vigorous action and hard fighting.

During the operations very effective assistance was given both to the infantry and cavalry by the armoured cars of the 17th Armoured Car Battalion. Seven cars were allotted to the 3rd Cavalry Division, of which three cars were detailed to the 6th and four to the 7th Cavalry Brigade; two cars were kept in corps reserve. The cars accompanying the 6th Cavalry Brigade were ordered at 9 a.m. to go forward and report on the situation at Maretz. One car broke its axle, but the other two proceeded to Maretz, where they were informed that our infantry and cavalry were checked in front of Gattigny Wood. The cars proceeded thither at once and engaged a party

The action of the armoured cars

of about 30 Germans with machine-guns near the cross roads immediately south of the wood ; these they scattered, killing four of the gunners
and capturing 10 machine-guns.   The cars then went towards Honnechy
where, in conjunction with some men of the South African Brigade,
they attacked the enemy in the railway cutting and in the
wood immediately west of the point where the railway crosses the
Roman road.   The cars then pushed on to Maurois, where the bridge
over the railway west of the village was blown up after one of the cars had
crossed it.   This car engaged parties of the enemy in Maurois and Honnechy,
and, near Honnechy Station, surprised and put to flight a guard on the
bridge, which it was preparing to demolish.   Then, after proceeding to
Busigny and killing five out of a party of twenty Germans, who were
going up the road with four trench mortars, it was rejoined by the car
which had been cut off by the destruction of the bridge at Maurois, and
returned to report.[1]   Although the four cars with the 7th Cavalry Brigade
did not have such an adventurous career, they gave effective help to the
3rd Dragoon Guards in the attack on Honnechy.

As a result of the day's fighting all the original objectives and, in
addition, a considerable amount of ground opposite the northern flank of
the army had been secured.   Fresnoy-le-Grand, Bohain,
Becquigny, Busigny Wood, Busigny, Proyart Wood,
Escaufort, Reumont, and Troisvilles had all been
occupied, while our outposts were in advance of these places.   The enemy
held Riquerval Wood, Vaux-Andigny, and La Haie Menneresse, and, further
north, a line from St. Souplet to St. Benin.   Our losses had been small.

The further objectives which Sir Henry Rawlinson had ordered to be
taken during the day had, however, not been secured.   The advance was,
therefore, ordered to be resumed at 5.30 a.m. on the 10th in order to gain
these objectives ; in addition, the XIII and II American Corps were to
push strong infantry patrols across the Selle in order to cover the passage
of our troops across that river.

The morning was dull with mist and rain which prevented any observation of the enemy's movements.   At 6 a.m. the 3rd Cavalry Division,
with the 1st Cavalry Division following behind it, led
the advance ; heavy hostile shell and machine-gun fire,
however, from the line of the Selle between Le Cateau
and Neuvilly, inflicted considerable casualties, and the advance of the
cavalry was checked.   Although our artillery opened fire and the armoured
cars moved forward in support, it was found necessary to withdraw the
7th Cavalry Brigade out of observation behind the ridges west of the Selle.
As the result of a reconnaissance, an advance in the direction of Briastre
was also deemed inadvisable, that village and Viesly being both found
to be strongly held by the Germans.   The resistance of the enemy had now
obviously become too strong to be overcome by cavalry action, and, after
the arrival of the infantry, the Army Commander ordered the withdrawal
of the whole of the Cavalry Corps.[2]   This brought the action of the

The result of the
fighting

October 10th : the
advance resumed ;
cavalry action

---

[1] It fired 2,500 rounds from its machine-guns during this run.

[2] During these three days' operations the cavalry captured over 500 prisoners, 10 guns, and
60 machine-guns, while their casualties amounted to 7 officers and 77 other ranks killed and 41
officers and 479 other ranks wounded or missing.

To face page 201.

Riquerval Wood

RIQUERVAL WOOD.

Oblique air photograph.

cavalry to an end for the time being. Though it had not found the resistance of the enemy sufficiently broken to permit of far-reaching operations in the vicinity of Valenciennes, it had given most effective assistance to the infantry.

Meanwhile, at 5.30 a.m. the infantry advanced close behind the cavalry. On the right on the IX Corps front, the 46th and 6th Divisions advanced each with one infantry brigade as advance guard. In *The infantry advance* addition to field artillery, each division was also supported by a mobile brigade of heavy artillery.[1] Although for the first 2,000 yards the troops made rapid headway, the enemy's resistance increased later, and by 12 noon the advance was definitely checked in front of the western edge of Riqerval Wood. This wood was watched by the 46th Division, while the 6th Division on the left gained touch with the Americans immediately south of Vaux-Andigny.

In the centre the 30th American Division again led the advance of the II American Corps, with the 120th and 119th Regiments of the 60th Brigade in line. The Americans captured the western outskirts of Vaux-Andigny, La Haie Menneresse, and St. Souplet after some fighting. Serious resistance was encountered, however, by the troops of the 60th Brigade, when they reached the west bank of the Selle, and vigorous machine-gun fire from the eastern bank of the river brought the advance to a standstill.

On the left the XIII Corps also made rapid progress until the slopes running down into the valley of the Selle were reached. At 11 a.m. the *The attacks of the 25th and 66th Divisions on St. Benin and Le Cateau* 25th Division, with the 74th and 75th Brigades leading, reached the high ground north-west of St. Benin, when it came under heavy fire from the village, which stands on a commanding knoll, and from the railway embankment between St. Benin and Le Cateau. The 25th Division then arranged to attack St. Benin, and at 2.40 p.m. the village was carried by the 74th Brigade with great dash, and the enemy was driven across the Selle. No further progress by the division was, however, possible, partly because the bridges over the Selle had all been destroyed, but chiefly owing to the heavy machine-gun fire from the railway on the east bank of the river, which appeared to be strongly held.

Further north the 66th Division had by noon secured the spur immediately west of Le Cateau, and patrols were sent forward into the western outskirts of the town, the 198th and 199th Brigades, however, which were leading, were considerably harassed by artillery fire from the high ground south-west of Forest. Arrangements were then made between the 66th and 25th Divisions for a concerted attack on the high ground immediately east of Le Cateau and the spur south-west of Forest; but, as it was found impossible for the 25th Division to complete its arrangements in time, the attack was carried out independently by the 66th Division. The assault was delivered at 5.30 p.m. by the 5th Connaught Rangers on the right and the 18th King's Liverpool on the left. The former battalion rushed the town with great gallantry, and a considerable number

---

[1] The mobile brigade of heavy artillery consisted of two 60-pounder and two 6-inch howitzer batteries.

of men of the 5th Connaught Rangers succeeded in establishing themselves in the deep railway cutting, which runs in a gentle curve round the eastern outskirts of the town. The latter battalion reached Montay, but found the banks of the Selle wired and was unable to cross the stream. As the 5th Connaught Rangers had both its flanks exposed, it was withdrawn during the night to the western portion of Le Cateau, and held the line of the Selle where it passes through the town. During the night St. Benin was taken over by the II American Corps.

Considerable progress had been made by the Fourth Army on the 10th, and numerous villages had been captured;[1] with the exception of a few posts on the western bank the enemy had been driven across the Selle. The enemy's resistance, however, had been strong enough to prevent our troops from securing all their objectives, and corps were accordingly instructed to organise attacks with a view to securing those still uncaptured; in the case of the IX Corps this meant Andigny-les-Fermes, and in that of the II American and XIII Corps the high ground east of the Selle which covered the passages over the river.

On no part of the front was any substantial advance made on the 11th. On the IX Corps front the 46th Division effected a lodgement in Riquerval Wood, but failed to penetrate it, while the 6th Division, after advancing about 1,500 yards towards the Andigny-les-Fermes–Bellevue ridge, could make no further progress. Further north the Americans and the XIII Corps were checked by heavy shell fire, and by rifle and machine-gun fire from the eastern bank of the Selle; the 118th American Regiment, however, completed the capture of Vaux-Andigny and La Haie Menneresse. In Le Cateau prisoners of the 17th Reserve Division were captured, and it was therefore clear that the enemy had reinforced this portion of their front with fresh troops. The result of the day's fighting proved conclusively that the Germans meant to make a stand behind the Selle; moreover, their artillery showed increased activity and seemed to be organised for a stubborn defence.

The events of October 11th

On the right of the Fourth Army the First French Army had been unable to advance beyond Seboncourt, while the Third British Army had reached a line running from the high ground overlooking Neuvilly and Briastre on the Selle, due west to Quiévy, and thence northwards to St. Hilaire-les-Cambrai and St. Aubert, all of which villages were in the hands of the enemy.

The exact dispositions of the enemy were uncertain, and the dull, misty weather of the preceding few days had made reconnaissance by aircraft very difficult. The task of locating the enemy's line had, therefore, to be undertaken chiefly by infantry patrols, whose work was rendered the more arduous by the fact that every movement was under direct observation from the high ground beyond the Selle. The results of the air and infantry reconnaissances showed that the enemy was holding trenches south of Vaux-Andigny and west of Molain, that between Molain and St. Benin new trenches had been dug east of the river, that from opposite St. Benin to Le Cateau Station the enemy held the line of the railway running immediately east of the Selle, and that various parts of the trench

[1] Between the Hindenburg Line and the Selle 12,088 French inhabitants had been liberated.

FRENCH INHABITANTS COMING BACK TO THEIR HOMES IN MARETZ.

By kind permission of the Australian Government.

lines had been wired. It was evident that the position was too strong to be rushed, and that it could only be taken by an organised attack, adequately supported by artillery.

It was important to organise a general attack without any delay. On October 11th, therefore, the Commander-in-Chief, after a conference with the Army Commanders, issued orders for the offensive to be resumed on a large scale. The Fourth Army was to establish itself on the general line Wassigny–Le Cateau, and, in co-operation with the First French Army, was to push forward strong advance guards to the line of the Sambre and Oise Canal. The Third Army was to establish itself on the line of the Selle and secure the passages across that river, while the First Army was to protect the left flank of the Third Army. The Cavalry Corps was to be again placed under the direct orders of General Headquarters, and was to be held in readiness to pursue vigorously in the general direction of Mons, should the enemy carry out a further retirement.

The orders from General Headquarters for the continuance of the offensive

The IX, II American, and XIII Corps were accordingly ordered to be ready to carry out a concerted attack on October 14th or 15th, and, in the meanwhile, to push forward as much artillery as the difficulties of ammunition supply would permit of being employed. Every effort was also to be made to ascertain the enemy's exact dispositions, and to establish a suitable " starting line " for the infantry prior to the attack. The date of the attack was postponed subsequently until October 17th, on account of the enormous difficulties experienced with regard to the bringing up of ammunition and supplies. Between the 8th and 11th of October the Fourth Army had covered an average distance of ten and a half miles on a front of seven and a half miles, while the XIII Corps had advanced some thirteen or fourteen miles, and the only main line of railway for supply ran through St. Quentin, Bohain, and Busigny. This line, which had to serve both the Fourth Army and the northern corps of the First French Army, had been considerably damaged by the enemy. Railway bridges had been demolished and craters blown in the line, and, what was still more difficult to deal with, a large number of delay action mines had been scattered along the permanent way. For at least a month these mines exploded at varying intervals, causing considerable anxiety to those responsible for supplying the army with food and ammunition.

The interval between October 11th and 17th was spent in completing the preparations for the attack. No change in the dispositions of the IX Corps was found necessary ; in the centre the 27th American Division relieved the 30th American Division ; in the XIII Corps the 50th Division, which had just received strong reinforcements to replace the casualties suffered in the heavy fighting at Gouy and Le Catelet, relieved the 25th Division on October 11th. Only a small number of tanks was available for the operation, as it was found necessary to withdraw the 3rd Tank Brigade Headquarters and the 3rd and 4th Tank Battalions to refit. The 5th and 1st Mark V Tank Battalions were allotted to the IX and XIII

The preparations for the attack

Corps respectively; the 301st American Mark V Tank Battalion was to co-operate with the American Corps; the 6th Whippet Battalion and 10th and 16th Mark V Tank Battalions were held in army reserve. The whole of the cavalry was moved further back, except the 5th Cavalry Brigade, which was split up, the 12th Lancers being thenceforward attached to the XIII Corps, and the Royal Scots Greys and 20th Hussars to the IX Corps and II American Corps respectively.[1]

Artillery was brought up as rapidly as the supply of ammunition permitted, and wire-cutting, counter-battery work, and the bombardment of important localities were carried on from the 12th onwards. All the enemy's communications, roads, and approaches were searched by artillery fire, while 6-inch guns, placed well forward, shelled the crossings over the Sambre and Oise Canal, the approaches to the canal at Oisy, Catillon, and Landrecies, and the approaches to others of the more important villages.

A German map was captured on October 13th, which indicated that the enemy had intended to construct certain lines of defence, on to which he was to have retired on October 18th. These positions were called Hermann Stellung I and II. Hermann Stellung I was to have consisted of a line east of the Selle from St. Souplet to Le Cateau; Hermann Stellung II was to have been constructed east of the Sambre and Oise Canal. A continuation of these lines, north of Le Cateau, was shown on a similar map captured by the Third Army about the same date.

On October 14th the weather cleared sufficiently for air reconnaissance, and nearly the whole country as far as Maubeuge was reconnoitred and photographed. The air photographs revealed the non-existence of either of the Hermann lines, except for certain lengths of trenches, protected in places by wire, between Vaux-Andigny and Le Cateau. A number of rifle pits in pairs on the high ground separating the Selle and the Sambre and Oise Canal were also shown.

The chief obstacle to the advance of the Fourth Army was the Selle. The valley of the river is bounded on either side by slopes which rise steeply to undulating country some 200 feet above the level of the stream. But, while the gentle and rolling slopes to the west of the river are devoid of cover or obstruction, those to the east are more abrupt in nature, and the country soon becomes very enclosed owing to the numerous orchards and grass fields, bounded by thick hedges, which restrict the view and make movement difficult. The river itself, between St. Souplet and Le Cateau, is under normal conditions from fifteen to eighteen feet wide and three to four feet deep, and runs through water meadows extending some 100 to 200 yards on either bank. Where it passes through the western edge of Le Cateau the banks are bricked up, the span being about twenty feet. A topographical feature of special importance, as affecting the operations, was the high spur running in a south-westerly direction from Forest towards Montay, from which excellent observation could be obtained up

The nature of the country; the Selle

---

[1] When the II American Corps was withdrawn after the Battle of the Selle, the 20th Hussars were also attached to the IX Corps.

THE SELLE, SOUTH OF LE CATEAU.

To face page 205.

THE SELLE AT THE SOUTHERN OUTSKIRTS OF ST. SOUPLET.

the valley of the river and over the plateau east of it, and from which enfilade fire could be brought to bear on any troops attacking across the river.[1]

Le Cateau itself, through which the Selle runs, was a provincial town of some 10,500 inhabitants and contained several large factories. The houses were solidly built, and deep cellars provided

Le Cateau   excellent shelter against bombardment. The railway embankment and cutting, east of the town, commanded all the exits and formed a natural position of exceptional strength. During the German occupation, the railway station had been largely used for the detrainment of troops, and numerous sidings had been constructed covering an area of some 200 yards wide and 500 yards in length. On the eastern side the yard was bounded by a bank 30 feet high, and the area was surrounded by goods sheds, factories, and other buildings strongly constructed and easily adaptable for defence. There was a mound some 30 feet high, resembling the spoil heap of a coal mine, about fifty yards east of the bank which bounded the goods yard, from which an exceptional command to the south was obtainable. This mound was surrounded by trees, and was thus almost hidden by their foliage from observation from the western bank of the Selle.

Certain difficulties faced the IX Corps with regard to its arrangements for the attack on the Bellevue spur. This spur ran in a north-easterly

The readjustment of direction from Andigny-les-Fermes towards Belle-vue the front Farm. The configuration of the ground made it (see Maps 13 and 14) inadvisable to attack this spur from the west, and Sir Walter Braithwaite decided to do so from the north-west. This necessitated a rearrangement of the boundary between the IX Corps and the II American Corps, in order to provide depth for the attacking troops to form up in. On the night of October 14th, therefore, the IX Corps took over the village of Vaux-Andigny from the II American Corps, thus extending its front by 1,200 yards.

On the XIII Corps front careful and repeated reconnaissance of the Selle south of Le Cateau disclosed the fact that, owing to recent heavy rains, combined with the damming of the stream by the enemy at St. Crepin, St. Benin, and at the southern exit of Le Cateau, the flooded area was rapidly extending, and the river itself was increasing considerably in depth. It was found that at no place on the front of the 50th Division was a crossing practicable without elaborate bridging operations, which would have had to be undertaken under close range machine-gun fire from the opposite bank. Further south, however, in the neighbourhood of St. Souplet the stream was much narrower, and on the front of the II American Corps presented no serious obstacle. In order, therefore, to enable the 50th Division to attack south of Le Cateau, Sir Henry Rawlinson arranged that the front of the XIII Corps should be extended some 2,000 yards southwards, including on the extreme south a stretch of about 500 yards of river, the crossing of which, though difficult, was not impracticable.

---

[1] It was on this high ground that the Germans placed the artillery, which caused such heavy casualties to the artillery of our II Corps, during the Battle of Le Cateau in August, 1914.

The IX Corps, after taking over the extra ground from the Americans, held a front of 7,000 yards, from a point on the Bohain–Aisonville road just south of Riquerval Wood to Vaux-Andigny inclusive. The forward boundary with the French ran in a north-easterly direction through the centre of the Andigny Forest and midway between the hamlets of Blocus d'en Haut and Blocus d'en Bas, the village of Mennevret being wholly in the French area. The II American Corps held some 4,000 yards of front from Vaux-Andigny exclusive to St. Souplet inclusive, while the frontage of the XIII Corps extended thence for 8,000 yards to Montay. It was only possible, however, for the XIII Corps to attack along certain portions of this front.

The dispositions of the troops

The objectives given to the corps were ambitious and comprised the capture of the whole of the ground lying between the Selle and the Sambre and Oise Canal, bounded on the south by the boundary with the French, and on the north by the Richemont river and the Bazuel–Catillon road, along which a defensive flank facing north-east was to be established. Le Cateau itself was included in the objectives.

The objectives

In all, four objectives were given. The first included Andigny-les-Fermes and the whole of the Bellevue spur, the villages of Molain, St. Martin Rivere, and St. Souplet, and an advance of some 2,000 yards east of the river between Molain and Le Cateau. The second objective included the villages of La Vallée Mulâtre and Arbre Guernon, Jonc de Mer Farm, La Roux Farm, and the town of Le Cateau, that is to say a further advance of some 1,500–2,000 yards. The third objective entailed an advance of 2,500–3,000 yards, and included the villages of Wassigny, Mazinghien, and Bazuel. Finally, if all went well, the troops were to try to reach the Sambre and Oise Canal between La Laurette and Catillon. The southern flank of the army was to be protected by the advance of the First French Army.

As in the case of previous attacks, it was not expected that the troops would be able to reach the furthest objective on the first day, but, in view of the demoralisation of the enemy, it was felt that the resistance might collapse at any moment, and that it was essential that every effort should be made to exploit any initial advantage gained to the utmost physical power of the men.

Our information as regards the enemy, though not as complete as on some previous occasions immediately prior to an attack, was favourable to a bold and ambitious plan. The fine weather on October 14th had been taken full advantage of, and air reconnaissance had shown that big changes in the organisation of the rear areas had taken place, which foreshadowed a further retirement. A score of new aerodromes had sprung up, the chief groups being those north of Bavai and Maubeuge. A number of hospitals had been erected at Maubeuge and near the important railway junction of Aulnoye. Moreover, a number of footbridges had been thrown over the Sambre and Oise Canal, on which all barge traffic south of Landrecies had ceased.

Information regarding the enemy

The enemy's power of resistance was not expected to be great. The pause of six days had undoubtedly given him a short breathing space in which to make some re-organisation in his order of battle. Owing, however, to the distance which separated the forces and to the presence of the Selle between the opposing lines, it had been difficult to secure prisoners, and our information, therefore, as to the number of divisions which were likely to oppose us on the 17th, was incomplete. It was estimated that we should be confronted by four comparatively fresh divisions and two exhausted ones. It was known that the Alpine Corps had been sent to Serbia, owing to the unconditional surrender of Bulgaria and the advance of the Allies in Macedonia, and that on the whole of the western front the Germans only had six fresh divisions at their disposal to meet all eventualities. It was probable, therefore, that the Second and Eighteenth Armies opposed to us would have to rely on their own resources for reserves ; this meant twelve exhausted divisions of which only one had had any real rest.

There were two excellent reasons, on the other hand, why the enemy must make every possible endeavour to check our further advance. He must if possible prevent us from coming within artillery range of the railway junction at Aulnoye, the destruction of which by our guns would effectively sever his main lateral line of communication between Sedan and Lille. He must also gain time for carrying out the retirement of his troops in the Lens and Laon areas, in both of which a retreat on a large scale had now commenced, Laon having been occupied by the French on October 13th.

It was clearly impossible for the tanks to render any assistance against the hostile trenches and wire in the early stages of the attack, and the enemy's positions were, therefore, subjected to a heavy preliminary bombardment of forty-eight hours, which commenced at 8 a.m. on October 15th. By dint of excellent organisation in the rear services and the hard work of all concerned, the artillery and ammunition situation had been much improved, with the result that, for the forty-eight hours' bombardment and barrage work, 33 field artillery brigades, and 20 brigades and 13 batteries of heavy and siege artillery, were in position by October 15th with sufficient ammunition available. The system of barrages for the attack was similar to that for previous attacks, the lifts up to the first objective being at three minute intervals. Here, there was to be a halt of thirty minutes, after which the barrage was to continue to advance at the same rate up to the second objective [1] ; field and heavy artillery were detailed to move forward and cover the advance when it continued beyond the second objective. In view of the unsuitability of the northern portion of the army front for tank action, the IX Corps was allotted the bulk of the tanks, the 16th Mark V Tank Battalion and the 6th Battalion of whippets operating with that corps, while the 301st American and 1st Mark V Tank Battalions remained with the II American and XIII Corps respectively. "Zero" was fixed for 5.20 a.m. on the 17th.

By the 16th, on the eve of the Battle of the Selle, all arrangement had been completed. Energetic patrolling had furnished us with full

The detailed arrangements for the attack

---

[1] This was rather a faster rate than usual.

information as regards the state of the enemy's defences, and the result of the preliminary bombardment had been reported as most effective. The moral of our troops had never been higher. They had, during the attacks of October 8th and 9th, seen the enemy in full flight and they knew that there were no more prepared defence lines to be overcome. Every day brought fresh news of the German retreat both in the Laon and Lens areas, and optimists were not lacking who prophesied that the war might end before Christmas.

CHAPTER XI

THE BATTLE OF THE SELLE, OCTOBER 17TH–19TH; AND THE EVENTS
TO OCTOBER 31ST

Maps 2, 13, 14, and 15

SIR WALTER BRAITHWAITE decided to attack with the 46th Division on the right and the 6th Division on the left, while the 1st Division, which had moved up from Bellenglise during the night of the 16th, was concentrated just north and west of Bohain. This last division was held in readiness to pass through the 6th Division and capture the second and third objectives, including the villages of Wassigny and La Vallée Mulâtre, after the 46th and 6th Divisions had secured the first objective. The attack of the IX Corps, owing to the lie of the ground, and to the position of Riqueval Wood in the south and of the Bellevue spur in the north, was complicated and required careful preparation, good preliminary staff work, and exceptional leadership from battalion and company commanders.

The plan of attack of the IX Corps

As it was not considered advisable to make a frontal attack against Riqueval Wood, it was arranged that one brigade of the 46th Division should neutralise the enemy on this front, while the other two brigades, making a flank attack in a south-easterly direction, should clear all the ground west of the Bellevue spur, including Andigny-les-Fermes, and cut off the defenders of the wood. It was intended that the advance of the troops of the IX Corps should continue north of the Andigny Forest and should join up east of it with the XV French Corps which was attacking along its southern edge, thus pinching it off. It was, therefore, arranged that, when the 46th Division had secured the first objective, it should form a defensive flank facing southwards, immediately south of the Regni-court–Andigny-les-Fermes road, in order to meet any hostile counter-attacks which might be delivered through the forest. Subsequently, should the attack progress favourably, it was to maintain touch with the French and " mop up " the forest as it advanced.

At the same time the 6th Division, also attacking in a south-easterly direction from Vaux-Andigny, was to capture the Bellevue spur and the remainder of the first objective as far as the northern corps boundary, including the high ground north-west of La Vallée Mulâtre.

The dividing line between the 46th and 6th Divisions ran along the valley from the village of Vaux-Andigny to Andigny-les-Fermes. The boundary dividing the 6th Division, and later the 1st Division, from the Americans ran from north of Vaux-Andigny in a slightly north-easterly direction to the village of Ribeauville.

The 46th Division formed up with the 137th, 139th, and 138th Bri-gades in line from south to north. The 137th Brigade held a front of about 2,500 yards, from the junction with the French to the northern edge of Riqueval Wood, with one bat-talion, the remaining two battalions being held in reserve. Its rôle was to deceive the enemy as to the direction of the real attack and to hold him by means of a " Chinese " attack[1] with dummy tanks and dummy figures. A special rolling barrage, in which the machine-gun company allotted to the brigade played a leading part, was to come down at " zero " and move through Riqueval Wood in an easterly direc-tion.

The dispositions of the 46th Division

The 139th and 138th Brigades, detailed for the main attack, held the line between Riqueval Wood and Vaux-Andigny. In order that these two brigades might start square with their objectives, which ran almost east and west just south of the Regnicourt–Andigny-les-Fermes road, it was arranged that they should form up along the Bohain–Vaux-Andigny road. As part of this line lay in the 6th Division area, special arrangements had to be made so that the forming up of the attacking troops of the 46th and 6th Divisions should not clash. The barrage to cover the advance of these two brigades also required special treatment. It was not possible to place the artillery which was detailed to cover the advance in positions from which it could put down a frontal barrage, because this would have involved occupying battery positions required by the 6th Division and the 30th American Division. The barrage, therefore, fired from positions north and north-west of Bohain, was oblique to the line of advance. It was to move forward at the rate of a hundred yards every three minutes, and was finally to rest for thirty minutes on the northern edge of the Andigny Forest, after which it was to cease.

The three tanks of the 16th Tank Battalion which were allotted to the 46th Division were to co-operate with the infantry, with a view to dealing first of all with a strong point situated about 1,500 yards east of

[1] This " Chinese " attack succeeded in deceiving the enemy, as ten minutes after " zero " he put down a heavy barrage on the outpost line of this brigade.

Guyot Farm and, subsequently, to working along a line of trenches west of Regnicourt. Thereafter, leaving one tank to deal with the hostile trenches in Riquerval Wood, the other two were to assist in " mopping up " Regnicourt and Andigny-les-Fermes.

The attack was launched at 5.20 a.m. in a thick mist which caused several machine-gun nests to be passed by unmolested by the leading troops. The 139th Brigade advanced on a one-

The attack of the 46th Division

battalion front, with the 1/8th Sherwood Foresters leading, supported by two companies of the 1/5th Sherwood Foresters. The remaining battalion and a half were held in brigade reserve. Owing to the dense mist and the oblique nature of the barrage there was some loss of direction. The leading companies advanced without difficulty on the right and left, but in the centre the advance was checked by the fire of some machine-guns in a small clearing north-west of Regnicourt. A prompt use of reserves, however, by the battalion commander of the 1/8th Sherwood Foresters in a flanking movement from the north, resulted in the capture of 140 prisoners and 27 machine-guns in the clearing.

The enemy took up a position in a line of trenches running along the Regnicourt–Andigny-les-Fermes road, and was not finally dislodged until our leading troops had been reinforced by the remaining two companies of the 1/5th Sherwood Foresters, and until an outflanking movement east of Regnicourt had been carried out with the assistance of a company of the 11th Essex of the 6th Division.

The enemy's final withdrawal into the forest resulted soon after 10 a.m. in the capture of the whole of its objective by the 139th Brigade, which still had the 1/6th Sherwood Foresters in reserve. About 11 a.m. the enemy attempted to launch a counter-attack from south-east of Regnicourt, but met with no success. The 137th Brigade, after its successful " Chinese " attack, received orders to push patrols into Riquerval Wood ; these patrols quickly got in touch with the 139th Brigade, and by 2.30 p.m. Riquerval Wood was clear of the enemy, and the 137th Brigade was in touch with the French on its right. By 3.30 p.m. it had reached the western edge of the Andigny Forest, and its patrols, which were still advancing supported by a battery, were meeting with little opposition.

Meanwhile, north of the 139th Brigade, the 138th Brigade attacked with two battalions in line, the 1/4th Leicestershire on the right, the 1/5th Lincolnshire on the left, and the 1/5th Leicestershire in reserve. The troops pressed forward rapidly and, in spite of the thick mist, had reached the Regnicourt–Andigny-les-Fermes road by 6.45 a.m. On the fog lifting some casualties were suffered from fire from the Bellevue spur, and there was a temporary check ; when this position, however, had been captured by the 6th Division soon after 9 a.m., the 138th Brigade was able to continue its attack against the village of Andigny-les-Fermes. The 138th Brigade captured this village about 11.30 a.m. in conjunction with the 1st Loyal North Lancashire of the 1st Division, which had moved forward through the 6th Division on its way to attack the second objective. Attempts were now made by the 137th Brigade to establish touch with the French along the Andigny-les-Fermes–Mennevret road, a company being detailed for the purpose, but, owing to a strong post which was held by the enemy in the wood, junction with the French on this road was not established until 5.30 a.m. on the following day.

By 7.30 p.m. the 46th Division had taken all its objectives, and its line ran from the Forester's House 1,000 yards west of Mennevret, where it was in touch with the French, to where it joined up with the 1st Division about 700 yards east of Andigny-les-Fermes. It held this line with all three brigades in line, of which the 137th Brigade was still fresh, while one battalion each of the 139th and 138th Brigades had only been slightly engaged.

The captures for the day by the 46th Division amounted to about 15 officers and 500 other ranks, chiefly belonging to the 5th Reserve Division, 2 field guns, and over 100 machine-guns.

Maj.-Gen. Marden arranged to attack with the 18th and 16th Brigades in line and the 71st Brigade in reserve. The attack was to be made under an artillery barrage, for which eight brigades of field artillery were available. The infantry advance was also to be covered by the fire of eighty machine-guns of the 2nd Life Guards Machine Gun Battalion and the 6th Machine Gun Battalion, which received orders to search the reverse slopes of the spurs in order to prevent enfilade fire up the valleys. Three tanks of the 16th Mark V Tank Battalion were allotted to each attacking brigade to assist in the attack on a trench line running north from Andigny-les-Fermes, in front of which it was thought that there might be uncut wire.

The attack of the 6th Division

The assembly of the 18th and 16th Brigades, and the execution of the attack itself, presented considerable difficulties. The " starting line " of the division was extremely limited, each brigade having a frontage of only 700 yards on which to form up, while the total frontage when the first objective was reached would be about 4,000 yards; the attack would, therefore, spread out fan-wise. These difficulties were further enhanced by both brigades having to debouch from the village of Vaux-Andigny, which might be shelled with gas prior to or immediately after the commencement of the attack, and by the fact that the " starting line " of the 18th Brigade, which was to attack the Bellevue spur, faced east-south-east, while its direction of advance was south-east.

The 18th and 16th Brigades moved forward to their preliminary assembly positions on October 16th and, before " zero," relieved the 71st Brigade, which up to that time had been holding the divisional front. The assembly of the attacking troops was carried out without a hitch, in spite of heavy shelling with high explosive and gas which began two hours before " zero," but luckily fell in rear of the assembly positions.

The 18th Brigade formed up on the line of the railway with its left at Vaux-Andigny station. The brigade was to attack on a two-battalion front, with the 11th Essex on the right, the 2nd Durham Light Infantry on the left, and with the 1st West Yorkshire in reserve in rear of the right flank. The part of the first objective assigned to the 18th Brigade lay between the village of Andigny-les-Fermes and a point 500 yards west of La Vallée Mulâtre. At " zero " the two leading battalions advanced, each with two companies in line and two companies in support. A certain amount of uncut wire was encountered which caused the infantry to lose the barrage, and, owing to this and the mist, the troops lost direction; the fighting that ensued became very confused. The tanks also lost direction and, joining the right company of the 11th Essex, proceeded with it in the direction of Regnicourt, where they took part in the capture of the village in conjunction with the 139th Brigade of the 46th Division, after which they proceeded to Andigny-les-Fermes, only to find that the troops of the 1st and 46th Divisions had already captured it. Meanwhile, the remainder of the 11th Essex was assisting to clear the Bellevue spur. Further north the 2nd Durham Light Infantry was checked on the northern slopes of the spur until reinforced by two companies of the 1st West Yorkshire from reserve, when its advance was continued. Thus, about 10.30 a.m. troops of the 18th Brigade and of the 1st Division, which was now arriving on the scene, reached the first objective together.

The 16th Brigade formed up with its right at the railway station of Vaux-Andigny; the 1st The Buffs was on the right, the 2nd York and Lancaster on the left, and the 1st Shropshire Light Infantry in reserve. This brigade, which started parallel to its objective and had the railway as a guide, kept direction and by 9.15 a.m. had reached its objective, except on the extreme right where it did not arrive until an hour later.

The 6th Division had, therefore, by 10.30 a.m. reached the first objective along its whole front, and the 1st Division was passing through. Owing to the fog, the fighting had been confused and in some places severe, as the enemy, consisting of portions of the 3rd Naval, 15th Reserve, and 24th Divisions, resisted with considerable determination. For the remainder of the day the front of the 6th Division was covered by the 1st Division, and a counter-attack from the direction of La Vallée Mulâtre was forestalled by the attack of the latter division.

Maj.-Gen. Strickland detailed the 1st and 2nd Brigades, on the right and left respectively, to carry out the attack on the second and third objectives, the leading troops of these two brigades "leap-frogging" the 6th Division during the half-hour pause of the barrage covering the first objective. The 1st and 2nd Brigades were to attack the second objective under a barrage and, when they had captured it, were to be covered by a protective barrage lasting for three hours. During this halt artillery and machine-guns were to be brought forward to furnish another barrage for the attack on the third objective.

The dispositions of the 1st Division

The dividing line between brigades ran east and west through Angin Farm to a point on the railway immediately west of La Vallée Mulâtre, whence the railway was to be the boundary as far as the southern outskirts of Wassigny. This gave the southern outskirts of La Vallée Mulâtre and the northern portion of the Andigny Forest to the 1st Brigade, and the greater part of La Vallée Mulâtre, the whole of Wassigny, and the high ground north of it to the 2nd Brigade. On the capture of Wassigny, however, the 1st Brigade was to take over the village and the ground as far north as the Wassigny–Oisy road from the 2nd Brigade.

Attached to the division for the operations were twelve whippet tanks of the 6th Tank Battalion and three tanks of the 16th Mark V Tank Battalion. To assist in the capture of La Vallée Mulâtre, the three tanks of the 16th Tank Battalion were allotted to the 2nd Brigade, one of these tanks being detailed to work south of the railway in the 1st Brigade area. The whippet tanks were to be held in reserve for exploiting to the Sambre and Oise Canal after the third objective had been taken. The arrangements for the assembly of the 1st and 2nd Brigades presented some difficulty, as both brigades had to pass through the troops of the 6th Division on a line 2,500 to 3,000 yards east of Vaux-Andigny. As the barrage only paused on this line for half an hour, it was necessary that the two brigades should follow close behind the troops of the 6th Division, when these advanced at " zero," without waiting for information as to the success or failure of the 6th Division attack ; in order to do this it was necessary to assemble in rear of and in touch with them, immediately west of Vaux-Andigny. But the attacks of the 6th and 46th Divisions both debouched from the neighbourhood of Vaux-Andigny, the 6th Division attacking east and south-east, and the 46th Division attacking south-east ; the tails of these two divisions, therefore, converged west of Vaux-Andigny. In addition to this, the direction of the American attack on the left of the 6th Division was considerably north of east, with the result that the tail of the 59th American Brigade which was to lead the attack, and the head of the 60th American Brigade which was to follow close behind it, both required to be in the area west of Vaux-Andigny. An assembly position in this neighbourhood was, therefore, required by troops of all four divisions concerned. Thanks to the harmony which reigned in the IX Corps, and between it and the American Corps, and to the excellent arrangements made by the 1st and 2nd Brigades, all difficulties were overcome, and the assembly was successfully completed.

The attacking troops advanced at 5.20 a.m. through the mist, which considerably hampered their movement. The 1st Brigade advanced with the 1st Loyal North Lancashire on the right, the 1st Cameron Highlanders on the left, and the 1st Black Watch in reserve; the 2nd Brigade moved forward with the 1st Northamptonshire on the right, the 2nd King's Royal Rifle Corps on the left, and the 2nd Royal Sussex in reserve. On the left the 2nd Brigade was unable to find the tracks through the gardens and hedges which it had reconnoitred and intended to use in order to avoid the main road through Vaux-Andigny, so the troops were compelled to use this road, upon which the enemy concentrated a considerable amount of artillery fire. The approach march to the " starting line " was continued in spite of this and of the fact that the 6th Division in its advance had passed by a number of machine-gun nests unnoticed owing to the fog. These met the troops of both the 1st and 2nd Brigades with heavy fire, as soon as they appeared east of Vaux-Andigny, and while still 2,000 yards from their " starting line."

During this approach march the 1st Loyal North Lancashire on the right, after assisting in the capture of the Bellevue spur, where the fire from strong machine-gun positions threatened at one time to check the entire advance, pushed troops forward into Andigny-les-Fermes in its efforts to get touch with the 46th Division and assisted the 138th Brigade to "mop up" this village. On the left of the 1st Loyal North Lancashire, the 1st Cameron Highlanders was at one time completely checked by machine-gun fire near the first objective. The situation here was retrieved by the successful action of a single platoon, which was dispatched by the battalion commander to work round by the railway on the left and outflank the enemy's position; the advance was also materially assisted by the close support of a section of 18-pounders.

The approach march of the 1st Northamptonshire was successfully conducted without special incident. The 2nd King's Royal Rifle Corps on the left of the line was heavily shelled in Vaux-Andigny, and, on emerging from the village, the battalion commander and adjutant found themselves alone in the mist with a handful of men, the rest of the battalion having disappeared. Within a short space of time, however, the whole battalion found its way to its correct position on the " starting line " and then proceeded to advance, still on compass bearings, towards the second objective. When the fog lifted the battalion found itself in its correct position with the 1st Northamptonshire on its right. The manner in which the four leading battalions of the 1st and 2nd Brigades, moving by compass bearing throughout the advance, maintained their cohesion and direction and reached their " starting line " on the first objective, practically up to time, constituted a very fine achievement.

Although all four battalions advanced from their " starting line " towards the second objective approximately according to the time-table, they lost touch with the barrage. In spite of this, however, they fought their way forward for about 1,000 yards, which brought the right of the division on to the objective, the centre east of La Vallée Mulâtre, and the left to the neighbourhood of the Wassigny–St. Souplet railway, some little distance short of the objective. La Vallée Mulâtre was captured by the 1st Northamptonshire, but some troops of the 29th German Division counter-attacked from the wood to the south-east and drove our men back to the centre of the village.

Thus about midday the 1st Division was approximately on the line of the second objective from Andigny-les-Fermes northwards, through the centre of La Vallée Mulâtre, to the railway north of the village, where touch was gained with the Americans. By this time the barrage programme was over, and any further progress by the infantry had to be made with the assistance of such artillery support as could be arranged by commanders on the spot. The enemy had fought well, and an advance, in these circumstances, would have been costly. Maj.-Gen. Strickland, therefore, decided to prepare for an organised attack on the front of both brigades in the evening.

This attack took place at 5.15 p.m., but the barrage was not as good as usual, owing to the short notice and to the difficulty of communicating with the batteries which had all been on the move. On the 1st Brigade front the 1st Loyal North Lancashire and 1st Cameron Highlanders reached the edge of the wood south-east of La Vallée Mulâtre. A heavy gas shelling in this area, however, forced the commanders on the spot to order a withdrawal practically to the "starting line." The 1st Northamptonshire again cleared La Vallée Mulâtre and established itself well east of it. North of the village a certain amount of progress was made, our troops at one time reaching the vicinity of Ribeauville, the hostile machine-guns in this neighbourhood prevented us, however, from maintaining all the ground gained.

The 3rd Brigade in reserve moved during the night to the valley just west of La Vallée Mulâtre, where it arrived at dawn on the 18th, and commanders reconnoitred forward in view of a probable continuance of the attack.

As the result of the day's operations the IX Corps had advanced its line to a depth of 4,500 yards; it had firmly established itself on the

The result of the day's fighting by the IX Corps

crest of the water-shed which divided the Selle and the Sambre valleys and was in an excellent position to continue its advance next day. It had engaged and defeated the 5th Reserve, 29th, and 81st Reserve Divisions, and portions of the 3rd Naval, 15th Reserve, and 24th Divisions. To accomplish this, it had employed three divisions, but of these one brigade of each division was still untouched.

The task of the II American Corps was to cross the headwaters of the Selle between Molain and St. Souplet and capture the important

The dispositions of the II American Corps

hamlet of Arbre Guernon and the villages of Mazinghien and Ribeauville. From reconnaissance of the ground it was clear that the attack on the first objective, which included Arbre Guernon and Bandival Farm, was likely to be the more arduous. The obstacle formed by the stream was made more formidable by the fact that the enemy held the hamlets of Molain and St. Martin Rivere and the eastern outskirts of St. Souplet, which lay astride the river; while the Le Cateau–Wassigny railway, which was admirably adapted for defence, barred the way to the high ground about Arbre Guernon.

Prior to the attack on the 17th the II American Corps had been holding the line with the 27th Division, but on October 16th, for the purpose of the operations, the 30th Division was introduced into the line between the 27th American Division and the IX Corps. The dividing line between the 27th and 30th Divisions ran in a north-easterly direction, leaving St. Martin Rivere, Molain, Ribeauville, and Mazinghien in the area of the 30th Division, and Arbre Guernon, Bandival Farm, La Roux Farm, and Jonc de Mer Farm in that of the 27th Division. The northern boundary of the corps ran from the northern outskirts of St. Souplet, past La Roux Farm, to the southern edge of Bazuel.

The 30th and 27th American Divisions, which were now very weak in numbers, each attacked on a front of two regiments with two regiments

The attack of the II American Corps

in support. The 30th American Division advanced with the 117th and 118th Regiments of the 59th Brigade in line followed by the 119th and 120th Regiments of the 60th Brigade in support. The 27th American Division advanced with the 53rd Brigade on the right, the 105th Regiment leading, and the 54th Brigade on the left, the 108th Regiment leading;

No. 85.

ToWASSIGNY

Railway
from St SOUPLET

MARSH MILL

St. Martin River

R. SELE

Old practise trenches

ST. MARTIN RIVERE.

Oblique air photograph.

No. 86.

ST. CREPIN AND BANDIVAL FARM.

Oblique air photograph.

the 106th and 107th Regiments followed in support, on the right and left respectively.

Ten tanks of the 301st American Tank Battalion were detailed to assist the 27th American Division, and twelve tanks the 30th American Division. The 20th Hussars were also attached to the II American Corps, one squadron with each division, and the remaining squadron in corps reserve. The goal of the leading regiments of both divisions was the second objective, after the capture of which the regiments in rear were to pass through and secure the third objective.

At 5.20 a.m. the divisions advanced to the attack assisted by the 301st American Tank Battalion, of which twenty tanks reached the " starting line." They succeeded in crossing the Selle without much difficulty, although some casualties were suffered from machine-gun fire which came chiefly from the direction of St. Martin Rivere. The enemy's main line of defence was along the line of the railway, and here severe fighting took place. The American infantry owing to the strong opposition could advance but slowly, and the barrage was in consequence lost. Notwithstanding this, the 30th Division pushed forward with the greatest determination, gained the first objective, and on the right even penetrated to the outskirts of Ribeauville.

On the left of the II American Corps front, owing to the mist, touch between the 27th American Division and the 50th Division was lost at an early hour. The 105th and 108th Regiments of the 27th American Division met with determined opposition, and were unable to fight their way forward past the railway east of St. Souplet and gain the first objective until some hours after " zero." After a short pause on the first objective the 27th American Division continued its advance and attacked Arbre Guernon, but the 204th German Division made a strong counter-attack against it and the 50th Division on its left, and the American troops were forced back almost to the line of the railway.

Not to be denied, however, the 53rd and 54th American Brigades again pressed forward and re-established their line along the Arbre Guernon–Le Cateau road, regaining touch with the 50th Division at 4.30 p.m. During the afternoon the 27th American Division, after heavy fighting, succeeded in driving the enemy out of Arbre Guernon, which it held in spite of vigorous attempts by the Germans to retake it. One thousand six hundred prisoners and 12 guns were taken during the day, and heavy losses were inflicted on the enemy in the severe fighting which took place. The Americans had been opposed by the 3rd Naval and 204th Divisions, as well as by portions of the 24th and 243rd Divisions.[1]

Sir Thomas Morland arranged for the attack of the XIII Corps [2] to be made by two divisions, the 50th Division on the right and the 66th Division on the left, with the 25th Division in reserve.

The dispositions of the XIII Corps   The dividing line between the 50th and 66th Divisions was the Honnechy–Le Cateau road as far as the southern exit of Le Cateau, thence north of the railway triangle, which was inclusive

---

[1] Of these, the 3rd Naval and 204th Divisions were comparatively fresh, and the former had only been brought into the line since the enemy's retreat to the Selle.

[2] The attack should be followed in detail on Map 14 in order to realise the difficulties.

F F

to the 50th Division, thence along the Le Cateau–Pommereuil road, inclusive to the 66th Division. The 25th Division remained in the Maretz area, with the 75th Brigade forward at Reumont.

The operation was to be divided into three phases. In the first phase, the 151st Brigade of the 50th Division, after forming up in depth on a narrow front, was to cross the Selle immediately north of St. Souplet, capture the railway embankment immediately opposite its point of crossing, and then fan out on the first objective along the Arbre Guernon–Le Cateau road. The right and centre battalions of the brigade, immediately after crossing the river, were to move north-eastwards on to the high ground which bounds the river valley on the east ; the left battalion was to turn due north, roll up the enemy's defences along the railway, and capture the extensive buildings and goods sheds about Le Cateau station.

In the second phase, the 149th Brigade was to pass one battalion over the crossings made by the 151st Brigade and one battalion over the demolished bridge at St. Benin. These two battalions, after passing through the right and centre battalions of the 151st Brigade, were to capture the second objective, namely the ridge running parallel to the first objective and about 2,000 yards further east. The third battalion of the 149th Brigade, following the right battalion of its brigade, was to turn northwards after crossing the railway and move on the railway triangle south-east of Le Cateau. In conjunction with the attack of the 149th Brigade, the South African Brigade of the 66th Division was to cross the river north of the town and establish itself along the railway as far north as the northern corps boundary, joining up with the 149th Brigade immediately north of the railway triangle.

The third phase was to be carried out by the 150th Brigade of the 50th Division, which was to pass through the 149th Brigade and capture Bazuel, while the South African Brigade was to conform by swinging forward its right, and was to establish itself on the ridge between Le Cateau and the Richemont River. Special parties of the 198th Brigade of the 66th Division were also detailed during this phase to " mop up " Le Cateau. Since the V Corps was not attacking simultaneously with the XIII Corps, careful arrangements were made to obliterate by smoke the enemy's observation from the high ground north-east of Montay. The V Corps also agreed to attract the enemy's attention on its front by vigorous artillery action, including a creeping barrage.

The ground afforded exceptional facilities for artillery and machine-gun support. In order to strengthen the machine-gun covering fire the machine-gun battalions of the 50th and 66th Divisions were reinforced by the machine-gun battalions of the 18th and 25th Divisions. Twelve tanks from the 1st Mark V Tank Battalion were allotted to the 50th Division, but it was no easy matter to get them across the Selle.

The initial front of attack of the 50th Division was restricted to a width of some 600 yards, and the whole success of the plan depended on breaking through the enemy's line on this frontage.

The attack of the 50th Division

The 151st Brigade (4th King's Royal Rifle Corps, 1st King's Own

Richmont Valley

Level Crossing

Valley of the Selle

← Line of Railway →

VIEW LOOKING EAST FROM THE HIGH GROUND ABOVE LE CATEAU.

Yorkshire Light Infantry, 6th Royal Inniskilling Fusiliers) and the 3rd Royal Fusiliers and 2nd Royal Dublin Fusiliers of the 149th Brigade were formed up north of St. Souplet,[1] ready to cross the river as soon as the barrage came down and bridges had been thrown across by the Royal Engineers. The remaining battalion of the 149th Brigade, the 13th Royal Highlanders (Scottish Horse), was in St. Benin, ready to cross the river. The 150th Brigade was in reserve immediately west of the railway embankment and was to advance, as soon as the second objective was captured, to the valley separating the first and second objectives, and there deploy for the attack on Bazuel.

The artillery and machine-gun barrage came down at 5.20 a.m. Under cover of it the bridging of the river was quickly accomplished by the Royal Engineers; within three minutes of " zero," twelve bridges were placed across the river north of St. Souplet by the 446th Field Company and a company of the 5th Royal Irish Regiment (Pioneers); while in the same time four bridges were thrown across the Selle at St. Benin by the 447th Field Company, assisted by two platoons of the pioneer battalion. This expeditious and satisfactory work avoided any delay. Moreover, the crossing of the infantry was obscured by the heavy mist and smoke of the barrage. During the night the enemy had fired a considerable number of gas shell along the whole length of the Selle Valley; there was, however, very little hostile shelling at " zero."

The first battalion to cross the river was the 4th King's Royal Rifle Corps; it was closely followed by the 1st King's Own Yorkshire Light Infantry and the 6th Royal Inniskilling Fusiliers. The attacking troops soon encountered strong opposition, both from the line of the railway and from the slope of the ridge east of the river. At 8.45 a.m. the 4th King's Royal Rifle Corps, with two companies of the 1st King's Own Yorkshire Light Infantry, had advanced no further than the western slopes of the spur immediately east of St. Crepin and the railway; at the same hour the other two companies of the 1st King's Own Yorkshire Light Infantry were fighting in the orchards on the top of the ridge due east of St. Benin. Further north the 6th Royal Inniskilling Fusiliers, which had turned north to roll up the enemy's line, was meeting with strong opposition from the station buildings.

About 9.30 a.m., owing to the 151st Brigade being checked short of the first objective by the resistance of the 204th and 243rd German Divisions, the battalions of the 149th Brigade, which had been detailed to capture the second objective, became embroiled in the fight. The 3rd Royal Fusiliers, moving up in rear of the 4th King's Royal Rifle Corps, formed a defensive flank facing south, as touch with the Americans had been temporarily lost, while the 2nd Royal Dublin Fusiliers advanced to support the 1st King's Own Yorkshire Light Infantry; the 13th Royal Highlanders was sent to reinforce the 6th Royal Inniskilling Fusiliers. About 11 a.m., when the mist lifted, the situation of the attacking troops could at last be definitely ascertained. The 4th King's Royal Rifle Corps was just west of the Le Cateau–Arbre Guernon

---

[1] On the night of October 16th the 151st and 149th Brigades had relieved the 150th Brigade in the line.

road, facing Le Quennelet Farm, with the 3rd Royal Fusiliers on its right, forming a defensive flank facing south-east across the head of the valley north of Bandival Farm, on the spur to the east of which were troops of the 27th American Division.   The companies of the 1st King's Own Yorkshire Light Infantry and 2nd Royal Dublin Fusiliers were intermingled, and were held in check by the enemy in the orchards on the Arbre Guernon–Le Cateau road, north of the 4th King's Royal Rifle Corps. The companies of the 6th Royal Inniskilling Fusiliers and 13th Royal Highlanders, also intermingled, were fighting round the station buildings and meeting with strong opposition.

As the 149th Brigade had thus been unable to advance against the second objective, the 150th Brigade (2nd Northumberland Fusiliers, 7th Wiltshire, 2nd Royal Munster Fusiliers) was brought forward to carry out this task, its place in reserve being taken by the 75th Brigade of the 25th Division, which was placed at the disposal of Maj.-Gen. Jackson.   With a view to preparing the way for the continuance of the attack, the massed heavy artillery of the corps put down an intense bombardment from 3 p.m. to 3.30 p.m. on the northern portion of the station buildings and on the railway triangle.   Our attack, however, was anticipated by two strong German counter-attacks which were made against the junction of the II American Corps and the 50th Division.   These counter-attacks struck the 3rd Royal Fusiliers, the 4th King's Royal Rifle Corps, and the 1st King's Own Yorkshire Light Infantry.   The latter battalion held its ground, but the two former, having suffered heavy casualties, were forced back off the top of the ridge down the western slopes.   These counter-attacks also drove back the American 27th Division.

In consequence of this the 150th Brigade was at 4 p.m. ordered to regain the lost ground and to make good the first objective.   This mission was entrusted to the 7th Wiltshire and the 2nd Royal Munster Fusiliers, who, rushing forward, carried with them the troops of the 4th King's Royal Rifle Corps and the 3rd Royal Fusiliers and by 4.30 p.m. had established themselves on the first objective.   About the same time the enemy was driven out of the station buildings, but still held the brickworks. The 50th Division, after this attack, held practically the whole of the first objective within its divisional boundaries.   On the right touch had been established with the 27th American Division at the farm buildings about 500 yards north of Bandival Farm, which the Americans had captured, while on the left the 66th Division had reached the line of railway, a short distance north of the main Le Cateau–Bazuel road.[2] This division was, however, unable to advance further until the railway triangle had been captured by the 50th Division.

By this time the infantry of the 50th Division was considerably disorganised, and, as it was impossible to extricate the battalions of any one brigade, Maj.-Gen. Jackson divided his line into three sections, each section being held by a group of three battalions.   The right group, consisting of the 3rd Royal Fusiliers, the 7th Wiltshire, and the 4th King's Royal Rifle Corps, held the line of the Arbre Guernon–Le Cateau road from the

---

[1] See page 217.   [2] See page 224.

southern corps boundary to the orchards.   The centre group, consisting
of the 1st King's Own Yorkshire Light Infantry, the 2nd Royal Munster
Fusiliers, and the 2nd Royal Dublin Fusiliers, held from the orchards inclusive to opposite the brickworks.   The left group, consisting of the 2nd
Northumberland Fusiliers, the 13th Royal Highlanders (Scottish Horse),
and the 6th Royal Inniskilling Fusiliers, held from opposite the brickworks to the divisional boundary north of the station.   This line was
firmly established, and at 8 p.m. the brickworks were captured with
100 prisoners.   The left group also attacked the railway triangle at
8 p.m., and the fighting continued in this part of the field throughout
the night.

An important part in the operations of the 50th Division was taken
by the tanks.   Of the twelve tanks of the 1st Mark V Tank Battalion
originally allotted to the division, only eleven were
available, and these were distributed between the
151st and 149th Brigades, four tanks accompanying
the right and left attacks; and three the centre.   After careful reconnaissance it had been ascertained that the only practicable place at which
the tanks could cross the Selle was where the St. Souplet–Arbre Guernon
road crosses the river.   Here, where the stream was only eight feet wide
and four feet deep, it was found that a crossing could be effected with
the help of " cribs " [1]; a route to the crossing-place was taped out on
the night of the 16th, and all the tanks, having arrived beyond the stream
shortly after " zero," proceeded to follow up the infantry.   Of the right
group, one tank speedily became bogged in the marshy ground, but the
other three tanks reached the first objective and " mopped up " several
machine-guns.   Of the centre group, the crew of one tank was overcome
by gas fumes and was unable to proceed; the other two reached
the first objective and became heavily engaged with hostile artillery and
machine-guns, one tank receiving six direct hits and catching fire.   Of
the left group, one tank was unable to cross the river, two were bogged,
while the remaining tank, after over-running two machine-gun posts,
put out of action the detachments of two field guns near the orchards.
It then proceeded to the vicinity of the station, where it disposed of two
trench mortars, after which it returned along the railway to St. Souplet.

The objective of the 66th Division was that part of the long ridge, west
of Bazuel, which lies between the Le Cateau–Pommereuil road and the
Richemont river.   The attack presented considerable
difficulties.   Le Cateau, east of the Selle, was in the hands
of the enemy and would have to be cleared; the
Selle, which was under the enemy's observation, could only be crossed
by bridges.   Furthermore, it had been decided that Le Cateau was to
be encircled by the 66th Division from the north and the 50th Division
from the south, the troops of the two divisions meeting at the eastern
exit of the town; as the troops of the 50th Division had considerably
further to go than those of the 66th Division, the synchronisation of the
attacks of the 66th and 50th Divisions required careful adjustment.

Tank action

The plan of attack of the 66th Division

---

[1] These were very strong hexagonal frames, constructed by the Tank Corps, which were dropped
into the obstacles and over which the tanks then crossed.

In order to ensure this the South African Brigade was ordered to start at 7.47 a.m., two hours and twenty-seven minutes after " zero." Attacking on a front of 900 yards, it was to cross the Selle by eight bridges, placed by the engineers across the river immediately north of Le Cateau. At 8.20 a.m., three hours after " zero," at which hour it was estimated that the attacking brigades of the 66th and 50th Divisions would have joined hands east of the town, the 198th Brigade was to begin clearing Le Cateau, starting from the north-east. After the capture of its objective by the South African Brigade, special instructions were issued to ensure the clearing up of the line of the railway and the formation of a defensive flank as far north as Montay. The South African Brigade in its attack was to advance in a south-easterly direction under a creeping barrage, with its right flank resting on the Faubourg St. Martin–Faubourg de Landrecies road, and, after gaining touch with the 50th Division near the Faubourg de Landrecies, was to move forward with its flank along the Le Cateau–Pommereuil road. The left of the brigade was to advance due east through Baillon Farm to the level crossing just east of it, where a strong point was to be established in order to protect the left flank of the division. After the line of the railway had been captured and contact obtained with the 50th Division, the advance was to be continued, pivoting on the level crossing, until the objective of the division was reached.

It was essential that the attack should be a surprise and that no indications should be given to the enemy that the bridging of the Selle north of Le Cateau was contemplated. With a view to diverting the enemy's attention from this part of the field, feints at bridging operations were carried out in Le Cateau, in order to make him believe that a direct advance through the town was intended.

The valley of the Richemont river was to be bombarded with gas shell on the night of the 16th up to 3 a.m. on the 17th, and at " zero " an intense bombardment, carried out for fifteen minutes by guns and howitzers of all calibres, was to be directed on the area lying between Le Cateau and Baillon Farm, to be followed by a slower rate of fire on the same area. A similar programme was also to be carried out by the 38th Division of the V Corps, immediately north of the Fourth Army. A proportion of smoke shell was to be used in the bombardment of the north-east and eastern outskirts of Le Cateau, on the area between the Selle and the railway north of Baillon Farm, and on the slopes of the spur north-east of Montay. At 7.29 a.m. a barrage was to be put down 300 yards in front of the infantry " starting line." This barrage was to remain stationary for fifteen minutes and was then to advance, at the rate of 100 yards every three minutes, straight through to a distance of 300 yards in front of the divisional objective, no halt being made on the railway line. Having paused for three hours beyond this objective, the barrage was again to advance on the right flank of the division in order to assist the advance of the 50th Division to its final objective. Six machine-gun companies were to supplement the artillery barrage.

By midnight on October 16th, when the final dispositions of the 66th Division had been completed, the 198th Brigade (6th Lancashire Fusiliers,

Richmont Valley

Line of railway

Level Crossing

Selle River.

THE SELLE JUST NORTH OF LE CATEAU, WHERE THE SOUTH AFRICAN BRIGADE CROSSED

5th Royal Inniskilling Fusiliers, 6th Royal Dublin Fusiliers) held the line on the right, with the 6th Royal Dublin Fusiliers and two companies of the 5th Royal Inniskilling Fusiliers ready to " mop up " Le Cateau. The remaining two companies of the 5th Royal Inniskilling Fusiliers were holding the line north of the South African Brigade, having relieved portions of that brigade between the Roman road and the northern divisional boundary. The 6th Lancashire Fusiliers were in divisional reserve in the valley west of Le Cateau : the South African Brigade was in the centre of the line with all three battalions along the western banks of the Selle [1] : the 199th Brigade was in divisional reserve north of Reumont.

On the night of the 16th parties of the 9th Gloucestershire (Pioneers) and the divisional engineers erected eight bridges immediately north of Le Cateau, completing them by 2 a.m. Opposite these bridges the South African Brigade was formed up by 5 a.m., with the 4th South African Battalion on the right, the 2nd South African Battalion on the left, and the 1st South African Battalion in close support. As soon as the bridges were laid, the South Africans pushed patrols across the stream and established themselves in rifle pits in the midst of the wire entanglements which had been erected by the enemy along the east bank of the river. In this dangerous situation, within fifty yards of the enemy's advanced posts, the brigade lay for three hours, protected from observation by the friendly mist, and escaping, by the very hazard of its position, from the hostile artillery and machine-gun fire, the bulk of which passed harmlessly overhead.

At 8.45 a.m. information was received that the 149th Brigade of the 50th Division had crossed the river, and the welcome order to advance was given. Rapidly crossing the stream the leading waves joined the advanced posts, penetrated the wire obstacles, and, pressing forward up the hill, vanished into the mist. Meanwhile, the second wave, after crossing the river, was temporarily checked by the obstacles on the further bank. Patrols were sent forward, but nothing could be seen of the leading waves. A report was sent back that the attack had failed, and, so substantial was the evidence, that a discussion was held between the divisional and brigade commanders as to the advisability of bringing back the barrage to its initial line in order to start the attack " de novo " with fresh troops. Fortunately, however, before any such drastic expedient could be decided on, a message was received that our troops had reached the railway cutting and were engaged in hand-to-hand fighting with the enemy.

The South African Brigade attack

After crossing the river the leading waves had encountered several lines of wire about thirty yards from the stream and parallel to it. On approaching the railway a still more formidable obstacle was met with in the shape of four to six belts of wire ; moreover, the railway cutting was lined with machine-guns and riflemen. With indomitable courage

---

[1] Some days prior to the attack, several attempts had been made to bridge the Selle between Le Cateau and Montay, which was here twenty feet wide and five feet deep, with the surface of the water five feet below the steep grass-covered banks. These attempts had been frustrated by machine-gun fire from several German posts immediately west of the Selle, but on the night of the 15th, the 1st South African Battalion had cleared the whole of the left bank of the river, as far as Montay, of the enemy.

the South African troops rose to the emergency. At one point, a shallow trench was found, evidently used by the enemy to communicate from the railway cutting to an advanced post; at another, a tortuous path through the wire for the use of his patrols was discovered; at another, a narrow passage was laboriously cut by hand. With dogged determination small parties of men, covered by Lewis gun fire, fought their way through and penetrated into the cutting, where very bitter fighting took place. Gradually, and with great difficulty, reinforcing troops dribbled up to support the points where penetration had been effected; slowly but surely the enemy's resistance was overcome, and by about 9.45 a.m. a considerable portion of the railway cutting was in our possession.

At 10.20 a.m. the 2nd South African Battalion reached its final objective on the crest of the ridge. It was unable to stay there owing to heavy machine-gun fire from both its left flank and right rear, and fell back on to the railway cutting, where it got in touch with the 4th Battalion on its right. By 12 noon the South African Brigade had captured the whole of the railway from a point 500 yards north of the railway triangle to the northern boundary of the XIII Corps, but it was found impossible to advance further east until the 50th Division had captured the railway triangle.

Meanwhile, at 9 a.m. two companies of the 6th Royal Dublin Fusiliers had followed the right battalion of the South African Brigade across the Selle and had begun to " mop up " Le Cateau. These companies were shortly afterwards reinforced by the remainder of the battalion, as it was important to capture all the strong points in the eastern part of the town as soon as possible, owing to the casualties they were causing to the South African Brigade. Further south two platoons of the 6th Royal Dublin Fusiliers also succeeded in crossing the river, and began working north to meet the remainder of the battalion; they were joined later by two companies of the 5th Royal Inniskilling Fusiliers.

The position remained practically unchanged during the day; at nightfall the 66th Division was holding the whole town of Le Cateau, from its southern exit to just north of its eastern exit, with the 198th Brigade, only two battalions of which had been engaged.[1] North of the 198th Brigade the South African Brigade held the line of the railway as far as the Roman road at Montay, with two companies of the 5th Royal Inniskilling Fusiliers prolonging the line to the northern corps boundary. The South African Brigade had fully employed two of its battalions, while the third battalion had also been engaged. In reserve, however, were the 199th Brigade and the 6th Lancashire Fusiliers, intact; the division was therefore in good condition to continue the battle.

The position attacked by the 66th Division, and especially by the South African Brigade, requires to be studied on the ground before the difficulties overcome by the initiative and leadership of the regimental officers and non-commissioned officers, and by the gallantry of all ranks, can be fully realised. None but the very best troops could have attempted, let alone have succeeded in, such an enterprise, and the crossing of the Selle

[1] The 66th Division had been opposed by the 177th Reserve Division and portions of the 44th Reserve Division.

at Le Cateau will always remain, like the struggle in Delville Wood in 1916, a lasting testimony to the fighting qualities of the South African soldier.

The attack of the 17th had broken the crust of the enemy's defence on the Hermann Stellung I. The most difficult part of the task set to the three corps had been carried out with the same skill **The result of the fighting on October 17th** and dash which had been so noticeable in previous attacks, and which had given rise to the belief that no task was now beyond their power. The passage of the Selle had been forced, and our troops were firmly established along the western portion of the ridge separating the Selle and the Sambre Valleys ; no serious physical obstacle now remained to retard our advance till the Sambre and Oise Canal was reached.

The Allied success had by no means been confined to the Fourth Army front. On the right of the IX Corps the First French Army had attacked in strength with the Oise as its objective. In spite of determined resistance and several counter-attacks, it had established a line west of Hauteville, along the western outskirts of Aisonville and Grougis, and west and north-west of Mennevret, and had captured over 1,200 prisoners.

A severe resistance had been expected, as it was clear that the situation of the enemy was becoming desperate, and that his hopes of an armistice depended largely on his troops being able to check our advance.[1] But the resistance was even more obstinate than had been anticipated.

It had been estimated that our advance would be opposed by four fresh and two exhausted divisions in the line. Our initial attack was actually opposed by five fresh and three fairly fresh divisions ; four of the fresh divisions, the 17th Reserve, 44th Reserve, 204th, and 243rd, held the line north of St. Souplet, while the 5th Reserve Division, also fresh, opposed the IX Corps in the Andigny-les-Fermes area. In the course of the morning yet another fresh division, the 29th, recently liberated by the evacuation of the Laon salient, counter-attacked at La Vallée Mulâtre.

The total of prisoners captured during the 17th amounted to about 4,500, taken from ten different divisions, of which the IX Corps captured 1,500, the II American Corps 1,800, and the XIII Corps 1,200. Over 20 guns were also captured.

---

[1] The following captured orders are of interest :—
Issued by an Artillery Sub-Group Commander of the 204th Division, on October 12th :—
" The Higher Command states that the possibility of an armistice being brought about depends on the battle coming to a standstill.
" All officers are to be informed. Other ranks are to be reminded that every gunner, whether gun number, telephonist, linesman, or observer, must carry out his duty day and night.
" The English must not cross the Selle on our front. The artillery must prevent them."
Issued by the Commander of an Artillery close-range group belonging to the 79th Reserve Division, undated :—
" The Higher Command have ordered that troops are to be made to understand clearly that the ' Hermann Stellung ' must be held at all costs.
" Reason—if the ' Hermann Stellung ' is held there are good prospects of carrying on peace negotiations, or, as the case may be, of arranging an armistice with the enemy.
" If, on the other hand, the ' Hermann Stellung ' is not held peace in the near future is out of the question."

G G

Sir Henry Rawlinson issued orders on the evening of October 17th for the attack to be continued next day.   The first objective given was

The army orders for the attack on October 18th

practically the same as the second objective of the 17th, while the second objective included Wassigny, Mazinghien, Bazuel, and the line of the Richemont River. Having captured this line, divisions were to exploit to the Sambre and Oise Canal.

Instructions were also received from General Headquarters on October 17th ordering the Fourth, Third, and First Armies to be ready

Further orders from General Headquarters

to carry out a general attack about October 21st, in co-operation with the First French Army, with a view to securing the line of the Sambre and Oise Canal, the western edge of the Mormal Forest, Ghissignies, Ruesnes, Querenaing, and up to the Scheldt (Escaut).

The attack ordered by the Army Commander was carried out on October 18th.   On the IX Corps front, the 46th Division held the line from its

October 18th; the attack of the IX Corps

junction with the French near the Forester's House to where it joined up with the 1st Division about 700 yards east of Andigny-les-Fermes.   The 1st Division covered the remainder of the corps front with the 1st and 2nd Brigades in line, the inter-brigade boundary being the line of the railway; the 3rd Brigade was in reserve in the valley immediately west of La Vallée Mulâtre.   The 6th Division was in corps reserve behind the 1st Division.   The 46th Division was to maintain touch between the left of the French advance and the right of the 1st Division, which was to carry out the main attack, until Wassigny was captured, when it would be " squeezed out " and go into reserve.   The hour at which the attack was to be resumed by the IX Corps on the 18th was left to be decided by Sir Walter Braithwaite with the II American Corps, as the 30th American Division was to attack in conjunction with the 1st Division.   It was finally decided that the 1st Division should attack at 11.30 a.m.

When the attack was launched the 126th French Division made such good progress through the Andigny Forest that, together with the 137th Brigade, which had taken over the whole front of the 46th Division, it completely cleared the forest during the afternoon.   The attack of the 1st Division, which employed the 1st Brigade on the right and the 3rd Brigade on the left,[1] was completely successful, and Wassigny and the line of the road from Wassigny cemetery to Ribeauville were captured.   The 1st Black Watch was on the right, while the 2nd Welsh, the 1st South Wales Borderers, and the 1st Gloucestershire continued the line northwards.   Shortly after nightfall the 1st Black Watch, which had captured Wassigny, gained touch with the 126th French Division at Blocus d'en Bas south-east of Wassigny, thus " squeezing out " the 46th Division, which then passed into corps reserve.

In the north the 1st Gloucestershire maintained touch with the 30th American Division during the day, and in the evening pushed into Ribeauville with the Americans.   In spite of the close nature of the country very useful reconnaissance work was done during the day by two

---

[1] The 3rd Brigade passed through the 2nd Brigade, which was holding the line, before " zero."

squadrons of the Royal Scots Greys, one of which was attached to the 1st and one to the 46th Division.

The opposition offered by the enemy throughout the day was considerably less than on the 17th, although our infantry had no tanks to assist them. This was due, no doubt, to the heavy losses he had sustained, and to the disorganisation of his units.[1] By the evening of October 18th the IX Corps had captured the objectives allotted to it in the face of weakening opposition, and was preparing to exploit its successes on the following morning.

The attack of the II American Corps was arranged so as to synchronise with the attacks of the corps on its flanks, hence the 60th Brigade of the 30th Division on the right commenced its attack

The attack of the II American Corps   in conjunction with the 1st Division at 11.30 a.m., while the 105th and 107th Regiments of the 27th Division attacked at 5.30 a.m. in conjunction with the 50th Division. The objectives of the 30th Division included the villages of Ribeauville and Mazinghien, while the Jonc de Mer Farm and the line of the Jonc de Mer stream were to be taken by the 27th Division.

The fighting in this part of the field was severe throughout the day. The infantry had no tanks to assist them, and, consequently, slow progress was made along the whole corps front. The troops of the 119th Regiment of the 30th American Division captured the village of Ribeauville in touch with the left of the 1st Division, and Mazinghien was entered by the American troops later in the evening, its capture being completed during the night of the 18th and the early morning of the 19th. Considerable opposition was also offered by the enemy at Jonc de Mer Farm, but this was captured about 2.45 p.m. by the 27th American Division, and the line was pushed forward soon afterwards to the Jonc de Mer stream. La Roux Farm, however, at the junction of the American and XIII Corps, remained in the hands of the enemy until captured by an enveloping movement from the north-east, carried out by troops of the 75th Brigade, temporarily attached to the 50th Division. By nightfall the II American Corps had captured all its objectives.

The 50th Division had on the evening of October 17th made arrangements for continuing the attack on the 18th ; this was to be carried out

The preparations for the attack of the XIII Corps   in two phases. The first phase had as its objective the ridge 2,000 yards east of the Arbre Guernon– Le Cateau road, which had been its second objective on the 17th. This was to be captured by an attack launched at 5.30 a.m., and was to be carried out by the three groups into which the 50th Division had been temporarily divided.[2] The second phase, timed to begin at 8.30 a.m., had as its objective Bazuel and the approximate line of the Bazuel– Baillon Farm road, that is the third objective of the 17th. This task was allotted to the 75th Brigade of the 25th Division, which for this operation remained under the orders of the 50th Division.

---

[1] Portions of the 15th Reserve, 22nd Reserve, 24th, 29th, and 221st Divisions opposed the advance of the IX Corps. Of these the 22nd Reserve, 29th, and 221st Divisions had just arrived and were relieving exhausted divisions.

[2] See page 220.

The 66th Division was ordered to synchronise its attack with that of the 50th Division, and to swing forward its right on to the top of the ridge east of Le Cateau, at the same time clearing the Faubourg de Landrecies of the enemy. No tanks were available for the operations of the XIII Corps, but the whole attack was to be covered with barrages similar to those of the preceding day.

At 5.30 a.m. the attack of the 50th Division was launched and was most successful from the outset. The first objective, the ridge west of Bazuel, was captured by the three groups of the division without much opposition, and touch was established with the 27th American Division. A party of the 2nd Royal Dublin Fusiliers, over-running their objective, even penetrated into Bazuel and captured a few prisoners. Here, a daring individual exploit by Sergeant Curtis of this battalion put out of action the teams of two hostile machine-guns, and resulted in the capture of four other machine-guns with their crews.[1] On the left some difficulty was experienced at the railway triangle, where fighting had continued throughout the night, and which was not completely cleared before " zero."

The attack of the 50th and 66th Divisions

After the capture of the first objective, the 75th Brigade " leap-frogged " the troops of the 50th Division about 8.45 a.m. and succeeded in establishing itself on the western slopes of the ridge, at the northern end of which stands Bazuel. Its right was, however, not in touch with the left of the 27th American Division, which was held up by a strong point at La Roux Farm. Seeing this, the commander of the 75th Brigade at once took steps to attack this post from the north-east, and captured it by 3 p.m., whereupon the American left swung forward into line. About 5 p.m. the 75th Brigade advanced and captured Bazuel, together with a 9·2-inch gun and a complete battery of 4·2-inch howitzers, whose teams had just arrived to remove the guns. Posts were then established east and north-east of the village.

Meanwhile, on the left, parties of the left group of the 50th Division, after clearing up the whole of the railway triangle, fought their way slowly up the railway and on to the Le Cateau–Pommereuil road. Here they gained touch with the 198th Brigade of the 66th Division, which had secured the ridge lying between Le Cateau and the Richemont River.

At the close of the day, therefore, the XIII Corps had gained all its objectives, and had pushed patrols forward of this line. The battle of the Selle, which was at an end so far as the XIII Corps was concerned, had resulted in the capture, by six brigades of this corps, of a carefully prepared and strongly garrisoned position on a front of 7,000 yards, the greater part of which was protected by a difficult obstacle.

All objectives allotted for the day having been captured early in the evening, and the resistance of the enemy having been broken, orders were issued by Sir Henry Rawlinson, late on October 18th, for the troops to advance to the line of exploitation given in the orders for the attack on October 17th. This line ran from the Arrouaise Farm, east of Wassigny, north-eastwards to the Sambre and Oise Canal near La Laurette, thence along the canal

The events of October 19th

---

[1] See Appendix E, No. 15.

To face page 229.

No. 89.

THE HIGH GROUND OVERLOOKING THE SAMBRE AND OISE CANAL.

Oblique air photograph.

to Catillon, and from there, along the Catillon–Bazuel road and the Richemont River, to Montay ; on the XIII Corps front this line had already been reached. In view of the severe defeat the enemy had suffered on the 17th and 18th, it was considered extremely probable that he would retire across the Sambre and Oise Canal during the night, especially as the result of the fighting on the front of the First French Army had been very successful. During the 18th the French had gained a line running east of Aisonville, Grougis, and Andigny Forest, and had captured over 1,000 prisoners.

The advance on October 19th, on the IX Corps front, was continued at 5.30 a.m. by the 1st Division, the enemy offering little opposition ; he had, as was anticipated, withdrawn the greater part of his troops beyond the Sambre and Oise Canal. By noon the whole of Wassigny was finally cleared, and our troops entered Rejet de Beaulieu, the French on our right occupying Tupigny and Hannappes. By nightfall the IX Corps had reached the line of the Oisy–Rejet de Beaulieu road, overlooking the canal, and was in touch with the French at Oisy and with the Americans north of Rejet de Beaulieu. Every attempt, however, to occupy the western bank of the Sambre and Oise Canal was met with heavy machine-gun fire from the eastern bank, and hostile artillery fire considerably increased during the day.

The II American Corps advanced at the same time as the IX Corps and, meeting with little opposition, occupied the high ground north-east of Mazinghien with the 60th Brigade and two battalions of the 59th Brigade of the 30th Division, while the 53rd and 54th Brigades of the 27th Division held the line of the St. Maurice Ravine. Between Bazuel and Montay the line of the XIII Corps remained unchanged, the enemy occupying the slopes running down to the right bank of the Richemont River.

The Battle of the Selle may be said to have terminated on the evening of October 19th, by which date the enemy had been driven by the First
French Army and the Fourth Army across the Sambre
The result of the Battle of the Selle and Oise Canal between Tupigny and Rejet de Beaulieu. On the Fourth Army front this represented an advance of 9,000 yards on a front of over seven miles. This success had been achieved in the face of strong opposition, and in spite of the urgent appeals of the German High Command to its troops to prevent our passage of the Selle at all costs. Between the morning of the 17th and the evening of October 19th, 5,139 prisoners, including 143 officers, and 60 guns were captured. The prisoners represented fourteen different divisions, eleven of which were fully engaged against the Fourth Army. Furthermore, our advance had brought the important railway junction of Aulnoye, which was only fourteen miles from Le Cateau, dangerously near the limit of our long-range guns. The southern flank of the enemy was, however, safe for the moment behind the Sambre and Oise Canal, and the centre of interest was for the time being transferred to the northern flank of the army.

The Battle of the Selle had scarcely been concluded before a conference was held by the Army Commander at which the outline of the next operation, foreshadowed on October 17th by the orders of the Commander-in-Chief,[1] was explained to Corps Commanders, and warning orders were issued as regards objectives and artillery action. The forthcoming operation was to be a com- *The army orders for the advance to be con- tinued on October 23rd* bined attack carried out by the Fourth, Third, and First British Armies, in which the Fourth Army was to establish a defensive flank facing east to protect the main operations which were to be carried out by the Third and First Armies, while further south the First French Army was to co-operate. October 23rd was the date given for the attack.

The task given to the IX Corps by Sir Henry Rawlinson was to advance to the line of the Sambre and Oise Canal, and capture Catillon, Ors, and the southern portion of L'Evêque Wood. The XIII Corps, in conjunction with the V Corps on its left, was at the same time to secure the line of the main Landrecies–Englefontaine road near the western edge of Mormal Forest, capturing Pommereuil, the northern part of L'Evêque Wood, Bousies, Fontaine-au-Bois, and Robersart. The northern boundary of the XIII Corps would run parallel to, and 500 yards south of, the Roman road from Montay to Englefontaine. An essential object of the operation was to secure artillery positions, from which the railway junction at Aulnoye could be kept under the fire of our long-range guns.

Sir Henry Rawlinson laid especial stress on the necessity of the most energetic measures on the part of the engineers and pioneers in the repair of bridges, and in the clearance of the roads of obstacles, which the enemy had created by an extensive system of demolitions and road mines. These troops accomplished their task with the utmost diligence and zeal, and our ultimate success was in no small measure due to their continuous efforts, and to those of the Labour Companies.

Corps Commanders were informed that the forthcoming attack would not be preceded by a preliminary bombardment, but that vigorous counter-battery work was to be maintained, while the enemy's communications were to be continually harassed, and special localities selected by corps were to be bombarded. *Artillery and tanks* Tanks were to be allotted: the 301st American Mark V Tank Battalion, which was now organised in three sections of five tanks each, to the IX Corps; the 10th Mark V Tank Battalion, organised in three companies of eight tanks each, to the XIII Corps. These two tank battalions were to be under the orders of the 2nd Tank Brigade.

As the Fourth Army was now covered along a considerable portion of its front by the Sambre and Oise Canal, it became possible to withdraw more troops into reserve. Orders were, therefore, issued for the II American Corps, which had been considerably weakened during the last three days' fighting, to be withdrawn to rest, its front being taken over by the IX Corps.[2] On relief, the II American Corps went into reserve near Amiens *The readjustment of the front*

[1] More detailed orders regarding objectives, barrages, etc., were issued on the 21st. The warning orders issued by Sir Henry Rawlinson at the conference were intended to enable corps and divisions to go ahead with their preparations. See p. 226.

[2] The II American Corps had received practically no reinforcements to make good its casualties since it joined the Fourth Army at the end of September, and its fighting strength was, therefore, very reduced.

No. 90.

From ENGLEFONTAINE

To LANDRECIES

THE ENCLOSED COUNTRY BETWEEN THE SELLE AND THE SAMBRE.

Oblique air photograph.

to rest and refit.   Since the end of September it had taken a very prominent and successful part in the operations of the Fourth Army.   Its losses had been severe,[1] but the spirit and keenness of all ranks had been maintained to the end, and it had thoroughly earned the praise it received from Sir Douglas Haig and Sir Henry Rawlinson.

By October 21st the necessary reliefs were completed, and the army front, from Oisy exclusive to Montay, was held by the IX and XIII Corps; the former with the 1st and 6th Divisions in line, and the 32nd and 46th Divisions in reserve; the XIII Corps with the 25th and 18th Divisions in line, and the 50th and 66th Divisions in reserve.   In view of the forthcoming operations certain alterations in boundaries became necessary.   These changes did not affect the boundary between the Fourth Army and the First French Army, but the IX Corps took over about 1,000 yards of front from the XIII Corps, while the V Corps of the Third Army also extended its front for a similar distance southwards.   As the result of this arrangement the dividing line between the IX and XIII Corps ran north of Bazuel and then forward in a north-easterly direction through the centre of L'Evêque Wood to the Forester's House ; thence, it bent still more eastwards to Landrecies.

The country, over which the advance had taken place since passing the St. Quentin Canal, was open, rolling down conspicuously devoid of cover,

The nature of the country

except for the villages and occasional woods, but, after crossing the Selle, the character of the country entirely changed.   East of the Selle the slopes became more abrupt, small streams ran in the valleys, and there were large tracts of woodland.   The pasture land between these tracts was cut up into innumerable small enclosures bounded by high, thick hedges, which, while constituting a serious obstacle to an infantry advance, at the same time afforded it excellent cover from view except at short ranges.   Pommereuil, Bousies, Fontaine-au-Bois, and Robersart were straggling villages, the houses of which were of a poor type and of no great defensive value. Bousies alone contained buildings of considerable strength, including a large factory.   L'Evêque Wood, covering an area of some four square miles, had been cleared of standing timber over three parts of its area, and the cleared spaces were covered with brambles and undergrowth. Apart from the difficulty of maintaining touch and direction, the passage of this wood did not present any serious obstacle, except by night or in a fog.

Detailed   orders   for   the   forthcoming   attack   were   issued   on October 21st.   On   the   right   the   IX   Corps   was   to   conform   to   the

The detailed orders for the attack on October 23rd (See Map 15)

advance   of   the   XIII   Corps,   and,   having   captured Catillon   and   Ors,   was   to   establish   a   defensive   flank facing south-east, along the line of the railway embankment   which   ran   parallel   to   the   Sambre   and   Oise Canal between Ors and the elbow in the canal 2,000 yards north-east of that village.   To ensure the closest co-operation in the attack between the left of the Fourth and the right of the Third Army, careful timings were laid down as to the hour at which the troops of the Fourth

[1] The losses of the corps amounted to 11,500 since it came into the line in September.

Army were to arrive at, and depart from, the various objectives. The barrage, which was to come down as usual 200 yards in front of the infantry "starting line," was to lift four minutes after "zero" and advance at the rate of 100 yards every four minutes, except through L'Evêque Wood, where special arrangements were to be made by the IX and XIII Corps. As the moon was full on the night of October 22nd, it was considered that it would be an advantage to launch the attack during the night instead of at dawn, as had been the custom hitherto, so that the unexpectedness of the hour would take the enemy by surprise. "Zero" for the Fourth Army was, therefore, fixed for 1.20 a.m., and, in order to synchronise the advance on the flanks of the V and XIII Corps, the V Corps agreed to start its troops at forty minutes after "zero," by which time the left of the XIII Corps would be up in line with them.

Sir Walter Braithwaite's plan was to attack with two divisions in line, the 1st Division on the right, and the 6th Division on the left. The rôle of the 1st Division was to gain ground towards the

The IX Corps plan   canal and to drive the enemy across it south of Catillon, while the 6th Division, conforming to the advance of the 25th Division, was to form an ever-lengthening defensive flank facing east, as that division gained ground. The 1st Division was to attack with the 2nd and 3rd Brigades in line and the 1st Brigade in reserve, and the 6th Division with the 18th and 71st Brigades in line and the 16th Brigade in reserve.

To the XIII Corps were allotted five objectives. First, the Pommereuil–Forest road; second, for the left division only, the Tilleuls Farm–Vert Baudet road; third, a line along the north-

The XIII Corps' plan   eastern edge of L'Evêque Wood and the western edge of Bousies; fourth, the spur east of Malgarni and the village of Bousies; fifth, from the spur east of Malgarni in a north-easterly direction to the junction of roads half a mile south-east of Fontaine-au-Bois, thence due north to the bend in the Landrecies–Englefontaine road, and along that road to the northern corps boundary.

Sir Thomas Morland arranged to attack with two divisions in line, the 25th Division on the right and the 18th Division on the left. The boundary between the two divisions ran through Garde Mill, along the north-western edge of L'Evêque Wood, through Tilleuls Farm to Bout du Monde.

On the 25th Division front the attack on the first objective was to be carried out by the 7th Brigade, with three battalions deployed in the front line. Owing to the weakness of the 7th Brigade, whose strength was under 700 rifles, one battalion of the 75th Brigade was placed at its disposal; this battalion was only to be used if absolutely necessary for the capture of the first objective. Then, when the 18th Division pushed forward in order to outflank L'Evêque Wood from the north, one battalion of the 75th Brigade was to advance along the northern edge of the wood, establishing posts at certain points to protect the right flank of the 18th Division. The remaining battalion of the 75th Brigade was to clear the north-eastern portion of the wood and establish itself on the

eastern edge of the wood. The 7th Brigade was to clear the western portion of the wood, using for this purpose, if it was still available, the battalion of the 75th Brigade which had been placed at its disposal.

The 74th Brigade was in turn to move along the northern edge of L'Evêque Wood, deploy behind the battalion holding the eastern edge, and carry forward the attack on to the fourth and fifth objectives.

In the case of the 18th Division, the capture of the first and second objectives, which included reaching the Tilleuls Farm–Vert Baudet road, was entrusted to the 53rd Brigade and the 54th Brigade, less the 6th Northamptonshire, while the 55th Brigade, with the 6th Northamptonshire attached, was to pass through and secure the third, fourth, and fifth objectives.

Of the twenty-four tanks of the 10th Tank Battalion at the disposal of the XIII Corps for the operation, sixteen were allotted to the 18th Division, which in turn sub-allotted four tanks each to the 53rd and 54th Brigades, and eight to the 55th Brigade. Eight tanks were allotted to the 25th Division, of which four were to assist in the capture of Pommereuil. An extra machine-gun battalion was lent to each of the 18th and 25th Divisions for barrage work, from the divisions in reserve, in order that a large proportion of the machine-guns of the two attacking divisions might be kept mobile, ready to move forward with the infantry. Arrangements were also made for the advance of field artillery brigades and sections of 6-inch howitzers to support the attack in the later stages, and three sections of 6-inch guns were held in readiness to move forward to positions selected on the map, from which they could engage Aulnoye railway junction as soon as the situation permitted.

On the south, when the IX Corps attacked, the enemy put down a heavy barrage mixed with gas, but this did not check the advance. On the right the 1st Division by 8 a.m. had reached the outskirts of Catillon and was sending patrols into the village. More stubborn opposition was experienced by the 6th Division, and severe fighting took place before the Richemont River was crossed. No ground was gained without fighting, and, on one occasion, a party of our troops was surrounded and only hacked its way out after hand-to-hand fighting. A certain amount of progress was made through L'Evêque Wood, but the 6th Division was unable to keep abreast of the 25th Division, which had to form a defensive flank to the south. Little further advance was made on the IX Corps front that day, and, although patrols made their way to the banks of the Sambre and Oise Canal, Catillon and Ors remained in the possession of the enemy.

The troops of the XIII Corps, after a very well organised night march, reached their assembly positions without a hitch. At 1.20 a.m. the attack started in bright moonlight. Considerable opposition was experienced from the mills and farms along the banks of the Richemont River, but this was gradually overcome, the garrisons being killed or taken prisoner. Unfortunately several machine-gun posts were passed by unnoticed by the leading troops, and these gave trouble to the troops detailed for the attack on the more distant objectives as they moved forward.

H H

On the front of the 25th Division the three battalions of the 7th Brigade led the attack, with the 1/8th Royal Warwickshire of the 75th

The 25th Division attack

Brigade in support. The heavy mist made it difficult to keep direction, and this caused a certain loss of cohesion among the attacking troops; the first objective was, however, gained without much difficulty. Then began the arduous task of clearing the northern half of L'Evêque Wood,[1] but, in spite of the hostile resistance and the thick undergrowth, this was successfully accomplished, except on the right, where the 6th Division had not been able to keep pace with the advance of the 25th Division; a defensive flank was, therefore, established through the wood along the line of the Bazuel–Malgarni road. Meanwhile the right flank of the 18th Division was protected by the 1/8th Worcestershire, of the 75th Brigade, which had moved along the northern edge of the wood and captured Tilleuls Farm and a battery of 4·2-inch howitzers. The 74th Brigade, which was to attack the fourth and fifth objectives, advanced from its assembly position on the Le Cateau–Busigny road behind the 75th and 7th Brigades. Its advance was delayed by a party of the enemy in a sunken road near Garde Mill, which had been missed by the artillery, and had been passed by the leading troops owing to there being a gap between the left of the 25th Division and the right of the 18th Division. The enemy was driven from this locality after some fighting, but so much time had been lost that the leading troops of the brigade did not reach Pommereuil until 10.30 a.m. The 74th Brigade then moved along the northern edge of L'Evêque Wood, and endeavoured to deploy along the eastern outskirts of the wood for the attack on the fourth and fifth objectives. One battalion, however, the 9th Yorkshire, became involved in the fighting for the clearing of the wood; also it was found that the eastern exits from the wood were raked by the enemy's fire from the Hermann Stellung II. This line ran parallel to the road running south-east from Bousies near the eastern boundary of the wood, and, although the trenches were not completed, the wire in front of it was very strong. It soon became obvious that the brigade could not be got into position before dark, and the attack was accordingly postponed until the following day.

The 18th Division attacked with the 53rd Brigade on the right and the 54th Brigade, less one battalion, on the left. The 53rd Brigade

The 18th Division attack

advanced with the 7th Royal West Kent on the right, the 10th Essex on the left, and the 8th Royal Berkshire in support. The Richemont River was crossed, and a dashing attack by a company of the 7th Royal West Kent secured Garde Mill together with 70 prisoners. The 7th Royal West Kent reached the first objective after overcoming all opposition, but the 10th Essex was held up by machine-gun fire when about 300 yards from the objective. The 8th Royal Berkshire, which was to " leap-frog " the leading battalions on the first objective, was checked when crossing the Richemont River by fire from a machine-gun post that the leading troops had missed, and the left company was held up for some time. The battalion then went on,

---

[1] During the fighting, Private Francis Miles, 1/5th Gloucestershire, by his courage and initiative was responsible for the capture of 16 machine-guns and 50 prisoners. See Appendix E, No. 36.

but became involved in the check sustained by the 10th Essex, and no progress could be made until the arrival on the left of the 54th Brigade with tanks turned the enemy's position and allowed the advance to be resumed. The 8th Royal Berkshire then secured the second objective, and established touch with the 25th Division on the right and with the 54th Brigade on the left.

The attack on the 54th Brigade front was led by the 2nd Bedfordshire. At the outset considerable resistance was encountered, and many prisoners were captured in the sunken roads north-east of Richemont Mill, which had been subjected to the enfilade fire of forty machine-guns from a position east of Le Cateau. The attack was carried on with fine determination, and White Springs was captured after stubborn fighting. The battalion then established itself on a track which it took to be the first objective, but was in reality 500 yards short of it. Here, the 11th Royal Fusiliers passed through and, advancing with great dash, captured eleven guns. One company went right through to the second objective, but, as both flanks were unsupported, it had to withdraw and come into line with the remainder of the battalion which had been checked by machine-gun fire. At 7.30 a.m., however, the 7th The Buffs of the 55th Brigade came up, and passed through the 11th Royal Fusiliers.

The 55th Brigade, with the 8th East Surrey and the 7th The Buffs leading, followed up the 54th Brigade so closely that it became involved in the fighting west of the second objective. The 8th East Surrey then captured Fayt Farm, and the 7th The Buffs Epinette Farm. As a result of this fighting these battalions were forty minutes behind schedule time in beginning the attack on the third objective. Determined resistance was encountered at Bousies, where the enemy had posts and machine-gun nests among the hedges which surrounded and intersected the village, and the opposition had to be beaten down yard by yard before the enemy, who lost heavily, was driven out of the village about 8 p.m. As touch with the brigade of the V Corps on the left had been lost, and on account of the darkness, it was found impossible to continue the advance on the remaining objectives, and a further attack was postponed until the following morning. The day had been a very successful one for the 25th and 18th Divisions, the latter division had made an advance of 8,000 yards and could claim the capture of 53 guns.

The day on the whole was not a happy one for the tanks. Owing to the indifferent light in the early stages of the attack a large number were "ditched" in passing over comparatively insignificant obstacles, the drivers being unable to see clearly what was in front of them. Much valuable work, however, was done by the tanks of the 10th Tank Battalion in the heavy fighting in Bousies.

The action of the tanks

At the end of the day the line held by our troops ran from the little hamlet of La Louvière, past Catillon Halt, along the western outskirts of Ors, through L'Evêque Wood to within 500 yards of Malgarni, and thence east and north of Bousies to the south-eastern edge of Vendegies Wood. As a result of the fighting 849 prisoners, including

The result of the day's fighting; army orders issued for the attack to be continued on October 24th

23 officers, were captured, of the 8th, 17th Reserve, 44th Reserve, 121st, 204th, and 243rd Divisions, and the 2nd Cyclist Brigade. Of these Divisions the 8th and 204th were in the act of relieving the 44th Reserve and 121st Divisions in the Bousies and Catillon areas respectively. It was resolved to give the enemy no respite, and both corps were ordered to resume the attack next morning at 4 a.m. for the purpose of securing the remaining objectives.

On the right of the IX Corps the 1st Division confined itself to patrolling the banks of the canal and the outskirts of Catillon. At the same time the 6th Division gained a footing in Ors and cleared the southern part of L'Evêque Wood. A few prisoners and some field guns and howitzers were captured. The 6th Division was still unable to reach its final objective on the extreme left flank, but it made sufficient progress in L'Evêque Wood to allow of the 25th Division withdrawing its defensive flank.

October 24th ; the IX Corps attack

The 74th Brigade, to which was attached the 1/8th Worcestershire of the 75th Brigade, carried on the attack of the 25th Division. The troops formed up in the eastern outskirts of L'Evêque Wood, but, as soon as they emerged into the open, they were met with heavy fire from the enemy's position west of Malgarni.[1] This position was carried in spite of the strong wire, and Malgarni was captured after severe hand-to-hand fighting in the orchards and houses. Fontaine-au-Bois was then occupied, and by 12 noon the 74th Brigade had established itself on the fifth and final objective. Patrols, which were sent out, found the enemy holding the line of the Landrecies–Englefontaine road in strength, and all attempts to dislodge him failed.

The XIII Corps attack

The 18th Division met with considerable difficulties. No tanks were available for the operation, and the 55th and 54th Brigades, which carried out the attack, were not able to keep up with the barrage on account of the enclosed and thickly-hedged country through which they had to pass. Along the whole front the enemy opposed our advance with great tenacity, and, in the wired defences amidst the hedges and orchards between Bousies and Robersart, the fighting was exceptionally strenuous and the advance slow. North-west of Robersart our troops were checked by five hostile machine-guns posted on the ridge on which stands Renuart Farm. Lieut. William Hedges of the 6th Northamptonshire promptly proceeded up the hill under cover, accompanied by a sergeant, and followed at some considerable distance by a Lewis gun section. Having gone as far as he could under cover, Lieut. Hedges dashed forward, killed the first enemy machine-gunner, and took two others prisoner. He then worked his way along the crest of the hill and served three other machine-gun posts in the same fashion. This dashing exploit broke down the enemy's resistance at this point and enabled our line to go forward.[2] Ultimately, after dogged fighting, our men pushed into Robersart, which was cleared by the end of the day. A German garrison, which held out in Renuart Farm, was outflanked by three companies of the 6th Northamptonshire, while the remaining company engaged the enemy's attention in front.

[1] Hermann Stellung II.   [2] See Appendix E, No. 24.

No. 91.

THE SOUTHERN OUTSKIRTS OF ENGLEFONTAINE AND MORMAL FOREST.

Oblique air photograph.

Some progress was made east of Robersart and Renuart Farm, but the final objective on the line of the main Landrecies–Englefontaine road was held in force by the enemy.

Thus, after two days' strenuous fighting,[1] the line of the final objective had been gained on most of the army front. The greater part

The result of the fighting on the 23rd and 24th of Catillon and Ors were still, however, held by the enemy as well as the south-east corner of L'Evêque Wood, while the 18th Division held a line just short of the main Landrecies–Englefontaine road. Eight German Divisions and a Cyclist Brigade had been defeated, and 27 officers, 1,213 other ranks, and 66 guns had been captured. In addition, the Aulnoye railway junction, so important to the enemy for movement of transport, troops, and supplies, was now within range of our 6-inch guns.

After the fighting of the 23rd and 24th there was a lull, during which the troops were rested and reorganised, while preparations were at once

Minor operations from October 25th to 31st begun for a resumption of the offensive. Infantry action until the end of the month was confined chiefly to active patrolling, but on October 26th the 18th Division, by throwing forward its left flank, co-operated with an attack of the V Corps, which resulted in the capture of Englefontaine and the establishment of our line from Petit Planty to the north-east corner of Englefontaine. On the left of the IX Corps a company of the 1st The Buffs of the 6th Division attacked and, after a first failure, secured part of the Happegarbes spur, which it held against the enemy's counter-attacks until relieved. On October 29th the 1st Division established itself along the western bank of the Sambre and Oise Canal from Oisy to the south of Catillon.

North and south of the Fourth Army the experiences of the enemy had been no more encouraging for him. In Flanders, by the end of Octo-

The progress north and south of the Fourth Army ber, the enemy had been forced back to the line of the Scheldt, and the Third and First Armies had advanced our line well to the north and east of the Le Quesnoy–Valenciennes railway. To the south the French had made good progress, had crossed the Serre and Peron rivers, and had reached the southern bank of the Oise near Guise.

In front of the Fourth Army the enemy was now making a stand on the line of the Sambre and Oise Canal and along the western edge of

A summary of the situation on October 31st Mormal Forest. His troops, however, were depressed by continuous defeat and exhausted by incessant fighting, while the moral of our own men was magnificent. The general attack was, therefore, only delayed by the Commander-in-Chief until such time as the preparations should be complete. One fresh, and five fairly fresh German divisions were transferred to other parts of the front from in front of the Fourth Army, and the 221st Division, which had been engaged three times by the Fourth Army, was now disbanded. Hence the enemy's reserves on the Fourth Army front were reduced by seven divisions. At the end of October it was estimated that

---

[1] The strong resistance experienced by the XIII Corps in the Bousies area was due to the fact that the enemy had been reinforced here by the 30th and 58th Divisions.

the Fourth Army was opposed by the equivalent of seven divisions, together with portions both of the Cyclist Brigade and the Jäger Division ; all these divisions, however, were believed to be exhausted and were supported only by three other equally exhausted divisions. It was believed that in the back areas the enemy had thirteen divisions at his disposal, of which the large majority had been recently withdrawn from the fighting and had suffered heavy casualties. On the whole of the western front, there was only one German division which had been resting for one month.

Whatever might be his ultimate intentions, it was essential for the enemy to maintain the line of the Sambre and Oise Canal as long as possible, and the importance of denying the passage of the canal to our troops was impressed by him on all ranks of his army.[1] At the same time, aeroplane reconnaissance made it clear that the Germans were removing aerodromes and destroying railways, and making preparations for a further retirement. If the passage of the Sambre and Oise Canal could be forced before their preparations for an orderly retirement could be completed, they must inevitably suffer disaster.

[1] The following Army Order, issued by the Crown Prince to the XVIII German Army, which was captured about October 29th, shows the intentions of the enemy :—

"The defence of the Canal position is of great strategical importance for the Army Group front. I reckon absolutely on the Army holding its new positions at all costs.

"The reserves at the Army's disposal should be engaged and utilised with a view to this. It must be clearly understood by all commanding officers that only a stubborn resistance will induce the enemy to discontinue his attack. Again I order that the canal front be strongly reinforced with machine-gun units. I insist upon no further withdrawal being undertaken without my authority.

"(Sd.) WILHELM, Crown Prince.

"The above is to be issued down to Regiments.

"(Sd.) BURKNER, Chief of Staff."

CHAPTER XII

THE CROSSING OF THE SAMBRE AND OISE CANAL, AND THE EVENTS LEADING UP TO THE ARMISTICE, NOVEMBER 1ST TO 11TH

Maps 1, 2, 16, and 17

The situation prior to the resumption of the Allied offensive—The orders from General Headquarters for a general advance—The preliminary operations by the IX Corps—The general plan for the attack on November 4th—The nature of the country; the Sambre and Oise Canal—The Mormal Forest—The country east of the Sambre and Oise Canal—The objectives of the attack—The IX Corps plan of attack—The XIII Corps plan of attack—The action of the artillery—The preparations for bridging the canal—The allotment of tanks—The assembly—November 4th; the IX Corps; the attack of the 1st Division; the crossing of the canal by the 2nd Brigade—The 1st Brigade crossing—The capture of Catillon by the 3rd Brigade—The further advance of the 1st Division—The result of the fighting by the 1st Division—The attack of the 32nd Division; the 14th Brigade force a crossing—The temporary check to the 96th Brigade—The capture of the Happegarbes spur—The further advance of the 32nd Division—The XIII Corps operations—The capture of Landrecies by the 25th Division—The 50th Division attack through Mormal Forest—The attack by the 18th Division—The armoured cars—The result of the fighting on November 4th —The pursuit; November 5th and 6th; the events on the IX Corps front—The events on the XIII Corps front—The pursuit continued on November 7th, 8th, and 9th—The IX Corps— The XIII Corps—The question of supply—Bethell's Force—The frontier of France reached on November 10th—The Armistice, 11 a.m., November 11th.

By the end of October the defeat of Germany appeared inevitable. In a long series of almost continuous battles her armies had been defeated with heavy losses in men and material, and it was becoming increasingly difficult for the German High Command to withdraw the troops in good order. Menaced by overwhelming defeat, German soldiers were no longer available to assist their Allies in other theatres of war; Turkey and Bulgaria had surrendered to the Allies, while Austria, bankrupt of leaders, plan, and organisation, was incapable of carrying on the war.[1]

The situation prior to the resumption of the Allied offensive

Within Germany itself the soaring hopes, aroused by the brilliant start of the March offensive, had given place to profound depression, as each week recorded a fresh withdrawal of the German forces. Internal conditions had grown desperate, and dreams of victory had given place to a sense of the complete futility of prosecuting a profitless war. The leaders of the nation were no longer trusted, and social agitators were given a sympathetic hearing.

Thus, while each military disaster made it difficult for the German

[1] Bulgaria signed an Armistice on September 29th, Turkey on October 31st, and Austria on November 3rd.

239

leaders to control the army, it was still more difficult to control the forces within Germany itself. Complete disaster could only be averted if the defeated armies could be withdrawn behind a line capable of checking the Allies during the winter months. Then it might be possible for Germany to bargain with the Allies, and arrange an armistice, the terms of which would allow her a voice in the settlement on more or less equal terms. It was, however, within the power of the Allied forces to shatter this last hope, if full use was made by Marshal Foch and Sir Douglas Haig of the enormous moral and strategic advantages which they had gained. An immediate attack upon the enemy's centre, the vital part of his line upon which depended the safety of his communications in the north and south, would anticipate his contemplated and inevitable withdrawal, and, if successful, would convert that withdrawal into a rout.

With this object orders were issued by Sir Douglas Haig on October 29th for the Fourth, Third, and First Armies to carry out a concerted
The orders from attack in the general direction of Maubeuge and Mons,
General Headquarters while on the right of the Fourth Army, the First French
for a general advance Army would co-operate by pushing forward in the direction of La Capelle.

A preliminary operation to secure Valenciennes was necessary before the general attack could be made, and this was successfully accomplished by the Third and First Armies by November 2nd. This victory compelled the enemy to withdraw on the Le Quesnoy–Valenciennes front, and rendered the position of his forces in the Tournai salient precarious, as our progress south of it had now turned the line of the Scheldt.

Preliminary operations were also undertaken by the Fourth Army in preparation for the general attack. The front of the Fourth Army
The preliminary opera- at the end of October extended from the Sambre and
tions by the IX Corps Oise Canal, north of Oisy, to its junction with the Third
(see Map 17) Army south of Englefontaine; of this the IX Corps held from the southern army boundary to the south-east corner of L'Evêque Wood, a front of some nine miles, while the XIII Corps held from L'Evêque Wood, to the junction with the Third Army, a distance of about six miles.

Before making any attempt to force the passage of the Sambre and Oise Canal it was necessary to secure complete control of all ground on its western bank. The chief points of tactical importance still held by the enemy west of the canal were Catillon, Le Donjon, Ors, and the Happegarbes spur south-west of Landrecies. Vigorous patrolling was therefore carried out by the IX Corps on November 1st, and by November 2nd the village of Ors and the whole western bank, from Ors to the elbow in the canal further north, had been cleared of the enemy. Further south, the enemy still retained Catillon and the circular strong point known as Le Donjon.

The most important point, however, held by the enemy on the western bank was the Happegarbes spur, which commanded the canal as far south as Catillon and of which the 32nd Division only held a part.[1]

---

[1] The 32nd Division relieved the 6th Division on the left of the IX Corps front on the night of October 30th.

THE SAMBRE AND OISE CANAL, SHOWING THE RESERVOIRS ON EACH SIDE.

In order to secure the whole of the spur it was attacked at 6 a.m. on November 2nd by the 15th Lancashire Fusiliers of the 96th Brigade, assisted by three tanks of the 10th Mark V Tank Battalion. After heavy fighting the spur was captured, together with 60 prisoners of the 6th battalion of the 2nd Cyclist Brigade.[1] Three hours later the position was counter-attacked by the enemy from the north-east; this attack was repulsed, but a second and stronger counter-attack, preceded by a violent bombardment in which a large quantity of gas shell was used, was carried out by the 6th Battalion reinforced by the 4th Battalion of Cyclists, and succeeded in forcing our men off the spur. A second attack by the 15th Lancashire Fusiliers, reinforced by two companies of the 16th Lancashire Fusiliers, regained possession of the spur on the morning of November 3rd. Two determined counter-attacks were again delivered by the enemy. The first was successfully beaten off, but a second was delivered by a strong force, consisting of the two Cyclist battalions reinforced by a regiment of the 1st Guard Reserve Division. Fighting of the most obstinate and bitter description took place, and at one time the battalion headquarters of the 15th Lancashire Fusiliers was almost surrounded. The gallant resistance of the battalion staff, however, kept the enemy at bay until night fell, when, owing to the casualties sustained, it was deemed advisable to withdraw to the "starting line."

It was now clear that, while the capture of the spur presented no great difficulties to resolute troops, its retention was a matter of considerable difficulty. Consequently, it was decided to abandon the idea of securing this ground before the main attack was launched, as it was considered that in a general advance the enemy would not be in a position to deliver local counter-attacks in such strength as he did on November 2nd and 3rd.[2]

These operations had prepared the way for the general attack which was to take place on November 4th. The attack of the British Armies

The general plan for the attack on November 4th
was to be delivered on a frontage of about thirty miles, from the Sambre and Oise Canal, immediately north of Oisy, to Valenciennes, and was to be extended to the south of Oisy for another twenty miles by the French. The general line of advance of the Fourth Army, on a frontage of about fifteen miles, was to be due east.

The nature of the country over which the advance was to be made was difficult. On the right there was the obstacle of the Sambre and

The nature of the country; the Sambre and Oise Canal
Oise Canal which had to be crossed at the outset. This canal runs from La Fère by Mont D'Origny, Vadencourt, and Etreux to Landrecies. From La Fère to Vadencourt it follows the course of the Oise, thence, swinging to the north near Etreux, it enters the Sambre valley near Oisy. At Landrecies the canal terminates and the canalised Sambre begins as a

---

[1] Both during this attack, and again on November 3rd and 4th, Sergeant Clarke, 15th Lancashire Fusiliers, displayed great gallantry and fine leadership. See Appendix E, No. 10.

[2] It is always a difficult question to decide whether a small preliminary operation of this description to capture some important tactical point is wise, or whether it is not better to include it in the general attack. Experience proves that, with few exceptions, it is better to wait for the general attack, when such points will be captured without difficulty.

separate waterway. The canal is of the ordinary type to be met with in France and Belgium and forms a considerable obstacle, being some seventy feet wide from bank to bank, and thirty-five to forty feet wide at water-level except at Lock No. 1, and at the locks at Catillon, Ors, and Landrecies, where it is seventeen feet wide. It contained at that time an average depth of six to eight feet of water and was nowhere fordable except at the bridges, which had been either demolished or prepared for demolition.

In addition to the obstacle offered by the canal itself, the low ground on both sides of the canal had been inundated by the Germans and much of it had been transformed into swamp. In some places the water was only ankle deep, but, north and south of Ors, there were small streams parallel to the canal swollen to a width of about fifteen feet and a depth of two to three feet; similar streams existed south of Catillon. Along each side of the canal between Oisy and Lock No. 1 there are wide reservoirs; at their northern end they are more than twice the width of the canal, and at that time contained a fair depth of water, but they are narrower and shallower further south. South of Catillon the enemy had felled the trees along the western bank of the canal for the double purpose of improving his field of fire and of forming an abattis.

Further north the area west of the Mormal Forest is of a peculiarly intricate and enclosed nature. The scattered and rambling villages of
Les Etoquies, Happegarbes, Rosimbois, Preux-aux-Bois,
The Mormal Forest and Hecq are surrounded by small orchards and pad-
docks, enclosed by thick, almost impenetrable, hedges, which restricted the view and greatly increased the difficulties of main-taining direction.

Mormal Forest itself covers an area of forty square miles, but much of it had been cut down for timber by the enemy during his occupation, and there were, therefore, numerous clearings; in those portions which were untouched by the axe the undergrowth was very dense and hampered movement. A number of streams have their source in the forest and run through narrow channels with steep banks into the Scheldt and Sambre valleys. In the centre, surrounded by small pastures and orchards, is the village of Locquignol, on which the numerous roads and tracks, almost all of which are unmetalled, mostly converge. In addition, many light railway tracks had been constructed by the enemy in order to transport the felled timber. The whole forest offered great oppor-tunities for resolute defence. Owing to its size, density, and good interior communications it was capable of sheltering considerable forces, whilst its large expanse made it difficult for artillery to deal with effectively.

The general configuration of the country, east of the Sambre and Oise Canal and south of Mormal Forest and the Sambre, consists of a series
, The country east of of parallel valleys, through which run the tributaries
the Sambre and Oise of the river Sambre, and which are separated by
Canal ridges affording excellent successive positions for rear-guard action. The whole area was intersected by wire and hedges, and cavalry or infantry could make only slow progress off the roads, to which the artillery would be entirely confined for any considerable movements or changes of position. The landscape bore a striking resemblance to

MORMAL FOREST, SHOWING SOME OF THE CLEARINGS.

Oblique air photograph.

that of a dairy-farming county in England. There was little or no cultivation, the fields being pasture land; scattered farmsteads were frequent, and the villages, for the most part tucked away in the valleys, were of a very much better type than those to be found in the Somme area before the war wrought its devastation.

In the instructions issued to the IX and XIII Corps Sir Henry Rawlinson laid down two main objectives to be secured. The first, or red line, extended approximately due north and south from east of Fesmy to east of Landrecies, and thence northwards through the Mormal Forest about 3,000 yards from its western edge. The attainment of this objective would in the south carry the attacking troops well beyond the canal, and would enable the engineers to repair or erect bridges across it without fear of interference, thus facilitating the forward communications.

The objectives of the attack

The second objective, or line of exploitation, ran east of Cartignies, Dompierre, and St. Remy Chaussée (see Map 16). This was some three miles short of the general objective defined by the Commander-in-Chief, namely the Avesnes–Maubeuge road, and was considered to be the limit of penetration that could be reached before a halt would be necessary in order to reorganise and complete the communications.

For the forcing of the Sambre and Oise Canal the IX Corps employed the 1st and 32nd Divisions on the right and left respectively. Although the attacks of both divisions were to be simultaneous, they were to be entirely independent as regards their detailed execution, each as it advanced arranging for the protection of its flanks, but establishing connection with the other immediately on crossing the canal and on the first objective (red line). The 46th Division was concentrated in corps reserve with its head on the line of the Mazinghien–Bazuel road. Its rôle, after the attack was launched, was to follow closely behind the 1st Division with a view to relieving that division either on the first objective, or immediately afterwards; the 46th and 32nd Divisions would then continue the advance to the second objective. For the IX Corps attack Sir Walter Braithwaite gave the 1st and 32nd Divisions two preliminary objectives before reaching the first objective laid down by the army.

The IX Corps plan of attack

(1) The bridgehead or blue-dotted line, which ran on the front of the 1st Division from the bridge at Petit Cambrésis along the road to Hautrève, thence to the eastern outskirts of Catillon, and, on the front of the 32nd Division, from Catillon through Petit Versaille to La Folie.

(2) The intermediate or blue line, which ran on the 1st Division front from the bridge at Petit Cambrésis to La Groise, excluding Fesmy and including Robelmètre, Grand Galop Farm, and Petit Galop Farm, and, on the 32nd Division front, from east of Mezières to Petit Versaille, including Locquignol Farm.

On the right Maj.-Gen. Strickland, commanding the 1st Division, which was holding a front of 7,000 yards from Oisy to north of Catillon, arranged for the 1st and 2nd Brigades to cross the canal south of Catillon under cover of a heavy barrage. This was to come down at " zero," simultaneously with a smoke screen which was to be put down immediately east of the canal to conceal the infantry crossing.[1] Each brigade was allotted one main crossing; the 2nd Brigade at the Lock No. 1, about two miles south of Catillon, the 1st Brigade at the bend in the canal north-west of Bois l'Abbaye. Once a crossing had been effected, the 1st and 2nd Brigades were to advance behind the creeping barrage and establish the bridgehead. There was to be a pause on the bridgehead line of one and a-half hours to allow time for artillery to move forward. The advance was then to be resumed to the intermediate line, from which, after fifteen minutes, the infantry on the flanks was to continue to move forward to the first army objective (red line).

Concurrently with the attack of the 1st and 2nd Brigades, the 3rd Brigade was to clear Catillon from the south under cover of an enfilade artillery and machine-gun barrage, after which it was to establish a small bridgehead east of the canal until such time as touch was definitely established with the 32nd Division further east.

Maj.-Gen. Lambert, commanding the 32nd Division, arranged that the 14th Brigade should cross the canal just south of Ors, and the 96th Brigade immediately south of the elbow in the canal north of Ors. Success depended on obtaining complete superiority of fire over the enemy holding the eastern bank of the canal, and arrangements were made for the crossing of the infantry to be covered by a powerful artillery barrage and smoke screen similar to those employed in the case of the 1st Division. After effecting a crossing the 14th and 96th Brigades were to reorganise before renewing the advance to the bridgehead line under the creeping barrage.[2] No barrage was arranged beyond the bridgehead line for the further advance to the first army objective (red line), the arrangements for the necessary artillery support being left to the brigade commanders concerned.

In view of the topographical features of the country south of the Sambre, offering as they did splendid opportunities for enfilade and oblique fire up the valleys which ran at right angles to the enemy's communications, the IX Corps sited two of its heavy artillery brigades well forward in the XIII Corps area to enfilade these valleys, which the enemy would undoubtedly make use of for sheltering troops and guns.

The task of the XIII Corps entailed an attack through the southern portion of Mormal Forest, the forcing of the canal crossings at Landrecies,

The XIII Corps plan of attack

and a total advance of approximately ten miles. Its first objective corresponded with the first objective laid down by the army, while, between this and the second objective, an intermediate objective following the Maroilles–Hachette Farm–Locquignol road was allotted to the divisions.

In view of the depleted strengths of his divisions and of the depth to which the advance was to be carried, Sir Thomas Morland decided to employ three divisions for the initial attack, each being on a comparatively

---

[1] The barrage was to lift off the eastern bank of the canal at three minutes after " zero," and then advance towards the blue-dotted line. Smoke screens for both 1st and 32nd Divisions were made by No. 1 Special Company, R.E., with 4-inch Stokes Mortars.

[2] The barrage was to remain on the eastern bank of the canal for five minutes; it was then to be lifted 300 yards and remain for thirty minutes, after which pause it was to advance at the rate of 100 yards every six minutes.

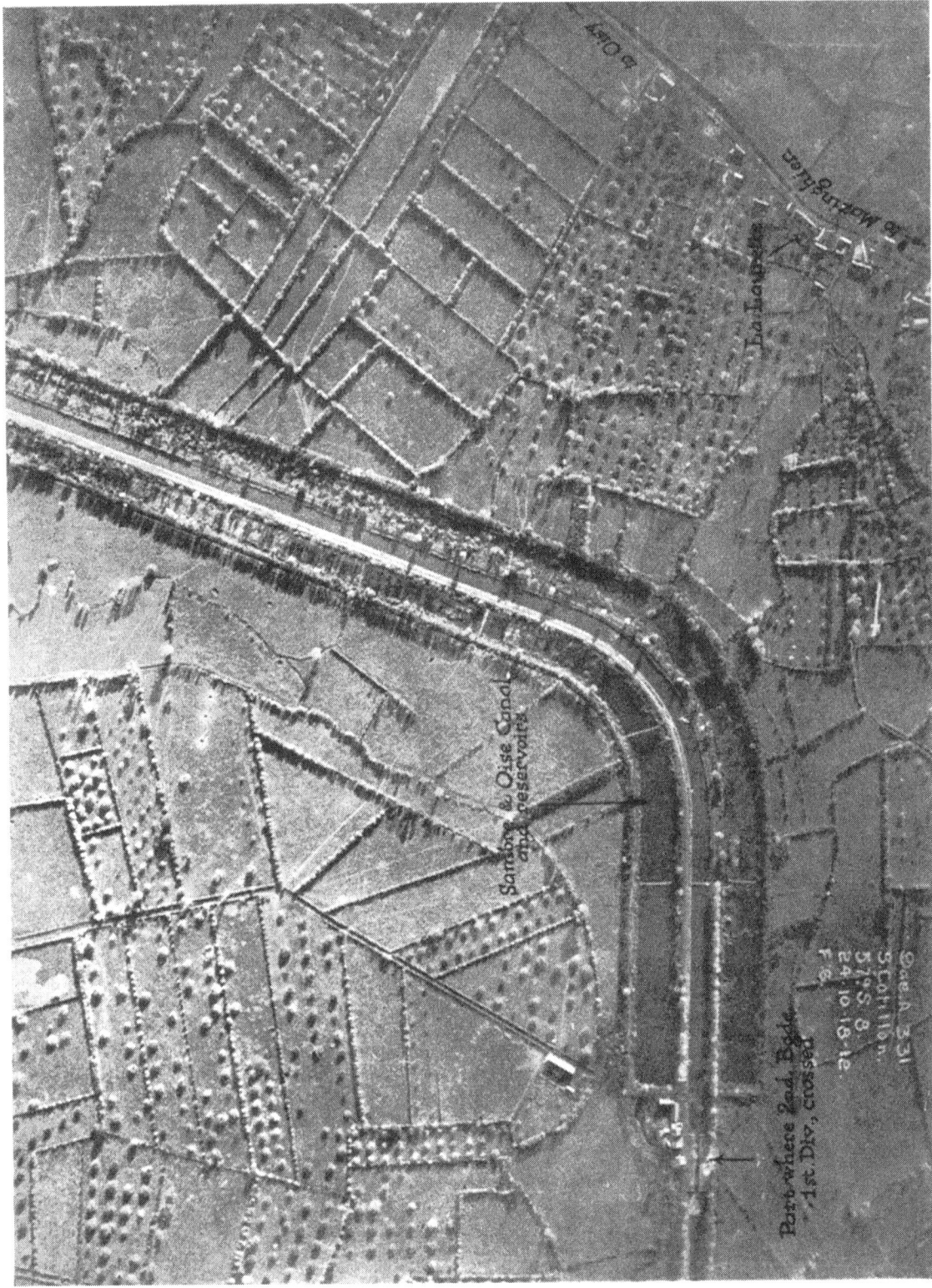

THE SAMBRE AND OISE CANAL BETWEEN CATILLON AND OISY, SHOWING THE LOCK-HOUSE
AT LOCK NO. I, WHERE THE 2ND BRIGADE, 1ST DIVISION, CROSSED.

Vertical air photograph.

narrow front, with one division in support.   On the right, the 25th Division was allotted the difficult task of forcing the passage of the canal opposite Landrecies, capturing that town, and pushing forward to the XIII Corps intermediate objective, which included the capture of Maroilles.   On this line the 66th Division was to pass through the 25th Division and secure the final line of exploitation.   The 50th Division, in the centre, operating on a front of 2,500 yards, was responsible for clearing the portion of the Mormal Forest between the northern boundary of the 25th Division and a line drawn approximately due west from the bend of the canal 2,000 yards west of Sassegnies.   The division was then to cross the canal and advance, in conjunction with the 66th Division, to the line of exploitation, or second objective laid down by the Army Commander.

On the left, the 18th Division, with an initial frontage of 3,000 yards, which narrowed rapidly as the advance progressed, was to attack through the Mormal Forest towards Sassegnies, establishing itself on the canal east and south of that village until its front was covered by the advance of the 50th Division.

Maj.-Gen. Charles, commanding the 25th Division, arranged to attack with the 75th Brigade in line, while the 74th and 7th Brigades were to "leap-frog" the 75th Brigade on the first objective (red line). Maj.-Gen. Jackson, commanding the 50th Division, ordered an advance on a two-brigade front, with the 149th and 150th Brigades leading, intending to pass the 151st Brigade through them when it was considered that the attack required fresh impetus.   Maj.-Gen. Lee, commanding the 18th Division, attacked on a two-brigade front, with the 54th and 53rd Brigades leading and the 55th Brigade "leap-frogging" them on the first objective. As it was expected that the enemy would offer strong resistance at Preux-aux-Bois, a convergent attack by the 50th and 18th Divisions from the south and north, wheeling inwards when they had passed the village and attacking it from both flanks and rear, was arranged by Sir Thomas Morland. The chief part in this attack was to be taken by the 54th Brigade as the village lay in the 18th Division's area.

The instructions for the artillery support of the XIII Corps attack were drawn up after a careful study of air photographs, and the artillery

The action of the artillery

barrage fire was modified to suit the peculiar conditions. Owing to the wooded nature of the country many areas were unsuitable for an 18-pounder barrage ; moreover, the undergrowth impeded the advance of the infantry and rendered turning movements necessary.   Certain areas or "blocks" were, therefore, kept under fire for definite periods, which allowed time for the infantry to work round them ; the fire was then lifted on to other areas which were treated in the same manner.   This fire was combined with a thin creeping barrage the advance of which was regulated on the usual principles.   This system of "block" barrages continued as far as the first objective, beyond which the infantry was to be supported by brigades of field artillery and 6-inch howitzers.

It was of paramount importance on this occasion that the attack should be a complete surprise to the enemy, otherwise the difficulties of crossing the canal would have been very greatly increased ; artillery action, therefore, remained normal, there being neither an increase nor diminution of artillery fire prior to "zero."[1]   In view of the close nature of the country, arrangements were made for pushing units of artillery and trench mortars far forward so that immediate artillery support would always be available for the infantry.

The provision of means for crossing the canal offered great scope for ingenuity, industry, and organisation.   There was none too much time

The preparations for bridging the canal

to complete the preparations, and the engineers of divisions and corps vied with each other in producing various patterns of light strong bridges for the passage of infantry and more substantial ones for guns and transport.

In the case of the 1st and 32nd Divisions, it was decided that the bridges for the use of the assaulting troops should be carried up bodily as bridges, so that no constructional work would be necessary on arrival at the canal bank.   The bridges for the leading troops of the 2nd Brigade to cross at Lock No. 1 were designed as single span bridges, as light as was consistent with their being able to support four to six men on them at one time.   They were fitted with a lever and a pair of wheels, so that they could be launched from the western abutments of the lock without requiring anyone on the far side to receive them.   The leading troops of the 1st Brigade used floating bridges carried on German steel floats.[2]   Four bridges of this type were made, and, owing to their lightness and shape, as well as their suitability for sliding over mud, they were perhaps the most effective pattern of all.   The several bays of each bridge were hinged together in such a way as to give the maximum flexibility in order to avoid any difficulty when passing them over the near bank of the canal.   The head of each bridge was fitted with a ladder to enable the infantry to scale the far bank.   The latter type of bridge was also used by the 32nd Division, which, in addition, constructed light footbridges by lashing petrol tins together.

The 25th Division arranged for infantry bridges to be thrown at three places at and on both sides of the Landrecies lock.   Rafts, consisting of sixteen petrol tins fixed to a timber framework, were accordingly designed by the engineers of the 25th Division.   This raft was primarily intended for ferrying the leading infantry across the canal,[3] and to each raft was fixed a paddle and towing lines so that it could be paddled or towed backwards and forwards across the canal.   As soon as the leading infantry was across, it was intended to form the rafts into light floating bridges[4]; these rafts were carried forward by hand by engineers and pioneers.   For crossing the lock at Landrecies, in the event of the lock gates being destroyed, the engineers of the 25th Division made two light trussed footbridges 22 feet long.

---

[1] For the attack on November 4th the Fourth Army employed 31 field artillery brigades, 19 brigades of heavy artillery, and 13 long-range siege batteries.

[2] These were light, hollow, metal cylinders made for this purpose by the Germans, and of which we had captured considerable numbers in their engineer parks.

[3] It weighed 95 lbs. and had a buoyancy of 230 lbs.

[4] A demonstration was carried out with six rafts on the Selle near Le Cateau on November 2nd which was witnessed by all battalions who were likely to carry out the crossing of the canal.

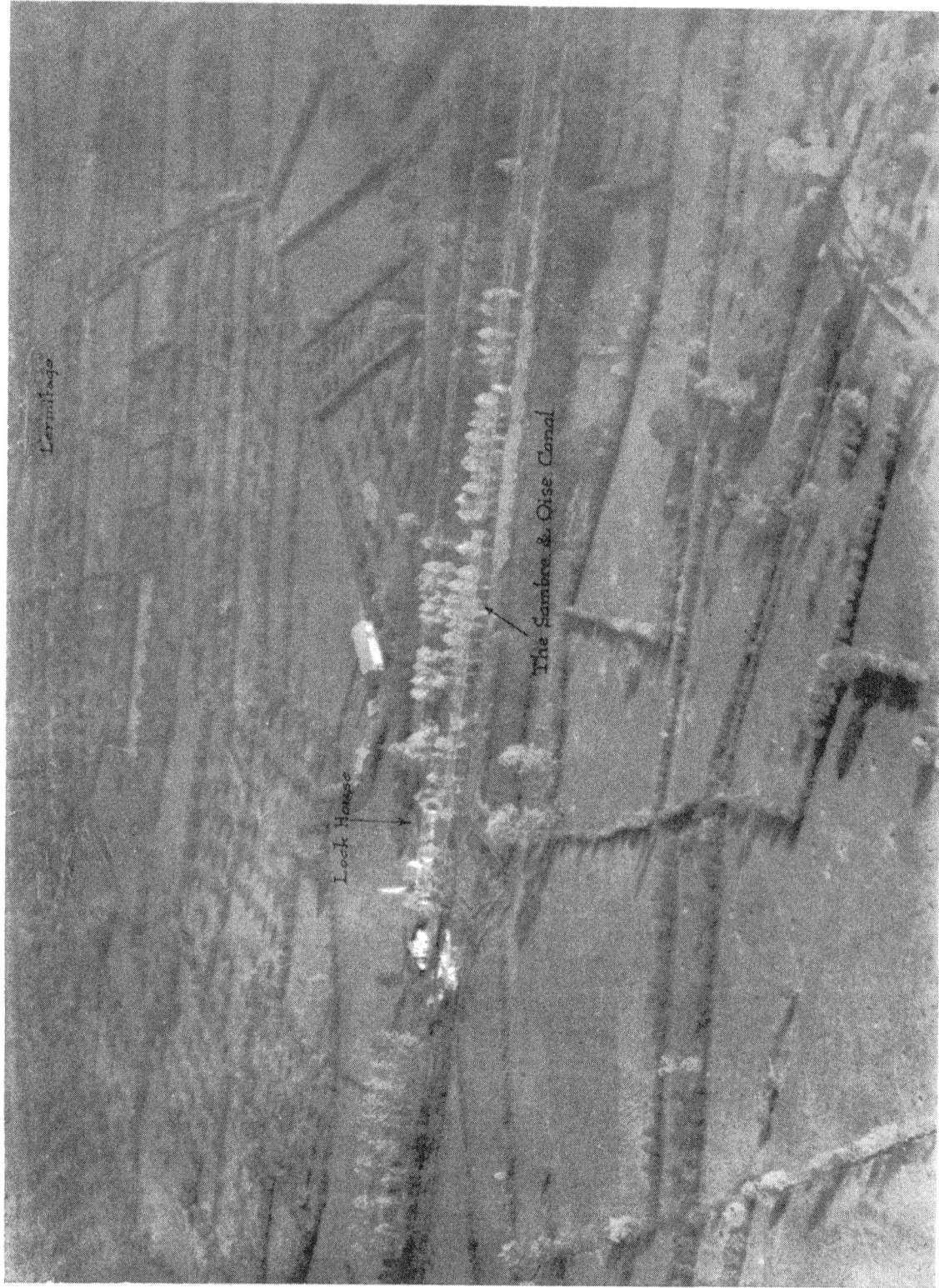

Ermitage

Lock House

The Sambre & Oise Canal

THE LOCK-HOUSE AT LOCK NO. I AND THE RESERVOIRS ON THE SAMBRE AND OISE CANAL.

As a last resort, in the event of the various types of bridges used by the infantry failing, lifebelts were issued to all troops engaged in the crossing of the canal, and a number of light portable Berthon boats were held in readiness.

For the operations the Fourth Army was allotted forty-two Mark V or Mark V star tanks of the 2nd Tank Brigade, nine armoured cars of the 17th Armoured Car Battalion, and eight supply tanks for carrying forward ammunition and bridging material.

The allotment of tanks

Of the Mark V and Mark V star tanks, the IX Corps was given the 10th Tank Battalion consisting of eleven tanks ; of these, three tanks were allotted to the 1st Division, two to the 32nd Division, and the remaining six were retained in corps reserve. The tanks operating with the 1st and 32nd Divisions were to assist in the attack on and the " mopping up " of Catillon and the Happegarbes spur respectively, subsequently assisting the infantry in establishing bridgeheads over the canal. The 9th and 14th Tank Battalions, consisting of fourteen and seventeen tanks respectively, were given to the XIII Corps ; of these, the 25th and 50th Divisions were allotted respectively four and ten tanks of the 9th Tank Battalion, and the 18th Division ten tanks of the 14th Battalion. The rôle of these tanks was to precede the infantry through the difficult and intricate orchard country along the western edge of the Mormal Forest and to force passages through the thick hedges, which would otherwise have delayed the infantry considerably. These tanks were not intended to enter the forest, but were ordered to rally when the infantry had penetrated into it and when the area outside the forest had been cleared. Certain tanks were, however, given the special task of " mopping up " Preux-aux-Bois in conjunction with the attack of the 50th and 18th Divisions. The XIII Corps retained in reserve seven tanks of the 14th Tank Battalion. Of the nine cars of the 17th Armoured Car Battalion, two were allotted to the 18th Division and two to the 50th Division to carry out reconnaissances in Mormal Forest. As far as possible the infantry was trained in co-operation with the tanks during the period of preparation, and the various units made elaborate arrangements with the personnel of the tanks which were to work with them in order to ensure satisfactory co-operation.

" Zero " for the IX Corps attack was fixed for 5.45 a.m. on November 4th, while that of the XIII Corps was half an hour later so as to conform with that of the Third Army. The assembly of the infantry and tanks was carried out during the night of the 3rd without a hitch, and a heavy ground mist in the early morning obscured their movements from the enemy.

The assembly

At 5.45 a.m. the barrage came down in front of the IX Corps along the eastern bank of the canal, and the assembled infantry of the 1st and 32nd Divisions moved forward to the attack.

November 4th ; the IX Corps ; the attack of the 1st Division ; the crossing of the canal by the 2nd Brigade

On the right the 2nd Brigade moved forward with the 2nd King's Royal Rifle Corps and the 2nd Royal Sussex on the right and left, followed by the 1st Northamptonshire in support. South of the reservoirs the 2nd Welsh of the 3rd Brigade held the line of the canal to the junction with the French north of Oisy.

It had been hoped to have a bridge erected over the lock within five minutes of " zero," but a small stream west of the canal proved a more serious obstacle than had been anticipated and caused some delay. A heavy hostile barrage fell on the western banks of the canal, and withering machine-gun fire from the lock-house and from the direction of Bois de l'Abbaye swept all approaches to the lock. So intense was the enemy's fire that even the stoutest troops hesitated, and it seemed impossible for any man to get to the lock and yet live. It was a situation that called for personal gallantry of the highest order; fortunately this was not lacking. Major Findlay,[1] of the 409th Field Company, quickly steadied and led forward his sappers and the leading infantry towards the lock. In spite of heavy casualties, the engineers and infantry responded magnificently to Major Findlay's example, and a bridge was placed across the lock. Meanwhile Lt.-Col. Dudley Johnson,[2] commanding the 2nd Royal Sussex, had come forward to see what progress had been made. He found that when any parties of infantry approached the fire-swept zone they were checked and thrown into confusion by the intensity of the enemy's fire. Recognising at once that delay would only increase casualties and demoralise the troops, Lt.-Col. Johnson quickly collected men to assist the sappers with the bridges and then personally led the assault forward. Again the enemy's fire broke up the bridging and attacking parties. The rear waves, which were now closing up, added to the congestion, and heavy casualties began to be suffered from the enemy's withering fire. Lt.-Col. Johnson made another great effort, reorganised his parties, and, under his gallant leadership, the attacking troops finally crossed the bridge and stormed the lock-house.

The whole of the 2nd Royal Sussex, followed by a large number of the 2nd King's Royal Rifle Corps, was soon across the canal and moving up the spur south of Bois de l'Abbaye. One company of the latter battalion, which was to have crossed further south by the existing footbridges over the reservoirs, found them badly damaged by shell fire and attempted to cross the reservoir by means of Berthon boats. This was impracticable in face of the hostile machine-gun fire, and the company, therefore, followed the remainder of its battalion over the canal by the lock bridge. The leading troops of the 2nd Brigade soon reached the line of the road running south from Bois de l'Abbaye, and, after a pause of twenty minutes to reorganise, moved forward to the bridgehead line, which they gained by 8 a.m., capturing a large number of prisoners of the 19th Reserve and 29th Divisions.

On the front of the 1st Brigade the 1st Cameron Highlanders and the 1st Loyal North Lancashire moved forward on the right and left respectively, simultaneously with the 23rd Field Company; the 1st Black Watch followed in support. Practically no resistance was encountered on the west bank of the canal, except for one machine-gun, the crew of which was disposed of by a sergeant of the 23rd Field Company. As soon as the barrage lifted off the east bank of the canal at three minutes after " zero," four floating

The 1st Brigade crossing

---

[1] See Appendix E, No. 17.   [2] See Appendix E, No. 26.

THE LOCK-HOUSE FROM THE WEST.

No. 97.

ANOTHER PART OF THE SAMBRE AND OISE CANAL, SOUTH OF CATILLON, SHOWING
THE BRIDGES BY WHICH THE 1ST BRIGADE, 1ST DIVISION, CROSSED.

To face page 249.

To Mézières

Sambre and Oise Canal

CATILLON FROM THE WEST.

Oblique air photograph.

bridges were pushed across the canal and were all in position by ten minutes after " zero." On the right the 1st Cameron Highlanders crossed without opposition in six minutes,[1] and very shortly afterwards both battalions were across the canal and re-forming before moving forward towards the bridgehead line. The enemy's retaliatory barrage, which had been slow in opening, fell west of the canal well behind the leading battalions, and the bridgehead line was reached with little difficulty by 8 a.m.

For the attack on Catillon the 3rd Brigade employed the 1st Gloucestershire, which prior to " zero " was assembled in the orchards

The capture of Catillon by the 3rd Brigade

south of the village. Though the thick ground mist made it difficult to keep direction, good progress was made. Of the three tanks of the 10th Tank Battalion with the 3rd Brigade, one broke down before the attack commenced, but the remaining two rendered valuable assistance. After some opposition in the outskirts of the village the southern portion was quickly cleared with the help of one of the tanks. The other tank made for the bridge over the canal, and in co-operation with the infantry destroyed a machine-gun cunningly concealed in a house near by.

In the meantime two companies of the 1st South Wales Borderers had approached Catillon from the west and assisted the 1st Gloucestershire to " mop up " the village. While this fighting was in progress an excellent artillery barrage had been maintained along the canal bank, preventing all escape, and, when it lifted to enable the infantry of the 3rd Brigade to move forward and secure the bridge crossings, fully 100 of the enemy crawled from the cellars of Catillon and surrendered. The bridge crossings were blocked with wire and various obstacles; these were surmounted, and soon after 8 a.m. six platoons of the 1st Gloucestershire were across the canal and were pushing forward to form a bridgehead and get in touch with the units on either flank.

When the protective barrage, which had been maintained in front of the bridgehead line, lifted at 9.30 a.m., the 2nd and 1st Brigades moved

The further advance of the 1st Division

forward towards the intermediate objective (blue line), and on the right the 1st Northamptonshire was brought up from support for the attack against Fesmy. The advance met with little opposition, and the intermediate objective north of Fesmy was secured shortly after midday, though in Fesmy itself the enemy was still holding out. Owing to the 66th French Division on the right being unable to move forward as fast as was expected, the flank of the 2nd Brigade became exposed and was reinforced by the 1/6th Welsh (Pioneers). A battalion of the 46th Division was also ordered up later.[2]

At 4 p.m. the 66th French Division attacked with a view to joining up with the 1st Division at La Justice, while simultaneously the 1st Northamptonshire advanced and captured Fesmy and Viéville. A patrol

---

[1] There was a competition between the two battalions as to which should be across the canal first. The Cameron Highlanders won by the narrow margin of half a minute.

[2] In order to avoid complicating Map 17, the movements of the 46th Division are not shown on it.

succeeded in penetrating as far as La Justice, but touch was not actually gained with the French, who had reached the western outskirts of Bergues-sur-Sambre. A flank was established from Viéville, south-east of Fesmy, to the canal, while the 2nd Welsh, which had captured the bridge at Pt. Cambrésis, held the canal and maintained touch between the French and the 2nd Brigade.

When the barrage moved forward on the 1st Brigade front, the 1st Cameron Highlanders and the 1st Black Watch, the latter having "leap-frogged" the 1st Loyal North Lancashire, advanced on the right and left respectively. At Robelmètre the 1st Cameron Highlanders were held up temporarily by shell fire, but the left company, avoiding the shelled area, reached the road south of Grand Galop Farm. The right company of the 1st Black Watch moved through Boyau de Leu and advanced to Grand Galop and Petit Galop farms, which they captured with 30 prisoners. The left company of the 1st Black Watch met with little resistance until Mezières was reached. Here the enemy attempted to fight, but was soon overwhelmed, and 50 prisoners were taken.

As the 1st Brigade was not in touch with the 32nd Division on the left, a company of the 1st Loyal North Lancashire moved forward to the Mezières–Catillon road and by 5.15 p.m. had established communication between the 1st Brigade and the 32nd Division at Malassise Farm.

As the result of the day's fighting the 1st Division had forced the difficult passage of the Sambre and Oise Canal, penetrating beyond it The result of the to a depth of over 4,000 yards and capturing the villages fighting by the 1st of Catillon, Mezières, La Groise, and Fesmy. The Division total casualties of the division were under 500, whereas 49 officers and 1,649 other ranks had been captured belonging to the 19th Reserve, 29th, and 200th Divisions, together with 20 guns of various calibres.

At 5.45 a.m., on the 32nd Division front, the 14th Brigade moved forward with the 5/6th Royal Scots on the right, the 1st Dorsetshire on The attack of the the left, and with the 15th Highland Light Infantry in 32nd Division; the reserve. The 96th Brigade on the left advanced 14th Brigade force a with the 2nd Manchester, 16th Lancashire Fusiliers, crossing and 15th Lancashire Fusiliers in line from right to left, and with two companies of the 2nd King's Own Yorkshire Light Infantry in reserve. The 97th Brigade, less two companies of 2nd King's Own Yorkshire Light Infantry, was held in reserve in the vicinity of St. Souplet.

When the artillery barrage lifted off the canal bank five minutes after " zero," the infantry occupied the whole of the western bank of the canal except south of Ors, where the 5/6th Royal Scots were checked by machine-gun fire from Le Donjon. A surprise attempt by the 1st Dorsetshire to force a crossing over the canal at Ors failed owing to the severity of the enemy's machine-gun and shell fire. The battalion effected a crossing, however, by means of a bridge of petrol tins south of Ors by twenty-five minutes after " zero "; luckily the enemy, while subjecting all the suspected points of crossing to an accurate fire, did not locate this bridge owing to the mist until it was too late, with the result that the 1st Dorset-shire crossed with but little opposition. Taking advantage of this crossing, two companies of the 5/6th Royal Scots gained the eastern bank of the canal, and by 8.15 a.m. they and the 1st Dorsetshire were firmly estab-lished along the road running parallel to the canal through Rue Verte and the eastern outskirts of Ors. The enemy defending Le Donjon was now threatened from the rear and was forced to surrender.

The 96th Brigade was not so successful in its attempt to cross just south of the elbow in the canal north of Ors. Only through the heroism of Major Waters and Sapper Archibald [1] of the 218th Field Company was it possible to get a bridge across. The whole area was swept with shell and machine-gun fire, and it seemed impossible for anyone to live on the bank of the canal. All the rest of the party were killed or disabled, yet these two gallant engineers carried on the work, while bullets splintered the wood they were holding and struck sparks from the wire binding the floats. Meanwhile, 2nd Lieut. Kirk [2] of the 2nd Manchester, in a splendid spirit of self-sacrifice, paddled across the canal on a raft and engaged the enemy with a Lewis gun. This gallant act cost him his life, but a bridge was erected, and two platoons of his battalion succeeded in crossing. Unfortunately, the bridge was almost immediately destroyed by shell fire, and, though repeated attempts were made to repair it, the undertaking had to be abandoned, and the remainder of the battalion took shelter from the enemy's fire behind the western bank of the canal until it received a message from the 1st Dorsetshire that it was possible to cross at Ors.

The temporary check to the 96th Brigade

Just below the elbow in the canal the Engineers and the 16th Highland Light Infantry (Pioneers) succeeded in erecting a bridge of small cork rafts; before, however, the leading troops of the 16th Lancashire Fusiliers could cross, the bridge was broken by concentrated artillery and machine-gun fire. The officer commanding this battalion, Lt.-Col. Marshall of the Irish Guards, [3] took charge of the situation and organised parties of volunteers for the repair of the bridge; the first party were all soon killed or wounded, nevertheless the bridge was finally erected. Lt.-Col. Marshall stood on the bank while the work was being carried out, and then attempted to rush across at the head of his battalion; he was killed almost at once. Over 200 casualties had now been sustained in the effort to cross the canal, and it was clear that any further attempts to cross on the 96th Brigade front would only result in purposeless loss of life. The troops of the 14th Brigade east of the canal were, therefore, ordered to stand fast until the 96th Brigade had succeeded in crossing by the bridges which had been erected by the 14th Brigade.

While these events were occurring further south the 15th Lancashire Fusiliers and the two companies of the 2nd King's Own Yorkshire Light Infantry attacked the Happegarbes spur, assisted by two tanks. The infantry and tanks worked through the village of Happegarbes, clearing up strong points and machine-gun nests, and then advanced parallel to the railway

The capture of the Happegarbes spur

[1] See Appendix E, Nos. 46 and 2.   [2] See Appendix E, No. 29.
[3] See Appendix E, No. 34.

embankment, where considerable opposition was encountered. By 7 a.m. the whole ground west of the Canal was finally cleared as a result of the excellent co-operation between the two arms.

Shortly after 8.30 a.m. the 96th Brigade began to cross the canal by the 14th Brigade bridges and cleared the area north-east of

The further advance of the 32nd Division

Ors. It was held up at La Motte Farm, but on the right reached the intermediate objective in conjunction with the 14th Brigade, which later joined up with the 1st Division north of Mezières.

During the afternoon the 15th Lancashire Fusiliers, holding Happegarbes, passed two companies across the canal south of Landrecies over the two footbridges which had been used by the 25th Division. These two companies at dusk held a position facing south, with their right on the canal 1,000 yards south-west of Landrecies and their left in touch with the 25th Division near Pont à Beaumetz.

During the day's fighting 238 prisoners of the 22nd Reserve, 54th, and 204th Divisions and Cyclist Battalions, 20 guns, and many machine-guns were captured by the 32nd Division, and a bridgehead had been firmly established. Thanks to the untiring energy of the 219th Field Company a transport bridge at Ors was completed by 1 p.m., and by means of this bridge a brigade of field artillery crossed the canal and was in action south of Ors by 4 p.m.

At 6.15 a.m., half an hour after the IX Corps launched its attack,

The XIII Corps operations

the XIII Corps began its advance, in conjunction with the V Corps operating through the northern portion of Mormal Forest.

The 75th Brigade of the 25th Division attacked, under a creeping barrage moving forward at the rate of 100 yards every six minutes, with the 1/5th Gloucestershire and the 1/8th Royal Warwickshire in line

The capture of Landrecies by the 25th Division

on the right and left respectively. The 1/8th Worcestershire followed in support, while the 108th Field Company and a company of the 11th South Lancashire (Pioneers) followed close behind the leading infantry carrying 80 rafts down to the canal, the majority of which reached it safely. At the same time, two companies of the 21st Manchester from the 7th Brigade " mopped up " the ground between the 25th and 32nd Divisions in conjunction with the troops of the 96th Brigade. By 8.15 a.m. the two companies of the 21st Manchester had cleared up this area and were in touch with the 32nd Division on the railway. Half an hour later the 1/5th Gloucestershire reached the canal bank south-west of Landrecies and had the good fortune to discover two footbridges, about 1,000 yards south-west of the town, which the enemy had not destroyed. The battalion streamed across these bridges at 9.30 a.m., closely followed by two companies of the 1/8th Worcestershire, and commenced to encircle Landrecies from the south. The 1/8th Royal Warwickshire on the left experienced stiff opposition in the vicinity of Faubourg-Soyeres. The enemy's resistance was, however, finally overcome largely owing to the gallantry of Lce.-Corp. William Amey, who rushed the château unaided and, after killing two Germans, held up

THE LOCK AND BRIDGE AT LANDRECIES

the remainder of the garrison till his comrades arrived.[1] With the capture of Faubourg-Soyeres the enemy's resistance in this part of the field was broken, and the 1/8th Royal Warwickshire reached the canal. As was anticipated, the road bridge near the lock in Landrecies was blown up, but the left company of the battalion discovered another enemy bridge intact about 500 yards further north. Shortly afterwards the remainder of the 1/8th Royal Warwickshire crossed at the lock gates, which had been rushed by a small party of the 182nd Tunnelling Company who overpowered the enemy demolition party while in the act of blowing them up. At the same time one company of the 1/8th Worcestershire crossed the canal by means of petrol-tin rafts between these two crossings. Thus, by midday, there were more than half a dozen crossings available for infantry, and the 106th Field Company then undertook the erection of two pontoon bridges near the lock, which, in spite of heavy shell fire, were completed soon after dark.

The failure of such an obstacle as the canal to stop our advance, doubtless exercised a demoralising influence on the Germans defending Landrecies. Attacked on three sides, from the south, west, and north, the resistance of the garrison, consisting chiefly of men of the Cyclist Brigade, was quickly overcome, and by noon the whole of the village had been cleared. The capture of Landrecies was an operation beset with many difficulties, but, thanks to good leadership, the bravery of the troops, and the skill and devotion of the divisional engineers and pioneers, the 75th Brigade met with the success and good fortune which such a well planned and boldly executed operation deserved.

About 1 p.m. the 74th Brigade commenced to cross the canal and, moving through Landrecies, advanced towards Le Preseau with the 11th Sherwood Foresters on the right, the 9th Yorkshire on the left, and the 13th Durham Light Infantry in support. To cover the right flank of the 74th Brigade the 75th Brigade established a defensive flank south of Landrecies to Pont à Beaumetz, where touch was later established with the 32nd Division. By nightfall the 74th Brigade had established itself along the line from Saule Bryante through Le Preseau to the canal.

The 50th Division began its advance at 6.15 a.m. with the 149th Brigade on the right, the 150th on the left, and the 151st in support. Eight of the ten tanks of the 9th Tank Battalion allotted to the division left their assembly position half an hour before the infantry began to advance and co-operated in the attack.[2] Though the enemy's artillery fire was not very heavy, falling chiefly in the vicinity of Fontaine-au-Bois and Robersart, the machine-gun fire was severe, the numerous hedgerows being infested with machine-guns. On account of this and the thickness of the mist, progress was much slower than was anticipated. The 149th Brigade found itself temporarily checked along the Landrecies–Englefontaine road, but by about 8 a.m. the opposition had been overcome

The 50th Division attack through Mormal Forest

[1] See Appendix E, No. 1.

[2] The crew of one of these tanks was put out of action by the enemy's gas shell on the way up to join the infantry, but was replaced by a scratch crew of Dublin Fusiliers which rendered an excellent account of itself.

with the assistance of the tanks, and the advance was resumed.   In this area the enemy had a very complete system of machine-gun defence, which constantly checked the advance of the 149th Brigade.   The value of the training carried out by the infantry with the tanks was very marked, and the final subjugation of this strong machine-gun defence must be ascribed to a very large extent to their excellent co-operation.

Meeting with less resistance, the 150th Brigade had reached the line of the Hirondelle Stream by 9 a.m.   At this time two companies of the 2nd Royal Munster Fusiliers attacked Preux-aux-Bois from the south in conjunction with an attack of troops of the 18th Division from the north and east.   Here the fighting continued for a long time, but did not interfere with the advance of the 50th Division.

By 11 a.m. the 149th Brigade had reached the northern portion of Faubourg-Soyeres, with their left in Mormal Forest and in touch with the 150th Brigade, which was disposed along the road running north from the Drill Ground through the forest about 1,000 yards from its western edge. The enemy's resistance, though still fairly strong in front of the 149th Brigade, was much weaker opposite the 150th, consequently Maj.-Gen. Jackson decided to move up the 151st Brigade, then in support near Bousies, to increase the pressure where the opposition was weakest.   While the 151st Brigade, however, was moving forward, the two leading brigades made good progress, and by 12 noon the whole of the first objective (red line) was in our hands.   All organised resistance appeared to be broken, and the only opposition encountered was from isolated machine-guns firing at fairly long range.   Half an hour later the leading battalions of the 151st Brigade " leap-frogged " the 150th Brigade and continued the advance on the left of the 149th Brigade, which had reached the railway east of Les Etoquies and was approaching the canal.   At dusk the 149th Brigade held the line of the canal from the bend north of Le Preseau, where it was in touch with the 25th Division, to near Cense Toury ; the 151st Brigade continued the line due north through Mormal Forest to Carrefour de l'Hermitage, where it joined up with the 18th Division.

Simultaneously with the advance of the 50th Division the troops of the 18th Division moved forward on the extreme left of the XIII Corps.

The attack by the 18th Division   On the right, the 54th Brigade attacked north of Preux-aux-Bois with the 6th Northamptonshire, while, south of this battalion, the 11th Royal Fusiliers stood fast until the village should be turned from the north by the 2nd Bedfordshire, who followed in support of the 6th Northamptonshire ; on the left, the 7th Royal West Kent led the advance of the 53rd Brigade against Hecq. The barrage was all that could be desired, whereas the enemy's artillery fire, although it came down three minutes after " zero," was weak and not effective.   Assisted by ten tanks of the 14th Tank Battalion, the 6th Northamptonshire and the 7th Royal West Kent made good progress in the face of considerable resistance.   By 8 a.m. these two battalions were north-east of Preux-aux-Bois and east of Hecq, although the Germans held out in both villages.   One tank, detailed to assist in the capture of Hecq, entered the village from the west, but almost immediately lost touch with the

Mormal Forest

Fler-aux-Bois

To Landrecies

From Englefontaine

PREUX AUX BOIS AND MORMAL FOREST.

Oblique air photograph.

7th Royal West Kent. It came into contact, however, with some troops of the 38th Division on the left and helped them by silencing a machine-gun nest on the outskirts of Englefontaine. Then, returning to Hecq, it re-joined the 7th Royal West Kent and proceeded to " mop up " strong points, capturing two machine-guns and two trench mortars in the northern end of the village. Before completing this task it was put out of action, but the crew, removing the machine-guns, successfully finished its fight with one of the strong points from outside the tank. The fighting in Hecq was severe and continued for several hours after the rest of the line had advanced. Even more determined was the struggle for the possession of Preux-aux-Bois. It was attacked from the north by the 2nd Bedford-shire, assisted by a company of the 11th Royal Fusiliers and a company of the 6th Northamptonshire. The 50th Division also co-operated by sending two companies of the 2nd Royal Munster Fusiliers to attack the village from the south. In the strenuous fighting that ensued before its capture important and valuable assistance was rendered by three tanks.[1]

The struggle in and around Preux-aux-Bois and Hecq delayed the advance of the two " leap-frogging " battalions of the 53rd Brigade which had been detailed to continue the advance east of those villages to the first objective (red line). However, two companies of the 8th Royal Berkshire eventually succeeded in pushing through on the north about noon, followed by the 10th Essex which moved up into line with them on their right some time later.

The advance was then resumed without incident until the line of the Route Duhamel was reached. Here there was a check, but the 55th Brigade, which had followed in rear of the 10th Essex and 8th Royal Berkshire, assisted them to push forward to the first objective, which was gained by 2.30 p.m. The general advance of the 55th Brigade, east of the first objective, commenced at 3.30 p.m. and proceeded rapidly. Slight opposition was encountered in the vicinity of Carrefour de l'Hermitage, but, by 7 p.m., our line was established 300 yards east of the Carrefour de l'Hermitage–Locquignol road.

A few armoured cars of the 17th Armoured Car Battalion co-operated with the 18th and 50th Divisions, and were most useful in the fighting which took place amongst the hedgerows and in the forest. Their
The armoured cars appearance along the muddy roads of Mormal Forest caused considerable confusion, with the result that a number of the enemy abandoned their machine-guns without firing a shot.

Thanks in a large measure to the heroism of subordinate leaders, both officers and men, the day's operations had been a brilliant success. The
The result of the passage of the Sambre and Oise Canal had been forced
fighting on November on a wide front from south of Catillon to Landrecies
4th in the face of a determined opposition; a bridgehead on a front of at least fifteen miles and to an average depth of three miles

[1] At one time one of these tanks, with three of its machine-guns out of action and its 6-pdr. guns badly jammed by the enemy's fire, found itself surrounded by Germans. These, pushing up the muzzles of the remaining machine-guns, climbed on to the top of the tank and endeavoured to throw bombs through the apertures, but they were prevented from doing so by the crew using their revolvers. The enemy was then driven off and the tank continued its task of " mopping up " the village.

had been established, while Mormal Forest had been penetrated to a depth of some 6,000 yards. Over 4,000 prisoners and nearly 80 guns had been captured. The IX and XIII Corps, which achieved such decisive results in the last organised attack by the Fourth Army and held the post of honour at the end of the campaign, received from the Commander-in-Chief and the Army Commander the praise which their work had so well deserved.[1]

Equally unsuccessful was the attempt of the enemy to check the advance of the Third and First Armies further north and that of the First French Army to the south. More important, however, than the gain of territory or the capture of prisoners and material, was the fact that on this vital portion of his front the enemy's resistance had been broken. The only hope that had remained to the enemy of preventing his military position from becoming desperate was to have held on to the line of the Sambre long enough to enable the German High Command to make preparations for a planned withdrawal to another line ; numerous captured German documents clearly showed this.[2] After this defeat, the German forces had no alternative but to fall back along the whole front, and the Allied pursuit only required to be pressed home in order to compel the enemy to accept whatever terms the Allies were prepared to offer.

Accordingly, the IX and XIII Corps were ordered to resume the advance towards Avesnes on the morning of November 5th. The heavy
The pursuit; November 5th and 6th; the events on the IX Corps Front drizzling rain, which was falling when the advance was resumed, restricted observation, and the rate of advance was slow. For the next few days the rain continued without cessation, and the surface of the roads and tracks was churned into mud and slush by the continuous traffic, thus increasing enormously the difficulties of the much tried transport services. During the night of November 4th the 46th Division moved across the canal, relieving the 1st and 14th Brigades of the 1st and 32nd Divisions respectively, astride the main Mezières–Catillon road, and the advance was resumed at 6.30 a.m. on November 5th.

On the extreme right the 2nd Brigade of the 1st Division still held a defensive flank round Fesmy, and, when the advance was resumed, occupied La Justice without opposition, gaining touch with the French who had advanced through Bergues-sur-Sambre. The subsequent advance of the 46th British Division and the 66th French Division enabled the 2nd Brigade to be " squeezed out," and it rejoined the 1st Division in reserve in the Wassigny area. On the front of the 32nd Division the enemy at La Motte Farm had withdrawn during the night and allowed the 97th Brigade, which took over the whole divisional front, to join up with the right of the XIII Corps south of Landrecies. Under cover of a thin cavalry screen provided by the 20th Hussars rapid progress was made on the IX Corps front. The cavalry successfully prevented the enemy's rear-

[1] Of all the British divisions engaged in the hundred days the 18th and 32nd were the only two that began and finished the campaign in the Fourth Army.
[2] One issued by General von Larisch, commanding the LIV Corps on October 19th, 1918, said :—
" The Army Group will accept the decisive battle on the Hermann Stellung (line of Sambre and Oise Canal). The Hermann Stellung *must be held* at any price. This is to be notified to all commanders down to and including Regimental Commanders."

guards offering any serious resistance and captured a number of guns, including two 8-inch howitzers in the village of Favril. By nightfall the 46th Division held the high ground 2,000 yards east of Le Sart-en-Thiérache and was astride the La Rivierette just north-west of Prisches. The 32nd Division held the spur about 2,000 yards east of Favril and was in touch with the 25th Division south of Maroilles.

On the morning of the 6th, owing to the difficulties of communication which were much increased by the enemy's systematic destruction of roads and bridges, it was impossible to renew the advance until 9.30 a.m. There was practically no fighting throughout the day; the 20th Hussars keeping in touch with the retreating enemy, while the advanced guards of the 46th and 32nd Divisions followed along the roads. Towards evening the 46th Division entered Cartignies and established an outpost line on the Petite Helpe. The 32nd Division cleared Grand Fayt before noon, but found the Petite Helpe a difficult obstacle. Two companies of the 10th Argyll and Sutherland Highlanders, however, crossed by a bridge erected by the 25th Division at Maroilles and worked southwards. In the meantime, the main body of the 97th Brigade forced its way across the river at the lock at Grand Fayt in spite of hostile machine-gun fire, and by 5 p.m. its leading infantry had passed through Le Foyaux and established an outpost line astride the ridge some distance further east. The IX Corps had thus gained the exploitation line, laid down by Sir Henry Rawlinson in his orders for the attack of November 4th, and was in touch with the First French Army on the right south of Cartignies, and with the XIII Corps on the left at the cross roads 1,500 yards east of Marbaix.

By the morning of November 5th two good pontoon bridges, suitable for carrying field artillery, were in position at Landrecies and Les Etoquies lock, and field artillery brigades were moved across the canal to support the advance of the 25th Division towards Maroilles and Marbaix. The advance of the XIII Corps was continued at 6.30 a.m., and an hour and a-half later the vanguard of the 25th Division was approaching the Petite Helpe in the face of slight opposition. By noon Maroilles had been captured, and our troops were advancing towards Taisnières-en-Thiérache and Noyelles.

The events on the XIII Corps front

Further north the 50th Division had completed the clearance of the south-eastern portion of Mormal Forest by 10.30. a.m. and had commenced to cross the canal by a footbridge south of Hachette Farm. The 149th Brigade was ordered to occupy Haute Noyelles and advance to the high ground at St. Roch Chapelle, followed by the 150th Brigade which was to move by Petit Landrecies to Leval. On the left of the army, the 18th Division had occupied the area west of the canal within the northern army boundary by noon, and was in touch with the V Corps, which held Berlaimont and was engaged in crossing the canal north of Leval. Owing to the swampy reaches of the Sambre and the enemy's opposition on the line of the Grande Helpe, the progress of the 50th Division towards Leval was slow, and, as the bridge at Noyelles had been blown up, there was some danger of touch being lost with the V Corps. To avoid this the 18th Division was instructed to keep in touch with the V Corps by moving patrols across the canal, and the 12th Lancers were ordered to move to Dompierre, Monceau, and Leval with a view to reducing the opposition in front of the 50th Division. Here, however, the resistance of the Germans, who belonged to the 121st and 241st Divisions, was too strong to be overcome by the cavalry. The enemy held the ground between Leval and Aulnoye in considerable strength, and at this point no further progress was made by our troops that day.

Further south, the 25th Division captured Basse Noyelles late in the afternoon, and at dusk the 50th Division secured a footing on the far bank of the Grande Helpe near Le Champ du Parc Farm. As soon as its front was covered by this advance the 18th Division was withdrawn and moved back to the vicinity of Le Cateau. The 66th Division, which had concentrated in the vicinity of Landrecies during the day, was warned to be ready to move to the Maroilles–Taisnières-en-Thiérache area and relieve the 25th Division.

The night of November 5th passed quietly, and the advance of the XIII Corps was resumed on the following morning at 7 a.m. The 25th Division pushed forward with the 74th Brigade on the right and the 7th Brigade on the left. The 50th Division directed the 149th Brigade on Leval to gain touch with the V Corps which was now fighting in the northern outskirts of that village, while the 150th Brigade was ordered to cross the Grande Helpe at Le Champ du Parc Farm, capture Haut Noyelles from the north, and, swinging eastwards, continue the advance on the right of the 149th Brigade.

Throughout the morning steady progress was made. All the available cars of the 17th Armoured Car Battalion co-operated with the XIII Corps and were of great assistance in dealing with enemy machine-gun nests on the roads which they patrolled.

By noon the leading infantry of the XIII Corps had reached the western outskirts of Marbaix and Taisnières-en-Thiérache, and Petit Landrecies and was advancing towards Leval which was still held by the enemy. Two hours later Marbaix had fallen, and by evening Dompierre, Monceau, and Leval had been occupied. Thus, by the evening of the 6th, the XIII Corps had also been able to gain the exploitation line of November 4th without serious difficulty.

On the afternoon of November 5th it had already become evident that the enemy was in full retreat, and, consequently, orders were issued by **The pursuit continued** Sir Henry Rawlinson for the IX and XIII Corps to **on November 7th, 8th,** continue the pursuit to the La Capelle–Avesnes–Mau- **and 9th** beuge road, including the town of Avesnes. The cavalry was to maintain touch with the enemy's rearguards, but the infantry was not to advance beyond this road. All tanks and armoured cars were withdrawn into army reserve in the vicinity of Landrecies for overhaul.

The 46th and 32nd Divisions resumed the advance at dawn on November 7th with the 20th Hussars well in advance. By the evening of the 7th the 46th Division had reached a line just west of **The IX Corps.** the La Capelle–Avesnes road, but the 32nd Division encountered considerable opposition near Avesnes. By dribbling forward small parties our troops succeeded in approaching to within a few hundred yards of the town, but every effort to enter Avesnes during the night was repulsed by heavy trench mortar and machine-gun fire. It was, therefore, arranged for the town to be attacked next morning by the 2nd King's Own Yorkshire Light Infantry. At 11 a.m. on November 8th the infantry, covered by a light barrage, rushed the enemy's posts and forced their way into the town; by the evening troops of the 32nd Division held Avesnes and Avesnelles with an outpost line 1,000 yards further east. During the day the 46th Division pushed patrols across the main La Capelle–Avesnes road and by nightfall had established an outpost line 2,000 yards beyond it, in touch with the French east of La Folie and with the 32nd Division south-east of Avesnes.

The 25th and 50th Divisions resumed the advance at 8 a.m. on November 7th. One and a-half hours later the vanguard of the 25th Division passed through Les Ardennes, with cavalry patrols at St. Hilaire-sur-Helpe where they encountered some fire from machine-guns along the Avesnes–Marbaix road; the 50th Division at this time was approaching St. Aubin. Throughout the remainder of November 7th considerable fighting took place. The numerous sunken roads, copses, and hedgerows concealed the enemy's machine-guns which covered the withdrawal of his rearguards. Slowly but surely, however, each centre of resistance was located and dealt with in turn. Particularly severe was the fighting in the 50th Division area in the village of Dourlers, which was captured by the 6th Royal Inniskilling Fusiliers supported by the 1st King's Own Yorkshire Light Infantry. At nightfall our outpost line was established 1,000 yards east of St. Hilaire-sur-Helpe, through La Croisette Farm, and along the eastern outskirts of Dourlers.

The XIII Corps

During the afternoon of November 7th the 66th Division moved up to the Marbaix–Taisnières-en-Thiérache area, and at dusk moved forward again and relieved the 25th Division with the 199th and 198th Brigades, while on the left the 151st Brigade covered the front of the 50th Division with all three battalions in line.

When the advance was resumed on the morning of November 8th, the 66th Division, though somewhat hampered by the intricate nature of the country north of Avesnes, gradually forced its way to the main Avesnes–Maubeuge road and emerged into more open country. Further north the 50th Division encountered considerable resistance, as the enemy had selected the line of the Avesnes–Maubeuge road as a rearguard position.[1] The vigour and determination of the attack, however, overcame all resistance, and by 9.30 a.m. the road was in our possession as far south as Les Trois Pavés. A prisoner captured in this locality by the 50th Division gave the information that his regiment, 500 strong, was assembled in Beugnies Wood with orders to counter-attack and regain the line of the Avesnes–Maubeuge road should it be lost. This proved to be correct, as at 11 a.m. troops of the 9th German division counter-attacked from south-west of the Beugnies Wood, while hostile artillery searched the ground in the vicinity of the road. The counter-attack was received with fire from every available machine-gun, Lewis gun, and rifle, and the hostile infantry was soon

[1] This was ascertained from a captured order.

dispersed. The German machine-gun detachments, however, continued to advance, but, after an obstinate fight which lasted for an hour and a-half, the 151st Brigade held its ground, and the enemy was completely repulsed. At 2.30 p.m. the 50th Division resumed the advance by moving forward the 149th Brigade through the 151st Brigade, and by 4.30 p.m. Semousies and Floursies had been captured. At nightfall, an outpost line was established along the spur running north-east from Bas Lieu, where touch was gained with the 32nd Division, and thence northward through the eastern outskirts of Semousies, Mont Dourlers, and Floursies.

On the evening of November 8th infantry patrols along the whole army front reported that touch with the enemy's rearguards had been lost. Accordingly, at dawn on the 9th, the cavalry—Royal Scots Greys, 20th Hussars, and 12th Lancers—moved forward and gained touch with them at Sivry and along the Thure. They were supported by infantry, which reached Sains-du-Nord, Semeries, Felleries, Solre-le-Château, and Solrinnes.

The dominant factor that decided the rate at which the pursuit of the enemy could be carried out was the question of supply. The main railway line between St. Quentin and Busigny had been The question of supply reconstructed, but the periodic explosions of delay action mines made it necessary frequently to use rail-heads further back, such as Vermand, Bellicourt, and Montigny Farm. From these railheads supplies and ammunition had to be carried up by motor transport. The long distances involved, and the gradual breakdown of the roads as the weather became worse and the traffic grew heavier, threw an enormous strain on the motor transport. In several cases lorries were on the road for seventy-two consecutive hours, and it was difficult for the workshops to cope with the abnormal work of repair rendered necessary by the constant wear and tear and the bad condition of the roads. In the forward area, where the roads had been destroyed by mine craters, the infantry had outstripped the forward limit of lorries, and it became necessary to use additional horse transport from the ammunition columns; it was quite obvious, therefore, that if the army continued to advance a complete breakdown in the supply organisation must result before long.

Consequently, on November 9th Sir Henry Rawlinson decided that the main bodies of corps should be distributed in depth on and west of the main La Capelle–Avesnes–Maubeuge road, with an Bethell's Force outpost line east of it. The enemy was in full retreat and no longer had the heart, or the power, to put up a strong resistance; only a comparatively small force was, therefore, necessary to keep in touch with him. Accordingly a mobile force was organised, chiefly from the 66th Division, and was placed under the command of Maj.-Gen. H. K. Bethell.[1]

---

[1] The detailed composition of Bethell's Force was as follows :—

5th Cavalry Brigade.
South African Brigade.
17th Armoured Car Battalion.
IX Corps Cyclist Battalion.
A/331 to B/331 Batteries, R.F.A.
1 Anti-Aircraft Section.

1 Coy. 100th Battalion Machine Gun Corps.
430th, 431st, 432nd Field Companies, R.E.
1 Coy. 9th Gloucestershire (Pioneers).
2 Squadrons, Royal Air Force.
2 Sections, D/331 Battery (4·5-in. howitzers).
1st South African Field Ambulance.

On the 10th November, the 199th Brigade was added to the force.

This force moved forward on the morning of November 10th and found the enemy in strength around Sivry and Hestrud. In accordance with

The frontier of France reached on November 10th

orders received from Army Headquarters, the attack was not pressed home, and at night Bethell's Force occupied a line which ran approximately north and south through Sivry and Hestrud. Next morning some ground was gained by our troops before the cessation of hostilities. The enemy held out stubbornly in the vicinity of Hestrud, but the 20th Hussars were gradually working their way through Sivry. Just before 11 a.m. the enemy launched a small counter-attack against our troops who were forcing him back out of Grandrieu, but its only result was to add six more to the total of Germans killed during the war.

The troops had been warned about 7 a.m. that hostilities were to cease at 11 a.m. The firing, however, which had been heavy all the morning continued until three minutes to 11 a.m., when it

The Armistice, 11 a.m., November 11th

ceased for a short period and then broke out in a final crash at 11 a.m.[1] Then all was silence. Combatants from both sides emerged from cover and walked about in full view. No further act of hostility took place, nor was there any attempt at intercourse on either side. In accordance with the instructions received from the Commander-in-Chief, our troops stood fast on the line which they had gained at 11 a.m. At that time the line held by Bethell's Force ran from Mont Bliart through Martinsart Wood, round the eastern edge of Grandrieu, along the river Thure to the western outskirts of Cousolre.[2]

Further north the Third, First, Fifth, and Second Armies had reached the general line Marpent—east of Mons–Jurbise–Lessines–Grammont.

The victory of November 4th and following days had finally broken the enemy's capacity for organised resistance. During the fighting he had reinforced his line in front of the Fourth Army with seven divisions from reserve ; but these had been repeatedly engaged since August 8th ; exhausted by heavy losses and insufficiently rested, they no longer possessed the fighting qualities necessary to stem the advance of victorious troops. It was the same all along the British front. The German officers had lost faith and shared with their men the general feeling of hopelessness,[3] and even of bitter blame towards the German High Command for uselessly prolonging the war. The moral of the great German Army had been shattered. In these circumstances the German nation had no option but to accept the terms of the Allies.

---

[1] The final act of a German machine-gunner, always our most formidable opponent throughout the war, is worthy of record. At two minutes to 11, a machine-gun, about 200 yards from our leading troops, fired off a complete belt without a pause. A single machine-gunner was then seen to stand up beside his weapon, take off his helmet, bow, and turning about walk slowly to the rear.

[2] The portion of the front just west of Mont Bliart and Sautain was the most easterly point reached by British troops at the time of the armistice.

[3] The following extract from a letter by a German company commander was typical of many :—

"The men have been in the same clothes, dirty, lousy, and torn for four weeks, are suffering from bodily filth and a state of depression due to living continuously within range of the enemy's guns, and in daily expectation of an attack. The troops are hardly in a fit state to fulfil the task allotted to them in the case of an attack."

So ends the story of the Fourth Army in its last campaign of the Great War. Between August 8th and November 11th it engaged and defeated 67 German Divisions, and this was accomplished by 24 British, Australian, Canadian, and American Divisions.[1] During this period 79,743 prisoners, including 1,848 officers, and 1,108 guns were captured, while the losses of the Fourth Army were 122,427 killed, wounded, and missing. This is probably a unique record, when it is remembered that no account is taken in these figures of the very large number of Germans who were killed and wounded.[2]

[1] Twelve British, 5 Australian, 4 Canadian, and 3 American. This does not include the 17th Division, which held the line for a few days in August, but took no part in any attack while with the Fourth Army. In addition to the twenty-four infantry divisions, the Cavalry Corps was engaged on the Fourth Army front, once as a corps of three divisions and once as a corps of two divisions. See Diagram III and Appendices C and D.

[2] Their losses must have been heavy, as the fighting was on occasion very severe, and the dead actually buried amounted to a large total.

DIAGRAM III.

To face page 262.

TARTAN DIAGRAM SHOWING THE EMPLOYMENT OF FORMATIONS IN THE FOURTH ARMY
DURING THE BATTLES OF THE HUNDRED DAYS.

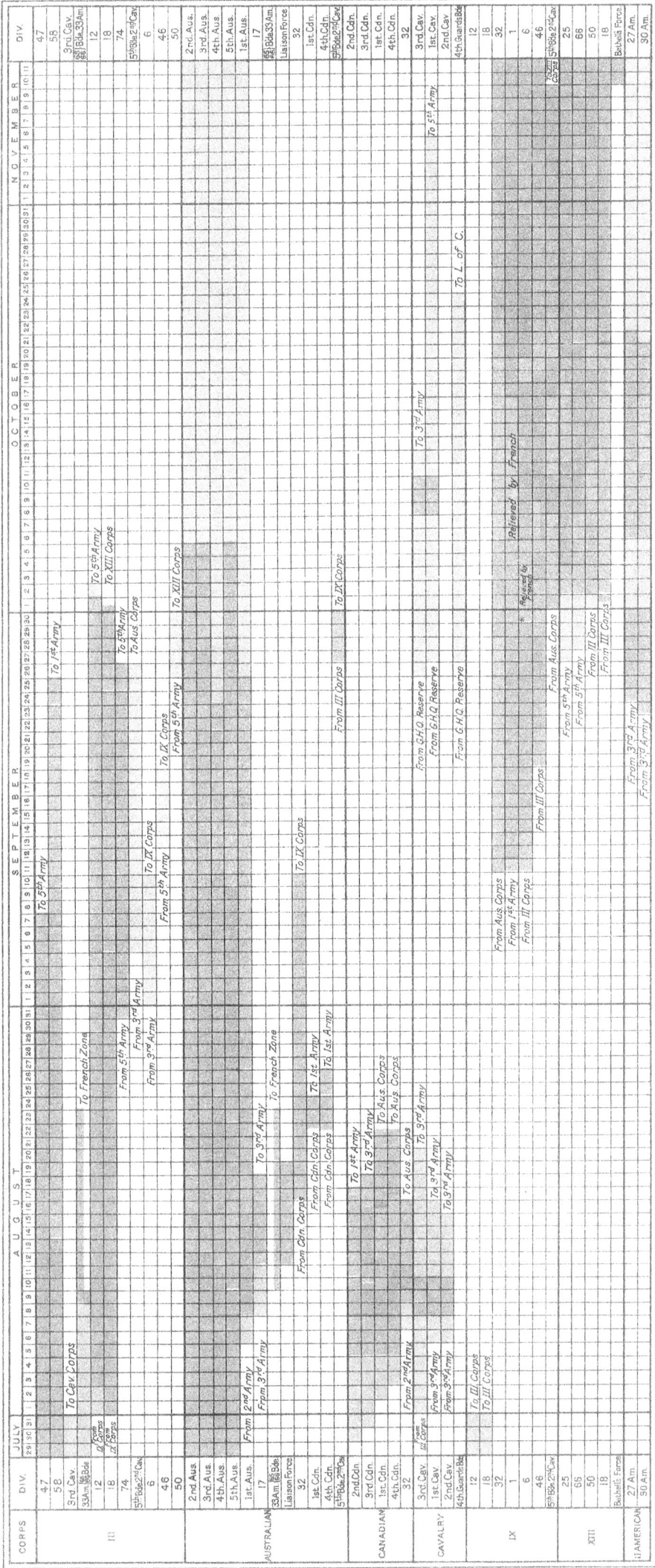

Ordnance Survey, 1919.

In Line   Corps Reserve   Army Reserve   G. H. Q. Reserve

CHAPTER XIII

CONCLUSION

Some tactical questions—The co-operation of all arms—Surprise—Flank attacks—Simultaneous attacks—Attack formations and the number of men required—Counter-attacks —"Zero"—The rate of advance of the barrage—The creeping barrage—Pre-war textbooks—Col. Henderson and the "human" side of war—Initiative and discipline.

MANY tactical questions of general interest arose during these operations, about the most important of which it may be worth recording the impressions left at the time, before they become less **Some tactical** vivid. No attempt has been made to elaborate them, **questions** but they will doubtless recall to soldiers many of their own experiences, and may perhaps assist others in thinking out future tactical developments.

Nothing perhaps was of greater moment, or affected the issue more, than the co-operation of the various arms in battle. The necessity for this co-operation, although as old as war itself, con- **The co-operation of all** tinues to grow in importance as each new war adds **arms** fresh inventions. Aeroplanes, tanks, gas, and Stokes mortars, all made their appearance for the first time in the Great War, and the result of their co-operation with the other arms, especially that of the tanks, had an all-important bearing on the result of the Allied Offensive of 1918. The remarkable number of heavy howitzers and long-range guns of large calibre that were used by the rival armies was another new development which materially altered the conditions of field warfare, but made no change in the principle of co-operation. Nor must the ever-growing importance of the machine-gun, Lewis gun, and the automatic rifle be forgotten. In all the reports of attacks and retirements, both on the German side and our own, the constant reference to the deadly effect of machine-gun fire became more and more noticeable, and the co-operation of both machine-guns and tanks with the infantry is likely to modify many of our ideas on minor tactics, as much as, or even more perhaps than did the appearance of masses of heavy artillery in the earlier stages of the war.

The question of surprise has been discussed in Chapter VIII.[1] It is referred to again here as it is important to emphasise the difference between a strategical and a tactical surprise, which have been **Surprise** sometimes confused. One may gain a strategical but not a tactical surprise, as was, for instance, the case on the III Corps front on the morning of August 8th. Here the Germans

[1] See page 150.

expected us to attack, in order to recover the ground lost on the 6th, but had no idea of the scope of the offensive that had been prepared. Or a tactical but not a strategical surprise may be gained, as on the front of the IX Corps on September 29th, when, although a general attack was expected, the date and hour of the attack were unknown to the enemy. Or, again, it is possible to gain both a strategical and tactical surprise, as was done on the fronts of the Australian and Canadian Corps on August 8th, when the offensive was entirely unexpected and found the enemy completely unprepared both strategically and tactically. As regards the tactical surprise by the IX Corps on September 29th, the fact that the First and Third British Armies attacked on September 27th, and that the bombardment by the Fourth Army commenced on the 26th, may have induced the Germans to think that the Fourth Army bombardment was only a blind, and that no attack was impending on that, perhaps the most strongly fortified, part of the Hindenburg Line.

A failure to attain a strategical surprise means that the enemy has adequate time to collect his reserves in rear of the threatened front and to make all the other necessary arrangements to meet the attack. This war has shown that an attack in such circumstances will not achieve decisive results, until the other side has either reached a stage of exhaustion or has lost its moral, or both. Under these latter conditions, a strategical surprise loses its importance, but a tactical surprise must always remain an advantage and will undoubtedly save casualties.

The question of whether a preliminary bombardment is advisable or not depends on what measure of surprise is required, and the question of whether such a bombardment is necessary or not is dependent on the nature of the defences which have to be overcome. The nature of the hostile defences, and especially the amount of wire, was really the deciding factor as regards this in 1915, 1916, and the early part of 1917, but the advent of improved tanks in large numbers rendered a surprise possible against almost any defences.

Some interesting flank attacks were made during the hundred days, notably those by the 9th Canadian Brigade at Rifle Wood on August 8th,[1]

Flank attacks by the 18th Division at Trones Wood on August 27th,[2] and by the same division at Frégicourt[3] and Ronssoy[4] on September 1st and 18th. Flank attacks, as opposed to purely frontal attacks, date back to the days of Frederick the Great, who first saw the advantage of such a manœuvre, and possessed troops sufficiently well drilled and disciplined to be able to carry it out. But Frederick the Great also knew the answer to this form of attack, when his opponents tried to turn the tables and attack him in flank. His answer to it, namely, to strike the manœuvring columns in flank,[5] holds good to-day, always provided that the manœuvre has been discovered in time, and that sufficient troops are at hand for the purpose. At Trones Wood, the Germans did counter-attack the outflanking battalions with some success. At Ronssoy, the attempt of one division to carry out

---

[1] See page 34.   [2] See page 90.   [3] See page 107.   [4] See page 131.
[5] For a description of Frederick the Great's methods and an excellent account of the battles of Rosbach and Leuthen, see Home's " Précis of Modern Tactics."

this manœuvre, when the remaining divisions were making a frontal attack on a wide front by time-table, was, it is suggested, a tactical mistake. In the circumstances which obtained on September 18th a straightforward frontal attack under a heavy barrage, such as was made by the 1st and 74th Divisions and the 1st and 4th Australian Divisions, would probably have met with more success. To judge of this, the attack must be studied in detail on the map or on the ground.

The advisability, or otherwise, of launching attacks simultaneously, when attacking on a wide front, has been a much debated question. Not doing so undoubtedly leads to the exposed flanks of forma-
Simultaneous   tions being enfiladed by the fire of the enemy's troops
attacks   and guns that have not yet been engaged, as occurred on
August 9th and 10th, and on several other occasions, and increases the chances of these attacks failing; this disadvantage would seem to decide the question. How often, however, has it been suggested that it is of the greatest importance to attract the enemy's attention off some point where the attacker wishes to make certain of success, and to engage the hostile reserves on other parts of the front before the attack on the most important objective is launched? In nine cases out of ten, the simultaneous attack will avoid complications and possible chances of mistakes and will lead to the best results; at least experience in the Great War points to this conclusion.

Throughout the war, military opinion has varied considerably as regards the best attack formation for infantry and the number of men, per
Attack formations   yard of front to be attacked, that it is advisable to
and the number of   employ. The discussion on this subject, it is safe to
men required   prophesy, will not end with the war, and it would be
rash to attempt to lay down even a guide when so much depends on the ground, the obstacles to be crossed, the machine-gun and artillery support, and the moral of the opposing forces. It may be said, however, that the employment of tanks must and will materially alter our ideas on the subject of both attack formations and the number of troops required. Also that to attack with too few troops is on occasion as likely to lead to heavy casualties as attacking with too many, and, in addition, may lead to failure, either through lack of driving power to overcome the enemy's resistance completely, or through lack of sufficient strength, when the objective has been gained, to repulse the enemy's counter-attacks.

Instructions were issued from time to time by General Headquarters giving a guide as to suitable frontages and formations, these being based on the latest experiences, but what was suitable then will almost certainly not apply to the next war in which we may be engaged. It may be of interest here to give some of the frontages allotted to troops in some successful attacks carried out during 1915, 1916, 1917, and 1918, with the chief factors that influenced the situation. (See Table on pp. 266–267.)

It has been an axiom in our army almost from the beginning of the war that, unless an immediate counter-attack to recover lost ground can be made with troops on the spot, it is advisable to postpone the counter-attack until complete preparations can be made for an organised attack, including artillery and machine-gun support. The advantages of an

M M

Formations, Date, and Place.	Frontage of Attack.	Troops Employed.	Depth of Objective.	Artillery and Machine-Gun Support.
Sept. 25th, 1915, Loos. 15th Division (IV Corps).	1,400 yards. Indefinite later.	1 division, of which 2 brigades attacked, each on a two-battalion front, and one brigade was in reserve.	Indefinite. 4,000 yards to Hill 70, which was reached. Infantry "starting line" 200–300 yards from enemy's front line.	1 gun to about 18 yards of front. 58 field guns and howitzers, about 20 heavy howitzers. Four days' slow bombardment, and discharge of gas cylinders 40 minutes before "zero."
July 1st, 1916, Montauban. 18th and 30th Divisions. (XIII Corps).	3,500 yards (i.e., 1,750 yards per division). 4,000 yards on final objective.	2 divisions, of which 4 brigades attacked, and 2 were in reserve.	Maximum, 2,400 yards, average, 2,000 yards. Infantry "starting line" 200–300 yards from enemy's front line.	1 gun to about 14 yards of front. No creeping barrage. 5 days' bombardment.
July 14th, 1916, Longueval Ridge. 9th, 3rd, 7th and 21st Divisions of XIII and XV Corps.	5,000 yards (i.e., 1,250 yards per division). 5,000 yards on first objective.	4 divisions, of which 6 brigades attacked and 6 were in reserve.	Maximum, 2,500 yards, average, 1,500 yards. Infantry "starting line" originally 1,500 yards on part of front; but reduced during night to 300 yards from enemy's front trench.	1 gun to about 6 yards of front. 48 hours' slow bombardment, finishing with 5 minutes' intense fire. No creeping barrage.
Sept. 15th, 1916, Flers. 14th, 41st, N.Z. Divisions. (XV Corps).	2,700 yards (i.e., 900 yards per division). Same on final objective.	3 divisions, of which 6 brigades attacked, and 3 were in reserve.	Maximum, 4,500. Average, 4,000. 3,000 yards actually captured. Infantry "starting line" 300–400 yards from enemy's front line.	1 gun to about 10 yards of front. Creeping barrage. No preliminary bombardment.
June 7th, 1917, Messines. 36th, 16th, 19th Divisions. (IX Corps.)	6,400 yards (i.e., 2,130 yards per division), narrowing down to about 2,000 yards on the corps front on the final objective.	3 divisions, of which 6 brigades attacked, and 3 "leap-frogged" the leading brigades on the 4th objective and captured final objective.	4,000 yards. Infantry "starting line" about 200–300 yards from enemy's front line.	1 gun to about 8¼ yards of front. 480 field guns and howitzers. 246 heavy howitzers. Artillery and machine-gun creeping barrage 7 days' bombardment.
July 4th, 1918, Hamel. 4th Australian Division.	6,000 yards increasing to 7,300 yards on final objective.	10 battalions, of which 6 attacked.	Maximum, 2,500 yards. Average, 2,000 yards. Infantry "starting line" 300 yards from enemy's front line.	1 gun to 25 yards of front. Creeping artillery and machine-gun barrage. No preliminary bombardment. 111 machine-guns for machine-gun barrage. 326 guns and heavy howitzers, of which 2/3 were on counter battery work.
August 8th, 1918. Battle of Amiens. 1st and 2nd Canadian Divisions. (Canadian Corps.)	5,000 yards (i.e., 2,500 yards per division) decreasing down to 3,500 on final objective.	2 divisions, each on a front of 1 brigade which "leap-frogged" each other in turn on the successive objectives.	Maximum, 12,000 yards (3 objectives, of which all were captured). "Starting line" 300 yards from enemy's front line.	1 gun to about 14 yards of front. Creeping artillery and machine-gun barrage. 192 machine-guns available. No preliminary bombardment.
Sept. 18th, 1918. Outer defences of Hindenburg Line. 1st and 4th Australian Divisions. (Australian Corps.)	7,500 yards (i.e., 3,750 yards per division) narrowing down to 6,000 on final objective.	2 divisions, of which 4 brigades attacked and the other 2 were in reserve and were not employed.	Maximum, 5,000 yards. (3 objectives, of which all were captured). "Starting line" 300–400 yards from enemy's front line.	1 gun to about 20 yards of front. 270 field guns and howitzers and about 100 heavy howitzers. Creeping artillery and machine-gun barrage. 256 machine-guns available. No preliminary bombardment.
Sept. 29th, 1918. Hindenburg Line (canal defences). 46th Division (IX Corps).	3,000 yards.	1 division on a brigade front with all 3 battalions in line, followed by two other brigades which "leap-frogged" the leading brigade when canal was crossed.	Maximum, 5,000 yards. "Starting line" 200–300 yards from enemy's front line.	1 gun to about 8 yards of front. Creeping artillery and machine-gun barrage by 108 field guns and 128 machine-guns. A 10 hours' gas bombardment, followed by 48 hours' bombardment by high explosive and shrapnel.

State of Enemy's Defences.	State of Enemy's Moral.	Degree of Surprise.	Tanks employed.	Remarks.
Very strong. Front, support, and reserve trenches. Fortified village of Loos.	Very good.	Expected.	Nil.	The 15th Division was the centre of three divisions of the IV Corps attacking, while the I Corps attacked simultaneously on its left. The supply of ammunition was still very limited.
Very strong. Front, support, and reserve trenches, and fortified village of Montauban.	Very good.	Expected.	Nil.	The XIII Corps, of two divisions, was on the right of the British attack by five corps. The French attacked on the right of the XIII Corps.
Very strong, but only front and support lines.	Temporarily reduced by previous fortnight's fighting, but still good.	Expected.	Nil.	The XIII and XV Corps carried out the main attack, with the III Corps on their left also attacking.
Fair. A good many trenches and some wire.	Good.	Expected	17 Mark I	This was the first time tanks were used. The XV Corps was the centre of three corps attacking.
Very strong. Numerous lines.	Very good.	Expected.	28 Mark IV	The IX Corps of three divisions was the centre of three corps attacking a salient. Six mines were fired on the corps front at " zero."
Poor.	Fair.	Complete surprise.	60 Mark V	An independent operation.
Poor.	Fair.	Complete surprise.	84 Mark V	The 1st and 2nd Canadian Divisions were the left and centre divisions of the Canadian Corps, which was the right corps of the three corps attacking. The French attacked on the right of the Canadian Corps.
Fair. Three lines and fortified villages and farms.	Fair. Getting worse.	Probably expected.	9 Mark V tanks and some dummy tanks.	The Australian Corps, attacking with 1st and 4th Divisions, was the centre of three corps attacking.
Very strong, with canal in front.	Poor.	Probably expected.	Nil, till canal had been crossed.	The 46th Division was the leading division of the IX Corps which was the right of three corps attacking.

immediate counter-attack have been proved time after time, and examples of the efficacy of such attacks were very common during the hundred days. The essence of success is that such a counter-attack should strike the enemy while still disorganised and exhausted after his assault, probably having lost many of his leaders, with his artillery fire slackening after firing a rapid rate of barrage fire, and before all his machine-guns told off for consolidation have arrived. Once this phase is over, the chances of success of a counter-attack decrease rapidly. The commander on the spot must, therefore, usually be the best judge of the most favourable hour to counter-attack, which will depend to a large extent on the position of his available reserves. The very successful counter-attack of the three brigades (two Australian and one British) at Villers Bretonneux on April 24th[1] may almost be described as an immediate counter-attack because, although it was not carried out until about twelve hours after the village was captured, it was made before the Germans had been able to organise their defence, and, owing to its being made under cover of darkness, it came as a complete surprise and found them unprepared.

The most effective hour at which to attack was also the subject of much discussion before and after August 8th. The question of surprise is a most important factor in this problem, and, when the various pros and cons are discussed, it must always be taken into consideration. To carry out a surprise attack in daylight in these days of aeroplanes is almost impossible except in bad weather, and it was found that the choice usually lay between " dawn " or " night " attacks. The advantage of constantly varying the hour of attack is obvious, but it may be found that, as in the case of the Fourth Army during the hundred days, other considerations will over-rule the advantage that might be gained by a greater variation of the hour. It was generally considered that for large forces night attacks, unless made in bright moonlight, are best avoided altogether, as their disadvantages greatly outweigh their advantages, especially as it was found that tanks in a night attack were of little assistance, even in moonlight. The almost unanimous opinion, especially as our experience increased, was that an hour before sunrise, just as the first streaks of light were showing in the sky, was the best time, and nearly every attack by the Fourth Army was made at that hour. Several moonlight attacks were made, notably one by the III and Australian Corps on August 24th,[2] and one by the XIII Corps on October 23rd.[3] Both were successful, but, although some advantage was undoubtedly gained from the change from the usual hour, their success was not so striking as to change the general opinion that the best time for " zero " was an hour before sunrise.

The dim light an hour before dawn enables the infantry to form up on its " starting line " without being observed; at the same time, within a few minutes of the assault commencing there is light enough for the infantry to see its way and to shoot. The tanks, to begin with, would have preferred even a little later, but their skill at manœuvring in the dark improved as the operations went on.

Counter-attacks

" Zero "

[1] See page 3.   [2] See page 83.   [3] See page 232 et seq.

It is possibly not realised with what care the " zero " hour was selected, and what stress units and formations placed on even five minutes one way or the other. Officers were detailed to ascertain by personal observation the exact amount of light that there was at certain hours, and exactly how much could be seen at different distances at such times. The visibility varied very much according to the time of year and the weather conditions, and the meteorological adviser had to be consulted as regards this aspect. The actual hour of " zero " was decided as late as was consistent with everyone being informed in sufficient time—but not too soon. It was usually sent out from Army Headquarters at noon on the day preceding the attack, if the attack was to be early in the morning.

The rate of advance of the barrage, and the advisability of arranging for halts in its advance, were questions on which opinions differed considerably at first, but experience caused the consensus of opinion to harden towards a rapid rate of advance to begin with, slowing down to a steadier rate once the attack was fairly launched. That is to say that for the first 200–300 yards the barrage should be timed to advance at the rate of 100 yards every two, or three, minutes, while the men were fresh, their nerves highly strung after a long night's waiting, and while the enemy was still stunned by the initial shock of our artillery fire. Then the rate of advance should be reduced to 100 yards every four minutes over good ground; to be further reduced to six, or even eight, minutes if there were any obstacles, or the ground was much cut up. It must be remembered, with regard to the above remarks, that the going was always good during the hundred days, when compared to what it was in Flanders in 1917 and in the later stages of the Somme in 1916.

The rate of advance of the barrage

That creeping barrages, both artillery and machine-gun, have come to stay there can be little doubt, and the infantry whose moral is sufficiently good to allow of its keeping close under the barrage, even at the cost of some casualties from its own artillery and machine-guns, will continue to win battles and suffer the least casualties in the end.

The creeping barrage

That the principles laid down in our pre-war military text-books were sound and stood the test of war few will dispute, and any changes that may be necessary in these books will be those affecting the method of application of those principles in the light of modern inventions. All these inventions are really for one ultimate purpose only, and that is to obtain superiority of fire over the enemy before our infantry comes to close quarters with the bayonet, so that our men may enter into this combat on advantageous terms.

Pre-war text-books

" Success in war," as our Field Service Regulations say, " depends more on moral than on physical qualities. Skill cannot compensate for want of courage, energy, and determination ; but even high moral qualities may not avail without careful preparation and skilful direction. The fundamental principles of war are neither very numerous nor in themselves very abstruse ; but the application of them is difficult and cannot be made the subject of rules. The correct application of principles to circumstances is the outcome of sound military knowledge, built up by study and practice till it has become an instinct."

One more line might be added to this—Knowledge breeds self-confidence in times of stress and adversity ; than this there is no more valuable quality in war.

Lord Roberts wrote in April, 1905, in his Memoir of Col. Henderson, which forms the introduction to " The Science of War," " The influence of

Colonel Henderson such a man must bear good fruit, and the more widely and the " human " his writings are read, and the more closely his teachings side of war " are followed, the more successful will be our would-be commanders and the better will it be for England when again she is forced to go to war."

Soldiers, and civilians, who desire to profit by the lessons which stand out in so many pages of this story should compare them with the deductions which Col. Henderson drew from his wide study of Military History, and especially of British Campaigns and of the Civil War in America. The following quotation well exemplifies his wonderful foresight :

" If I see in the future an English General at the head of an Army far larger than that which drained the life blood of Napoleon's Empire in the Peninsula, if I see our Colours flying even over a wider area than in the year which preceded Waterloo, you may think I am over sanguine ; but to my mind the possibility exists, and with it the probability that the forces which are employed upon the counter-stroke will be constituted, at least in part, as were the Armies of the American Civil War. Our men will not all be Regulars. They will come straight from civil life, and to civil life they will return." [1] His imagination, far from being over sanguine, was, as events have proved, well within the mark.

It is in his knowledge and appreciation of the " human " side of war, as opposed to the mechanical or material side, that lies perhaps the greatest value of Col. Henderson's writings. His chapters are full of reference to the qualities, good and bad, of the officers and men who served Wellington, Lee, and Grant, and the effect that such qualities had on the result of the campaigns in which they were engaged. Discussions on the characters and characteristics of the various commanders invariably form part of his account of the campaigns which he describes. As he says, " In Military History the very highest ideals may be found ; and here again I would advise students of campaigns to mark the influences of the characters of great soldiers in difficult operations, and to learn how determination, perseverance, and the fixed resolve to conquer has enabled them to triumph over obstacles before which men of weaker fibre would have turned aside. To keep these points always before our minds, the influence of moral, and the influence of individual character is the true way of studying Military History." [2]

There is nothing, perhaps, more striking in this narrative of the events of the hundred days than the value of individual initiative, and the manner in which the action of one or two men, who instinctively grasped the situation and the best means of dealing with it, affected the whole

[1] " The Science of War," p. 310. [2] Ibid., p. 313.

course of events. Numerous instances of this have been recorded in these pages, but many more still remain untold. It is largely a matter of character. In some men this power of initiative is born, in others it has been developed by the surroundings in which they have lived, and has thus become a habit which enables them to deal instinctively with difficult situations and command men. No other Army in Europe during the Great War drew its officers from more varied conditions than did ours, or from so many careers in which individuality, resource, and leadership were qualities which were essential to success. History has shown that this is one of the great characteristics of the British race. It is this power of leadership, of dealing with the unexpected on the spur of the moment, that has made the British Empire what it is. It is a characteristic that as a nation we can never afford to lose, or with its loss will fall the edifice of which it is the foundation. It is an asset that in every walk of life, and especially in the fighting services, we must continue to cultivate and encourage.

Initiative and discipline

A well-organised war machine is a wonderfully powerful weapon, especially when directed by the hands of capable leaders, but, when plans miscarry, and days of difficulty and disaster have to be faced, it is the character and initiative of the individual, and that power over men which compels them to follow whither the commander leads, that are the dominating factors in the final struggle. This war has, in a great measure, been a fight to a finish between a marvellous war organisation and a free people filled with pride of race. The campaign of 1918 was the final round of this titanic struggle, in which victory eventually went to the individual as against the machine.

One lesson more ; the superiority of British discipline, based on mutual confidence and respect between officers and men, over Prussian discipline, based on fear of punishment. We have heard much during the past five years of the marvellous results of Prussian discipline, and how no other army could have kept together so long under the trials and hardships that it was called upon to endure. British discipline has now proved that it has no equal in the armies of Europe ; it has stood the hard test of war and has emerged triumphant. It has passed through times of stress and hardship, of retreat and apparent disaster ; times which have strengthened rather than weakened the bonds that held it together. The British Army of to-day is imbued with the same spirit and the same ideals as the old army of 1914. Its faith in those ideals is all the stronger because they have been tested and not found wanting.

The British officer of the future must be under no misapprehension as to how these ideals have been attained in the past ; if he wishes to lead his men and not to drive them, to receive their willing obedience without recourse to threats of punishment, and to gain their confidence and respect. He must realise that example is the soul of British discipline, and that it is more effective than punishment ; that in order to set that example he must have both character and knowledge. Character can be cultivated, it is based on unselfishness, loyalty, and determination ; knowledge can only be attained by hard work.

In conclusion I venture to dedicate this book to the soldiers from

Great Britain, Ireland, and the Dominions who by their self-sacrifice and dogged determination in defence, and by their initiative, resource, and unequalled gallantry in attack, turned days of disaster and alarms into weeks of success and victory.

History records many glorious pages in the annals of the British Army, but it is safe to prophesy that never will the name of the British soldier stand higher than in the last eight months of the greatest war the world has ever known, when the fate of the British Empire, and all for which it stands in the world, trembled in the balance.

THE FOURTH ARMY COMMANDER AND THE ARMY HEADQUARTERS STAFF.

1. Lieutenant-Colonel V. Vivian.
2. Brigadier-General E. C. F. Gillespie.
3. Major-General H. C. Holman.
4. Major-General C. E. D. Budworth.
5. Major-General A. A. Montgomery.
6. General Sir Henry Rawlinson, Bart.
7. Major-General R. U. H. Buckland.
8. Major-General Sir M. W. O'Keefe.
9. Colonel W. J. Tatam.
10. Colonel T. Ogilvie.
11. Colonel R. G. Earle.

12. Major E. A. Parker.
13. Lieutenant-Colonel H. S. Rogers.
14. Colonel J. W. Yardley.
15. Colonel F. M. Westropp.
16. Lieutenant-Colonel R. M. Luckock.
17. Major G. D. Roberts.
18. Lieutenant-Colonel V. M. Napier.
19. Captain H. Lightstone.
20. Lieutenant-Colonel W. P. H. Hill.
21. Lieutenant-Colonel J. Craik.
22. Major Lord Hamilton of Dalziel.

23. Colonel R. S. Hamilton.
24. Lieutenant-Colonel O. R. Millman.
25. Lieutenant-Colonel F. B. Legh.
26. Colonel F. J. Childers.
27. Major W. E. L. Cotton.
28. Captain R. de Luce.
29. Lieutenant the Hon. P. M. Methuen.
30. Lieutenant the Earl of Dalkeith.
31. Lieutenant-Colonel G. T. Dalby.
32. Captain L. Jennings.
33. Captain R. C. Berkeley.

34. Lieutenant-Colonel E. T. Potts.
35. Captain P. J. Murray.
36. Captain H. L. Wilson.
37. Major A. P. W. Wedd.
38. Captain D. W. Furlong.
39. Captain H. Pawle.
40. Captain J. J. W. Herbertson.
41. Major J. H. T. Priestman.
42. Captain P. Renondeau.
43. Major C. Burn-Callender.
44. Captain H. O. Cooper.

45. Captain S. Haden.

APPENDICES

(A).—Comparative Table for the months of March to November, 1918, showing captures, casualties, and reinforcements of the Fourth Army.

(B).—Table giving the battle casualties suffered, and the prisoners captured by the Fourth Army in the operations between August 8th and November 11th, 1918, shown by corps.

(C).—Table showing the losses in prisoners suffered by German divisions and the number of times these divisions were engaged by the Fourth Army between August 8th and November 11th, 1918.

(D).—Table showing the rate of absorption of German divisions between August 8th and November 11th, 1918.

(E).—V.C. Stories.

(F).—The Fourth Army Orders of Battle for August 8th, September 29th, and November 4th, 1918.

(G). Table showing the daily ammunition expenditure by the Fourth Army from August 8th to November 11th, 1918.

(H). Extracts from captured German orders issued during the first half of September, 1918.

(J). Notes on machine-gun organisation and tactics.

(K) The adventures of a whippet tank on August 8th.

N N

APPENDIX A

COMPARATIVE TABLE FOR THE MONTHS OF MARCH TO NOVEMBER, 1918, SHOWING CAPTURES, CASUALTIES, AND REINFORCEMENTS OF THE FOURTH ARMY

PERIOD.	CAPTURES. Prisoners. O.	Prisoners. O.R.	Guns. M.Gs. and T.Ms.	Guns.	CASUALTIES. Killed. O.	Killed. O.R.	Missing. O.	Missing. O.R.	Evacuated. Wounded. O.	Wounded. O.R.	Sick. O.	Sick. O.R.	Reinforcements. O.	Reinforcements. O.R.
1918. March¹ ..	4	113	—	—	33	196	40	285	412	9,963	49	1,347	—	—
April	28	1,118	17	—	120	1,372	59	1,840	732	14,909	289	6,947	1,022	16,584
May	16	674	177	—	53	957	19	570	271	4,428	392	9,348	420	9,986
June	5	309	55	—	31	596	5	60	132	2,738	365	7,432	807	18,020
July	42	1,797	241	3	44	711	9	79	168	3,879	279	7,851	459	8,593
August ..	684	29,752	2,148	456	415	5,263	84	2,516	1,936	40,782	592	16,695	1,407	37,360
September..	547	20,981	1,232	245	313	4,262	47	3,123	1,010	22,313	364	9,735	1,259	23,666
October ..	516	20,112	1,078	197	303	3,683	38	3,195	962	18,250	445	12,020	1,568	31,174
November..	101	4,981	1,015	210	62	884	8	747	188	3,564	428	14,369	897	23,897
TOTALS ..	1,943	79,837	5,963	1,111	1,374	17,924	309	12,415	5,811	120,826	3,203	85,744	7,839	169,280

81,780

247,606

177,119

¹ For March 28th—31st only.

APPENDIX B

TABLE GIVING THE BATTLE CASUALTIES SUFFERED AND THE PRISONERS CAPTURED BY THE FOURTH ARMY IN THE OPERATIONS BETWEEN AUGUST 8TH AND NOVEMBER 11TH, 1918, SHOWN BY CORPS.

Formation.	Killed.		Wounded.		Missing.		Total.		Prisoners captured.
	O.	O.R.	O.	O.R.	O.	O.R.	O.	O.R.	
III Corps	280	3,534	1,146	21,275	52	4,369	1,478	29,178	13,700
Australian Corps.. ..	248	3,267	1,193	20,383	29	1,379	1,470	25,029	22,854[1]
Canadian Corps	147	1,814	500	9,324	13	1,041	660	12,179	8,785[1]
Cavalry Corps	24	176	118	1,325	7	185	149	1,686	3,000[1]
IX Corps	207	2,720	854	14,607	36	2,456	1,097	19,783	16,713
XIII Corps	154	2,087	621	11,891	11	1,855	786	15,833	8,745
II American Corps	86	1,358	235	8,609	9	1,541	330	11,508	5,946
British troops attached II American troops	9	67	47	1,131	—	7	56	1,205	—
TOTALS	1,155	15,023	4,714	88,545	157	12,833	6,026	116,401	79,743

[1] A certain number of prisoners captured by the cavalry are also included among those captured by the Canadian and Australian Corps, owing to the Cavalry Corps having had no prisoners' cage. These figures are, therefore, not quite accurate.

276

APPENDIX C

TABLE SHOWING THE LOSSES IN PRISONERS SUFFERED BY GERMAN DIVISIONS, AND THE NUMBER OF TIMES THESE DIVISIONS WERE ENGAGED BY THE FOURTH ARMY, BETWEEN AUGUST 8TH AND NOVEMBER 11TH, 1918.

This list does not pretend to be absolutely accurate, owing to the difficulty of obtaining the necessary information.

Division.	Number of times engaged.	Officers.	Other Ranks.	Division.	Number of times engaged.	Officers.	Other Ranks.
Alpine Corps ...	2	28	640	38th Division ...	2	39	1,198
Jäger Division ...	2	14	657	41st ,, ...	2	47	2,518
1st Guard Res. Div.	1	7	171	[1]43rd Res. Div. ...	1	11	1,036
1st Res. Div. ...	3	63	2,091	44th ,, ,, ...	1	8	79
2nd Cyclist Bde....	2	19	800	54th Div. ...	4	36	1,428
2nd Guard Div. ...	4	42	2,784	[1]54th Res. Div. ...	1	22	1,052
2nd Division ...	1	58	1,483	58th Div. ...	1	3	474
3rd Naval Div. ...	1	14	376	75th Res. Div. ...	1	42	2,187
5th Bav. Div. ...	2	24	846	79th ,, ,, ...	2	36	2,174
5th Res. Div. ...	1	—	714	81st ,, ,, ...	1	—	20
6th Cav. Div. ...	1	—	131	82nd ,, ,, ...	1	4	354
6th Bav. Div. ...	1	?	?	83rd Division ...	1	2	282
8th Division ...	2	15	670	84th ,, ...	1	5	612
9th ,, ...	1	?	?	87th ,, ...	1	15	958
11th ,, ...	1	8	529	107th ,, ...	1	68	1,609
13th ,, ...	2	46	3,367	[1]108th ,, ...	1	39	2,386
14th Res. Div. ...	1	26	1,285	[1]109th ,, ...	1	25	1,522
[1]14th Bav. Div. ...	2	98	2,846	117th ,, ...	2	48	2,891
15th Res. Div. ...	2	15	1,267	119th ,, ...	3	70	2,859
17th ,, ,, ...	1	26	1,268	121st ,, ...	5	30	1,671
18th Division ...	1	?	?	185th ,, ...	2	72	2,017
19th Res. Div. ...	1	1	61	192nd ,, ...	1	25	1,125
20th Division ...	1	7	201	197th ,, ...	1	17	623
21st ,, ...	3	70	2,429	200th ,, ...	1	—	8
21st Res. Div. ...	1	32	1,517	201st ,, ...	1	3	217
22nd ,, ,, ...	2	—	13	204th ,, ...	4	51	1,549
24th Division ...	2	18	1,478	208th ,, ...	1	5	163
25th ,, ...	2	25	857	221st ,, ...	3	30	1,252
25th Res. Div. ...	2	11	495	[1]225th ,, ...	2	66	3,527
26th ,, ,, ...	1	4	155	232nd ,, ...	2	65	1,525
27th Division ...	1	45	1,374	[1]233rd ,, ...	1	?	?
29th ,, ...	1	1	38	241st ,, ...	1	34	1,859
30th ,, ...	2	?	?	243rd ,, ...	5	33	1,693
34th ,, ...	1	23	997	Odd Units ...	—	38	1,981
				TOTAL	—	1,729	76,420

[1] These divisions were disbanded in August or September.

Total of 67 Divisions, of which 38 were engaged once, 20 twice, 4 three times, 3 four times, and 2 five times. Some of these divisions were also engaged on a varying number of occasions by other armies between August 8th and November 11th.

APPENDIX D

TABLE SHOWING THE RATE OF ABSORPTION OF GERMAN DIVISIONS BETWEEN AUGUST 8TH AND NOVEMBER 11TH, 1918.

The dates given are those on which the divisions were identified by prisoners. On some occasions divisions had been some days in the line before their presence was ascertained.

The majority of divisions mentioned in the table were employed wholly against the Fourth Army; a certain number, however, were engaged astride the boundaries of the Fourth Army and the Third British and First French Armies.

The number in brackets after each division shows whether it was engaged by the Fourth Army, on the date referred to, for the 1st, 2nd, 3rd, 4th, or 5th time.

Aug. 8th, 1st day.	Aug. 9th, 2nd day.	Aug. 10th, 3rd day.	Aug. 11th, 4th day.	Aug. 13th, 6th day.	Aug. 18th, 11th day.	Aug. 22nd, 15th day.	Aug. 23rd, 16th day.	Aug. 24th, 17th day.	Aug. 26th, 19th day.	Aug. 27th, 20th day.
1 54 Res. Div. [1] 1 27 Div. [1] 1 108 Div. [1] 1 43 Res. Div. [1] 1 13 Div. [1] 1 41 Div. [1] 1 109 Div. [1] 1 117 Div. [1] 1 225 Div. [1] 1 14 Bav. Div. [1] 1 192 Div. [1]	1 Res. Div. [1] 82 Res. Div. [1] 10 Div. [1] 119 Div. [1] 233 Div. [1] (portions) 243 Div. [1]	5 Bav. Div. [1] 79 Res. Div. [1] 121 Div. [1] 221 Div. [1]	Alpine Corps [1] (1 regiment) 26 Res. Div. [1] (portions) 38 Div. [1] 204 Div. [1]	Alpine Corps (fully engaged) 21 Div. [1]	185 Div. [1]	13 Div. [2] 25 Div. [1] 233 Div. (fully engaged) [1]	225 Div. [2] 243 Div. [2]	41 Div. [2] 83 Div. [1]	87 Div. [1] 117 Div. [2]	2 Guard Div. [1]

Aug. 29th, 22nd day.	Sept. 2nd, 25th day.	Sept. 3rd, 26th day.	Sept. 4th, 27th day.	Sept. 5th, 28th day.	Sept. 6th, 29th day.	Sept. 9th, 32nd day.	Sept. 13th, 36th day.	Sept. 5th, 38th day.	Sept. 17th, 40th day.	Sept. 18th, 41st day.
14 Bav. Div. [2] 14 Res. Div. [1] 232 Div. [1]	243 Div. [3]	25 Div. [2]	Alpine Corps [2]	5 Bav. Div. [2] 6 Cav. Div. [1] 119 Div. [2]	201 Div. [1]	21 Div. [2]	1 Res. Div. [2]	25 Res. Div. [1] 79 Res. Div. [2]	2 Guard Div. [2]	185 Div. [2] 197 Div. [1]

1 Divisions in line on August 8th, from north to south.

APPENDIX D—continued

Sept. 19th, 42nd day.	Sept. 20th, 43rd day.	Sept. 22nd, 45th day.	Sept. 23rd, 46th day.	Sept. 24th, 47th day.	Sept. 26th, 49th day.	Sept. 30th, 53rd day.	Oct. 1st, 54th day.	Oct. 2nd, 55th day.	Oct. 3rd, 56th day.	Oct. 4th, 57th day.
121 Div. [2]	2 Div. [1] 75 Res.Div. [1]	232 Div. [2]	8 Div. [1]	11 Div. [1]	54 Div. [1]	21 Div. [3]	2 Guard Div. [3] 25 Res.Div.[2] 84 Div. [1] 221 Div. [2]	119 Div. [3] 241 Div. [1]	21 Res.Div.[1] 34 Div. [1]	2 Guard Div. [4]

Oct. 5th, 58th day.	Oct. 6th, 59th day.	Oct. 8th, 61st day.	Oct. 11th, 64th day.	Oct. 12th, 65th day.	Oct. 17th, 70th day.	Oct. 18th, 71st day.	Oct. 19th, 72nd day.	Oct. 22nd, 75th day.	Oct. 23rd, 76th day.	Oct. 24th, 77th day.
24 Div. [1] 121 Div. [3]	20 Div. [1] 25 Res. Div. [2] 38 Div. [2]	Jäger Div. [1] 2nd Cyclist Bde. [1] 30 Div. [1] 204 Div. [2] 208 Div. [1]	5 Res. Div. [1] 17 Res. Div. [1] 54 Div. [2]	15 Res. Div. [1] 81 Res. Div. [1]	3 Naval Div.[1] 24 Div. [2] 29 Div. [1] 44 Res. Div. [1] 243 Div. [4]	22 Res.Div.[1] 54 Div. [3] (portions) 121 Div. [4]	221 Div. [3]	8 Div. [2]	2nd Cyclist Bde. [2] 204 Div. [3]	19 Res.Div.[1] 58 Div. [1]

Nov. 1st, 85th day.	Nov. 2nd, 86th day.	Nov. 4th, 88th day.	Nov. 5th, 89th day.	Nov. 6th, 90th day.	Nov. 7th, 91st day.	Nov. 8th, 92nd day.	Nov. 9th, 93rd day.
Jäger Div. [2] (portions)	54 Div. [4]	Jäger Div. [2] (complete) 1 Guard Res. Div. [1] 22 Res.Div. [2] 200 Div. [1] 204 Div. [4]	121 Div. [5] 243 Div. [5]	15 Res. Div. [2]	1 Res. Div. [3]	9 Div. [1] 18 Div. [1]	6 Bav. Div.[1]

APPENDIX E

V.C. STORIES.

(Given in the words of the original recommendations.)

1. L/Cpl. W. Amey	.. .. ..	1/8th Bn. Royal Warwickshire Regt., T.F.
2. Sapper A. Archibald	.. ..	Royal Engineers.
3. Lieut. J. C. Barrett	.. ..	1/5th Bn. Leicestershire Regt., T.F.
4. Pte. R. M. Beatham	.. ..	8th Bn. Australian Infantry.
5. T/Capt. A. W. Beauchamp-Proctor		Royal Air Force.
6. L/Cpl. A. Brereton	.. ..	8th Bn. Canadian Infantry.
7. Lieut. J. Brilliant..	.. ..	22nd Bn. Canadian Infantry.
8. Cpl. A. H. Buckley	.. ..	54th Bn. Australian Infantry.
9. Pte. G. Cartwright	.. ..	33rd Bn. Australian Infantry.
10. Sgt. J. Clarke	.. .. ..	15th Bn. Lancashire Fusiliers.
11. L/Cpl. W. H. Coltman	.. ..	1/6th Bn. North Staffordshire Regt., T.F.
12. Cpl. F. G. Coppins ..	.. ..	8th Bn. Canadian Infantry.
13. Pte. J. B. Croak	.. ..	13th Bn. Canadian Infantry.
14. Pte. W. M. Currey	.. ..	53rd Bn. Australian Infantry.
15. Sgt. H. A. Curtis ..	.. ..	2nd Bn. Royal Dublin Fusiliers.
16. Pte. T. Dineson	.. ..	42nd Bn. Canadian Infantry.
17. A/Major G. de C. E. Findlay	..	Royal Engineers.
18. Lieut. A. E. Gaby ..	.. ..	28th Bn. Australian Infantry.
19. Cpl. H. J. Good	.. ..	13th Bn. Canadian Infantry.
20. L/Cpl. B. S. Gordon	.. ..	41st Bn. Australian Infantry.
21. Cpl. A. C. Hall	.. ..	54th Bn. Australian Infantry.
22. Sgt. T. J. Harris ..	.. ..	6th Bn. Royal West Kent Regt.
23. Pte. J. Harvey	.. ..	1/22nd Bn. London Regt., T.F.
24. Lieut. F. W. Hedges	.. ..	The Bedfordshire Regt.
25. 2nd Lieut. G. M. Ingram ..	..	24th Bn. Australian Infantry.
26. A/Lt.-Col. D. G. Johnson..	..	South Wales Borderers.
27. Sgt. W. H. Johnson	..	1/5th Nottinghamshire and Derbyshire Regt., T.F.
28. Lieut. W. D. Joynt	.. ..	8th Bn. Australian Infantry.
29. 2nd Lieut. J. Kirk ..	.. ..	10th Bn. Manchester Regt.
30. L/Cpl. A. Lewis	.. ..	6th Bn. Northamptonshire Regt.
31. Sgt. A. D. Lowerson	.. ..	21st Bn. Australian Infantry.
32. Lieut. L. D. McCarthy	.. ..	16th Bn. Australian Infantry.
33. Pte. R. Mactier	.. ..	23rd Bn. Australian Infantry.
34. A/Lt.-Col. J. N. Marshall	..	1st Bn. Irish Guards.
35. Lieut. J. Maxwell ..	.. ..	18th Bn. Australian Infantry.
36. Pte. F. G. Miles ..	.. ..	1/5th Bn. Gloucestershire Regt., T.F.
37. Cpl. H. G. B. Miner	.. ..	58th Bn. Canadian Infantry.
38. Pte. J. Ryan	.. ..	55th Bn. Australian Infantry.
39. Sgt. G. Sexton	.. ..	13th Bn. Australian Infantry.
40. Sgt. R. Spall	.. ..	Princess Patricia's Canadian Light Infantry.
41. Sgt. P. C. Statton ..	.. ..	40th Bn. Australian Infantry.
42. Lieut. J. E. Tait	.. ..	78th Bn. Canadian Infantry.
43. Lieut. E. T. Towner	.. ..	2nd Australian Machine Gun Bn.

44. A/Lt.-Col. B. W. Vann ..	1/8th Bn. Nottinghamshire and Derbyshire Regt., T.F.
45. Major B. A. Wark ..	32nd Bn. Australian Infantry.
46. A/Major A. H. S. Waters	Royal Engineers.
47. L/Cpl. L. C. Weathers ..	43rd Bn. Australian Infantry.
48. T/Capt. F. M. F. West ..	Royal Air Force.
49. Pte. J. P. Woods ..	48th Bn. Australian Infantry.
50. Sgt. R. L. Zengel ..	5th Bn. Canadian Infantry.

1. No. 307817 L/Cpl. WILLIAM AMEY, 1/8th Battalion, The Royal Warwickshire Regt., T.F. (Birmingham).

On November 4th, 1918, during the attack on Landrecies, this non-commissioned officer displayed most conspicuous and outstanding gallantry. The attack commenced in a fog resulting in many hostile machine-gun nests not being mopped up by the leading troops. This non-commissioned officer with his section, having lost touch with his company, attached himself to another company which was held up by heavy machine-gun fire, and carried out the following deeds of gallantry :—
On his own initiative, he led his section to attack a machine-gun nest in the face of heavy fire. With great bravery he forced the garrison to retire to a neighbouring farm, finally causing them to capitulate, and capturing about 50 prisoners and several machine-guns. Later, single-handed, he attacked a hostile machine-gun post situated in a farmhouse. Exposed to heavy fire, he advanced unhesitatingly, killed two of the garrison and drove the remainder into a cellar until assistance arrived. Again later and unaided, he attacked a Château in Faubourg-Soyères, which was strongly held, and holding up the line of advance. With determination and disregard for personal safety he rushed the Château, killing two Germans and holding up the remainder until reinforced. This gallant action was instrumental in the capture of a further 20 prisoners, and cleared away the last of the opposition in this sector. Throughout the day, the conduct of L/Cpl. Amey, in the face of much opposition, and danger, was of the highest type and beyond all praise. The work done by him not only resulted in clearing up a critical situation, but was instrumental in the saving of many lives.

2. No. 213078 Spr. ADAM ARCHIBALD, 218th Field Company, Royal Engineers (Leith).

For courage of the very highest order and the most exemplary devotion to duty and disregard of personal safety on November 4th, 1918, near Ors. This sapper was one of a party building a floating bridge across the canal. He was foremost in the work under a very heavy artillery barrage and machine-gun fire. The latter was directed at him from a few yards' distance while he was working on the cork floats. Though the fire was such that it seemed impossible that anyone could live under it, he persevered in his task and his example and efforts were such that the bridge, which was essential to the success of the operations, was completed very quickly. Just as his work was finished he collapsed from the effects of gas poisoning. The heroism of this sapper was beyond all praise. That anyone should have lived through such close and accurate fire is little short of miraculous.

3. Lieut. JOHN CRIDLAN BARRETT, 1/5th Battalion, The Leicestershire Regt., T.F. (Leamington Spa).

For most conspicuous gallantry and devotion to duty on the morning of September 24th, 1918, during the attack on Pontruet. On emerging from the smoke barrage Lieut. Barrett found himself faced by Forgan's trench which was very strongly held by the enemy, with five machine-guns on his immediate front. Without hesitation, he collected all the available men and charged the nearest group of machine-guns. He was wounded while making the charge, but gained the trench. He himself destroyed two guns and attacked another gun team with bombs. When his supply of bombs

o o

gave out he sent for a Lewis gun and got it into action ; in doing this he received two bullet wounds in the right arm. Seeing that his men were firmly established in the trench he climbed out into the open and made a reconnaissance, but was unable to get in touch with the remainder of the battalion which was occupying the village in rear of his position. On returning to the trench he found that he was becoming exhausted from loss of blood ; he therefore called up his non-commissioned officers, gave them exact instructions as to where they would find the battalion, and ordered the party to cut its way out. He refused help and started to crawl back, but was wounded a fourth time so severely that he was unable to move, and had to be carried out. It was due to the courage and coolness displayed by this gallant officer, in spite of his wounds, that any of the party were extricated from a very difficult situation.

4. No. 2742 Pte. ROBERT MATTHEW BEATHAM, 8th Battalion, Australian Infantry, Australian Imperial Force.

For conspicuous gallantry and devotion to duty during the attack north of Rosières, east of Amiens. On August 9th, 1918, Pte. Beatham showed such heroism and courage that he inspired all officers and men in his vicinity in a wonderful manner. When the advance was held up by heavy machine-gun fire, Pte. Beatham dashed forward and assisted by one man bombed and fought the crews of four enemy machine-guns, killing ten of them and capturing ten others. The bravery of the action greatly facilitated the advance of the whole battalion and prevented casualties. In fighting the crew of the first gun he was shot through the right leg but continued in the advance. When the final objective was reached and fierce fighting taking place, he again dashed forward and bombed the machine-gun that was holding off our men, getting riddled with bullets and killed in doing so. His heroism and self-sacrifice were not in vain, and, as his bombs knocked out the enemy machine-gun, our men were enabled to advance.

5. Temp. Capt. ANDREW WEATHERBY BEAUCHAMP-PROCTOR, D.S.O., M.C., D.S.C., The Royal Air Force, 84th Squadron.

For conspicuous valour and devotion to duty between August 8th, 1918, and October 8th, 1918, this officer proved himself victor in twenty-six decisive combats, destroying twelve enemy kite balloons, ten enemy aircraft, and driving down four other enemy aircraft completely out of control. Between October 1st and October 5th, 1918, he destroyed two enemy scouts, burnt three enemy kite balloons, and drove down one enemy scout completely out of control. On October 1st, 1918, in a general engagement with about twenty-eight machines, he charged one Fokker biplane near Fontaine, and a second near Flamicourt ; on October 2nd, he burnt a hostile balloon near Selvigny ; on October 3rd, he drove down, completely out of control, an enemy scout near Mont D'Origny, and burnt a hostile balloon ; on October 5th he destroyed a third hostile balloon near Bohain. On October 8th, 1918, while flying home at a low altitude, after destroying an enemy two-seater near Maretz, he was painfully wounded in the arm by machine-gun fire, but, continuing, he landed safely at his aerodrome, and, after making his report, was admitted to the hospital. In all he has proved himself conqueror over fifty-four foes, destroying twenty-two enemy machines, sixteen enemy kite balloons, and driving down sixteen enemy aircraft completely out of control. Besides these, his work in attacking enemy troops on the ground, and in reconnaissance both during the withdrawal following on the battle of St. Quentin from March 21st, 1918, and during the victorious advance of our Armies commencing on August 8th, has been almost unsurpassed in its brilliancy and as such has made an impression on those serving in his squadron, and those around him, that will not be easily forgotten.

6. No. 830651 Pte. (A/L.-Cpl.) ALEXANDER BRERETON, 8th Battalion, Canadian Infantry (90th Rifles), Manitoba Regt.

For outstanding and conspicuous valour and devotion. On August 9th, 1918, during the attack on the Amiens defence line, a line of hostile machine-guns opened fire suddenly on L/Cpl. Brereton's platoon when it was in a very exposed position where there was no possibility of taking cover. Realising the necessity for instant action, he at once rushed one of the machine-gun posts without waiting for orders. He bayoneted the man operating the gun and shot the first man who attempted to approach it; whereupon nine others surrendered to him. The platoon was then enabled to advance and capture the five remaining posts, where they killed fifteen and captured thirty of the enemy, and subsequently went on to their final objective. L/Cpl. Brereton's action was a splendid example of resource and bravery. It undoubtedly saved the lives of many of his comrades and turned a critical situation into a brilliant success.

7. **Lieut. John Brilliant, M.C., 22nd Battalion (French Canadian), Quebec Regt.**

For most conspicuous gallantry and almost superhuman devotion to duty during the operations of the 8th and 9th August, 1918, in the attack and twelve miles advance from the vicinity of Villers Bretonneux to east of Méharicourt. Lieut. Brilliant was in charge of a company which he led during the two days with absolute fearlessness and extraordinary ability and initiative. At about 1 p.m. on August 9th, 1918, one mile east of Caix, just after that day's attack had begun, his company's left flank was held up by an enemy machine-gun. Lieut. Brilliant rushed and captured the machine-gun, himself killing two of the enemy crew. Whilst doing this, he was wounded in the thigh, but refused to be evacuated. A little after 3 p.m. the same day, his company was held up by heavy machine-gun fire from a machine-gun nest in the houses in the northern part of Vrély. He reconnoitred the ground personally, organised a party of two platoons and rushed straight for the machine-gun nest. Here 150 Germans and 15 machine-guns were captured, Lieut. Brilliant himself killed five Germans and was wounded a second time, in the shoulder. He had his wound dressed immediately and again refused to be evacuated. About 6 p.m. the same day, after his company had reached a line east of Méharicourt, this gallant officer saw a field gun firing on his men over open sights from the Bois de Maucourt. He immediately organised and led a rushing party towards the gun. After progressing about 600 yards, Lieut. Brilliant was seriously wounded in the abdomen. In spite of this third wound, he continued to advance for some 200 yards more when he fell unconscious from exhaustion and loss of blood. Lieut. Brilliant's wonderful example throughout the day fired his men with enthusiasm and fury which largely contributed towards the battalion's notable achievements.

8. **No. 1876 Cpl. Alexander Henry Buckley, 54th Battalion, Australian Infantry, Australian Imperial Force.**

For most conspicuous gallantry and devotion to duty at Péronne during the operations on September 1st and 2nd, 1918. After passing the first objective, his half company and part of the company on the flank were held up by an enemy machine-gun nest. With one man he rushed the post, shooting four of the occupants and taking twenty-two prisoners. Later, on reaching a moat, another machine-gun nest commanded the only available footbridge. Whilst this was being engaged from the flank, this non-commissioned officer endeavoured to cross the bridge and rush the post, but was killed in the attempt. Throughout the advance he had displayed great initiative, resource, and courage, being a great inspiration to his men. In order to avert casualties amongst his comrades and to permit of their advance, he voluntarily essayed a task which practically meant certain death. He set a fine example of bravery and of self-sacrificing devotion to duty.

9. **No. 726 Pte. George Cartwright, 33rd Battalion, Australian Infantry, Australian Imperial Force.**

For most conspicuous valour and devotion to duty. On the morning of August 31st, 1918, during the attack on Road Wood, south-west of Bouchavesnes, near

Péronne, Pte. Cartwright displayed exceptional gallantry and supreme disregard for personal danger in the face of a withering machine-gun fire. Two companies were held up by a machine-gun firing from the south-western edge of the wood. Without hesitation this man stood up, and, walking towards the gun, fired his rifle from his shoulder. He shot the No. 1 gunner, another German manned the gun and he killed him; a third attempted to fire the gun, and him he also killed. Pte. Cartwright then threw a bomb at the post and on its exploding he rushed forward, captured the gun and nine Germans. Our line then immediately rushed forward loudly cheering him. This magnificent deed had a most inspiring effect on the whole line; all strove to emulate his gallantry. Throughout the operation Pte. Cartwright displayed wonderful dash, grim determination, and courage of the highest order.

10. No. 37721 Sgt. JAMES CLARKE, 15th (Service) Battalion, The Lancashire Fusiliers (Rochdale).

During the attack at Happegarbes on November 2nd, 1918, this non-commissioned officer was in command of a platoon. He led his men forward with great determination, and on being held up by heavy machine-gun fire he rushed forward through a thick and strongly held hedge, captured in succession four machine-guns, and single-handed bayoneted the crews in spite of a very heavy and point blank fire from the guns. Later, he led the remnants of his platoon and captured three more machine-guns and many prisoners. In the later stages of the attack on the same day, finding the platoon held up by a nest of enemy machine-guns, he personally led a tank to this point over very exposed ground, and the opposition was broken down. Continuing the attack on November 3rd, after capturing many prisoners and gaining his objective, he found his flank being turned by the enemy. He at once organised a defensive flank, posting each man so that the enemy was successfully held. On November 4th in the attack on the Oise–Sambre Canal this non-commissioned officer came under heavy fire from the opposite bank of the canal. He rushed forward with a Lewis gun and team in the face of an intense barrage, brought the gun into action, effectively silenced the enemy's fire, and enabled the rest of his company to advance and gain their objectives. Throughout the whole of these operations this non-commissioned officer acted with magnificent bravery and total disregard of personal safety, and by his gallantry and high sense of duty he set a magnificent example and greatly inspired all ranks.

11. No. 241028 Pte. (L/Cpl.) WILLIAM HAROLD COLTMAN, D.C.M., M.M., and Bar, 1/6th Battalion, The Prince of Wales's (North Staffordshire Regt.), T.F. (Winshill, Burton-on-Trent).

For most conspicuous bravery, initiative, and self-sacrifice in attack. During the operations at Mannequin Hill north-east of Sequehart, on October 3rd and 4th, 1918, this non-commissioned officer, a stretcher bearer, did most conspicuous acts of bravery in rescuing and carrying, on his back, on three successive occasions, badly wounded men who had been left behind when we were compelled to retire after a heavy enemy counter-attack. Hearing that there were wounded men lying further to the front who had not been attended to, he went forward alone—and on his own initiative—into the valley north of the Hill in the face of fierce enfilade fire, found the wounded, dressed them, and carried each one to his stretcher squad in the rear of our line, thus saving their lives. In that action alone this very gallant non-commissioned officer dressed and carried wounded for 48 hours without rest; his efforts did not cease until the last wounded man had been attended to.

12. No. 1987 Cpl. FREDERICK GEORGE COPPINS, 8th Battalion, Canadian Infantry (90th Rifles), Manitoba Regt.

For conspicuous and exceptional valour, gallantry, and devotion. On August 9th, 1918, during the attack east of the Amiens defence line on Hatchett Wood, Cpl. Coppins' platoon came unexpectedly into the zone of fire of numerous machine-guns in Hatchett Wood. They were unable to advance or retire and, as they were on the forward slope, there was no available cover. It was apparent that the platoon would be annihilated unless the enemy machine-guns were silenced immediately. Cpl. Coppins at once appreciated the situation. Without hesitation, and on his own initiative, he called on four men to follow him and leaped forward in the face of a terrific machine-gun fire. This act alone attracted the enemy's fire, which was concentrated on his small party, thus saving the others lying on the ground. Cpl. Coppins with his comrades rushed straight for the machine-guns. The four men with him were killed ; Cpl. Coppins was wounded in the ankle. Despite his wound he reached the hostile machine-guns and called on the crews to surrender. They refused. He then killed the man operating the first gun and three of the crew—four others immediately surrendered. This act of outstanding bravery was the means of saving many lives of the men of his platoon, and enabled the platoon to advance. Despite his wound he continued with his platoon to the final objective—5,000 yards distant—and only left the line when it had been made secure and when ordered to do so by his Commanding Officer. The heroism of Cpl. Coppins undoubtedly saved the lives of many of his comrades and ensured the success of the attack by his platoon.

13. No. 445312 Pte. JOHN BERNARD CROAK, 13th Battalion, Canadian Infantry, Quebec Regt.

On August 8th, 1918, during the attack on the Amiens defence line, Pte. Croak, after being separated from his section, encountered a machine-gun nest in Ring Copse which he first bombed unassisted, and then jumped into the post, making prisoners of the crew and capturing the gun. Shortly afterwards he was severely wounded in the right arm but refused to desist. In a few minutes his platoon, which he had rejoined again, encountered a very strong point containing several machine-guns, and were forced to take cover. Croak, however, seeing an opportunity, dashed forward alone, and was almost immediately followed by the remainder of the platoon in a brilliant charge. Croak was the first to arrive at the trench, into which he led the men, capturing 3 machine-guns and bayoneting or capturing the entire garrison. His perseverance and courage were undoubtedly responsible for taking the strongest point in the whole day's advance. Pte. Croak was again severely wounded in the knee and died in a few minutes.

14. No. 1584A Pte. WILLIAM MATTHEW CURREY, 53rd Battalion, Australian Infantry, Australian Imperial Force.

During the attack on Péronne on the morning of September 1st, 1918, Pte. Currey displayed most conspicuous gallantry and daring. During the early stage of the advance the battalion was suffering heavy casualties from a 77 mm. field gun that was firing over sights at a very close range. Pte. Currey without hesitation rushed forward and, despite a withering machine-gun fire that was directed on him from either flank, succeeded in capturing the gun single-handed after killing the entire crew. Later, when continuing the advance, an enemy " strong point " containing 30 men and two machine-guns was noticed which was holding up the advance of the left flank. Pte. Currey crept around the flank and engaged the post with a Lewis gun, causing many casualties. Finally he rushed the post single-handed, killing four, wounding two, and taking one prisoner, the survivors running away. It was entirely owing to his gallant conduct that the situation was relieved, and the advance enabled to continue. After the final stage of the attack it was imperative that one of the companies, that had become isolated, should be withdrawn. This man at once volunteered to carry the message, although the ground to be crossed was very heavily shelled and continuously swept by machine-gun fire. He crossed the shell and bullet swept area three times in the effort to locate the company, and on one occasion his box respirator was shot through by machine-gun bullets, and he was gassed. Nevertheless, he remained on duty, and, after finding the isolated company, delivered the message, and returned with very valuable information from the company commander. Owing to the gas poisoning from which he was suffering Pte. Currey had shortly afterwards to be evacuated. Throughout the operations his striking example of coolness, determination, and utter disregard of danger had a most inspiring effect on his comrades, and his gallant work contributed largely to our success.

15. No. 14017 Sgt. Horace Augustus Curtis, 2nd Battalion, The Royal Dublin Fusiliers (Newlyn, East Cornwall).

For conspicuous gallantry and devotion to duty east of Le Cateau on the morning of October 18th, 1918. During an attack on an enemy position his platoon came unexpectedly under the intense hostile fire of many machine-guns. Knowing that the attack would be a failure unless the enemy guns were silenced, Sgt. Curtis without hesitation rushed forward through our own barrage and the enemy machine-gun fire. He reached the enemy position, and killed and wounded the teams of two guns. Through his extraordinary bravery and prompt action the teams of four other guns surrendered to him. A train-load of reinforcements was in the immediate vicinity, from which many of the enemy were detraining. He shot at the driver and succeeded in capturing over a hundred prisoners by the time his comrades reached him. His outstanding gallantry and disregard of personal safety inspired all near him to greater keenness and effort, which resulted in the attack on the whole battalion front being a complete success.

16. No. 2075467 Pte. Thomas Dineson, 42nd Battalion (Royal Highlanders of Canada), Quebec Regt.

During the action of Parvillers, August 12th, 1918, he was the outstanding man of his company during ten hours hand-to-hand fighting, which resulted in the capture of over a mile of strongly garrisoned and stubbornly defended German trenches. Five times in succession he rushed forward alone, and single-handed put hostile machine-guns out of action, accounting for twelve of the enemy with bomb and bayonet. His aggressiveness and resourcefulness inspired his comrades at a very critical stage of the action.

17. Capt. (A/Major) George de Cardonnell Elmsell Findlay, D.S.O. M.C., Royal Engineers, 409th (Lowland) Field Company, Royal Engineers, T.F. (Balloch, N.B.).

For very conspicuous gallantry and devotion to duty during the forcing of the Sambre–Oise Canal at the lock two miles south of Catillon on November 4th, 1918. Major Findlay with his company was in charge of the bridging operations at this crossing and, although wounded, remained at duty until these operations were completed. He was with the leading bridging and assaulting parties, who came under a heavy fire while trying to cross the dyke which intervened between the forming up line and the lock. The casualties were severe and the advance was stopped. Major Findlay, under a heavy and incessant fire, collected what men he could and repaired the bridges. During this time the casualties continued to be very heavy, all the officers of the Royal Engineers Company and 45 per cent. of the other ranks had become casualties. In spite of being wounded himself, Major Findlay continued his task, and, after two unsuccessful efforts owing to his men being swept down, he eventually placed the bridge in position across the lock, and was the first man to cross. It was his cool and gallant behaviour that ensured him volunteers from different units at this critical time, when men became casualties almost as soon as they joined him in the fire swept zone. He remained on duty, though wounded, at this dangerous spot until 10 p.m. that day, there being no other officer to superintend further work on the bridges. Without this officer's gallantry and devotion there can be no doubt that this most important crossing could not have been effected. The value of the crossing at this point is well known.

18. Lieut. Alfred Edward Gaby, 28th Battalion, Australian Infantry, Australian Imperial Force.

During the attack east of Villers Bretonneux, near Amiens, on the morning of August 8th, 1918, this officer led his company with great dash, being well in front. On reaching the wire in front of the enemy trench, strong opposition was encountered.

The enemy was holding a strong point in force about 40 yards beyond the wire, and commanded the gap with four machine-guns and rifles. The advance was at once checked. Lieut. Gaby found another gap in the wire, and, entirely by himself, approached the strong point, while machine-guns and rifles were still being fired from it. Running along the parapet, still alone, and at point blank range, he emptied his revolver into the garrison, drove the crews from their guns, and compelled the surrender of 50 of the enemy with four machine-guns. He then quickly reorganised his men and led them on to his final objective, which he captured and consolidated. On the morning of August 11th, 1918, during an attack east of Framerville, near Amiens, Lieut. Gaby again led his company with great dash on to the objective. The enemy brought heavy rifle and machine-gun fire to bear upon the line, but in the face of this heavy fire Lieut. Gaby walked along his line of posts, encouraging his men to quickly consolidate the line. While engaged on this duty he was killed by an enemy sniper.

19. No. 445120 Cpl. HERMAN JAMES GOOD, 13th Battalion, Canadian Infantry, Quebec Regt.

On August 8th, 1918, in Hangard Wood, Cpl. Good's company was held up by heavy machine-gun fire from three machine-guns in a strong point, seriously delaying the advance near the start of the operation. Cpl. Good, seeing the seriousness of the situation, dashed forward alone, killing several of the garrison and capturing the remainder. Later on, while alone, he encountered a battery of 5·9 guns which were in action at the time. Collecting three men of his section, he charged the battery and captured the entire crews of three guns, who continued to fire point blank at them until the four men were within a very short distance of the guns.

20. No. 23 Pte. (L/Cpl.) BERNARD SIDNEY GORDON, 41st Battalion, Australian Infantry, Australian Imperial Force.

During the operations of August 26th and 27th, 1918, east of Bray, this non-commissioned officer showed most conspicuous gallantry and devotion to duty in the face of the enemy. He led his section through heavy enemy shelling to its objective, which he consolidated. Then, single-handed, he attacked an enemy machine-gun which was enfilading the company on his right, killed the man on the gun, and captured the post, which contained an officer (Captain) and ten men. After handing these over at company headquarters he returned alone to the old system of trenches in which were many machine-guns, entered a communication trench and proceeded to mop it up, returning with 16 prisoners in one squad and 14 in another, together with two machine-guns. Again he returned to the system, this time with a trench mortar gun and crew, and proceeded to mop up a further portion of the trench, bringing in 22 prisoners, including an officer and three machine-guns. This last capture enabled the British troops on our left to advance, which they had not been able to do owing to machine-gun fire from these posts. His total captures were thus 2 officers and 61 other ranks together with 6 machine-guns, and, with the exception of the trench mortar assistance, it was absolutely an individual effort and done entirely on his own initiative.

21. No. 2631 Cpl. ARTHUR CHARLES HALL, 54th Battalion, Australian Infantry, Australian Imperial Force.

For most conspicuous gallantry, brilliant leadership, and devotion to duty during the operations at Péronne on September 1st and 2nd, 1918. A machine-gun post in the enemy front line was holding up the advance; alone this non-commissioned officer rushed the position, shot four of the occupants as he advanced, and captured nine others and two machine-guns. Then crossing the objective with a small party, he reconnoitred the approaches to the town covering the infiltration of the remainder of the company. During the mopping up he continuously, in advance of the main party, located enemy points of resistance and personally led parties to the assault. In this way he captured many small parties of prisoners and machine-guns. On the morning of September 2nd, during a heavy barrage on the newly consolidated position, a man of his platoon was severely wounded. Seeing that only immediate medical attention could save him, Cpl. Hall volunteered and carried the man out of the barrage, handed him to a stretcher bearer, and immediately returned to his post. This company was heavily engaged throughout the day, only one officer remaining unwounded. The energy and personal courage of this non-commissioned officer undoubtedly contributed largely to the success of the operation. Throughout the operations he showed utter disregard for danger, and under trying conditions behaved in a most gallant and skilful manner. His daring, coolness, and self-sacrificing devotion to duty compelled the admiration and confidence of all associated with him.

22. No. 358 Sgt. THOMAS JAMES HARRIS, M.M., 6th Battalion, The Queen's Own (Royal West Kent Regt.) (Lower Halling, Kent).

For conspicuous gallantry and devotion to duty near Morlancourt on August 9th, 1918. During the attack of the battalion the advance was much impeded by hostile machine-guns concealed in the crops and shell holes. Sgt. Harris led his section against one of these, capturing it, and killing seven of the enemy. Later, on two successive occasions, he attacked, single-handed, enemy machine-guns which were causing heavy casualties and holding up the advance. He captured the first gun and killed the team, but was himself killed when attacking the second one. It was largely due to the great courage and initiative of this non-commissioned officer that the advance of the battalion was continued without delay and undue casualties. Throughout the operations he showed a total disregard for his own personal safety and set a magnificent example to all ranks.

23. No. 681139 Pte. JACK HARVEY, 1/22nd Battalion (County of London), The London Regt. (The Queen's) T.F. (Camberwell).

For most conspicuous gallantry and disregard of personal danger on September 2nd, 1918, during the advance north of Péronne. The advance of his company was held up by intense machine-gun fire ; this man at once rushed forward a distance of fifty yards alone through our barrage, and, in the face of heavy enemy fire, rushed a machine-gun post, shooting two of the team and bayoneting another. He then destroyed the gun and continued to work his way along the enemy trench, and single-handed rushed an enemy dug-out containing 37 Germans, whom he compelled to surrender. By these two acts of great gallantry he saved his company heavy casualties and enabled the whole of the attacking line to advance ; throughout the entire operation he showed the most magnificent courage and determination, and, by the splendid example he set to all ranks, materially assisted in the success of the operation.

24. Lieut. FREDERICK WILLIAM HEDGES, The Bedfordshire Regt., attached 6th (Service) Battalion, The Northamptonshire Regt. (Hounslow).

For conspicuous gallantry and initiative during operations north-east of Bousies on the afternoon of October 24th, 1918. During the morning this officer, who was detailed to leap-frog his company to the final objective, handled his company in a very skilful manner, maintaining direction under the most difficult conditions. His company was on the right of the brigade front. He advanced a considerable distance to a point where his further advance was held up by about six machine-gun posts on the hill opposite the line. Early in the afternoon this officer made up his mind to clear out these enemy posts. Later, accompanied by one sergeant and followed at some considerable distance by a Lewis gun section, he proceeded up the hill under cover of a hedge, and killed the first machine-gunner and took two others prisoner. He then worked his way along the crest of the hill and dealt with three other machine-gun posts in a similar manner, taking the feed blocks out of the guns, his total being six machine-guns and fourteen men. The direct result of this officer's action was that the whole line which had been held up since the morning was enabled to advance, thus having a great effect on subsequent operations.

25. 2nd Lieut. GEORGE MORBY INGRAM, M.M., 24th Battalion, Australian Infantry, Australian Imperial Force.

During the attack on Montbrehain, east of Péronne, on October 5th, 1918, this officer was in charge of a platoon. About 100 yards from the jumping-off trench severe enemy machine-gun fire was encountered from a strong post which had escaped our artillery fire, and the advance was thus held up. Lieut. Ingram dashed out, and, under cover of the fire of a Lewis gun, rushed the post at the head of his men. This post contained nine machine-guns and 42 Germans, who fought until our men were within three yards of them. They were killed to a man—Lieut. Ingram accounted for no less than 18 of them. A number of enemy posts were then observed to be firing on our men from about 150 yards further forward and the company moved forward to attack them, and severe casualties were sustained. The company commander had been badly wounded, and the company sergeant-major and several others who attempted to lead the advance killed. Our barrage had passed on, and no tanks were near. Lieut. Ingram quickly seized the situation, rallied his men in face of murderous fire, and led them forward with magnificent courage and resolution. He himself rushed the first post, shot six of the enemy, and captured the machine-gun, thus overcoming a very serious resistance. By this time the company had been reduced from 90 to about 30 other ranks, but this officer, seeing enemy fire coming from a quarry to his left front, again led his men forward and rushed the quarry. He jumped into the quarry amongst enemy wire and his men followed and proceeded to mop up a large number of the enemy who were in bivouacs there. He then observed an enemy machine-gun firing from the ventilator of a cellar through a gap in the wall of a house about 20 yards away. Without hesitation and entirely alone he scrambled up the edge of the quarry, ran round the rear of the house, and, entering from the far side, shot the enemy gunner through the ventilator of the cellar. He fired several more shots into the cellar, then, seeing some enemy jumping out of the window of the house, he burst open the door, rushed to the head of the stairs leading into the cellar, and forced 62 of the enemy to surrender. He now found he was out of touch with the company on his left flank, so went out alone and made a personal reconnaissance under heavy fire, and succeeded in gaining touch with the left company, which had lost all its officers. Having returned to his company he placed a post on his left flank to ensure its safety, and then reconnoitred and established two posts on his right flank. All this was done in the face of continuous machine-gun and shell fire. Throughout the whole day he showed the most splendid qualities of courage and leadership and freely exposed himself again and again with utter contempt of danger. By his example he encouraged his men to keep up such constant fire on the enemy, who were reinforcing in large numbers, that not only did he levy a large toll of casualties on them, but was responsible for destroying counter-attacks on his front. He personally inflicted 40 casualties on the enemy, exclusive of the large number of prisoners he captured.

26. Capt. (A/Lt.-Col.) DUDLEY GRAHAM JOHNSON, D.S.O., M.C., The South Wales Borderers, attached 2nd Battalion, The Royal Sussex Regt.

For very conspicuous gallantry and leadership during the forcing of the Sambre Canal on November 4th, 1918. The 2nd Infantry Brigade, of which the 2nd Battalion, The Royal Sussex Regiment, formed part, was ordered to cross by the lock, south of Catillon. This was a very strong position and before the bridges could be placed over the lock, a steep bank leading to the lock and waterway about 100 yards this side of the canal had to be crossed. It was also overlooked by houses on the far side of the canal. The assaulting platoons and parties of the Royal Engineers, carrying bridges, moved towards the canal at zero hour, from their hidden assembly area about 250 yards from the lock. On their arrival at the waterway they were thrown into confusion by a heavy barrage and machine-gun fire, and heavy casualties were caused, the remnants withdrawing from the barrage. At this moment Lt.-Col. Johnson, commanding 2nd Battalion, The Royal Sussex Regiment, came up to see the progress made. He grasped the situation quickly, hurriedly collected men to man the bridges

P P

and assist the Royal Engineers, and personally led the assault forward. In spite of his efforts the heavy fire again broke up the assaulting and bridging parties. Owing to the delay the situation at this moment was becoming serious, as the succeeding waves were closing up and getting congested. Without any hesitation, Lt.-Col. Johnson again reorganised the platoons and bridging parties, and again led them at the lock, this time succeeding in effecting a crossing, after which all went well. During all this time Lt.-Col. Johnson was under a very heavy fire, which, though it nearly annihilated the assaulting columns, left him untouched. His conduct was a fine example of great valour and remarkable coolness and intrepidity, and this, added to his splendid leadership and the offensive spirit that he had inspired in his battalion, was entirely responsible for the successful crossing. In addition to securing the success of the right brigade of the First Division, there can be no doubt that the result of Lt.-Col. Johnson's action very materially assisted the advance on the left flank of the division, which might otherwise have been jeopardised.

27. No. 306122 Sgt. WILLIAM HENRY JOHNSON, 1/5th Battalion, The Sherwood Foresters (Nottinghamshire and Derbyshire Regt.), T.F. (Worksop).

For most conspicuous gallantry at Ramicourt on October 3rd, 1918. When his platoon was held up by a nest of enemy machine-guns at very close range, this non-commissioned officer worked his way forward under very heavy fire, and single-handed charged the post, bayoneting several gunners and capturing two machine-guns. During this attack he was severely wounded by a bomb but continued to lead forward his men. Shortly afterwards the line was again held up by machine-guns, and Sgt. Johnson rushed forward alone and attacked the post single-handed. With wonderful courage he bombed the garrison, put the guns out of action, and captured the teams. He showed throughout the attack most exceptional gallantry and devotion to duty.

28. Lieut. WILLIAM DONOVAN JOYNT, 8th Battalion, Australian Infantry, Australian Imperial Force.

For conspicuous gallantry and devotion to duty during the attack on Herleville Wood, near Chuignes, near Péronne, on August 23rd, 1918. Early in the advance Lieut. Joynt's company commander was killed. He immediately took charge of the company and led them with courage and skill. A great deal of the success of the operation in this portion of the sector was directly due to his magnificent work. When the advance was commenced the battalion was moving into support to another battalion. On approaching Herleville Wood the troops of the leading battalion lost all their officers and became disorganised. Under very heavy fire and having no leaders they appeared certain to be annihilated. Lieut. Joynt grasped the situation and rushed forward in the teeth of very heavy machine-gun and artillery fire over the open. He got the remaining men under control and worked them into a piece of dead ground until he could re-form them. He manœuvred his own men forward and linked them up with the men of the other battalion. He then made a personal reconnaissance and found that the fire from the wood was holding the whole advance up, the troops on his flank suffering very heavy casualties. Dashing out in front of his men he called them on, and by sheer force of example inspired them into a magnificent frontal bayonet attack on the wood. The audacity of the move over the open staggered the enemy, and Lieut. Joynt succeeded in penetrating the wood and working through it. By his leadership and courage a very critical situation was saved, and on this officer rests to the greatest extent the success of the brigade's attack. When the battalion on our left was held up on Plateau Wood and was suffering severe casualties, Lieut. Joynt, with a small party of volunteers, worked right forward against heavy opposition, and by means of hand-to-hand fighting forced his way round the rear of the wood, penetrating it from that side and demoralising the enemy to such an extent that a very stubborn and victorious defensive was changed into an abject surrender. He was always in the hardest pressed parts of the line and seemed to bear a charmed life. He was constantly ready to run any personal risks and to assist flank units.

He continually showed magnificent leadership and his example to his men had a wonderful effect on them, causing them to follow him cheerfully in his most daring exploits. He continued to do magnificent work until he was badly wounded in the legs by shell fire.

29. **2nd Lieut. JAMES KIRK, 10th (attached 2nd) Battalion, The Manchester Regt. (Heaton Moor).**

North of Ors on November 4th, 1918, whilst attempting to bridge the Oise Canal, this officer showed most conspicuous bravery, absolute fearlessness, and supreme devotion to duty. In order to cover the bridging of the canal he took a Lewis gun and four magazines, and paddled himself across the canal on a raft under a most intense machine-gun barrage. The bank bristled with machine-guns. He set up his Lewis gun at 10 yards range and fired off the whole of his ammunition. Further ammunition was paddled across to him on the raft and he continued firing, covering the Royal Engineers in their task. He was wounded in the arm and the face, but still fired continuously from a most exposed position until he was shot through the head and fell dead over his gun. It was his supreme contempt of danger and his magnificent self-sacrifice which prevented many casualties, and enabled two platoons to cross the bridge before it was destroyed. He deliberately faced certain death to save the men of his platoon, and inspired them and all who saw him by the example of his most magnificent devotion.

30. **No. 45062 L/Cpl. ALBERT LEWIS, 6th (Service) Battalion, The Northamptonshire Regt. (Whitney, Hereford).**

On the morning of September 18th, 1918, this non-commissioned officer was in charge of a section which he had successfully kept together. He was on the right of the line and the battalion started to advance to attack Ronssoy, where the east and west barrage opened. The battalion advanced to a point where the enemy machine-gun fire was so intense that it was practically impossible to get forward. The barrage went on and the battalion was temporarily held up. This man, working with his section on the right amongst the ruins, observed two enemy machine-guns opposite him enfilading the whole battalion. On his own initiative he crawled forward single-handed, got within bombing range, and successfully bombed the teams manning the enemy's guns. The enemy left their guns and ran out of their emplacement. L/Cpl. Lewis thereupon used his rifle with good effect and the whole team surrendered. He had wounded six and captured four of the enemy, unwounded. By his courage and determination in putting out of action two enemy machine-guns he undoubtedly enabled the battalion to advance, and so contributed largely to the success which followed. Later, on September 21st, 1918, during another attack, this non-commissioned officer displayed splendid power of command. When his company was caught in the enemy barrage, he was the first to rush them through it until they came under heavy fire from enemy machine-guns, whereupon L/Cpl. Lewis immediately began to place them out in shell holes. While doing this he was killed. Throughout he showed a splendid disregard of danger, and his leadership at a critical period was beyond all praise.

31. **No. 2358 Sgt. ALBERT DAVID LOWERSON, 21st Battalion, Australian Infantry, Australian Imperial Force.**

At Mont St. Quentin, north of Péronne, on September 1st, 1918, this non-commissioned officer displayed courage and tactical skill of the very highest order during the attack on this village. Very strong opposition was met with early in the attack and every foot of ground was stubbornly contested by the enemy located in very strong positions. This non-commissioned officer's example during the fighting was of the greatest value. He moved about, regardless of the heavy enemy machine-gun fire, directing his men, encouraging them to still greater effort, and finally led them on to the objective. On reaching the objective, he saw that the left attacking party had not met with success, and that the attack was held up by an enemy strong point heavily manned with 12 machine-guns. Under the heaviest sniping and machine-gun fire, Sgt. Lowerson rallied seven men around him into a storming party, and deployed them to attack the post from both flanks, one party of three being killed immediately. He himself then rushed the strong post, and, with effective bombing, inflicted heavy casualties on the enemy, and captured the post containing 12 machine-guns and 30 prisoners. Though severely wounded in the right thigh, he refused to leave the front line until the prisoners had been dispatched to the rear, and the organisation and consolidation of the post by our men had been completed. When he saw that the position was thoroughly secure, he returned to the rear, but refused to leave the battalion, until forced to evacuate two days later by the seriousness of his wound. This act was the culminating point of a series of most gallant performances by this non-commissioned officer during the fighting extending over a week. His leadership and example had a continual influence on the men serving under him, whilst his prompt and effective action at a critical juncture allowed the forward movement to be carried on without delay, thus ensuring the success of the attack.

32. Lieut. LAWRENCE DOMINIC McCARTHY, 16th Battalion, Australian Infantry, Australian Imperial Force.

This officer is especially brought to notice for his wonderful gallantry, initiative, and leadership on the morning of August 23rd, 1918, when an attack was being made near Madame Wood, west of Vermandovillers (north of Chaulnes). The objectives of this battalion were attained without serious opposition. The battalion on the left flank was less fortunate. Here several well-posted machine-gun posts were holding up the attack and heavy fire was being brought to bear on our left flank. When Lieut. McCarthy realised the situation he at once engaged the nearest machine-gun post; but still the attacking troops failed to get forward. This officer then determined to attack the nearer post. Leaving his men to continue the fire fight, he, with two others, dashed across the open and dropped into a disused trench which had been blocked. One of his two men was killed whilst doing this. He was now right under the block over which the enemy machine-gun was firing. The presence of head cover prevented the use of bombs. He therefore tunnelled a hole through the bottom of the block, through which he inserted his head and one arm. He at once shot dead the two men firing the gun. He then crawled through the hole he had made, and by himself charged down the trench. He threw his limited number of Mills bombs among the German garrison and inflicted some more casualties. He then came in contact with two German officers, who fired on him with their revolvers. One of these he shot dead with his revolver, the other he seriously wounded. He then charged down the trench using his revolver and throwing enemy stick bombs, and captured three more enemy machine-guns. At this stage, some seven hundred yards from his starting point, he was joined by the non-commissioned officer whom he had out-distanced when he crawled through the hole in the trench block mentioned above. Together they continued to bomb up the trench, until touch was established with the Lancashire Fusiliers, and in the meanwhile yet another machine-gun had been captured. A total of five machine-guns and 50 prisoners (37 unwounded and 13 wounded) was captured, while Lieut. McCarthy during his most amazing and daring feat had, single-handed, killed 20 of the enemy. Having cleared up a dangerous situation, he proceeded to establish a garrison in the line. Whilst doing this he saw a number of the enemy getting away from neighbouring trenches. He at once seized a Lewis gun and inflicted further casualties on them. The determined and daring conduct of this gallant officer saved a critical situation, prevented many casualties, and was mainly, if not entirely, responsible for the final objective being taken.

33. No. 6939 Pte. ROBERT MACTIER, 23rd Battalion, Australian Infantry, Australian Imperial Force.

On the morning of September 1st, 1918, during the operation entailing the capture of Mont St. Quentin, this man stands out for the greatest bravery and devotion to duty. Fifteen minutes before zero two bombing patrols were sent to clear up several enemy strong points close to our line, but they met with very stubborn resistance and no success, and the battalion was unable to move on to its jumping off trench. Mactier, single-handed and in daylight, then jumped out of the trench from the leading company, rushed past the block, closed with and killed the machine-gun garrison of eight men with his revolver and bombs, and threw the enemy machine-gun over the parapet. He rushed forward another twenty yards and jumped into another strong point held by a garrison of six men, who immediately surrendered. Continuing to the next block through the trench, an enemy gun, which had been enfilading our flank advancing troops, was swung on to him, but he jumped out of the trench into the open and disposed of this third post and gun crew by bombing them from the rear. Before he could get into this trench he was killed by enemy machine-gun at close range. In the three posts which Mactier rushed 15 of the enemy were found killed and 30 taken prisoners. It was entirely due to this man's exceptional bravery and determination that the battalion was able to move on to its jumping-off trench and carry out the successful operation of capturing the village of Mont St. Quentin a few hours later.

34. Lieut. (A/Lt.-Col.) JAMES NEVILLE MARSHALL, M.C., 1st Battalion, Irish Guards (attached 16th (Service) Battalion, The Lancashire Fusiliers).

For most conspicuous gallantry, determination, and leadership in the attack on the Sambre–Oise Canal near Catillon, on November 4th, 1918. A partly constructed bridge composed of small cork rafts had been thrown over the canal by the Royal Engineers and Pioneers, but before the advanced troops of Lt.-Col. Marshall's battalion could cross, the bridge came under a concentrated fire of artillery and machine-guns and was broken. On hearing of this Lt.-Col. Marshall at once came up, took charge of the situation, and organised parties of volunteers for the repair of the bridge. All the first party of volunteers were quickly killed or wounded, but so great was the personal example of the commanding officer that other volunteers instantly took their places. Throughout the repair of the bridge Lt.-Col. Marshall, standing on the bank, encouraged and assisted the men under a hurricane of heavy fire without any regard to his own safety. When the bridge was repaired Lt.-Col. Marshall attempted to rush across at the head of his battalion and was killed while so doing. The forcing of the line of the canal was of vital importance, and the gallantry displayed by all ranks at this spot was largely due to the personal example given by Lt.-Col. Marshall. He had been wounded ten times during the war and fell in the last great fight in which the Division was engaged.

35. Lieut. JOSEPH MAXWELL, M.C., D.C.M., 18th Battalion, Australian Infantry, Australian Imperial Force.

On October 3rd, 1918, he took part as a platoon commander in an attack on the Beaurevoir–Fonsomme Line near Estrées, north of St. Quentin. His company commander was severely wounded soon after the jump off, and Lieut. Maxwell at once took charge of the company. When the enemy wire was reached, they were met by a hail of machine-gun fire and suffered considerable casualties, including all other officers of the company. The wire at this point was six belts thick, each belt being 20 to 25 feet wide. Lieut. Maxwell pushed forward single-handed through the wire, and attacked the most dangerous machine-gun. He killed three of the crew and captured the remaining four men in the post together with a machine-gun. His company followed him through the wire and captured the trenches forming their objective. Later, it was noticed that the company on his left was held up in the wire by a very strong force on the left flank of the battalion. He at once organised a party and moved to the left to endeavour to attack the enemy from the rear. Heavy machine-gun fire met them. Lieut. Maxwell again dashed forward single-handed at the foremost machine-gun, and with his revolver shot five of its crew, so silencing the gun. Owing to the work of this party, the left company was then able to work a small force through the wire and eventually to occupy the objective and mop up the trenches. In the fighting prior to the mopping up, an English-speaking prisoner who was captured stated that the remainder of the enemy were willing to surrender. Lieut. Maxwell and two men with this prisoner, walked to a post containing more than 20 Germans, who, instead of surrendering, seized and disarmed them. Lieut. Maxwell waited his chance and then with an automatic pistol, which he had concealed in his box respirator, shot two of the enemy and with the two men escaped. They were pursued by rifle fire, and one man wounded. However, Lieut. Maxwell organised a small party at once, attacked, and captured the post. Throughout the day, this young officer set a most remarkable example of personal bravery, tempered with excellent judgment and aggressive decision. There is no doubt that, had it not been for his personal dash, the operation could not have succeeded as quickly as it did. He handled a most involved situation with very fine leadership.

36. No. 17324 Pte. FRANCIS GEORGE MILES, 1/5th Battalion, The Gloucestershire Regt., T.F. (Coleford, Gloucestershire).

For conspicuous gallantry and splendid initiative in attack. On October 23rd, 1918, during the advance against the Bois l'Evêque, his company was held up by a line of enemy machine-guns in the sunken road near the Moulin J. Jacques. Pte. Miles alone, and on his own initiative, made his way forward for a distance of 150 yards under exceptionally heavy fire, located one machine-gun, and shot the man firing the gun. He then rushed the gun and kicked it over, thereby putting it out of action. He then observed another gun firing from 100 yards further forward. He again advanced alone, shot the machine-gunner, rushed the gun, and captured the team of eight. Finally, he stood up and beckoned on his company, who, following his signals, were enabled to work round the rear of the line, and to capture 16 machine-guns, one officer, and 50 other ranks. The courage, initiative, and entire disregard of personal safety shown by this very gallant private soldier enabled his company to advance at a time when any delay would have seriously jeopardised the whole operation in which it was engaged.

37. No. 823028 Cpl. HARRY GARNETT BEDFORD MINER, 58th Battalion, Canadian Infantry, 2nd Central Ontario Regt.

For valour during the operations against the German lines on August 8th, 1918. Cpl. Miner was with his company in the initial attack on the German outpost line. He received a severe wound in the head and shoulder at the commencement of the operations but refused to withdraw. He then rushed a German machine-gun post single-handed, killed the entire crew, and turned the gun, which he had captured, on the enemy. Afterwards he, with two others, attacked another German machine-gun post and succeeded in putting the gun out of action. He then rushed a German bombing post, which was about twelve strong, single-handed. He bayoneted two of the garrison and put the remainder to flight. At this post he was mortally wounded, by German cylindrical stick bombs. He died of wounds the same day, in the Casualty Clearing Station.

38. No. 1717 Pte. JOHN RYAN, 55th Battalion, Australian Infantry, Australian Imperial Force.

For conspicuous gallantry and devotion to duty, and for saving a very dangerous situation in particularly gallant circumstances during an attack against the Hindenburg defences on September 30th, 1918. In the initial assault on the enemy's positions this soldier went forward with great dash and determination, and was one of the first men of his company to reach the trench which was their objective. Seeing him rush in with his bayonet with such exceptional skill and daring, his comrades were inspired and followed his example. Although the enemy shell and machine-gun fire was extremely heavy, the enemy trench garrison was soon overcome. In the assault the attacking troops were weakened by casualties, and, as they were too few to cover the whole front of attack, a considerable gap was left between the 55th Battalion and the unit on its left flank. The enemy counter-attacked soon after the objective was reached, and a few succeeded in infiltrating through the gap and taking up a position of cover in rear of our men, where they commenced bombing operations. The section of the trench occupied by Pte. Ryan and his comrades was now under fire from front and rear, and for a time it seemed that the enemy was certain to force his way through. The situation was critical and necessitated prompt action by someone in authority. Pte. Ryan found that there were no officers or non-commissioned officers near, they had become casualties in the assault. Appreciating the situation at once, he organised the few men nearest him, and led them out to attack the enemy with bomb and bayonet. Some of his party fell victims to the enemy's bombs, and he finally dashed into the enemy position of cover with only three men. The enemy were three times their number, but by skilful bayonet work, they succeeded in killing the first three Germans on the enemy's flank. Moving along the embankment, Pte. Ryan alone rushed the remainder of the enemy with bombs. While thus engaged he fell wounded, but his dashing bombing assault drove the enemy clear out of our positions. Those who were not killed or wounded by his bombs fell victims to our Lewis gunners as they retired across " No Man's Land." A particularly dangerous situation had been saved by this gallant soldier, whose display of determined bravery and initiative was witnessed by the men of the two attacking battalions, who, inspired and urged by it, fought skilfully and bravely for two days.

39. No. 6594 Sgt. GERALD SEXTON, 13th Battalion, Australian Infantry, Australian Imperial Force.

In the attack near Le Verguier, north-west of St. Quentin, on September 18th, 1918, Sgt. Sexton displayed the most conspicuous bravery and performed deeds which, apart from their gallant nature, were in a great measure responsible for the battalion's success. On the southern edge of the village of Le Verguier the enemy fought very hard, and serious opposition had to be crushed. During the whole period of the advance Sgt. Sexton was to the fore dealing with enemy machine-guns by firing from the hip as he advanced, rushing enemy posts, and performing feats of bravery and endurance which are better appreciated when one realises that all the time he fired his Lewis gun from the hip without faltering, or for a moment taking cover. Immediately the attack began, Sgt. Sexton's Lewis gun section was confronted by an enemy machine-gun. He called out to his section to follow, rushed the machine-gun, and killed the crew. He then called out to the rest of the company to follow, but they had not gone far before they encountered some bombers and riflemen about 70 yards in front of the company. Sexton rushed the trench, firing his gun from the hip, and killed or took prisoner all the members of the post. Continuing, he entered a copse and killed or took prisoner another party of the enemy. The advance continued over the ridge at Le Verguier to where Sexton was met by Lieut. Price, who pointed out a party of the enemy manning a bank and a field gun in action which was causing casualties and holding up a company. There was also a trench mortar in action. Sgt. Sexton did not wait, but firing a few short bursts as he advanced, and calling out to his section to follow, rushed down the bank and killed the gunners on the field gun. Dashing out on to a flat under fire from two hostile machine-guns directed on him, he killed 12 more of the enemy. Paying no heed to the machine-gun fire he returned to the bank and after firing down some dug-outs induced about 30 of the enemy to surrender. Owing to his action the company on the left of the battalion was able to continue the advance, where they had been definitely held up and were suffering from the effects of the field gun. When the advance was continued from the first to the second objective, the company was again held up by two machine-guns on the right and one on the left. In conjunction with a platoon, Sexton engaged the machine-gun on the left, firing all the while from the upright position, a fearless figure which, according to eye-witnesses, inspired everyone. (To have taken cover would have been more prudent, but Sexton realised that prompt action was essential and did not wait to lie down.) Silencing this gun he turned his attention to the two machine-guns on the right and silenced them. He then moved forward into a trench, killing quite a number of the enemy, and advancing along a sap took a few prisoners. Further on he was responsible for a few more small posts. When the final objective was reached he was given a responsible post on the left of his company, whence he engaged a machine-gun which was firing across the company front, and thus enabled his company to dig in. This completed, he went forward down a sunken road and captured several more prisoners.

40. No. 475212 Sgt. ROBERT SPALL, Princess Patricia's Canadian Light Infantry, Eastern Ontario Regt.

On the night of August 12th to 13th, 1918, near Parvillers, during an enemy counter-attack which cut off the whole of his platoon, this non-commissioned officer took a Lewis gun and standing on the parapet fired upon the advancing enemy, inflicting most severe casualties. He then came down the trench directing the men into a sap seventy-five yards from the enemy. Picking up another Lewis gun he again climbed the parapet and with his fire held up the enemy. While holding up the enemy at this position he was killed. This non-commissioned officer deliberately gave his life in order to extricate his platoon from a most difficult situation, and it was owing to his bravery that the platoon was saved.

41. No. 506 Sgt. PERCY CLYDE STATTON, M.M., 40th Battalion, Australian Infantry, Australian Imperial Force.

For most conspicuous gallantry and initiative in action near Proyart on August 12th, 1918. The platoon commanded by Sgt. Statton reached its objective, but the remainder of the battalion was held up by heavy machine-gun fire. He skilfully engaged two machine-gun posts with Lewis gun fire, enabling the remainder of his own battalion to advance. The advance of the battalion on his left had been brought to a standstill by the heavy enemy machine-gun fire, and the first of our assaulting detachments to reach the machine-gun posts were put out of action in taking the first gun. Armed only with a revolver, in broad daylight, Sgt. Statton at once rushed four enemy machine-gun posts in succession, disposing of two of them and killing five of the enemy. The remaining two posts retired and were wiped out by Lewis gun fire. His act had a very inspiring effect on the troops who had been held up ; they cheered him as he returned. By this daring exploit he enabled the attacking troops to gain their objective. Later in the evening, under heavy machine-gun fire he went out again and brought in two badly wounded men. Sgt. Statton set a magnificent example of quick decision and determined gallantry.

42. Lieut. JAMES EDWARD TAIT, M.C., 78th Battalion, Canadian Infantry, Manitoba Regt.

For bravery in the face of the enemy in the " Llandovery Castle " operations in front of Amiens, August 8th to August 12th, 1918. On August 8th, in the first phase of the attack, the advance was checked by a terrific machine-gun fire from Beaucourt Wood. Lieut. Tait rallied his company and led them forward with consummate skill and dash under a hail of bullets. One cleverly concealed machine-gun continued to cause us many casualties. Lieut. Tait, taking a rifle and bayonet from a casualty, dashed forward alone and killed the German gunner single-handed. Inspired by his example his men rushed the wood, which yielded 12 machine-guns and 20 prisoners, besides many slain. His glorious action cleared the way for his battalion to advance. Again, in the second phase of the battle when the enemy counter-attacked our positions in Hallu under intense artillery bombardment, he displayed outstanding courage and leadership and continued to direct and encourage his men after he was hit by a shell, until his death.

43. Lieut. EDGAR THOMAS TOWNER, M.C., 2nd Australian Machine Gun Battalion, Australian Imperial Force.

On September 1st, 1918, in the attack on Mont St. Quentin, near Péronne, this officer was in charge of four Vickers guns operating on a front of 1,500 yards. During the early stages of the advance an enemy machine-gun was causing casualties to our advancing infantry. Locating the gun, Lieut. Towner dashed ahead alone and succeeded in killing the crew with his revolver, capturing the gun, and then, by turning it against the enemy, inflicted heavy casualties on them. Advancing then past a copse from which the enemy were firing, he brought his gun into action, placing his fire behind the enemy and cutting them off. On their attempting to retire before the advancing infantry, and finding they were prevented by this machine-gun fire, the party of 25 Germans surrendered. He then reconnoitred alone over open ground exposed to heavy machine-gun and snipers' fire, and by his energy, foresight, and the promptitude with which he brought fire to bear on further enemy groups, enabled the infantry to reach a sunken road. On moving his guns up to the sunken road, he found himself short of ammunition, so went back across the open under heavy fire and obtained a German gun and brought it and boxes of ammunition into the sunken road. Here he mounted and fired the gun in full view of the enemy, causing them to retire further and enabling infantry on the flank, who were previously held up, to advance. Enemy machine-gunners having direct observation flicked the earth round and under his gun, and played a tattoo along the top of the bank. Though one bullet went into his helmet and inflicted a gaping scalp wound he continued firing. Subsequently he refused to go out to have his wound attended to, as the situation was critical and his place was with his men. Later in the day the infantry were obliged to retire slightly, and one gun crew with the first wave having become casualties, the gun was left behind. Lieut. Towner seeing this dashed back over the open, carried the gun back in spite of terrific fire and brought it into action again. He continued to engage the enemy wherever they appeared, and put an enemy machine-gun out of action. During the following night he insisted on doing his tour of duty along with the other officers, and his coolness and cheerfulness set an example which had a great effect on the men. To steady and calm the men of a small detached outpost he crawled out among the enemy posts to investigate. He remained out about an hour, though enemy machine-guns fired continuously on the sector and the Germans were moving about him. He moved one gun up in support of the infantry post and patrolled the communication saps which ran off this post into the German line during the remainder of the night. Next morning after his guns had assisted in dispersing a large party of the enemy, he was led away utterly exhausted, 30 hours after being wounded. The resourcefulness and courage of this officer undoubtedly saved a very difficult situation and was a very large factor in the success of the attack.

44. Capt. (A/Lt.-Col.) BERNARD WILLIAM VANN, M.C., late 1/8th Battalion, The Sherwood Foresters (Nottinghamshire and Derbyshire Regt.), T.F., attached 1/6th Battalion, The Sherwood Foresters (Nottinghamshire and Derbyshire Regt.), T.F.

For most conspicuous gallantry, devotion to duty, and fine leadership during the attack at Bellenglise and Lehaucourt on September 29th, 1918. This officer showed very great courage and skill in leading his battalion across the Canal du Nord through a very thick fog, and in spite of heavy fire from field and machine-guns. On reaching the high ground above Bellenglise, the whole attack was held up by artillery fire from the front and by very heavy machine-gun and rifle fire from the right flank. Realising that everything depended on the advance going forward with the barrage, Col. Vann rushed up to the firing line and with the greatest gallantry led the whole line forward. By his prompt action and absolute contempt for danger the whole situation was changed, the men were encouraged, and the line swept forward. Before the final assault he completely reorganised the whole line and personally led one company from one flank to the other in face of the heaviest machine-gun fire. Later, by himself, he rushed the team of a field gun firing at point blank range. He shot with his revolver one of the gunners who was on the point of firing and clubbed two others. The success of the day was in no small degree due to splendid gallantry and fine leadership displayed by this officer. Col. Vann was killed near Ramicourt on October 3rd, 1918, when leading his battalion in a further attack. This very gallant officer had been wounded on six previous occasions. He invariably showed the utmost contempt for danger and, by his splendid example, largely inspired his men with his own magnificent spirit. This gallant officer was a clergyman of the Church of England.

45. Major BLAIR ANDERSON WARK, D.S.O., 32nd Battalion, Australian Infantry, Australian Imperial Force.

During the period September 29th to October 1st, 1918, in the operations against the Hindenburg Line at Bellicourt, and the advance through Nauroy, Etricourt, Magny-la-Fosse, and Joncourt, Major Wark, in command of the 32nd Battalion, displayed most conspicuous gallantry, and set a fine example of bravery, energy, coolness, and control under extremely difficult conditions. On September 29th under heavy artillery and machine-gun fire at very close range from all sides and in a dense fog Major Wark, finding that the situation was critical, moved quickly forward alone, and obtained sufficient information regarding the situation in front to be able to lead his command forward. The American troops, which had formed the first waves of the attack, were by this time held up and, having suffered heavy losses, were considerably disorganised, Major Wark quickly organised 200 of them, attached them to his leading companies and pressed forward. By his prompt action in the early stages of the battle he restored the situation and enabled the supporting troops to advance. Still moving fearlessly at the head of his leading companies, and at most times far out in advance attended only by a runner, he cheered on his men, and they swept through the Hindenburg defences towards Nauroy. Pushing quickly through Nauroy and mopping up the southern portion of the village, the process yielding 50 prisoners, the battalion swung towards Etricourt. Still leading his assaulting companies, he observed a battery of 77 mm. guns firing point blank into his rear companies and causing heavy casualties. Calling on a few of his men to follow him, he rushed the battery, capturing the four guns and ten of the crew ; the remainder of the crew fled or were killed. Moving rapidly forward with only two non-commissioned officers, he surprised and captured 50 Germans near Magny-la-Fosse. Quickly seizing this opportunity, he pushed one company forward through the village and made good the position. Having captured his objective for the day, he made personal reconnaissance to see that his flanks were safe and found his command in a very difficult and dangerous position, his left flank being exposed to the extent of 3,000 yards on account of the 31st Battalion not being able to advance. After a strenuous day's fighting he set about the selection and reorganisation of a new position, effected a junction with the British troops on the right and 31st Battalion on the left, and made his line secure. At 6 a.m. on September 30th he again led his command forward to allow of the troops on the right being able to advance. The men were tired and had suffered heavily, but he personally led them, and his presence amongst them inspired them to further efforts. On October 1st, 1918, his battalion was ordered to advance at very short notice. He gave his orders for the attack, and led his troops forward in person. A nest of machine-guns was encountered, causing heavy casualties to his men. Without hesitation and regardless of risk, he dashed forward practically into the muzzles of the guns, and, under exceptionally heavy fire, he silenced them, killing or capturing the entire crews. Joncourt and Mill Ridge were then quickly captured and his line consolidated. His men were practically exhausted after the three days' heavy fighting, but he moved amongst them from post to post, across country swept by heavy and continuous shell and machine-gun fire at point blank range, urged them on to further efforts, and the line was made secure. Throughout he displayed the greatest courage and devotion to duty, coupled with great tact and skill. His work together with the reports based on his own personal observation which he forwarded, were invaluable to the brigade. It is beyond doubt that the success achieved by the brigade during the heavy fighting on September 29th and 30th, and October 1st, was due to this officer's gallantry, determination, skill, and great courage.

46. Temp. Capt. (A/Major) ARNOLD HORACE SANTO WATERS, D.S.O., M.C., 218th Field Company, Royal Engineers.

For most conspicuous gallantry and devotion to duty on November 4th, 1918, near Ors. This officer was in command of the field company whose task it was to throw a bridge across the Oise-Sambre Canal. As soon as the operations began, the enemy swept the canal with artillery and machine-gun fire, the latter being at point blank range, smashing the bridge that was being commenced and inflicting heavy casualties on the building party. Major Waters, hearing that all his officers were killed or wounded, advanced through the heavy enemy artillery barrage, and personally supervised the completion of the bridge. He was working on the cork float in the canal under fire from enemy machine-guns on the opposite bank only 30 yards distant, and the bullets were striking sparks from the wire binding the floats. Timbers that he was actually handling were struck repeatedly and it appeared impossible that he could escape being killed. He completed the bridge himself after all his men had been killed or wounded or had collapsed from gas poisoning. Having finished the task he returned to our side of the canal and led the first party of infantry over the bridge. That the attempt was successful was entirely due to his extraordinary bravery and example.

47. No. 1153 Pte. (L/Cpl.) LAWRENCE CARTHAGE WEATHERS, 43rd Battalion, Australian Infantry, Australian Imperial Force.

On September 2nd, 1918, during operations north of Péronne, L/Cpl. Weathers was one of an advanced bombing party operating well forward of our attacking troops. Just before the attack reached its final objective it was held up by the enemy, who occupied a trench in great numbers. After an hour's continuous fighting L/Cpl. Weathers went forward alone in the face of heavy enemy fire and located a large body of Germans. He immediately attacked them with bombs and killed the senior officer ; then made his way back to our lines, and, securing a further supply of bombs and taking three men with him, he went forward and again attacked under very heavy fire. On reaching the enemy position he jumped up on to the parapet of the trench and threw bombs amongst the Boches. He then signalled for his comrades to come up, and the remainder of the enemy, seeing this, surrendered. When counted, the number of prisoners totalled 180 and three machine-guns. The bravery of this non-commissioned officer cleared a very difficult situation and the fearless way in which he attacked confused the enemy, and resulted in the successful capture of the final objective with a minimum number of casualties to our troops.

48. Lieut. (Temp. Capt.) FERDINAND MAURICE FELIX WEST, M.C., The Royal Munster Fusiliers (S.R.) and The Royal Air Force, 8th Squadron.

For unparalleled pluck and endurance. This officer has flown in France for over five hundred hours. On August 8th, 1918, he had a bad accident in the fog. In spite of this he went out on tank contact patrol on August 9th. He scattered by machine-gun fire enemy infantry, who were surrounding four of our tanks. His machine was riddled, but he brought it down safely in our front line, when he proceeded at once to the tank company commander and reported the situation. On August 10th, 1918, he went far over the enemy lines, and fired from a low altitude at enemy troops in Roye, when he was attacked by seven enemy aircraft. At the outset of the fight one of his legs was severed by an explosive bullet, and fell into the controls, from which he lifted it, and, although wounded in the other leg, he manœuvred his machine so that his observer was able to get several good bursts in to the enemy machines and drive them off, and then by sheer grit and determination he brought his machine over our lines, and safely landed himself and his observer. When he regained consciousness, he insisted on writing his report. The valour displayed by this officer has throughout been a magnificent example to his flight, which he has inspired with his devotion, courage, and power of endurance.

49. No. 3244 Pte. JAMES PARK WOODS, 48th Battalion, Australian Infantry, Australian Imperial Force.

For conspicuous gallantry and initiative during the operations near Le Verguier, north-west of St. Quentin, on September 18th, 1918. Pte. Woods was one of a party of three men sent out to patrol the right flank of the battalion, which was at that time in the air. He discovered an enemy strong point garrisoned by about 25 men with four heavy and two light machine-guns. This strong point, which was at the junction of four fire trenches covering the approaches to Bellenglise, was so situated that it commanded the greater part of our position while, if in our hands, it would give us observation over the whole of the canal defences. Pte. Woods, appreciating the great importance and the necessity for its immediate capture, attacked it at once. He wounded one man with his bayonet, captured another, and drove out the remainder of the garrison. One of the patrol was now wounded, and Pte. Woods, although slightly gassed, defended the post with the help of the remaining man. When the enemy discovered that they were only opposed by two men they attempted to recapture the strong point. At least thirty men took part in this counter-attack, advancing down three of the trenches and over the open. Pte. Woods was thus attacked from both flanks and from the front. He jumped upon the parapet and, although exposed to heavy fire from machine-guns, rifles, and bombs, opened fire on the advancing enemy. By this means he inflicted several casualties, and, by his dogged determination held off the enemy until help arrived, when the attack was repulsed with heavy loss. The capture of the strong point enabled the battalion to gain touch with the troops on its flank. The initiative, bravery, and grasp of the situation displayed by Pte. Woods resulted in the capture of a very important position at comparatively slight cost. He set a splendid example of courage and determination throughout the whole operation.

50. No. 424252 Sgt. RAPHAEL LOUIS ZENGEL, M.M., 5th Battalion, Canadian Infantry, Saskatchewan Regt.

For most conspicuous gallantry and devotion to duty during an attack made on the enemy's positions east of Warvillers on August 9th, 1918. This non-commissioned officer with his platoon was protecting the battalion right flank. He was leading his platoon gallantly forward to the attack, but had not gone far when he realised that a gap had occurred on his flank, and that an enemy machine-gun was firing at close range into the advancing line. He immediately grasped the situation, and, rushing forward about 200 yards ahead of the platoon, tackled the machine-gun emplacement, killing the officer who was directing the fire of this gun, killing the machine-gun operator, and wounding another of the crew, the remainder beating a hurried retreat. By his boldness and quick action, he undoubtedly saved the lives of many of his comrades. Sgt. Zengel's platoon was now in advance of our general line, and came under the fire of one of our own tanks. He immediately went towards the tank, signalling that his party were friends and directed it towards the enemy's strong points. Later, when the battalion was held up by heavy machine-gun fire, he took up a most advantageous position on the crest of a mound, where he could obtain observation of the various enemy machine-gun emplacements and strong-points, and direct destructive fire on the occupants. While he was doing this an enemy shell exploded a short distance away from him, rendering him unconscious for a few minutes. When he recovered, however, he picked up his rifle, and again directed harassing fire on the enemy. This non-commissioned officer showed the highest qualities of leadership, and was responsible for the saving of many of his comrades' lives. His work throughout the attack was excellent, and by his utter disregard for personal safety, and by the confidence he inspired in all ranks, he greatly assisted in bringing the attack to a successful issue.

APPENDIX F

THE FOURTH ARMY ORDERS OF BATTLE FOR AUGUST 8TH, SEPTEMBER 29TH, AND NOVEMBER 4TH, 1918.

Explanation of Abbreviations.

A.A. ...	...	...	Anti-Aircraft.
A.T. Co.	...	...	Army Troops Company.
Aux. ...	...	...	Auxiliary.
E. and M. Co.		...	Electrical and Mechanical Company.
Howr. ...	...	...	Howitzer.
M.T. Co.	...	...	Mechanical Transport Company.
Pdr. ...	...	...	Pounder.
(T) Co....	...	...	Tunnelling Company.

COMPOSITION OF HORSE, FIELD, AND GARRISON ARTILLERY BRIGADES.

[1]*Horse Artillery Brigade, with Cavalry Divisions.*
    3–13 pdr. Batteries (18–13 pdrs.).

Field Artillery Brigade (18 guns and 6 howitzers).
    3–18 pdr. Batteries (18–18 pdrs.).
    1–4·5″ Howr. Battery (6 howrs.).

8″ Howitzer Brigade (24 howitzers).
    3–6″ Howr. Batteries (18 howrs.).
    1–8″ Howr. Battery (6 howrs.).

9·2″ Howitzer Brigade (24 howitzers).
    3–6″ Howr. Batteries (18 howrs.).
    1–9·2″ Howr. Battery (6 howrs.).

Mobile Brigade (12 guns and 12 howitzers).
    2–60 pdr. Batteries (12 guns).
    2–6″ Howr. Batteries (12 howrs.).

Mixed Brigade (12 guns and 24 howitzers).
    2–60 pdr. Batteries (12 guns).
    2–6″ Howr. Batteries (12 howrs.).
    1–8″ Howr. Battery (6 howrs.).
    1–9·2″ Howr. Battery (6 howrs.).

AUGUST 8TH.

A. FOURTH ARMY. Gen. Sir H. S. Rawlinson, Bart., G.C.V.O., K.C.B., K.C.M.G.

M.G.G.S.	Maj.-Gen. A. A. Montgomery, C.B.
D.A. and Q.M.G.	Maj.-Gen. H. C. Holman, C.B., C.M.G., D.S.O.
G.O.C., R.A.	Maj.-Gen. C. E. D. Budworth, C.B., C.M.G., M.V.O.
C.E.	Maj.-Gen. R. U. H. Buckland, C.B., C.M.G.
D.M.S.	Maj.-Gen. Sir M. W. O'Keefe, K.C.M.G., C.B.
D.D.S. and T.	Brig.-Gen. E. C. F. Gillespie, C.B., C.M.G.
Chief Signal Officer	Col. R. G. Earle, D.S.O.
Labour Commandant	Col. T. Ogilvie, C.M.G.
D.D.O.S.	Col. R. S. Hamilton, C.M.G., D.S.O.
D.D. Remounts	Col. J. W. Yardley, C.M.G., D.S.O.
D.D.V.S.	Col. W. J. Tatam, C.M.G.

Army Troops.
    5th Brigade, R.A.F.[2] Brig.-Gen. L. E. O. Charlton, C.M.G., D.S.O.

        15th Corps Wing.[3] Lieut.-Col. J. A. Chamier, D.S.O., O.B.E.
            8 Squadron (A. W. B.) (working with Tank Corps).
            9 Squadron (R.E. 8).

---

[1] Army Brigades, R.H.A. attached to the Fourth Army during the period August 8th to November 11th were composed of 18 pdr. batteries, with the exception of the 16th Brigade which was organised similarly to the R.H.A. Brigades with Cavalry Divisions.

[2] The 9th Brigade R.A.F. from General Headquarters assisted the R.A.F. of the Fourth Army during this operation.

[3] The other four squadrons of the Corps Wing are shown with the Corps they worked with.

22nd Army Wing. Lieut.-Col. T. A. E. Cairnes, D.S.O.
  24, 41, and 84 (S.E. 5), 23 (Dolphin), 80, 201, and 209 (Camel), 48 (Bristol Fighter) Squadrons.
  83 (F.E. 2B), 101 (F.E. 2B), 205 (D.H. 4) Bombing Squadrons.

5th Balloon Wing. Lieut.-Col. W. F. MacNeece, D.S.O.

4th Aircraft Park.   4th Air Ammunition Column.   4th Reserve **Lorry Park.**

Artillery.
  Half 471 Siege Battery, R.G.A. (14″ gun on railway mounting).
  Half 543 Siege Battery, R.G.A. (12″ gun on railway mounting).

A.A. Defence. Lieut.-Col. R. Bruce Hay, D.S.O.
  " F," " G," " P," and " Q " A.A. Batteries.
  50th (Field Searchlight) Co., R.E.
  6, 7, 16, 17, 29, and 30 A.A. Searchlight Sections, R.E.
  No. 6 A.A. Company.

5th Field Survey Battalion. Lieut.-Col. F. B. Legh, M.C.
  13, 14, 15 and 24 Observation Groups.
  " A," " B," " G," " K," and " O " Sound Ranging Sections.

Fourth Army Signal Company.
  43, 45, 48, and 53 (Motor) Airline Sections.
  " BL " and " BR " Cable Sections.
  No. 4 Telegraph Construction Co., R.E.
  No. 4 Signal Construction Co., R.E.

213 A.T. Co., R.E.
254 (T.) Co., R.E.
353 E. and M. Co.
No. 3 Water Boring Section.
No. 6 Pontoon Park.
4th Army Troops M.T. Co.

B. CAVALRY CORPS. Lieut.-Gen. Sir C. T. McM. Kavanagh, K.C.B., C.V.O., D.S.O.
  B.G.G.S...   ..   ..   Brig.-Gen. A. F. Home, C.M.G., D.S.O.
  D.A. and Q.M.G.   ..   Brig.-Gen. J. C. G. Longmore, C.M.G., D.S.O.
  G.O.C., R.A.   ..   ..   Brig.-Gen. H. S. Seligman, D.S.O.
  C.R.E.   ..   ..   Lieut.-Col. W. H. Evans, D.S.O.

6 Squadron, R.A.F. (R.E. 8).

3rd Tank Brigade. Brig.-Gen. J. Hardress-Lloyd, D.S.O.
  3rd Tank Bn. ⎱ Whippets.
  6th Tank Bn. ⎰

Corps Signal Troops ⎰ Cavalry Corps Signal Squadron.
                      ⎱ Cavalry Corps Wireless Squadron.
                        " AD " and " GG " Cable Sections.
Cavalry Corps Bridging Park, R.E.
Cavalry Corps Troops M.T. Co.

1st Cavalry Division. Maj.-Gen. R. L. Mullins, C.B.
  G.S.O. 1 ..   ..   ..   Lieut.-Col. R. E. Cecil, D.S.O.
  A.A. and Q.M.G.   ..   Lieut.-Col. J. Blakiston-Houston, D.S.O.

1st Cavalry Brigade.	*2nd Cavalry Brigade.*
(Brig.-Gen. H. S. Sewell, D.S.O.)	(Brig.-Gen. A. Lawson, C.M.G.)
2nd Dragoon Guards.	4th Dragoon Guards.
5th Dragoon Guards.	9th Lancers.
11th Hussars.	18th Hussars.
" I " Battery, R.H.A.	" H " Battery, R.H.A.
(6–13 pdr. guns).	(6–13 pdr. guns).
1st Cavalry Machine Gun Squadron.	2nd Cavalry Machine Gun Squadron.
1st Signal Troop.	2nd Signal Troop.

9th Cavalry Brigade.
(Brig.-Gen. D'A. Legard, D.S.O.)
8th Hussars.
15th Hussars.
19th Hussars.
" Y " Battery, R.H.A.
   (6–13 pdr. guns).
9th Cavalry Machine Gun Squadron.
9th Signal Troop.

7th Brigade, R.H.A., and Ammunition Column.
1st Field Squadron, R.E.
1st Signal Squadron.
H.Q. 1st Cavalry Divisional R.A.S.C.
1st Cavalry Divisional M.T. Co.
1st Cavalry Divisional Aux. (Horse) Co.
1st, 3rd, and 9th Cavalry Field Ambulances.
1st, 10th, and 39th Mobile Veterinary Sections.

2nd Cavalry Division.   Maj.-Gen. T. T. Pitman, C.B., C.M.G.
    G.S.O. 1 ..   ..   .. Lieut.-Col. M. Graham, D.S.O.
    A.A. and Q.M.G.   .. Lieut.-Col. Hon. G. V. A. Monckton-Arundell, D.S.O.

3rd Cavalry Brigade.	*4th Cavalry Brigade.*
(Brig.-Gen. J. A. Bell-Smyth, C.M.G.)	(Brig.-Gen. C. H. Rankin, C.M.G., D.S.O.)
4th Hussars.	6th Dragoon Guards.
5th Lancers.	3rd Hussars.
16th Lancers.	1/1st Oxfordshire Hussars.
" D " Battery, R.H.A.	" J " Battery, R.H.A.
(6–13 pdr. guns).	(6–13 pdr. guns).
3rd Cavalry Machine Gun Squadron.	4th Cavalry Machine Gun Squadron.
3rd Signal Troop.	4th Signal Troop.

5th Cavalry Brigade.
(Brig.-Gen. N. W. Haig, C.M.G.)
2nd Dragoons (Royal Scots Greys).
12th Lancers.
20th Hussars.
" E " Battery, R.H.A.
   (6–13 pdr. guns).
5th Cavalry Machine Gun Squadron.
5th Signal Troop.

3rd Brigade, R.H.A., and Ammunition Column.
2nd Field Squadron, R.E.
2nd Signal Squadron.
H.Q. 2nd Cavalry Divisional R.A.S.C.
2nd Cavalry Divisional M.T. Co.
2nd Cavalry Divisional Aux. (Horse) Co.
2nd, 4th, and 5th Cavalry Field Ambulances.
7th, 8th, and 9th Mobile Veterinary Sections.

3rd Cavalry Division.   Maj.-Gen. A. E. W. Harman, D.S.O.
    G.S.O. 1 ..   ..   .. Lieut.-Col. G. P. L. Cosens, D.S.O.
    A.A. and Q.M.G.   .. Lieut.-Col. T. W. Pragnell, D.S.O.

6th Cavalry Brigade.	*7th Cavalry Brigade.*
(Brig.-Gen. E. Paterson, D.S.O.)	(Brig.-Gen. A. Burt, D.S.O.)
3rd Dragoon Guards.	7th Dragoon Guards.
1st Royal Dragoons.	6th (Inniskilling) Dragoons.
10th Hussars.	17th Lancers.
" C " Battery, R.H.A.	" K " Battery, R.H.A.
(6–13 pdr. guns).	(6–13 pdr. guns).
6th Cavalry Machine Gun Squadron.	7th Cavalry Machine Gun Squadron.
6th Signal Troop.	7th Signal Troop.

Canadian Cavalry Brigade.
(Brig.-Gen. R. W. Paterson, D.S.O.)
Royal Canadian Dragoons.
Lord Strathcona's Horse.
Fort Garry Horse.
Royal Canadian H.A. Brigade,
    (two batteries of 4–13 pdr. guns).
Canadian Cavalry Machine Gun Squadron.
Canadian Signal Troop.

4th Brigade, R.H.A., and Ammunition Column.
3rd Field Squadron, R.E.
3rd Signal Squadron.
H.Q. 3rd Cavalry Divisional R.A.S.C.
3rd Cavalry Divisional M.T. Co.
3rd Cavalry Divisional Aux. (Horse) Co.
6th, 7th, and Canadian Cavalry Field Ambulances.
13th, 14th, and " A " Canadian Mobile Veterinary Sections.

C. III Corps. Lieut.-Gen. Sir R. H. K. Butler, K.C.M.G., C.B. (From August 11th to
    September 11th, Lieut.-Gen. Sir A. J. Godley, K.C.B., K.C.M.G.)

B.G.G.S...	Brig.-Gen. C. G. Fuller, D.S.O.
D.A. and Q.M.G. ..	Brig.-Gen. J. F. Doyle, C.M.G., D.S.O.
G.O.C., R.A.	Brig.-Gen. C. M. Ross-Johnson, C.B., C.M.G., D.S.O.
C.E.	Brig.-Gen. A. Rolland, D.S.O.

Corps Cavalry and Cyclists.
    1/1st Northumberland Hussars
    XXII Corps Cavalry Regt. } Temporarily attached.
    XXII Corps Cyclist Bn.

Corps Heavy Artillery. Brig.-Gen. A. E. J. Perkins, C.B.
    47, 71, and 89 (8″ Howr.) Brigades, R.G.A.
    23 (9·2″ Howr.) Brigade, R.G.A.
    27, 51, and 76 (Mixed) Brigades, R.G.A.
    85 (Mobile) Brigade, R.G.A.
    189, 312, and 449 (6″ gun) Siege Batteries, R.G.A.
    243 (12″ Howr.) Siege Battery, R.G.A.
    V/III Heavy Trench Mortar Battery, R.G.A.

35 Squadron, R.A.F. (A.W.B.)
10th Tank Bn. (Mark V).
Corps Signal Troops { " C " Corps Signal Co.
    Nos. 6 and 76 (Motor) Airline Sections.
    " LZ," " WE " and " SS " Cable Sections.
No. 2 (2nd Life Guards) Bn., Guards Machine Gun Regt.
No. 1 Siege Co., R.A., R.E.
216 and 574 A.T. Cos., R.E.
180, 253, and 256 (T.) Cos., R.E.
III Corps Troops M.T. Co.

12th (Eastern) Division. Maj.-Gen. H. W. Higginson, C.B., D.S.O.
    G.S.O. 1 .. .. .. Lieut.-Col. J. D. Belgrave, D.S.O.
    A.A. and Q.M.G. .. Lieut.-Col. F. R. Burnside, D.S.O.

35th Infantry Brigade.	*36th Infantry Brigade.*
(Brig.-Gen. B. Vincent, C.M.G.)	(Brig.-Gen. C. S. Owen, C.M.G., D.S.O.)
7th Bn., Norfolk Regt.	9th Bn., Royal Fusiliers.
9th Bn., Essex Regt.	7th Bn., Royal Sussex Regt.
1/1st Bn., Cambridgeshire Regt.	5th Bn., Royal Berkshire Regt.
———	———
35th Trench Mortar Battery.	36th Trench Mortar Battery.

37th Infantry Brigade.
(Brig.-Gen. A. B. Ingledon-Webber, C.M.G., D.S.O.)
6th Bn., The Queen's (Royal West Surrey Regt.).
6th Bn., The Buffs (East Kent Regt.).
6th Bn., The Queen's Own (Royal West Kent Regt.).

37th Trench Mortar Battery.

Divisional Artillery. Brig.-Gen. H. M. Thomas, C.M.G., D.S.O.
62nd and 63rd Brigades, R.F.A.
X/12 and Y/12 Trench Mortar Batteries, R.A.

12th Divisional Ammunition Column.

Divisional Engineers. Lieut.-Col. A. T. Shakespear, D.S.O., M.C.
69th, 70th, and 87th Field Cos., R.E.
12th Divisional Signal Co.
5th Bn., Northamptonshire Regt. (Pioneers).
No. 12 Bn., Machine Gun Corps.
12th Divisional Train.
12th Divisional M.T. Co.
36th, 37th, and 38th Field Ambulances.
23rd Mobile Veterinary Section.

Attached Troops.
25th Divisional Artillery. Brig.-Gen. K. J. Kincaid-Smith, C.M.G., D.S.O.
169th and 232nd Army Brigades, R.F.A.

18th (Eastern) Division. Maj.-Gen. R. P. Lee, C.B.
G.S.O. 1 .. .. .. Lieut.-Col. G. Blewitt, D.S.O., M.C.
A.A. & Q.M.G. .. .. Lieut.-Col. R. H. L. Cutbill, D.S.O.

53rd Infantry Brigade.
(Brig.-Gen. M. G. H. Barker, D.S.O.)

10th Bn., Essex Regt.
8th Bn., Royal Berkshire Regt.
7th Bn., The Queen's Own (Royal West Kent Regt.).

53rd Trench Mortar Battery.

54th Infantry Brigade.
(Brig.-Gen. L. W. de V. Sadlier-Jackson, C.M.G., D.S.O. (From August 24th, 1918, Brig.-Gen. J. A. Tyler, C.M.G.)

11th Bn., Royal Fusiliers.
2nd Bn., Bedfordshire Regt.
6th Bn., Northamptonshire Regt.

54th Trench Mortar Battery.

55th Infantry Brigade.
(Brig.-Gen. E. A. Wood, D.S.O.)
7th Bn., The Queen's (Royal West Surrey Regt.).
7th Bn., The Buffs (East Kent Regt.).
8th Bn., East Surrey Regt.

55th Trench Mortar Battery.

Divisional Artillery. Lieut.-Col. T. O. Seagram (acting).
82nd and 83rd Brigades, R.F.A.
X/18 and Y/18 Trench Mortar Batteries, R.A.

18th Divisional Ammunition Column.

Divisional Engineers. Lieut.-Col. C. B. O. Symons, D.S.O.
79th, 80th and 82nd Field Cos., R.E.
18th Divisional Signal Co.
8th Bn., Royal Sussex Regt. (Pioneers).
No. 18 Bn., Machine Gun Corps.
18th Divisional Train.
18th Divisional M.T. Co.
54th, 55th, and 56th Field Ambulances.
30th Mobile Veterinary Section.

R R

Attached Troops.
　5th Army Brigade, R.H.A.
　18th, 86th, and 175th Army Brigades, R.F.A.

47th (London) Division (T.).　Maj.-Gen. Sir G. F. Gorringe, K.C.B., K.C.M.G., D.S.O.
　G.S.O. 1 ..　　..　　.. Lieut.-Col. B. L. Montgomery, D.S.O.
　A.A. and Q.M.G.　　.. Lieut.-Col. S. H. J. Thunder, D.S.O., M.C.

140th Infantry Brigade.	*141st Infantry Brigade.*
(Brig.-Gen. H. B. P. L. Kennedy, C.M.G., D.S.O.)	(Brig.-Gen. W. F. Mildren, C.M.G., D.S.O.)
1/15th Bn., London Regt.	1/18th Bn., London Regt.
1/17th Bn., London Regt.	1/19th Bn., London Regt.
1/21st Bn., London Regt.	1/20th Bn., London Regt.
140th Trench Mortar Battery.	141st Trench Mortar Battery.

142nd Infantry Brigade.
(Brig.-Gen. R. McDouall, C.M.G., D.S.O.)
1/22nd Bn., London Regt.
1/23rd Bn., London Regt.
1/24th Bn., London Regt.

142nd Trench Mortar Battery.

Divisional Artillery.　Brig.-Gen. E. N. Whitley, C.M.G., D.S.O.
　235th and 236th Brigades, R.F.A.
　X/47 and Y/47 Trench Mortar Batteries, R.A.

47th Divisional Ammunition Column.

Divisional Engineers.　Lieut.-Col. A. B. Carey, C.M.G., D.S.O.
　517th, 518th, and 519th Field Cos., R.E.

47th Divisional Signal Co.
1/4th Bn., Royal Welsh Fusiliers (Pioneers).
No. 47 Bn., Machine Gun Corps.
47th Divisional Train.
47th Divisional M.T. Co.
1/4th, 1/5th, and 1/6th (London) Field Ambulances.
1/2nd (London) Mobile Veterinary Section.

58th (London) Division (T.).　Maj.-Gen. F. W. Ramsay, C.M.G., D.S.O.
　G.S.O. 1 ..　　..　　.. Lieut.-Col. C. M. Davies, D.S.O.
　A.A. and Q.M.G.　　.. Lieut.-Col. A. G. P. McNalty, C.M.G., D.S.O.

173rd Infantry Brigade.	*174th Infantry Brigade.*
(Brig.-Gen. C. E. Corkran, C.M.G.)	(Brig.-Gen. A. Maxwell, D.S.O.)
2/2nd Bn., London Regt.	6th Bn., London Regt.
3rd Bn., London Regt.	7th Bn., London Regt.
2/4th Bn., London Regt.	8th Bn., London Regt.
173rd Trench Mortar Battery.	174th Trench Mortar Battery.

175th Infantry Brigade.
(Brig.-Gen. H. W. Cobham, D.S.O.)
9th Bn., London Regt.
2/10th Bn., London Regt.
12th Bn., London Regt.

175th Trench Mortar Battery.

Divisional Artillery.　Brig.-Gen. J. McC. Maxwell, C.B., D.S.O.
　290th and 291st Brigades, R.F.A.
　X/58 and Y/58 Trench Mortar Batteries, R.A.

58th Divisional Ammunition Column.

Divisional Engineers. Lieut.-Col. A. J. Savage.
503rd, 504th, and 511th Field Cos., R.E.

2/1st Wessex Signal Co.
4th Bn. Suffolk Regt. (Pioneers).
No. 58 Bn., Machine Gun Corps.
58th Divisional Train.
58th Divisional M.T. Co.
2/1st, 2/2nd, and 2/3rd Home Counties Field Ambulances.
58th (London) Mobile Veterinary Section.

Attached Troops.
50th Divisional Artillery. Brig.-Gen. W. Stirling, D.S.O.
108th Army Brigade, R.F.A.

[1] *74th (Yeomanry) Division.* Maj.-Gen. E. S. Girdwood, C.B.
G.S.O. 1 .. .. .. Lieut.-Col. A. C. Temperley, D.S.O.
A.A. and Q.M.G. .. Lieut.-Col. R. B. Cousens, D.S.O.

229th Infantry Brigade.	*230th Infantry Brigade.*
(Brig.-Gen. R. Hoare, D.S.O. From September 15th, 1918, Brig.-Gen. F. C. Thackeray, D.S.O., M.C.)	(Brig.-Gen. A. A. Kennedy, C.M.G.)
16th (Royal 1st and Royal North Devon Yeo.) Bn., Devon Regt.	10th (Royal East and West Kent Yeo.) Bn., The Buffs.
12th (West Somerset Yeo.) Bn., Somerset L.I.	15th (Suffolk Yeo.) Bn., Suffolk Regt.
14th (Fife and Forfar Yeo.) Bn., Royal Highlanders.	16th (Sussex Yeo.) Bn., Royal Sussex Regt.

229th Trench Mortar Battery.　　　230th Trench Mortar Battery.

231st Infantry Brigade.
(Brig.-Gen. C. E. Heathcote, C.M.G., D.S.O.)
25th (Montgomery and Welsh Horse Yeo.) Bn., Royal Welsh Fusiliers.
24th (Pembroke and Glamorganshire Yeo.) Bn., Welsh Regt.
10th (Shropshire and Cheshire Yeo.) Bn., King's Shropshire Light Infantry.

231st Trench Mortar Battery.

Divisional Artillery. Brig.-Gen. L. J. Hext, C.M.G.
44th and 117th Brigades, R.F.A.
X/74 and Y/74 Trench Mortar Batteries, R.A.

74th Divisional Ammunition Column.

Divisional Engineers. Lieut.-Col. W. R. Izat, D.S.O.
5th Field Co., Royal Anglesey, R.E.
5th Field Co., Royal Monmouth, R.E.
439th Field Co., R.E.

74th Divisional Signal Co.
1/12 Bn. Loyal North Lancashire Regt. (Pioneers).
No. 74 Bn., Machine Gun Corps.
74th Divisional Train.
74th Divisional M.T. Co.
229th, 230th, and 231st Field Ambulances.
59th Mobile Veterinary Section.

33rd (Illinois) American Division. Maj.-Gen. George Bell, Jnr.
Chief of Staff .. .. Col. W. K. Naylor.

---

[1] The 74th Division did not join the Fourth Army until September 1st, and remained with it until September 26th, when it was transferred to another Army.

65th Infantry Brigade.
(Brig.-Gen. E. L. King.)
129th (3rd Illinois) Regt. (1st, 2nd, and 3rd Bns.).
130th (4th Illinois) Regt. (1st, 2nd, and 3rd Bns.).

123rd (5th Illinois) Machine Gun Bn.

66th Infantry Brigade.
(Brig.-Gen. P. A. Wolf.)
131st (1st Illinois) Regt. (1st, 2nd, and 3rd Bns.).
132nd (2nd Illinois) Regt. (1st, 2nd, and 3rd Bns.).

124th (5th Illinois) Machine Gun Bn.

108th Engineer Regt.
108th Field Signal Bn.
122nd Machine Gun Bn.
108th Train Headquarters.
108th Sanitary Train.
129th and 130th Field Ambulance Cos.

D. CANADIAN CORPS. Lieut.-Gen. Sir. A. W. Currie, K.C.B., K.C.M.G.
     B.G.G.S...   ..   ..   Brig.-Gen. N. W. Webber, C.M.G., D.S.O.
     D.A. and Q.M.G.   ..   Brig.-Gen. G. J. Farmar, C.B., C.M.G.
     G.O.C., R.A.   ..   Maj.-Gen. E. W. B. Morrison, C.B., C.M.G., D.S.O.
     G.O.C., C.E.   ..   Maj.-Gen. W. B. Lindsay, C.M.G., D.S.O.

Corps Cavalry and Cyclists.
Canadian Light Horse.
Royal North-West Mounted Police.
Canadian Cyclist Bn.

Corps Heavy Artillery. Brig.-Gen. R. H. Massie, C.M.G.
12 and 40 (8″ Howr.) Brigades, R.G.A.
98 (9·2″ Howr.) Brigade, R.G.A.
79 and 83 (Mixed) Brigades, R.G.A.
29, 41, and 86 (Mobile) Brigades, R.G.A.
3rd Canadian Brigade, R.G.A.
192, 434, and 525 (6″ gun) Siege Batteries, R.G.A.
493 (12″ Howr.) Siege Battery, R.G.A.

5 Squadron, R.A.F. (R.E.8).

4th Tank Brigade. Brig.-Gen. E. B. Hankey, D.S.O.
     1st Tank Bn. (Mark V star.)
     4th Tank Bn. ⎫
     5th Tank Bn. ⎬ Mark V.
     14th Tank Bn. ⎭

1st and 2nd Canadian Motor Machine Gun Brigades.

Corps Signal Troops ⎰ Canadian Corps Signal Co.
                   ⎰ Nos. 1 and 2 Canadian (Motor) Airline Sections.
                   ⎱ " CE," " CF," " CG," and " CH " Cable Sections.

No. 4 Siege Co., Royal Anglesey, R.E.
144 A.T. Co., R.E.
182 (T.) Co., R.E.
1st Tramways Co., Canadian Engineers.
1st Canadian Infantry Works Bn.
13th Bn., Canadian Railway Troops.
No. 8 Pontoon Park.
A.A. Searchlight Co., Canadian Engineers.
Canadian Corps Troops M.T. Co.
Canadian Motor Machine Gun M.T. Co.
Canadian Engineers M.T. Co.

1st Canadian Division. Maj.-Gen. A. C. Macdonell, C.B., C.M.G., D.S.O.
     G.S.O. 1 ..   ..   ..   Lieut.-Col. J. L. R. Parson, D.S.O.
     A.A. and Q.M.G.   ..   Lieut.-Col. J. S. Brown, C.M.G., D.S.O.

1st Canadian Infantry Brigade.
(Brig.-Gen. W. A. Griesbach, C.M.G., D.S.O.)
1st Canadian Bn. (Western Ontario Regt.).
2nd Canadian Bn. (Eastern Ontario Regt.).
3rd Canadian Bn. (Toronto Regt.).
4th Canadian Bn. (1st Central Ontario Regt.).

1st Canadian Trench Mortar Battery.

2nd Canadian Infantry Brigade.
(Brig.-Gen. F. O. W. Loomis, C.B., C.M.G., D.S.O.)
5th Canadian Bn. (Saskatchewan Regt.).
7th Canadian Bn. (British Columbia Regt.).
8th Canadian Bn. (Manitoba Regt.).
10th Canadian Bn. (Alberta Regt.).

2nd Canadian Trench Mortar Battery.

3rd Canadian Infantry Brigade.
(Brig.-Gen. G. S. Tuxford, C.B., C.M.G.)
13th Canadian Bn. (Royal Highlanders of Canada) (Quebec Regt.).
14th Canadian Bn. (Royal Montreal Regt.) (Quebec Regt.).
15th Canadian Bn. (48th Highlanders of Canada) (1st Central Ontario Regt.).
16th Canadian Bn. (The Canadian Scottish) (Eastern Ontario Regt.).

3rd Canadian Trench Mortar Battery.

Divisional Artillery. Brig.-Gen. H. C. Thacker, C.M.G., D.S.O.
  1st and 2nd Brigades, C.F.A.
  V/1C Heavy Trench Mortar Battery.
  X/1C and Y/1C Trench Mortar Batteries.

1st Canadian Divisional Ammunition Column.

1st Brigade, Canadian Engineers. Col. A. MacPhail, D.S.O.
  1st, 2nd, and 3rd Bns., Canadian Engineers.
  1st Pontoon Bridging Transport Unit, Canadian Engineers.

1st Canadian Divisional Signal Co.
No. 1 Bn., Canadian Machine Gun Corps.
1st Canadian Divisional Train.
1st Canadian Divisional M.T. Co.
1st, 2nd, and 3rd Canadian Field Ambulances.
1st Canadian Mobile Veterinary Section.

Attached Troops.
  5th Canadian Divisional Artillery. Brig.-Gen. W. Dodds, C.M.G., D.S.O.
  77th Army Brigade, R.F.A.

2nd Canadian Division. Maj.-Gen. Sir H. E. Burstall, K.C.B., C.M.G., A.D.C.
  G.S.O. 1 ..   ..   .. Lieut.-Col. W. R. Bertram, D.S.O.
  A.A. and Q.M.G.   .. Lieut.-Col. P. J. Montague, D.S.O., M.C.

4th Canadian Infantry Brigade.
(Brig.-Gen. R. Rennie, C.B., C.M.G., M.V.O., D.S.O.)
18th Canadian Bn. (Western Ontario Regt.).
19th Canadian Bn. (1st Central Ontario Regt.).
20th Canadian Bn. (1st Central Ontario Regt.).
21st Canadian Bn. (Eastern Ontario Regt.).

4th Canadian Trench Mortar Battery.

5th Canadian Infantry Brigade.
(Brig.-Gen. T. L. Tremblay, C.M.G., D.S.O.)
22nd Canadian Bn. (Canadian Français). (Quebec Regt.).
24th Canadian Bn. (Victoria Rifles of Canada) (Quebec Regt.).
25th Canadian Bn. (Nova Scotia Rifles) (Nova Scotia Regt.).
26th Canadian Bn. (New Brunswick Regt.).

5th Canadian Trench Mortar Battery.

6th Canadian Infantry Brigade.
(Brig.-Gen. A. Ross, D.S.O.)
27th Canadian Bn. (Manitoba Regt.).
28th Canadian Bn. (Saskatchewan Regt.).
29th Canadian Bn. (British Columbia Regt.).
31st Canadian Bn. (Alberta Regt.).

6th Canadian Trench Mortar Battery.

Divisional Artillery. Brig.-Gen. H. A. Panet, D.S.O.
5th and 6th Brigades, C.F.A.
V/2C Heavy Trench Mortar.
X/2C and Y/2C Trench Mortar Batteries.

2nd Canadian Divisional Ammunition Column.
   2nd Brigade, Canadian Engineers. Col. S. H. Osler, D.S.O.
   4th, 5th, and 6th Bns., Canadian Engineers.
   2nd Pontoon Bridging Transport Unit, Canadian Engineers.

2nd Canadian Divisional Signal Co.
No. 1 Bn. Canadian Machine Gun Corps.
2nd Canadian Divisional Train.
2nd Canadian Divisional M.T. Co.
4th, 5th, and 6th Canadian Field Ambulances.
2nd Canadian Mobile Veterinary Section.

Attached Troops.
   150th Army Brigade, R.F.A.

3rd Canadian Division. Maj.-Gen. L. J. Lipsett, C.M.G., D.S.O.
   G.S.O. 1 ..   ..   .. Lieut.-Col. Hon. C. M. Hore-Ruthven, C.M.G., D.S.O.
   A.A. and Q.M.G.   .. Lieut.-Col. H. E. Boak, D.S.O.

7th Canadian Infantry Brigade.
(Brig.-Gen. H. M. Dyer, C.M.G., D.S.O.)
Princess Patricia's Canadian Light Infantry (Eastern Ontario Regt.).
The Royal Canadian Regt. (Nova Scotia Regt.).
42nd Canadian Bn. (Royal Highlanders of Canada).
49th Canadian Bn. (Edmonton Regt.) (Alberta Regt.).

7th Canadian Trench Mortar Battery.

8th Canadian Infantry Brigade.
(Brig.-Gen. D. C. Draper, D.S.O.)
1st Canadian Mounted Rifle Bn. (Saskatchewan Regt.).
2nd Canadian Mounted Rifle Bn. (1st Central Ontario Regt.).
4th Canadian Mounted Rifle Bn. (1st Central Ontario Regt.).
5th Canadian Mounted Rifle Bn. (Quebec Regt.).

8th Canadian Trench Mortar Battery.

9th Canadian Infantry Brigade.
(Brig.-Gen. D. M. Ormond, D.S.O.)
43rd Canadian Bn. (Manitoba Regt.).
52nd Canadian Bn. (Manitoba Regt.).
58th Canadian Bn. (2nd Central Ontario Regt.)
116th Canadian Bn. (2nd Central Ontario Regt.).

9th Canadian Trench Mortar Battery.

Divisional Artillery. Brig.-Gen. J. S. Stewart, D.S.O.
9th and 10th Brigades, C.F.A.
V/3C Heavy Trench Mortar Battery.
X/3C and Y/3C Trench Mortar Batteries.

3rd Canadian Divisional Ammunition Column.

3rd Brigade, Canadian Engineers. Col. H. F. Hertzberg, D.S.O., M.C.
7th, 8th, and 9th Bns., Canadian Engineers.
3rd Pontoon Bridging Transport Unit, Canadian Engineers.

3rd Canadian Divisional Signal Co.
No. 3 Bn., Canadian Machine Gun Corps.
3rd Canadian Divisional Train.
3rd Canadian Divisional M.T. Co.
8th, 9th, and 10th Canadian Field Ambulances.
3rd Canadian Mobile Veterinary Section.

Attached Troops.
104th and 179th Army Brigades, R.F.A.
8th Army Brigade, C.F.A.

4th Canadian Division.   Maj.-Gen. Sir D. Watson, K.C.B., C.M.G.
G.S.O. 1 ..   ..   .. Lieut.-Col. E. de B. Panet, C.M.G., D.S.O.
A.A. and Q.M.G.   .. Lieut.-Col. K. R. Marshall, D.S.O.

10th Canadian Infantry Brigade.	*11th Canadian Infantry Brigade.*
(Brig.-Gen. R. J. F. Hayter, C.M.G., D.S.O.)	(Brig.-Gen. V. W. Odlum, C.B., C.M.G., D.S.O.)
44th Canadian Bn. (New Brunswick Regt.).	54th Canadian Bn. (2nd Central Ontario Regt.).
46th South Saskatchewan Bn. (Saskatchewan Regt.).	75th Canadian Bn. (1st Central Ontario Regt.).
47th Canadian Bn. (Western Ontario Regt.).	87th Canadian Bn. (Canadian Grenadier Guards) (Quebec Regt.).
50th Canadian Bn. (Calgary Regt.) (Alberta Regt.).	102nd Canadian Bn.(2nd Central Ontario Regt.).
10th Canadian Trench Mortar Battery.	11th Canadian Trench Mortar Battery.

12th Canadian Infantry Brigade.
(Brig.-Gen. J. H. McBrien, C.M.G., D.S.O.)
38th Canadian Bn. (Ottawa Regt.) (Eastern Ontario Regt.)
72nd Canadian Bn. (Seaforth Highlanders of Canada) (British Columbia Regt.).
78th Canadian Bn. (Nova Scotia Highlanders) (Nova Scotia Regt.).
85th Canadian Bn. (Winnipeg Grenadiers) (Manitoba Regt.).

12th Canadian Trench Mortar Battery.

Divisional Artillery.   Brig.-Gen. W. B. M. King, C.M.G., D.S.O.
3rd and 4th Brigades, C.F.A.
V/4C Heavy Trench Mortar Battery.
X/4C and Y/4C Trench Mortar Batteries.

4th Canadian Divisional Ammunition Column.

4th Brigade, Canadian Engineers.   Col. H. T. Hughes, C.M.G.
10th, 11th, and 12th Bns., Canadian Engineers.
4th Pontoon Bridging Transport Unit, Canadian Engineers.

4th Canadian Divisional Signal Co.
No. 4 Bn., Canadian Machine Gun Corps.
4th Canadian Divisional Train.
4th Canadian Divisional M.T. Co.
11th, 12th, and 13th Canadian Field Ambulances.
4th Canadian Mobile Veterinary Section.

32nd Division.   Maj.-Gen. T. S. Lambert, C.B., C.M.G.
G.S.O. 1 ..   ..   .. Lieut.-Col. A. E. McNamara, C.M.G., D.S.O.
A.A. and Q.M.G.   .. Lieut.-Col. J. P. B. Robinson, D.S.O.

14th Infantry Brigade.	*96th Infantry Brigade.*
(Brig.-Gen. L. P. Evans, V.C., D.S.O.)	(Brig.-Gen. A. C. Girdwood, D.S.O.)
5/6th Bn., Royal Scots (T.).	15th Bn., Lancashire Fusiliers.
1st Bn., Dorset Regt.	16th Bn., Lancashire Fusiliers.
15th Bn., Highland Light Infantry.	2nd Bn., Manchester Regt.
14th Trench Mortar Battery.	96th Trench Mortar Battery.

97th Infantry Brigade.
(Brig.-Gen. J. R. Minshull-Ford, D.S.O., M.C.)
1/5th Bn., Border Regt.
2nd Bn., The King's Own Yorkshire Light Infantry.
10th Bn., Argyll and Sutherland Highlanders.

97th Trench Mortar Battery.

Divisional Artillery. Brig.-Gen. J. A. Tyler, C.M.G.
161st and 168th Brigades, R.F.A.
X/32 and Y/32 Trench Mortar Batteries, R.A.

32nd Divisional Ammunition Column.

Divisional Engineers. Lieut.-Col. G. C. Pollard, C.M.G., D.S.O.
206th, 218th, and 219th Field Cos., R.E.

32nd Divisional Signal Co.
16th Bn., Highland Light Infantry (Pioneers).
No. 32 Bn., Machine Gun Corps.
32nd Divisional Train.
32nd Divisional M.T. Co.
90th, 91st, and 92nd Field Ambulances.
42nd Mobile Veterinary Section.

E. AUSTRALIAN CORPS. Lieut.-Gen. Sir J. Monash, K.C.B.
B.G., G.S.	.. ..	Brig.-Gen. T. A. Blamey, C.M.G., D.S.O.
D.A. and Q.M.G.	..	Brig.-Gen. R. A. Carruthers, C.B., C.M.G.
G.O.C., R.A.	.. ..	Brig.-Gen. W. A. Coxen, C.M.G., D.S.O.
C.E.	.. .. ..	Brig.-Gen. C. H. Foott, C.M.G.

Corps Cavalry and Cyclists.
13th Regt., Australian Light Horse.
Australian Cyclist Bn.

Corps Heavy Artillery. Brig.-Gen. L. D. Fraser, C.B., C.M.G.
5, 14, and 68 (8″ Howr.) Brigades, R.G.A.
8 and 69 (9·2″ Howr.) Brigades, R.G.A.
77 and 93 (Mixed) Brigades, R.G.A.
9 and 21 (Mobile) Brigades, R.G.A.
73 Army Brigade, R.G.A. (H.Q. only).
222, 499, and 504 (6″ Gun) Siege Batteries, R.G.A.
50 (6′ Gun on Naval Mounting) Siege Battery, R.G.A.
494 (12″ Howr.) Siege Battery, R.G.A.
V/Australian Heavy Trench Mortar Battery, A.F.A.

3rd Squadron, Australian Flying Corps (R.E. 8).

5th Tank Brigade. Brig.-Gen. A. Courage, D.S.O., M.C.
2nd Tank Bn. ⎫
8th Tank Bn. ⎬ Mark V.
13th Tank Bn. ⎭
15th Tank Bn. Mark V star.
17th Armoured Car Bn.

⎧ Australian Corps Signal Co.
Corps Signal Troops ⎨ Nos. 1 and 2 Australian (Motor) Airline Sections.
⎩ Nos. 1 and 2 Australian Cable Sections.

648 Field Co., R.E.
146, 238, and 567 A.T. Cos., R.E.
1st A.T. Co., Australian Engineers.
1st and 2nd (T.) Cos., Australian Engineers.
No. 11 Pontoon Park.
6th Australian (Corps Troops) M.T. Co.

1st *Australian Division.* Maj.-Gen. T. W. Glasgow, C.B., C.M.G., D.S.O.
  G.S.O. 1 ..   ..   ..   Lieut.-Col. A. M. Ross, D.S.O.
  A.A. and Q.M.G.   ..   Lieut.-Col. H. G. Viney, C.M.G., D.S.O.

1st *Australian Infantry Brigade.*	2nd *Australian Infantry Brigade.*
(Brig.-Gen. I. G. Mackay, D.S.O.)	(Brig.-Gen. J. Heane, C.B., C.M.G., D.S.O.)
1st Australian Bn.	5th Australian Bn.
2nd Australian Bn.	6th Australian Bn.
3rd Australian Bn.	7th Australian Bn.
4th Australian Bn.	8th Australian Bn.
1st Australian Trench Mortar Battery.	2nd Australian Trench Mortar Battery.

3rd *Australian Infantry Brigade.*
(Brig.-Gen. H. G. Bennett, C.B., C.M.G.)
9th Australian Bn.
10th Australian Bn.
11th Australian Bn.
12th Australian Bn.

3rd Australian Trench Mortar Battery.

Divisional Artillery. Brig.-Gen. S. M. Anderson, D.S.O.
1st and 2nd Brigades, A.F.A.
X/1A and Y/1A Trench Mortar Batteries, A.F.A.
1st Australian Divisional Ammunition Column.

Divisional Engineers. Lieut.-Col. W. A. Henderson, D.S.O.
  1st, 2nd, and 3rd Australian Field Cos.
1st Australian Divisional Signal Co.
1st Australian Pioneer Bn.
No. 1 Australian Bn., Machine Gun Corps.
1st Australian Divisional Train.
1st Australian Divisional M.T. Co.
1st, 2nd, and 3rd Australian Field Ambulances.
1st Australian Mobile Veterinary Section.

2nd *Australian Division.* Maj.-Gen. C. Rosenthal, C.B., C.M.G., D.S.O.
  G.S.O. 1 ..   ..   ..   Lieut.-Col. C. G. N. Miles, C.M.G., D.S.O.
  A.A. and Q.M.G.   ..   Lieut.-Col. J. M. A. Durrant, C.M.G., D.S.O.

5th *Australian Infantry Brigade.*	6th *Australian Infantry Brigade.*
(Brig.-Gen. E. F. Martin, C.M.G., D.S.O.)	(Brig.-Gen. J. C. Robertson, C.M.G., D.S.O.)
17th Australian Bn.	21st Australian Bn.
18th Australian Bn.	22nd Australian Bn.
19th Australian Bn.	23rd Australian Bn.
20th Australian Bn.	24th Australian Bn.
5th Australian Trench Mortar Battery.	6th Australian Trench Mortar Battery.

7th *Australian Infantry Brigade.*
(Brig.-Gen. E. A. Wisdom, C.B., D.S.O.)
25th Australian Bn.
26th Australian Bn.
27th Australian Bn.
28th Australian Bn.

7th Australian Trench Mortar Battery.

Divisional Artillery. Brig.-Gen. O. F. Phillips, D.S.O.
    4th and 5th Brigades, A.F.A.
    X/2A and Y/A2 Trench Mortar Batteries, A.F.A.
2nd Australian Divisional Ammunition Column.
Divisional Engineers. Lieut.-Col. J. M. Corlette, D.S.O.
    5th, 6th, and 7th Australian Field Cos.
2nd Australian Divisional Signal Co.
2nd Australian Pioneer Bn.
2nd Australian Bn., Machine Gun Corps.
2nd Australian Divisional Train.
2nd Australian M.T. Co.
5th, 6th, and 7th Australian Field Ambulances.
2nd Australian Mobile Veterinary Section.

Attached Troops.
    298th Army Brigade, R.F.A.

3rd Australian Division. Maj.-Gen. J. Gellibrand, C.B., D.S.O.
    G.S.O. 1 ..   ..   .. Lieut.-Col. C. H. Jess, D.S.O.
    A.A. and Q.M.G.   .. Lieut.-Col. R. E. Jackson, D.S.O.

9th Australian Infantry Brigade.
(Lieut.-Col. J. E. C. Lord, D.S.O., (acting).
33rd Australian Bn.
34th Australian Bn.
35th Australian Bn.
36th Australian Bn.

9th Australian Trench Mortar Battery.

10th Australian Infantry Brigade.
(Brig.-Gen. W. R. McNicoll, C.M.G., D.S.O.)
37th Australian Bn.
38th Australian Bn.
39th Australian Bn.
40th Australian Bn.

10th Australian Trench Mortar Battery.

11th Australian Infantry Brigade.
(Brig.-Gen. J. H. Cannan, C.B., C.M.G.)
    41st Australian Bn.
    42nd Australian Bn.
    43rd Australian Bn.
    44th Australian Bn.

11th Australian Trench Mortar Battery.

Divisional Artillery. Brig.-Gen. H. W. Grimwade, C.B., C.M.G.
    7th and 8th Brigades, A.F.A.
    X/3A and Y/3A Trench Mortar Batteries, A.F.A.
3rd Australian Divisional Ammunition Column.
Divisional Engineers. Lieut.-Col. H. Bachtold, D.S.O., M.C.
    9th, 10th, and 11th Australian Field Cos.
3rd Australian Divisional Signal Co.
3rd Australian Pioneer Bn.
No. 3 Australian Bn., Machine Gun Corps.
3rd Australian Divisional Train.
3rd Australian Divisional M.T. Co.
9th, 10th, and 11th Australian Field Ambulances.
3rd Australian Mobile Veterinary Section.

Attached Troops.
    16th Army Brigade, R.H.A.
    23rd and 189th Army Brigades, R.F.A.
    3rd and 12th Army Brigades, A.F.A.

4th Australian Division. Maj.-Gen. E. G. Sinclair-Maclagan, C.B., D.S.O.
    G.S.O. 1 ..   ..   .. Lieut.-Col. J. D. Lavarack, D.S.O.
    A.A. and Q.M.G.   .. Lieut.-Col. R. Dowse, D.S.O.

4th Australian Infantry Brigade.
(Brig.-Gen. E. A. D. Brockman,
C.M.G., D.S.O.)
13th Australian Bn.
14th Australian Bn.
15th Australian Bn.
16th Australian Bn.

4th Australian Trench Mortar Battery.

12th Australian Infantry Brigade.
(Brig.-Gen. R. L. Leane, D.S.O., M.C.)

45th Australian Bn.
46th Australian Bn.
48th Australian Bn.

12th Australian Trench Mortar Battery.

13th Australian Infantry Brigade.
(Brig.-Gen. S. C. E. Herring, D.S.O.)
49th Australian Bn.
50th Australian Bn.
51st Australian Bn.

13th Australian Trench Mortar Battery.

Divisional Artillery. Brig.-Gen. W. L. H. Burgess, C.M.G., D.S.O.
10th and 11th Brigades, A.F.A.
X/4A and Y/4A Trench Mortar Batteries, A.F.A.

4th Australian Divisional Ammunition Column.

Divisional Engineers. Lieut.-Col. R. J. Dyer, D.S.O.
4th, 12th, and 13th Australian Field Cos.

4th Australian Divisional Signal Co.
4th Australian Pioneer Bn.
No. 4 Australian Bn., Machine Gun Corps.
4th Australian Divisional Train.
4th Australian Divisional M.T. Co.
4th, 12th, and 13th Australian Field Ambulances.
4th Australian Mobile Veterinary Section.

5th Australian Division. Maj.-Gen. Sir J. J. Talbot-Hobbs, K.C.B., V.D.
G.S.O. 1 ..   ..   Lieut.-Col. J. Peck, D.S.O.
A.A. and Q.M.G.   ..   Col. J. H. Bruche, C.M.G.

8th Australian Infantry Brigade.
(Brig.-Gen. E. Tivey, C.B., D.S.O.,
V.D.)
29th Australian Bn.
30th Australian Bn.
31st Australian Bn.
32nd Australian Bn.

8th Australian Trench Mortar Battery.

14th Australian Infantry Brigade.
(Brig.-Gen. J. C. Stewart, D.S.O.)

53rd Australian Bn.
54th Australian Bn.
55th Australian Bn.
56th Australian Bn.

14th Australian Trench Mortar Battery.

15th Australian Infantry Brigade.
(Brig.-Gen. H. E. Elliott, C.B., C.M.G., D.S.O., D.C.M.)
57th Australian Bn.
58th Australian Bn.
59th Australian Bn.
60th Australian Bn.

15th Australian Trench Mortar Battery.

Divisional Artillery. Brig.-Gen. A. J. Bessel-Browne, C.B., C.M.G., D.S.O.
13th and 14th Brigades, A.F.A.
X/5A and Y/5A Trench Mortar Batteries, A.F.A.

5th Australian Divisional Ammunition Column.

Divisional Engineers. Lieut.-Col. L. F. S. Mather, D.S.O.
8th, 14th, and 15th Australian Field Cos.

5th Australian Divisional Signal Co.
5th Australian Pioneer Bn.
No. 5 Australian Bn., Machine Gun Corps.
5th Australian Divisional Train.
5th Australian Divisional M.T. Co.
8th, 14th, and 15th Australian Field Ambulances.
5th Australian Mobile Veterinary Section.

Attached Troops.
    14th Army Brigade, R.F.A.
    76th Army Brigade, A.F.A.

17th (Northern) Division. Maj.-Gen. P. R. Robertson, C.B., C.M.G.
  G.S.O. 1 ..   ..   .. Col. E. M. Birch, C.M.G., D.S.O.
  A.A. and Q.M.G.   .. Lieut.-Col. A. E. J. Wilson, D.S.O.

50th Infantry Brigade.	*51st Infantry Brigade.*
(Brig.-Gen. G. Gwynn-Thomas, C.M.G., D.S.O.)	(Brig.-Gen. R. M. Dudgeon, D.S.O., M.C.)
10th Bn., West Yorkshire Regt.	7th Bn., Lincolnshire Regt.
7th Bn., East Yorkshire Regt.	7th (Westmoreland and Cumberland Yeo.) Bn., Border Regt.
7th Bn., Dorsetshire Regt.	10th Bn., Sherwood Foresters (Nottinghamshire and Derbyshire Regt.).
50th Trench Mortar Battery.	51st Trench Mortar Battery.

52nd Infantry Brigade.
(Brig.-Gen. W. Allason, D.S.O.)
10th Bn., Lancashire Fusiliers.
9th Bn., West Riding Regt.
12th (Duke of Lancaster's Yeo.) Bn., Manchester Regt.

52nd Trench Mortar Battery.

Divisional Artillery. Brig.-Gen. P. Wheatley, C.M.G., D.S.O.
    78th and 79th Brigades, R.F.A.
    X/17 and Y/17 Trench Mortar Batteries, R.A.
17th Divisional Ammunition Column.

Divisional Engineers. Lieut.-Col. F. A. Ferguson.
77th, 78th, and 93rd Field Cos., R.E.
17th Divisional Signal Co.
7th Bn., York and Lancaster Regt. (Pioneers).
No. 17 Bn., Machine Gun Corps.
17th Divisional Train.
17th Divisional M.T. Co.
51st, 52nd, and 53rd Field Ambulances.
29th Mobile Veterinary Section.

SEPTEMBER 29TH.

A. FOURTH ARMY. Gen. Sir H. S. Rawlinson, Bart., G.C.V.O., K.C.B., K.C.M.G.
                  Staff as for August 8th.

Army Troops.
  5th Brigade, R.A.F. Brig.-Gen. L. E. O. Charlton, C.M.G., D.S.O.
    15th Wing. Lieut.-Col. J. A. Chamier, D.S.O., O.B.E.
      8 Squadron (A.W.B.) } Working with Tank Corps.
      73 Squadron (Camel) }
    22nd Wing. Lieut.-Col. T. A. E. Cairnes, D.S.O.
      24, 84, 85, and 92 (S.E. 5), 23 (Dolphin), 46, 80, and 208 (Camel), 20 (B.F.) and 205 (D.H. 9) Squadrons.
    5th Balloon Wing. Lieut.-Col. F. F. M. Roxby.
    4th Aircraft Park. 4th Air Ammunition Column. 4th Reserve Lorry Park.

Artillery.
  Half 471 Siege Battery, R.G.A. (14″ gun on railway mounting).
  Half 543 Siege Battery, R.G.A. (12″ gun on railway mounting).

Tanks.
  2nd Tank Bn. (G.H.Q. Reserve).

A.A. Defence. Lieut.-Col. R. Bruce Hay, D.S.O.
  " F," " G," " P," and " Q " A.A. Batteries.
  50th (Field Searchlight) Co., R.E.
  1, 7, 16, 17, 36, 69, 3 Canadian, and 4 Canadian Searchlight Sections, R.E.
  No. 66 A.A. Co.

5th Field Survey Battalion. Lieut.-Col. F. B. Legh, M.C.
  2, 13, 14, and 24 Observation Groups.
  " A," " B," " G," " K," " O," and " R " Sound Ranging Sections.

Fourth Army Signal Company.
  43, 45, 48, and 53 (Motor) Airline Sections.
  " BL " and " BR " Cable Sections.
  No. 4 Telegraph Construction Co., R.E.
  No. 4 Signal Construction Co., R.E.

213 A.T. Co., R.E.
353 E. and M. Co. (less two advanced sections).
" B " and " Z " Special Cos., R.E.
No. 3 Water Boring Section.
No. 8 Pontoon Park
4th Army Troops M.T. Co.

B. CAVALRY CORPS (G.H.Q. Reserve). Lieut.-Gen. Sir C. T. McM. Kavanagh, K.C.B., C.V.O., D.S.O.
  B.G.G.S... .. .. Brig.-Gen. A. F. Home, C.M.G., D.S.O.
  D.A. and Q.M.G. .. Brig.-Gen. J. C. G. Longmore, C.M.G., D.S.O.
  G.O.C., R.A. .. .. Brig.-Gen. H. S. Seligman, D.S.O.
  C.R.E. .. .. .. Lieut.-Col. W. H. Evans, D.S.O.

6 Squadron, R.A.F. (R.E. 8).

4th Guards Brigade. Brig.-Gen. Hon. L. J. P. Butler, C.M.G., D.S.O.
  4th Bn., Grenadier Guards.
  3rd Bn., Coldstream Guards.
  1/1st Bn., Honourable Artillery Co.
  ————
  4th Guards Light Trench Mortar Battery.
  A/58 Battery, R.F.A.

Household Machine Gun Brigade.
  No. 1 (1st Life Guards) Bn., Guards Machine Gun Regt.
  No. 3 (Royal Horse Guards) Bn., Guards Machine Gun Regt.
  XVIII Corps Cyclist Bn.
  Corps Signal Troops { Cavalry Corps Signal Squadron.
                      { Cavalry Corps Wireless Squadron.
                      { " AD " and " GG " Cable Sections.
  Cavalry Corps Bridging Park, R.E.
  Cavalry Corps Troops M.T. Co.

1st Cavalry Division.
  As for August 8th.

3rd Cavalry Division.
  As for August 8th.

C. III Corps. Lieut.-Gen. Sir R. H. K. Butler, K.C.M.G., C.B.
    B.G.G.S...   ..   ..   Brig.-Gen. C. G. Fuller, D.S.O.
    D.A. and Q.M.G.   ..   Brig.-Gen. A. F. Doyle, C.M.G., D.S.O.
    G.O.C., R.A.   ..   ..   Brig.-Gen. C. M. Ross-Johnson, C.B., C.M.G., D.S.O.
    C.E.   ..   ..   ..   Brig.-Gen. A. Rolland, D.S.O.

Corps Cavalry.
    1/1st Northumberland Hussars.

Corps Heavy Artillery. Brig.-Gen. A. E. J. Perkins, C.B.
    47 (8″ Howr.) Brigade, R.G.A.
    27 and 76 (Mixed) Brigades, R.G.A.
    189 and 545 (6″ gun) Siege Batteries, R.G.A.
    243 (12″ Howr.) Siege Battery, R.G.A.
    V/III Heavy Trench Mortar Battery, R.G.A.

35 Squadron, R.A.F. (A.W.B.)
Corps Signal Troops { "C" Corps Signal Co.
Nos. 6 and 76 (Motor) Airline Sections.
"LZ" "WE" and "SS" Cable Sections.
283rd A.T. Co., R.E.
No. 100 Bn., Machine Gun Corps.
III Corps Troops M.T. Co.

12th (Eastern) Division.
    As for August 8th, except that the 25th Divisional Artillery and the 169th and 232nd Army Brigades, R.F.A., were no longer attached.

18th (Eastern) Division.
    As for August 8th, except that the 5th Army Brigade, R.H.A., and the 18th, 86th, and 175th Army Brigades, R.F.A., were no longer attached. The 74th Divisional Artillery was, however, under the 18th Division at this time.

D. IX Corps. Lieut.-Gen. Sir W. P. Braithwaite, K.C.B.
    B.G.G.S...   ..   ..   Brig.-Gen. A. R. Cameron, C.B., C.M.G.
    D.A. and Q.M.G.   ..   Brig.-Gen. J. C. Harding-Newman, C.M.G.
    G.O.C., R.A.   ..   ..   Brig.-Gen. G. Humphreys, C.B., C.M.G., D.S.O.
    C.E.   ..   ..   ..   Brig.-Gen. R. A. Gillam, D.S.O.

Corps Cyclists.
    9th Cyclist Bn.

Corps Heavy Artillery. Brig.-Gen. G. B. Mackenzie, C.M.G., D.S.O.
    5, 12, and 14 (8″ Howr.) Brigades, R.G.A.
    69 and 98 (9·2″ Howr.) Brigades, R.G.A.
    79 and 83 (Mixed) Brigades, R.G.A.
    21 (Mobile) Brigade, R.G.A.
    498 and 499 (6″ gun) Siege Batteries, R.G.A.
    50 (6″ gun on naval mounting) Siege Battery, R.G.A.
    80 (12″ Howr.) Siege Battery, R.G.A.
    No. 1 (12″ Howr.) Siege Battery, R.M.A.
    V/IX Heavy Trench Mortar Battery, R.G.A.

9 Squadron, R.A.F. (R.E. 8).

3rd Tank Brigade. Brig.-Gen. J. Hardress-Lloyd, D.S.O.
    6th Tank Bn. (Whippets).
    5th Tank Bn. (Mark V).
    9th Tank Bn. (Mark V).

Corps Signal Troops { "E" Corps Signal Co.
Nos. 11 and 81 (Motor) Airline Sections.
"AA," "BT," and "SV" Cable Sections.
No. 2 (2nd Life Guards) Bn., Guards Machine Gun Regt.
No. 4 Siege Co., Royal Anglesey, R.E.

216, 221, 567, and 574 A.T. Cos., R.E.
180, 253, 254, and 256 (T.) Cos., R.E.
No. 1 Special Co., R.E. (Mortars).
IX Corps Troops M.T. Co.

1st Division. Maj.-Gen. E. P. Strickland, C.B., C.M.G., D.S.O.
    G.S.O. 1 ..   ..   ..   Lieut.-Col. E. N. Tandy, C.M.G., D.S.O.
    A.A. and Q.M.G.   ..   Lieut.-Col. H. H. Spender Clay, C.M.G., M.C.

1st Infantry Brigade.
(Brig.-Gen. L. L. Wheatley, C.M.G., D.S.O.)
1st Bn., The Black Watch (Royal Highlanders).
1st Bn., Loyal North Lancashire Regt.
1st Bn., The Queen's Own Cameron Highlanders.

1st Trench Mortar Battery.

2nd Infantry Brigade.
(Brig.-Gen. G. C. Kelly, D.S.O.)
2nd Bn., Royal Sussex Regt.
1st Bn., Northamptonshire Regt.
2nd Bn., King's Royal Rifle Corps.

2nd Trench Mortar Battery.

3rd Infantry Brigade.
(Brig.-Gen. Sir W. A. I. Kay, Bt., C.M.G., D.S.O.)
(From October 6th, 1918, Brig.-Gen. E. G. St. Aubyn, D.S.O.)
1st Bn., South Wales Borderers.
1st Bn., Gloucestershire Regt.
2nd Bn., The Welsh Regt.

3rd Trench Mortar Battery.

Divisional Artillery. Brig.-Gen. H. F. E. Lewin, C.M.G.
  25th and 39th Brigades, R.F.A.
  X/1 and Y/1 Trench Mortar Batteries, R.A.

1st Divisional Ammunition Column.

Divisional Engineers. Lieut.-Col. C. E. P. Sankey, D.S.O.
  23rd, 26th, and 409th Field Cos., R.E.

1st Divisional Signal Co.
1/6th Bn., The Welsh Regt. (Pioneers).
No. 1 Bn., Machine Gun Corps.
1st Divisional Train.
1st Divisional M.T. Co.
1st, 2nd, and 141st Field Ambulances.
2nd Mobile Veterinary Section.

Attached Troops.
  5th Army Brigade, R.H.A.
  298th Army Brigade, R.F.A.

6th Division. Maj.-Gen. T. O. Marden, C.B., C.M.G.
    G.S.O. 1 ..   ..   ..   Lieut.-Col. T. T. Grove, D.S.O.
    A.A. and Q.M.G.   ..   Lieut.-Col. P. Hudson, D.S.O.

16th Infantry Brigade.
(Brig.-Gen. H. A. Walker, C.M.G., D.S.O.) (From October 10th, 1918, Brig.-Gen. W. G. Braithwaite, C.B., C.M.G., D.S.O.)
1st Bn., The Buffs (East Kent Regt.).
1st Bn., King's Shropshire Light Infantry.
2nd Bn., York and Lancaster Regt.

16th Trench Mortar Battery.

18th Infantry Brigade.
(Brig.-Gen. G. S. Craufurd, C.M.G., C.I.E., D.S.O., A.D.C.)
1st Bn., West Yorkshire Regt.
11th Bn., Essex Regt.
2nd Bn., Durham Light Infantry.

18th Trench Mortar Battery.

71st Infantry Brigade.

(Brig.-Gen. P. W. Brown, D.S.O.)

9th Bn., Norfolk Regt.

1st Bn., Leicestershire Regt.

2nd Bn., Sherwood Foresters (Nottinghamshire and Derbyshire Regt.).

71st Trench Mortar Battery.

Divisional Artillery. Brig.-Gen. E. F. Delaforce, C.M.G.

　　2nd and 24th Brigades, R.F.A.

　　X/6 and Y/6 Trench Mortar Batteries, R.A.

6th Divisional Ammunition Column.

Divisional Engineers. Lieut.-Col. H. A. L. Hall, M.C.

　　12th, 459th, and 509th Field Cos., R.E.

6th Divisional Signal Co.

11th Bn., Leicestershire Regt. (Pioneers).

No. 6 Bn., Machine Gun Corps.

6th Divisional Train.

6th Divisional M.T. Co.

16th, 17th, and 18th Field Ambulances.

6th Mobile Veterinary Section.

32nd Division.

As for August 8th, except that Brig.-Gen. Sir G. Armytage, Bt., C.M.G. ,D.S.O., took over command of the 97th Infantry Brigade on October 6th, 1918, and Lieut.-Col. E. F. G. Dillon, D.S.O., had succeeded Lieut.-Col. A. E. McNamara, C.M.G., D.S.O., as G.S.O. 1, of the Division.

46th (North Midland) Division (T.). Maj.-Gen. G. F. Boyd, C.M.G., D.S.O., D.C.M.,

G.S.O. 1 .. 　　.. 　　.. Lieut.-Col. C. F. Jerram, D.S.O.

A.A. and Q.M.G. 　　.. Lieut.-Col. R. Duckworth, D.S.O.

137th Infantry Brigade.	*138th Infantry Brigade.*
(Brig.-Gen. J. V. Campbell, V.C., C.M.G., D.S.O.)	(Brig.-Gen. F. G. M. Rowley, C.M.G., D.S.O.)
1/5th Bn., South Staffordshire Regt.	1/5th Bn., Lincolnshire Regt.
1/6th Bn., South Staffordshire Regt.	1/4th Bn., Leicestershire Regt.
1/6th Bn., North Staffordshire Regt.	1/5th Bn., Leicestershire Regt.
137th Trench Mortar Battery.	138th Trench Mortar Battery.

139th Infantry Brigade.

(Brig.-Gen. J. Harington, D.S.O.

1/5th Bn., Sherwood Foresters (Nottinghamshire and Derbyshire Regt.).

1/6th Bn., Sherwood Foresters (Nottinghamshire and Derbyshire Regt.).

1/8th Bn., Sherwood Foresters (Nottinghamshire and Derbyshire Regt.).

139th Trench Mortar Battery.

Divisional Artillery. Brig.-Gen. Sir Hill Child, Bt., C.M.G., D.S.O., M.V.O.

　　230th and 231st Brigades, R.F.A.

　　X/46 and Y/46 Trench Mortar Batteries, R.A.

46th Divisional Ammunition Column.

Divisional Engineers. Lieut.-Col. H. T. Morshead, D.S.O.

　　465th, 466th, and 468th Field Cos., R.E.

46th Divisional Signal Co.

1/1st Bn., Monmouthshire Regt. (Pioneers).

No. 46 Bn., Machine Gun Corps.

46th Divisional Train.

46th Divisional M.T. Co.

1/1st, 1/2nd, and 1/3rd (North Midland) Field Ambulances.

1/1st (North Midland) Mobile Veterinary Section.

Attached Troops.
    16th Army Brigade, R.H.A.
    5th Army Brigade, R.F.A.
    14th Army Brigade, R.F.A.
    23rd Army Brigade, R.F.A.
    232nd Army Brigade, R.F.A.

E. XIII CORPS. Lieut.-Gen. Sir T. L. N. Morland, K.C.B., K.C.M.G., D.S.O.
    B.G.G.S...   ..   ..   Brig.-Gen. I. Stewart, D.S.O.
    D.A. and Q.M.G.   ..   Brig.-Gen. S. W. Robinson, D.S.O.
    G.O.C., R.A.   ..   ..   Brig.-Gen. R. A. C. Wellesley, C.B., C.M.G.
    C.E.   ..   ..   Brig.-Gen. C. A. Elliott, D.S.O.

Corps Cyclists.
    13th Cyclist Bn.

Corps Heavy Artillery. Brig.-Gen. J. D. Sherer, D.S.O.

Corps Signal Troops   { " N " Corps Signal Co.
                  Nos. 35 and 95 (Motor) Airline Sections.
                  " H " and " VV " Cable Sections.

XIII Corps Troops M.T. Co.

25th Division. Maj.-Gen. J. R. E. Charles, C.B., D.S.O.
    G.S.O. 1 ..   ..   ..   Lieut.-Col. D. F. Anderson, D.S.O.
    A.A. and Q.M.G.   ..   Lieut.-Col. Hon. E. P. J. Stourton, D.S.O.

7th Infantry Brigade.	*74th Infantry Brigade.*
(Brig.-Gen. C. J. Hickie.)	(Brig.-Gen. H. M. .Craigie-Halkett, D.S.O.)
9th Bn., Devonshire Regt.	9th Bn., Yorkshire Regt.
20th Bn., Manchester Regt.	11th Bn., Sherwood Foresters (Nottinghamshire and Derbyshire Regt.).
21st Bn., Manchester Regt.	13th Bn., Durham Light Infantry.
7th Trench Mortar Battery.	74th Trench Mortar Battery.

75th Infantry Brigade.
(Brig.-Gen. M. E. Richardson, D.S.O.)
(From October 1st, 1918, Brig.-Gen. C. W. Frizell, D.S.O., M.C.)
1/8th Bn., Royal Warwickshire Regt.
1/5th Bn., Gloucestershire Regt.
1/8th Bn., Worcestershire Regt.

75th Trench Mortar Battery.

Divisional Artillery. Brig.-Gen. K. J. Kincaid-Smith, C.M.G., D.S.O.
    110th and 112th Brigades, R.F.A.
    X/25 and Y/25 Trench Mortar Batteries, R.A.

25th Divisional Ammunition Column.

Divisional Engineers. Lieut.-Col. R. J. Done, D.S.O.
    105th, 106th, and 130th Field Cos., R.E.
25th Divisional Signal Co.
25th Divisional Train.
25th Divisional M.T. Co.
75th, 76th, and 77th Field Ambulances.
37th Mobile Veterinary Section.

50th Division. Maj.-Gen. H. C. Jackson, D.S.O.
    G.S.O. 1 ..   ..   ..   Lieut.-Col. E. C. Anstey, D.S.O.
    A.A. and Q.M.G.   ..   Lieut.-Col. A. C. H. Duke, D.S.O.

149*th Infantry Brigade*.
(Brig.-Gen. P. M. Robinson, C.M.G.)
3rd Bn. Royal Fusiliers.
13th Bn. (Scottish Horse), Royal Highlanders.
2nd Bn., Royal Dublin Fusiliers.

149th Trench Mortar Battery.

150*th Infantry Brigade*.
(Brig.-Gen. G. Rollo, D.S.O.)
2nd Bn., Northumberland Fusiliers.
7th Bn., Wiltshire Regt.
2nd Bn., Royal Munster Fusiliers.

150th Trench Mortar Battery.

151*st Infantry Brigade*.
(Brig.-Gen. R. E. Sugden, D.S.O.)
6th Bn., Royal Inniskilling Fusiliers.
1st Bn., King's Own Yorkshire Light Infantry.
4th Bn., King's Royal Rifle Corps.

151st Trench Mortar Battery.

Divisional Artillery. Brig.-Gen. W. Stirling, D.S.O.
250th and 251st Brigades, R.F.A.
X/50 and Y/50 Trench Mortar Batteries, R.A.
50th Divisional Ammunition Column.

Divisional Engineers. Lieut.-Col. P. de H. Hall, M.C.
7th, 446th, and 447th Field Cos., R.E.
50th Divisional Signal Co.
5th Bn., Royal Irish Regt. (Pioneers).
No. 50 Bn., Machine Gun Corps.
50th Divisional Train.
50th Divisional M.T. Co.
1/1st, 1/3rd, and 2/2nd Northumbrian Field Ambulances.
1/1st Northumbrian Mobile Veterinary Section.

66*th Division*. Maj.-Gen. H. K. Bethell, C.M.G., D.S.O.
G.S.O. 1 .. .. .. Lieut.-Col. F. P. Nosworthy, D.S.O., M.C.
A.A. and Q.M.G. .. Lieut.-Col. F. J. Lemon, D.S.O.

198*th Infantry Brigade*.
(Brig.-Gen. A. J. Hunter, D.S.O., M.C.)
6th Bn., Lancashire Fusiliers.
5th Bn., Royal Inniskilling Fusiliers.
6th Bn., Royal Dublin Fusiliers.

198th Trench Mortar Battery.

199*th Infantry Brigade*.
(Brig.-Gen. G. C. Williams, D.S.O.)
18th Bn., (Lancashire Hussars Yeo.)
The King's (Liverpool Regt.).
9th Bn., Manchester Regt.
5th Bn., The Connaught Rangers.

199th Trench Mortar Battery.

South African Infantry Brigade.
(Brig.-Gen. W. E. C. Tanner, C.M.G., D.S.O.)
1st Bn., South African Infantry.
2nd Bn., South African Infantry.
4th Bn., South African Infantry.

South African Trench Mortar Battery.

Divisional Artillery. Brig.-Gen. A. Birtwistle, C.M.G., D.S.O.
330th and 331st Brigades, R.F.A.
X/66 and Y/66 Trench Mortar Batteries, R.A.
66th Divisional Ammunition Column.

Divisional Engineers. Major S. H. Morgan, M.C. (Acting).
430th, 431st, and 432nd Field Cos., R.E.
66th Divisional Signal Co.
9th Bn., Gloucestershire Regt. (Pioneers).
66th Divisional Train.
66th Divisional M.T. Co.
2/2nd and 2/3rd (East Lancashire), and South African Field Ambulances.
1/1st (East Lancashire) Mobile Veterinary Section.

F. AUSTRALIAN CORPS.   Lieut.-Gen. Sir J. Monash, K.C.B.
      B.G.G.S... .. .. Brig.-Gen. T. A. Blamey, C.M.G., D.S.O.
      D.A. and Q.M.G. .. Brig.-Gen. R. A. Carruthers, C.B., C.M.G.
      G.O.C., R.A. .. .. Brig.-Gen. W. A. Coxen, C.M.G., D.S.O.
      C.E. .. .. .. Brig.-Gen. C. H. Foott, C.M.G.

Corps Cavalry and Cyclists.
      5th Cavalry Brigade (attached).   Brig.-Gen. N. W. Haig, C.M.G.
      13th Regt., Australian Light Horse.
      Australian Cyclist Bn.

Corps Heavy Artillery.   Brig.-Gen. L. D. Fraser, C.B., C.M.G.
      68, 71, and 89 (8″ Howr.) Brigades, R.G.A.
      18 and 23 (9.2″ Howr.) Brigades, R.G.A.
      51 and 93 (Mixed) Brigades, R.G.A.
      9, 41, and 85 (Mobile) Brigades, R.G.A.
      73 Army Brigade, R.G.A. (H.Q. only).
      222, 312, 449, and 504 (6″ gun) Siege Batteries, R.G.A.
      494 (12″ Howr.) Siege Battery, R.G.A.
      V/Australian Heavy Trench Mortar Battery, A.F.A.

3rd Squadron, Australian Flying Corps (also worked with II American Corps).

5th Tank Brigade.   Brig.-Gen. A. Courage, D.S.O., M.C.
      3rd Tank Bn. (Whippets).
      8th Tank Bn. } Mark V.
      13th Tank Bn. }
      16th Tank Bn. Mark V star.
      17th Armoured Car Bn.
Corps Signal Troops { Australian Corps Signal Co. / Nos. 1 and 2 Australian (Motor) Airline Sections. / Nos. 1 and 2 Australian Cable Sections.
146 and 238 A.T. Cos., R.E.
1st A.T. Co., Australian Engineers.
1st and 2nd (T.) Cos., Australian Engineers.
No. 2 Advanced Section 353 E. and M. Co.
No. 11 Pontoon Park.
No. 4 Special Co., R.E. (less 1 section).
6th Australian (Corps Troops) M.T. Co.

The 58th Divisional Artillery and the following Army Brigades, R.F.A., were attached to divisions of the Australian Corps :—
      65, 84, 86, 104, 108, and 150.

1st Australian Division.
      As for August 8th.

2nd Australian Division.
      As for August 8th, except that the 298th Army Brigade, R.F.A., was no longer attached to the division.

3rd Australian Division.
      As for August 8th, except that Brig.-Gen. H. A. Goddard, D.S.O., had taken over command of the 9th Brigade ; that the 36th Bn. had, owing to lack of reinforcements, been amalgamated with another battalion in the division ; the 16th Army Brigade, R.H.A., and the 23rd and 189th Army Brigades, R.F.A., were no longer attached to the division.

4th Australian Division.
      As for August 8th.

5th Australian Division.
      As for August 8th, except that the 60th Bn. had, owing to lack of reinforcements, been amalgamated with another battalion in the division.

APPENDIX F

G. II AMERICAN CORPS. Maj.-Gen. G. W. Read.
      Chief of Staff .. .. Col. George S. Simonds.
  412th Telegraph Bn.
  Attached Troops.
      3rd Squadron Australian Flying Corps (also worked with Australian Corps).
VII Corps, R.A., H.Q. Brig.-Gen. K. K. Knapp, C.M.G.
VII Corps, H.A., H.Q. Brig.-Gen. F. H. Metcalfe, D.S.O.
4th Tank Brigade. Brig.-Gen. E. B. Hankey, D.S.O.
    1st Tank Bn. (Mark V star.)
    4th Tank Bn. ⎫
    301st American Tank Bn.⎰(Mark V.)
  1st Siege Co., Royal Anglesey, R.E.
  144 and 288 A.T. Cos., R.E.
  182 (T.) Co., R.E.
  No. 1 Advanced Section 353 E. and M. Co.
  27th American Division. Maj.-Gen. F. O'Ryan.
      Chief of Staff .. .. Lieut.-Col. S. H. Ford.

53rd Infantry Brigade.	*54th Infantry Brigade.*
(Brig.-Gen. A. H. Blanding.)	(Brig.-Gen. P. D. Pierce.)
105th Regt. (1st, 2nd, and 3rd Bns.).	107th Regt. (1st, 2nd, and 3rd Bns.).
106th Regt. (1st, 2nd, and 3rd Bns.).	108th Regt. (1st, 2nd, and 3rd Bns.).
105th Machine Gun Bn.	106th Machine Gun Bn.

  102nd Engineer Regt.
  102nd Field Signal Bn.
  104th Machine Gun Bn.
  102nd Train Headquarters.
  106th and 107th Ambulance Sections.
  105th and 106th Field Hospital Sections.
30th American Division. Maj.-Gen. E. M. Lewis.
      Chief of Staff .. .. Col. John K. Herr.

59th Infantry Brigade.	*60th Infantry Brigade.*
(Brig.-Gen. L. D. Tyson.)	(Brig.-Gen. S. L. Faison.)
117th Regt. (1st, 2nd, and 3rd Bns.).	119th Regt. (1st, 2nd, and 3rd Bns.).
118th Regt. (1st, 2nd, and 3rd Bns.).	120th Regt. (1st, 2nd, and 3rd Bns.).
114th Machine Gun Bn.	115th Machine Gun Bn.

  105th Engineer Regt.
  105th Field Signal Bn.
  113th Machine Gun Bn.
  105th Train Headquarters.
  118th and 119th Ambulance Sections.
  118th and 119th Field Hospitals.

NOVEMBER 4TH.

A. FOURTH ARMY. Gen. Sir H. S. Rawlinson, Bart., G.C.V.O., K.C.B., K.C.M.G.
      Staff as for August 8th.
  Army Troops.
    5th Brigade, R.A.F. Brig.-Gen. L. E. O. Charlton, C.M.G., D.S.O.
      15th Wing. Lieut.-Col. J. A. Chamier, D.S.O., O.B.E.
        3rd Squadron, Australian Flying Corps, 6 (R.E.8), 8 (A.W.B.) and 73
        (Camel) Squadrons (working with Tank Corps).
      22nd Wing. Lieut.-Col. T. A. E. Cairnes, D.S.O.
        24, 84, 85, and 92 (S.E. 5), 23 (Dolphin), 46, 80, and 208 (Camel), 20
        (Bristol Fighter), 211, and 218 Squadrons.
      5th Balloon Wing. Lieut.-Col. F. F. M. Roxby.
      4th Aircraft Park. 4th Air Ammunition Column. 4th Reserve Lorry Park.

Artillery.

Half 456 Siege Battery, R.G.A. (9·2″ gun on railway mounting).
Half 471 Siege Battery, R.G.A. (14″ gun on railway mounting).
Half 543 Siege Battery, R.G.A. (12″ gun on railway mounting).
374 Siege Battery, R.G.A. (no guns).

Tanks.

2nd *Tank Brigade.* (These Headquarters worked with both IX and XIII Corps).
1 Co. 14th Tank Bn. (Mark V).
17th Armoured Car Bn.

A.A. Defence. Lieut.-Col. R. Bruce Hay, D.S.O.
" F," " G," " P," " Q," and " Z " A.A. Batteries.
50th (Field Searchlight) Co., R.E.
6, 7, 16, 17, 29, 36, and 69 A.A. Searchlight Sections, R.E.
No. 6 A.A. Co., 44th Garrison Bn., Royal Fusiliers.

5th Field Survey Bn. Lieut.-Col. F. B. Legh, M.C.
2, 13, 14, and 24 Observation Groups.
" A," " B," " G," " K," " O," and " R " Sound Ranging Sections.

Fourth Army Signal Co.

43, 45, 48, and 53 (Motor) Airline Sections.
" BL " and " BM " Cable Sections.
No. 4 Telegraph Construction Co., R.E.
No. 4 Signal Construction Co., R.E.

546 and 648 Field Cos., R.E. (less H.Q. and two sections).
213 A.T. Co., R.E.
353 E. and M. Co. (less 2 advanced sections).
No. 3 Water Boring Section.
Nos. 8 and 11 Pontoon Parks.
4th Army Troops M.T. Co.

B. IX Corps. Lieut.-Gen. Sir W. P. Braithwaite, K.C.B.

B.G.G.S...	..	Brig.-Gen. A. R. Cameron, C.B., C.M.G.
D.A. and Q.M.G	..	Brig.-Gen. J. C. Harding-Newman, C.M.G.
G.O.C., R.A. ..	..	Brig.-Gen. G. Humphreys, C.B., C.M.G., D.S.O.
C.E.	..	Brig.-Gen. R. A. Gillam, C.M.G., D.S.O.

Corps Cavalry and Cyclists.

5th Cavalry Brigade (less 1 Regt.). Brig.-Gen. N. W. Haig, C.M.G.
9th Cyclist Bn.

Corps Heavy Artillery. Brig.-Gen. G. B. Mackenzie, C.M.G., D.S.O.

12, 14, 68 and 71 (8″ Howr.) Brigades, R.G.A.
18, 69, and 98 (9·2″ Howr.) Brigades, R.G.A.
51, 79, 83, and 93 (Mixed) Brigades, R.G.A.
9, 21, and 41 (Mobile) Brigades, R.G.A.
222, 498, and 499 (6″ gun) Siege Batteries, R.G.A.
50 (6″ gun on naval mounting).
80 and 494 (12″ Howr.).
No. 1 (12″ Howr.) Siege Battery, R.M.A.
V/IX Heavy Trench Mortar Battery, R.G.A.

9 Squadron, R.A.F. (R.E. 8)
10th Tank Bn. (Mark V).
Corps Signal Troops { " E " Corps Signal Co.
Nos. 11 and 81 (Motor) Airline Sections.
" AA," " BT," and " SV " Cable Sections.

No. 3 (Royal Horse Guards) Bn., Guards Machine Gun Regt.
648 Field Co. (less 2 sections).
No. 4 Siege Co., R.A., R.E.
146, 221, 238, and 567 A.T. Cos., R.E.
253, 254, and 256 (T.) Cos., R.E.
1st (T.) Co., Australian Engineers.
No. 1 Adv. Section, 353 E. and M. Co.
No. 1 Special Co., R.E. (4″ Stokes' Mortars).
IX Corps Troops M.T. Co.

1st Division.
> As for September 29th, except that the 23rd Army Brigade, R.F.A., was attached to the division.

6th Division.
> As for September 29th.

32nd Division.
> As for September 29th, except that the 16th Army Brigade, R.H.A., and the 5th and 14th Army Brigades, R.F.A., were attached to the division.

46th (North Midland) Division (T.).
> As for September 29th, except that Lieut.-Col. W. Garforth, D.S.O., M.C., had taken over command of the Royal Engineers, and that there were no Army Brigades, R.F.A., attached.

C. XIII CORPS. Lieut.-Gen. Sir T. L. N. Morland, K.C.B., K.C.M.G., D.S.O.
  B.G.G.S... .. .. Brig.-Gen. I. Stewart, D.S.O.
  D.A. and Q.M.G. .. Brig.-Gen. S. W. Robinson, D.S.O.
  G.O.C., R.A. .. .. Brig.-Gen. R. A. C. Wellesley, C.B., C.M.G.
  C.E. .. .. .. Brig.-Gen. C. A. Elliott, D.S.O.

Corps Cavalry and Cyclists.
  1/1st Northumberland Hussars.
  18th Cyclist Bn.
  No. 11 Group of Sharpshooters (Lovat's Scouts).

Corps Heavy Artillery. Brig.-Gen. J. D. Sherer, D.S.O.
  47 (8″ Howr.) Brigade, R.G.A.
  23 (9·2″ Howr.) Brigade, R.G.A.
  27 and 76 (Mixed) Brigades, R.G.A.
  85 (Mobile) Brigade, R.G.A.
  73 Army Brigade, R.G.A. (H.Q. only).
  189, 312, 449, 504, and 545 (6″ gun) Siege Batteries, R.G.A.
  243 (12″ Howr.) Siege Battery, R.G.A.
  V/XIII Heavy Trench Mortar Battery, R.G.A.

35 Squadron, R.A.F. (A.W.B.).

12th Lancers (from 5th Cavalry Brigade) attached.

9th Tank Bn. (Mark V).

14th Tank Bn. (less 1 company), (Mark V).

Corps Signal Troops { " N " Corps Signal Co. / Nos. 35 and 95 (Motor) Airline Sections. / " H " and " VV " Cable Sections.

No. 1 Siege Co., Royal Anglesey, R.E.

144, 283, 288, and 574 A.T. Cos., R.E.

180 and 182 (T.) Cos., R.E.

No. 2 Adv. Section, 353 E. and M. Co.

XIII Corps Troops M.T. Co.

18th (Eastern) Division.
  As for September 29th, except that the 74th Divisional Artillery was no longer under the 18th Division, and the 65th and 84th Army Brigades, R.F.A., were attached. Lieut.-Col. K. C. Weldon, D.S.O., and Lieut.-Col. A. P. B. Irwin, D.S.O., had taken over command of the 54th and 55th Brigades respectively.

25th Division.
  As for September 29th, except that the 25th Bn., Machine Gun Corps, and the 11th Bn. South Lancashire Regt. (Pioneers) had joined the division. The 150th Army Brigade, R.F.A., was attached.

50th Division.
  As for September 29th, except that the 86th and 104th Army Brigades, R.F.A. were attached.

  Lieut.-Col. A. K. Grant, D.S.O., had succeeded Lieut.-Col. E. C. Anstey, D.S.O., as G.S.O. 1 of the division.

66th Division.
  As for September 29th, except that the 100th Bn., Machine Gun Corps, had joined the division as Machine Gun Bn., and that Lieut.-Col. Q. S. Davies, D.S.O., had assumed command of the Royal Engineers.

D. AUSTRALIAN CORPS. Lieut.-Gen. Sir J. Monash, K.C.B.
      B.G.G.S...   ..   .. Brig.-Gen. T. A. Blamey, C.M.G., D.S.O.
      D.A. and Q.M.G.   ..   Brig.-Gen. R. A. Carruthers, C.B., C.M.G.
      G.O.C., R.A. ..   .. Brig.-Gen. W. A. Coxen, C.M.G., D.S.O.
      C.E.   ..   ..   .. Brig.-Gen. C. H. Foott, C.M.G.

Corps Cavalry and Cyclists.
    13th Regt., Australian Light Horse.
    Australian Cyclist Bn.

Corps Heavy Artillery. Brig.-Gen. L. D. Fraser, C.B., C.M.G.
    V/Australian Heavy Trench Mortar Battery, A.F.A.

Corps Signal Troops $\left\{\begin{array}{l}\text{Australian Corps Signal Co.}\\ \text{Nos. 1 and 2 Australian (Motor) Airline Sections.}\\ \text{Nos. 1 and 2 Australian Cable Sections.}\end{array}\right.$

3rd, 6th, and 12th Army Brigades, A.F.A.
1st A.T. Co., Australian Engineers.
2nd (T.) Co., Australian Engineers.
6th Australian (Corps Troops) M.T. Co.

1st Australian Division.
    As for September 29th.

2nd Australian Division.
    As for September 29th.

3rd Australian Division.
    As for September 29th, except that the 37th and 42nd Bns. had, owing to lack of reinforcements, been amalgamated with other battalions in the division. Brig.-Gen. C. H. Jess, D.S.O., had assumed command of the 10th Brigade on October 7th and Lieut.-Col. E. H. Harrison had become G.S.O. 1 of the division.

4th Australian Division.
    As for September 29th.

5th Australian Division.
    As for September 29th, except that the 29th and 54th Bns. had, owing to lack of reinforcements, been amalgamated with other battalions in the division.

II AMERICAN CORPS (*27th and 30th American Divisions*).
    As for September 29th, except that no British troops were attached, as the corps was resting in back areas.

APPENDIX G

Table showing the daily ammunition expenditure by the Fourth Army from August 8th to November 11th

Date.	Guns.							Howitzers.						
	13 pdr. A.A.	13 pdr. R.H.A.	18 pdr.	60 pdr.	6".	12".	14".	4.5".	6".	8".	9.2".	12".	14".	15".
August.														
8th	305	—	281,697	27,627	3,936	26	—	60,500	57,329	10,576	6,553	369	—	—
9th	404	9,100	100,346	9,578	1,629	54	—	20,675	18,611	4,315	3,218	132	—	—
10th	1,047	997	124,701	12,756	1,562	—	—	35,330	20,472	4,064	2,385	—	—	—
11th	1,493	886	65,363	10,579	1,162	—	—	12,663	15,213	1,354	571	22	—	—
12th	1,728	1,943	42,672	8,748	744	—	—	10,592	14,181	509	154	4	—	—
13th	496	1,008	34,510	8,368	1,117	—	—	8,710	15,691	262	272	—	—	—
14th	1,120	146	20,254	4,781	1,020	—	—	5,797	9,341	519	464	20	—	—
15th	1,425	569	14,489	5,167	971	—	—	4,111	9,171	510	268	5	—	—
16th	699	849	16,590	6,970	830	—	—	3,991	11,372	1,009	813	10	—	—
17th	1,868	666	23,150	9,754	1,321	6	2	7,443	16,792	2,300	1,572	80	2	—
18th	418	699	27,885	8,459	1,409	20	—	6,235	20,646	1,987	1,461	83	—	—
19th	703	925	39,589	7,020	989	20	—	9,998	15,503	2,120	1,094	61	—	—
20th	359	75	32,693	8,119	954	—	—	9,009	14,090	2,563	1,128	116	—	—
21st	43	101	24,405	7,556	723	—	—	7,330	14,274	2,357	1,153	75	—	—
22nd	770	—	125,710	10,463	1,496	14	—	31,840	22,088	4,274	2,603	160	—	—
23rd	1,290	2,353	71,506	13,380	1,657	36	15	16,260	31,242	6,533	4,347	183	—	—
24th	1,098	433	91,780	13,176	1,775	12	—	20,306	29,146	5,094	2,280	78	—	—
25th	561	433	72,542	10,419	1,014	—	12	17,839	22,573	3,576	1,709	69	—	—
26th	561	144	72,542	10,419	1,021	—	12	17,839	22,573	3,576	1,709	69	—	—
27th	404	936	37,338	10,211	2,006	—	—	10,655	17,236	2,575	626	12	—	—
28th	873	500	46,103	8,484	3,516	36	—	10,570	11,149	1,297	786	58	—	—
29th	389	—	23,427	6,085	875	16	—	5,370	9,072	230	250	—	—	—
30th	446	1,666	22,348	7,829	1,217	—	—	4,920	6,891	391	220	—	—	9
31st	—		56,579	7,801	805	—	—	12,417	16,217	446	270	—	—	—
Totals	18,500	24,429	1,468,219	233,749	33,749	240	41	350,400	440,873	62,437	35,906	1,606	2	9

AMMUNITION EXPENDITURE.

DATE.	GUNS.								HOWITZERS.				
	13 pdr. A.A.	13 pdr. R.H.A.	18 pdr.	60 pdr.	6".	20cwt.	12".	14".	4·5".	6".	8".	9·2".	12".
September.													
1st	775	6,341	80,349	10,931	769	—	—	—	18,940	19,208	1,414	1,129	—
2nd	857	3,046	72,354	8,946	1,070	—	—	—	18,730	19,551	1,207	681	—
3rd	1,185	1,674	17,158	9,518	839	—	—	—	3,398	19,346	1,574	1,160	—
4th	1,031	1,529	19,288	8,661	903	—	—	—	5,884	17,688	1,611	1,694	—
5th	2,490	129	16,489	9,505	787	—	—	—	5,906	16,097	2,042	943	24
6th	169	1,601	27,253	5,220	606	—	—	—	4,458	8,537	514	100	—
7th	1,159	1,144	21,383	1,702	434	—	—	—	4,297	4,512	364	74	—
8th	1,479	—	12,377	1,585	328	—	—	—	2,956	2,321	222	50	—
9th	1,865	—	16,988	1,708	358	—	—	—	2,932	2,218	374	132	—
10th	2,194	—	11,009	1,455	423	—	—	—	2,619	2,340	209	32	—
11th	431	—	6,259	1,944	187	—	—	—	2,050	4,046	384	20	—
12th	469	—	10,769	1,681	41	—	—	—	2,484	2,445	309	36	—
13th	875	—	5,631	1,297	34	—	—	—	1,290	2,659	310	40	—
14th	452	—	11,824	2,590	409	249	—	—	3,551	6,562	630	90	—
15th	1,045	172	10,869	4,091	383	—	—	—	2,864	8,136	1,133	151	8
16th	1,577	94	7,594	3,108	399	—	—	—	2,312	8,268	1,124	275	30
17th	569	7,626	14,902	4,875	375	255	—	—	3,918	6,637	1,245	249	83
18th	1,576	861	267,813	13,563	621	—	—	—	63,329	32,129	4,498	3,367	99
19th	1,864	1,342	70,585	10,485	796	93	—	—	16,980	17,865	2,820	2,031	73
20th	1,523	434	70,047	8,537	493	—	—	—	17,145	17,323	2,385	1,623	92
21st	2,129	795	69,143	9,986	884	—	—	—	16,826	18,285	2,985	2,076	37
22nd	1,986	795	47,599	6,770	608	—	—	—	10,353	10,695	2,678	1,353	6
23rd	1,986	5,382	47,599	6,770	608	—	—	—	10,353	10,695	2,678	1,222	10
24th	1,970	3,891	77,557	6,341	295	—	—	—	16,505	17,844	2,018	1,288	2
25th	3,468	—	57,399	6,863	581	—	—	—	13,521	14,467	2,415	1,616	—
26th	1,908	—	41,901	3,370	426	—	—	—	12,012	6,549	1,212	991	23
27th	1,092	—	78,065	5,778	595	—	—	—	13,038	20,877	2,338	978	—
28th	1,510	1,800	57,393	15,147	2,126	—	31	22	20,662	44,063	7,131	4,471	450
29th	534	6,231	244,502	23,801	2,404	—	42	26	67,656	63,271	9,764	7,768	805
30th	522	—	40,446	11,024	1,794	—	20	1	7,136	18,330	3,549	2,876	277
TOTALS	40,690	44,887	1,532,545	207,252	20,576	597	93	49	374,105	442,964	61,137	38,516	2,019

AMMUNITION EXPENDITURE

Date.	Guns.								Howitzers.				
	13 pdr. A.A.	13 pdr. R.H.A.	18 pdr.	60 pdr.	6".	3" 200wt.	12".	14".	4·5".	6".	8".	9·2".	12".
October.													
1st	207	1,773	40,296	7,685	1,077	—	—	—	11,978	13,452	2,167	1,306	58
2nd	197	2,139	29,085	6,135	1,110	—	21	—	3,826	9,577	1,321	993	140
3rd	1,215	6,682	117,542	8,939	1,289	—	—	—	23,461	21,002	1,696	1,249	69
4th	1,026	1,177	66,746	8,539	719	—	—	—	13,804	13,021	795	415	16
5th	1,137	1,835	58,225	6,945	735	—	—	—	13,287	11,029	1,397	352	5
6th	660	659	35,486	5,345	375	—	—	—	7,630	8,646	867	400	—
7th	2,512	—	26,974	6,232	390	164	—	17	8,454	14,400	1,727	802	25
8th	1,022	3,900	156,837	7,443	970	—	—	5	37,050	21,367	2,323	1,628	—
9th	997	2,261	65,563	6,629	627	—	—	—	13,621	10,601	1,012	1,032	—
10th	1,029	492	8,694	3,550	118	—	—	—	3,219	3,800	—	70	—
11th	1,273	1,262	19,749	2,990	497	—	—	—	4,220	3,316	319	70	—
12th	1,049	3,614	9,279	3,177	443	—	—	—	2,239	2,840	307	—	—
13th	785	1,103	18,986	3,824	75	—	—	—	5,094	4,385	95	84	—
14th	—	126	9,075	4,838	963	—	—	—	2,284	3,106	146	239	—
15th	829	225	11,248	5,685	794	193	—	—	3,992	7,850	792	497	—
16th	1,298	472	11,579	5,180	481	—	—	—	6,336	9,792	572	2,522	—
17th	60	3,245	149,675	11,020	1,176	—	—	—	28,527	28,368	2,711	863	—
18th	200	—	65,996	8,409	879	—	—	—	14,702	10,112	1,423	407	—
19th	693	118	24,871	5,231	377	—	—	—	5,913	6,613	268	—	—
20th	844	—	11,715	2,893	502	—	—	—	2,293	1,617	60	160	—
21st	—	—	9,407	2,937	417	—	—	—	3,056	1,934	47	50	—
22nd	138	5,400	5,162	1,947	224	—	—	—	1,380	2,410	80	1,506	—
23rd	465	6,229	111,671	9,753	445	—	—	—	29,232	20,033	1,757	489	—
24th	446	—	25,423	5,504	499	—	—	—	5,065	7,041	524	359	—
25th	191	—	10,116	5,847	308	—	—	—	1,720	3,952	275	370	—
26th	216	—	9,583	2,813	757	—	—	—	2,358	3,543	500	634	—
27th	924	—	6,248	2,496	902	—	—	—	1,234	4,003	580	563	—
28th	506	—	11,278	2,533	1,177	—	—	—	3,486	8,078	629	435	—
29th	628	—	7,158	2,396	1,440	—	—	—	2,832	5,890	463	330	—
30th	1,368	—	11,284	1,616	696	—	—	—	4,759	5,230	245	244	—
31st	—	—	10,328	1,868	687	—	—	—	3,145	4,483	160	—	—
TOTALS	21,915	42,712	1,155,279	160,399	21,149	357	21	22	270,197	271,471	25,258	18,069	313

AMMUNITION EXPENDITURE.

DATE.	GUNS.					HOWITZERS.			
	13 pdr. A.A.	13 pdr. R.H.A.	18 pdr.	60 pdr.	6".	4·5".	6".	8".	9·2".
November. 1st	322	—	13,781	1,679	676	5,017	4,224	576	1,061
2nd.. ..	693	—	8,811	1,787	421	1,812	3,540	604	770
3rd	693	—	8,811	1,787	421	1,806	3,540	604	770
4th	308	—	103,435	10,129	731	28,724	30,983	3,478	3,257
5th	110	5,413	62,286	7,951	1,365	9,478	12,979	1,851	1,771
6th	—	—	7,701	2,339	—	3,680	206	329	270
7th	—	—	131	—	—	20	—	—	—
8th	—	—	1,453	1,000	263	1,008	100	—	154
9th	—	—	1,470	—	—	622	—	—	—
10th	—	—	3,373	—	—	955	—	—	—
11th.. ..	20	—	1,730	—	—	56	—	—	—
TOTALS ..	2,146	5,413	212,982	26,672	3,877	53,178	55,572	7,442	8,053
GRAND TOTALS	83,251	117,441	4,369,025	628,072	79,351	1,047,880	1,210,880	156,274	100,544

APPENDIX H

Extracts from captured German Orders issued during the First Half of September, 1918

C.G.S. of the Field Army.
II No. 10144. Secret op.

G.H.Q.
3/9/18.

An increase has recently taken place in the number of complaints received from home that men on leave from the front create a very unfavourable impression by making statements actually bordering on high treason and incitement to disobedience. Instances such as these drag the honour and respect of the individual as well as of the whole Army into the mud, and have a disastrous effect upon the moral of the people at home.

No doubt such expressions often emanate from a certain irritation which changes into an explicable anger at the sight of the superficiality, war-weariness, and despondency which is unfortunately so widely prevalent at home. In order to counter this, it will suffice to bring home to the men by careful teaching the consequences of such action, especially if it is pointed out that, while travelling through the country, the soldier generally only sees the surface, and that the honest toil and the severe struggle which is going on at home is not apparent to him. It seems, however, as though some people were consciously adopting a line of conduct hostile to the State. Energetic steps must be taken to stop this.

I therefore request that :—

(1) All ranks be instructed on this point.
(2) Suspects be deprived of their leave.
(3) Men be informed that the home authorities have been instructed to take immediate action in such cases, with the result that offenders will be immediately returned to their unit, where they will be punished and, possibly, posted to a military prisoner company.

(Sd.)   Ludendorff.

Order of 1st Reserve Division, dated September 15th, 1918.

" Cases have occurred of men describing recent occurrences on the front in the gloomiest fashion, and of the local inhabitants obtaining knowledge of this. Such occurrences can only be attributed to notoriety-seeking chatterers, entirely devoid of conscience. Troops are to be instructed most earnestly in the danger which lies in the spreading of false and exaggerated accounts of events. The passing on of such stories to members of the population hostile to us borders on high treason. A corresponding punishment will be awarded in every single case, and the extreme penalties allowed by law will be inflicted."

Order of 38th Division, dated September 8th, 1918.

Instructions are given regarding march discipline, saluting, and dress :—

" Every opportunity and all means must be used to restore the old discipline among the troops.

" I expect this short reminder of our long-established principles to be sufficient to awaken in all officers and N.C.O.'s an understanding of the value of strict discipline and that the end in view will always be realised, *i.e.*, keeping the troops well in hand in all circumstances."

Order of 94th Infantry Regiment (38th Division), dated September 15th, 1918.

" I expect the battalion, as hitherto, to do its duty and discharge its obligations also during this period of stationary warfare in the responsible position in which it is placed.

" To secure better rationing for the next four days, I have granted every company 200 marks out of the canteen funds.

" Every commander and every man is to be most minutely instructed in the importance of holding the outpost and forward zones as long as possible and of retaking them if lost. In case of an attack on a large scale, the main line of resistance must be held absolutely intact.

" Company commanders are personally responsible for carrying out this order.

" For bringing in a prisoner a reward of 100 marks is offered."

Draft of an order from the 119th Division for inclusion in regimental orders, dated September 16th, 1918.

" There will be a lecture and conference for all officers and N.C.O.'s at the earliest possible date, with the object of pointing out how immeasurably important it is that the troops should now hold their ground more than ever, and that there can be no question of going back a single step farther.

" We want to show the British, the French, and the Americans that any further attacks of theirs on the Siegfried Line will be completely broken, and that this line is an impregnable rampart—with the result that the Entente Powers will condescend to consider the peace terms which are absolutely necessary to us before we can end this war. In other words, each step backward now means a lengthening of the war ; a successful stand, on the other hand, will give us the prospect of an early peace. Every man has got to be clearly convinced of these facts and company officers must be constantly telling their men this. I wish all commanding officers to take similar steps."

Extract from an order of the 1st Reserve Division, dated September 16th, 1918 (the Division was then in line near Bellenglise), issued down to companies in the 59th Reserve Infantry Regiment.

" At the present moment the enemy has gained the initiative. He must and will continue his attacks. In cases where he does not aim at far-reaching objectives, he will attack in order to keep us in a state of uncertainty and to tie down our forces.

" The enemy will not consider that the wire and trenches of the Siegfried Line constitute any extraordinary obstacle to his further advance, as his great successes have strengthened his consciousness of superiority, while the strength and condition of our troops cannot be unknown to him.

" An attack on our front, even on a large scale, is, therefore, quite possible and by no means improbable. If the enemy is actually planning such an attack, his endeavour can only be to carry it out as soon as possible, before we have settled down in our old system of trenches and to enable him to get the Siegfried Line behind him. There can be no doubt that he possesses the means to overcome the difficulties which confront him.

" We must, therefore, count on a hostile attack, and also that it may be delivered at any time.

" We must also make up our minds that, in view of our general situation and to prevent further harm being done to the moral of the troops, the attack, when it comes, must be completely repulsed.

" It is, therefore, the more necessary that all arms and auxiliary services should be employed and utilised to their fullest extent in view of the fact that the infantry needs all the support imaginable.

" In these circumstances, the defence cannot now be organised, systematically step by step, so as to secure careful and thorough work, but the organisation must be rather carried out simultaneously in all spheres, and so rapidly that we are able, at all times, to meet any attack with confidence.

" To secure this, the utmost exertions are required especially on the part of the commanders whose duty it is to make preparations for operations, and energetic measures are necessary.

" Wherever the defences, in consequence of this fact, are at first only of a temporary nature, they must, if the enemy leave us sufficient time, continually be improved and strengthened in accordance with the principles laid down for the defensive battle.

" I expect that full justice will be done to these considerations, and I draw attention to the fact that, here too, negligence and omissions have more serious results than mistakes in the choice of material."

(Sd.) COUNT VON WALDERSEE.

APPENDIX J

Notes on Machine Gun Organisation and Tactics

It is difficult to realise the enormous strides that have been made in the development of the Machine Gun Corps both as regards numbers and tactics since 1914. We began the war with only two machine-guns per infantry battalion; moreover, at that time, the infantry had no Lewis guns or other pattern of automatic small arm. Very early in the war this paucity of machine-guns was fully realised, and great efforts were made to increase the supply. Thus, by the early part of 1916, machine-guns were organised in companies of 16 guns, at the rate of one company to each infantry brigade. The next stage in development was reached early in 1918 when the Brigade Machine Gun Companies were organised into battalions of four companies, 16 guns each, with a Lieutenant-Colonel in command. One battalion was allotted to each division, and senior Machine Gun Corps officers were attached to General Headquarters, and to the headquarters of armies and corps, to assist the General Staff in all questions relating to the organisation and tactical employment of machine-guns. The principal results of these changes may be summarised as follows :—

(1) The discipline of the machine-gunners improved rapidly as the result of the presence of senior officers in the Machine Gun Corps.

(2) The recognition of their corporate unity naturally promoted " Esprit de Corps."

(3) It became possible to arrange for the co-ordination and collective action of the machine-guns within the division, and even within corps.

In the battle of the Somme in 1916 there was very little collective action or weight of fire power from the machine-guns, whereas in 1918, in the operations described, many instances occurred of the collective use of machine-guns on a large scale, especially at the capture of the outer defences of the Hindenburg Line, and later in the attack on the main Hindenburg Line itself. There is no question that the deluge of machine-gun bullets, which rained down on the enemy positions in 1918, had a large share in the success of the operations. In addition to this heavy covering fire, machine-guns were also invariably detailed for the close support of the advancing infantry, and there are countless instances of the good work performed by these forward guns.

In order to explain the method of their employment the action of the machine-guns supporting the attack of the 4th Australian Division on September 18th is here given in some detail as being typical of the employment of machine-guns during the hundred days.[1] For this operation the 4th Australian Division had at its disposal the 4th and 5th Australian Machine Gun Battalions, of 64 guns each. These were organised under three categories, " rear " or " barrage " guns, " support " guns, and " forward " guns.

The 64 " rear " guns were found by the 5th Australian Machine Gun Battalion, whose task was to supplement the artillery barrage supporting the infantry advance to the first objective, and subsequently to maintain a protective barrage beyond that objective until the advance was continued. On completion of their task they remained in their barrage positions, which are shown in yellow circles on the map, to provide the necessary defence in depth. The preliminary arrangements for these 64 " barrage " guns entailed very heavy work in bringing up ammunition, oil, water, and other stores, the selection and preparation of gun positions, and the arrangements for communications.

[1] See Map No. 19.

334

The " support " guns, consisting of two machine-gun companies, 32 guns, were furnished by the 4th Australian Machine Gun Battalion. These guns moved forward ten minutes after " zero," followed the infantry as the latter advanced to the first objective, and from there supplemented the artillery barrage covering the further advance to the second objective. The guns were brought up in limbered wagons to their assembly positions in rear of the infantry " starting line," beyond which they were carried by hand. On arrival at the first objective, the guns were grouped in batteries of four in positions previously selected on the map from which to cover the advance to the second objective. On the right, the machine-gunners, moving forward in the mist to these positions, found some of the trenches on the first objective, which had apparently been missed by the infantry, still held by the enemy. These were captured without difficulty, and all the " support " guns were in the positions shown by red circles on the map, and laid on to their barrage lines, within an hour of arrival.

The " forward " guns, 32 in number, were provided by the remaining two companies of the 4th Australian Machine Gun Battalion, one company working with each attacking brigade ; their task was to provide the requisite fire in close support of the infantry as it advanced. These machine-guns with their ammunition and stores were carried on limbered wagons up to the infantry " starting line," beyond which pack animals were used.[1]

After the first, second, and part of the third objective had been captured, it was decided to postpone the completion of the task allotted to the division until 11 p.m., and orders were issued for machine-gun co-operation.[2] The " support " guns were ordered up from their positions on the first objective, marked with red circles on the map, to positions on the second objective, marked with green circles on the map, from which they were to fire a barrage at 11 p.m. All the guns were in position and ready to fire by 9 p.m., having advanced 4,000 yards during the day's fighting.

From the examination of prisoners there is no doubt that the machine-gun barrages on the 18th had had a great moral and material effect, and had aided the 4th Australian Division very materially in attaining all its objectives with abnormally few casualties.

The ammunition expenditure of the 4th and 5th Australian Machine Gun Battalions during the 18th amounted to the enormous total of 354,750 rounds. Of these, 342,000 were expended by indirect, and the remainder by direct fire.

---

[1] The pack animals were able to get forward to the third objective, only one being killed and eight wounded during the advance.

[2] For the account of the attack of the 4th Australian Division, see pp. 128 *et seq.*

APPENDIX K

The Adventures of a Whippet Tank on August 8th

The experiences of a whippet tank of " B " Company of the 6th Tank Battalion will give some idea of the work which the tanks performed during the operations. This tank, under the command of Lieut. Arnold and with a crew of two men, was one of the company of tanks detailed to accompany the leading troops of the 1st Cavalry Division in the attack on August 8th. At " zero " it proceeded across country south of the Amiens–Chaulnes railway together with the other tanks of " B " Company. After proceeding some distance it found itself ahead of the other whippets and near some Mark V tanks ; these were being followed by infantry, and were under fire from a German battery situated between Bayonvillers and Warfusée-Abancourt, the fire from which put out of action two Mark V tanks. Seeing this, Lieut. Arnold engaged the battery by running diagonally across its front, narrowly escaping being hit. Having passed out of view of the battery behind a belt of trees he manœuvred to attack the battery from the rear, and, when he charged it, the artillerymen to the number of about 30 abandoned the guns and attempted to escape, but all were accounted for. The whippet then moved on, accounting for a large number of Germans, who were in full retreat and appeared quite demoralised, and assisting two cavalry patrols to advance by killing some Germans who were holding them up on the edge of a cornfield. Shortly afterwards Lieut. Arnold found another cavalry patrol checked by some Germans who were firing over the parapet of a railway bridge, so he drove his tank up on to the railway embankment until he could obtain a clear view of the bridge, when he opened fire on the enemy, killing some and driving the others away. The whippet, now quite alone, proceeded eastwards to a small valley between Bayonvillers and Harbonnières, shown as containing hutments on the maps issued for the use of the tank commanders. On entering the valley a large number of Germans were discovered packing their kits preparatory to flight, of these at least 60 were killed. The whippet then pursued the retiring enemy, engaging them at ranges of from 200–600 yards, but, being alone, was the target for heavy rifle and machine-gun fire. Up to this time all had gone well, but now the petrol from some spare tins on the roof, which were perforated by bullets, began to run into the inside of the tank. The fumes, combined with the intense heat, made it necessary for the crew to breathe through their box respirators. Nothing daunted, the whippet again advanced eastward at 2 p.m. and ran into a stream of motor vehicles, horse transport, and crowds of infantry all retiring in confusion. A lorry was put out of action by shooting the driver, and heavy casualties were inflicted on the infantry at ranges of from 400–500 yards ; indescribable confusion was caused amongst the mass of horse and motor transport. The enemy's rifle and machine-gun fire now grew so intense that it was difficult to return the fire. Finally, the left-hand revolver port was shot away, and the fumes and heat combined became so bad that Lieut. Arnold ordered the driver to turn about and withdraw ; unluckily at this moment two concussions were felt, and the tank burst into flames. The two men reached the door and collapsed ; Lieut. Arnold was almost overcome, but managed to open the door and drag out his comrades. To add to their difficulties the ground on which they were lying was running with burning petrol, and they were forced to make a rush to get further away. In this rush one of the crew was killed by a bullet, and Lieut. Arnold and the other man were enveloped in flames, which they tried to extinguish by rolling over on the ground. Meanwhile a number of Germans were approaching from all sides ; the first arrival wounded Lieut. Arnold in the arm with his bayonet, the second knocking him senseless with the butt of his rifle. On recovering consciousness he found himself surrounded by an infuriated mob, who kicked him mercilessly. The subsequent treatment of this officer was equally brutal, as, on refusing to give information to a German officer during his examination, he was struck in the face, and later received five days' solitary confinement in a room with no window.

The story of this gallant exploit, typical of the work of the Tank Corps throughout the operations, was supplied by Major-Gen. Hugh Elles, the Commander of the Tank Corps, to whom the Fourth Army owes much, not only for his assistance during the hundred days, but for the high moral with which he had infused the officers and men of the Tank Corps.

INDEX

NOTE.—For formations, units, etc., not referred to in the Index, see details in Appendix F.

A

Abbeville, 13, 139
Ablaincourt, occupied, Aug. 28 : 91
Accroche Wood, sector, 17 ; captured, Aug. 8 : 40
Achiet, captured, Aug. 22 : 72
Aerodromes, German, new, Oct. 14 : 206 ; evacuation of, Oct. 6 : 191 ; withdrawal of, Oct. 31 : 238
Aeroplane Patrols (see also Contact Patrols), services of, 19
Aeroplanes, surprise attack in daylight rendered difficult by, 268
  British, bombing attacks and bomb-dropping by, 25, 157, 189
    Used to drown noise of tanks, 24, 28, 125, 156, 157
  British and German, numbers brought down, etc., on various dates, see Royal Air Force, Work of
  German, attacks by, on British cavalry, Oct. 8–9 : 197, 198 n.
Ailette river, 72 n.
Air Photographs, issue of, prior to Aug. 8 : 25 & n., 26 ; value of, 16, 123, 204 ; artillery instructions based on, Nov. 4 : 245
Air Reconnaissance, see R.A.F., Work of, see also Contact Patrols
Aisonville, 206, 225, 229
Aizecourt-le-Haut, 97, 108, 109
Albert I., King of the Belgians, success of, Sept. 28–9 : 9, 138 n., 145
Albert, Aug.–Sept. : 13, 16, 21, 22, 67 n., 82, 112, 140 ; captured, Aug. 22 : 73, 74, 76
  Defences near, British, 5
    German, 15
  German withdrawal from (Aug.), 14, 86, 112
Albert–Bapaume road, Aug. 23 : 82
Albert–Méaulte road, Aug. 22 : 76
Allaines, Sept. 1–2 : 106, 109, 110
Allason, Brig.-Gen. W., D.S.O., G.O.C. 52nd Inf. Brig., 316
Allied Armies, see each Army
Allonville, Aug. 8 : 40
America, U.S., Civil War in, lessons of, as drawn by Henderson, 270
American Forces, see also under Armies, Component Parts, and in Appendix F
  Arrival of, effect on German moral, 70
  Attack on St. Mihiel Salient, Sept. 12, success of, 137
  Soldiers, characteristics shown by, 6, 10 n., 67, 103, 162 & n., 163, 168, 217, 231
Americans, isolated parties in advance of British line, Sept. 30 : 171
Amey, L/Cpl. W., V.C., 252-3, 280, 281

Amiens, situation in front of, at end of March, and in April, 2, 3 n.
  British defences constructed April–July : 5, 175
  German advance on, March : 2
  German defences before, state of, July : 5, 15
  Last German attempt on, 2, 4
  Rest areas near, 139, 175, 176, 189
Amiens, Battle of, 1, 44 ; plans for, 6, 7, 18 sqq. ; concentration of troops for, 7, 19, 27, 28, 29 ; attack of Aug. 8 : 31 sqq. ; progress of, Aug. 9–11 : 52 sqq. ; events from Aug. 12 : 64 sqq. ; results, 9, 68–70, 121
Amiens, Defences
  Inner, 15, 16
  Outer, 15, 16, 66, 73
    Attacked, Aug. 8–10 : 22, 23, 39, 40, 43, 46, 56
    Occupied, 45, 57, 61
Amiens-Brie road, Aug. 8–26 : 42, 43 n., 54, 61, 67, 79, 87
Amiens-Chaulnes railway, 32 n., 36, 40, 54
Amiens-Roye road, Aug. 1 sqq., 14, 15, 17, 20, 21-2, 33, 39, 44, 53, 66
Ammunition
  Daily expenditure by Fourth Army Aug. 8–Nov. 11 : Appendix G, 328
  Expenditure of, in attack on Hindenburg Line, 154
Ammunition dumps, German, emptied, Oct. 6 : 191
Ammunition supplies by aeroplane, Aug. 8 : 24 & n.
  Difficulties concerning, 63, 154, 203, 204, 207
Ancre river, July, Aug., Sept. : 5, 13, 21, 22, 46, 49, 55, 115 ; German defences on, 15 ; German withdrawal behind, 14 ; attack N. of, 71, 72, 73 ; crossing of, 74, 76 ; marshes of, 73, 76, 82
Anderson, Brig.-Gen. S. M., D.S.O., G.O.C. 1st Aus. Divl. Artillery, 313
Anderson, Lieut.-Col. D. F., D.S.O., G.S.O. 1, 25th Div., 321
Andigny Forest, Oct. 8–18 : 192, 206, 209, 210, 211, 213, 226, 229
Andigny-les-Fermes, Oct. 9–17 : 199, 202, 205, 206, 209, 210, 212, 213, 215, 225, 226 ; capture of, 211
Andigny-les-Fermes-Bellevue Ridge, Oct. 11 : 202
Andigny-les-Fermes-Mennevret road, Oct. 17 : 211
Angin Farm, Oct. 17 : 213
Anstey, Lieut.-Col. E. C., D.S.O., G.S.O. 1, 50th Div., 321
Anti-Aircraft Defence, see Appendix F, 302, 317, 325
Anvil Wood, Aug. 31–Sept. 1 : 99, 100, 101, 104, 106

Corps—*cont.*
British—*cont.*
Infantry—*cont.*
XXII, and the transfer of the Canadian Corps, 19
Commander of, in temp. command of III Corps, Aug. 11 : 65 *n.*
Canadian
Commander of, at conference, July 21 : 18
Composition and Commander of, Aug. 8 : 12
German divisions opposed to, 17
Operations of, in the Battle of Amiens : frontage of attack, Aug. 8 : 21 ; method of advance, 22, and synchronisation of, 23 ; tanks allotted to, for Aug. 8 : 23, 33 ; Cav. Div. and R.A.F. Squadron allotted to, 24 ; assembly of, for attack, 28 ; plan of attack and objectives, 32, 33, 35 ; progress of, 32 *n.*, 33 ; results of day's fighting by, 39, 40, 189 ; pause in advance, 40 ; advance continued, 46, 49 ; task allotted to, for Aug. 9 : 51 ; advance on Aug. 9 : 52 *sqq.* ; orders for Aug. 10 : 57 ; advance on Aug. 10 : 57–59 ; 32nd British Div. allotted to, 57 ; objective of, for Aug. 11 : 61 ; action on front of, Aug. 11 : 62 ; German forces opposing, Aug. 12–15 : 64 *& n.* ; reliefs effected, and patrols pushed out by, 64 ; withdrawn into reserve, Aug. 17, 20 : 65, 66, 85
Training of, with tanks, 21 *n.*
Transfer of, to Fourth Army, how camouflaged, 19
French
XV, Sept. 30 : 171 ; attack of, Oct. 3 : 179–80 ; advance and attacks of, Oct. 4, 17 : 185, 209–10, 211
XXXI, frontage held by, Aug. 8 : 22 ; advance of, 39 ; attack by, 50
XXXVI, reliefs effected by, Aug. 24, night, 85 ; objectives, Sept. 18 : 123, 126 ; successes of, Sept. 24, 25 : 143, 144
German
Alpine, *see under* Divisions, German
XI, position of, early Aug., 17
XIV, position of, early Aug., 17
LI, position of, early Aug., 17
H.Q. Staff of, surprised at Proyart, Aug. 8 : 42
LIV, Orders issued to, Oct. 19, on the holding of the Hermann Stellung, 256 *n.*
Machine Gun, moral maintained by, 112
Corps Commanders, Gen. Rawlinson's Conference with, on Aug. 11 : 63 *sqq.*
Cosens, Lieut.-Col. G. P. L., D.S.O., G.S.O. 1, 3rd Cav. Div., 303
Counter-attack, immediate, value of, instances of, 3, 4, 62, 267–8
Value of surprise in, 268
Counter-attacks
British, at
Hallu, Aug. 11 : 62
Mannequin Hill, Oct. 3 : 179
Trones Wood, Aug. 27 : 90, 264
Villers Bretonneux, April 24 : 4
by 1st Div., Sept. 24 : 143
by 32nd Div., Aug. 11 : 62
German, in
August, 48, 49, 61, 62, 63, 64, 74, 77–8, 83, 84, 90, 94, 99, 100, 102
Sept., 118, 119, 120, 127 *& n.*, 129, 135, 141, 142, 143 *n.*, 144, 163, 171 *& n.*, 175, 190
Oct., 173, 176, 178, 183, 184, 187, 188, 190, 194, 211, 215, 217, 220, 225, 237
Nov., 241, 259–61

Counter-attacks—*cont.*
German—*cont.*
Anticipated at Somme crossings, Aug. 30 : 97
Forestalled, various dates, 61-2, 84, 134 *n.*, 172 *n.*, 213
Lack of means to deliver, Aug. 22 : 72 *n.*
in Mass formation, 62
Met by bayonet charge, 143 *& n.*
Reserves for, lack of good concealment for, Sept. 29 : 149 *& n.*
Undelivered, 172 *n.*, 174 *n.*
Counter-offensive, allied, plans for, 7, and crisis of, 9
Country between Somme and Luce, nature of, 15
Courage, Brig.-Gen. A., D.S.O., M.C., G.O.C. 5th Aus. Tank Brig., 312, 323
Courcelles, Aug. 22 : captured, 72
Cousens, Lieut.-Col. R. B., D.S.O., A.A. & Q.M.G. 74th (Yeo.) Div., 307
Cousolre, Nov. 11 : 261
Coxen, Brig.-Gen. W. A., C.M.G., D.S.O., G.O.C. R.A., Aus. Corps, 312, 323, 327
Craigie-Halkett, Brig.-Gen. H. M., D.S.O., G.O.C. 74th Inf. Brig., 321
Craufurd, Brig.-Gen. G. S., C.M.G., C.I.E., D.S.O., A.D.C., G.O.C. 18th Inf. Brig., 319
Crépey Wood, Aug. 9, 10 : 55, 59, 60, 63
Cribs, for helping tanks to cross obstacles, 221 *& n.*
Croak, Pte. J. B., V.C., 36 *n.*, 280, 285
Croix-Fonsomme, Oct. 8–9 : 193, 197
Crucifix, The (Bray-sur-Somme), Aug. 22 : 77
Cubitt, Maj.-Gen. T. A., G.O.C. 38th Div., 74 *n.*, 82
Curlu, Aug. 28 : 92
Currey, Pte. W. M., V.C., 104 *n.*, 280, 285
Currie, Lieut.-Gen. Sir A. W., K.C.B., K.C.M.G., G.O.C. Cdn. Corps, 12, 32-3, 53, 308
Curtis, Sgt. H. A., V.C., 228, 280, 286
Cutbill, Lieut.-Col. R. H. L., D.S.O., A.A. & Q.M.G. 18th (Eastern) Div., 305

D

Dados Loop, Sept. 21-2, 23, 29 : 140, 141, 142, 168
Damery, Aug. 10, 12, 17, 21 : 58, 61, 62, 66 ; captured, 64
Damery-La Chavatte–Fransart–Chilly–Rainecourt–Proyart–Etinehem–Amiens outer defences–Dernancourt, British line on, Aug. 21 : 66
Damery-Parvillers, 62
Davies, Lieut.-Col. C. M., D.S.O., G.S.O. 1, 58th (London) Div. (T.), 306
Davies, Lieut.-Col. Q. S., D.S.O., C.E. 66th Div., 327
Dawn attacks, 268
Debeney, General, G.O.C. First French Army, 11 *n.* ; placed under Haig's orders, and to co-operate with Fourth Army, 12
Defence in depth, 74, 119, 120
Delaforce, Brig.-Gen. E. F., C.M.G., G.O.C. 6th Divl. Artillery, 320
Delay Action mines, 203, 260
Delville Wood 1916 : 225
1918, Aug. 27 : 90, 91
Demuin, 15, 32, 33 ; Aug. 8 : captured, 35, 39
Deniécourt, Aug. 28 : occupied, 91
Dernancourt, Aug. 9, 10, 27 : 51, 56, 57, 61, 66, 74
Despatches of F.M. Sir D. Haig *cited*, on German demoralisation after Nov. 4 : 10 ; on reasons for extending N. the front of attack, Aug. 21 : 71–2 ; on importance of British attack on Sept. 29 : 137 *n.* ; on the shattering of the German last defences, 190

Florina Trench, Aug. 31, Sept. 1 : 100, 101, 103, 104
Floursies, 260
Fluquières, 117
Foch, General (made Marshal, 5 & n.), and the plan of attack of the Fourth Army, 5, 7, 11 n., 12, 18, 19, 240 ; arrangement with, for front of Cdn. Corps to be taken over by First French Army, Aug. 17–22 : 66
 and Sir D. Haig, convergent attacks delivered by, Sept. 26–9 : 9 ; attack on Hindenburg Line decided on, Sept. 22 : 137 ; support given by, to Fourth Army, Oct. 3 : 178
Folemprise Farm, Sept. 30, Oct. 2 : 169, 180, 182 ; captured, 174
Folies, Aug. 9 : captured, 53
Fontaine-aux-Bois, Oct. 23–4, Nov. 4 : 230, 231, 232, 253 ; captured, 236
Fontaine-les-Cappy, Aug. 26–7 : 87, 88, 89
Fontaine Uterte, Oct. 3, 4, 8 : 180, 184 ; gained, 195
Footbridges, German, over Sambre and Oise Canal, 206
Foott, Brig.-Gen. C. H., C.M.G., C.E. Aus. Corps, 312, 323, 327
Ford, Lieut.-Col. S. H., Chief of Staff, 27th Amer. Div., 324
Foreign Legion, The, at Villers Bretonneux, April 24 : 4 n.
Forest, Oct. 10–11 : 201, 204
Forester's House, the, in
 Andigny Forest, Oct. 17, 18 : 212, 226
 L'Evêque Wood, Oct. 21 : 231
Fort Garry Horse, Oct. 9 : attack by, 198
Foucaucourt, 16 ; Aug. 8, 23, 27 : 42, 79, 88 ; captured, 89
Fouquescourt, Aug. 10–11 : 58, 59, 61, 62
Framerville, Aug. 8–9 : 42, 45, 55, 57
France, frontier of, reached by Fourth Army, Nov. 10 : 261
Francilly-Selency, Sept. 18 sqq. : 126, 135, 138, 142
Franco-American attack towards Mezières, date fixed for, 138 n.
Franco-British liaison force, Aug. 8 : 35
Fransart, 66
Fraser, Brig.-Gen. L. D., C.B., C.M.G., G.O.C. Heavy Artillery, Aus. Corps, 312, 323, 327
Freckles Wood, Aug. 31 : 101
Frederick the Great, methods of, in employing and meeting flank attacks, 264 & n. ; spirit of, as influencing the moral of his forces, 10 n.
Frégicourt, Aug. 30, Sept. 1 : 96 sqq., 107, 108, 264
Freideburg, — von, order issued by, Aug. 27 : 69 n.
French Armies, see each, under Army, French
 Front, shortening of, Aug. 11–20 : 66
 High Command, Third French Army withdrawn by, 66
 Inhabitants of Bohain, plight of, Oct. 9 : 197 n.
 Liberated between the Hindenburg Line and the Selle, 202 n.
 Offensive on the Marne, July 18 : 5, 17 & n., 68 n., 70
Fresnoy-en-Chaussée, Aug. 8 : 38–9, 44, 51
Fresnoy-le-Grand, Oct. 6, 8, 9 : 191, 193, 197 ; occupied, 200
Fresnoy-le-Grand-Bohain railway, 197
Fresnoy-le-Petit, tactical importance of, Sept. 11 : 120 ; objective on Sept. 18 sqq. : 123, 125, 127, 135, 136, 139, 142 ; captured, 143

Fresnoy-le-Petit–Berthancourt–Le Verguier–Grand Priel Woods–Hargicourt–Ronssoy–Basse Boulogne–Epéhy–Peizières, high ground near German first line of defence, 120
Fresnoy-le-Petit–Thorigny–Le Tronquoy road, Sept. 29 : 153
Fricourt, Aug. 25 : captured, 85
Frise, 16 : Aug. 27–8 : 89 ; captured, 92
Frizell, Brig.-Gen. C. W., D.S.O., M.C., G.O.C. 75th Inf. Brig., 321
Froissy Beacon, Aug. 23 : captured, 81
Frontage, length considered suitable to allot to a division at various dates, 6 & n.
Frontages allotted to troops in successful attacks, 1915–18, with chief factors influencing the situation, 265–268 ; Tables, 266–7
Frontal attack, 265
Fuller, Brig.-Gen. C. G., D.S.O., B.G.G.S. III Corps, 304, 318
Fuses, instantaneous, used for
 Road shelling, Aug. 25 : 86 & n.
 Wire-cutting, Sept. : 154

G

Gaby, Lieut. A. E., V.C., 40, 280, 286–7
Gailly, Aug. 8 : captured, 43
Garde Mill, Oct. 23 : 232, 234
Garenne Wood, Aug. 23 : 81
Garforth, Lieut.-Col. W., D.S.O., M.C., C.E. 46th Divl. Engineers (T.), 326
Gas, BB., British use of, 144, 153
 Yellow Cross or Mustard, German use of, 3 & n., 26, 144 n., 153
Gas-shelling
 British
  Sept. 26–7 : 144 & n., 153 ; Oct. 5, 16 : 222
 German
  Aug., Sept., Oct., Nov. : 3 & n., 26, 47, 49, 64, 67 n., 74, 83, 85, 116, 131, 132 n., 186, 212, 215, 219, 241
Gattigny Wood, Oct. 9 : 198, 199
Gauche Wood, Sept. 18 : captured, 134
Gellibrand, Maj.-Gen. J., C.B., D.S.O., G.O.C. 3rd Aus. Div., 40, 314
General Headquarters, see also Haig
 Instructions from, Aug. 17 : 65 & n., 66
Generalship, art of, 2, 10 n., 269–70, 271
Genève, Oct. 4 : 184
Gentelles-Cachy plateau, British batteries on, 15, 28
German advance on Amiens, the final attempt to capture, April 24 : 2 sqq.
 Armies, see under Armies, German
 Artillery, see Artillery, German
 Casualties, passim
 Counter-attacks, see Counter-attacks
 Defeat, way opened for, 9 ; the climax, 256, 261
 Defences, at
  Amiens, 15–16, 73 et alibi
  Hamel, 6
  Hindenburg Line, 120–1 sqq., 147 sqq.
  St. Souplet- Le Cateau, 202, 204
 Disorganisation, by attacks of Aug. 8, Sept. 29–Oct. 8 : 32, 177, 196
 Forces (see also Man-power), strength of, in Sept., 121, maximum of, 113
 Intelligence, examination by, of prisoners, 27 n.
 Losses in prisoners, see also Prisoners, German, and Appendices A, B, and C, 275–7
  Aug. 8–21 : 70
  Aug. 8–Sept. 28 : 145
  Aug. 8–Nov. 11 : 262, Appendix C, 277

Moonlight attacks, Aug. 24, Oct. 23 : 83, 233 *sqq.*, 268

" Mopping up," defined, 42 & *n.*

Moral in war, Henderson *cited* on, 1–2, 10 *n.*, 270

Influence of, to be noted in studying military history, 270

British, increase in, April–July and after, 1, 5, 9, 69, 101–2, 145–6, 208, 237, 253

Confederate, 10 *n.*

German, progressive deterioration in, July 18 *sqq.* : 5, 6, 7, 9, 10 *n.*, 16 *n.*, 17 & *n.*, 51, 52, 69 & *n.*, 72, 112–13, 121, 122, 125, 126, 137 *n.*, 145, 154, 159, 160 & *n.*, 161 *n.*, 172 *n.*, 174 *n.*, 190, 206, 237, 253, 260, 261

Ludendorff, *cited* on, 10 *n.*

Orders issued on, by

von Freideberg, Aug. 27 : 69 *n.*

von der Marwitz, Aug. 25 : 69 *n.*

Retained by Alpine Corps and other units, 112

Moral effect of tanks, 131, German witness to, 16 *n.*, 69 *n.*

Morcourt, Aug. 8, Oct. 8 : 194 ; captured, 43

Moreuil, 15 ; Aug. 8 : 11 *n.*, 22 ; captured, 8, 50, 51

Moreuil to the Ancre, front on which decided to attack, Aug. 8 : 21

Moreuil Wood captured, Aug. 8 : 50

Morgan, Major S. H., M.C., A/C.E. 66th Divl. Engineers, 322

Morgemont Wood, Aug. 8 : 36

Morlancourt, July, Aug. : 11 *n.*, 74 ; extension of III Corps front to, 14 ; German troops near, 16 *n.*, 17, attack by, 27 ; attack on, *ib.*

Morland, Lieut.-Gen. Sir T. L. N., K.C.B., K.C.M.G., D.S.O., G.O.C. XIII Corps, 139, 175, 184–5, 188, 196, 217, 232, 244, 245, 321, 326

Mormal Forest, Oct. 18, 23–4, Nov. 1–4 : area and features of, 242 ; attacks on, 226, 230, 237, 243, 244, 245, 247, 252, 254, 255, 256 ; part cleared, 257

Morrison, Maj.-Gen. E. W. B., C.B., C.M.G., D.S.O., G.O.C. R.A., Cdn. Corps, 308

Morshead, Lieut.-Col. H. T., D.S.O., C.E. 46th (North Midland) Divl. Engineers (T.), 320

Morval, Aug. 30, Sept. 1 : 96 ; attacked by Third Army, 103, 107

Mound, The, at Le Cateau, 205

Moyenneville, 72

Mullins, Maj.-Gen. R. L., G.O.C. 1st Cav. Div., 44, 302

Munster Fusiliers, Royal, *see* Royal Munster Fusiliers

Mustard Gas, *see* Gas, Yellow Cross

N

Napoleon I., 270

Moral of his forces, 10 *n.*

Views of, on value of moral, 2

Waterloo strategy of, 3

Nauroy, Sept. 22–9, Oct. 1–3 : 149, 152, 160, 162, 164, 165, 174 *n.*, 180, 184 : effect of artillery fire on, 154

Naylor, Col. W. K., Chief of Staff, 33rd (Illinois) Amer. Div., 307

Nesle, railway centre at, Aug. : 25, 58, 61, 84 & *n.*, 91 *n.*

Neuville-Vitasse, Aug. 24 : 86

Neuvilly, Oct. 9–11 : 199, 200, 202

Neuvilly–Troisvilles road, Oct. 9 : 199

Neville's Cross, Oct. 5, 8 : 187, 194

Newton mortars used for wire-cutting, Sept. 27 : 154

Night attacks, pros and cons of, 268

Night movements, to ensure secrecy, 19

Norfolk Regt.

7th Batt., Aug. 8, Sept. 18 : 48, 133

9th Batt., Oct. 9, at Bohain, 197

Northamptonshire Regt.

1st Batt., Sept. 24 : defence by, 143 ; attack by, Oct. 17 : 214, 215, 216 ; crossing the Sambre and Oise Canal, Nov. 4 : 247 ; at Fesmy, etc., 249

6th Batt., Aug. 22, Sept. 18 : 76, 133 *n.* ; Oct. 23–4 : 233, 236 ; Nov. 4, at Preux-aux-Bois, 254, 255

North Staffordshire Regt.

1/6th Batt., at the St. Quentin Canal, Sept. 29 159 ; at Mannequin Hill, Oct. 3 : 179 *n.*

Northumberland Fusiliers

2nd Batt., Oct. 3 : 182 ; at the Selle, Oct. 17 : 220, 221

Northumberland Hussars, Aug. 8, Sept. 6–7 : 47 & *n.*, 116

Nosworthy, Lieut.-Col. F. P., D.S.O., M.C., G.S.O. 1, 66th Inf. Div., 322

" Notes on Wellington," by Henderson, referred to, 1, 10 *n.*

Nottinghamshire and Derbyshire Regt., *see* Sherwood Foresters

Noyelles, Nov. 5 : 257

Noyon, Aug. : 18, 84 ; captured, 91 ; Germans in full retreat from, *ib.*

Nurlu and Nurlu heights, Aug. 30, Sept. 2–6 : 97 ; attacks on, 108, 110, 111, 116 ; pivot of German retreat, 113

O

Observing for artillery, by R.A.F. Corps Squadrons, 24, 50 ; *see also* R.A.F., work of

Oder Trench, Aug. 31 : 100, 101

Odlum, Brig. Gen. V. W., C.B., C.M.G., D.S.O., G.O.C. 11th Cdn. Inf. Brig., 311

Offensives, convergent and simultaneous, decided for Allies, 137

Offoy, Somme crossings near, 61

Ogilvie, Col. T., C.M.G., Labour Commandant, Fourth Army, 301

Oise river, 68–9, 147, 225, 237

Oisy, Oct., Nov. : 204, 213, 229, 231, 237, 240, 241, 242, 243, 248

Oisy-Rejet de Beaulieu road, Oct. 19 : 229

O'Keefe, Maj.-Gen. Sir M. W., K.C.M.G., C.B., D.M.S. Fourth Army, 301

Old British main line of resistance in 1917, and March 1918, held by Germans, Sept. : 118 & *n.*, 120

Outpost Line held by Germans, Sept. : 120, 124, 136

Reserve line of March 1918, reoccupied, Sept. 11 : 120

" Old Contemptibles," The, retreat of, in 1914, 10

Old Copse, Sept. 19 : 136

Omignon river, Sept. 8 : 117, 118

Ommiécourt-les-Cléry, Aug. 29–31, crossing the Somme at, 93, 94, 99, 101

Ormond, Brig.-Gen. D. M., D.S.O., G.O.C. 9th Cdn. Inf. Brig., 310

Ors, Oct. 23–4, Nov. 1–4 : 230, 231, 233, 235, 236, 237, 244, 250, 251, 252 ; captured, 240

O'Ryan, Maj.-Gen. F., G.O.C. 27th Amer. Div., 324

Osler, Col. S. H., D.S.O., C.E. 2nd Cdn. Div., Ammunition Column, 310

Quarry, near Trones Wood, Aug. 27 : 90 n.
Quarry Farm, Aug. 31–Sept. 1 : 102, 106
Queen's Own, see Royal West Kent Regt.
Queen's Own Cameron Highlanders, see Cameron Highlanders
Queen's, The, see Royal West Surrey Regt.
Quennemont Farm, Sept. 11–29 : attacks on, 120, 124, 129, 130, 137, 140–1, 149, 163, 164, 166, 167
Quennemont Farm–Gillemont Farm line, Sept.11–29 : 120, 124 ; attacks on, 140–1, 144, 157, 163
Quennet Copse, Sept. 21, 29 : 140, 166, 167
Querenaing, Oct. 17 : 226
Quid Copse, Sept. 18 : 133, 134
Quiévy, Oct. 11 : 202

R

Rafts, used at Sambre and Oise Canal crossing, 246 & n., 253
Raids by Australians, effect of, on German moral, 5–6
Railway centres bombed by R.A.F., 25, 189 et alibi
Junctions, see Aulnoye, and Le Cateau
Lines available for Fourth Army, 13, 121 n. ; see also Railway Centres, Junctions,Stations, etc.
Damage sustained by, 203, 260
Ridge, Oct. 1 : occupied, 174–5
Rainecourt, Aug. 11, 21 : 66 ; captured, 63
Rambourlieux Farm, Oct. 9 : 199
Ramicourt, Oct. 1–4 : 174, 176, 177, 179, 182, 185
Ramsay, Maj.-Gen. F. W., G.O.C. 58th (London) Div. (T.), 46, 74, 306
Rancourt, Aug. 31, Sept. 1 : 102, 112 ; captured, 107
Rankin, Brig.-Gen. C. H., C.M.G., D.S.O., G.O.C. 4th Cav. Brig., 303
Rawlinson, Gen. Sir H. S., Bt., G.C.B., G.C.V.O., K.C.M.G., A.D.C., G.O.C. Fourth Army, 301, 316, 324
British Representative at Versailles, again becomes G.O.C. Fourth Army, 2 n.
Concern of, to secure Somme bridges intact, Aug. 29 : 93 & n.
Conference with commanders held by
July 21 : 18
Aug. 4 : 18–19
Aug. 11 : 63
Oct. 19 : 229–30
Co-operation with, of the First French Army, 11 n., 12
Decision of, as to
Barrage line, for Sept. 29 : 157
Capture of Hamel, July 4 : 6
Retaking Villers Bretonneux, April 24 : 3
Securing Quennemont and Gillemont Farms and the Knoll, Sept. 20 : 137
Orders issued by (in order of date) for
Attack on Aug. 8 : 18 sqq.
Continuance of advance on Aug. 9–10 : 51, 57–8, 61
Combined attack by III Corps and Aus. Corps on Aug. 23 : 77
Battle of Mont St. Quentin, Aug. 30 sqq.: 97
Pursuit by III Corps and Aus. Corps on Sept. 5 sqq. : 113, 114
Attack on Outer Defences of Hindenburg Line on Sept. 18 : 123–5
Readjustment of Fourth Army front, Sept. 21–5 : 138 & n., 139
Attack on Hindenburg Line on Sept. 29 : 138 & n., 149–50 sqq.

Rawlinson, Gen. Sir H. S.—cont.
Orders issued by (in order of date) for—cont.
Cavalry concentration for Sept. 29 : 156–7
Operations on Sept. 30 : 169
Attack on the Masnières–Beaurevoir–Fonsomme line on Oct. 3 : 177–8
Attack on Oct. 8 (advance to Le Cateau), 193–4
Resumption of offensive on Oct. 9 : 197
Further objectives on Oct. 9 : 199, 200
Continuance of attack on Oct. 18 (Battle of the Selle), 226
Advance to line of exploitation, Orders for attack on Oct. 17, to take effect on Oct. 19 : 228
Combined attack on Oct. 23 : 230 & n.
Continuance of attack on Oct. 24 : 236
Attack of Nov. 4 : 243, 256
Continuance of pursuit on Nov. 7–9 : 258
Plans (in order of date), for
Attack on Aug. 8 : approved by C.-in-C., 7, 11–12 ; the original proposal, 11 n.
Forcing passage across the Somme, Sept. 3 : 113
Operation to gain possession of Outer Defences of Hindenburg Line, Sept. 11 : 121–2 ; approved by C.-in-C., 122
Praise given by, to
II Amer. Corps, Oct. 19 : 231
IX and XIII Corps, Nov. 4 : 256
Report of, to C.-in-C. on the general situation on Sept. 11 : 120–1
Read, Maj.-Gen. G. W., G.O.C. II Amer. Corps, 324 ; Aus. Corps front taken over by, Oct. 6 : 189 ; working with Gen. Monash, Sept. 29 : 139, 151
Regiments
American
105th, Sept. 29 : 162 ; Oct. 17–18 : 216, 217, 227
106th, Oct. 17 : 217
107th, Oct. 17–18 : 217, 227
108th, Oct. 17 : 216, 217
117th, Sept. 29 : 162 ; Oct. 7, 17 : 194, 216
118th, Oct. 11, 17 : 202, 216
119th, Oct. 10, 17, 18 : 201, 216, 227
120th, Oct. 9, 17 : 201, 216
130th, Aug. 8 : 47
131st, Aug. 9, 10, 12–20 : 55, 56, 57, 60 ; forming part of liaison force, 65 n., 67
132nd, Aug. 20 : 67
British, see under their respective designations
German
Emperor Francis Joseph's Prussian Guards, at Trones Wood, Aug. 27: 90
1st Guard Grenadier, counter-attack by, foiled, poor moral of, Sept. 30 : 172 n.
Regnicourt, Oct. 17 : 210, 211, 213
Regnicourt–Andigny-les-Fermes road, Oct. 17 : 210, 211
Reinforcement train captured, Aug. 8 : 45
Rejet de Beaulieu, Oct. 19 : 229
Rennie, Brig.-Gen. R., C.B., C.M.G., M.V.O., D.S.O., G.O.C. 4th Cdn. Inf. Brig., 309
Renuart Farm, Oct. 24 : flank attack on, 236, 237
Reports, conflicting, secrecy secured by, early Aug., 19
Reserve Hindenburg Line, see Hindenburg Reserve Line
Reserves, German, absorption of, see Appendix D, 278–9
Reticence of British prisoners, German tribute to, 20 n., 27 n.
Reumont, Oct. 9, 17 : 199, 218, 223 ; secured, 200
Reverse fire, German, Sept. 29 : 164
Rheims, July 15 : German attack on, 4, 5

3 A*

Lightning Source UK Ltd.
Milton Keynes UK
UKHW050704170619
344547UK00009B/356/P